D0152303

DATE DUE			
10/3/05			
OCT 3 0 2012			

HIGHSMITH #45114

Hellenism and Empire

Hellenism and Empire

Language, Classicism, and Power in the
Greek World AD 50–250

SIMON SWAIN

CLARENDON PRESS · OXFORD

Oxford University Press, Great Clarendon Street, Oxford, OX2 6DP
Oxford New York
Athens Auckland Bangkok Bogota Bombay Buenos Aires
Calcutta Cape Town Dar es Salaam Delhi Florence Hong Kong Istanbul
Karachi Kuala Lumpur Madras Madrid Melbourne Mexico City
Nairobi Paris Singapore Taipei Tokyo Toronto Warsaw
and associated companies in
Berlin Ibadan

Oxford is a registered trade mark of Oxford University Press

Published in the United States
by Oxford University Press Inc., New York

British Library Cataloguing in Publication Data
Data available

Library of Congress Cataloging in Publication Data
Hellenism and empire : language, classicism, and power in the
Greek world, AD 50–250 / Simon Swain.
Includes bibliographical references and index.
1. Greek literature, Hellenistic—History and criticism. 2. Greek
language, Hellenistic (300 B.C.–600 A.D.)—Social aspects—Greece.
3. Politics and literature—Greece—History. 4. Literature and
society—Greece—History. 5. Nationalism—Greece—Historiography.
6. Civilization, Greceo-Roman. 7. Greece—Relations—Rome.
8. Rome—Relations—Greece. 9. Power (Social sciences)
10. Imperialism. 11. Classicism. 12. Hellenism. I. Title.
PA3081.S93 1996   880.9'001—dc20   95–4765
ISBN 0–19–815231–0

1 3 5 7 9 10 8 6 4 2

Printed in Great Britain on acid-free paper by
Bookcraft (Bath) Midsomer Norton

For 87

ACKNOWLEDGEMENTS

It is a pleasure to thank the following for their assistance and inspiration at various times: Stephen Colvin, Harriet Jordan, Fergus Millar, John Moles (to mutual benefit), Vivian Nutton, Chris Pelling, and the staff of the Ashmolean and Bodleian Libraries for their care and consideration in supplying the books and articles that another book needs. Many others, including Greg Woolf and Chris Howgego, have supplied help knowingly or unknowingly. Special thanks are due to Ewen Bowie, Simon Price, Harry Sidebottom, and most of all to Donald Russell for being so very generous with their time; it is appreciated and remembered. Finally, thanks are due also to All Souls College, Oxford, for feeding the book so well.

S.S.

Woodstock
October 1994

CONTENTS

ABBREVIATIONS

Abbreviations of journals, etc., are based on those used in the annual bibliographical publication, *L'Année philologique*, and other standard works. The following are not otherwise explained in the text, notes, or Bibliography.

AE	*L'Année épigraphique*
BE	J. and L. Robert, 'Bulletin épigraphique' (cited by item and by year of its appearance in *REG*)
BGU	*Berliner griechische Urkunden*
CIL	*Corpus Inscriptionum Latinarum*
CMG	*Corpus Medicorum Graecorum*
CPJ	*Corpus Papyrorum Judaicarum*
DK[6]	H. Diels and W. Kranz, *Fragmente der Vorsokratiker*[6]
Ehrenberg–Jones	V. Ehrenberg and A. H. M. Jones, *Documents Illustrating the Reigns of Augustus and Tiberius*[2]
FD	*Fouilles de Delphes*
FGrH	F. Jacoby, *Die Fragmente der griechischen Historiker*
FIRA	S. Riccobono *et al.*, *Fontes iuris Romani antejustiniani*[2]
Heitsch	*Die griechischen Dichterfragmente der römischen Kaiserzeit*
IG	*Inscriptiones Graecae*
IGBulg	*Inscriptiones Graecae in Bulgaria repertae*
IGR	*Inscriptiones Graecae ad res Romanas pertinentes*
IK	*Inschriften griechischer Städte aus Kleinasien*
ILS	H. Dessau, *Inscriptiones Latinae Selectae*
IOSPE	B. Latysev, *Inscriptiones antiquae orae septentrionalis Ponti Euxini Graecae et Latinae*
Kaibel, *Epigr. gr.*	G. Kaibel, *Epigrammata Graeca ex lapidibus conlecta*
Kassel–Austin	R. Kassel and C. Austin, *Poetae Comici Graeci*
Kock	Th. Kock, *Comicorum Atticorum Fragmenta*
LSJ[9]	H. G. Liddell, R. Scott, H. Stuart Jones, *A Greek-English Lexicon*
MAMA	*Monumenta Asiae Minoris Antiqua*

McCrum–Woodhead	M. McCrum and A. G. Woodhead, *Select Documents of the Principates of the Flavian Emperors*
OGIS	W. Dittenberger, *Orientis Graeci Inscriptiones Selectae*
Paroemiographi Graeci	E. L. von Leutsch and F. G. Schneidewin, *Corpus Paroemiographorum Graecorum*
PIR²	*Prosopographia Imperii Romani²*
PLRE	*Prosopography of the Later Roman Empire*
PMG	D. L. Page (ed.), *Poetae Melici Graeci*
P.Berol.	Berlin Papyri
P.Gen.	*Les papyrus de Genève*
P.Giess.	*Griechische Papyri im Museum des oberhessischen Geschichtsvereins zu Giessen*
P.Oxy	*Oxyrhynchus Papyri*
PSI	*Papiri greci e latini*
RE	Pauly–Wissowa–Kroll, *Real-Encyclopädie der classischen Altertumswissenschaft*
RIC	H. Mattingly, E. A. Sydenham, *et al.*, *The Roman Imperial Coinage*
RPC	A. Burnett, M. Amandry, P. P. Ripollès, *Roman Provincial Coinage*
SEG	*Supplementum Epigraphicum Graecum*
Select Papyri	A. S. Hunt and C. C. Edgar, *Select Papyri*, ii
SIG³	W. Dittenberger, *Sylloge Inscriptionum Graecarum³*
Smallwood	E. M. Smallwood, *Documents Illustrating the Principates of Gaius, Claudius and Nero*
SVF	H. von Arnim, *Stoicorum Veterum Fragmenta*
TAM	*Tituli Asiae Minoris*
Walz	Chr. Walz, *Rhetores Graeci*, i–ix

Aelius Aristides is cited by the text of F. W. Lenz and C. A. Behr (Leiden, 1976–80) for works i–xvi, and by the incomplete edition of B. Keil (Berlin, 1898) for works xvii–liii.

Galen's works are cited by volume and page of C. G. Kühn's edition (Leipzig, 1821–33; repr. Hildesheim, 1965), unless otherwise specified.

Internal references from one chapter to another are by (abbreviated) chapter title and footnote number (e.g. 'Language', n. 22, 'Galen', n. 3). In many cases the reference is to the text in the vicinity of the footnote.

Introduction

This book is concerned with Greek culture and society between AD 50 and 250, the period known to us from the biographer and sophist Philostratus as the 'second sophistic'.[1] My aim is twofold. First, I want to explore the identity of the Greeks of this time with respect to their ancestors, the 'ancient Greeks', who were the source of their moral and political authority. The focus will be on the male Greek elite, that is, the restricted group in control of economy, culture, and government whose activities and beliefs are reasonably well known to us, and on the world of Old Greece and Asia Minor, where the culture in which I am interested was best represented and where populations most clearly expressed their relationship with the Greece of the classical or mythological age. In the second part of the book I want to consider from the standpoint of Greek culture how the leading Greek intellectuals of the second sophistic viewed Rome and Roman power in Greece and the Greek world.

Periodization is naturally problematic. It too often reflects examination syllabuses rather than real cultural or political boundaries. However, the world of the Greek elite in the second sophistic age is distinctive. In political terms it benefited particularly from the prosperity and stability of the High Roman Empire and from its largely philhellene emperors. The political ambitions of the elite were channelled through symbolic gifts of property and money to the Greek cities (the practice known as benefaction or 'euergetism'), and the cities were equally responsive to their notables' desire for status and recognition. As with other elements of the second

[1] *Lives of the Sophists* (henceforth *VS* = *Vitae Sophistarum*), 481. It is called 'second' sophistic to distinguish it from the 'first' sophistic of the 5th c. BC. Philostratus' *Lives* are dedicated to Antonius Gordianus as proconsul (*VS* 480 *anthupatos*; *hupatos* at 479 is here the equivalent of *hupatikos*, 'consular'; cf. Mason 1974: 167), who is probably the elder Gordian, proconsul of Africa in 237–8 (so Avotins 1978a; cf. Rothe 1989: 5–6). On Philostratus' own use of the phrase see below.

sophistic, there is nothing concretely new here. It is rather the prevalence or intensity of such practices that marks them off in this
period and establishes them as a speciality of the civic politics of
the age. Culturally the period is distinct for its renaissance of Greek
letters and for its emphasis on Hellenic culture and speech as the
emblems of civilization, and I shall be saying more about these
below. It is this cultural confidence that Philostratus captures so
well in his *Lives*. The individual biographies of the rhetorical stars
of the second sophistic—which commences for Philostratus in the
time of Nero—are often not concerned with rhetorical talent, but
with display and wealth and with the status of practitioners, in
other words with their position as cultural and political leaders of
the civic elite in the Greek East. It is for this reason that Philostratus'
term 'second sophistic' can be used as a convenient shorthand for
the period as a whole rather than being restricted to the declamatory rhetoric then in vogue as he himself has in mind.[2] The Greek
elite's cultural power at this time is in stark contrast with its lack
of overall political independence and effective political representation. Whether or not Greeks felt this and how far their views of
Rome were affected by the possibility of participating in Roman
government, as a small fraction of the elite did, albeit in increasing
numbers, from the end of the first century, are questions to be
considered in the course of the book.

The dates AD 50 and 250 are only approximate. Economic and
cultural activity did not suddenly arise in the Greek world in the
mid-first century, and it certainly did not cease in the mid-third.
Nevertheless, it can be argued that there are reasonably clear breaks
with the periods before and after. The Greeks of the second and
first centuries BC, the period during which Rome first became
a power in the Greek East, were not overly prosperous. The
Mithridatic war and the Roman civil wars at the end of the Republic fell particularly hard on an already depressed Greek world; many
decades later Plutarch and Pausanias still expressed anger over the
suffering of Greece at this time. Leading Greek intellectuals were

[2] Over-use of the Philostratean definition of 'second sophistic' (and the resulting
concentration on the personnel of the *VS*) is rightly objected to by Brunt 1994
(taking his cue from Wilamowitz 1900 on the continuity of Greek rhetoric from the
classical age and on Philostratus' tendentious presentation of a wholly revived art;
cf. Swain 1991a: 149, 151); but Brunt's consequent doubting of a Greek renaissance
(as if this too were an invention of Philostratus—rather than an indisputable fact) is
a good example of performance rhetoric in itself.

drawn to Rome to find Roman patrons. Thus there is a significant difference between the major Greek authors of the late Republican/Augustan period like Philodemus, Diodorus, Nicolaus, Dionysius, Strabo, and others, who did important work in Rome, and the leading writers of the later first century and after, beginning with Plutarch and Dio of Prusa. The dislocation between the two sets reflects a quite different cultural landscape. The leaders of Greek intellectual life in the second sophistic period were part of a world that did not need Rome. This is clear if one considers the professional speakers, or rhetors, whose cultural activity was so prominent during the second sophistic. In the early first century a number of such rhetors were established in Rome, as the elder Seneca recalls in his *Controversiae* and *Suasoriae*; whereas at the time of the second sophistic, although Rome and the West were places which certainly attracted the rhetors and sophists (as the most successful rhetors and teachers of rhetoric were known), the centre of the sophistic was very firmly in the world of old Greece, where Athens was dominant, and in the rich city states of Asia Minor.

As regards the years after 250 there is again a perceptible break. The middle and later decades of the third century were a time of political, military, and economic instability for the Roman empire. How this actually affected local power, prestige, and intellectual life in the Greek East is not at all clear. The major problem is that our sources are so poor. There is no Plutarch or Philostratus to guide us. Indeed, with one exception no contemporary Graeco-Roman narrative survives intact. The exception, the obscure *Thirteenth Sibylline Oracle*, shows an interesting attitude, if it is read impartially without preconceived ideas of a general 'crisis'. The *Oracle* was written in two parts by two authors, the first and largest presenting an Emesene perspective of the years from Gordian III to 253, the second additional section representing the view from the rich caravan city of Palmyra in the 260s. The text is a catalogue of Rome's military failures, especially against the resurgent Persian empire of Shapur I. It dwells on the disasters suffered by the cities of Syria in the Persian invasions. Even so, in its final analysis the crisis is one for Rome rather than for Emesa and Palmyra, whose powers and successes are exuberantly hailed. There is no sign here of the death of the city as an institution. We may then wonder whether the Greek world proper, especially in the urban centres of Asia Minor and Old Greece, responded differently when it too was exposed to barbarian pressure. Many seem to have retained their confidence in Greek culture. It is at any rate to a familiar 'Hellenic virtue and freedom' that the Athenian aristocrat Herennius Dexippus appealed when he galvanized his countrymen to drive off the occupying Herulian forces in 267. More importantly this same intellectual confidence is alive and well when it 're-emerges' in the fourth century, albeit in a quite different framework. However, though blanket talk of 'crisis' is undoubtedly going too far, in between there were significant changes.[3]

For a start, it is very noticeable that the epigraphic record, which is so important in attesting the diffusion of second sophistic life and the interconnection of culture and power in the eastern cities, is greatly diminished from the second half of the third century onwards. This presumably signals a considerable reduction in the number of local and national festivals which are such clear signs of cultural activity in the second sophistic, since their benefactors and participants liked their contributions to be commemorated on stone. A particularly alarming sign for the life of the cities is the disappearance of inscriptions celebrating new gifts of buildings or the establishment of funds for distributions or games. Finance may have become difficult. Indeed, we know that there was a marked debasement of the imperial coinage and that inflation was a serious problem, at least from the time of Aurelian. The total disappearance of the eastern city mints (so prolific in the second sophistic period) between 250 and 300 is presumably due (again, in part) to this financial crisis.[4]

There are political changes too. The restored Roman empire of the Tetrarchs and Constantine was a far more monarchical, bureaucratic, centre-oriented affair than the High Empire. Although this is the culmination of a trend visible from the time of Augustus

[3] Dexippus, *FGrH* 100 F28. 6 (the speaker is not necessarily Dexippus); Millar 1969: 24–8. On the Gothic invasions of Asia Minor in the 250s and 260s see e.g. Mitchell 1993: i. 235–8 (also on Shapur's Syrian incursions), with literature; beware, however, the element of drama (in an otherwise very sane book), by no means uncommon on this subject, imported into the epigraphical evidence—for example, if Stratonicea was worried enough about the possibility of barbarian invasion to seek an oracle from Zeus Panamarus, the oracle itself clearly affirms that the good times will continue (*IK* xxii. 1 [Stratonikeia ii. 1] 1103); again, if Dorylaeum reused the statue bases of a recent local benefactor to help build its walls, should we really diagnose a virtual collapse of civic pride?

[4] Epigraphic record: MacMullen 1988: 3–7 (with warnings against overinterpreting this and other symptoms of 'decline'). Finance: cf. Howgego 1985: 71–2, 99.

himself, there is no doubt that it was intensified by the long period of Roman military and political difficulty. It is probably due to this centralization that the honorific verse inscriptions we do find in the cities from this time onwards more often celebrate high-ranking imperial officials than those from the local elite. Men's minds were drawn upwards away from their homelands. From the end of the third century leading citizens were increasingly allowed to ignore the local obligations that had previously been enjoined on them by law.[5] Another major change from the earlier period is the steady Christianization of the Empire. The Greek religious heritage is as important as other cultural traditions in the period of the second sophistic, when pagan cults were flourishing as never before. After Constantine this world no longer received imperial support. Thus, although the traditional urban culture of Libanius in fourth-century Antioch resembles that of second-century Athens or Smyrna, it is avowedly less confident in the face of Christian culture, the removal of prominent citizens to the new court and senate at Constantinople, and the vigorous use of Latin in the administration and law of the eastern Empire, problems the Greek elite of the second sophistic did not have to contend with.

For sure, writing and rhetoric went on in the years after 250, with men like the famous orator Callinicus of Petra, whose career spanned the 260s and 270s, and the philologist Cassius Longinus, who was executed by Aurelian in 273.[6] Nevertheless, high-level pagan Greek culture does seem to have lost its way for a while. The cessation of the epigraphical record coincides with a lack of really major authors. Plotinus, who died at Rome about 270, is one exception. His pupil Porphyry, who died after 300, is another, but also an indicator of how the land would henceforth lie. When the intellectual life of the Greek city reappears to us in the fourth century, it is split between pagans and Christians. In this environment Hellenic culture meant pagan culture. The two were combined in the new philosophy of Neoplatonism, which Porphyry had distinguished from its Middle Platonist antecedents by disseminating and expounding the complex works of his great master. And just as Porphyry had felt obliged to write fifteen books *Against the Christians*, so the story of late Hellenism is the story of its slow

[5] Robert 1948*a* on the honorific epigrams; Millar 1983 on changes in exemptions.
[6] Callinicus: *FGrH* 281; Longinus: Russell 1964: pp. xxiv–xxx, Kennedy 1972: 637–41.

strangulation by Christianity, a very different scenario from the easy days of the second sophistic. Now too the distinctive cultural centres of our period, Athens and Asia Minor, were largely displaced by Constantinople, Antioch, and Alexandria (a city which was distanced from the main concerns of the second sophistic by its Macedonian origin and its cultural bias towards science and philosophy).[7]

Philostratus did not know that the cultural and political world he recorded in the *Lives of the Sophists* was not to endure.[8] That he wrote near its end is a neat coincidence, for it enables us to look back two hundred years with his fund of anecdotes and comments. But if we did not have his *Lives*, we would still be able to identify the years 50–250, the period that runs approximately from the birth of Plutarch to the death of Philostratus, as one with its own recognizable political and cultural integrity. The pattern of cultural production that is the visible form of this integrity directly reflects the special confidence of the Greek elite at this time. This confidence was due to their perceived closeness to the classical Greeks. The importance this relationship had for them is quite unparalleled before the second sophistic. Afterwards it quickly lost power as Greek society was transformed into the world of late antiquity. For an important part of this process was the emergence and triumph of a rival, more powerful creed which denied the worth of non-Biblical history and myth; the complex issues thrown up by this change and by the decay of Hellenism are reasons enough for bringing the present work to a close in the age of Philostratus.

Although it is possible to view the confidence of the second sophistic elite as a purely cultural matter, because it is largely expressed in the cultural forum, we are really dealing with a feeling of great political importance touching on the sources of power and the rights to exercise it. We are concerned, in short, with the cultural-political identity the Greek elite now adopted. The value of this identity lay in the sanction of a successful past whose glories were

[7] It is a defect of Anderson 1993 that it fails to distinguish culture from letters, with the result that 'second sophistic' refers to all Greek culture AD, including the world of the 4th c. and beyond.

On Alexandria 'between' Macedon and Greece cf. 'Past' n. 7, 'Arrian' nn. 47–49.

[8] Compare and contrast Giorgio Vasari—in his biographies of the Renaissance artists he does discuss the possibility of the decay of the arts from their present high point and imagines an organic cycle of death as well as *renascità*, 'renaissance' (i. 243 Milanesi); cf. below 'Language', text after n. 21, on Dionysius of Halicarnassus.

unimpeachable. It found two complementary modes of organization, one an extraordinary example of linguistic formalism with its own very particular rules which sought to settle the question of what correct, classicizing language might look like, the other a more general classicism characterized by looser and more flexible formulations which reflect the fact that the Greek past was not the preserve of the Greek elite alone but was open to use by other groups including non-Greeks. It is clear that there were attendant risks in this project. The search for cultural and political authority involved idealizing the past, and the result of this idealization was that it was always open to negotiation to say what the past actually was (an especial difficulty in the matter of language, as the multiplication of rule books shows), and to say what authority it conferred on whom (particularly since non-Greeks could appropriate the Greek past or even suggest that modern Greeks had no real connection with it). These problems are unsurprising, but they should not obscure the general cohesion and the relative security of the identity the Greeks gave themselves in the period before Christianity.

I shall begin the first part of the book by discussing the elite's obsession with language, because it is the clearest way in which they expressed themselves as a stable grouping, and has been very little studied in this regard.[9] I will be focusing on the phenomenon of 'atticism', the name given to the process whereby the style and language of authors writing in the dialect of classical Athens became the foundation for virtually all *belles-lettres* in this (and later) periods. Atticism looked to an ideal of correct Greek within an already widely polarized language situation with clearly established differences between educated and non-educated Greek. The value of studying it lies in the fact that it is a disclosure of social and political events quite as much as an expression of literary tastes. I shall move from language to the general meaning of the past. Here I shall be concerned partly with the elite's internal political and cultural strategies and partly with the important implications of their relationship with the past for their relationship with Rome. Following on from this I shall complete the discussion of Greek identity under Rome by considering key aspects of a group of texts known as the Greek novels. These flourished for the first time in

[9] The reason for this is probably that it falls between 'history' and 'literature', that unhelpful but still common division in classical civilization studies, and possibly because its technical aspect (which I have minimized) initially disguises its importance.

the second sophistic (and very probably not after it). The remarkably homogeneous content of these fictions allows us to investigate their role as a medium for articulating the values and aspirations of the contemporary elite to whom they appealed. It is noteworthy in this context that the novels are set in the free Greek world of the classical and Hellenistic periods before Rome. They are a particularly good way of bringing together literature and political society.

It may come as a surprise to some to find that the search for this society will not be following the usual historiography of institutions and governmental apparatuses and their accessory materials, and in particular that it avoids the now common *Stadt und Fest* approach to the history of the Greeks under Rome, which studies them largely through the epigraphic and numismatic record of their communal displays. There is clearly a very great deal to be learned by examining, for example, the festivals and processions of the civic calendar or the role of benefactors and the mechanism of provisioning. But the identity of the Greek elite in the second sophistic will not be revealed in this way, for such things present merely the surface expression of the dominant cultural system, not the organizing principles which inform it. This is where identifying the role of language formalism and history, the past, becomes important. There is of course no generally accepted terminology in which the operation of such matters can be mentioned. But it may be helpful here, though unfamiliar to some, to compare the operation of 'discursive practices' or 'structures' like medicine or law. To define these may seem hard, but we can readily take note of their particular functions and areas of work, and of their possession of an internal stability and coherence around which gather various sorts of surface statements and events in both public and private life. Thus paying a traffic fine or buying an aspirin are not isolated moments but part of a complex nexus of interrelated matters, to participate in which is to reassert the guiding intentions of the discourse in question. Language and the past functioned in a similar manner. To consult a lexicon of 'pure' Greek or to promote the cult of an eponymous ancestor was to connect with a large number of related surface statements or events whose significance is easy to miss in isolation, but which can be seen in perspective to combine and express the elite's identity as rightful inheritors of the classical world.

In suggesting this comparison with 'discursive structures' I am not offering a traditional structuralist analysis of the period, as some may be thinking. For with structuralism, which is essentially anti-historical, culture too often arrives still-born and immobile. But the search for structures is useful as long as we remember that they arise from particular historical and real-time contexts. In this sense we can speak of structures inhering in a given culture and giving it an identity. Different combinations will dominate at various times for different social groups. Among the ancient Greeks cultural/political identity had in fact long turned on the power of language and the power of the past. But it is in the second sophistic that it particularly organized itself through these. There is, then, an in-tensification here, a much more conscious feeling of being Greek which found in language and classical culture its clearest means of articulation. The reasons behind this have to do with internal and external political relations, and will be explored in due course.

It has become axiomatic today to speak of the 'Graeco-Roman world' and to assume that the High Roman Empire was an age of more or less unitary politics and culture. There are certainly very many parallels of form and content between the two cultures throughout the period, allowing and encouraging interconnections. This is due to the Romans' successful and original employment of Greek cognitive and educational structures from Republican times onwards. But it was Romans who boasted of being 'utraque lingua doctus', not Greeks. So far as the Greeks of our period were con-cerned, there was indeed just one culture: that culture was Greek and Greek only. They were more than happy if others took their culture on board. At the same time there is no doubt that its im-portance lay primarily in constructing their own identity without regard to others.[10] It must be asked, though, who these Greeks were? There are no hard and fast rules to set out in answer. I shall return to the matter again, but some points may be made now. The ancient Greeks were never organized in a 'nation'. Patriotism was restricted for most of the time to politically separate and often mutually hostile city-states (*poleis*). The very wide spread of these cities in the Hellenistic period following the conquests of Alexander

---

[10] Cf. Dihle 1994: 45–6, on the absence of 'Graeco-Latin bilingualism' in the eastern half of the Empire (though Dihle's own use of 'Graeco-Roman' tends to follow a traditional perspective, as the structuring of his great literary survey by emperors' reigns suggests). On the relationship between the two languages see fur-ther 'Language' nn. 59–68.

the Great, together with the obvious degree of intermarriage between imported and indigenous populations (following a pattern set much earlier in the Aegean itself and in the western mediterranean Greek colonies), makes a cultural definition of Greeks, involving especially the employment of Greek as a first language, far more acceptable to us than a racial definition. However, as we shall see, there were many in our period not only in Old Greece and Asia Minor, but in Egypt, Cyrenaica, and elsewhere, who held themselves to be descendants of Greeks. Whether they were or not is irrelevant. The numerous examples of cities trying to pass themselves off as ancient Greek foundations from the historical or mythological eras show well enough the importance of 'blood' (biological or imaginary) and the political value of claiming such an ancestry. How many of the inhabitants of these cities, yet alone others, *felt* Greek is not answerable for understandable reasons of lack of evidence, and also because this type of question is too closely bound up with the modern idea of nationality, which is inapplicable to the ancient Greek world.

The importance of claiming Greek descent is one reason why I have largely avoided using the fashionable word 'ethnicity' and its cognates (which come too close to abolishing the imaginary biology the Greeks held dear). Another is that ethnicity is in fact a term whose meaning no one (including cultural anthropologists) can properly agree on and which in technical and general usage is often practically restricted in application to non-western minorities (who may indeed be non-white immigrants to western countries). In British English at any rate it is not an expression of how people see themselves, whereas most or perhaps all can talk of their (cultural or national) identity.[11] Naturally, 'identity', a term drawn from psychology, has much in common with 'ethnicity' and all other classifying terminology; its advantage to me—apart from the fact that it is in general use—lies in 'its primary emphasis on perception of the self',[12] since it is precisely the *consciousness* of being Greek that I wish to emphasize. As important is the fact that my main

---

[11] Cf. Tonkin *et al.* 1989: 11–20 (with literature), on the development of 'ethnicity' in the aftermath of the Nazi era, its continuing affinity with the discredited 'race', and its marginalizing character. I have used 'ethnic' and 'ethnocentric' once or twice in colonialist, segregatory contexts.

[12] Epstein 1978: p. xii (Epstein employs both 'identity' and 'ethnic identity' in these studies).

interest is in the Greek elite and its members' collective identity as Greeks. It would certainly be odd to construe *their* consciousness as a matter of ethnicity rather than cultural-political identity, even if one thought it obligatory or possible to use this sort of terminology about the Greeks in general.[13]

One more point: the matter of who was Greek is additionally complicated by the fact that many modern languages, including English, habitually follow the Romans in discarding the word the Greeks used of themselves, 'Hellenes'. In a very real way we too condemn the ancient (and modern) Greeks to be seen through western eyes by refusing them their own name.[14] Since 'Greek' and 'Greece' are nevertheless the proper English language equivalents of *Hellēn*, *Hellēnikos*, and *Hellas*, I have used them in preference to 'Hellene' etc. in general description, retaining the latter terms in more culturally significant contexts (e.g. in opposition to 'barbarian', or in the word 'Hellenism').

It is with all these thoughts in mind that in the second part of the book I shall be studying attitudes towards Rome displayed by the leading intellectuals of the second sophistic from Plutarch and Dio of Prusa to Philostratus and Cassius Dio. This is not simply an examination of the relation between Greek culture and Roman power. Some general remarks about this will be made in the first part of the book. Rather, the aim of this second part is to concretize our understanding of the relationship by looking at authors whose social, cultural, and political identities are reasonably well known, who discuss Greek and Roman relations generally or from a personal viewpoint, and whose feelings can be gauged from the large amount of material left to us in their works. There are naturally omissions (and perhaps inclusions) which will annoy or surprise some readers. There is no discussion of Athenaeus and only briefer treatments of Arrian, Appian (who will be taken together with Arrian), and Cassius Dio. The reason for this is simply that these

---

[13] This to my mind is a problem in e.g. Smith 1986, who imports from French the idea of the *ethnie* to characterize pre-modern groups, including the Greeks, as forerunners of modern nations: too often this *ethnie* looks like an elite affair only. It is of course quite possible for a ruling group to possess an ethnic/racial identity that is different from that of their subjects—cf. e.g. Greeks in Egypt or Syria; tension of this sort is not of much interest to me here (though cf. 'Novel' nn. 54–60), and I assume—which is all one can do—that the elite in the Greek city did not think it was any more 'Greek' in descent than those it governed (cf. 'Past', text before n. 62).

[14] Cf. 'Past' n. 35.

authors do not have much to say about the relationship *between* Greece and Rome (despite, in varying degrees, their obvious interest in Rome itself). Epictetus is omitted for a similar reason, as is Maximus of Tyre. The main authors considered are Plutarch, Dio of Prusa, Aelius Aristides, Lucian, Pausanias, Galen, and Philostratus. They have much to say about Rome and, importantly, their comments are very often embedded in a Greek context. These authors were largely concerned with matters Greek, of both past and present, and the bulk of their writings was about the Greek world and its culture. That is why they are so valuable for interpreting Greek views of Rome, not only in terms of how the Greek inheritance fared under Roman power, but also in particular for their attitudes towards contemporary politics and society.

I am well aware that recovering the personal views of (ancient) authors is a hazardous operation. The project concerns opinions, which are variable and mutable, both in expression and in interpretation. It will no doubt be felt by some that the search for such opinions is futile. If all statements are reducible to 'rhetoric', we cannot even begin to find the 'true' view the Greek elite held about Rome, for all their works are 'open' and 'intertextual'—thus there is no author as such—and all views they contain are relative—thus (e.g.) Plutarch's view of Rome, if recoverable, is not worth having (nor is that of anyone else). This objection would certainly be voiced by some members of the literary academy who are interested in the narratological reading of literary texts, that is, in the deployment of structuralist techniques of analysis to writing. Another objection would appeal to some ancient historians. It will be said that we can examine gravestones and honorary inscriptions, or wine bottles and die-stamps safely because they supply objective and disinterested 'data' that cannot be extracted from literary texts; hence there is no point in studying the latter.

Views like these are neither completely silly, nor absolutely valid. 'Objective' sources of information (to take this first) are very rarely just that: they too often serve particular social, economic, or cultural demands (in expression *and* in interpretation). The supposition that disinterested history can be written from them is really dubious, and the notion that epigraphic texts in particular contain unbiased information accumulated for historians' usage would be merely surprising, if it were not so widely credited. For statements (of whatever form) made in the public domain are as dangerous for us as those in literary texts—and possibly more so, because (as I shall have occasion to remark again) we generally have fewer controls over their intellectual provenance or context.

It may well be that narratological demands have contributed to some historians' suspicions of literary evidence, whether consciously or unconsciously. For Greek historians of the archaic and classical periods literary texts must have a paramount status. These historians have to rely on their Herodotus and Thucydides to a degree many Roman historians would find quite embarrassing. For the latter the greater possibility of making epigraphical, numismatic, or archaeological enquiry, together with the availability of other non-literary 'documentary' evidence like Justinian's *Digest*, has led not only to more independence from literary texts but to a downgrading of these as sources of information. This is wrong. It is certainly important to acknowledge that much modernist literary work is genuinely progressive. No one would want to go back to the state of affairs where literary texts were only read 'literally'. On the other hand, it is as well to be aware of the implications and limits of the newer literary school and not to become unduly concerned by its theses. It is of course legitimate to read texts as a closed system abstracted from the real world.[15] But that is not the only licit approach. Neither historians nor literary scholars need in fact be afraid of recognizing that the views of ancient authors exist (not just those of modern readers), nor should they be shy of trying to isolate them, even if it is impossible to be definite, and to use them to illuminate the societies they came from. The approach I have adopted in such matters is, where possible, to remain sensitive to the context both of the text and of the historical background (so far as we can discern it), and ultimately to allow myself occasionally the privilege of belief.[16]

---

[15] Which is only one of many ways in which 'modern' literary analysts bear a remarkable resemblance to the traditional critics they so deplore.

[16] I shall return to some of these points in the Conclusion. Two important studies of the second sophistic which have appeared since this book was written may be mentioned here: Gleason 1995 and esp. Schmitz 1997.

PART ONE

Greeks

I

Language and Identity

In this first chapter I want to examine the language consciousness
of the Greek elite in the second sophistic period, concentrating on
the phenomenon of atticism, its causes, and its meaning. In the next
chapter I shall be considering how various individuals encouraged
or responded to the pressures of language purism. Here I shall be
concerned with the political and social meaning of atticism in general terms. The search for this will involve looking at the development of the so-called *koine* or 'common' language in the Hellenistic
age, at the stylistic classicism and atticism championed by Dionysius
of Halicarnassus in Augustan Rome, and at the later combination
of this stylistic atticism with the linguistic purism and formalism of
the second sophistic. Changes in the Greek language, the political
situation of the Greek elite under the High Empire, and the question of their reaction to Rome are other topics to be considered.

THE ORIGINS OF PURISM

Language is one of the most important areas in which cultural groups
may adopt definitions for themselves and/or against others. The
Greeks had always been highly conscious of their language and the
distinctiveness it granted them from non-Greeks whom they called
barbaroi. This onomatopoeic term originally signified those whose
language was not Greek (cf. 'barbarophone' at *Iliad* ii. 867), but
because of the importance of language in defining cultural behaviour it quickly became (and remained) an evaluative description of
non-Hellenic behaviour and attitudes.[1] The special place of language in Greek self-definition in the archaic and classical periods is

---

[1] See e.g. Jüthner 1923; Toynbee 1969; Dubuisson 1982*a*; Hall 1989: 3 ff. following Baslez 1984: 183–201; *RAC* Suppl. I.5/6 (1992), 811–95 (Speyer and Opelt); ib.
895 ff. (Schneider).

signalled by the fact that, while the Greeks of this time borrowed
extensively from the older cultures of Egypt and the Near East in
the sciences and arts, even recognizing the technical apparatus of
the alphabet as a Phoenician import, in the one area of language
they were remarkably exclusive. This is the more striking given
Greek's prehistorical assimilation of a significant amount of non-
Indo-European vocabulary—something which occurred again much
later in the medieval period—and, of course, its own great internal
variation as we see it in the dialects of archaic and classical times.[2]

Dialectal variation did not remain important for long. For a new
common Greek arose that largely displaced the old dialects. This
new form was a development of the Attic dialect and was of the
greatest importance for general spoken and written Greek over the
next millennium and thereafter. Language purism in the second
sophistic is certainly in part a reaction against it. To explain the
origin of this common Greek we must look to the period of Athens' political influence over the Ionian Greeks in the Aegean islands
and the littoral of Asia Minor in the fifth and fourth centuries BC.[3]
For it seems that at this time there was a linguistic exchange between Attic and its closely allied Ionic sister-dialect. Apart from
population movements and general contacts Ionic Greek's possession of an old and varied prestige literature in the arts and sciences
must have been a factor in its influence over Attic. The result of this
exchange was that certain peculiarities of Attic were suppressed
where the corresponding features of Ionic were common to other
dialects. There was an acccompanying redistribution of vocabulary.
It is also noteworthy that Athens officially adopted the Ionic alphabet at the end of the fifth century, recognizing a trend already
apparent in private inscriptions. Literary Attic continued to reproduce the distinctive sounds of pure Attic—though even here there
was a good deal of contamination and an avoidance of archaic features. But it is reasonable to believe that in the spoken language
Ionic forms were admitted to a far greater extent. The pedigree and
diffusion of this Attic-Ionic were such that, when Alexander the
Great gave Greeks control over the domain of the Persian empire
at the end of the fourth century, it was this Greek that necessarily
emerged as the general language of communication and civilization

[2] Meillet 1935, Palmer 1980 (including Linear B) offer good general surveys.
[3] For this picture see López Eire 1981.

in the new Greek East (where it displaced Aramaic) and throughout the old Greek world. This *koine* ('common' sc. dialect), as it is
known, endured throughout antiquity to serve eventually as the
basis of the demotic forms of modern Greek.

The term *koine* is used nowadays in a variety of meanings. For
the Hellenistic period it describes both literary and non-literary
prose (the language of Polybius, of inscriptions, etc.). Its application to Greek under the Roman empire is even more confusing.
Here *koine* can refer to anything that is not in atticizing Greek—
that is, not in a Greek which imitates the Attic literary standard of
the classical age—and is therefore non-belletristic, whatever its
quality; it does not matter whether it comes from an educated (e.g.
Galen) or a non-educated pen (e.g. the Gospels). The term is, then,
a handy but unsatisfactory and idealized shorthand for several complex linguistic situations in which the actual language to be attributed to any individual at a particular time depends on various
diachronic, social, local, and cultural determinants.[4] In antiquity
itself '*koine*' often in fact indicated the ideal language of the educated class. It is used in this sense by, among others, the grammarians, for whom it is the equivalent of what they also call *sunêtheia*,
'general usage', again an abstracted ideal to which elite usage came
closest.[5] But in the second sophistic period, when the literary language of the elite turned away from the written *koine* of authors
like Polybius and Strabo towards linguistic and stylistic imitation
of the writers of classical Athens, *koine* Greek became for many a
sign of intellectual inadequacy. The *koine* was now deemed unsuitable for literary creation, and the word became a derogatory label
for language situated anywhere between the Hellenistic literary
standard (which remained, however, the main province of research
by grammarians like Apollonius Dyscolus and his son Aelius
Herodian for whom Attic was a dialect) and the 'vulgar', spoken
language (without any real interest in what this was at any one time
or place).[6] Good writing now could only be in a language which
was at least classicizing and preferably atticizing in its vocabulary
and syntax. Of these terms 'atticism' and 'classicism', the first is
used by ancient Greek authors themselves, both for stylistic and

[4] Information on the range and diffusion of *koine* Greek can be extracted from
Bubeník 1989. See also now Brixhe and Hodot 1993 (and other essays in the same
volume), with recent bibliography.
[5] See Versteegh 1987: 256–64.   [6] Maidhof 1912; Versteegh 1987: 267.

linguistic purism. The second is another essentially modern word (derived from Latin).[7] It means the wider imitation of the culture and especially the literature of the classical period, including but not restricted to that of Athens. As we shall see, there was keen debate in our period about what classical models were suitable for imitation. The key point to remember is that Athens at all times remained the cynosure of Greek classicism. It was Athenian society and culture that led the way, and those who identified themselves most strongly with it set the pace and direction of second sophistic elite culture. In matters of language the particular prestige of Athens ensured that the main term in use for language purism had to be atticism.

The cultural roots of this movement lie in the calls to imitation (*mimêsis*) of the style of classical Athenian authors which were made at the end of the first century BC, especially by the critic and historian, Dionysius of Halicarnassus. This was the original meaning of the term *attikismos*,[8] and I shall return to Dionysius and his atticism (which also has a political side) below. In the second sophistic stylistic atticism was joined by a dominant grammatical and linguistic atticism (also called *attikismos*, or *attikisis*), which was an imperative to restrict vocabulary to the linguistic thesaurus of the Attic authors (including some of the poets). It is important to understand that the difference between educated *koine* and classicizing/atticizing Greek was at no time comparable with the difference between educated and non-educated Greek. We are really dealing with different degrees of a single linguistic continuum ranging between educated *koine* (the *sunêtheia* of the grammarians) and the ideal standard of fifth- and fourth-century BC literary Attic Greek upon which educated usage was always dependent, even in the Hellenistic period.[9] (The extent to which the non-educated language had broken away from this continuum in our period will be discussed below.) Those who called themselves 'atticists' (*attikistai*) were a group within this continuum which perceived itself as enjoying the greatest proxmity to classical Attic. This linguistic atticism was never a perfect copy of Attic Greek (which, of course, had its own internal variations). As we shall see, atticizing authors (including

[7] Cf. Gelzer 1979: 3–13.

[8] Dionysius of Halicarnassus, *On Imitation* fr. vi. v (ii. 211 Usener–Radermacher).

[9] On this idea cf. Versteegh 1987: 254–5. Palm's 1955 study of Diodorus gives a good idea of this educated *koine* (which he calls 'Normalprosa').

those studied in this book) incorporated many non-Attic features in their language. Further, atticizing Greek was not used at all times, but was rather a refinement of educated speech for certain sorts of prestige literary and speech occasions. All Greeks continued to use a *koine* (reflecting their class and education) in non-belletristic writing and, so far as we may surmise, in their conversation. Those like Plutarch and Galen who thought of themselves more as philosophers and thinkers than as littérateurs did not feel overly bound by the rules of the linguistic purists. If we prefer to call people like them classicists, we should not forget that they along with the rest felt the pull of stylistic and linguistic atticism.

The aim of *attikismos*, stylistic and linguistic, was to differentiate the leaders of Greek letters and speech from the broad mass of Greek speakers in order to signal clearly that they had command of the best sort of Greek. It was the expression of a certain sort of consciousness, a distinction to do with the maintenance of cultural superiority. It is closely connected in the second sophistic with classicism in architecture, political constitutions, even personal names, again focusing on but not restricted to Athens. The meaning of this wider engagement with the past will be studied later. The importance of atticism in language and literature is simply that language was the best way to reproduce the past in a culture that placed such enormous value on the classical heritage and on oral communication. It made the elite of the second sophistic the direct heirs in their very words of the leaders of free Greece and of the first city in free Greece. We shall see that the effect of having the right sort of language was as political as it has been in more recent times.

DIONYSIAN STYLISTICS

Before we can turn to the second sophistic itself we must pay attention to the stylistic evaluation of the classical Athenian authors by Dionysius of Halicarnassus and the rhetorical academy of his time, for this is where the atticism of the second sophistic takes its ultimate origin. This preference for an Attic style had little to do with the intensive study of the Athenian language that had been going on among grammarians since the third century BC. Research into the Attic dialect by men like Istros the Callimachean,

Eratosthenes, and Aristophanes of Byzantium in the mid-third century no doubt helped to entrench the lexical superiority of Attic.[10] But their work was apparently not concerned with recommending the imitation of Athenian authors by living orators. Consider their contemporary, the orator Hegesias: for the later atticists of the rhetorical school he was regarded as the arch-representative of the affected and corrupt style of oratory (which Romans, as we shall see, labelled 'Asiatic' or 'Asian'), the very antithesis of the purity and simplicity that were seen as the hallmarks of atticism; yet he apparently thought of himself as an imitator of Lysias who made the real Attic writers look 'practically rustic' in comparison.[11] Hegesias lived at a time when grammatical study did not really influence the schools of rhetoric. It was not until the second sophistic that grammatical atticism exerted any real influence on the world of Greek rhetoric. But at Rome—paradoxically—grammatical theories of language purity had a rather different history, and this must be explored before turning back to Greek developments, for Roman tastes clearly had some influence on the Greeks' new-found interest in the Athenian classics, which Dionysius discovered at the time of Augustus.

In the Greek educational system grammar and rhetoric, the preparatory and higher stages of elite education, were taught consecutively by different practitioners. At Rome, especially for Greek studies, it seems they were taught in tandem by the same man.[12] The result was that grammar assumed a greater place in rhetorical theory at Rome than it had ever had among the Greeks. In the Greek world the Stoics alone had developed grammar and rhetoric together, fusing the notion of *Hellênismos*—the concern to reproduce the 'good Greek' of canonical authors—with a technical theoretical grammar.[13] It is this combination that seems to have had an

---

[10] Dihle 1977: 167–8.

[11] See Dionysius of Halicarnassus, *On the Composition of Words* 18 (ii. 79 U.–R.); Cicero, *Brutus* 83. 286 for Hegesias' own view; and below, n. 19 on 'Asian'. Already in the 2nd c. BC Agatharchides was adversely contrasting the tasteless style of Hegesias' remarks on the destruction of Thebes and Olynthus with the soberer comments of the Athenian orators (Photius, *Library* cod. 250, 446a–447b; Norden 1909: i. 135–9 for analysis of the style)—but these remarks on the appropriate tone for reporting disasters are not comparable with the wide-ranging, conscious programme of Attic imitation established by Dionysius and his contemporaries.

[12] Dihle 1957: 178 ff. (summarized in id. 1994: 23).

[13] See Diogenes Laertius, *Lives of the Philosophers* vii. 42, 55 ff. on Diogenes of Babylon (first half of the 2nd c. BC).

initial influence at Rome. Diogenes of Babylon, who was especially concerned with the formulation of Stoic thought on language, became famous there for his part in the 'philosophers' embassy' of 156/155 BC. The older Roman purists in matters of language were in fact nearly all Stoics.[14] Since Romans lacked models in their own language, their grammatically-minded orators turned to purifying Latin through a rigorously 'analogical' approach to language (known as *proportio*), essentially the application of a grammatical straitjacket. That is another story.[15] Good models may not have been available for Roman orators in Latin: they were in Greek. The search for Greek models to imitate is indeed one of the most noticeable and productive features of Latin at this time. In rhetoric the Athenian masters were unavoidable. And from their favoured reading in Greek Roman orators particularly associated with the quest for a pure Latin came to dub themselves the 'Attici'.

Late first-century BC Rome was a centre for Greek intellectual activity. Since Dionysius of Halicarnassus and his friend Caecilius of Caleacte, the initiators of Greek stylistic atticism, were active at Rome, it is reasonable to assume that they were directed towards their exclusive stylistic recommendations of the Athenian orators by current Roman taste.[16] The matter is in fact more complex than it seems. Most of Caecilius' work has perished, but the titles and fragments left to us show that his concerns were much the same as those of Dionysius, of whose efforts much remains.[17] In addition to his well-known twenty-book account of early Roman history down to the First Punic War, Dionysius wrote a collection of important rhetorical studies.[18] In the introduction to his series of essays on six of the classical Athenian orators he attributes to 'the highly educated and noble' Roman elite responsibility for the revival of sober rhetorical taste, that is Attic taste, and for the abandonment of the debauched 'Asian' manner of speech (*On Ancient Orators* 2–3

---

[14] Dihle 1957: 179 ff.; Kennedy 1972: 62–3.

[15] Well told by Dihle 1977: 170 ff. suggesting the influence of Philoxenus.

[16] See e.g. Schmid 1887–97: i. 1–26; Kennedy 1972: 350 ff., 366 ff.; Tonnet 1988: i. 304–5, 313. 'Atticism' itself occurs in a letter of Cicero to Atticus (*To Atticus* iv. 19. 1; the word is in Greek), where Cicero refers to 'that Latin *attikismos*' of C. Vestorius; but this is no more than a humorous and punning reference to the supposed purity of Vestorius' Latin language, and has nothing to do with Greek stylistic or linguistic purism.

[17] Kennedy 1972: 366 ff.; *Suda* κ 1165; the fragments are edited by E. Ofenloch (1907).

[18] In general see Bonner 1939.

[i. 4–6 Usener–Radermacher]). The antithesis of 'Asian' and 'Attic' does indeed reflect a stylistic debate that was Roman, not Greek, in origin. The terms are opposed by Cicero and his contemporaries, as we see from Cicero's *Brutus* and *Orator*; whereas in the Greek rhetorical and grammatical tradition 'Asian', where used, indicated geographical origin and was not a mark of stylistic criticism. Nor in fact does 'Asian' have any importance to Dionysius as a stylistic marker outside this preface (where the statement that the danger has arrived only 'yesterday or the day before' from Mysia, Phrygia, or Caria and the reference to 'many fine treatises which show the hard work of both Romans and Greeks' is suggestive enough of the Roman influence at this point). For in reality these remarks are not much more than a nod in the direction of Roman friends and patrons.[19]

If we examine the matter more carefully, we can see that Dionysius did not need to define his own interests through those of the Roman 'Attici' of the previous generation.[20] Consider the matter of language. Greek grammatical exegesis of the Attic language clearly had some imput into the stylistic atticism that was now arising in Greek rhetorical studies; but, as has been said, it is not until the

---

[19] Mysia, Phrygia, or Caria: cf. Cicero, *Orator* 8. 25; 'treatises': *On Ancient Orators* 3 = i. 6. 5 U.–R. (for criticism of asianism—but not named as such—see e.g. *On the Composition of Words* 18 = ii. 79. 9 ff. U.–R., and here below); cf. Caecilius' *How the Attic Style Differs from the Asian* and *Against the Phrygians*.

For the Roman debate see Radermacher 1899 (positing a reaction against Greek ideas of style); Heck 1917; Gelzer 1979: esp. 13–19; Kennedy 1972: 241–2; Bowersock 1979: 59–65. It is picked up in Strabo's and Theon's remarks about Hegesias (*Geography* xiv. 1. 41 [C 648]; *Progymnasmata* ii. 71. 10 Sp.), and later in Plutarch's misguided comment that Mark Antony embraced asianism (*Antony* 2. 8).

On the Greek side, Schmid's premiss in *Der Atticismus* that Greek atticism was constantly battling against a rampant asianism always lacked evidence, as Wilamowitz 1900 demonstrated. This old debate about the contribution of 'Asian' and 'Attic' rhetoric to the second sophistic is summarized by Boulanger 1923: 58–69 and Desideri 1978: 524–36, and is explored in detail by Goudriaan 1989: 595–677, 735–7. As Pernot 1993: i. 379 n. 239 observes (in the course of an important discussion of types of stylistic effect or tone in second sophistic Greek that *we* may call 'Asian'), it was never legitimate to oppose atticism and asianism anyway, because 'l'asianisme est une esthétique' and not 'une langue et une culture' like atticism.

[20] Cf. Gabba 1991: 24–34. For a different, prosopographically reductionist view of the matter, see Bowersock 1979: 68–70. Dionysius and Caecilius were presumably aware of the imitators of Thucydides and Isocrates in the previous generation of *Greeks*, to whom Philodemus briefly refers (*On Rhetoric* 151. 19–22 Sudhaus); though there is, again, no reason to suppose direct influence from these on their own campaign; the same goes for the sort of intra-school imitation we see in the Platonic *spuria* (whenever these were actually written).

second sophistic that atticizing language purism and atticizing rhetorical style combined as a recognizable unit (which quite clearly
owed nothing then to any Roman influences). Thus Caecilius'
lexicon of 'elegant usage' (*kallirhêmosunê*) no doubt built on the
labours of the Hellenistic grammarians. But neither Caecilius (as
far as we can tell) nor Dionysius (as we can see) had any interest
in producing orators from first principles and abstract rules of language, as the Roman 'Attici' did. There was no 'grammaticalization'
of language yet. That language was not of the greatest importance
to Dionysius is a crucial difference between him and the Romans.
His mission was rather to guide speakers to imitate the real orators
of classical Athens by practical example. A crucial task here was the
formation of a canon of authors with a bibliography of genuine
writings. The work of the great Alexandrian scholars like Callimachus and of others in the Pergamene school was unsatisfactory
in this regard, as Dionysius observes in the only remaining work of
either man in this area, the *On Deinarchus* (1 = i. 297 U.-R.). Again,
the purist concerns of the Roman 'Attici' were never interested in
this sort of project—nor could they be. Hence we should not get
unduly excited about their influence on Dionysius' stylistic choices.

We would in fact do better to take note of Dionysius' political
motives in advocating pure style, where he again appeals to Roman
example, but for rather different reasons. In *On Ancient Orators*
he makes it plain that good Attic style—the 'Attic Muse'—was
'ancient and indigenous' to very many cities (i.e. Greek cities),[21]
although it appeared to have been disenfranchised after Alexander
by a style of oratory that was devoid of philosophical content and
pandered to 'the mobs' (1 = i. 3–4 U.-R.). The revival of Attic was,
says Dionysius, due to 'time', that is, to the plans of some god or
to the natural, cyclical order of things, or to human endeavour
(2, 4 = i. 4. 20 ff., 6. 13 ff. U.-R.). It was Rome's role to be the particular 'cause and origin of such a change' by showing through the
example of her own excellent taste—which her empire made influential—that Attic style was proper to a properly run city. The explicit
political slant is striking. Dionyius crows that 'that mad style of
rhetoric' has now been totally marginalized (3 = i. 6. 14 ff. U.-R.).
His invocation of Rome here is certainly as a conservative member
of the Greek elite who well understood the political benefits the

[21] Cf. Gelzer 1979: 33.

Empire accorded his class; but there is one important difference from the usual picture. In his *History of Early Rome* Dionysius spent a great deal of time proving to his own satisfaction that Rome was actually a Greek city in almost all respects (both by race and by conduct). In the *History* Rome (and not simply early Rome) achieves the status of an archetypal Greek city constructed according to the conservative views of the fourth-century Athenian orator Isocrates, whose beliefs Dionysius held dear.[22] When Dionysius focuses in *On Ancient Orators* on the contravention of such politics by the 'Asian' style of oratory, we are dealing with a matter of personal political concern to him, not one he has inherited from the Roman 'Attici'. Rome's political preferences for 'the sensible' over 'the unintelligent' combine with her encouragement of Attic good taste to exemplify the proper purpose of civic oratory (3 = i. 5. 26 U.–R.). In sum Dionysius' interest lay in these alignments of rhetoric and politics and not in Roman culture, except in so far as the best Greek culture was appropriate to the ideal Greek city.

Dionysius' idea of rhetoric as the key instrument of political government—both in the technical-administrative sense and in the ideological one—is hardly new. We observe, though, that the notion of correct political control through correct rhetoric is now more conscious, more closely defined, and this seems to bear out Dionysius' claims to originality in the matter. The parallel between his encouragement of the revived 'philosophic' rhetoric on the pure Attic model and Isocrates' own moral crusade to bring back the pure Athens of Solon and Cleisthenes is clear enough, for example, from his essay on Isocrates which offers ringing applause of his hero's conservative political credos (*Isocrates* 5–9 = i. 61–71 U.–R.). When Dionysius asks, 'Who would not become a patriot and a supporter of the democracy [as presented by Isocrates] . . . after reading his *Panegyricus*?', we see a combination of Hellenism and conservatism (referred to, as often, as 'democracy') that finds much common ground within the second sophistic.[23] Dionysius was

[22] Greek origin: *History* i. 5. 1, 89. 1–2, 90. 1. Dionysius is particularly resourceful in asserting that the Trojan element in Rome's make-up (i. 45. 1–60. 3) was also Greek, and specifically Peloponnesian and Attic, in origin (i. 61. 1–62. 2 naming Phanodemus, *FGrH* 325 F13; see Jacoby in *FGrH* IIIb [Suppl.] i. 186 citing Strabo xiii. 1. 48 [C 604]). The construction of Rome along these lines is now fully examined in Gabba 1991; it is worth noting that Dionysius was presenting this idea primarily to a Greek audience (Gabba: 80 on ii. 63. 1 and xvi. 4. 1).

[23] *Isocrates* 5 (i. 61. 10 U.–R.) τίς γὰρ οὐκ ἂν γένοιτο φιλόπολίς τε καὶ φιλόδημος, κτλ;

interested in recreating an image of the past according to a particular elite viewpoint and in applying this in the present. Actual past
events are not especially important. So, when he expresses regret
that we cannot fully appreciate the wonders of Demosthenes' Greek
'because we have no feelings about the events', whereas the Athenians and other Greeks were being addressed 'on real issues of
relevance to them' (*Demosthenes* 22 = i. 177. 8–9 U.-R.), his regret
is tempered by an optimism that the spirit of Demosthenes or
Isocrates can be revived today by imitating the style of their works.
That is what he is encouraging us—the Greek elite—to do.

THE RISE OF THE PURISTS

In the second sophistic the style of Demosthenes and the political
views of Isocrates (allied to those of Plato) are still the preferred
options, and 'democracy' the name often given to an undemocratic
system of government. What particularly distinguishes this later
period from the time of Dionysius is that to the existing concern
with the style of speech there was joined an obsession among the
elite with the language of speech. Classicism was now fundamental
in constituting the elite's identity, as it had not been before, and
language was quite literally the clearest way of expressing this.
Dionysius himself did atticize in language in some key areas (for
example in his greater use of the optative, a hallmark of atticism),
but overall his work contains many examples of 'Hellenistic' usages
(i.e. vocabulary and syntactical formations not found in the Attic
authors).[24] The high point of the atticizing movement did not arrive
until the second and third centuries. This concern with language
did not, of course, happen overnight. The linguistic features which
mark a text as atticist are found already (in lesser numbers) in
Plutarch and (to a greater extent) in Dio of Prusa, and so we are
dealing with a progressive development from the age of Dionysius
and Caecilius.[25] Literary and stylistic reasons can certainly help to

[24] See Lasserre 1979: 144–7 (with literature), 155, 157; cf. Palm 1955: 201–2.
[25] Dio: Schmid 1887–1897: i. 72–191. Plutarch: id. iv. 635–85 (an extensive discussion of atticist vocabulary taking Plutarch as a reference point); Weissenberger 1895:
3–37; Ziegler 1951: 931–2 on Plutarch's atticism, 932–5 on his rigorous avoidance of
hiatus; cf. 'Plutarch' n. 8. Note that Schmid himself considered Herodes Atticus the
first fully atticist author (i. 192–215).

explain the rise of the atticizing movement; but social-linguistic and political causes also suggest themselves. Galen for example testifies to the pressure to atticize that was felt by those who 'happen simply to be either rich or just well-off'.[26] One thing we can be sure of: Rome was not a source of inspiration; but she may well have been a source of reaction, as we shall see. The second sophistic was centred in the Greek East and, though Romans supported atticizing tastes in Greek language and literature, no influence is attributed to them by Greeks—as indeed we should expect in a movement so conscious of its Greekness.

Literary and stylistic motives behind linguistic atticism are obvious. Once Attic style had been established, the textual power supporting it struck alternatives dead. No one was seriously going to imitate Polybius, however highly his historical worth was valued, when they had Xenophon and Lysias to follow. Given this, sooner or later the relationship between educated *koine* and the Greek of the canonical models would no doubt anyway have become closer. But second sophistic atticism amounts to something greater than a natural progression. It is terribly self-conscious and aware of the superiority it enjoyed through its nearness to the classics. Dionysius makes it plain enough that the attractions of good reading were not the main reason for imitation of Attic literature. Indeed, when we see that knowledge of a certain type of literature is confined to a narrow section of society and that this class holds economic and political power, the innocent comforts of good literature can only be seen as part of the reason. Fashion, taste, and pleasure are always relevant in assessing attitudes to literature. They must not be forgotten. But the Attic texts were studied particularly as texts to compose from, as the rhetorical handbooks state.[27] What one has read and what one can oneself write say a lot about one's position in the world. In the second sophistic we see not the discovery of this commonsensical observation, but its intensified employment.

---

[26] *On the Order of his Own Books* xix. 60. 20–21; below, 'Practice' nn. 59, 64.

[27] The chief of these in the second sophistic period are the *Progymnasmata* (i.e. the basic rhetorical exercises) of Aelius Theon (i AD) and Ps.-Hermogenes (? ii); various works of Hermogenes himself (ii); Ps.-Aristides *Rhetoric* (? ii); the *Anonymus Seguierianus* (? ii–iii); Apsines, *Art of Rhetoric* (iii); the two works on epideictic attributed to Menander (iii); Ps.-Longinus, *Art of Rhetoric* (iii). Even a work of criticism which comes close to a modern outlook, the Ps.-Longinus, *On the Sublime* (written some time in i), is aimed at 'political men' (1. 2). See Kennedy 1972: 614–41, Russell 1964, esp. id. 1983, Pernot 1993: esp. ii. 800–11 for editions and discussion.

Language was taken up as the badge of the elite because it particularly showed the possession of wealth and leisure by taking the classics as its point of reference. Mastering Attic Greek must have been always a matter of much greater effort than was required for reading. Thus, whether composition was for political or literary reasons, the language used and the stylistic imitation involved were statements of differentiation from the mass of the population and from anyone else not skilled in their employment.

The urge to be different must, then, be explained against more concrete factors than the pleasure of the text. One of these factors relates to real changes in the Greek language at this time. As has been said, rather than classifying the Greek of certain texts of the Hellenistic and imperial periods as *koine* and assuming that this has no relationship with Attic, even if it is from an educated pen, it is far more accurate to locate most written texts within a single linguistic continuum whose high point is the fossilized Attic of 'the books' (as the rhetoricians called the classics). In certain usages and contexts approximation to the high form was not required or desirable. We might term writing in this sort of language 'non-belletristic' or 'non-literary', meaning that such texts originate in written or spoken environments that do not possess the generic machinery or internal stability to produce Greek very close to the Attic standard. They are, nevertheless, still in a relationship with it. We see the non-belletristic standard most clearly in our period in the lectures of Epictetus and in the (more artistic) *Meditations* of Marcus Aurelius. Both texts are the products of highly educated and intelligent men; but close imitation of Attic was not required because the authors spoke or wrote in a philosophical context without thought of publication. This is perfectly clear with Epictetus' *Discourses*, which were in fact written up by Flavius Arrian, for Arrian employs a consistently atticizing Greek in his own works.[28] Galen's many writings in what he calls 'the common dialect' are another excellent example of non-atticizing but highly educated Greek. His subject matter did not 'generate' atticism (though this

---

[28] Epictetus: Melcher 1906. Marcus: Ghedini 1926, Zilliacus 1936.

It might seem paradoxical to cite Marcus, a Roman. But it was of course possible for Romans—or anyone else—to atticize (see below, 'Practice' nn. 4–10, 11–31, 'Past' n. 49, on Favorinus, Lucian, Claudius Aelian; Antoninus Liberalis, the author of a short collection of metamorphoses, may be another Roman example). As it happens, Marcus' Greek is a good example of the normal educated standard.

did not keep him from worrying on the matter).[29] A much 'lower'
form of Greek can be seen in early Christian texts like the Gospels
and the *Didache* and of course in voluminous numbers of papyri
from Graeco-Roman Egypt. In many of these we are on the bor-
derline between texts that have some claim on education and those
that have none. Such texts offer a clue to the rise of linguistic atticism, for they reflect the fact that the contemporary language of the
economically unprivileged groups to which their authors and
audiences were close was unstable and prone to phonological, morphological, and syntactical change, since it was less securely pegged
to a recognized (but irrelevant) standard. For reasons which can
only be guessed at—for example, the social diffusion of Hellenism,
increasing contact with other languages in the Empire—the pace of
change in the living Greek language accelerated after the first century AD. The end result was the modern demotic tongue, which was
formed essentially by the eighth or ninth century (though not used
in literature for many centuries after that). It was contact with the
changing Greek of the non-educated mass that educated Greek
wanted to avoid. Those with the competence to atticize, i.e. to write
in the 'high' literary language, had a particular interest in so doing.

It is worth reminding ourselves of the scale of these changes in
the living language. By the first/second century AD, if not before,
the vowel system of ancient Greek had lost all quantitative distinction. Most diphthongs had disappeared. These changes are probably connected with the important shift from a pitch to a stress
accent that affected all forms of Greek and was complete by the
fourth century AD.[30] The consonant system was also undergoing
alteration in the first few centuries. Here the pace of change is less
clear. On evidence from texts in the Jewish catacombs at Rome and
other items the major development of the aspirated voiceless plosives ϕ, θ, χ to the fricatives of the present day (in phonetic terms
$[p^h] > [f]$; $[t^h] > [\theta]$; $[k^h] > [\chi]$) can be placed in the first to third
century with $[p^h]$ leading the way, and though good evidence from

---

[29] 'Common dialect'—e.g. *On the Differences of the Pulse*, viii. 584. 18; see below,
'Practice' nn. 55–69. The 'remarkably unpolished' *koine* of Vettius Valens' *Anthology* of astrology (Dihle 1994: 289), written between 152 and 162, is another good
example of 'generic' restrictions, here with a less accomplished result.

[30] Allen 1968: 89, 119; id. 1973: 268; Gignac 1976: 325. Teodorsson 1974 argues
that quantitative distinction in the Attic dialect was eradicated as early as 350 BC—
but see Threatte 1980: 385–7 who concludes that the change is unmistakable in
Attica only from 100 AD.

Egypt of continuing confusion between the aspirated voiceless plosives and voiceless plosives ([pʰ] vs. [p], etc.) is counter-proof for
the early Roman period there, it is clear from Latin borrowings of
Greek words that φ had generally acquired a fricative value before
the end of the second century. The voiced plosives β, δ, γ were also
acquiring a fricative pronunciation ([b] > [v], [d] > [ð], [g] > [ɣ]).
These changes do not seem as early, except for [b] > [v] (on good
Egyptian and Latin evidence).[31] Morphological and syntactical
changes are most visible in the abandonment of the dual in nouns
and verbs, the gradual loss of the dative in nouns, and the optative
in verbs. The last change and the expansion of the subjunctive made
the complex modal sentences of classical Greek impossible to reproduce.[32] Changes in pronunciation and stress must have affected
all (though there is a little evidence to suggest that a 'scholarly'
pronunciation of the old aspirates continued in the schools).[33]
Morphological and syntactical change clearly developed first among
those with no call on the educational system. It is impossible to
date it with accuracy because texts which show, for example, the
loss of the dative may really reveal the loss not of the dative itself—
which has already disappeared—but the loss of the writer's ability
to link up with the high standard.

That the Greek of the educated class was endangered by such
changes is shown well enough by what did happen eventually to
the language of all classes. In our period careful study and reproduction of literary-educative texts helped to preserve the speech of
the elite. The imperative to imitate was one thing; to understand
how to do so successfully another that must have demanded increasing amounts of instruction. It was no doubt at least partly as
a response to this need that grammatical studies became influential
in rhetoric. The two dovetailed neatly because Attic Greek, as has
been observed, had long been the focus of the grammarian. Presumably both technical grammar (the detailed analytical study of
language that probably began in the late first century BC) and the

[31] Leon 1927: 210 ff., 227; Allen 1968: 21–4 (aspirates), 28–30 (voiced plosives);
Gignac 1976: 68 (β), 71 (γ), 75 (δ), 100 (aspirated plosives); Biville 1990: 189 ff. on
Latin evidence for the fricative value of φ, 283 ff. on γ and β. Threatte 1980: 469–70
suggests that in Attica the aspirated plosives kept their original values until quite late
in the Roman period.
[32] On this and other features of the non-belletristic *koine* see Meillet 1935: 267–
89; Costas 1936: 58–71; Radermacher 1947: 23 ff.; Browning 1983a: 29–43.
[33] Allen 1968: 22–3.

older Alexandrian tradition of critical exegesis played a part in preserving language confidence and purity, as we see in the grammar attributed to Dionysius Thrax.[34] The input of grammatical systematics into the atticizing movement itself is most noticeable in the many lexicons of Attic usage that were written in our period.[35] The aims, contents, and contexts of these works naturally differ. Some prescribe the right sort of vocabulary and (to a lesser extent) correct syntax, others are mainly proscriptive and negative in outlook. It is in the way of texts like these to reduce a complex linguistic situation (where varying shades of literary and non-literary Greek coexist) to a simple binary antithesis between right 'Attic' and wrong non-'Attic' usage. With the probable exception of Moeris, who seems to have some slight idea of a greater diversity (and to whom I shall return), the lexicographers, like the grammarians themselves, were not at all interested in popular, 'uneducated' speech. Their aim was to make the language of an already highly literate class more exclusive, and perhaps to enable and encourage others to join this class (for the possibility of recruitment is important to any elite). Rhetorico-grammatical theory was not interested in telling the elite how to talk to their slaves or to do their accounts. Its concern was with speech and writing within its own jurisdiction (as it were) over higher culture. It addressed itself to the twin problems of selecting correct variants from the expected language competence (i.e. the

[34] Dionysius Thrax: below, n. 60. As a superb example of technical grammar note the *Catholic Prosody* of Aelius Herodian (known as ὁ τεχνικός), a work presented to Marcus Aurelius which gave rules for accentuating no less than 60,000 words, which task its author hails as 'the conclusion of almost the whole of grammatical method' (i, p. 6. 1–2, 7. 19 Lentz). On the importance of this work in preserving understanding of the pitch system of accentuation, cf. Dihle 1994: 252. The 48 books *On Metres* by the Alexandrian grammarian Hephaestion (probably also connected with the Antonine royal family: *Augustan History, Verus* 2. 5), which was the culmination of centuries of research on classical verse forms, and which survives in the author's one-book epitome (ed. Consbruch), partly fulfilled a similar need arising from the disappearance of vowel quantity. Cf. also Kaster 1988 on the role of the grammarian in the Latin language in late antiquity (though this is for the most part a prosopographical account).

[35] Surviving in part or as a whole are works by Ammonius, Aelius Dionysius, Pausanias, Phrynichus, Pollux, Moeris, Ps.-Herodian *Philetaerus*, and the so-called *Antiatticist*; there were many others now and later including specialist works on particular authors (e.g. Apollonius' *Homeric Lexicon* [AD i] or Timaeus Sophistes' *Platonic Lexicon* [AD i/iv]). A brief survey of the lexicons can be found in Serrano Aybar 1977: esp. 93–8; for editions and discussion see e.g. Latte 1915, Erbse 1949, Argyle 1989, and below, 'Practice' nn. 35–54.

total language knowledge) of the educated and of identifying the occasions when such variants should be used.[36]

The conscious linguistic distinctiveness of atticism certainly has a political aspect. Since the possession of classical texts was necessarily restricted more and more to those who had the resources to learn how to read them, classical culture and the possession of the Greek heritage became an elite preserve and increasingly so as the Greek of the uneducated changed further. The statements of Dionysius about the utility of atticist culture for *politikoi*, a term which effectively means the members of the ruling section of society, are clear. They represent assumptions repeated by very many second sophistic texts. An 'educational divide' is familiar in all societies. It was certainly at work in classical Greece, even in the Athenian democracy. But in the second sophistic the gap between the educated and the non-educated is far more explicit than before. Those with education now label themselves 'the educated'/'the cultured' (*hoi pepaideumenoi*), or regularly use other words (rhetors, sophists, philosophers, *philologoi*) to show they are superiors in culture. The last term, meaning 'lovers of language and literature' (though it is not restricted to these areas), is particularly revealing. It is essentially a claim to amateurism like that made by the English eighteenth-century figure of the Critic and signals the casual, polymorphous expertise of men to whom no sector of cultural life is foreign.[37] Here, then, we are concerned with internal Greek social stratification and with a restrictive education system which furthered the result of other social divisions.

It is as well to be sure where the atticizing movement itself stood in this system. An earlier and quite influential view held that atticists formed a sectarian movement which appealed to only a few Greeks capable of understanding them and particularly to the more educated

[36] Cf. Frösén 1974: 12–14 (noting, however, that the lexicons do not suggest which language should be used in which language situations; this is the job—amongst other things—of the handbooks).

[37] On *paideia* as an index of superiority in epigraphy see Panagopoulos 1977: 226–30; Frézouls 1991: 144–5. For the *philologos* see Kuch 1965: 79–115 (and on the Critic Eagleton 1984: 22, whose words I borrow).

Romans. They were totally at variance with contemporary spoken language.[38] This is an extreme assessment. Since atticizing Greek was simply an extension of its users' own spoken language, anyone with some claim on the educated standard would have been able to follow atticizing language to some extent, and this is consistent with the atticist authors' expressed concern to have large audiences, which they claim were not always made up of *pepaideumenoi*.[39] It has also been argued—on the basis of particular syntactical constructions, especially usage of the optative mood in conditional clauses—that the atticists positively embraced the 'vernacular'.[40] This is quite wrong. If the atticists departed from genuine Attic usage in the optative—as they did—it is because perfect reproduction of Attic Greek was never part of their agenda. They were hunting after an ideal, a mirage, and so long as they believed their language was Attic, that was enough. When we find similar 'incorrect' optative forms in non-literary texts, all we see is atticizing grammatical theory exercising its influence in the 'vernacular' language recorded in writing.[41] It is quite clear that the classical optative had in fact largely disappeared in all its functions from the spoken language. This is reflected in writings like the Gospels which were not concerned to approximate to the Attic standard. By contrast the optative was reintroduced (in all its classical functions) by the atticists for its value in achieving the much sought-after 'Attic' literary quality of 'simplicity'.[42] Atticizing Greek was about the repristination of linguistic features, phonological, morphological, or syntactical, that

[38] Schmid 1887–97: i. 21–6.

[39] Cf. Dio of Prusa, *Or.* xii. 84; Aristides, *Orr.* xxxiv. 37–47, li. 29–34; Lucian, *Apology* 3; Philostratus, *VS* 619, 627.

[40] Higgins 1945 (focusing especially on the non-Attic patterning εἰ + optative + indicative); Higgins was vigorously opposed by Anlauf 1960. For a fair summary of their arguments see Reardon 1971: 80–96; a not unjustified criticism of their methodologies is offered by Frösén 1974: 95 ff. (Frösén's own self-consciously methodological investigation has a large bibliography relevant to this and other problems.)

[41] Cf. Tonnet 1988: i. 312 ('préjugés linguistiques dont l'école était responsable').

[42] See Ps.-Aristides, *Rhetoric* §106 (114 Schmid), a 2nd-c. text (cf. Schmid 1917–18: 244, identifying as author the Zeno known from *Suda* ζ 81) which takes Xenophon as its model; cf. Lesbonax the grammarian on optatives in final clauses (absent in Arrian, *Discourses of Epictetus* [iii. 1. 37 is corrupt] and the New Testament) as 'an Attic [figure]' (in Valckenaer's edition of Ammonius [1822], 173). Debrunner and Scherer 1969: §194 give figures for its massive reuse in final clauses (Polybius 7%, Diodorus 5%, Plutarch in the *Lives* 49%, Arrian 82%, Appian 87%, Herodian 75%, Josephus 32%, 4 Maccabees 71%; cf. Hein 1914: 1–6 (figures, earlier literature); for final clauses see Diel 1894: 17–25; cf. Radermacher 1947: 56 on practice exercises.

were becoming or had become obsolete.[43] Stylistic reasons were often behind the selection of particular atticizing features (rather than a real hunt for perfect Attic prose).[44] The degree of exclusivity depended on who you were; but essentially atticism was another step on in educational differentiation from the mass.

To understand better the meaning of language division in second sophistic Greek society I am going to turn for comparison to the 'language question' in modern Greece. For until recently modern Greece was plagued by a not dissimilar phenomenon. On one side stood those who advocated as the national language the *dhimotiki* ('demotic') form, i.e. some sort of standardized version of the Greek that had developed naturally from *koine* (and in itself representing a diverse linguistic situation). On the other side were those who championed the *katharevousa* or 'purified' form, an atticizing version of Greek starting from demotic but improved by the addition of much classical vocabulary and grammar. The idea of *katharevousa* arose during the struggle for Greek independence among the followers of the great nationalist and classical scholar, Adamantios Korais. As a vehicle for expressing their national feeling Korais wanted to give the Greeks a language based on their spoken tongue but elevated to a proper intellectual standard.[45] The overall political significance of language in the nationalist struggle must be read against the general connection between language use and choice and the growth of national movements in the modern period.[46] In Greece internal political division soon hijacked any possibility of discovering

[43] Noticeable are the adoption of characteristically Attic *-rr-* (for *-rs-*) and *-tt-* (for *-ss-*), *gignomai* for *ginomai*, etc., Attic rules of contracting vowels, the Attic conjugation of irregular verbs like 'be' and 'know', the so-called 'Attic' second declension, troublesome third-declension nouns like *naus* (this e.g. was replaced by *ploion* in the spoken language), extensive reuse of the dative (essentially reduced in non-educated writing to signifying indirect objects), a revival of the long-dead dual, archaic uses of the infinitive, and a liking for the optative. Almost all of these features are absent from modern demotic Greek.
  On individual authors (Plutarch, Dio, and especially Lucian, Aristides, Aelian, and Philostratus) Schmid 1887–97 remains valuable; see on Plutarch above, n. 25; on Lucian below, 'Practice' n. 11; on Aristides Pernot 1981: especially 117–46; and on Arrian Tonnet 1988: i. 299–351 (very useful on atticism in general).
[44] So, Arrian deliberately avoids ἵνα + subjunctive in final clauses in his own works (but not in the *Discourses of Epictetus*) because, though perfectly good 'Attic', it was also the living construction (Tonnet 1988: i. 344–5).
[45] See Kedourie 1971: 37–48 (a good general sketch); Jeffreys 1985: esp. 50–5 on the influence of the French revolutionary regime's suppression of non-standard French.
[46] See e.g. Morgan 1983: 69–74; Sussex 1985; Patterson 1985; esp. Hobsbawm 1990: 51–63, 106–19; and Anderson 1991: 67–82.

a truly national tongue. For it is ironic that after independence Korais' great idea quickly became another means of entrenching the power of the conservative ruling class centred on the Phanariot nobility from Constantinople.[47] The battle between the language camps raged throughout the nineteenth and twentieth centuries, long after the Phanariots ceased to exist as a political force, and it was only in the years after the restoration of democracy in Greece in 1974 that demotic has finally acquired permanent governmental support. The leaders of the last non-democratic regime, that of the colonels, were particularly arch-classicizers.[48]

Western influence on the history of the new Greece and on its cultural and linguistic identity is also of interest for our comparison with the second sophistic, where Roman philhellenes' support for Attic taste was certainly appreciated by Greeks (as, for example, Philostratus' *Lives of the Sophists* shows well enough). For the most part the Greeks had referred to themselves from the time of late antiquity as 'Romans', a politico-religious designation opposed to 'Hellene' which in the Christian Roman empire had come to mean 'pagan', and they were thus forced to yield any sense of an internal identity based on their heritage.[49] The notion of 'Hellenism' as a Periclean, Isocratean, Spartan ideal was reinstituted in the eighteenth and nineteenth centuries by the liberators of Greece and their western backers, for whom 'Greece' was a distillate of the language and literature, history, and thought of the archaic and classical period from Homer to Demosthenes. Greeks then found themselves caught between an internal 'Romeic' identity, which had been theirs in the Byzantine and Venetian/Turkocratic periods, and an externally imposed 'Hellenic' one that now afforded them freedom and respect on the classical model thoughtfully brought to their attention once again by western liberals.[50] The result has been a deep cultural schizophrenia which continues to mar Greek life to the present day. Linguistic polarization is the clearest expression of this. It is not surprising that *katharevousa* should have been appropriated and promoted as the new national speech by the political 'right'.[51]

[47] In general see Householder 1962; Sotiropoulos 1977; Mouzelis 1978: 136; Browning 1983*a*: 100–18; esp. Herzfeld 1987: 51 ff.

[48] Clogg 1972.

[49] Except of course in the case of the late antique pagans: Bowersock 1990: 9–10.

[50] Herzfeld 1982: 1–23, id. 1987: 101 ff., 111–12; cf. also Just 1989.

[51] With the notable exception of General Metaxas (dictator 1936–41).

Although the right's ideology was one of national unity and hence in theory the extension of the 'national' language to all Greeks within a certain time, so artificial a language could only ever be mastered by those with the leisure and economic power to do so and in practical terms was never likely to be anything other than a mechanism for controlling the masses. That this was clear to all concerned is shown by the fact that opponents of this imposed linguistic formalism were branded as 'slavophiles' and 'communists', tags reflecting not only political abuse but wider fears on the part of the classicizers that the Greeks might not be genetic heirs of the ancient Greeks after all and that the demotic tongue would show it.[52]

It has been widely remarked that the modern Greek language question is an excellent example of 'diglossia'. This is the name given in socio-linguistics to the situation where there exists side by side with a language's primary dialects a highly codified, often more complex variety which is sanctified by a large and respected body of literature from an earlier period or another language group, learned through formal education, and used for written and formal spoken purposes but not by any social class for ordinary conversation.[53] In modern Greece linguistic purism pushed diglossia to the extreme by proposing to make the *katharevousa* serviceable even as the language of conversation—though this could never be so for the majority. To speak of 'diglossia' carries the risk, of course, of abstracting what are real political and cultural attitudes into the safe world of technical analysis (which too easily serves governing attitudes).[54] It enables us to realize that we are dealing with a common and readily classifiable phenomenon; but it is only useful if we remember that language division is likely to be a carefully constructed sign of a much deeper political divide.

Atticism as we see it in the second sophistic fits the general definition of diglossia very well as a particular language which depends on the status of ancient texts and is a symptom of internal political division. What comparisons can we then make between the modern and ancient Greek language situations? Let us take the differences first. In the second sophistic the educated language was suitably

[52] For opposing sides of this bitter 'survivalist' debate see Jenkins 1963: 21–42 and Browning 1983*b*: 119.
[53] As defined by Ferguson 1972: 245; and e.g. Kahane and Kahane 1979.
[54] So rightly Herzfeld 1987: 112.

distinct from the language of the masses in its intellectual range to be acceptable to the elite as the language in which they could converse, promulgate laws, decrees, and honours, and write private letters or works of a technical or philosophical nature. Atticism was a label to be worn only on certain literary and rhetorical occasions which advertised the elite's ability to demonstrate its particular proximity to the classics.[55] Second, on a linguistic level atticizing Greek had its fair share of archaisms and hypercorrections; but it did not in any way share the massive incongruities of the *katharevousa*. Atticism certainly produced grammatical and lexical absurdities—but these were thoroughly ridiculed at the time by other atticists—'Attic' simplicity being always an estimable goal, as we shall see. With *katharevousa*, on the other hand, it often seemed as if purification would reach unchecked further and further heights of idiocy. This difference between ancient and modern depends upon a further one, that the study of the Attic language had been continuous from classical times till the second sophistic, whereas *katharevousa* was an entirely artificial introduction. Another important contrast is that in antiquity there was no expressed desire to generalize acquaintance with atticizing Greek, no intention to claim it as a 'national' language. If one accepts that this was a genuine aim of some of the modern linguistic conservatives (rather than always a matter of internal party politics), it is not one which would have been understood in ancient times where the notion of 'nationalism' in the modern sense did not exist (with the possible exception of the Jewish people). The ancient world lacked the ethnico-linguistic blocks in defined or desired political borders that are the foundation of modern nations and their nationalist sentiments. On the other hand, ancient atticism did operate within the familiar normative cultural divide of Hellene–barbarian as the language *par excellence* of the Greek elite whenever it should wish for it, and in this sense it was a form of commentary relevant not only to Greeks, but also to non-Greeks who lacked the ability to use it.

Differences aside, there are important areas of contact between the two language situations. First, there can be no doubt that *katharevousa* has played a great part in perpetuating the power of an educated and conservative grouping in control of administration

---

[55] Cf. Browning 1978: 105–6 distinguishing Byzantine and atticist diglossia from the modern type in this way.

and economy. The condemnation of the demotic as 'Turkish' or 'Slavic' because of its borrowings from those languages was not simply due to a desire to create a truly Greek language through innocent academic analysis: the result of such obloquy was practical in that those who had not mastered *katharevousa* were denied responsibility or power.[56] In the second sophistic period the education system was totally and unashamedly elitist. In this system Attic language and literature were dominant and inescapable as the high standard. That does not mean that all of those who had gone through the system were atticists *tout court*. But education in Attic texts cannot have failed to inculcate a strong bonding among those who had it and a sense of superiority over those who did not—and indeed we see both of these strongly displayed by the authors to be studied in this book. The linguistic competence of the elite was far broader than it was for the rest. The grammatico-rhetorical theories promoting atticism were fully conscious of this.

Second, what of foreign influences? As we have seen, Roman taste for Attic authors and the articulation of Latin stylistic battles in terms of 'Attic' and 'Asiatic' had certainly had some influence on Dionysius of Halicarnassus and his generation. Here, there again seems to be a parallel with the modern western philhellenes whose neo-classicism encouraged Greek neo-classicism, though as we have also seen Dionysius' stylistic recommendations had a thoroughly Greek pedigree. In the second sophistic period there are again parallels between Roman and modern western philhellenism. It is as true for the Romans of this period as it was for those of the Republic that philhellenism meant not 'love of Greece', but love of the ideal of Greece rather than its contemporary reality. Importantly, Roman philhellenism was not simply dependent on the Greeks' own classicizing tastes (though Romans were no doubt heavily influenced by their Greek education in this respect). For Rome actively encouraged classicism in the Greek world with real political and economic benefits.[57] Both Roman and modern philhellenes searched for an ideal Hellas, found it, and rewarded it with their aid, positing 'survivals' of classical culture which functioned as a bridge to the ideal Greece they knew of.[58] How did the Greeks react to this? The ancient Greeks certainly played up to the Romans'

---

[56] Herzfeld 1987: 52–3. Costas 1936: 130–7 offers a hearty defence of linguistic elitism.

[57] See below, 'Past', esp. nn. 15–25.   [58] Cf. Herzfeld 1987: 49–76.

philhellenism. As we shall see, they were well aware of the value of exploiting their heritage (for example in the 'museum' cities of Athens and Sparta). Modern Greeks were also happy to pander to western rhetoric. But moderns differ from the ancients in that, while the former showed themselves quite capable of adapting neo-classical requirements to their own internal political strategies, especially in language, the ancients did not of course have to look for outside inspiration in the first place, and this is true of language in particular.

This point may be developed. One of the most difficult questions to answer is whether Greek classicism was an assertion of Greekness as a reaction against a Rome whose power the emperors had made permanent. No doubt in certain contexts this was the case, and the subject will be treated later. With regard to the question of language, the atticizing movement probably did involve rejection of Latin influence on Greek, for as I have said it was a source of comment on anyone unable to atticize as well as a source of author-ity and identity for those who could.[59] We can take the matter back to the time of the late Republic when, not long before Dionysius and Caecilius, detailed technical analysis of the Greek language began in the work of grammarians like Tyrannion, Asclepiades, and Tryphon. The reason why more traditional exegesis of the language chose this moment to crystallize into formal linguistic science is not clear. But the rise of Latin as a world language where before there was only Greek has not implausibly been seen as one factor at work behind the new subject.[60] The work of the grammarians, lexicographers, and handbooks in the second sophistic was one of building defences around educated Greek. Internal politics and the dangers of linguistic change in the non-educated language are the major reasons for the project; but the existence of Latin is surely another. It is very noticeable that educated Greek in our period almost totally avoids terms transcribed or translated from or calqued on the basis of Latin words and phrases—though these occur with some frequency in non-literary writing.[61] Although there are only

[59] Browning 1983a: 44, cf. Sotiropoulos 1982: 12 ff.; Zgusta 1980: 127.

[60] Di Benedetto 1958: 202; for other references and discussion of the ideas of Di Benedetto, Pinborg (1975; a useful survey), Siebenborn 1976, and others on the rise of language science in the 1st c. BC, see Taylor 1987a: 8–11 on the vexed dating of the grammar by or attributed to Dionysius Thrax.

[61] Latin in the *koine*: Magie 1905 (official terms); Hahn 1906: 208–65 (Latinisms, including literary texts; see below, 'Arrian' n. 53, on Appian's Greek); Cameron

a few explicit statements about the need to avoid Latin words in particular (rather than barbaric Greek),[62] it is quite plain that Latin influence was being deliberately limited. Greeks were obviously very aware of Latin. It was the official language of the army and the Roman law and must have been frequently heard in the context of the administration. There is no reason to believe, as was once held, that Rome was interested in promoting Latin over Greek, though there are some examples of a protectionist attitude towards Latin.[63] Rather, there is ample evidence for official use of Greek by Roman administrators in Greek language areas.[64] This favourable treatment perhaps stopped Greek from acting as a spur to some form of proto-nationalism, as vernacular languages have often been in modern independence or nationalist contexts. The area of Latin culture and literature in particular is hardly different here. It is true that, as Romans developed their own cultural aspirations, Latin literature asserted its independence and equivalent worth to Greek, admitting to no more than a technical inferiority in comparison with its rival. Cicero was particularly vigilant in this matter.[65] Under the Empire we find Quintilian noting the dangers of too much early study of Greek.[66] Latin was bolstered by the establishment of a chair at Rome of Latin (as well as Greek) rhetoric by Vespasian; and there is certainly a concern with the quality of the language among the Latin archaizers of the second century. But there was no real hostility to Greek in our period.[67]

This is not, however, the issue. Educated Greek resisted Latin because it was contaminating the purity of the language; that Latin

1931 (list of technical terms without dates); Zilliacus 1935 (good evidence for the penetration of Greek by the time of the late Empire); Viscidi 1944 (basic thematic and chronological categorization); Mason 1970, id. 1974 (amplifying Magie). All of these studies show well enough the relative lack of penetration into the realm of higher culture.

[62] Cf. below, 'Practice' nn. 33–4, text after nn. 62, 74, and 'Philostratus' nn. 41–2, for Athenaeus on the borrowings *miliarion* and *decocta*, the *Philetaerus* on *miliarion* and *argentarion*, Galen on *nepeta*, Sextus Empiricus on the 'barbarian' *panarion*, and Apollonius and Philostratus on the 'barbarism' of Greeks using Latin names.

[63] Dubuisson 1982*b*.

[64] Kaimio 1979: 59–167; cf. Zgusta 1980: 132–3.

[65] Various aspects: Horsfall 1979; Dubuisson 1981; Kaimio 1979: 262 ff. Cicero: Trouard 1942: esp. 52–9; Petrochilos 1974: 23–33, 141 ff.; Dubuisson 1982*b*: 187.

[66] *Education in Oratory* i. 1. 13–14.

[67] Vespasian—Suetonius, *Vespasian* 18, Cassius Dio lxvi. 12. 1a, Herzog 1935: 14. Latin archaism—Marache 1952 (arguing correctly for the separation of Latin archaism from Greek atticism, cf. Bowie 1974: 167). Cf. Russell 1990*b*: 1–17.

words were used in non-educated Greek made this clear enough. There is no need to think in terms of an active opposition. Greeks may indeed have spoken Latin better than we imagine. One of the conversations reported in Plutarch's *Table Talks* suggestively shows them humorously making up etymologies of Latin words, reflecting the old idea that Latin really was a dialect of Greek.[68] But in their own speech they wanted the encroachments of Latin as little as an educated Frenchman welcomes those of English.

Similar considerations about the establishment of the Greeks' identity and their relationship with Rome will emerge in Chapter 3 from the examination of the wider function of the past in our period, to which the role of language is complementary. But before discussing this, we must first look at some of the operations and contexts of atticism among the Greek elite through the eyes of key individuals of the age.

---

[68] *Table Talks* viii. 6, 726e; cf. e.g. the use of Latin by Greeks at a birthday party in Rome for 'a young man of Asia', which was attended by Aulus Gellius (*Attic Nights* xix. 9. 7), or Pliny the Younger's egocentric claim that Greeks were learning Latin on account of their 'love' of his poems (*Letters* vii. 4. 9); see recently Holford-Strevens 1993: 203–7. Plutarch's casual remark at *Platonic Questions* 1010d that 'nearly all men are familiar with [χρῶνται] the speech of the Romans' implies an expected awareness rather than actual use (which is contested by Philostratus, *Life of Apollonius* v. 36, below, 'Philostratus' n. 48). See also Kramer 1993: 237–40 on Greeks' awareness that the language of the Romans was Latin rather than 'Roman' (which is what they normally call it).

The idea that Latin was drawn from the Aeolic dialect of Greek originated in the late Republican period (Gabba 1963; Schöpsdau 1992), and the affinity of the two languages—with the assumption that Latin derived from Greek—was commented on into late antiquity: Dubuisson 1984: 59–63, Schöpsdau ibid. (it was not accepted by Plutarch himself—below, 'Plutarch' n. 23).

2

The Practice of Purism

INTRODUCTION

I want now to turn to some practical effects of the atticizing movement and to explore how key individuals reacted to it or promoted it.[1]

I have already noted that atticism looked to a mythically pure standard. There was an inherent instability because exact reproduction of classical Attic was an unattainable ideal. Just as no one could ever agree as to what precisely constituted *katharevousa* or demotic in modern times,[2] so in the second sophistic the rhetorical-grammatical academy could never establish exactly how or how far the style of Xenophon or the vocabulary of the orators might and should be isolated and made one's own. The result was an ever-increasing amount of advice and competition between the experts as to who prescribed and who followed the rules best, a contentiousness brilliantly captured by Philostratus in his *Lives of the Sophists*. Philostratus' association of prestige in atticizing culture and high political and civic status, often involving contacts with the Roman elite, is easily confirmed.[3] But rather than looking at obvious atticists like Philostratus or Aelius Aristides or retelling Philostratus' entertaining anecdotes about the activities of the sophistic stars, I want to focus here on three types of intellectual who offer contrasting perspectives on language status. First I shall consider Favorinus and Lucian, both of whom make a play of coming from non-Greek backgrounds (respectively Arelate in the province

---

[1] Cf. recently Anderson 1993: 86–100, esp. Schmitz 1997: 67–96.

[2] See Mirambel 1937 for an interesting analysis of the scale of the modern problem between the Wars.

[3] Bowersock 1969 remains the most important study of this; see also Bowie 1982; Rothe 1989; Swain 1991*a*; Flinterman 1993: 31–55. On Philostratus' own atticism see Schmid 1887–97: iv. 1–576.

of Gallia Narbonensis and Samosata in the province of Syria), but
having nevertheless acquired a perfect knowledge of Greek language and literature. Lucian is particularly interesting for the fun he
has with the atticists (which I shall also illustrate briefly from
Athenaeus' *Sophists at Dinner*), and for his paranoia about language
purity. Second, I want to look at some of the lexicographers who
made the rules Favorinus and Lucian took such care to follow.
Finally I shall turn to Galen. He is extremely valuable for assessing
the influence of atticism on the elite at large, since although he had
good reason as a doctor and philosopher to resist the call to atticize,
he felt compelled to show that he was sufficiently well educated to
do so, had he wished.

THE USES OF PURISM: FAVORINUS, LUCIAN, ATHENAEUS

In the *Corinthian Oration*, which survives among the speeches of
his teacher Dio of Prusa, the philosopher and sophist Favorinus
tells an audience in Corinth of his successful strivings to be first in
Greek language and culture.[4] Favorinus, whose wealth qualified him
to be priest of the local imperial cult, claims to have abandoned
property and political standing 'so that one thing should happen to
him above all else—to seem Greek and to be Greek!' (25). Even
though Narbonensis had a flourishing Greek cultural tradition,[5]
Favorinus clearly felt obliged to connect himself with the authentic
Greek culture of old Greece. For this endeavour he deserved, he
says, a statue 'among you because, though Roman, he became Greek
(as your own country has),[6] among the Athenians because he atticizes
in his speech, among the Lacedaemonians because he loves the
gymnasium, and among all because he practices philosophy, has
already roused many of the Hellenes to practice it with him, and
has attracted to it not a few of the barbarians [i.e. in Gaul]' (26). We
may believe Favorinus when he says he had spent much money and
lost hope of a political career in the pursuit of Greek culture.
Apuleius makes a comparable assessment of the cost of education.[7]

[4] *Corinthian Oration* (Ps.-Dio, *Or.* xxxvii) 25–7 'not only the language, but also
the thought, manners, and dress of the Greeks'. On Favorinus see Barigazzi 1966;
for a rather different view of his life Swain 1989a.
[5] Bannert 1977: 87–91.
[6] Contrast Pausanias' views at 'Pausanias' nn. 72–3.
[7] See below, 'Pausanias' n. 5.

By philosophy Favorinus means Platonic philosophy, as we know from the fragments of his works and from the reports of others. Part of the reason why Platonism (blended with Stoic ethics and Pythagorean mysticism) dislodged alternative philosophical systems in the second and third centuries to emerge as the only intellectual alternative to Christianity in later antiquity is without doubt its possession of core texts that were also classics of Athenian literature.[8] Thus Platonic philosophy and atticizing speech complement each other very closely in Favorinus' efforts to constitute himself as a Greek. The physical archaism of Sparta completes the picture.[9]

The scale of Favorinus' claim was bound to have repercussions. He was a controversial figure (this speech itself concerns the Corinthians' destruction of one of his statues), and as Philostratus' *Life* shows (*VS* 489–92) had run-ins with a number of people including the emperor Hadrian and the great sophist Antonius Polemo. His rivalry with the latter was a struggle reflecting the 'love of glory' that specially makes a man a sophist (*VS* 491). Favorinus' atticism came in for particular attack, since it was the foundation of his claims. In his lexicon of words and phrases to be avoided in good writing the exceptionally strict atticist Phrynichus subjects the sophist to acute criticism because of his errors in Greek.[10] As we shall see, Galen also unkindly and somewhat hypocritically attacked Favorinus for his failure to atticize fully. It is worth asking whether this has anything to do with Favorinus' proficiency in Latin, as we see it in the pages of Aulus Gellius. Perhaps he remained too western for some after all. For himself, though, atticizing culture was all.

Lucian also believed he had obtained a secure grasp on Athenian language and literature.[11] Like Favorinus he was immensely competitive and made enemies with ease. His own character and other people's reactions to him seem to have a lot to do with his interesting cultural background from a family that was not among the super rich and which was very probably Semitic rather than Greek.

[8] Cf. Russell 1973: 63; in general de Lacy 1974; Dillon 1977.
[9] On this cf. 'Past' n. 16.
[10] See *Selection of Attic Verbs and Nouns* 218 Fischer 'I am amazed that Favorinus who thought he was the first of the Hellenes used [this]'; for other attacks on Favorinus see Fischer 1974: 139 (index), and see below, n. 45.
[11] See especially *Double Indictment* 27, *Dream pass.*; below, 'Lucian' nn. 41–9. On his atticism consult Bompaire 1994; Schmid 1887–97: i. 216–432; Deferrari 1916 (the verb); Chabert 1897 (less helpful).

The way to combat these disadvantages was to make himself as Greek as he possibly could. Lucian gives us a fine but rather apocryphal version of his education in the autobiographical *Dream, or Life of Lucian*. Favorinus' remarks about barbarians in the *Corinthian Oration* served to remind his audience of the labour he had expended in learning Greek as a westerner. Lucian's numerous allusions to his own barbarian origin are far more bitter and self-conscious. They refer especially to his Greek language.[12] This is not simply a question of a bad accent.[13] Lucian was worried about making mistakes in Greek to an extent that verges on paranoia and he was intensely aware of the rules which guaranteed respect in second sophistic society. This is plain above all in three essays that attack (probably) real enemies, first in the *Lexiphanes* for excesses in atticism, a vice Lucian dubs 'hyperatticism',[14] second in the *Teacher of Rhetoric* for promising short cuts to rhetoric where none exist, and third in *The Uneducated Book Collector* for general ignorance and pretence of learning.

'Lexiphanes' means 'Word-flaunter' and may well be a nickname for the arrogant sophist Philagrus of Cilicia.[15] He has written a symposium in imitation of Plato but has used words that are not properly Attic, including many crass neologisms, or are now totally obsolete.[16] Lucian employs the doctor Sopolis to cure the sophist of his problem. Sopolis has a significant name—'City-Saver' (perhaps

[12] *Double Indictment* 27; *Fisherman* 19; *False Critic* 1, 11; cf. *On Hirelings* 10. See below, 'Lucian' nn. 5, 39, 50.

[13] On the reception of which we know little; cf. Aulus Gellius, *Attic Nights* xix. 9. 2, Philostratus *VS* 594; Millar 1968: 127.

[14] Apparently introduced into literature by him: *Lexiphanes* 25, cf. *Demonax* 26.

[15] A plausible suggestion made by Jones 1972a: 475–8 on the basis of *Lexiphanes* 3, 'I am *philagros*' (literally 'fond of the country', a neologism—Casevitz 1994: 79). For Philagrus' verbal arrogance see *VS* 578 ('when a foreign word [*ekphulon*, i.e. not enrolled in an Athenian tribe; cf. e.g. Phrynichus, *Selection* 233 F.] escaped him . . . , and Amphicles said . . . "In which of the greats is this used?", he replied, "In Philagrus!" ').

[16] See Casevitz 1994. Cf. e.g. the epigram of Ammianus (first half of the 2nd c.; below, 'Past' n. 87) at *Greek Anthology* xi. 157:

> Ὠγαθὲ καὶ μῶν οὖν καὶ ποῖ δὴ καὶ πόθεν, ὦ τᾶν
> καὶ θαμὰ καὶ φέρε δὴ καὶ κομιδῇ καὶ ἴθι
> καὶ στόλιον, μάλιον, πωγώνιον, ὤμιον ἔξω
> ἐκ τούτων ἡ νῦν εὐδοκιμεῖ σοφία.

The obsolete, Platonizing atticisms of vv. 1–2 (which are unrenderable) are juxtaposed with neologistic forms describing the rhetor's dress and hair in v. 3; or, again, Lucilius (under Nero) at *Greek Anthology* xi. 142.

suggesting the importance of proper rhetoric to civic life)—and a significant profession, for, as we shall see when we come to Galen, doctors were especially averse to the more obscure side of atticism. Lucian urges instead the clarity and simplicity which are constantly stressed in the atticizing books of style and language as the qualities needed for successfully imitating the ancients. His warnings of excessive archaism for the sake of parading one's learning are paralleled by the remarks made in the second- or third-century essay *On Mistakes in Declamation* (the tenth chapter of the Ps.-Dionysius of Halicarnassus *Art of Rhetoric*).[17] Lucian's *Teacher of Rhetoric* is rather similar to *Lexiphanes*. Here again the Teacher, who is perhaps to be identified with the lexicographical sophist Julius Pollux of Naucratis,[18] uses obsolete Attic words supported by invented citations to cover his errors (16–17).

More interesting than Lucian's attacks are his defences of his own Greek. Take first the remarkable essay called *A Slip of the Tongue During a Greeting*, in which he defends himself for greeting a Roman governor at the governor's levee with the word *hugiainein* ('good health'). This greeting was in fact appropriate for evening time and Lucian should have said *chairein* ('have joy'). Worse, *hugiainein* could also be interpreted as an invitation to sound mental health.[19] Meeting a great man was likely to be a stressful occasion and particularly so for those who had invested heavily in correct diction. When the wrong word came out, 'I began to sweat and go red and was completely at a loss. Some of those present thought it was delirium,[20] naturally enough, while there were others who thought I was talking nonsense because of my old age and others who thought I had a bad hangover from yesterday' (1). Lucian's error is a classic case of what we call 'parapraxis', that is, the psychological state where the sliding and hiding of meaning in the subconscious mind breaks to the surface in a moment of strain. Interestingly he warns of a similarly embarrassing disjunction of

[17] ii. 365. 9 ff. U.–R.; expounded by Russell 1979: 128–9.
[18] A suggestion made by the scholiasts (174, 180 ed. Rabe) on the basis of *Teacher of Rhetoric* 24.
[19] For puns involving the reversal of these greetings see Cassius Dio lxix. 18. 3 (the story of Fronto and Turbo); Plutarch, *Agesilaus* 21. 10; Athenaeus, *Sophists at Dinner* 289d; Aelian, *Varied History* xii. 51 (on the famous megalomaniac Menecrates of Syracuse).
[20] Cf. Galen's case of a rhetor who declaimed during a phrenitic attack (*First Commentary on Book One of Hippocrates' Prorrheticus* xvi. 566. 14).

thought and speech in his essay on Greek scholars who take paid
employment in the houses of rich Romans. They are liable to be
called upon in company to answer the host's enquiries on literature—only to be laughed at when they provide answers to different questions (*On Hirelings* 11). In so tightly rule-bound a society
as the atticizers made for themselves dysphasia was an inevitable
and terrible hazard.[21]

Similar evidence for the place of correct Greek comes from
Lucian's attack on *The False Critic*. Lucian's enemy here is probably the great rhetor and sophist Hadrian of Tyre.[22] The essay is a
remarkably sustained piece of personal abuse against the Critic for
laughing at the way Lucian had used the word *apophras*
('unpropitious'). Lucian had been called 'a barbarian in speech'.[23]
The background is typically sophistic. Lucian had earlier ridiculed
the Critic when he had tried to pass off an old work as an extempore composition. Now the Critic was paying him back (5–9). The
difference, according to Lucian, is that Lucian was in the right both
times. Editors note that Lucian could have appealed to the usage of
the famous Athenian comic poet Eupolis.[24] Such a defence might
have been felt too narrow (to judge from Lucian's attack on the
Critic's Greek vocabulary in general—9, 24—and his atticism in
particular—29). In any case the word used by Lucian had not passed
outside 'the borders of Attica' (11).[25]

Two other works, the first by Lucian, the other probably not,
humorously illustrate this linguistic phobia. Lucian's *Judgement of
the Vowels* is a court case—a favourite format of his—between the
letter Sigma and the letter Tau.[26] Sigma accuses Tau before the vowels

---

[21] Which is not to say that the tension of public performance was not common
to all speakers (cf. Pliny, *Letters* vii. 17. 13), but that the sophist's or rhetor's difficulties were due to his very particular claim to have invested in the Greek past
(cf. Philostratus *VS* 541 on the weariness this caused Polemo).

[22] Jones 1986: 113–14 plausibly (cf. §21 'only one person would have been your
helper [*boêthos*] . . . a man among the best of the Romans' with Hadrian's host at
Rome, Flavius Boethus; cf. below, 'Lucian' n. 107, 'Galen' n. 9). One other possible
link between Hadrian and Lucian may be mentioned: both wrote declamations on
the tyrant Phalaris (Lucian, *Phalaris* i–ii, *Suda* α 528) and, though Phalaris was a
stock figure (cf. Demetrius, *On Style* 292, the *Letters of Phalaris*), Lucian's humorous pieces may have been aimed at his rival.

[23] *The False Critic* 1. Apparently Lucian had applied the word to the Critic himself, whereas it normally qualifies the word for 'day' (cf. 23, 28, 31, 32).

[24] Cf. fr. 309 Kock (= 332 Kassel–Austin).

[25] Ironically Lucian's idea of the word's meaning seems to have been affected by
the Latin notion of the *dies ater*: see Mikalson 1975.

[26] See Baldwin 1973: 58; note Wolanin 1990 (in Polish).

of stealing from him all words which contain a double tau. The combination -*tt*- for -*ss*- (simplified to *t*- for *s*- initially) was a peculiarity of the Attic and Boeotian dialects of classical Greek. But even in the classical period itself some Athenian authors, notably Thucydides and the tragic poets, preferred to use the Ionic and general Greek form -*ss*-, perhaps in order to avoid a sound that was too narrowly Athenian. The *koine* dropped the distinctively Attic -*tt*- altogether.[27] It was to be expected that the atticists would revive it. Their affectation is Lucian's initial point of mirth.[28] Typically Sigma claims that -*tt*- is not Athenian at all. Rather, he first detected Tau's 'avarice' at the house of a comic poet called Lysimachus who 'claimed to come from the middle of Attica', but was in fact a 'Boeotian by descent' (7).[29] A series of examples follow,[30] including other genuinely atticizing forms (*ksun* for *sun*, -*rr*- for -*rs*-) and some humorous ones (11). Lucian had no doubt spent a considerable time learning these features in early life and enjoyed making fun of them knowing that his own usage conformed to atticist strictures.

Finally, the *Solecist* (alternatively known as *The False Sophist*) may also be by Lucian. It seems, however, that this rather loosely organized work, which criticizes some of Lucian's own usages, is not genuine.[31] That is encouraging, for though it draws on Lucian (it is a dialogue between 'Lucian' and a 'sophist'), it means that someone else appreciated the humour to be extracted from atticism. It is the atticists' attempts to legislate correctness in language that afford the many entertaining examples of grammatical and syntactical errors the work has fun with.

More gentle humour can be found in the generation after Lucian in Athenaeus' *Sophists at Dinner*. This work, at times highly entertaining, at times horribly dull, uses the symposium form to discuss all manner of human conduct connected with appetite.

[27] Cf. Meillet 1935: 297; López Eire 1981: 386.
[28] Cf. Phrynichus, *Selection* 177 F. (use the -*tt*- forms 'so you appear to be an ancient Attic [writer]'); Tonnet 1988: i. 316–17. Only Aristides, thoroughly imbued as he was with Plato and Demosthenes, uses the form successfully; see Schmid 1887–98: ii. 83–5 on him and others.
[29] The Athenian comic poets habitually used the -*tt*- forms. Lysimachus is unknown (as is his township, 'Cybelus') and is presumably an invention, but cf. *RE* Suppl. x (1965), 381–2 s.v. Lysimachos. See also below on the 'Heracles of Herodes' at 'Past' n. 47.
[30] Such as *basilitta* based on the non-Attic *basilissa* ('queen')—hence 'showing particular shamelessness' (8; cf. Phrynichus, *Selection* 231 F., Threatte 1980: 539 on the non-Attic form in epigraphy).
[31] Cf. Hall 1981: 298–307.

Taxonomy (of food, utensils, luxury, women) is important throughout, and there is an underlying concern with language. In one
passage two of the principal characters, the stereotypical Cynic
philosopher Cynulcus and the self-confessed pedant Ulpianus,
battle it out about neologisms and atticisms. Cynulcus is irked by
Ulpianus' constant testing of his fellow-diners as to whether a word
'is used or not used [i.e. by the ancients]' (97c).[32] Cynulcus is particularly pleased to be able to catch Ulpianus using the word
phainolês, 'cloak', in the (now normal) masculine gender, since it
had earlier been feminine (as in the Latin borrowing *paenula*).
Ulpianus is also criticized for his preposterous etymological usages,
which for example make him take *achrêstos* ('useless') in the sense
of 'unused' (97d–e). According to Cynulcus there is a whole tribe
of sophists—the *Oulpianeioi*—who display the same faults. A contemporary, Pompeianus of Philadelphia, is named as another 'word-
hunter' (which is Ulpian's soubriquet); but Cynulcus can quote
older examples of the game of etymological word playing too. It is
typical of the Ulpianites that they substitute the made-up word
ipnolebês for *miliarion* from the Latin *miliarium* (the machine for
heating water in the baths),[33] while at the same time Ulpian is happy
to use the word *chortazô* 'fatten up, feast, fill full' in the sense of
korennumi 'satisfy', a usage Cynulcus seems to take as an affected
metaphor (which it perhaps was in origin), but which also coincides
with the general aversion in the *koine* from the athematic verbs in
-*mi* and the particular replacement of *korennumi* by *chortazô* in the
spoken language (severely damaging, therefore, Ulpianus' atticist
credentials).

For the moment Ulpianus defends himself by quoting instances
of *chortazô* from the poets (99e–100a). Later he attempts to get his
own back when Cynulcus asks for a drink of *decocta* (the Latin
word for the cold water drink invented by Nero).[34] Ulpianus

---

[32] κεῖται, οὐ κεῖται;—for which he is nicknamed (according to the epitomator of
the first book) Keitoukeitos.

[33] The engineer Hero of Alexandria (*c*.100) found no difficulty in using the correct term (*Pneumatics* ii. 34–5 ed. Schmidt, i. 304 ff., with notes and illustrations) for
an object that must have been rather familiar to the eastern elites; but *ipnolebês* is
used (of course) in Lexiphanes' symposium (Lucian, *Lexiphanes* 8), and the anonymous *Philetaerus* (or *Companion*) suggests *ipnion* for 'what they now call a *miliarion*'
(216 Dain; a rare diminutive of *ipnos* 'oven'; cf. 194 on *argurothêkê* for Latin
argentarion, 'silver chest').

[34] Cf. Pliny, *Hist. Nat.* xxxi. 40. Cf. Galen, *On the Method of Healing* x. 467. 16–
468. 1.

immediately upbraids him for 'barbarizing'. Cynulcus offers an interesting apology: 'staying at present, my dear sir [*ô lôste*, a typical atticism], in imperial Rome, I follow the speech of the country in accordance with its normal usage [*sunêtheia*].' Cynulcus compares the employment by classical authors who 'have the best Greek' of Persian words 'because they were normally used'. Macedonian expressions too entered Attic. In any case, says the philosopher with ironic deprecation, no one's speech is completely pure (121e–122e). It is not surprising that a Cynic should be given the task of defending non-atticist usage. But in fact it is worth noting that Ulpianus also is not an extreme atticist along the lines of a Phrynichus. Any ancient source for a word will do. And Athenaeus himself, with his broad interests, naturally could not be overly bound by atticist restrictions.

THE CHOICE OF TEXTS: SOME LEXICOGRAPHERS

I turn from these humourists to the lexicographers and first to Moeris, perhaps the most interesting among them on account of the threefold distinction between Attic, Hellenic, and 'common' usage which he employs in some of his entries.[35] Moeris was a strict atticist in aim, and since his work was apparently influenced by the views of Phrynichus it is probably right to date him to the early third century. Although his lexicon is vitiated by brevity, unintelligibility, and error, compounded by a poor manuscript transmission, its schema—difficult to define though it is—is still of great worth as evidence of the evaluative language distinctions of the period. Most of the entries in his lexicon distinguish the usage of 'the Hellenes' from that of 'the Attic [writers]' or rarely 'the ancients', and the vast majority concern lexical rather than syntactical usage. A preliminary point of interest is Moeris' differentiation on four occasions between 'primary Attic' and 'secondary Attic', an unusual and rather unconvincing overscrupulousness.[36] In five entries Attic lexical usage is distinguished from a joint Hellenic and 'common' usage and in five others Hellenic and 'common' are then distinguished themselves.[37] 'Hellenic' usage is surely that of the educated

---

[35] I refer to Bekker's old edition (1833; for textual criticism see Wendel 1928).

[36] 194. 29, 197. 28, 208. 15, and 213. 2 (where a 'middle [? Attic]' is mentioned).

[37] Respectively 189. 32, 193. 35, 204. 15, 204. 17, 205. 14; 196. 4, 202. 11, 205. 3, 208. 33, 209. 17 (on these see Maidhof 1912: 54 = 330–62 = 338).

Greeks of Moeris' own time. This is suggested (and the difficulty
of assessing precisely what Moeris means must be borne in mind)
by the occasional substitution of 'we' against Attic for 'Hellenes'
against 'Attic'.[38]

All of this makes Moeris a slightly more subtle lexicographer
than his colleagues. But his aims are similar. In comparing 'Hellenic' and 'Attic' usage Moeris wished to extend his readers' language competence for occasions when atticizing speech was required.
(Naturally he does not feel the need to say when this might
be.) 'Common' usage probably meant for him the language of the
lower end of the linguistic continuum of educated/semi-educated
speakers.[39] Moeris was aware that 'common' forms often coincided
with those of educated speakers—hence 'common' and 'Hellenic'
could be identified and, indeed, 'common' alone (?presumably signalling 'common' and 'Hellenic') could be contrasted with 'Attic'.[40]
But in referring to 'common' forms, either in vocabulary or grammar, as distinct from both Hellenic and Attic, Moeris is of course
stigmatizing the language of those who used them in respect of
both competence and performance.[41] It is no surprise to find a form
Moeris labels 'common' occurring in literary authors of quality.[42]
Rule books like his were necessary precisely because the rules were
not and could not be definitively formulated. With his inconsistencies and mistakes in Attic he is a good example of how the atticists'
desire to be perfect could quite easily go wrong. A problem inherent in all such attempts at codification is the conflict with the goal
of possessing a naturally faultless Greek. Moeris and the others
represent a process of negotiation between the ideological imperative to atticize and the cultural conditions of the real world which
made rule books necessary. It was a game where compromise,

---

[38] 194. 24, 206. 30, 208. 7, 209. 19 (see below, n. 41), 214. 10.

[39] Maidhof 1912: 61 = 337; cf. Versteegh 1987: 272 n. 13.

[40] e.g. 197. 5, 198. 2, *et al.*

[41] 196. 4 ἐξίλλειν Ἀττικοί, ἐξείργειν Ἕλληνες, ἐκβάλλειν κοινόν, 208. 33 ῥιγῶν Ἀττικοί,
ῥιγοῦν Ἕλληνες, ῥιγοῖν κοινόν (Maidhof's text). Thus I see no reason to equate 'common' usage with that signalled by 'we' (as suggested by Wendel in *RE* xv. 2 [1932],
2504); the only possible vulgar 'we' example is 209. 19 σωδάριον Ἕρμιππος τὸ ὑφ'
ἡμῶν σουδάριον, but this Latin word *sudarium* (the evidence from 'Hermippus' is
clearly corrupt; see Kassel–Austin ad fr. 93) for equipment familiar from the baths
is listed as the form now in use by Pollux (*Onomasticon* vii. 71), and so was presumably felt acceptable enough (cf. Ps.-Herodian, *On Dichrona* ii, p. 13. 24 Lentz).

[42] Cf. 205. 3 Οἰδίπουν Ἀττικοί, Οἰδίπουν καὶ Ἕλληνες, Οἰδίποδα κοινῶς, where the
last given form is that used in Plutarch, Arrian, and Pausanias (whereas Aristides has
the Attic/Hellenic form).

adjustments, and trade-offs were constant, sometimes with surprising results, though never confessed.

One area to be taken account of seriously was sources. Not all Attic authors were of the same quality. Phrynichus is one of the most exact of the atticists in this regard. His surviving *Selection of Attic Verbs and Nouns* (*Eklogê rhêmatôn kai onomatôn Attikôn*), addressed to an imperial *ab epistulis graecis* called Cornelianus,[43] is an aggressive work written, as the author says in his preface, against those who dared to claim sources for their incorrect usages. It seems reasonably certain that the lexicon ascribed to the so-called 'Antiatticist' was one of those Phrynichus had in his sights.[44] 'Antiatticist' is something of a misnomer, for while the author of this short work is not a strict atticist, he is nevertheless a classicist in taste, citing as precedents non-Attic classical poets like Simonides, Sappho, and Pindar along with a wide variety of Attic comedy and prose (including Aristotle, Theophrastus, and Theopompus). The Antiatticist was governed by the same desire for language purity as Phrynichus, but had different views of how to achieve it. This was anathema to Phrynichus, who pictured himself 'fighting on behalf of atticism' (332 Fischer). Although Phrynichus warns against the use of *hapax legomena* (402 F.), his major objections are against anything he sees as contaminating good Attic. All other dialects, including Homeric Greek, are firmly rejected. Menander is scathingly denied a place in the thesaurus of educated speech (e.g. 393 F.). Phrynichus' ideal is to speak like Aristophanes, Cratinus, and Eupolis, or Plato, Thucydides, and Demosthenes (114, 286 F.). Mistakes of his great (and not so great) contemporaries, including professionals like Stoic philosophers, forensic orators, and doctors, are criticized with special vigour.[45]

[43] *Selection*, Pref. p. 61 Fischer; it is usually assumed that 'the kings of the Romans' who appointed Cornelianus are Marcus and Commodus (Bowersock 1969: 54–5), but the probable chronology of Phrynichus' own life (see below, nn. 46, 48) makes Marcus and Lucius more likely and, if this is right, the date of the *Selection* must be put in the early 160s.

[44] Latte 1915: 373–84 with Fischer 1974: 39–41, 45–6; the 'Antiatticist' is edited by Bekker in *Anecdota graeca*, i. 75–116, iii. 1074–7.

[45] See e.g. 396 F. on Polemo: 'so very important then is knowledge of words, when we see even the pinnacle of the Hellenes stumbling.' Apart from Favorinus (above, n. 10) and Polemo, Antiochus of Aegeae, Alexander Clay-Plato, Lollianus, Dio ('the philosopher', 22 F.), and Plutarch are among those named. For these and the rest see Fischer 1974: 138–41 (index). Sensible remarks on Phrynichus' aims, likes, and dislikes in both the *Selection* and the *Sophist's Stock-in-Trade* can be found in de Borries 1911: pp. xxiv–xxxv.

For Phrynichus' ideal blend of prose and comic authors cf. Ps.-Dionysius of

Surely more interesting than the negative *Selection* was the *Sophist's Stock-in-Trade* (*Preparatio sophistica*), of which there remains an abridgement, fragments, and a summary by Photius (*Library*, cod. 158). In this lengthy work of thirty-seven books (as poor Photius laments) Phrynichus undertook to provide guidance on vocabulary, grammar, and style for literature, rhetoric, and conversational purposes, as well as for satirical writing (*skôptikai laliai*) and, interestingly, for the language of love (*erôtikoi tropoi*). Particular attention was again paid to sources. Non-Attic forms were athetized. We are not surprised to learn from Photius that Aristides—the most successful atticizer of them all—received high praise in the preface to the eleventh volume. The *Sophist's Stock-in-Trade* was first published in books dedicated to various friends, and then republished with a dedication to 'Commodus Caesar' as 'king'.[46] Phrynichus' career used to be seen as one of rivalry with his contemporary Pollux over imperial attention. The *Selection* was thought to have made criticisms of Pollux's encyclopaedic treasury of words, the *Onomasticon*, which Pollux then answered in retreatments in the final book of his work (all of which was also dedicated to Commodus).[47] But, though Pollux's idea of valid sources has more in common with the Antiatticist than with Phrynichus (a fact which reflects the breadth of his interests), there is no real evidence of rivalry.[48] It is probably to the general pressure to be first in language

Halicarnassus, *Art of Rhetoric* ii. 386 U.–R. (Aristophanes, Cratinus, Eupolis, Menander, Lysias, Demosthenes, Aeschines, Antiphon), and below, n. 65 on Galen. The Old Comedy had the dual advantages of a purely Athenian pedigree and a wide vocabulary.

[46] This must be after 180 when Commodus was sole ruler. Phrynichus will have been a very old man by now—he was already calling himself old (i.e. at least fifty) and ill by the fifth book of the *Sophist's Stock-in-Trade* (Photius, *Library* cod. 158, 100b), which was the second book to be written after his friend (Ti. Claudius) Aristocles (perhaps of a similar age: cf. ibid. *sumpaistês*) had been adlected to the Senate (very probably) under Pius (Avotins 1978b: 189–90).

[47] Commodus is not described as 'lord' till *Onomasticon* iii Pref. (*kurios*); on the chronology see Avotins 1975: 320–1; for another view Swain 1990c: 215–16. Amongst other works Pollux composed the wedding hymn for Commodus' marriage to Bruttia Crispina (*Suda* π 1951).

[48] See Fischer 1974: 43–4, Avotins 1978b: 190–1 on the curiously influential thesis—in reality a house of cards—advanced by Naechster 1908; common words treated in their very different works simply reflect the common teaching of the schools and common usage. Even if the *Selection* was written in 177–80 (as is usually thought; but see above, n. 43), it is difficult to see that Pollux had time to notice and answer its criticisms—to do so would mean (if we assume that Book iii, where Commodus is first addressed as *kurios*, was published at the earliest in 177) that Books vi and vii (whence most of the retreatments in Book x are taken) were rushed into publication (there is no need to take Pollux's depreciatory 'at speed' in viii Pref. too seriously).

and literature that we should ascribe Phrynichus' excessively self-conscious atticism. Of additional interest is Photius' notice that Phrynichus was an 'Arabian'. This may not be right, for the *Suda* says he was a Bithynian.[49] But if it is (and the two statements need not be contradictory—sophists moved around a good deal), Phrynichus would resemble Lucian in being a non-Greek speaker by birth who had to learn the rules through hard work and who was understandably opposed to and frightened of anyone (or, in Lucian's case, anyone else) who challenged them, however indirectly.

Homer was a particular danger to the atticists. For if atticism rested its claims on the antiquity of the Athenian classics, it should follow that Homer was a better candidate; if it rested its claims on the quality of Attic literature, Homer and other texts of central importance to Greek education and reading could demand inclusion as equally meritorious models. 'Some say', says the treatise *On Solecism and Barbarism* attributed to Aelius Herodian, 'that the poet *is* pure Greek [*Hellênismos*]', because of his use of all the dialects.[50] The sceptical philosopher Sextus Empiricus, who was no friend of the atticists or of the grammatico-rhetorical academy, notices extreme analogical grammarians who (he alleges) equated purity of language with the language of Homer, something which would 'lead to laughter if we try it in our Greek' (*Against the Grammarians* i. 202–9). The problem was posed by the prominent second-century grammarian Telephus of Pergamum, who prospered according to his fellow-citizen Galen for nearly a hundred years through careful living.[51] Telephus was a committed local patriot who wrote several books on Pergamum and the history of its kings (the name of whose mythical ancestor he bore).[52] Loyalty to Rome is shown by two books *On the Sebasteion [Temple of Augustus] at Pergamum* and by his appointment as a tutor of the emperor Lucius Verus (*Augustan History, Verus* 2. 5). In matters of language he produced several books on Attic syntax and authors. But he seems to have particularly favoured Homer for his research, and one of his Homeric works—*That Homer alone of the Ancients uses Pure Greek*—is part of the tradition (ultimately depending on the Homeric

[49] Photius, *Library* cod. 158, 100a; *Suda* φ 764.
[50] 311. 5 ed. Nauck 1867. Cf. Dio of Prusa, *Or.* xii. 66, Ps.-Plutarch, *On Homer* ii. 8–14 (pp. 9–15 Kindstrand), Maximus of Tyre xxvi. 4 Hobein.
[51] Galen, *On Safeguarding Health* vi. 333. 12–334. 5, 379. 15–16. For Telephus' works see *Suda* τ 495, Jacoby, *FGrH* 505.
[52] On the mythological Telephus (and the alternative Pergamus) and his role at Pergamum in our period see Strubbe 1984–6: 260–1.

criticism of the Alexandrians) that threatened to uncover the instability of atticism and the rhetorical school that supported it.[53] Atticist response to the challenge was either, like Phrynichus, to explicitly reject Homer and all dialectal intrusion or, like Moeris, to appropriate the poet as a proto-Attic author (a more risky enterprise).[54] Fortunately for the atticists the power of Athenian letters and the status of Attic-Ionic as the basis of the *koine* made it impossible for non-Attic texts actually to take their place.

PURISM WITHOUT ATTICISM: THE CASE OF GALEN

Drawing the boundaries of atticism in terms of what texts one was allowed to imitate was one problem. Another was on what occasions atticizing Greek should be employed. If one confined oneself to literary activity—like Lucian, for example—there was no problem with atticizing in all one's writings, whereas the *politikoi*, the politically influential or active members of society who are addressed in the handbooks of rhetoric, would no doubt have made appropriate distinctions. When they made speeches to the people, they probably benefited more from the sentiments of the Attic texts they studied than from the language in which they were expressed; when they wrote up their texts afterwards, as we see in the case of Dio of Prusa and Aelius Aristides, they were free to atticize. It is important to bear this in mind when we read an author like Philostratus who never gives the impression that atticizing Greek could ever be inappropriate. In the writing of technical or official texts educated *koine* continued as the correct mode of expression. The status of Attic was, however, so great that not to imitate it—even with good reason—could lead to a real or a perceived slur.

A man who was particularly aware of this was the medical writer and philosopher Galen, whose opinions and perspective on the matter are of immense interest. Galen was someone who set enormous store by education and counted himself extraordinarily

---

[53] ὅτι μόνος ὁ Ὅμηρος τῶν ἀρχαίων ἑλληνίζει (*Suda* s.v.). On the correctness of Homeric Greek and the textual-critical Alexandrian academy see Siebenborn 1976: 30–1.

[54] Phrynichus, *Sophist's Stock-in-Trade* 110. 19, 126. 5 de Borries, *Selection*, 42 *et al.* F.; Moeris 198. 6 *et al.*, cf. Aristides, *Or.* i. 328, Ps.-Plutarch, *On Homer* ii. 12 (p. 12 Kindstrand), 'he especially uses the Attic dialect'.

fortunate to have been well educated by his father.[55] He 'had been reared on the texts of the ancients'.[56] His problem was that medical writing was no outlet for belletristic atticism. The major reason for this was that medicine's canonical works—the Hippocratic texts of the fifth and fourth centuries BC—had been written in the Ionic dialect. Later primary works were written in the *koine*. There were no prestige models from classical Athens to form a point of reference; whereas Ionic had still to be mastered in order to read the Hippocratics. The production of Ionic medical lexicons, like Galen's own *Hippocratic Glossary*, which names and draws on rivals going back to Bacchius of Tanagra in the Hellenistic period,[57] or of later medical works written in Ionic, like those of Aretaeus of Cappadocia (first century AD), does not represent the same phenomenon as the virtuoso display of Ionic that we find in occasional pieces by Lucian, Arrian, and others. Galen took a major interest in the philosophy of language, and as a formidable logician (who held that the logics of the philosophical Schools were inadequate to the needs of science) he was particularly interested in problems of definition and formal demonstration.[58] For him philosophy was naturally propaedeutic to a medical task that was often concerned with the logical reduction of opponents' positions and the defence of one's own. Language was particularly important because Galen's taxonomic works demanded precise knowledge of the identity of any given referent. This need was often a cause of irritation between him and the atticists. The latter with an eye on status and fame called things by the wrong names and caused serious confusion.[59] The grammatico-

[55] *On the Order of his Own Books* xix. 59. 4–15.
[56] *On the Differences of the Pulse* viii. 587. 8.
[57] Note Ilberg 1888: esp. 342–54 on the sources.
[58] See esp. *On the Method of Healing* i–ii (Hankinson 1991); *On Sophisms in Language* (Edlow 1977). It was for the power of his logic that a Christian tract alleged he was 'perhaps even being offered obeisance' by heretics at the start of the 3rd c.: see 'Galen' n. 49.
[59] Many passages are collected in Herbst 1911; see e.g. *On the Powers of Foods* vi. 584. 5–586. 9: *sukamina*, 'mulberries', should not be confused with *mora*, the name given to them by the Athenians of 600 years ago (cf. Pollux *Onomasticon* vi. 46 'Aeschylus termed them *mora*') but by no one, not even at Athens, today: 'this is written not for those who have chosen to atticize in their speech ... but particularly for doctors, who are not much concerned with atticisms, and indeed for others who live like logical beings and have chosen to care for body and soul rather than honour, glory, wealth, and political power ... I well know that the clearer word is more useful to them and I shall write the names they use even if they were not current among the ancient Greeks, etc.' (note the equation of atticism with social and political

rhetorical theory of the Stoics was a constant bugbear.[60] Galen held understandably enough that clear usage was useful 'not only for doctors . . . but also for those whose profession is speaking [good] Greek' (*Third Commentary on Hippocrates' Prognosis* xviiib. 307. 14–308. 3).

Inexactness in language was a charge that Galen levelled particularly at the eclectic-pneumatic physician Archigenes of Apamea, who had been a well-known figure at Rome in the reign of Trajan. In his *On the Differences of the Pulse* Galen aimed at a more systematic classification of the pulse than Archigenes had achieved. The second book of this work begins with a memorable passage where Galen battles over the definition of various terms to do with the pulse and *inter alia* defends his own use of the current language of the Greeks as the clearest medium of expression (viii. 566. 1–590. 4, esp. 583. 4 ff.). The passage starts with an alleged confrontation between Galen and two sophists, a younger one who wanted to throttle him and an older one with a magnificent beard whose ears flapped like a donkey's as Galen sermonized. The style is fast and triumphant. Galen argues that words must be firmly related to things they represent, and that people must be consistent in the language they use. This 'common' language, says Galen employing the term positively like a grammarian, is perhaps an Attic dialect, though Attic has suffered many changes, or a different one altogether. In another work, *On the Composition of Drugs by Type* (xiii. 407. 8–408. 9), he again notes the many changes undergone by Attic and sees these as justifying present-day general usage. In any case, 'Attic men themselves followed the prevailing usage' (cf. Cynulcus in Athenaeus), and 'all those with the greatest reputation among the Greeks for skill in language follow the custom of their own time'. The standard-bearers in this passage are the more recent medical writers: 'we too employ the prevailing usage.' This, however, as

standing and how 'ancient Greeks' signifies those writing in Attic); ibid. vi. 633. 5–8 'those who practice that damnable pseudo-culture require us to call [the *krambê*, 'cabbage'] a radish [*raphanos*], as if we were conversing with the Athenians of 600 years ago and not with the Greeks of today, all of whom habitually apply the word *raphanos* to another plant' (Helmreich's text); *On the Composition of Drugs by Places* xiii. 8. 15–9. 4 (the disputed meaning of *siraion* [a decoction] among Atticists and others); *On Unnatural Tumours* vii. 729. 17–19: modern doctors use the form *kêlê* ('tumour', 'rupture') for tumours of the testicles rather than the Athenian *kalê* (recommended by Phrynichus, *Sophist's Stock-in-Trade* 81. 18 de Borries).

[60] Pearcy 1983.

Galen asserts in *On the Differences of the Pulse* (583. 1–2, 587. 1–7), is certainly not the speech of sailors, traders, innkeepers, bath-keepers, and tax collectors, for Galen's father was 'exact in the language of the Greeks, and as a teacher and a tutor was a Greek'.

This stress on the Greekness of Galen's speech finds expression in his call to keep his 'most pleasing and most humane' Greek free of contamination. Using Cilician, Syrian, and Gallic words alongside Athenian ones is unacceptable. Galen is not a master of all languages. More than this, 'barbarian' tongues are horribly deformed. They sound like the noises made by animals and they distort the face as they are spoken (585–6).[61] It would be interesting to know what Galen thought about Latin in this respect. As we shall see, there is absolutely no reason to suppose he thought of the Romans as barbarian. He has cause to mention Roman names and words in many of his works, and was naturally at home with the prevailing Roman terms for measures.[62] But in one passage he expresses his 'amazement' that the younger Andromachus (in the late first century) should have used the Roman word *nepeta* instead of the Greek *kalaminthê* ('catmint') when everything else in his pharmacological treatise was written in good Greek (*On Antidotes* xiv. 44. 4–10). The point is sharpened by the preceding quotation of the elder Andromachus' correct usage (xiv. 40. 9 = Heitsch LXII, 139). The objection is, again, against the mixing of languages, not against Latin in itself; but it is noteworthy all the same. As we shall see, Galen lived in Rome for over thirty years, but in many ways he remained aloof from Roman life. Purity of Greek is a good example of this.

Galen's attitude towards atticism is, then, quite complex. He was strongly drawn to the idea of purity in language (where Greekness was to be maintained at all costs), he had been reared on the canonical texts, and was thus well equipped to write atticizing Greek. But he rejected this course because he saw no reason to use any other form of Greek than the excellent language he had learnt as a child, the general language of communication. The common, educated dialect was the only way to ensure comprehension among the experts: why use a different language for writing? And yet Galen,

[61] For the comparison, which begins with Aristophanes, see Deichgräber 1956*a*: 32 n. 1.

[62] See e.g. *On the Composition of Drugs by Type* xiii. 435. 1 ff., 893. 4 ff. (*librae, unciae, sextarii*).

who was at all times concerned to advertise his genius, could not, of course, simply reject and ignore atticism. His many attacks on the atticists confess the power and standing of their position. Thus he himself had also to display his competence in Attic Greek. In a passage in the *Thrasybulus* Galen stresses how important it is to learn the Attic dialect thoroughly and to have a secondary knowledge of Ionic, Doric, and Aeolic (*Thrasybulus* v. 868. 1–869. 7).[63] More revealing comments come in a short work written late in his life on how best to read through his works. A final question that had puzzled the addressee was what to do with Galen's lexicon of Attic vocabulary (*On the Order of his Own Books* xix. 60. 11–61. 20). Galen says that many others were also asking what this huge work in forty-eight books was about. 'Unlike some people nowadays who are giving out orders, we do not require everyone to atticize in speech, just because they are doctors or philosophers and geometers and musicians and lawyers or even if they are none of these but happen simply to be either rich or just well-off.' The association between the requirement to atticize and professional and financial standing is to be noted.[64] Atticism, says Galen combatively, is simply not a part of culture at all. He had written the lexicon because doctors and philosophers are today changing the senses of 'Greek words'. A guide book to the vocabulary of 'the Attic authors' was thus made necessary. (Note the familiar shift from 'Greek' to 'Attic'.) Further, he had written another work *On Correctness* (i.e. of vocabulary), and he ends *On the Order of his Own Books* by saying 'it is best to read this before all the others'. At the end of his other bibliographical work, the *On his Own Books*, Galen again lists the forty-eight books on *The Vocabulary of Attic Authors*. In addition he shows us his close involvement with Attic language and literature. He mentions three books on Eupolis, five on Aristophanes, and two on Cratinus, which were collections of the 'political words' used by these poets, and amongst other works a book on *False Attic Usages* and something *On Clarity*

---

[63] The quotation of Homer that follows reinforces a curious similarity between this passage and Dio of Prusa, *Or.* xi. 23–4 (including the same notice on the meaning of *limên*, 'harbour', in Thessalian Greek). On the three non-Attic dialects cf. *On the Differences of the Pulse* viii. 585. 9–11.

[64] Cf. again *On the Powers of Foods* vi. 584. 6 ff. 'this is written not for those who have chosen to atticize in their speech [and who care for] honour, glory, wealth, and political power'; above, n. 59.

and Obscurity (Peri Saphêneias kai Asapheias).[65] These last two sound like checks on hyperatticism of the sort Lucian ridicules ('clarity' being an atticist catch-word). *On Correctness* no doubt also sought to check the more extreme atticists by attacking the principles of etymology, to which Galen was strongly opposed.[66] They are part of the confrontation with atticism that is seen above all in the work he mentions also in *On the Order of his Own Books* entitled *Against Those who Criticize Solecisms in Language.*

It is easy to accuse Galen of hypocrisy in matters of language. The forty-eight books on Attic usage jar with a comment he makes in a hectoring lecture surviving in Arabic about the useless rich who spend their time hunting etymologies and investigating 'how words were used in the past'.[67] Elsewhere Favorinus is taken to task in an attack on his philosophy because he had used the (non-Attic) Stoic terminology of cognition—'although he was accustomed to change each of his words into the Attic language'. On another occasion Galen says he does not care if Favorinus prefers to solecize.[68] These sets of remarks are, of course, carefully contextualized. The charge of hypocrisy is not the best way of explaining Galen's attitude to atticism. Most of his writing was necessarily constituted, inasmuch as it was medical and technical, in a non-atticist framework. But Galen could not leave it like this. He could not and would not ignore the atticists who abused him so 'variedly' when he spoke his own good Greek.[69] He answered them by appropriating their notions of purity and clarity (for he alone knew how to define properly the meanings of words), by grounding his knowledge of

[65] *On his Own Books* xix. 48. 8 ff. (the title *False Attic Usages* rests on Mueller's emendation at *Scripta minora*, ii ad loc. with p. xci). For 'political words', i.e. good, correct vocabulary suitable for elite speakers, cf. Schmid 1887–97: iv. 219, Rothe 1989: 175, on the *politikos logos* prized by the rhetoricians. There is a good discussion of Galen's grammatical and rhetorical works by Deichgräber 1956a: 3–26, who rightly brings them to bear to explain Galen's praise of Aristophanes in *On the Medical Names* (Meyerhof and Schacht 1931: 31–2), another work which is directly concerned with correct language usage. On poetry in particular cf. de Lacy 1966 on the role of poetic quotations in *On the Opinions of Hippocrates and Plato.*
[66] For its contents see *On the Opinions of Hippocrates and Plato* v. 214. 5–13 (the particular reference is to Chrysippus).
[67] *How to Recognize the Best Doctor* 129. 21 in the translation from the Arabic of Iskandar 1988. Cf. the Ulpianite 'word-hunters' in Athenaeus. See also Nutton 1990: 252–3.
[68] *On the Best Teaching* i. 41. 12–42. 6; *On the Differences of the Pulse* viii. 587. 13.
[69] *On the Differences of the Pulse* viii. 588. 1–5.

language in the same texts that they used, and by using non-Attic words as he thought necessary. Like them he made it quite plain that his own usage was far removed from that of the ordinary man. Thus for all his differences from the atticists he perhaps best of all shows their tight grip on the Greek elite and the inability of even a very great individual to resist the purifying call.

Two figures may be briefly compared with Galen. A hundred years before him Plutarch of Chaeroneia saw the current vogue of wearing 'the thin, light coat of Lysias'—a humorous allusion to that orator's noted Attic plainness—and the stress on reproducing the style rather than the content of Plato and Xenophon as signs of superficiality and stupidity.[70] In a familiar stylistic gesture he pays tribute to the 'simple clarity of genuine atticism' (fr. 186 Sandbach). Here Plutarch, like Galen, borrows the phraseology of his contemporaries but is far away from the meaning it had for most of them. The influence of the atticizing movement which was beginning in his time is certainly evident in his own usage.[71] But his wide interests and prodigious reading in classical and Hellenistic literature encouraged him to use a vocabulary far greater than most atticists ever had from their approved authors, as well as syntactical and grammatical forms they deplored.[72] Whether this would have changed, had Plutarch lived in the heyday of the sophistic, we cannot say. One philosopher who did live in this period and rejected the atticizers' rules is the sceptic Sextus Empiricus, a physician of the 'empirical' school who is best regarded as a contemporary of Galen. In *Against the Grammarians* and *Against the Rhetors* (= *Adversus mathematicos* i–ii) he too upholds general usage (*sunêtheia*) against the claims of linguistic purism (*Hellênismos*) and the requirements of the analogists and etymologists (atticists by other names). Like Galen he was concerned with the problem of how referents are to be signed.[73] Sextus has his own professional philosophical concerns at heart in his thoughts on language as well as his un-sceptically active hostility to the arts in general.[74] As with Galen, it is interesting to find that he does nevertheless display some interest in purism. Different sorts of speech should, he says, preserve their integrity (*Against the Grammarians* 176). More

---

[70] *How to Listen to Lectures* 42d–e; *How to Detect Progress in Virtue* 79d.
[71] See 'Language' n. 25.   [72] Cf. Phrynichus, *Selection* 160, 243 F.
[73] See Desbordes 1982; Dalimier 1991.   [74] Fortuna 1986.

revealing is his advice that, if one is speaking to *philologoi*, 'a more sophisticated, scholarly usage [*asteioteran kai philologon sunêtheian*]' is to be hunted after (235); if one is speaking to one's slaves, use vocabulary appropriate to them: for example, instead of the Greek *artophorion*, 'bread basket' (apparently a non-Attic word), slaves should be asked for the *panarion* (= Latin *panarium*), 'even if it is barbarian' (234). One of the *sunêtheiai* ('customary usages') which has its appropriate place is 'the ancient usage' of the Athenians (228). So although Sextus is not an atticist, he is intensely aware of the social function of language (cf. 5). If his sceptical suspension of judgement fails him in matters of social class, this failure at least allows us to see once more the importance of language differentiation in the Greek society of this period.

To sum up. The nature of our evidence makes it all too easy to take language purism as a purely literary affair without meaning or function in the real world. It is our job to look further and to appreciate the essential unity behind intra-elite wrangles of the kind we have been looking at. These rivalries, which are so clearly attested in our period in the great multiplication of grammatical and rhetorical aids, reflect partly the genuine difficulty of isolating and reproducing a linguistic ideal and partly the importance of this ideal to the enjoyment of authority and to control over its sources. Although other labels could be used to assert purity of language (cf. Galen's borrowing of the grammarians' 'common' educated standard, or claims to *Hellênismos*, 'good Greek'), the status of the classical Athenian texts ensured that 'atticism' was the most forceful and significant term in use. And while it was possible to disagree as to which classical texts should be imitated, those like the Antiätticist who advocated a wider variety of sources must always have stood in the shadow of the atticists, whose aims, if not methods, they shared. The attention commanded by classicizing/atticizing Greek is particularly striking given the continuing use of the non-classicizing educated standard for many everyday purposes. But it is not surprising if we recall the importance the ancient elite accorded the literary-cultural events for which classicizing language was appropriate and, more than this, the intense pleasure they derived from their *paideia*, their 'education' in classical literature and moral/political thought, and from the distinction such education enacted between themselves as the heirs of the classics and the masses, whose stake in the past was necessarily limited.[75]

Language, then, functioned as a badge of elite identity. As we saw in the preceding chapter, it seems likely that real changes in living speech were an important factor behind the rise of purism and the accompanying intensification of the usual social and political divisions. The rise of Latin was also noted there as an external factor which led to the erection of barriers around educated Greek. Over and above these, classicizing/atticizing language must certainly be understood in conjunction with the general role of the classical past in shaping Greek identity under Rome. It is to the meaning of this wider classicism that I now turn.

[75] I may add here that another group disadvantaged by this 'logocentrism' was undoubtedly women (of whatever social class), for in general only elite males enjoyed the privileged access to the education system which sustained classicizing Greek and all that went with it. However, lack of evidence about the precise effect of linguistic and other forms of classicism on the position of women discourages proper examination of the subject, though relevant comments about male attitudes will be made in the discussion of changing male views of fidelity and marriage at 'Novel' nn. 61 ff. (see also 'Conclusion' nn. 1, 8–9, 'Past' n. 48).

3

Past and Present

INTRODUCTION

The phenomenon of atticism leads naturally to a discussion of the wider relationship between the Greek past and the present in the second sophistic. This is a more complicated matter. Atticism is of course a part of the general reinvention and recreation of the classical age that is so striking in our period. But, as has been noted, the atticists never sought to control the language of the non-elite as the promoters of *katharevousa* did in modern times, cynically or otherwise. With atticism we are dealing with something of concern to the elite only (even though elite–mass relations are an essential element in it). History and tradition are different creatures. Actual reinvention and recreation of foundation legends and myths was no doubt in the hands of the elite (I shall be looking at some examples of this control below). But the statements of literary texts, the historical themes of the sophists and rhetors, historical references and assumptions in political oratory, the presence of semi-historical and historical tales in the ever popular entertainment of the pantomime, evidence from the competitions, festivals, and visual arts of this era, together with the 'sub'-literary pseudo-histories of Alexander the Great and other historical figures all suggest that 'ordinary' people had some knowledge of history and a sense of the tradition of the Greek world and its culture which was independent of the elite. This permeation of the past through the various social layers naturally made it into an object of political interest over the whole arena of civil society, among the tribes, ephebes, cults, schools, assemblies, processions, and all the other institutions of the ancient Greek world that allowed government to rest on a wide base of consent. The major beneficiary of the general respect for tradition was again the male establishment class. For, as has been remarked, in our period more than ever they took care to associate themselves with the traditions and history of their cities and of the Greek world as a whole, and by tying themselves to the leaders of classical Greece furthered their own claims to rule in the present.

THE USES OF HISTORY

The emphasis on the past as a source of authority was not only of internal political importance. The accent on Greek tradition was also of interest to Rome and certainly has implications for the Greeks' relationship with the ruling power. Many media in which the past was a particular focus were encouraged and licensed by Roman government—for example, the prolific festivals which celebrated ancient gods and city founders, or quasi-political institutions like Hadrian's panhellenic council, or the granting to cities of old or old-sounding names. Rome's attitude is hardly surprising. Romans had been nursed on Greek literature and tradition since long before the inception of the Empire; indeed, the Greek language was certainly familiar to them by the time of their political involvement in Greece at the end of the third century BC.[1] They came to Greece as philhellenes, not to admire what they found there passively and uncritically, but to shape it according to their pre-existing idea of what Greece was. In terms of imperial policy they had no special interest in the provinces of the contemporary Greek world. Under the Empire the demilitarized zone of Old Greece, the Roman province of Achaia, was indeed probably less advanced in its infrastructure and economic development than many other areas, while the prosperity of Provincia Asia owed nothing specifically to Roman guidance.[2] What the Greek world did offer to Roman visitors and officials in addition to what other provinces could provide was a history the Romans were familiar with. Romans expected to find the past when they journeyed to Greece in their pursuit of culture. If they did not find it, they could always lament its decline and proceed to reconstruct the Greece they had been taught to imagine, just as the modern philhellenes were to do many centuries later. As Pliny puts it to his friend Maximus, 'Reflect that in being sent to Provincia Achaia you are being sent to

---

[1] Dubuisson 1985: 262–3, id. 1992: 188.
[2] On the decline of Old Greece see Larsen 1938; Kahrstedt 1954; Alcock 1993. The surveys of Sartre 1991: 199–238 (Greece), 257–308 (Asia Minor) are also useful.

that true and pure Greece ... Reverence its ancient glory and its present old age ... It is Athens you are approaching, Lacedaemon you are ruling ... Remember the past of each city without despising it because it is this no more.'[3]

The Greek past functioned as a common framework of communication between the Greeks and their rulers. Because of this it was not free to take on any guise it chose. Like any ideological formation serving particular interests, it was a necessarily distorted form of communication marked by certain lacunas, repetitions, and equivocations. Thus some explicit emphases of Greek freedom were known by the Greeks to be unwelcome to Rome, if expressed in the wrong context. Correspondingly, properly contextualized declamatory themes taken from the Persian or Peloponnesian Wars could be endlessly recycled for both Greek and Roman consumption in perfect safety.[4] Equivocation and hesitancy about the meaning of the past shows clearly in the integration of Romans in festivals

[3] On travel to Greece for study see Daly 1950 on the Republican period; cf. for the 2nd c. Aulus Gellius *Attic Nights* i. 2. 1 'qui Roma in Graeciam ad capiendum ingenii cultum concesserant'; Apulius, *Apology* 72, *Florida* 18 (86, 162, 167 Valettte). The best Roman imaginary Greek landscape is Virgil's Arcadia: see Snell 1953 (but note Jenkyns 1989). On the modern views see Tsigakou 1981 (with many illustrations of how the Greek countryside should look; cf. the Roman taste for the idealized countryside, especially as we see it in 1st-c. BC and AD wall painting: see e.g. Strong 1988: 68–70); Herzfeld 1987: 49–76; Angelomatis-Tsougarakis 1990: 85–100, 118–45.

Pliny the Younger's advice to Maximus is in *Letters* viii. 24. For a harsh verdict on the present-day realities see Tacitus, *Annals* ii. 55. 1. The exploration of Cicero's love of the ancient Greeks and contempt for the moderns in Trouard 1942 reveals Romans' underlying feelings well enough, and there is further useful discussion, mostly on the late Republican period, in Petrochilos 1974 and Wardman 1976. For percipient analysis of the views of Cicero, Pliny the Elder (cf. Wallace-Hadrill 1990: 92–6), Pliny the Younger, and others see now Woolf 1994, and further below, n. 35. Note also Russell 1990*b*: 1–17 on the Romans' fascination with Greek literature and rhetoric in the Antonine period (cf. 'Introduction' n. 10).

[4] See below, 'Plutarch' nn. 95–6, for Plutarch's recommendation that Greek politicians under Rome should avoid making populist references to the Persian Wars before the *dêmos* ('people', as often, in the sense of the non-elite); and for the Persian wars as common property of Greeks and Romans, hence functioning occasionally as a channel of communication between them, see now Spawforth 1994*a* (which is, however, mainly concerned with the Roman perspective). Cf. also 'Plutarch' nn. 125–7 on the Greeks' sometimes hostile application to Rome of the terminology used to describe the old Persian empire.

Note the rather different phenomenon of Romans expressing their own political discontents through Greek myths: Tacitus, *Annals* vi. 29. 5 (cf. Cassius Dio lviii. 24. 4, Suetonius, *Tiberius* 61. 3), id. *Dialogue on Orators* 3; Juvenal, *Satires* iv. 65; Cassius Dio lxi. 16. 2² (cf. lxiii. 9. 4, 22. 6); *Augustan History, Two Maximini* 8. 5.

such as the procession of Salutaris at Ephesus, where the festive march celebrating the Ephesians' Greek identity is licensed by Roman governors and validates not only local power but also Roman rule by carrying Roman statues in its midst and by taking place on days devoted to the cult of the emperors.[5]

It might be expected that the Greeks' obsession with the past would have had some nationalistic import along the lines of the nationalist movements of new nations and regimes in modern times, for the histories of such peoples have often been carefully packaged in accordance with official ideologies and objectives.[6] If nationalism means the feeling and practice of self-consciousness and self-assertion of a racially or culturally identifiable group inhabiting (or striving to inhabit) a politically defined territory, then the comparison fails, since the ancient Greeks lacked the modern idea of 'nation' (whatever this means in particular modern situations): it was not clear who was a Greek by race (though many Greeks did claim a Greek patriliny), nor did national borders exist within which all 'Greeks' were gathered (something which has been a particular stumbling block for modern Greeks). That said, and despite a long history of political segmentation built round local rather than 'national' patriotism, the Greeks continued to be fully conscious in our period of an essential shared cultural identity, mediated through a common language, that was defined not simply by its own coherence but at all times by differentiation from the *barbaroi* who lacked Greek culture and speech. In the authors I shall be examining later the Hellene/barbarian opposition, which had been developed long before in the classical period, is alive and kicking. Romans were apparently conceived of as a *tertium quid*, an unstable position that was neither one nor the other. Pan-Greek cultural consciousness fostered by the educational system was naturally strongest among the elite whose internal identity as Hellenes was tightly focused by classicism and atticism on the history of the classical period in general and that of Athens in particular, a history which offered both a focus of allegiance and a source of commentary. This is not to say that a man of Halicarnassus or Nicomedia necessarily felt 'Athenian' (though in the case of Arrian of Nicomedia this does indeed

    [5] See Rogers 1991: 83, 114.
    [6] Of the many studies of modern examples see e.g. Smith 1976: 4, 16–17, id. 1986: 174–208; Morgan 1983; Clogg 1985; many of the original texts collected in Kedourie 1971 reflect this need. The work of Halbwachs and others on the construction of 'collective memory' is also relevant to these enquiries; see recently e.g. Connerton 1989.

seem to have been the case); but to suggest that to know of Sophocles, Xenophon, and Demosthenes as well as Homer, Pindar, and Herodotus and to be familiar with the stories they told was to feel part of a group whose homogeneity and status was guaranteed by hundreds of years of internal and external recognition. In this sense 'race' was not as problematic as it is for us. Many claims to Greek ancestry were made and easily accepted, if Greek culture and speech could be proved, through the familiar ploy of extending or creating a genealogy of descent. It is noticeable that the deployment of Greek ancestry worked better—or was perhaps more plausible—in the nearer Greek East, especially in Anatolia. Other cities, perhaps lying farther away, might be able to claim Macedonian paternity (which was not the same) or might not bother at all, in which case the inhabitants could be or could feel rejected by the cultural insiders of the Greek world, as we shall see with Lucian of Samosata.[7]

Articulating local patriotism through local history, real or recreated, was a natural part of this Hellenism. The feelings of rivalry and hostility towards neighbouring cities which were so prevalent in the second sophistic period and which certainly made use of tradition do resemble modern manifestations of nationalism on the surface. The key difference is that there was no united pan-Greek political action behind them. These are the local squabbles of neighbours living in the same street. For anyone not used to the idea it must be particularly striking that there was never any concerted action against Rome. The reason for this is that the Greek establishment was protected by the Romans and was integrated into the Empire by Rome's willingness to confer her citizenship on rich provincials who wanted it and to allow them to participate in her government.[8] We should not imagine that this produced an

[7] Membership of the Panhellenion, in which Greek ancestry was an important qualification (see below, n. 22), is attested so far only in the provinces of Achaia, Macedonia, Thrace, Crete-Cyrene, and Asia: see Spawforth and Walker 1985: 79–81. On Macedonian origin cf. Strubbe 1984–6: 273–4 (suppression/acknowledgement of Macedonian origin), and see also below, 'Arrian' nn. 47–9, on Appian (and below here in text).

[8] How many of the eastern elite actually did have citizenship is a matter of dispute. It is often assumed that there was a progressive increase in the number of provincial *cives* and that Caracalla's Empire-wide extension of the citizenship in 212 was a natural consequence of this. However, it is clear from the epigraphical record that a large number of new citizens was created by the *Constitutio Antoniniana*. These citizens, who bear Caracalla's gentilicium *Aurelius*, include members of the elite, and this at least modifies the traditional picture. See Follet 1976: 63–105, Buraselis 1989: 120–48, and of older work Sasse 1958, Sherwin-White 1973: 380–94.

undifferentiated 'mediterranean' ruling class. For Greeks the consciousness of being Greek remained extremely strong. Overall this means that we should be wary of assuming, as many have, that prosopographical contacts between Greeks and the Roman world necessarily indicate a generally close integration between the two without enquiring further into individuals' attitudes in such situations.[9] For it hardly needs to be said that personal identity is not a homogeneous mass. It is quite wrong to assume the priority of one area of a man's life—such as his Roman career—without at least asking whether other areas may not have been more important. It may be possible to get a clearer picture of the complex matter of how individuals see themselves by enquiring, where opportunity arises, after their political, cultural-cognitive, and spiritual identities ('who do you vote for?', 'what books do you read?', 'where do you go to church?', etc.). I do not mean to pretend that these things are discrete in any individual or society. They are of course overlapping and interconnected. But these are the important areas in which individuals express themselves as part of social groupings and the attempt to discern and evaluate them should be made. Choices in political allegiances, for example, often seem out of step with what one reads or the religion one adopts. A man may appear British in his cultural-cognitive outlook and love the Church of England; simultaneously he can support the idea of a federal Europe. For most of the time there is no essential incompatibility between such views, and they can easily be held in tandem without conflict. It is indeed only the crude discourse of nationalism, subconsciously absorbed and so difficult to dislodge, that pits groups against other groups, and leads to the stark assumption that the Greek elite must have been pro-Roman in all respects, since they could not otherwise have supported Rome at all.

Cognitively and spiritually those who are studied in detail in this book were avowedly Greek (with the possible exception of Lucian, whose Semitic background apparently led to doubts about his exact place in Greek culture, and Appian, for whom Macedon was also an important personal reference point). Yet at the same time many of these and other members of the elite accepted a Roman political identity. This was both political-administrative in the sense that

---

[9] On some of the dangers of prosopography see Stone 1987: 57–65; Carney 1973; Graham 1974.

they were very often Roman citizens or (in the case of a small minority) had a Roman career, and also political-ideological in the sense that Rome's interest in elite rule coincided with their own. But their loyalty to the idea of Greece was also political in ideological terms (something I shall be coming back to). On the wider political plane there is a degree of contradiction between their Greek and Roman identities. This is not surprising. For it is precisely when a people is under foreign domination that choices have to be made between acceptance or resistance and about preferences within these alternatives. The Greeks sometimes found these choices difficult—though it is easy, by selecting or ignoring passages of literary texts and by relying on the (in fact) heavily contextualized evidence of public discourse in the epigraphic record, to suggest otherwise. Certainly, in the case of the intellectuals studied in this book it seems clear that even those who were involved in Roman government did not put their Roman identity before their Greek one.

Why was it, then, that Rome supported local traditions in the Greek world and encouraged Greeks to identify with their past? Better modern comparisons than the new nations are offered by examples of societies still under colonial rule where traditions have been invented or at least encouraged to move in a certain direction by the colonial rulers with the tacit or explicit connivance of the local elites. In these cases the past served the convenience of the colonial administration. At the same time local elites filtered their own power through a history acceptable to the rulers with the aim of furthering their own position and entrenching their own identity. We find, for example, in British Africa cases where tribal units were invented thereby 'restoring' ethnic boundaries as they had supposedly existed in order to assist the efficiency of the administration and its ideology of *Volksmission*. It is reported that local chiefs were able to manipulate the 'tribes' to their own advantage. Again in British Africa there are studies of how unwritten customary law was rigidified in a form the administrators could work with. The effect of such changes was not only to help the colonial power but also to advantage the vested interests which happened to be in control locally at the time of the codification. That is, the past was being put at the service of present-day power arrangements among both the ruling and the ruled elites. To take another example, there is clear evidence from British India of collusion (probably

not too strong a word) between the imperial government and leading status groups. In particular the imperial courts' tendency to
respect Sanskrit texts lead to the 'Brahminization' of Indian law
whereby unwritten, more flexible village law systems were sub-
jected to the text-based classical Indian system of jurisprudence.[10]
Here, as in the case of the Greeks, an ancient written culture with
a prestige language commanded respect from the ruling power which
was consequently keen to further the position of those already in
control by preferencing the impulses of their traditions. The appeal
of recreating the past in ways like this is not always restricted to
elites. Although it is very difficult to gauge the feelings of the
ordinary population, there is no reason to think that recreation of
tradition would necessarily be seen by them as a repressive strategy.
The assertion of (reinvented) traditions can be widely supported in
the popular imagination, as for example in the quite extraordinary
case of the Highland Tradition of Scotland,[11] or it can be greeted by
equal amounts of enthusiasm and suspicion, as in the story of the
reinvention of Greece by the nineteenth-century patriots and the
western Philhellenes.[12]

These examples are merely suggestive of the many voices the past
has as it serves different interests simultaneously. In the case of the
ancient Greek world and Rome we must again be sensitive to the
possibility that benefit was available for rulers and ruled along
the same lines. The past assisted the local Greek elites to secure
their power by allowing them to claim a connection with the
recognized leaders of the great days of their countries; tradition
was also what the Romans wanted to find in the Greek world. The
difficulties of interpretation in particular cases are immense. Take
for example an inscription from Erythrae celebrating the advent of
the city's eponymous hero, who is responsible for restoring its
'good government, wealth, and morality' (*IGR* iv. 1540 = *IK* ii
[Erythrai ii], 224). This 'New Erythros' very likely signals the presence of the emperor Lucius Verus, who tarried in the cities of the
Asian littoral on his way to the Parthian War in 162/3.[13] On one

[10] Africa: Colson 1975: 74–83; Iliffe 1979: 318–41; Ranger 1983. India: Derret
1961: 28 ff.; Rudolph and Rudolph 1965: 32 ff.
[11] A key particular of which—the filibeg—was apparently invented by an English
Quaker industrialist: Trevor-Roper 1983.
[12] Herzfeld 1987; St. Clair 1972 on the Philhellenes themselves.
[13] Robert 1981: esp. 354–5. The Sibyl's cave in which the text stood was (?)
restored under Marcus and Lucius by a certain Marcus [Clau]dius P[-]: *IK* ii (Erythrai
ii), 225–6.

level the inscription, a pronouncement of the local sibyl, is a token of the integration of an eastern city into the Empire. On the other hand it bristles with local patriotism as it stresses her parentage and her loyalty to Erythrae, where she has lived for 'thrice three hundred years'. No Roman is named; indeed, as we will be seeing in literary texts of Plutarch and others, the era of prosperity is attributed to a Greek god, here specifically to the local hero. We must ask ourselves whether most people who went into the sibyl's cave and read this text would have really seen in it a reference to Rome rather than to their homeland. If they thought of both, is it really likely that Rome had a greater place in their hearts than Erythrae? Surely not. This sibyl's statements are, of course, in harmony with the feelings of those who governed Erythrae with Rome's support. 'Good government, wealth, and morality' would naturally be read by them as the results of their efforts now sanctioned by L. Verus. At the same time it was possible for other readers to integrate Rome into the local myth, if they knew of Verus' visit. But unless one did know of it, the text could surely be read only as an affirmation of local dignities.

There are numerous examples in the second sophistic of cities reasserting or recreating the roles of founders and civic myths.[14] We should certainly understand the function of these figures as one of dignifying not just the community in question but the rule of its establishment class by appeal to the mythological and literary network of the classical and archaic age (with which there might well be no long-standing connection). Again, there are links with Roman philhellenism. It is nice to find Lucian observing the importance of the 'public and official lies' used by cities and peoples about their past. At *Lovers of Lies* 3–4 he says these fabrications are not only designed to make cities appear 'grander'. If they were suppressed, the 'guides' would starve, 'since foreigners [i.e. tourists] wouldn't want to hear the truth, even for free!' Pausanias similarly reports that guides at Argos know the truth but cannot change the minds of 'the many' who want to hear what they already believe (ii. 23. 6). Romans are certainly included here. Tourist enjoyment

---

[14] Cf. e.g. in western Asia Minor the cases of Nacoleia, Synnada, and Dorylaeum with Jones 1940: 49–50, Robert 1980: 240, 412, Andrei 1984: 134. There are informative general discussions by Andrei 1984: 128–35, Weiss 1984 (good on coin evidence), Frézouls 1991 (the Asian cities), Mitchell 1993: i. 207–10, and esp. Strubbe 1984–6. Robert 1975: 162–88 is a very suggestive investigation of how a city can lock into the world of Greek myth (whose full potential is revealed to us by the poets—here Nonnus).

of the past cannot easily be disentangled from more obviously political aspects, for visitors often have preconceptions of the places
they go to, which stem from certain cultural-political positions, as
in the case of the Romans in Greece.[15]

Athens and Sparta were particularly good at presenting themselves to visitors as 'museum' cities. Sparta capitalized on the famous
'Lycurgan' education system with its brutal, visual rituals, and retained through its myths an influence in the world that was entirely
disproportionate to its economic strength. The revival of the Doric
dialect (apparently on the basis of continuing spoken forms) to
record dedications to Artemis Orthia is the literary side of a very
physical archaism.[16] In the case of Athens there are numerous examples of the city appealing to Romans for sympathy on the basis
of its past glories.[17] Athens was also of course the city offering the
clearest source of identity for the prevailing culture of the Greek
elite.[18] Aelius Aristides' *Panathenaicus* is a particularly prominent
example of the praise she attracted. The physical reorganization of
Attic history in terms of actual stone-by-stone movement of some
temples (or parts of temples) from the countryside into the city of
Athens and from within the city to the centre in the time of Augustus
and later is a good example of the creation of the 'museum' as an
institution performative of cultural identity. The resiting of at least
one of the temples seems also to have had a politico-religious di-
mension aimed at Rome.[19] A more obvious example of an appeal to
Roman philhellenism can be seen in the constitutional reforms at
Athens under Roman rule. Building on earlier changes Hadrian's

[15] Cf. Casson 1974: 229–99 for a general account of ancient tourism; Hunt 1984:
391–408 lists passages of secular and pagan religious tourism.

[16] Cartledge and Spawforth 1989: 190–211. Tourists included Plutarch, who witnessed the rituals (*Lycurgus* 18. 2, *Aristides* 17. 10), and Pausanias, who describes the
buildings (iii. 11. 1–18. 5). Dialect: Debrunner and Scherer 1969: §67 (with reference
to modern Tsakonian). Artemis Orthia: Woodward 1929: nos. 43 ff. (from Hadrian
onwards; NB not all of these are in the revived dialect forms—contrast nos. 50–1
from the same year).

[17] Plutarch, *Sulla* 13. 5, cf. Florus, *Epitome* i. 40. 10; Appian, *Civil Wars* ii. 88.
368; Tacitus, *Annals* ii. 53. 3–4, cf. *Histories* ii. 4. 1.

[18] See esp. Bowie 1974: 195–7. Note Lucian's criticism of the verb *Athêniô*, 'long
for Athens', at *The False Critic* 24.

[19] Cf. Thompson and Wycherley 1972: 160–8; Shear 1991: 362; Alcock 1993: 191–
5. On the 'museum' and its function for both colonial and new-nationalist regimes
see Anderson 1991: 178–84; many suggestive essays on the comparable role of sites
and institutions in contructing the identity of modern France can be found in Nora
1984–92.

constitution clearly made the Athenian state more archaic and elitist by vesting greater powers in the council of the Areopagus, the traditional body that had held power in pre-democratic Athens. This was to the advantage of Rome and the local elite.[20] With British East Africa in mind we may wonder (*mutatis mutandis*) who gained from the establishment of a thirteenth tribe named after the emperor between AD 121/2 and 124/5, which again benefited rulers and ruled by tying present-day power arrangements into the traditional civic-political structure of the city.[21]

The Panhellenion, the pan-Greek council instituted at Athens by Hadrian in 131/2, is another good example of this sort of thing. The new council was very much focused on the Greek past. Documents relating to the entry of cities like Magnesia ad Maeandrum, Cibyra, and Cyrene show that prospective members had to demonstrate good long-term relations with Rome and Greekness in respect of race and culture. The primacy of Athens, Sparta, and Argos in the Greek heritage was particularly important in the demonstration of this Greekness (in which, it may be observed, the old Greek subdivisions of 'Ionian' Athenians and 'Dorian' Peloponnesians had long since ceased to bear meaning). Emphasis was laid on proving a respectable background by promoting eponyms, local cults, and foundation legends. Some states, such as Cibyra, manufactured false claims—in Cibyra's case that it was both a colony of the Lacedaemonians and kin of the Athenians.[22] The reasons why the Panhellenion was established are not fully known. Nor is it known why some cities were members and some not. We can at least understand its desired ideological function as a representation of the living experience of the Greek elite with respect to the past. Although Roman citizenship was not a requirement of delegates, Roman power was present in the form of the cult of Hadrian

---

[20] Geagan 1967; Oliver 1968: 21–5; esp. Follet 1976: 116–25. The spirit of the reforms is suggested by Eusebius (198 Helm²) and Syncellus (659 Dind.) who speak of Hadrian's laws as recalling those of Dracon and Solon (cf. Graindor 1934: 73 on the 'illusion de la πάτριος πολιτεία').

[21] Date: Follet 1976: 121. Above, n. 10.

[22] See Oliver 1970: 94 ff., nos. 5, 6, 7; Touloumakos 1971: 42–6; Follet 1976: 125–35; esp. Spawforth and Walker 1985 and 1986, and recently Wörrle 1992: 337–49. Cibyra: *OGIS* 497 (a better text of Oliver no. 6); cf. Strubbe 1984–6: 259, 276 on its 'hero' Cibyras and the mythological links created through him with Cidrama and Tabae, 281 on its place in the Panhellenion (for Strabo xiii. 4. 17 [C 631] the ancestry is basically Lydian). Synnada also claimed Dorian and Ionian ancestry: Strubbe 269–70, Spawforth and Walker 1986: 89.

'Panhellenios'. For Rome the council was presumably another way
of tying the Greek elite into the Empire. We are not dealing with
some abstract philhellenic eccentricity on the part of Hadrian. Rather,
we have a superb example of Rome recreating the Greek past in its
idealized form, of making Greece how it should be. It is perhaps
for this reason that the Panhellenion was never particularly popular
with the Greeks themselves.[23] Hadrian's policies towards the
Amphictyonic league and in particular towards Delphi itself (another
tourist centre where the 'museum' of the Greek past was frequently
tampered with by Roman visitors) offer many parallels.[24]

One other well-known example of recreation might be quoted,
since I shall have cause to mention it again later. This is the case of
Alexander of Abonuteichos in Paphlagonia, the man attacked by
Lucian as the charlatan who invented the healing cult of the snake-
god Glycon. One of the interesting things about Lucian's account
in the *Alexander* is that he presents the cult as a danger to Rome
and to anyone who lacks the philosophical education needed to
resist its snares. A part of this is Alexander's attempt to claim a false
pedigree for Abonuteichos by associating it with the major Ionian
shrines and with the Milesian foundation of Sinope (*Alexander* 11,
29). The alleged antiquity of the god called the 'New Asclepius'
was indispensable to the establishment of the cult. Archaeological
evidence confirms its success which, as Lucian indicates, was of
great commercial importance and paved the way for the emperor to
allow Abonuteichos to change its name to the more respectable
'City of Ion' after the eponym of the Ionians (*Alexander* 23, 58);
the name is attested on coins from the 160s and survives in today's
Inebolu. Recreation here is taken as far as it can be. The results
are familiar. Approval by Rome, local dignification and thus rivalry
with other nearby centres, 'especially Amastris' (25).[25] This last
element, city rivalry, is, as has been remarked, a widespread phenomenon. We see the use to which local cults and local history

[23] See Spawforth and Walker 1985: 80–1 (who suggest that the absence, for example, of the major Asian cities is due to the nature of our evidence; that is always
possible). The notion that the Panhellenion played a major role in encouraging civic
classicism—Robert 1980: 412, Strubbe 1984–6: 280–282—is quite wrong.
[24] Jacquemin 1991: 229–31; tampering: Daux 1975, id. 1976.
[25] Note the satellite town of Amastris called the 'City of Doros' after the mythical
ancestor of the Dorians: Robert 1980: 414. On Lucian's *Alexander* see below, 'Lucian'
nn. 91–108.

were put against neighbours clearly also, for example, in the disputes of Nysa and Magnesia ad Maeandrum and Tarsus and Aegeae.[26]

Civic classicism depended to a large extent on the industry of intellectuals. We know that local history was especially popular in the second sophistic period. It was often based upon etymological research (an important tool of the language purists). This could happily derive the name of Tralles from the hero Tralleus or Nacoleia from the nymph Nacole or could connect Iconium with the 'icon' or image of the Gorgon. Examples may be multiplied.[27] In these efforts Telephus of Pergamum, whom we met earlier, is joined by men like the medical writer and local historian Hermogenes of Smyrna, who wrote origins of Asian and European cities, a history of Smyrna, and some sort of catalogue (*pinax*) of Romans and Smyrnaeans, and the great sophist P. Anteius Antiochus of Aegeae, whose *On My Fatherland* no doubt celebrated the local cult of Asclepius in the manner of the Maximus of Aegeae mentioned by Philostratus at the beginning of the *Life of Apollonius*. Antiochus' speech successfully renewing Aegeae's hereditary ties with Argos happens to survive commemorated on stone, while Philostratus reports to us his famous defence of the Cretans' rights regarding the Tomb of Zeus (*VS* 569 'debating brilliantly with scientific and theological lore of every kind').[28] Plutarch's pride in obtaining the right to wear crowns for two (?local) clans who descended from the Heracleidae is part of the same process.[29] No doubt any respectable town would have had local experts ready to produce books on its history, political or otherwise, as we know from inscriptional testimonies and as, for example, Galen found when he visited the city of Hephaestias on Lemnos.[30] The purely antiquarian aspect of this research should not be ignored. We see it on a wider scale in the works of men like Cephalion and Jason of Argos, whose universal

[26] Robert 1977a: 75–6, 107 ff., 119 ff.; Strubbe 1984–6: 263 on the similarity of Tarsus' and Aegeae's mythological origins.

[27] Bowie 1974: 184–8. Etymology: Strubbe 1984–6: 258–9, 270–3.

[28] Hermogenes: *IK* xxiii (Smyrna i), 536; *FGrH* 579; Bowie 1974: 186–7. Antiochus: *FGrH* 747; Robert 1977a: 119–29; it is possible that the defence of the Cretans was simply a declamation (Kohl 1915: no. 162), but cf. again Lucian, *Lovers of Lies* 3. Maximus: below, 'Philostratus' n. 24.

[29] *On God's Slowness to Punish* 558b on the Lykormai and the Satilaioi; on Plutarch and the Heracleidae see n. 58.

[30] Inscriptions: Strubbe 1984–6: 285–7; Galen, *On the Temperament and Power of Simple Drugs* xii. 174. 2–6.

histories were restricted to the Greek world down to Alexander.[31] Another good example of the trend is A. Claudius Charax of Pergamum, consul at Rome in 147, who wrote over forty books of *Hellenic and Italic Histories*. Myth and prehistory dominate in the surviving fragments (which mention early Rome).[32] Charax also wrote two books on Augustus and seven on Nero and his successors, and it may be right to suggest that in his literary work he is making a link between the glorious Greek past and the glorious Roman present, in which he shared. But a comparison with Arrian or Cassius Dio, about whom we know so much more, would encourage us to read Charax's Roman researches in the light of his Roman career and personal political ambitions and to suggest that his identity as a Greek was ultimately more important to him.[33]

Whatever the feelings of these particular men are, it is important to see antiquarian and historical research as a crucial element in the Greeks' affirmation of their Greek identity. It is well known that the Greeks' interest in their own past contrasts strikingly with their lack of interest in Rome's past and present and in the Greek world under Roman rule. This is a marked feature of much second sophistic writing and it obviously represents a reaction to Rome of some sort. If we look at the Greek past in its function as a channel of communication between Greeks and Romans, there is no problem with the Greeks' accent on their history. Romans as tourists or as administrators were expected to be interested, as for example Aristides assumed in the case of the two Roman governors he treated to his 'tour' of Smyrna.[34] On the other hand we should be aware that Greeks' devotion to the Greek past occupies quite different ideological territory from Rome's. Rome's philhellenism was, as it were, the transcendental part of her government of the Greek world, her way of making Greece what she wanted. Within Roman society itself there was always a danger that philhellenism would show its variance with itself that was due to its use of a past not its own; which explains the residual anti-Greek feelings of men like Florus

---

[31] *FGrH* 93, 94; Bowie 1974: 177–8.   [32] Andrei 1984.

[33] Contrast the more avowedly Roman perspective of Hadrian's freedman Aelius Phlegon of Tralles (*FGrH* 257), whose chronographical *Olympiads* (from 776 BC) gave far more space to recent events, especially Hadrian's reign (the period from Tiberius to Trajan being hurried through; cf. Jacoby at *FGrH* iid, p. 838); this is not surprising. Phlegon's *On Long Livers* F 37 includes a huge 'prosopographical' extract from the Italian census returns.

[34] *Orr.* xvii and xxi; below 'Aristides' nn. 148–51.

or Fronto.[35] For the Greeks the Greek past had in comparison a
stable meaning because it was theirs.[36] The strong and pervasive
feeling that they possessed the only culture and history worth having does tempt us to ask whether there was anything anti-Roman
here. This is a question I shall come back to.

THE LIVING PAST

Just as atticizing Greek turned out to be aiming for an ideal image
of the Attic dialect and to be quite happy with its own perception
of the model under imitation, so the endless rewritings of the Greek
past in our period were free to deviate from the known events of
history because for much of the time an idealized sense of the past,
not its reality, was the necessary goal. This emerges strongly in the
historical declamations of the rhetors and sophists and from other
works of pseudo-history. In assessing the past in this manner I do
not wish to deny or to downgrade the pleasure that reading or
hearing such texts gave, but to suggest that the greatest importance
lies in examining the cultural expectations which, once interiorized,
determine why texts are pleasurable. In the second sophistic this
means appreciating the sense of the past and the self-identity that
was wrapped up in it. I want at this point to turn to two examples
of such texts. In these past and present are telescoped. History and
myth are discovered to be surprisingly alive and the characters
of the past become tied up with the feelings of the present day
observer. Just as Plutarch says that his biographies of the great men
of the past are a mirror in which he seeks to see himself the better
(*Aemilius* 1. 1–2), so in these stories subject and object fuse together
and the observer is privileged to be transported to an ideal time.
   The story of Herodes Atticus, the leading sophist of second-

[35] Florus, *Epitome* i. 24. 13 'let Athens not be too pleased with herself' (comparing Rome's naval victory over Antiochus III at Myonnesus in 190 with Athens' over
Xerxes at Salamis). Fronto, *Ad M. Caes.* iii. 3. 3 (p. 38 v.d.H.²) on Herodes Atticus
as 'graeculum et indoctum'; cf. Dubuisson 1991 on the enduring pejorative associations of Latin *graecus/graeculus* (which are recognized by Plutarch, *Cicero* 5. 2, 38.
4, *Cato Major* 9. 2, and Athenaeus, *Sophists at Dinner* 50f.; see below, 'Cassius Dio'
nn. 22–4, on a probable usage in Cassius Dio).
[36] Contrast *SIG*³ 799 from Cyzicus: Antonia Tryphaena (of the Bosporan and
Thracian royal houses; Magie 1950: ii. 1368 n. 51) 'has dedicated our city's restoration as a thank-offering in memory of Augustus, concerning herself not with our
history as an ancient foundation of [the hero] Cyzicus, but pointing to the recent
favour of Agrippa, etc.' This could not have been uttered in the second sophistic.

century Athens and consul in 143, and the figure known as the 'Heracles of Herodes', is one of the most memorable in Philostratus' *Lives of the Sophists* (552–4).[37] We can probably believe Philostratus when he says his account goes back to a letter of Herodes to (Ti. Claudius) Julianus, suffect consul in or shortly after 154 and also of eastern origin.[38] It seems reasonably clear that this 'Heracles of Herodes' is the same figure as the Sostratus mentioned at the beginnning of Lucian's *Demonax*. There Lucian says he actually saw Sostratus and that in physical and philosophical prowess he was comparable to the philosopher Demonax. He tells us that he had in fact written a separate work on the man focusing on his hardiness and on his activities protecting and assisting rural travellers.[39] As far as Lucian is concerned Sostratus was born in Boeotia and lived out on Mount Parnassus in central Greece. Philostratus mentions but rejects the idea of Boeotian birth. Instead, his hero (who is not given his own name) tells Herodes that he is a son of the hero Marathon. Philostratus' account turns this Heracles into a mythological figure with familiar fairy-tale attributes of size, beauty, and dietary peculiarities. His hero is also something of a philosopher, stressing the need to suppress 'bad' myths like the story of the house of Pelops, which he has witnessed from the heights of Parnassus (cf. the Lucianic version) being performed in a tragic play at Delphi. But the most original feature of Philostratus' Heracles is his complete command of Attic Greek. Speaking as 'Agathion' ('The Good One')—a (really existing) name given him by the local farmers of Marathon and, note, Boeotia—he tells Herodes that unlike the city of Athens the 'midland' or 'interior' (*mesogeia*) of Attica remains uncorrupted by the speech of barbarian immigrants and so 'its tongue picks out notes of the purest Attic'. This concern for Attic purity is expressed through a reminiscence of a morose political tract of the fifth century BC attributed in the tradition to that favourite second sophistic author, Xenophon.[40]

What does Philostratus' account mean? First, it is clear that Sostratus/Heracles is historical: not only does Lucian claim to have

---

[37] Kindstrand 1979–80; Ameling 1983: ii. 155–8.

[38] Swain 1991*a*: 155; Julianus: Halfmann 1979: no. 94, id. 1982: 636 (the exact *origo* is unknown).

[39] Cf. Jones 1986: 98–100.

[40] Ps.-Xenophon (the 'Old Oligarch'), *Constitution of the Athenians* 2. 8. On Xenophon's popularity see Appendix A, 'Arrian' nn. 24, 26–28.

met him along with Demonax (and the *Demonax* depends for its success on personal acquaintance), but the title 'Heracles of Herodes' indicates some real degree of familiarity between the man and Herodes Atticus (who emerges from Philostratus' account in the *Lives* as someone who is fond of collecting companions and admirers). But the title also reflects on Herodes himself: if the hero-figure was his Heracles, he was Zeus. There may be a parallel here with the well-known story of the megalomaniac physician Mene-crates of Syracuse, who called himself 'Zeus' and made his former patient and aide Nicostratus of Argos his personal 'Heracles'.[41] Second, the descent of Heracles from the hero Marathon will be Herodes' fiction, since Herodes had a large estate in that part of Attica and officially termed himself *Marathônios*. In Philostratus' account it is Herodes who voices the denial of his 'earthborn' Boeotian descent: 'but Herodes says he heard him saying that his mother was a woman strong enough to drive oxen and that his father was Marathon.' Herodes' conversion of his Heracles into an Attic superman is connected to the greatest compliment of all—to Herodes' Greek. The perfect speech of Heracles mirrors Herodes' own and his desire to let everyone know it.[42]

There is no need, of course, to suppose that Lucian's version of the story is any more 'real'. Whatever the tale of Sostratus/Heracles was originally about (and madness is one plausible suggestion),[43] both Lucian and Philostratus/Herodes made it serve as a vehicle for their own interests. It may be that these were not so different. Lucian's *Demonax* portrays as its hero the free-speaking figure of the philosopher, who as a product of the moneyed and educational establishment (cf. *Demonax* 3) could confront the local and the Roman elite for their own moral good with almost total impunity. Demonax used a thoroughly well-rehearsed discourse, which both he and his targets perceived as a socially acceptable method of letting off steam when the rich, powerful, and educated got it wrong.[44]

---

[41] See Athenaeus, *Sophists at Dinner* 289a–290a, who also mentions the 'Heracles of king Antiochus'; Jones 1986: 99 with n. 56.

[42] Herodes liked to be known as 'king of words', 'tongue of the Athenians', etc.: Philostratus, *VS* 586, 598; Marcellus of Side in Kaibel, *Epigr. gr.* 1046. 36–7 (= *IGR* i. 194; Ameling 1983: ii, no. 146).

[43] Cf. Hartke 1951: 29 n. 4.

[44] On the typology cf. Hahn 1989; even Cynicism was brought within this ambit—ibid. 174–5; Griffin 1993: 258 (though Aristides, *Or.* iii. 672 expresses a rather different view).

Demonax affirms normative Hellenic values; the parallel *Sostratus*, with its accent on hard work and virtue, presumably did the same in its own way.[45] Philostratus and Herodes also used the story to put flesh on the ideology of Hellenism. Their figure had the sort of mythological pedigree members of the elite liked to aspire to.[46] He spoke the same language as they did. Yet in adapting the story for their purposes certain inconsistencies were bound to show through. Heracles (whose anonymity made him a better vehicle) functions as a sort of liminal figure between the past and the present. The ideal 'interior' he represents is a utopia, and like any other utopia its construction involved danger. For in the real world, while a lack of archaism entailed a failure to differentiate the educated elite from the masses, too much archaism could lead to marginalization and obscurity. In not completely suppressing the Boeotian connections of Heracles-Agathion it is almost as though Philostratus/Herodes is alive to this problem. Consider Lucian again. His fear of hyper-atticism was literally one of going 'over' (*huper*) the borders of the Attic language.[47] In the *Judgement of the Vowels* hyperatticism is traced to a man who was 'apparently Boeotian by descent' but who 'claimed to come from the middle of Attica' (7). Boeotia was always stereotypically archaic and primitive in Athenian eyes. In Lucian's skit excessive use of the Attic feature *-tt-* for *-ss-* is seen as Boeotian because it was a feature shared with that dialect. In the Heracles story, then, the attractions of the pure (the Attic) and the danger of the antiquated and rustic (the Boeotian) seem to combine in a way that represents a danger true for all atticists. Couched as it is in the fascinating discourse of the pastoral (which in itself was so beloved by the ancient elites), and with a hint of the Cynic superman thrown in, the story offers a particularly neat representation of the second sophistic's quest for a Greek identity.[48]

The Heracles-Agathion tale has resonances in a certain sort of

[45] And without the ambiguity present in, for example, Lucian's *Anacharsis*, which also strongly associates physicality—here the gymnasium—with the Hellenic heritage; see Branham 1989: 82–104.

[46] Cf. e.g. Cartledge and Spawforth 1989: 162–5 on elite Spartan families; and below, n. 56, on Plutarch.

[47] The metaphor is used in *The False Critic* 11, cf. *Double Indictment* 14.

[48] It ends, note, on a 'phallogocentric' tone, suggesting the intersection of word-power and sexual-power (cf. e.g. Artemidorus, *Interpretation of Dreams* i. 45) when Agathion rejects a bowl of milk prepared—and thus contaminated—by a woman: 'learning this was true, [Herodes] realized that the man's nature was divine' (*VS* 554).

modern anthropology that takes as its examples small, isolated, pseudonymous communities whose 'typicality' often serves the assumptions of the dominant group writing the story rather than reflecting the polyphony of the world at large. In both cases a kind of 'survivalism' is at work—the truly pure specimen is only to be found somewhere tucked out of the way where the trained eye will recognize his worth. In the case of Herodes and Philostratus anthropology has come home and the trained eye has found a reflection of itself: an atticist will discover Attic Greek in the Attic countryside.[49]

Dio of Prusa's *Borystheniticus* (*Or.* xxxvi), my second main example of a text which explores the relationship between the past and the present, offers interesting parallels. The overall subject of this highly polished speech is natural order and good government in heaven and on earth. Dio's remarks are couched in the form of a recollection of what he had said on these matters during a visit to the city of Borysthenes, the old and also the literary name of the isolated city of Olbia, which had been founded at the top of the Black Sea by Milesian colonists in the seventh century BC. I shall have more to say later on the important cosmological beliefs Dio expresses in the main part of this speech and on the relevance of these to his view of the Caesars and the possibility of divine monarchy on earth. What concerns us now are the speech's thoughts on Hellenism.

Aelius Aristides names Borysthenes as one of the outposts of the Hellenic world that will grieve for earthquake-stricken Smyrna (*Or.* xviii. 10). The picture Dio draws in the first part of the *Borystheniticus* is also of a city on the edge of the Greek world (1–17). Over the years it has been subject to numerous incursions by the barbarian Scythians. Nevertheless, it maintains a fierce devotion to Hellenic culture. Dio meets a young nobleman called Callistratus who is 'very handsome and tall with many Ionic features in his appearance' (8). He is associated racially with the original colonists and possesses the sort of archaic beauty that Dio elsewhere regrets

[49] Cf. the final words of the last preserved of the *Letters of Rustics* by the thoroughgoing atticist Claudius Aelian (Schmid 1887–97: iii): 'if these letters seem to you too clever for the countryside to supply, do not marvel—for we are not Libyan or Lydian farmers, but Athenian ones' (*ep.* 20). In the words of Philostratus Aelian, who was Roman by birth, 'talked Attic Greek like the Athenians of the *mesogeia*' (*VS* 624).

Greeks

is appreciated today by only a few and then for no noble reason (*Or.* xxi. 1–2). Callistratus also has lovers. Dio says the practice is an archaic one inherited from the founding city. His strong criticism here (8) and elsewhere is a matter I shall return to.[50] Dio wittily moves on from Callistratus as a man who is *philomêros* ('lover of thighs'/'lover of Homer') to stress the Borysthenites' devotion to Homer himself and to Achilles, whom they worship. 'Although they no longer have good Greek because they live among barbarians, still almost all of them know the *Iliad* by heart' (9).[51] Dio 'jests' with Callistratus that the *sententiae* of the archaic Milesian poet Phocylides are more instructive than the Homeric epics (10 ff.). Intending to expand on Phocylides' lines concerning the best city he steps back in the narrative to praise 'the truly Hellenic character' of the Borysthenites. 'A philosopher would have been extremely pleased at the sight because all of them had long hair and full beards in the ancient style, as Homer describes the Greeks.' Only one man shaved in order 'it was said' to flatter the Romans (16–17). A little after this an old man called Hieroson interrupts Dio and demands a more philosophical talk. The lack of culture among most of the 'so-called Greeks' who come to Borysthenes ('in reality more barbarous than ourselves, traders and shop keepers') encourages him to tell Dio that 'some but not many' of the Borysthenites are 'lovers of Plato', even if 'it is incongruous for a barbarous speaker to take particular delight in associating with the most Hellenic and wisest of poets' (26).

According to the heading in the manuscripts the *Borystheniticus* was delivered in Dio's home city. The extensive analogy Dio draws in the speech between earthly and cosmic harmony is present in another speech to the Prusans in which Dio aims to persuade them to live in concord with their neighbours (*Or.* xl. 35–41). Thus a general call to good government may be part of the message the audience was expected to take away from the *Borystheniticus*. But the setting of the tale in Borysthenes and the characterization of that city are also significant. Certainly Dio wants his audience to see him as a famous philosopher whom men in far-away places are waiting to hear: if the Borysthenites listened, so should the Prusans (cf. 61). But the particular appeal of Borysthenes (rather than any

[50] See 'Novel' n. 79, 'Dio' nn. 95, 99–109.
[51] Cf. the epic names (including Achilles) in *IOSPE* i². 206, 207, 237, *et al.*; on the cult of Achilles see Jones 1978*a*: 62.

other distant city) seems to lie in its archaic Hellenism. Dio explores the ambiguity of this spirit. In general it is remarkably pleasing to a philosopher like himself.[52] But in certain respects it can be gently ribbed (as in the excessive devotion to Homer and Achilles) or condemned (the archaic sexual practices). It is praiseworthy for having remained uncorrupted in the midst of so many barbarians (the gratuitously anti-Roman comment at 17 is significant in regard to this purity, as is the probability that Olbia was not under Roman control at the time of Dio's visit);[53] but it has not advanced since the seventh century—as only its discoverer, Dio, can point out. Above all Borysthenes is only just viable as a city (4–6), which makes Dio's discourse on the ideal city typically ironic. We see, then, the same tension here as in Philostratus' account of Agathion between the idealization of the past and the need to live in the present.

The Agathion tale and the *Borystheniticus* show us how key members of the elite looked into the mirror of history. For most it was not, of course, possible to meet living men of the past in real life. That did not matter, for the men of the past could always be summoned to one's side in the realm of the imagination. Plutarch thought a great deal in this wise. The volume of his surviving work makes his opinions well worth exploring. He looked on the great men who were his subjects in the *Parallel Lives* as dinner guests whom he would enjoy getting to know one by one (*Aemilius* 1. 2). Recalling the famous deeds of such men gave an intense pleasure and was useful for improving one's own character. 'We may imagine how great was the joy and delight and rapture that dwelt in the actual authors of actions whose memory, after five hundred years and more, has not lost the power to gladden the heart', he says of the deeds of Alexander, Pelopidas, Themistocles, and others.[54] It is not surprising that Plutarch thought we should ask ourselves, if the need arose, 'What would Plato have done here? What would Epaminondas have said? How would Lycurgus have appeared, or Agesilaus?' These men were again 'mirrors' to adjust ourselves in.[55]

---

[52] Cf. Apollonius of Tyana's fictional pleasure at rediscovering the Eretrians who had been deported by the Persians over five hundred years before, even though they have forgotten their Greek, in Philostratus, *Life of Apollonius* i. 23–4.

[53] See below, 'Dio' n. 107.

[54] *That Not even a Pleasant Life is Possible according to Epicurus* 1099e–f (cf. *Dion* 50. 4).

[55] *On Progress in Virtue* 85a. Cf. generally on recalling the past to achieve contentment now *Marius* 46. 2, *On Contentment* 473b–e, *On Bashfulness* 536c (etc.).

Plutarch traced back the ancestry of his own family (or one closely related to it) to the mythological and archaic heroes of Boeotia and Phocis and knew the family felt 'entitled to a greater share than others in Boeotia' because of it.[56] He naturally approved of the maintenance of ancestral privileges accorded, for example, to the descendants of Themistocles, Cimon, and Pindar. At the Theban festival of the Theoxenia the presentation to the family of Pindar was especially delightful: 'who could fail to be pleased and charmed by an honour that was so Hellenic and simple in its imitation of the ancients?'[57] He particularly identified with the mythological Heracleidae (and hence with Sparta) as the true Greeks and strongly reproves Aratus of Sicyon, who had distinguished himself in his early career as a great Greek patriot, for bringing Antigonus Doson and the Macedonians back into the Peloponnese in order to thwart the Spartan king.[58]

It is certainly true that the moral meaning of the past is upper-most in Plutarch's mind for most of the time. It is on this basis that Roman examples are as useful to his great ethical project in the *Parallel Lives* as Greek ones. That said, there is also a genuine strain of exclusively Greek patriotism in Plutarch's thought. This is expressed with great force in the dogmatic essay *On the Malice of Herodotus*, where he warns his readers of Herodotus' treachery against the Greeks and of his readiness to level accusations against them of cowardice and betrayal during the Persian Wars. The fair-ness Plutarch demands from the historian amounts in fact to noth-ing other than a one-sided support for Greeks, whatever their faults, and the work stands as an emotional common defence of all Greeks against an author Plutarch damns with the word *philobarbaros*, 'pro-barbarian' (857a).[59] There is no need to doubt that Plutarch's patriotism was quite similar to that of many other Greeks in his time. He was certainly able to combine this feeling with a genuine

[56] *On God's Slowness to Punish* 558a; cf. Jones 1971a: 8, 40, Einarson 1952, 1955 on this and other passages.

[57] Respectively *Themistocles* 32. 6, *On God's Slowness to Punish* 558c, 557f–558a (cf. Plutarch's lost *Life of Pindar* = fr. 9 Sandbach).

[58] See *Agis/Cleomenes* 37, *Agis/Cleomenes-Gracchi* synkrisis 2. 5, *Aratus* 38. 5–7 (cf. 16. 4, 24. 2 his freeing of Acrocorinth was 'the last, most recent deed of the Greeks').

[59] *Philobarbaros* apparently occurs only in Plutarch (cf. the rhetorical piece *On the Fortune or Virtue of Alexander the Great* II 344b 'Fortune was pro-barbarian and anti-Alexander [*misalexandros*]'). On Plutarch's stereotyping of *barbaroi* see Nikolaides 1986.

admiration of Rome and her great men and achievements. Indeed, as we shall see, he probably believed Roman rule was ordained of God in order to bring peace and prosperity to the world. But in assessing Plutarch in particular we should always remember that his ultimate goal is the self-knowledge that prepares us for a life based on virtue. One of this priest of Apollo's favourite sayings was the 'Pythian rule' which was displayed high on the temple of Apollo at Delphi, the famous 'Know Thyself'. A man whose fellow-citizens descended from those who drove out 'the barbarians' from his beloved Chaeroneia (*Cimon* 1. 1, cf. *Demosthenes* 2. 2) had no doubt about the place of his own identity within the Greeks' collective memory.

THE POLITICAL PAST

The fascination with the past in the second sophistic was above all a way for all Greeks, and especially members of the elite, to invoke the dictum 'know thyself'. Constant rewriting of the classical period was their way of defining and asserting a group identity. It is time to ask whether this was in any way 'anti-Roman'? The question is not an easy one to answer because it is loaded with the modern idea of national groups ('the Americans' versus 'the Japanese', 'the French' versus 'the Germans', etc.) and carries with it a whole set of political actions which such groups will take against each other (recall of ambassadors, imposition of tariffs, going to war); whereas the constitution of group identity in the ancient Greek world had nothing to do with nationhood, but was rather a cultural-political idea and not a political act as such. We must ask instead what implications an identity of this sort had for the Greeks *vis-à-vis* Rome. It should be remembered that the Greeks had always been fascinated by their own history, and understandably so. Dwelling on the glories of the past—like other aspects of second sophistic culture—was not in itself a new phenomenon. It is (again) the intensification of the attitude that is so striking now. It is surely right to see this intensification, this level of obsession with the past and the past's function as a 'discursive structure', partly as a reaction to Roman rule. Let it be said again that there is no cause to speak of a general hostility towards Rome on the part of the Greeks. For many of them, indeed, a desire to know their own past and the feel they had for it did not preclude them from taking a sympathetic and active interest in Rome, Romans, and Roman history.[60] On the other hand, the majority of Greeks whose testimony we can call on had no deep interest in Rome's past or culture. They may have been Roman citizens; we may be able to trace their contacts with prominent Romans through literary or inscriptional evidence. All this is excellent proof of the penetration of Roman influence in the Greek world. But with regard to the feelings of such Greeks themselves we cannot assume more than a political identification with the ruling power for particular reasons.

Greeks identified with Rome politically because Rome encouraged them and needed them (or their friends and colleagues), because there were solid benefits to be gained from Roman citizenship, and because they appreciated the benevolent regime of the Antonines. But cognitively and spiritually none of this means the Greeks did not remain Greeks, whereas there is an enormous amount of evidence to prove that they did. The second sophistic is the name given to manifestations of this intensified feeling of Greekness. It is wrong to simply categorize it as a 'cultural phenomenon' and leave it at that, for 'cultural' is far too innocent and passive a word. Rather, we must certainly read it in political-ideological terms too, while shying away from connotations of 'political' that are too active. The Greeks were well aware that particular political acts of the past were not going to be repeated today in the Roman peace.[61]

---

[60] It is worth noting again that Rome was sometimes fitted into the Greek past by making the most important of her inhabitants Trojans and/or Arcadians (see above, 'Language' nn. 22, 68 [Latin as Aeolic Greek: the Arcadians were held to have spoken Aeolic], and below, 'Pausanias' n. 84). Nothing much was made of these ideas in our period (indeed, it has been well observed how one text, which is almost certainly from this time, the *Library* of Apollodorus, studiously avoids mentioning Rome in its summary of the Greek myths: Bowie 1974: 189–90). There is nothing comparable in the Greek world with the hostile identification of Rome with Esau and Edom which is common in Talmudic and other Jewish texts (Fuchs 1938: 68–73; de Lange 1978: 269–71; Hadas-Lebel 1984).

[61] Cf. Plutarch, *Political Advice* 814a on 'the magistrates in our cities who stir up the masses by foolishly urging them to imitate the deeds, spirit, and actions of their ancestors, when these are out of keeping with the present times and conditions'; Dio *Or.* xi. 150 (no need to be patriotic about the Trojan war—'there is no fear that any of the inhabitants of Asia will ever come against Greece. For both Greece and Asia are subject to others'); Lucian, *Teacher of Rhetoric* 10, where the bad teacher of rhetoric asks what is the use of studying the speeches of Demosthenes and Aeschines 'as if they were tremendously useful . . . and that too in a time of peace when no Philip is advancing and no Alexander giving orders'; Aristides, *Or.* xxiii. 53 (the objection of irrelevancy in peacetime to his examples from classical history); Dionysius of Halicarnassus, *Demosthenes* 22 (above, 'Language', text after n. 23).

It was the feeling, the spirit of their history and heritage that they were investing in. This was never political like a demonstration, a riot, or a sit-in. Nevertheless, in a society where it was possible to indicate priority in time and priority of authority by a single word (*archê*), the stability of intention to seem Greek and to be Greek with the past constantly in mind has a clear underlying political significance. Its surface expression is visible in the various ways of organizing Greek society around the idea of the past. This certainly has internal political relevance; but it also comments on Roman rule. It may be recalled that from the early classical period the Greeks had consciously defined themselves against others whom they called *barbaroi*. In our period it was Rome—now permanently established as their political master and cultural rival—which particularly challenged them to say who they were. This is surely a key reason behind the intensified awareness of their Greekness. It also accounts for its mode of expression. For since Greek identity could not be grounded in the real political world, it had to assert itself in the cultural domain and do so as loudly as possible. The result of this is that, however close individuals got to Rome, overall we notice a certain distance, a resistance to integration, that may surprise anyone used to the modern view that the second sophistic is a facet of Roman history rather than Greek.

THE INVENTION OF HISTORY: RHETORS AND SOPHISTS

Dio of Prusa knew what the past was for when he tells his audience in his political speeches that he is using classical examples because he is addressing Hellenes (*Orr.* xliii. 3, xliv. 10, xlviii. 8, l. 2). 'I particularly want you', he tells the Prusans, 'to have a character that is Hellenic' (xliii. 3). On one level to tell your audience it is as Greek as you is simply a way of getting it to listen; but it is also an affirmation that both you and the audience have something to say to one another. Greek culture is the shared medium. Galen, perhaps predictably, chose to disparage 'the useless traditions of the past' in his lecture on how to recognize the best doctor. In a textbook the 'pleasure' of Herodotus could be scorned in comparison with the value of learning the nature of the hand.[62] Yet even Galen,

---

[62] Iskandar 1988: 129. 20; *On Anatomical Procedures* ii. 393. 7–10; Nutton 1990: 251–2.

as we have seen, prided himself on his familiarity with the great literature of the past and certainly thought of himself as the culmination of Greek medical tradition. This potent combination of knowledge of Greek culture and pleasure in showing it can be seen most clearly in the great public speakers of the second sophistic, the rhetors and sophists. To these great mediators between past and present I now turn.

The study of rhetoric was the commonest form of higher education followed by the elite. Many of its members would have gone through the stage of learning the basic exercises (or *progumnasmata*) that gave practice in narrative, description, comparison, refutation, confirmation, praise, blame, and the other recognized building blocks of speeches and written works.[63] These exercises revolved round continuous reading and writing from the classical texts. More advanced training was available after the *progumnasmata* stage to those who wanted it. For though opportunities for public speaking were diminished in comparison with the democratic Athens of the classical period, there remained many occasions when the educated class were obliged or pleased to speak in public. Speeches of welcome to dignitaries, memorial or funeral orations, addresses at weddings, speeches honouring the gods, competitions at festivals, in other words the types of speech filed under the heading 'epideictic' or display oratory, were always needed. The two other advanced categories of speech-making defined in classical times, forensic or judicial oratory and political or deliberative oratory, also remained in use. As a work like Plutarch's *Political Advice* makes clear, politicians might not be free to say what they wanted to the people, but public speech was the primary method of ruling them.

Important treatments of epideictic were written and survive.[64] But the major interest of the rhetorical schools was in judicial and deliberative oratory. Much effort was expended on instructing

[63] On the basic training see Clark 1957: 157–212; Bompaire 1976; Kennedy 1983: 54–73.

[64] Ps.-Dionysius of Halicarnassus, *Art of Rhetoric*, chs. 1–7 ed. Usener–Radermacher, ii. 255–92; and the two treatises under the name of Menander of Laodicea, best consulted in the edition of Russell and Wilson 1981 (who go into the question of authorship). See now the comprehensive examination of Pernot 1993 (but see 'Aristides' n. 111). Menander makes one particularly interesting comment—that today it is 'virtually useless' to praise a city for its fine laws, as tradition requires, because everything, including law, is controlled by Rome (60. 14–16, 67. 11–12, 68. 13–14 Russell–Wilson), a situation he plainly regrets (Modrzejewski 1982: 350).

students in what was called 'stasis' theory, that is, how to identify the issue involved in a case as it results from the 'stance' adopted by the speaker. Stasis theory was one of the three main so-called 'tasks' of the orator, the other two being 'invention' (how to compose and utilize arguments in the right order) and the theory of 'forms' (which was concerned with classifying different types of style).[65] The theoretical side of later Greek rhetoric is immensely complex. In this we see the culmination of a trend that began many centuries before; but it is in the time of the Empire that such detail became an indispensable part of the schools' profile. The earliest treatise of *progumnasmata* is that of Theon in the first century, while the crucial stasis theory, which was originally developed by Hermagoras in the middle of the second century BC, was elaborated in a lasting form by the definitive work of Hermogenes in the second half of the second century. This growth in sophistication should obviously be connected with the growing popularity and practice of oratory itself, especially the taste for *meletai* or 'declamations' (formal set-pieces on forensic or deliberative topics, literally 'practice exercises'). Not surprisingly, different systems of classification existed in tandem, just as there were different ideas of language purity. But all systems depended on the orators' need for academic assurance as they battled individually with rivals to be first in Greek letters and language and strove collectively to maintain the glory of their culture and Greekness.

From Hermogenes' work *On Staseis* and from its commentators and from Sopater's *Division of Questions*, a fourth-century work based partly on Hermogenes' stasis system and partly on that of his rival Minucianus, which treats at length eighty-two themes arranged by stasis, and from other works we have many examples of the fictitious forensic or deliberative cases which so appealed to the elite.[66] Not a few of these drew their subjects from Greek history; I shall come on to this type shortly. Those that do not are set in a world which is imagined as being vaguely in the past, and which is peopled by standard figures. These are the rich man, the poor man,

[65] Heath 1994; Kennedy 1983: 52–101; Martin 1974: 28 ff., 52 ff., 329 ff.; Russell 1983: 40–73; Wooten 1987 (a useful translation of Hermogenes' influential work on stylistic classification, *Peri Ideôn*).

[66] On Sopater see Innes and Winterbottom 1988: 1 ff. Apart from his main treatments a further eleven themes are referred to in detail and still others by allusion (eid. 2 n. 3).

and the war hero (*aristeus*), who confront each other in various permutations of character and relationship as fellow-citizens or family members. They are mentioned by Philostratus as the key elements of second sophistic oratory (*VS* 481). Their world is thoroughly Greek. They live in a democratic city with an assembly and a council. The poor are always honest, the rich invariably cruel, and the figure of the tyrant and the dangers of war never very far.[67] The political set-up of the city is obviously influenced by the classical Athenian model, though there are some notable changes.[68] The appeal of this world to the rhetors lay in the wide range of potential conflicts it offered. These only the central figure of the rhetor could solve with his entertaining skill (the cases are sometimes little different from character comedy) and with a laudable morality, if he happened to champion the poor against the rich and defended the city's democracy. The real position of the poor in the cities of the Roman empire and the absence of Athenian-style democracy might make this rhetorical city seem a rather cynical place. But we should bear in mind that the rich often did see themselves as protectors of the city and were, after all, essential to its well-being. They no doubt derived immense satisfaction from the benefactions, financial and otherwise, which they made to the citizens (who were not simply 'the poor'), and from the fact that the citizens, as Dio of Prusa puts it, could acclaim them 'all day long as war-heroes [*aristeis*], Olympians, saviours, and feeders [*tropheas*]'. Again, the elite liked to style their regimes as democratic.[69] The rhetoricians' moral game should certainly be connected with their wish to counter philosophers' objections to their unprincipled art. But for most of their pupils practising the role of civic protector in the schools was an entertaining way of practising for the real life of a superior.

Historical declamations allowed the elite not only to practise as leaders but to practise as the leaders of the great age of Greece.

[67] See the fine account of all this in Russell 1983: 21–39.

[68] Such as the provision, for the most part, of a single 'general' (the name of the executive officer in many Greek cities in our period) in place of the ten generals of classical Athens, and the lack of interest in the large democratic juries: Russell 1983: 22–3.

[69] Dio, *Or.* xlviii. 10. On these acclamations, especially the last (which had its corollary in accusations of hoarding), see Robert 1949*a*, 1960*a*. Euergetism and its satisfactions: generally Veyne 1990: 131–56, but see also Sartre 1991: 147–66 stressing the role of benefaction in civic life as a whole; on the games the public wanted from the rich in this context see recently Wörrle 1988, Mitchell 1990. Democracy: cf. below, 'Plutarch' n. 113, 'Aristides' nn. 101, 107.

Over the purely fictional types they had the pleasurable advantage of allowing the treatment of real situations well-known to rhetor and audience alike. Historical figures could even be put to comic use just as the stock ones sometimes were.[70] The themes used in historical declamations come almost exclusively from the mythological and classical period of Greece down to and including the age of Alexander.[71] Over 350 different subjects have been listed, and there were doubtless more. The history of Athens, especially in the age of Demosthenes, predominates.[72] These themes allowed rhetors to display their virtuosity by reworking real events or by freely inventing against a known background. Some examples may be helpful. In his *Art of Rhetoric* Philostratus' friend Valerius Apsines of Gadara can invite his declaimer to call for an expedition against those who took the Persian side in Xerxes' invasion of Greece (i[2]. 219. 9 Spengel–Hammer) or can imagine Demosthenes, acquitted in a trial over his role in the battle of Chaeroneia, now being tried again because he will not come forward to speak (i[2]. 222. 8–9 Spengel–Hammer). The former theme is quite plausible (Herodotus ix. 86 reports a similar decision taken against Thebes), the latter pure fantasy.[73] Again, Hermogenes imagines a case involving a

[70] Cf. Lucian's *Phalaris* i–ii. On humour with the stock-characters see esp. Libanius, *Declamation* xxvi (vi. 511 ff. Foerster) with Russell 1983: 91–6, and xxviii (vi. 573 ff. Foerster) where a parasite, having missed his supper, 'gives himself up' and demands an end to his life. (It is no matter that these examples are from the fourth century.)

[71] Exceptions are unimportant: see Russell 1983: 107 for semi-philosophical themes on Epicurus.

[72] Kohl 1915 remains the standard catalogue. On the popularity of Demosthenes in the second sophistic see Drerup 1923: 144–66.

The popular entertainment of the pantomime (Robert 1930; Kokolakis 1959; Jones 1986: 68–77), which had much in common with performance rhetoric, also drew heavily on mythological and historical themes, with the pantomimist being expected to know 'everything beginning with Chaos itself and the original birth of the world right down to the story of Cleopatra the Egyptian' (Lucian, *On the Dance* 37); though myth predominated (with very many Athenian themes—40), pseudo-history is found (37, 54, 58). See *RE* xviii.3 (1949), 847–9 (Wüst) with the additions of Kokolakis 1959: 51–4; cf. also Kokolakis 1960: 94–5 nn. 107–8 on the links between the pantomimists and the declaimers (which are noted by Lucian at *On the Dance* 65).

Note too the second sophistic's taste for pseudonymous epistles some of which are, again, 'historical'—such as the letters attributed to Phalaris, Themistocles, and Chion of Heraclea—and certainly build on the basic exercises of the schools (cf. Rosenmeyer 1994 with bibliography).

[73] Cf. Apsines i(2). 222. 13–14 Spengel–Hammer on Isocrates. The declaimers amused themselves with situations where rhetors were banned from speaking because of their success: viii. 408. 1–3, 411. 1–3 Walz.

conflict between Demosthenes' demand for immediate action against
Philip of Macedon and a law requiring three days debate before
going to war (*On Staseis* 7, p. 76. 7 Rabe). This theme is based on
no more than a hint in Demosthenes' much loved oration *On the
Crown* (xviii. 169). Not even a hint was necessary to make Sopater
dream up a situation based on the notorious Megarian Decree.
Pericles is sick with plague and a law is passed offering anyone who
cures him a gift of his own naming; a Megarian treats him and
'demands the lifting of the Megarian Decree' (*Scholia to Hermogenes
On Staseis* iv. 252. 24 ff. Walz).

The invention of history was kept within certain limits. So,
Hermogenes, in a discussion of various cases where a proper 'stance'
was difficult, says it is 'implausible' to imagine Socrates being accused of running a bordello, 'impossible' to have the tiny island of
Siphnos and the insignificant city of Maroneia debating their rights
to rule Greece, and simply 'bad invention' to propose Cleon be
sent out to replace Nicias in Sicily when he had already been dead
for some years.[74] Syrianus stresses that the laws of Athens and Sparta
must be used appropriately to avoid such 'bad invention': it was no
good having the Spartan ephor Sthenelaidas charged with not paying the resident alien tax at Athens.[75] It is plain that most historical
declamations were not so implausible and that speakers did keep in
mind an authentic historical background. The proper way to go
about it can be seen in Aelius Aristides' surviving declamations
(*Orr.* v–xvi).[76] The facts did not stifle inventiveness, as is shown
well by the *tour de force* of treating the same subject twice using
different language.[77] There is naturally a close relationship between
pure declamations of this sort and the speeches inserted by historians aiming at a like verisimilitude. In the case of one surviving
declamation, the *On Policy* attributed in the manuscripts to Herodes
Atticus, the speaker's attempt to persuade the people of Larissa to
ally with Sparta against Archelaus of Macedon has even persuaded

[74] *On Staseis* 1, pp. 33–4 Rabe, cf. Syrianus, *Commentary on Hermogenes On
Staseis* ii. 40. 17–24 Rabe, Marcellinus, *Scholia to Hermogenes On Staseis* iv. 173.
20–5 Walz.
[75] Syrianus, *Scholia to Hermogenes On Staseis* iv. 72. 6 ff. Walz.
[76] On *Orr.* v–vi see Pernot 1981.
[77] See Aristides' two Demosthenic speeches of alliance with Thebes (*Orr.* ix–x),
Alexander Clay-Plato's two *Scythians* at *VS* 572–3 (with Russell 1983: 84–6), and
Marcellinus' remarks on Aristides' two speeches on Critias (iv. 173. 4–11 Walz).

some moderns to take it for a real speech dealing with the real fifth-century issues it set out to mimic.[78]

It seems likely that historical themes were more usual than purely fictional ones in public performance. This shows in a comparison between the school curriculum and the corpus of a public orator. Just under half of Libanius' fifty-one practice declamations are historical, the other half being based on the fictional scenarios (*plasmata*) of the standard types.[79] Sopater's *Division of Questions* has only thirteen historical themes out of eighty-two.[80] In the work of Aelius Aristides we find no examples among his surviving speeches that use the stock characters and apparently only one attributed to him in his fragments.[81] Aristides may have practised privately with the stock characters, but when he delivered declamations in public, it was historical themes he chose. At *Or.* xxiii. 1 he condemns *plasmata* as a waste of time. Whether this means other speakers did employ them regularly in public is unclear. No doubt some did (Philostratus gives a few examples). We should remember, of course, that men like Aristides had many other concerns in making speeches. In Aristides' surviving corpus of fifty-one genuine works only eleven are fictions on historical themes (*Orr.* v–xvi).[82] In discussing the role of the speaker in society Aristides has other things in mind. The rhetor was trained to preserve himself, his friends, his city, and its allies (*Or.* ii. 376). Thus 'we praise national festivals, narrate men's deeds and wars, compose stories, and contend in the courts', and naturally honour the gods in the same language (*Or.* xlv. 4). Advice, consolation, and reconciliation are other stated uses of

[78] Cf. Albini 1968: 11–12 (Albini rightly puts the work in the second sophistic); Ameling 1983: i. 119–20. Herodes, if he is author, would have got his information from Thrasymachus' *For the Larisseans* (DK[6] 85 B2).

[79] Libanius, vols. v–vii Foerster (who holds nos. xviii, xxxiv, xl, xliii, xlv, xlix, li to be spurious; of these only xviii is an historical theme).

[80] Two further historical themes are found among themes mentioned in passing (viii. 129. 4 ff., 324. 14 ff. Walz).

[81] Behr 1981–6: i. 421, no. 104 (= Philostratus *VS* 583), 'The Mercenaries are asked to give back their Land' (cf. Sopater, *Division of Questions* viii. 325–6 Walz). A variation on a stock theme is mentioned by others in a dream at *Or.* l. 65.

[82] Other surviving historical declamations from our period are: (i) Polemo's pair of speeches (ed. H. Hinck 1873) where the fathers of Cynegeirus and Callimachus contest the right to hold the funeral oration for the *aristeus* at Marathon (cf. Herodotus vi. 114); (ii) two of the three short orations ascribed to Lesbonax of Mytilene (ed. Kiehr 1907, nos. i, iii; probably 2nd c.; Lesbonax is not in the *VS*); (iii) the Larissean speech attributed to Herodes Atticus (cf. above); (iv) Lucian's Phalaris speeches (cf. above).

rhetoric (iii. 672). Political scheming should no longer be on the rhetor's agenda 'because he can see things are different' (ii. 430, cf. xxiii. 3). But it is interesting to note that in *Or.* xxiii, *To the Cities, On Concord*, Aristides says that it is his 'continual practising' that has put him in good shape to speak on serious subjects (xxiii. 4).[83] In the context of a speech like this, where precedents drawn from history are important (xxiii. 41–52), 'practising' (as the Greek word *meletê* and its cognates suggests) will refer to declamation, and so in Aristides' case to historical declamation. His preferences for history seem to reflect a general tendency shared by Philostratus who is far less interested in his subjects' non-historical works.[84] Of the eleven or twelve separate works he mentions in his biography of Aristides (which includes speeches lost from the corpus), no less than nine or ten are on historical themes (*VS* 581–5).[85] In the *Lives of the Sophists* as a whole, of approximately seventy-nine individual speeches distinguishable by title, subject, or occasion, thirty-five have named themes from Greek classical history. Within this group Philostratus' preference for themes about Demosthenes and his age matches the interests of the handbooks.[86]

The relationship that developed with the past in this way could be quite personal. Aristides reports his dream communications with Plato, Lysias, Sophocles, and others (*Or.* l. 57, 59, 60). Antonius Polemo set up a statue of Demosthenes in the Asclepieum at Pergamum following a dream. Philostratus mentions that the sophist Ptolemy of Naucratis was nicknamed 'Marathon' because of his fondness for recalling the famous battle in his 'Attic themes' (*VS* 595). He reminds us that our period does in fact show a well attested increase in the personal use of classical and mythological names.[87] These are powerful symbolic associations. For the real

---

[83] Cf. Gascó 1992 on the coexistence of the two sorts of rhetoric.

[84] So Kennedy 1974: 19.

[85] 'Eleven or twelve': it is difficult to be sure in every case when Philostratus refers to individual speeches.

[86] Cf. Kohl 1915: 203–328 on Demosthenes and his era (36% of the total) with Philostratus' thirteen Demosthenic themes out of thirty-five (37%).

[87] Polemo—Habicht 1969: no. 33, cf. Phrynichus, *Selection* 396 F.; the epigrammatist Ammianus (Robert 1968*a*: 282–3), who attacks Polemo's activities as a corrupt judge (*Greek Anthology* xi. 180, 181), lampoons a comparable dedication by the rhetor Athenagoras (ibid. xi. 150).
Names: Bowie 1974: 199–200; Touloumakos 1971: 55–60. Cf. the steadily increasing use of Hebrew Patriarchal names in Egypt in the period before the Trajanic revolt (reported in *CPJ* i. 84–85), in this context clearly a form of proto-nationalism.

importance of the declamations (both the *plasmata* and the historical themes) is their affirmation of Greekness and the constant assumption that being Greek and possessing Greek culture is all that matters. Education played its part in this not simply by transmitting texts and allowing them to be read but also by itself establishing continuity. It is not surprising that the structure of Philostratus' *Lives* depends to a large extent on the idea of a progression between teachers and pupils which preserved Hellenism from one generation to the next.[88] Further, Philostratus' insistence on 'sophist' rather than the general 'rhetor' as the appropriate description of his subjects is again partly to do with this feeling of continuity.

For although it is not always easy to draw a distinction between the two terms among contemporaries, one clear meaning of 'sophist' was a rhetor involved in teaching.[89] Pollux's *Onomasticon* is informative here. It begins its section on sophists with the alternatives 'teacher, educator, interpreter, guide, leader', and then tells us how to describe the fee-earning capacity of sophists and gives various words for their pupils and their pupils' fees (iv. 41–51 Bethe). By contrast rhetors are defined by their skill and by their role in society as politicians, panegyrists, counsellors, etc., who serve the city on embassies and guard its laws. Unlike sophists, who can be criticized as tricksters, money-grabbers, flatterers, and hunters of pupils, the rhetor for Pollux can only be blamed for failing to help the city and its people (iv. 20–38 Bethe). Philostratus himself notes in a tongue-in-cheek passage that the sophist 'spends most of the day deep in study with boys' and hence may be rather shy in public (*VS* 614). Sextus Empiricus certainly has teaching in mind (coupled for him by inability to practise) when he rubbishes *hoi sophisteuontes*, 'those who practise as sophists' (*Against the Rhetors* 18–19). Galen was also thinking of teaching (and official teaching at that) when he calls Hadrian of Tyre a 'rhetor who was not yet [in the 160s] a

[88] Philosophers also sought to establish links between the present and the past in this way, either through the idea of 'succession' (as used by Epicureans), or by tying themselves to the fountainhead of their doctrine, which is one reason (if not the reason) for the use of the term *Platônikos* among Middle Platonist philosophers; see Glucker 1978: 206–25, 364–73. Plutarch bolstered the link between himself and Plato by still speaking of 'Academics', though the Academy, along with its Stoic and Peripatetic rivals, had ceased to exist as an institution in the 1st c. BC (Dillon 1988; esp. Glucker 1978: 257–80, cf. 280 ff. on Favorinus).

[89] Brandstaetter 1894: 236–57, esp. 239–40; Jeuckens 1907: 47–9; Bowie 1982: 39. On the 'chameleon' nature of the term cf. Anderson 1990.

practising sophist [*oupô sophisteuôn*]' (*On Precognition* xiv. 627. 14).[90]
This sense of sophist should also be understood in Phrynichus'
Sophist's Stock-in-Trade, and it occurs in inscriptions.[91] Thus when
the terms 'sophist' and 'rhetor' are coupled, as they are for example
on an Ephesian inscription for Claudius Dionysius of Miletus and
an Athenian one for Hordeonius Lollianus, the same distinction
may be read.[92]

Naturally there was a good deal of overlap between sophist and
rhetor depending on the particular stress one wanted to achieve.
Herodes Atticus honoured his own teacher Secundus as 'rhetor and
guide', and the emperor Antoninus Pius treats both rhetors and
sophists as teachers and the terms as interchangeable when he advises the *koinon* of Asia of the number of immunities that will be
allowed these groups in the cities.[93] Declamation was important to
those who taught and to those who did not.[94] Over and above this,
'sophist' could be used as a qualitative term. This is plainly a major
sense of the word in Philostratus' *Lives*. Philostratus suggests at the
end of his introduction that the ancients used 'sophist' of a rhetor
who was distinguished by the brilliance of his rhetoric and reputation and that philosophers who excelled in eloquence were also
given the title (*VS* 484). He clearly accepted this definition for his
modern subjects, whether philosophers (Dio of Prusa, Favorinus)
or (as most of them are) declaimers. This view of the sophist is a
way of connecting the moderns with the sophistic oratory of fifth-
and fourth-century Athens. Thus the biography of the first of the
modern sophists, Nicetes (511–12), who flourished in the time of
Nero, is juxtaposed with the account of Aeschines, to whom is
attributed the origin of the fictional declamation now in favour
(481, 507). The biographies of the eight philosophers from the fourth

[90] Cf. Swain 1991*a*: 161.

[91] T. Flavius Alexander: *FD* iii. 4, no. 474 (with Jones 1972*c*: 265–7; cf. *VS* 604–5).
Soterus: *IK* xv (Ephesos v), 1548 (cf. *VS* 605). Theodotus: *IG* ii² 3813 (cf. *VS* 566–7).

[92] Dionysius: Keil 1953: 6–7 (*IK* xvii. 1 [Ephesos vii. 1], 3047; *VS* 521–6). Lollianus:
IG ii² 4211 (*VS* 526–7). But a man might be known particularly, say, as a sophist (as
Lollianus is in a memorial of his daughter, *IK* xiii [Ephesos iii], 984) or as a rhetor
(as Dionysius is at *IK* xii [Ephesos ii], 426).

[93] Herodes: *SEG* xxiii. 115 = Ameling 1983: ii, no. 183 (*kathêgêtês*, 'guide', suggests 'a personal teacher': Glucker 1978: 127–34). Pius: *Digest* xxvii. 1. 6. 2 (possibly
not Pius' own phrasing, of course).

[94] Cf. Plutarch, *How to Stay Healthy* 131a, where the typical rhetor is driven on
by fame and ambition, the sophist by fees and rivalry; the sophist is exemplified by
Plutarch's friend Niger who, 'being engaged in sophistic teaching [*sophisteuôn*]' in
Gaul, was forced to declaim when a rival sophist turned up. For suggestive examples
of the contexts of rhetorical performance see Anderson 1989.

century BC to the second century AD (from Eudoxus to Favorinus)
who 'have the reputation of sophists', with which the *Lives* begins
(484–92), presumably again owe their existence (at least in part) to
this desire to make the 'second sophistic' look almost as old as the
'first sophistic' of Gorgias and the other early sophists.[95] The lives
of these classical sophists, together with those of Isocrates and
Aeschines, form the next section of the work (492–510). In the
imaginary community of the rhetorical schools sophists are in fact
hardly mentioned. In the progymnasmata and the declamations it is
the rhetor who reigns supreme. Thus in its discussion of mistakes
in declamation the Ps.-Dionysius *Art of Rhetoric* notes that one
should ignore the 'lectures of the sophists' and look to the 'practice
of rhetoric in reality' (ii. 371. 22–372. 2 Usener–Radermacher).
Philostratus is not interested in this. Rather than associating his
subjects with the canonical forensic and political orators who to a
large extent provided the inspiration and the language for their
declamations and with whom they identified on a personal level, he
preferred to link them with the name that most clearly signified
prestige, power, and money. In this he was thinking of the sort of
brilliant virtuosity Apuleius ascribes to Hippias of Elis, 'first of all
in the abundance of his talents, second to none in eloquence . . . no
less an object of view for his costume than of wonder for its work-
manship' (*Florida* ix [137 Valette]).

The appearance of 'sophist' on honorary and funerary inscriptions from about the second half of the first century (whatever the
precise meaning of the term in each case) goes some way to supporting Philostratus' contention (*VS* 511) that this period saw the
emergence of public speakers who claimed to be the heirs of the
classical sophists.[96] On the other hand the prejudice created against
the sophists by Plato and Isocrates meant that for others (like
Plutarch, Dio of Prusa, and Galen) 'sophist' remained a thoroughly
objectionable term.[97] Among the sophists of Philostratus' *Lives*
Aelius Aristides repudiates it strongly and, like his model Isocrates,

[95] Brancacci 1985: 89–90 (cf. Flinterman 1993: 31–4 on Brancacci's idea that
Philostratus particularly identified with these 'filosofi-sofisti').
[96] Cf. Goudriaan 1989: 51–61 on this and on the earlier re-establishment of the
word in rhetorical discussions such as Philodemus' *On Rhetoric*; Bowersock 1969:
10; Norden 1909: i. 379 n. 1 (in the context of his ideas about 'asianism'). Sopater
in the 4th c. traced the revival of rhetoric—with an eye on the development of stasis
theory—to the period of Hadrian and Marcus (v. 8. 13 ff. Walz).
[97] Plutarch: Jeuckens 1907: 49 ff.; Dio: Desideri 1978: 242–3 n. 65a; Galen: below,
'Galen' n. 80. All three preferred to think of themselves primarily as philosophers.

argues in *Orr.* ii (*To Plato, On Rhetoric*) and xxxiv (*Against Those who Lampoon* [*The Mysteries of Oratory*]) that he is concerned with a higher, philosophic rhetoric not open to Plato's charges of flattering the mob and distortion of the truth. Conscious of Plato's strictures against the sophists' love of fees he openly despises those who taught for money (*Orr.* ii. 342, iii. 98–9, xxviii. 127, xxxiii. 19). Above all Aristides based his rhetoric on an appropriation of the cardinal virtues and the (Stoic) formula of the best man as the best speaker.[98] Yet Philostratus insists on referring to him as a sophist who accepted remuneration (*VS* 583, 585, 605). It is as if he is afraid to allow even one of his subjects to escape from his chosen taxonomy, though he is virtually unable to connect any of them with the literature of the fifth-century sophists (who, it may be said, barely figure either in the reading of the schools).[99] In an age when the tangible symbols of dress and appearance and the concrete presence of benefaction were of such importance in ranking society's insiders, it seems Philostratus not only wanted his subjects to rank high in ostentation and civic display (cf. especially *VS* 587 on Hadrian of Tyre, 605–6 on Damianus) and to be able to define themselves decisively against the stereotypically shambolic figure of the philosopher (*VS* 567), but felt in addition that their special *éclat* could be guaranteed best of all by reference to the magical figures of the sophists of old.

[98] See Sohlberg 1972: 193–200, 256–76. On 'sophist' in Aristides see below, 'Aristides' n. 4.

[99] Gorgias is said to influence Lollianus (*VS* 518) and Proclus (604); Hippias Proclus (604); and Critias Herodes Atticus (564). In the schools only Gorgias is cited to any extent (and even then not very much nor very favourably; he occurs a number of times, for example, in Hermogenes and his commentator, Syrianus); his stylistic jingles can certainly be observed in the prose of Plutarch, who nevertheless joined others in attacking him (Philostratus, *Letters* 73; Plutarch fr. 186 Sandbach, part of which is quoted at 'Practice' n. 71), and in other authors (see Pernot 1993: i. 371 ff., 381 ff.).

4

The Greek Novel and Greek Identity

INTRODUCTION

The key point about the rhetors and sophists with whom I finished the last chapter is that they and their audiences spent much of their time living in the same composite Greek world of the past. This imaginary world, where subject and object and past and present were seamlessly joined, was a vital component of a completely new genre of Greek literature that flourished in the second sophistic, the Greek novel. It is to the implications of this new arrival for the contemporary meaning of the past that I now turn.

Several varieties of prose fiction survive from the ancient world. My concern here is not with folktale or fairy stories but only with the novel, which is marked out by its unmistakable combination of abstract form and lived experience. A number of long prose fiction texts from the first three centuries AD (and possibly later) can be classified as novels. They form a homogeneous group in terms of content, and for this reason they are susceptible of close analysis for what they tell us about their authors' and readers' likes, dislikes, and expectations. The major surviving works of Achilles Tatius (*Leucippe and Clitophon*), Chariton (*Chaereas and Callirhoe*), Heliodorus (*Ethiopian Story*), Longus (*Daphnis and Chloe*), and Xenophon of Ephesus (*Ephesian Story*)—the so-called 'ideal' Greek novels—are joined by two novels known for the most part from lengthy summaries (Antonius Diogenes' *The Incredible Things beyond Thule*; Iamblichus' *Babylonian Story*) and by several fragments of novels (notably the longer pieces of Lollianus' *Phoenician Story*, the *Metiochus and Parthenope*, the *Ninus*, and the shorter remains known as *Antheia, Apollonius, Calligone, Chione, Iolaus,*

Sesonchosis, and *Tinouphis*).[1] Variety is a hallmark of all novels at all times. But what is remarkable about the ideal novels is how much they have in common. All are distinctive for offering a similar basic story-line of adventure and romance between two young members of the urban elite leading to or in the context of marriage, for the setting of this story in the past time familiar to us from the world of declamation, and for the interplay between the town and the countryside where their dangers and challenges must be faced.

The extent to which the surviving ideal novels are representative of the genre is, of course, arguable. We can say only that the summaries and fragments confirm or at least do not seriously contradict the familiar picture. Of the summary novels Iamblichus' *Babylonian Story* is a tale of love and revenge with many of the literary features of the ideal novels (such as separations, supposed deaths, learned digressions), though it is consciously set not in the world of the Greek past but in the legendary past of Mesopotamia, that is, near to the probable Emesene homeland of its author, who claims it is a translation of a Babylonian story. The work is best seen as parasitic on the popularity of the 'true' Greek novel, and its firm dating to *c.*170 suggests that it was designed to cater for audience interest in the land of Marcus' and Verus' Parthian war.[2] Antonius Diogenes' story is more like the real thing, if perhaps a rather exotic version of it. Its prefatory statements, as reported by Photius, show a piling on of novelistic features, and this and other elements of the summary strongly suggest that it was a pastiche of the ideal novel, playful or satirical as it may be. We should compare it with Lucian's satire on travel and wisdom-seeking literature, the famous *True Story*.[3]

The fragmentary novels are far more difficult to define because of the brevity of the texts surviving to us. The key characteristic that has guided editors in determining whether a fragment is

[1] Translations and basic bibliography for the main texts and fragments can be found in Reardon 1989; for the *Antheia* fragment see Rattenbury 1933: 247–8, Zimmermann 1936 (to be used with care): 78–84, no. 9; for *Apollonius* see Rattenbury 1933: 248–9, Zimmermann 1936: 50–2, no. 5; for *Tinouphis* see Haslam 1981. *Ninus* and *Apollonius* are re-edited by Kussl 1991 (along with other possibly novelistic fragments including the *Herpyllis*, where the name could well be restored as 'Dercyllis', so connecting the piece with *The Incredible Things beyond Thule*). For the papyrological remains of the novels see Stephens and Winkler (forthcoming).
For the dates of the main novels see Appendix A.
[2] On Iamblichus' dates and background see below, 'Lucian' nn. 24–29.
[3] Cf. Swain 1992*a*.

novelistic is the presence of a romantic element. It is clear that *Ninus* and the *Metiochus and Parthenope* match the ideal novels well (though *Ninus* for all its sophistication lacks the familiar 'bourgeois' heroes).[4] *Antheia*, *Apollonius*, *Calligone*, and *Chione* contain nothing at variance with the main novels and, as they stand, fit well with them. By contrast Lollianus' *Phoenician Story* and the *Iolaus* fragment are far more 'racy' in content and could, again, be satirical. The *Phoenician Story*, which is written in fairly good atticizing Greek, seems to show a parallel with Apuleius' *Metamorphoses* (*Golden Ass*) and so, presumably, with the lost original of the heavily epitomized Ps.-Lucian *Lucius or Ass*, upon which Apuleius built. But we cannot exclude the possibility that Lollianus' text as a whole did after all purvey the normative values of the ideal novels.[5] The rough *Iolaus* fragment with its mixture of prose and verse and obscenity has reminded editors of Petronius' *Satyricon* and is perhaps a different species.[6] The short *Tinouphis* fragment (featuring adultery, escape from execution, and a magician) may be similar. But *Sesonchosis* with a more familiar romantic scene looks like an inferior *Ninus*, having again an eastern prince as hero.

Most of these pieces, then, fit well enough with the ideal type represented by the surviving works of Achilles Tatius, Chariton, Heliodorus, Longus, and Xenophon. Clearly, other sorts of novels were written. But there is no good cause to dispute the obvious predominance of the ideal type, and it is these texts and their common interests that are the focus of the present chapter. There are, of course, differences among these novels, as we should expect. For though there is a similar story at the base of all of them, it should be stressed that there are very wide variations as to how the plot is executed and with what degree of skill and ingenuity.[7] The best examples—Longus and Heliodorus—show well enough that second sophistic literature can be just as 'good' as classical material.

---

[4] On *Ninus* see Appendix A; on *Metiochus and Parthenope* see Maehler 1976; and on the date, below, Appendix A.

[5] On Lollianus and the *Ass* story/Apuleius see Jones 1980: 251–3, and esp. Winkler 1980 where parallels are drawn also with Achilles Tatius (it should be remembered, though, that there is no hint of a metamorphosis in Lollianus).

On the *Ass* and the ideal novels see below, n. 36.

[6] On Iolaus and Petronius (there is no reason to think of a dependent relationship) see Parsons 1971 (cf. *P.Oxy* 42 [1974], no. 3010).

[7] Good surveys/treatments of structures and plots can be found in Perry 1967; Reardon 1971: 309–403, id. 1991; Hägg 1983; Anderson 1984; Holzberg 1986; Billault 1991; and esp. Fusillo 1991 (1989).

Further, the language and the literary structure and range of allusion in the surviving novels leaves no doubt that their authors—even the less sophisticated Chariton and Xenophon (whose text is surely the victim of an epitomizer)—were highly educated products of the schools, fully able to call on the rhetorical techniques of their training.[8] There is no good reason to question the current realization that the readership of the novels was to be found primarily among the establishment class. The very low number of papyri of novels hardly justifies talk of a 'mass market' readership, and the manuscript tradition of our novels shows nothing akin to the complex variant recensions of truly popular tales like the *Alexander Romance*, the *History of Apollonius King of Tyre*, or the Aesop story. Nor is there any reason (for modern male scholars) to confine novel readers to women or young people (with the implication that the novels were irrelevant and superficial). We shall never be able to quantify the readership of the Greek novel; but its quality and rank should not have been doubted.[9]

REFLECTIONS OF SOCIETY

My interest in the novels focuses on what they tell us about Greek society in the second sophistic. In this regard the question of the novel's origin is acute: why did the Greeks of the elite class find it so satisfying to reinvent the age-old polarities of man and woman, town and country, Greek and non-Greek, in a universe that consciously ignored the present day? For, though there are problems of chronology (since we know next to nothing of the authors' lives), it cannot be seriously questioned that the novel flourished in the second sophistic period and arose at its beginning or not very long before. The most important explanations of why it became prominent

---

[8] Xenophon epitomized: Bürger 1892.

[9] On the readership see now Wesseling 1988; Bowie 1994; Stephens 1994; Morgan 1995; cf. Reeve 1971: 538. On women in particular see Egger 1988, 1994; Elsom 1992.

'Mass market'—Winkler in Reardon 1989: 171. Very small numbers of Egyptian papyri (signalling the fact that the novels were never part of the school curriculum) are known from our period for Chariton (Molinié 1989: 42, 49) and Achilles Tatius (Garnaud 1991: pp. xxiii–xxv, xxviii; Willis 1990); they are no guide to real popularity.

Alexander Romance: Merkelbach 1977; *History of Apollonius King of Tyre* (in Latin but originally a Greek text): Kortekaas 1984; Aesop: Holzberg 1992.

have to do with the consciousness of urban Greek society in the Roman Empire, with its level of confidence, and its need for self-reflection. This is what we must investigate. For the ideal Greek novel is recognizably a symptom of a particular social and cultural formation. We may compare it to the rise of tragedy in fifth-century BC Athens and recall the part that literature played in the Athenians' civic ideology. It may be suggested that in our period the Greek novel made a similar ideological contribution for the socially rather more restricted group who now held the reins of power. Chariton's tale of *Chaereas and Callirhoe* is probably the earliest of our complete novels; its comparatively simple plot (which recurs *mutatis mutandis* in the others) and its avoidance of strict atticizing language make a first-century AD date the most plausible. It is particularly easy to dissect Chariton's text and to discover its literary ingredients (epic, tragedy, historiography).[10] But to do so is to engage with the crux of the problem. For whatever view we take of the literary ancestors of this or that novel,[11] we are left with the question of why the novel flourished when it did in the second sophistic. We can explain the place of every part, but not account for the origin of the whole. Thus social and cultural factors are to be sought instead.

One such explanation has paid attention to the concept of the individual at the time of the novel's appearance. It has been suggested that in the Hellenistic world created by Alexander and expanded by Rome the inhabitants of the great eastern metropolises experienced a profound isolation and loneliness. These feelings were catered for by the representation of the individual in the pages of the novel, for readers wanted to read about people like themselves.[12] Although this theory was developed in the mistaken belief that the first novels were written in the first and second centuries BC, it was

---

[10] On Chariton's date and literary history see Appendix A.

[11] Cf. Rohde 1914 (Alexandrian love elegy and fantasy travel literature blended by the sophists); Schwartz 1896 (historiography); Lavagnini 1921 (embellishment of local legends); Anderson 1984: esp. 1–24 (non-Greek near eastern fiction); Fusillo 1988 (epic). For general surveys see Giangrande 1962; Reardon 1971: 311–18, 329 ff. on the role of translations from Egyptian literature; Hägg 1983: 109–24, 243–5.

[12] Perry 1967 (from original lectures of 1951): 175; Reardon 1971: 322–4; Hägg 1983: 90; Konstan 1994: 221 ff.; cf. Toohey 1992: 273–5 (lovesickness in the novels exemplifies a trend towards melancholia in the High Empire); and see further below, nn. 22, 27.

Individualism was certainly an important factor in the popularity of the modern English realist novel: see the classic account by Watt 1957 (esp. 9–34, 60–92).

clearly meant to account also for the particular popularity of the genre in the second sophistic. Interestingly, it owes much to views first expressed during the early and middle part of this century about the spiritual health of the ancient world during the early Empire. It was suggested that traditional systems of religion were breaking down at this time, that people were no longer sure where they stood in society, and that cults arose to satisfy a feeling of rootlessness which was eventually assuaged by Christianity. The distinctive personality of Aelius Aristides was taken as a prime example of these disturbing trends. Aristides spent much of his life afflicted by mental or physical illness and in thrall to the instructions of the healing god, Asclepius of Pergamum, which were mediated to him through dreams. His illness is documented by him in the six *Sacred Tales*, a work extraordinary both for its content, which describes the trouble and the god's commands, and for its form, which is paralleled in its snakes and ladders narrative only by the complex first half of Heliodorus' *Ethiopian Story*.[13] The illness Aristides suffered from was taken as emblematic of an all-pervasive hypochondria. This, together with the excessive devotion to cults suggested (among other things) by his special relations with Asclepius, encouraged the view that the second century was in E. R. Dodds' words an 'Age of Anxiety'.[14]

No one today should hold that this picture is true. For a start, there is nothing to indicate that Aristides' problems were like those of everyone else.[15] The school of anxiety made much of the discussion of ill health in the correspondence of Marcus Aurelius and Cornelius Fronto; but that reveals only that it was acceptable for friends to mention health problems.[16] There is no cause to think of a world-wide hypochondria on this basis. Determining the meaning of illness in the past is, of course, a very difficult task. The historical and geographical consciousness of illness changes with time and by culture. Our concept of hypochondria, a mental state of belief in persistent (but unreal) physical disease, belongs in origin to the epistemological conditions of the early modern period when

[13] Cf. below, 'Aristides' n. 29.

[14] Dodds 1965 (39–45 on Aristides; cf. e.g. Nestle 1934: 149–54); Bowersock 1969: 71–5 (Aristides, Marcus, Fronto); Reardon 1973.

[15] So Smith 1984: 47–8.

[16] Fronto may well have had bad health (Champlin 1980: 141) as did Marcus (Rutherford 1989: 120). References to illness in the correspondence may be found in Haines' Loeb edition of Fronto, ii. 333.

the body was finally relieved of responsibility for mental disorder and states like hypochondria and hysteria were moved from the parts of the body that gave them their names and lodged firmly in the mind. If Aelius Aristides looks like a hypochondriac to us, he did not to contemporaries (who failed to segment the rational and the irrational by our criteria). Galen classified him simply as someone whose health was ruined by hard work. He would not have thought that Aristides' devotion to the healing god was extraordinary, for he considered himself to be in his service too. As for the rhetor's dreams (which have especially attracted psychoanalysis), there is no cause to generalize. Indeed, dreams would seem to be the last place to go to discover a balanced view of any society.[17]

Second, the 'Age of Anxiety' was discovered in the middle decades of the twentieth century at least partly because this period itself was felt to be such a time.[18] Dodds is not the only scholar to have been saddened by the twentieth century and to have read his dolour back into the period that Gibbon—in his day—called the 'most happy and prosperous' known to man.[19] Comparable to Dodds's position are earlier statements about the 'decay' of Roman religion and the importation of foreign, 'oriental' cults in an era of individual psychological crisis and the breakdown of civic and familial structures.[20] The main problem behind these assessments was, perhaps, for (mostly) rationalist scholars to explain satisfactorily to themselves the eventual triumph of Christianity. From this school of thought arose the thesis that the novels themselves were charged with oriental religious meaning and represented in particular the stories of Isis and Osiris, an idea which failed to find much favour either at the time or in later elaborations which have presented the

[17] Galen's view: below, 'Aristides' n. 28, 'Galen' n. 66 (on the place of Asclepius, increasingly important in this period in personal identity, see Kee 1982). Aristides' (and others') dreams: 'Aristides' nn. 33–5.

[18] Dodds 1965: 3 'In calling it "an Age of Anxiety" I have in mind both its material and its moral insecurity; the phrase was coined by my friend W. H. Auden, who applied it to our own time, I suppose with a similar dual reference' (Dodds refers to Auden's dramatic poem of this title, which was published in 1948); cf. id. 1951: esp. 253–5, 1977: 188.

[19] Gibbon 1896–1900: i. 28–82 (quotation 78).

[20] Among others Cumont 1929 (1st edn. 1905): 19 ff., esp. 23–4; Nestle 1934: 62–7; Festugière 1954: 87 on Aelius Aristides: 'Poor Katherine Mansfield died in a sanatorium near Paris very much like the sanctuary of Pergamum'; id. 1955 (French edn. 1946): p. vii 'Man is unhappy . . . Pessimism is natural', 13 (the individual as a lonely cypher [so also Dodds 1951: 243] such as we find 'in London or Paris').

novels as mystery texts of various gods with overt messages for
initiates only.[21] The most extreme assessment of the novel as an
'Ausdruck von Umbruchs- und Krisenzeiten', voiced as it was in
an essay that combined admiration of Napoleon with an equation
of feminism, 'Dekadenz', and 'Nihilismus', involved a similar
retrojection of contemporary suspicions.[22]

The case for ancient anxiety has been vastly overstated. Far from
being in crisis or decline civic cults based on the traditional pantheon of Greek mythology were flourishing in the second sophistic. Newer cults completed rather than damaged what was a truly
vibrant paganism serving the community as a whole. Our perception of a disturbing trend towards mysticism and salvationism seems
to be unknown to the ancients themselves.[23] Among the elite a
sense of belonging to and helping one's local community was as
strong as ever, and there is absolutely no sign of difficulties with
the city as an institution. Indeed, the abundant epigraphic and
archaeological evidence from the Greek East makes it clear that the
mid-first to the mid-third century was the most successful period
of urbanization known anywhere in the ancient world.[24] Although
it was during this period that the very rich began to take greater
powers for themselves and to enshrine them in law at the expense
of even the poorer members of the elite, if the rich embarked on an

[21] Kerényi 1927; Merkelbach 1962: Vorwort ('Die antike Liebesromane hängen
eng mit den Mysterien des sinkenden Altertums zusammen'), id. 1988 (specifically
on Longus; cf. below, n. 41); Henrichs 1972: 28 ff. (on Lollianus). Against these
views see the excellent discussion and summary of earlier opinion in Reardon 1971:
318–19, 393–9; Winkler 1980 (on Lollianus). The novels' interest in religious matters
simply reflects the pervasive nature of religion in ancient society at all periods.

[22] Altheim 1951: 45–53, 60–4 (quotation 64), Napoleon and feminism 53 ff. (for
some protest against this Nietzschean picture see Anderson 1984: 97–8, who also
takes note of the imaginings of Scarcella 1972 on Heliodorus and that great modern
edifice, the Third-Century Crisis). Konstan's speculations on the 'transnational culture
of the Roman Empire' and the consequent decline of the cities, and comparisons
with the 'decentredness' of 'late capitalist global society' (1994: 226–9) follow the
same logic.

[23] On the vibrancy of pagan religion see MacMullen 1981, esp. Lane Fox 1986:
27–261; for the vitality of e.g. local cults of Apollo, Parke 1985: 69 ff., 142 ff. See also
Branham 1989: 163–77 on the sophisticated, unworried humour of Lucian in his
Assembly of the Gods and *Tragic Zeus*, where he includes remarks on newcomers
such as Mithras 'the Mede'.

[24] In the Greek East the health of the urban scene is shown to us particularly well
by the number of cities, large and small, which minted coins at various times in the
period (some 500 mints are known, with a peak of nearly 250 in operation under
Severus and Caracalla): see Johnston 1984a: 250 (NB these figures are approximate).

equestrian or senatorial career, they nevertheless continued to display an 'astonishing attachment' to their home towns.[25] It was at the end of the third century that immunity from local obligations first began to be acquired by those in imperial service. Until then the *polis* remained the locus of expression for the potent ambitions of the great, whose society was held together by the extensive networks of family and patronage established there.[26]

It is naturally possible to find signs of discontent in the closely rule-bound society the Greek elite constructed for itself in the second sophistic period, for, as has been remarked, the particular identity these Greeks gave themselves as the heirs of the classics certainly involved unsatisfactory contradictions and anomalies. But overall we must recognize a profound satisfaction with being Greek and living and continuing to live in the traditional Greek city.[27]

THE SETTING I: THE PAST

The answer to the question of the novel's origin lies not in reading it as a reflection of unhappiness, individual or otherwise, but in seeing it as another outlet for the cultural ideals and formulas of the elite, as another expression of their cultural hegemony. A strikingly similar ethical and political discourse runs through the novels. As with the declamations, we must understand that the entertainment value of these texts depends on the operation of certain key assumptions. First, that the Greek world of the past—a world without Rome—is the only possible setting; second, that the city is the

---

[25] Greater power: Garnsey 1970, id. 1974: 241. Continuing local patriotism: Quass 1982: 189, 207; cf. Eck 1980.

[26] Immunity: Millar 1983. Ambition: Brown 1978: 27–46.

[27] Mention should be made here of Toohey's interesting suggestions (1988, 1990, 1992) that the period of the High Empire marks the 'discovery' of a related group of negative affective emotions, (respectively) boredom, depression, and lovesickness. Worthwhile as his studies are, he does not to my mind prove his thesis on the rather slim evidence he adduces (cf. 1990: 160 'too selective to allow any firm conclusions'). His case is not assisted by hints about the unhappiness of the 'service aristocracy' under the Empire at a time of increasing urbanization. This looks like a strange blend of Foucault and Veyne with the positivist school of individual anxiety and isolation (a blend which unfortunately finds favour also with Konstan 1994). See further above, nn. 12, 22 (lovesickness in the novel; Konstan and isolation), and below, nn. 62, 83 (Foucault and Veyne).

centre of Hellenic civilization, the place from which the heroes
leave to face the dangers of the country and to which they return
to find themselves once more in the bosom of their loved ones; and
third, that the heroes should be two young people from the urban
elite who are constantly obsessed with the values of faithfulness
and marriage (and thus with the continuation of their own kind).
To these matters I now turn. With regard to the past in the novel
I am naturally building on the conclusions of the previous chapter.
The countryside and its meaning will also be treated fairly briefly,
since the subject is well known and easy to understand. The role of
the heroes picks up on changes in Greek society that were fairly
new in the period when the novel was being born and for this
reason I shall discuss it at greater length.

The past setting of the novels has close parallels with the world
of the declamation. Some of them are explicitly 'historical', that is,
they use known persons from history as primary or secondary
characters. Others have the feel of a Greek world independent,
indeed oblivious of Rome. Of the fragmentary texts *Metiochus and
Parthenope*, *Ninus*, and *Sesonchosis* are clear examples of the 'historical' type. *Ninus* uses well-known semi-historical figures from
exotic Babylon. *Sesonchosis* deals with another semi-real 'oriental',
in this case, an Egyptian king (or a conflation of two) known from
Herodotus (Sesostris), Diodorus Siculus (Sesoosis), and others.
Metiochus and Parthenope is set on the Samos of Polycrates, who
seems to be the father of Parthenope; Metiochus is the historical
eldest son of Miltiades, and thus chronologically wrong for
Polycrates and another character, the philosopher Anaximenes who
died about 525.[28] None of this would have worried the author (who
was plainly an admirer of Herodotus). Of the fully surviving novelists Chariton's relations with history have long been noted. His
work is set in the early fourth century, for the father of his heroine
Callirhoe is the famous late fifth-century Syracusan general
Hermocrates. Asia, where much of the story takes place, is under
Persian rule, and Dionysius' control of Miletus, though actually
'unhistorical', may be compared with what we know of the power
of the Hecatomnid dynasty who ruled Caria (Chariton's homeland)
on the Great King's behalf. There are of course inconsistencies,
notably that the reign of Artaxerxes (i.e. Artaxerxes II, who came

---

[28] *Sesonchosis*: O'Sullivan 1984. *Metiochus and Parthenope*: Maehler 1976.

to the throne in 404) coincides with the lifetime of Hermocrates who died in 407.[29]

The other surviving novels are not connected to particular figures. Their characters wander in a much larger version of the fictional world created in the schools. The narrative requirement of geographical freedom sometimes means that this world is the Hellenistic one after Alexander. Local patriotic factors may also be behind some of the settings authors chose. Achilles Tatius' *Leucippe and Clitophon* is set after the founding of Alexandria, from which city he himself is said to have come.[30] Egyptian troops have a commander with a common Greek name, Charmides (iv. 1), answering to a 'satrap' (iv. 11. 1, 13. 4). That this is not simply the stylistic, atticizing use of 'satrap' to signal the Roman governor is shown by the fact that Byzantium and Thrace are independent and at war with each other throughout the novel (i. 3. 6, ii. 24. 2–3, vii. 12. 4, viii. 18. 1), a war won not by the armies of Rome (which is nowhere mentioned) but by the 'epiphany of the gods' (viii. 18. 1, cf. ii. 14).[31] *Daphnis and Chloe* by Longus is entirely without indication of historical time; but there is again no hint of Roman power, even during the brief war between independent Mytilene and Methymna (which recalls Thucydides iii. 18. 1–2).[32] Heliodorus' *Ethiopian Story* has more in common with Chariton's approach to history. It is imagined as happening before the foundation of Alexandria and during the Persian domination of Egypt. Care is taken to preserve the fiction of government by the satrap Oroondates and his officer Mitranes (e.g. ii. 24. 2). There are two notable anachronisms involving references to real people and events: first, the garden of the Epicureans at Athens at a time after Epicurus' death (i. 16. 5; Epicurus died c.270); second, mention of the famous courtesan of

---

[29] On the historical background see Plepelits 1976: 15–20; Scarcella 1981: 344 ff.; Baslez 1992 on anachronisms like v. 1. 3, where the Euphrates marks the 'starting point' of the Great King's territory. Note recently Jones 1992*b* on Chariton's possible reading of Hellenistic history, and Hunter 1994 on the relation between historical background and plot.

[30] *Suda* α 4695.

[31] 'Satrap' is nevertheless stylistic (there are no Persians in Achilles Tatius); cf. below, 'Plutarch' nn. 125–6. Plepelits 1980: 18–27 tries inconclusively to demonstrate an imperial setting (he is no doubt right in suggesting that Achilles Tatius was influenced by some aspects of the contemporary world [cf. n. 51], but his citation of Tacitus, *Annals* xii. 63. 3, to explain the Romeless Thracian war hardly supports his case); Garnaud 1991: pp. ix–x also thinks the novel is set in the Roman Empire.

[32] Longus' Lesbian topography is similarly indefinite: Bowie 1985*b*: 86–91.

Naucratis, Rhodopis, who flourished about 575, before the Persian dominion (ii. 25. 1).[33] The *Ephesian Story* of Xenophon of Ephesus is set after the founding of Alexandria, Ephesus, and Antioch (ii. 9. 1), but is surely not supposed to be 'really' as late as has been suggested on the basis of the references to Perilaus as the man 'in charge of the peace', i.e. as eirenarch (ii. 13. 3, iii. 9. 5), an office well known in Roman Asia Minor from the first century AD, and by its mention of the 'commander' (*archôn*) of Egypt (iv. 2. 1 *et al.*), which has been taken as a reference to the Roman prefect. Xenophon is far less chary about admitting the contemporary world. But it is still a thoroughly Greek scene that forms the background to his novel. As in all our other texts, including the fragmentary novels, there is no mention here of Rome or Romans, and Perilaus' office has become part of the Greek world, just as it does for Xenophon's contemporary Aelius Aristides when he narrates his struggle against nomination to the post in the *Sacred Tales*.[34]

In his work on the origins of the modern historical novel (which effectively begins with Scott's *Waverley* in 1814) Lukács argued that the historical novel arose when the realist English social novel of the eighteenth century had become outmoded by capitalism's ever-increasing mystification of reality and by its consequent need to appropriate history in order to provide ideal humanist forerunners of the contemporary struggle.[35] His severely reductionist treatment stands as a warning to anyone engaged in explaining the origin of literary forms against pursuing historicism too far. Yet, even so, there are some points of contact between his schema and the rise of the ideal Greek novel. For here we are again dealing with a very particular new form of literature whose writers and audience (so far as we can tell) were members of a particular economic elite. We do not have to use the same terminology as Lukács to see that the past setting of the ancient Greek novel appealed to the Greek elite because of the role of the past in their ideology of power. They enjoyed the past in the novel for exactly the same reasons they enjoyed it in the world of declamatory oratory and in civic life. In the novel

[33] On Heliodorus' historical anachronisms see Morgan 1982: 236 n. 46.
[34] Below, 'Aristides' nn. 57 ff.
[35] Lukács 1962: 251, 300 ff. *Waverley* in fact refers to comparatively recent events (the '45), but later novels like *Ivanhoe* are properly 'historical'. For Scott's real aims in reinventing Scottish history (which were of no interest to Lukács) see Kidd 1993: 247–67.

this pleasure is somehow even more apparent. We might have expected at least some of the novels we are interested in to have been set in the real Roman world where their writers and audiences lived. That this is not the case strongly suggests that readers wanted their social and ethical concerns to be played out in a world entirely of their own.

This can be demonstrated in another way too, for in the one complete example of a non-ideal novel, the epitomized *Lucius or Ass*, the present-day setting is an intrinsic part of the (im-)moral colouring of the text, whose humour is concerned with anything but the normative values which the elite of our period held dear.[36] Nothing can be said about the setting of the other possibly non-ideal novels (which are, of course, only short fragments of narrative). If fully non-ideal novels similar to the *Ass* were set in the classical or Hellenistic periods, the shape of our evidence would still have to change a great deal before we could say that such texts were a dominant type. As things stand, the conclusion may be drawn that the normative values of the elite, which we see in the ideal novels, required a setting in a world away from Rome.

THE SETTING II: THE RURAL

As important as ever to the Greeks of this time was the division between the 'us' of the cities and the 'them' of the *chôra*, the 'countryside'. In the novel this difference is connected with the familiar Greek division between Hellene and barbarian, since much of the non-urban scene takes place in Egypt. The land in the novels encodes

[36] The ribald story of Lucius' transformation into an ass and his subsequent lowlife adventures revels in magic and sex without any hint of romantic love, and combines this with an explicitly contemporary setting in the Roman province of Macedonia in the early to mid-second century (for this date note first that Thessaly is very probably in provincia Macedonia: at *Ass* 26 Thessalian bandits are taken to the Roman governor, surely the Macedonian governor at Thessalonica who features at the end of the work; Thessaly was probably in Macedonia from AD 67 or not long after: see Bowersock 1965*a*: 285 ff.; second, Apuleius' *Metamorphoses* shows that the longer version of the *Ass* was in existence by the 170s or so). The realism of the setting is all part of the discomfort of the hero, who is an author and friend of sophists (2, 55) and a Roman citizen (16, 55). The Thessalian countryside is full of bandits (16, 22) who are fought by large numbers of (Roman) soldiers (26); these troops are billeted in the city (45; probably Beroea, where Ammianus xxxi. 11. 2 reports a fixed garrison in the late Empire), mistreat the locals for not understanding the 'Italian language' (44), and secure the collaboration of the local authorities (45).

key emotive responses, being at once beautiful and safe and constructed in man's image, and at once alien and menacing. The countryside of the villas, those 'pieces of cities broken off', and of the
rural estates of the rich in the ancient world was often enough
viewed through what we might call a 'ruralist' ideology, and the
way it is talked of coincides with the way power was exercised
there. We may recall that the exploitative energies of the ancient
city were principally focused on taxing its territory and taking the
peasants' food.[37] Thus the population of the country is likely to be
alien (though not invariably so), or alternatively to be seen in ideal
terms through the eyes of the urban rich longing to share its pure
living. Nature, whether is it hard, cruel, and exacting (as often), or
beautiful, innocent, and sublime, is always spoken of with adora-
tion by those who do not have to live by it. What comes through
most of all in the novelistic countryside is its unreality. It is not a
place where anyone actually lives and works. Further, its pervasive
inferiority is the reverse of life in the city.[38]

The role of the countryside is well exemplified in Longus' *Daphnis
and Chloe*. This sophisticated text is perhaps the best of the ancient
novels in literary terms, since it is the only one that consciously
develops its heroes' characters against real time (which is that of the
changing seasons).[39] It is especially concerned with the countryside
because its heroes are exposed urban aristocrats who are brought
up there as foundlings by peasant farmers. Further, *Daphnis and
Chloe* has a close relationship with pastoral poetry and is heavily
imbued with the language and style of Theocritus.[40] Along with
Heliodorus' *Ethiopian Story* it is also the most religious of the
novels, celebrating the power of Eros, here the cosmogonical deity
who is eternally young.[41] It thus demands to be read on several
levels and is clearly aimed at a readership able to respond to this.

[37] Cf. below, 'Galen' n. 31.
[38] See in general MacMullen 1974: 28–56 (quotation on villas 45–6); on the novel
Saïd 1987 (an excellent article). Cf. Sales 1983: 15–109 on the politics of pastoral in
early modern English literature.
[39] On the unsatisfactory time–space relationship in the other novels see the stimu-
lating remarks of Bakhtin 1981: 86–110 (cf. 141 on biography).
[40] Excellent recent explications of these and other aspects: Hunter 1983; Zeitlin
1990. On infant exposure in Longus see Kudlien 1989: 39 ff.
[41] Merkelbach 1988 clearly restates (with the aid of a useful review of Dionysiac
religion) his earlier belief that *Daphnis and Chloe* should be interpreted as a mystery
text of Dionysus, but his thesis again fails to convince; see above, nn. 21 ff. See
Chalk 1960 on Longus' religiosity (but, again, the allegorizing goes too far).

The father of modern scholarship on the novel, E. Rohde, condemned Longus as a sham sophist whose fake naïvety and urban construction of the rural amounted to 'canting affectation'.[42] Longus' rehabilitation came with G. Rohde's attempt to present him as a genuine lover of the purity and spirituality of eternal Nature, an approach which encouraged the development of the religious interpretation of his novel.[43] Also brought into the equation was D. H. Lawrence's vitalist metaphysics, the spirit or Life championed by F. R. Leavis and the Scrutineers, which formed an indefinable link between past and present and acted as a crucial weapon in their disavowal of technological dehumanization.[44] Longus, though, was not in fact trying to rescue his readers from the horrors of industrialization and the 'commodification' of cultural life which so worried the Scrutineers and their associates. It was not anxiety that Longus was grappling with. Rather, the world he created is intensely comforting for his readers. The countryside is seen through the eyes of a townsman, peopled by good and bad peasants, who are prone to victimization by urban elite thugs (ii. 12–20) and are at the beck and call of the urban rentier, Dionysophanes (iv. 1 ff.).[45]

Longus is the only one of the fully surviving novelists to include a preface telling us what he thought he was doing in his text. Its connection with the rest of the work requires sensitive analysis, for the story that follows is alleged to be the exegesis of a painting, perhaps one of the dedications made by Daphnis and Chloe at the end of the novel. That is not our concern here. Of interest now is Longus' statement at the end of the preface that his work has a propaedeutic function: 'it will remind the one who has loved, and prepare by its teaching [*propaideusei*] the one who has not' (Pref. 4). Longus' story is really about the education of Daphnis and Chloe, not just in terms of their sexual behaviour and readiness for matrimony, but also the discovery of their proper roles as landlords, which they assume after the recognition scene. They then continue to live 'the life of a shepherd . . . while owning numerous flocks of sheep and goats' (iv. 39. 1). It is doubtful that any part of this education (including Chloe's painful loss of virginity—iii. 19. 2–3, iv. 40. 3) is consciously made problematic by the author, as has

---

[42] Rohde 1914: 549–52.
[43] Rohde 1937; cf. Effe 1982: 69–70 on the ideas of Chalk and Merkelbach.
[44] Altheim 1951: 25, 41–5.
[45] Cf. Saïd 1987: 162–71; Vieillefond 1987: cxcvi–cciv.

been suggested.[46] As the schools knew, 'the root of education is bitter, but the fruits are sweet'.[47] To announce that one's text is part of a programme of *paideia* is to situate it precisely within elite society, not to question its validity.[48]

For the most part the countryside is much safer in *Daphnis and Chloe* than in the other novels where the heroes are more firmly associated with urban life. But even here pirates (disguised as *barbaroi*) interrupt the pastoral scene (i. 28–30). In the other texts the countryside is the place of bullying, burning, looting, and of course kidnapping and attempted rape. Pirates and bandits are featured heavily by the novelists because they foreground perfectly the virtuous innocence of the trysting teenagers trying to reach home. Their presence reflects wider fears, of course. At the time of the Empire outlaws were thought of as organized terrorists with their own codes and martial laws and ceremonies, in other words as a sort of mirror-image of the state itself.[49] How far bandits actually existed in our period is another matter.[50] They are, in any case, a necessary constituent in the novel. In Xenophon, Achilles Tatius, Heliodorus, and Lollianus especially we find similar groups. The Egyptian *boukoloi* or 'herdsmen' in Achilles Tatius and Heliodorus are particularly well organized (see e.g. *Leucippe and Clitophon* iii. 9, *Ethiopian Story* i. 6–7). No doubt the fictional *boukoloi* were intended to evoke memories of the real *Boukoloi* who terrorized Alexandria in 171/2.[51] It is noteworthy that the

[46] See Winkler 1990 urging us not to commit ourselves to 'the premises and protocols of the past' (126).

[47] Hermogenes, *Progymnasmata*, p. 7. 13–15 Rabe; Libanius, *Progymnasmata* viii. 82 ff. Foerster; Aphthonius, *Progymnasmata* ii. 23–5 Sp.

[48] Cf. also Chariton's remarks at the beginning of his last book: 'I think this last book will give the greatest pleasure to my readers. For it cleanses away the grim events of the earlier ones. There is no more piracy, slavery, lawsuits, fighting, suicide, war, or conquest in it; rather lawful love and legal marriage' (viii. 1. 4–5, alluding to Aristotle *Poetics* 1449[b]28).

[49] Notable examples: Spartacus (Plutarch, *Crassus* 8–11), Claudius (Cassius Dio lxxv. 2. 4), Bulla (Dio lxxvii. 10. 1), Maternus (Herodian i. 10); see the fine study of Shaw 1984; further Hopwood 1989 on Cilicia; cf. Winkler 1980 on the bandits' initiation scene in Lollianus fr. B1 recto.

[50] Pausanias never mentions encountering any trouble in his peregrinations in old Greece (but cf. above, n. 36, on bandits in the different terrain of Thessaly in the Ps.-Lucian *Lucius or Ass*).

[51] Cassius Dio lxxi. 4; cf. Scarcella 1981: 352–64; Shaw 1984: 42. But the date of 200 attached to the earliest papyrus of Achilles Tatius has been taken to indicate that he wrote around the middle of the century (see Appendix A), and this is consistent with a recent papyrological find which shows that the *Boukoloi* 'were there all along' (Bowersock 1994: 53).

terrorists in our novels are often nobles driven to break the law for love or economic survival. Callisthenes in Achilles Tatius, Thyamis in Heliodorus, Hippothous in Xenophon, conform to this 'Robin Hood' pattern. What greater threat could be imagined to the elite than conspirators of this type? We are taken back to the most famous conspiracy of all, Catiline's, which achieved archetypal status.[52] Better than Catiline's fate was the prospect that the misfits would come home and settle down. This was possible in the ideal novels, where movement within and without the boundaries of civilization is a major part of the attraction. Hence we can look forward to the rehabilitation of Callisthenes in Achilles Tatius (viii. 17), Hippothous in Xenophon (v. 15), and Thyamis in Heliodorus (vii. 1–9).[53]

A notable feature of the people heroes are likely to come across in the countryside is their race, especially in Heliodorus.[54] Thyamis' rehabilitation in the *Ethiopian Story* is doubly rewarding, for he is not only a hardened bandit, but is also, though Hellenized in manners (i. 19. 3), an Egyptian by birth and unable to speak Greek (ibid.). The inherent contradictions and narrative difficulties caused by this linguistic handicap require it not to be pursued too rigorously. As the story progresses Thyamis appears to have no difficulty communicating with Greek speakers. That said, Heliodorus is particularly keen on stressing barbarians' difficulties with the Greek language as well as their desire to know it and to imitate Greece's finery.[55] Greeks hardly expect to find a civilized man in the wilds of the orient (i. 8. 6 'A Greek? O gods!', exclaim Theagenes and Chariclea on discovering Cnemon).[56] The Ethiopians themselves are acceptable on account of the righteousness of their king Hydaspes, who along with the Ethiopian intellectual elite is presented as philhellene in accordance with the normal utopian image of Ethiopia in ancient literature (ix. 25 *et al.*).[57] The Persian satrap's

[52] See Winkler 1980: 172. On noble bandits see Hobsbawm 1985: 41–57.

[53] See Winkler 1980: 175 n. 97.

[54] Scobie 1973: 19–34; Kuch 1989; Bowie 1991; Saïd 1992 (contrasting Heliodorus with Philostratus' more rigorously Hellenizing *Life of Apollonius*).

[55] Cf. ii. 12. 4 (Thermouthis, Thyamis' lieutenant; though he understands Theagenes' threat at ii. 13. 3 well enough); vii. 12. 5, 14. 2, 19. 3 (Arsace, wife of the satrap Oroondates); viii. 15. 3 (Bagoas, Oroondates' eunuch, 'spoke Greek haltingly with a good deal of slovenly usage'; there is no attempt to reproduce this faulty Greek); see Morgan 1982: 258–60.

[56] Cf. ii. 21. 5 where Calasiris, mistaken by Cnemon for a Greek, asks Cnemon, 'How does a man who's a Greek in speech come to be in Egypt?'.

[57] Ethiopia as utopia: Morgan 1982: 248. Heliodorus was also thinking of the important contemporary power of Aksum (cf. *Ethiopian Story* x. 27. 1), as Morgan notes (242).

wife Arsace puts the matter in a nutshell when she introduces
Theagenes to her court: 'He is every inch a Greek and is afflicted
with the contempt they feel for us there' (vii. 19. 2). Outside
Heliodorus such stereotyping is introduced only occasionally, perhaps because the other narratives are set more in the Greek world
(in Longus, of course, no action occurs outside Lesbos). Chariton
and Achilles Tatius comment as necessary. The Persian eunuch
Artaxates in *Chaereas and Callirhoe* thought 'like a eunuch, a slave,
a barbarian' (vi. 4. 10). In Achilles Tatius we do at least find the
expected categorization of the notorious *boukoloi*: the shoreline
'was full of frightening, wild men, all of them big and black in
colour (not the absolute black of the Indians, but more like a bastard Ethiopian), their heads were shaven, their bodies gross, but
they were quick on their feet, and all spoke a barbarous tongue'
(*Leucippe and Clitophon* iii. 9 ff.).

These remarks and others like them certainly build on and perpetuate the ethnocentric boundaries between 'us' and 'them' that
are familiar in all Greek literature.[58] And familiarity rather than
unexpected horror is the source of the entertainment in these stories. The concentration on Egypt is due to its position in Greek
history and literature as the most familiar of all foreign places.[59]
Thus it is that a self-styled 'Phoenician' like Heliodorus, whose
social position at Emesa tells us he was probably an Arab (albeit
thoroughly Hellenized), can make free use of the traditional opposition of Hellene and barbarian.[60] For him, as for the others, it is an
affirmation of the values of urban Hellenic society in an age of
urbanized living.

THE SETTING III: FIDELITY AND MARRIAGE

I turn now to the heroes of the ideal novels. It is not difficult to see
why young people are the main characters in these stories. They are

[58] Cf. Winkler 1980: 180.

[59] Galen's denunciation of Egyptians, as reported by Arabic sources, for their
blackness, form, odour, skewed brains, and enlarged genitalia is an extreme example
of a regular Hellenocentric racism: see Nutton 1993: 26.

[60] Social position: 'a Phoenician man from Emesa, his clan that of the Descendants
of the Sun' (x. 41. 4); see further below, Appendix A. Cf. Kerényi 1927: 47–54,
250 ff. on Heliodorus' use of Egypt (as part of his thesis of the influence of Egyptian
religion in the novel). Heliodorus' heroine Charicleia is of course an Ethiopian by
birth, but functions throughout as a Greek (e.g. *Ethiopian Story* viii. 17. 3, x. 7. 5)
and is consequently, though notoriously, light-skinned (x. 14. 3–7).

typically impressionistic, naïve, brave, optimistic, etc. More important for the novel's appeal may be the sexual and moral message such heroes carried. The Greek novel is notable for its accent on the sexual fidelity of the protagonists, on virginity (almost exclusively, of course, for females), for its presentation of a general reciprocity between the male and the female, and for its stress on marriage as the proper forum for a successful emotional and physical relationship between the lovers.[61] These ethics assume great importance among male elite Greeks in our period and, as I have said, I shall accordingly treat this area of the novel at greater length than I have the place of the past and the role of the countryside. Clearly, one can go back to Penelope and Odysseus to find the archetype of the happy marriage. Many other examples could be cited before the age of the novel. The interesting development in our period is that the idea of 'conjugality', that is, of a marriage according at least in theory a proper integration of the wife and of the husband together as a couple (as opposed to the meticulously distinct position held by the spouse in Xenophon's *Oeconomicus*), now seems to have become a subject of serious discussion and thought among men conducted in tandem with a depreciation of the traditional male homoerotic relationship ('Greek pseudo-homosexuality').[62]

This new conjugality has a Stoic feel, as can be seen from Stobaeus' selections from Antipater of Tarsus' influential *On Marriage*, a text of the mid-second century BC which resonates through Musonius Rufus and Seneca in the first century AD, Epictetus and Plutarch in the first and second centuries, and on to the Stoic Hierocles in the time of Hadrian, for whom men and women in marriage were

[61] These aspects are well documented by Konstan 1994: 14–98. Note that only in Heliodorus is male virginity a way of life before marriage (cf. the virginity test for both heroes at *Ethiopian Story* x. 7–9). See also below in text after n. 70 on Clitophon's *parthenia* in the *Leucippe and Clitophon*.

[62] See Foucault 1988: 72–80, 147–85, 189–232 (Foucault builds on the ideas of Veyne 1978 about the senatorial aristocracy, cf. Veyne 1987: 133–49, and see below, n. 83, on the irrelevance of these particular ideas to the Greek elite); Scarcella 1993: 64 ff.; cf. Brown 1988: 12–16. Goldhill 1995 attacks Foucault for failing to emphasize the extent to which debate went on—but the key point is that the debate occurred, not that it found these matters difficult (whih no one has denied). See also Richlin 1992*b*: pp. xiii–xxxiii for bibliography and mostly justified protest about the typically Foucauldian androcentrism inherent in much modern scholarship on ancient 'sexuality' (including Foucault 1988); second sophistic ethics, however, are a male matter, as we shall be seeing.

The term 'Greek pseudo-homosexuality' was coined by Devereux 1967 (a paper that appears rather unsatisfactory today); Dover 1978 remains the best discussion of the matter; see also below in text.

naturally *sunduastikoi*, 'living as pairs'/'conjugal'.[63] The merits and
demerits of taking a wife had long been the subject of discussion by
the Greek male, turning on the compensations available to him for
his loss of freedom at marriage. Traditional debate of this sort,
profoundly or relatively misogynistic, is carried on till the end of
antiquity. But from the Stoicizing ethics of our period there emerges
a new premiss to the discussion, that marriage is a duty to the city
and that the wise man will make it an essential part of his life. In
the texts that take their departure here, the discussion of marriage
as a binary system dependent upon a mutual sexual fidelity and
pleasure offers something quite different from classical analyses of
the economy of marriage, where the relationship between husband
and wife, however respectful or shared, is pretty well an entirely
one-sided combination of male moderation and female virtue. The
main point to bear in mind is not that the idea of the loving family
was suddenly discovered in our period (any more than its reality
was effected);[64] but that married love was now given an intellectual
credibility lacking before and that at least among some male thinkers a traditional commendation of wifely virtue was joined by a
male restraint rooted in the marriage relation as an act of self-
obligation rather than a matter of external injunction.

In the classical period the areas of sexual relations that were
problematical to male authors were the question of pederasty and
the conception of young male beauty as the best earthly reminder
of the absolute. This problematic achieved its most sophisticated
exposition in surviving literature in Plato's *Phaedrus* and *Symposium*. It was argued that sexual intercourse had no part in the philosophical relationship where the older male lover (the *erastês*) gazed
for inspiration on the beauty of his younger friend (the *erômenos*).

[63] To this ensemble should probably be added Ps.-Aristotle, *Economics* iii (ed.
Wartelle; the work is known only from a late medieval Latin translation), which has
a similarly unclassical feel in its presentation of the husband's fidelity and self-
restraint. Antipater—in Stobaeus, *Anthology* iv. 507–12, 539–40 Hense (*On Marriage* 25, 103) = *SVF* iii, pp. 254–7, nos. 62–3. Hierocles—in Stobaeus, *Anthology* iv.
502–3 (*On Marriage* 22) = pp. 52–3 ed. von Arnim (1906); Hierocles' use of
'syndyastic' has an ethical value absent from Aristotle's use of the word at
Nicomachean Ethics 1162ª17 (where it is simply matter-of-fact description).

[64] Note Saller and Shaw 1984: 134 ff. arguing against Veyne 1978 on the basis of
Roman tombstone evidence from the Republican era; similarly Garnsey and Saller
1987: 132–3; plenty of evidence of enduring *conjugalis amor* is supplied by Treggiari
1991: 220–61. None of this affects the changed belief in *how* the marriage relation
should function.

Realizing perhaps that the requisite Socratic forbearance was alien
to most bodies, Plato went on in his *Laws* to ban homoerotic love
altogether.[65] During the second sophistic Platonism became the most
influential philosophic creed. It was naturally subject to innovations, and among other things it is clear that later Platonizing thinkers
rejected the possibility of Socratic love and preferred to predicate
the harmony of the city on the harmony of the married home and
its offspring. We see this shift plainly in Plutarch's essays, in his
personalized *Consolation* to his wife, in the *Advice on Marriage*,
and above all in the *Essay on Love* (the *Amatorius*). It is not that
Plutarch is *not* a conservative in his view of the place of the woman
in marriage (or elsewhere)—he certainly is.[66] The point is that the
relationship of man and wife is now intellectualized with the aim of
producing mutual contentment (albeit seen from the male point of
view). Thus in the *Advice on Marriage* (which to be sure is heavily
dependent on traditional views) the young husband Pollianus will
be the philosophical guide of his new wife Eurydice in a 'partnership for life', which is based on mutual love of personalities with
sexual fidelity and pleasure at its heart (138c, 138f, 143d–e, 144b).
In the charming *Essay on Love* the pro's and con's of homosexual
and heterosexual love are debated vigorously against the dramatic
background of a fictional erotic kidnapping—with a difference.[67] A
rich widow, Ismenodora, has fallen in love with a handsome youth,
Bacchon, and, since marriage between them meets with disapproval,
she with the help of her friends abducts him in the street. Here
there is an inversion of a familiar theme of erotic and pederastic
story-telling (seen for example in our period in the first four of the
short *Love Stories* ascribed to Plutarch). The dramatic situation
leads to the debate, the main point of which as it reaches its end is
that spiritual and sexual love can only be properly conjoined within
marriage. 'For married couples,' says Plutarch at 769a, 'sexual relations are a foundation of affection, a communion as it were in a
great mystery. The pleasure may be momentary, but the honour,
grace, and mutual love and trust arising therefrom day by day proves

[65] *Laws* 636c, 838–41; these and the other passages are discussed clearly in Buffière
1980; see also Dover 1978: 153–68.
[66] Le Corsu 1981: 273–4; Patterson 1991 and Treggiari 1991: 224–6 on the *Advice
on Marriage*.
[67] See Buffière 1980: 481–541 (also on Ps.-Lucian, *Amores*); Foucault 1988: 193–
210. Brenk 1988 offers a rather different, allegorical reading of the piece. The translation below is that of Russell 1993: 279.

the Delphians right when they gave Aphrodite the name Harma—
"harmony"—and Homer right when he used the word *philotês*—
"loving friendship"—of this association.' The main objection finally
raised against the male lover and his male beloved centres on the
lack of reciprocity between them, their essential inequality. The
Essay on Love makes it plain that institutional differences like age
and wealth do not come between true lovers.

The picture Plutarch gives us may be compared to that painted
in real life in a series of fine mosaics from Antioch and its suburb
Daphne, which date to the late second or early third century. These
show prince Ninus gazing lovingly at a portrait of his intended
Semiramis and Metiochus and Parthenope regarding one another
with mutual love in their eyes. Art historians would no doubt wish
to speak of the absent-minded intensity of their faces, their faraway
gaze, and their melting looks.[68]

Some other passages which evaluate the merits of homosexual-
pederastic and heterosexual love may be mentioned. These discussions are unequal in their aims and content. We should not forget
that the ideal novels themselves are the main vent for the new sexual
ethics. Nevertheless, they support the belief that 'illicit' sex with
boys or sex outside marriage was now no longer sanctioned and
that the security of the city was felt to depend on what Musonius
calls the 'rampart' (*peribolê*) of marriage.[69] We shall also not be
surprised to notice that theoretical respect for wives did not extend
to women in general (the new conjugality was not about the equality of the sexes), nor to find that pederasty and homosexuality
continued to be popular. The first of these discussions, Achilles
Tatius' *Leucippe and Clitophon* ii. 35–8, is really about sexual love
only. In it the hero's description of the female body during sexual
intercourse is longer and more physical than the praise of the young
male body, as we should expect in a novel.[70] Clitophon avowedly
introduces the debate as a piece of entertainment to distract two
homoerotic friends whose lovers have died (ii. 35. 1). It is 'with a

---

[68] See Hägg 1983: 19–23 with figs. 4–6; especially Quet 1992*a* (with full bibliography).

[69] Musonius fr. xiv = Lutz 1947: 92. 34. I refrain from drawing parallels with early
Christian thought on chastity and marriage, which was in fact travelling a very
different path from that recommended by the pagan moralists (cf. Lane Fox 1986:
340–51).

[70] Wilhelm 1902 sets the discussion in a typological framework; for the sexual
syncrisis cf. *Greek Anthology* v. 19, 208, 277, 278; Hunter 1983: 70–1; and see now
esp. Goldhill 1995: 66–102.

smile' that he asserts that 'male-directed love is becoming quite usual' (ii. 35. 2). More significant is the fact that he can speak on the joys of female sex because, as he reveals somewhat apologetically, he has associated with prostitutes (ii. 37. 5, 38. 1). Yet to Leucippe he remains adamant that he too remains for her in a state of *parthenia*, 'virginity' (v. 20. 5, viii. 5. 7, cf. vi. 16. 3).

A more interesting, more important discussion is the carefully constructed *Amores* attributed to Lucian and written perhaps not later than AD 250.[71] In the style of Lucian himself we have here a framing dialogue in which Lycinus (Lucian's own *nom de plume*) relates to his bisexual friend Theomnestus the fierce debate he had heard on love at Cnidus between the heterosexual Charicles of Corinth and the homosexual rhetor, Callicratidas of Athens. Charicles' remarks are the plainer of the two and are clearly Stoicizing (19–28). Callicratidas' speech is Platonist, rather baroque, and twice as long (30–49). It ends with a ringing approbation of ideal Socratic non-sexual love between the male lover and his beloved (48–9). The Socratic case for the higher, metaphysical form of love, the ultimate form of male friendship, is alive in our period in the shape of four of the 'talks' (*dialexeis*) of the bland philosophical orator Maximus of Tyre, who was active in Rome in the last quarter of the second century (*Dialexeis* xviii–xxi).[72] We also find it expressed in the introductions to Platonic doctrine by Alcinous and Apuleius.[73] The reassertion of the possibility of Socratic love is no doubt in part a reaction against continuing aspersions on Socrates' motives (for example in Lucian's fun at *Lives for Sale* 15, or in Alciphron's 'socratizing' at *Letters of Courtesans* iv. 17. 3). None of these texts represent any original thought. In the *Amores* the final message is in fact the impracticable nature of the Socratic position. When Lycinus is asked by the disputants to give his verdict as judge between them, he tells Theomnestus that he sided with Callicratidas in so far as 'wise men' alone are permitted to love boys (for there is no real virtue in women). Theomnestus then laughs at the sanctimony of the pederast's 'highbrow speech' and

[71] Date: Jones 1984 (on internal evidence). On the structure of the work see Foucault 1988: 211–27.
[72] On these see Trapp 1986: 138–42.
[73] Alcinous, *Didaskalikos* 33 ed. Whittaker–Louis; Apuleius, *On Plato and his Teaching* ii. 13–14 ed. Beaujeu; note the emphasis these texts place on the need for reciprocity between *erastês* and *erômenos*.

makes it plain that in real life homosexual relations involve sex
(51–4).

Books v and xiii of Athenaeus' *Sophists at Dinner* are also ger-
mane to these issues. I start with Book xiii.[74] The subject of this
book is male sexual interest in women as prostitutes and in boys.
As with the rest of the *Sophists at Dinner* it is difficult to isolate
contemporary interests and views from what is inherited from the
literary traditions of the classical and Hellenistic periods, for the
whole work is a parade of its author's familiarity with Greek culture. Nevertheless, some progress can be made towards bringing
Athenaeus within the thinking of his time. He introduces Book xiii
by saying that 'wives [*gametai*]' and 'prostitutes [*hetairai*]' were
often in the diners' conversation. The opening remarks are alleged
to be drawn from the speech of the host, Larensius (that is, P.
Livius Larensis), in praise of wives (555b).[75] The statements we
have are actually an account of what 'our married women' are not
like (557e), and hence an excuse to tell the usual lurid stories about
the behaviour of women and of men towards them. The rest of the
book takes its cue from this. Most of it is a monologue by the
grammarian Myrtilus, interspersed with criticisms of his morality
by the satirical Cynic Cynulcus (whose views on language we have
already encountered). Myrtilus begins with an attack on pederasty
practiced by philosophers, especially the Stoics (563d–566e). Having been abused by Cynulcus because he is in fact a pornographer
of women himself (*pornographos* is used here for the first time),
Myrtilus launches forth again (571a–610b), asserting his own morality, 'cataloguing' female prostitutes at length (573b ff.), and dis-
coursing on the popularity of pederasty in the classical past
(601a–605d). He condemns prostitutes, not prostitution, objecting
to their effect on men rather than to men's use of them.[76] Myrtilus'
attitude to pederasty seems different, since here it is those who
practice it, specifically the philosophers, as well as those who permit it (cf. 572b–c), who are taken to task. It is 'you philosophers'
who 'have sex contrary to nature' (605d, cf. 602f; Plato, *Laws* 841d).
For Myrtilus the 'beauty of a woman' is the best guarantee of sexual
arousal (608a–610b).

[74] On the representation of women here see Henry 1992: esp. 261–5.
[75] Larensis: *PIR*² L 297.
[76] Arguments in favour of prostitution were offered in antiquity: they are refuted by
Dio of Prusa vii. 138–40, and the subject was a theme in the schools: Kohl 1915: 224.

It is difficult to make very much of this. The statement that 'many prefer love-affairs with boys to those with women' (601e) is probably not a contemporary comment (as the tense might imply), since Myrtilus is led to it by a passage of Pindar and follows it with the traditional practices of the Cretans and the Euboeans. On the other hand, when he says that in the past those who professed love (*erôtikoi*; cf. 599e) were not thought 'vulgar' (601a), the context is firmly homoerotic (Aeschylus' *Myrmidons*, Sophocles' *Niobe*). This does look like an allusion to contemporary feelings. It is noticeable that no one defends either pederasty or its philosophical supporters when they are attacked in Book xiii.[77] Further, despite the porno-graphic, grinding detail of the catalogue of prostitutes (for which Athenaeus/Myrtilus is to be universally admired: 610b), the under-lying assumption is that this sort of sex is wrong (cf. 571b–c). With regard to pederasty we can take matters further by recalling the strong anti-philosophical streak in Book v of the *Sophists at Dinner*. This book is dedicated to 'assisting and nourishing' the soul by considering the high moral standard Homer adopts in his pre-sentation of eating and social intercourse (cf. also i. 8d–17d). Homer's superiority emerges strongly in syncrisis with the philosophers, especially Plato and also Xenophon. Anything bad in Homer is intentionally a bad example, whereas Plato and the other philo-sophers present us with disgusting manners in general and with pederasty in particular (which is attacked several times: 187c–f, 188a, 188d, 219d–220a). This is certainly in accordance with contem-porary values.[78]

As a final passage we may consider the ending of the second, declamatory half of Dio of Prusa's *Euboean Oration* (*Or.* vii). Here, following a discussion of what occupations are fit for the urban poor (103–24) and an assertion that his speech has shown how the poor can live respectably (125–32), Dio completes his survey of urban activities with a virulent attack on prostitution, pederasty, adultery, and sex before marriage (133–52). Although Stoic ideas of marriage and procreation as intrinsic parts of the wise man's

---

[77] Though note at 561a ff., esp. 561c–562a (before Myrtilus' first onslaught), the philosopher Pontianus on the chaste Eros of Zeno and others (cf. Schofield 1991: 35 ff.).

[78] So also Heraclitus, *Homeric Questions* 76. 11–15 ed. Buffière (probably 1st c. AD): Homer at all times upholds conjugal relations whereas Plato's dialogues are filled with pederasty; cf. Ps.-Aristotle, *Economics* iii, pp. 43–5 Wartelle.

political duties are behind these thoughts, the fascination with female virginity before marriage (142) and with pederasty (148–52) must be read against the new moral climate we have been discussing. The elegant first half of the *Euboean Oration*, where Dio tells the story of good rural life on Euboea, culminating with a description of a simple marriage, has often in fact been claimed as novelistic. It is not, for a number of reasons (lack of characterization and the very small role of romance being among them). It is rather that Dio shares the same moral outlook with the novelists, though his tone is quite different. The stridency of the economic and moral messages in the *Euboean Oration* reminds us to some extent of a manifesto. Although Dio is explicitly not sketching a new constitution (125), he does claim that what he is saying is 'useful for choosing an appropriate public policy' (127, cf. the comparison with Plato's *Republic* at 130–2). He calls on the magistrates to implement his advice (136–7, 140; cf. similarly on matters of marriage Plutarch, *Solon* 20. 6–8). Thus nowhere is it made clearer than in this speech that the new sexual ethics form an essential part of the government of the city. Of particular relevance to this is the fact that, while the economic programme Dio advances focuses only on the problems of the poor, his moral programme begins by addressing both poor and rich (133) and then concentrates on the rich. It is their virgin daughters who are at risk (142–5) and whose bastard children must be exposed or live as slaves (146–8). Above all (*eien dê*) it is their sons who are at risk, the ones who will become magistrates, judges, and generals (148–52). These final remarks accord with the vehement opposition to male homoerotic relationships expressed by Dio elsewhere, an opposition which is closely connected with his encouragement of ancestral Greek dignity.[79]

We may compare the Greek novels. In these there are one or two homosexual relationships (notably Cleinias and Charicles in Achilles Tatius' *Leucippe and Clitophon* i. 14 *et al.*, cf. Menelaus at ibid. ii. 34; Hippothous and Hyperanthes in Xenophon's *Ephesian Story* iii. 2; and Berenice and Mesopotamia in Iamblichus' *Babylonian Story* 17 = Photius, *Library* 94, 77a 20–2). That these have a minor

[79] See below, 'Dio' nn. 99, 109. Dio's remarks about moral behaviour in the big city led von Arnim (1898: 457) and others to argue that the *Euboean Oration* was delivered at Rome: a version may well have been, but the nature and style of Dio's points, especially regarding sexual conduct, are best understood in a Greek context (cf. Russell 1992: 13 n. 18 for a more balanced approach to the question of venue).

role in comparison with the major heterosexual interest is not because of the literary influence of Homer (as has been suggested), for there is no clear reference to homoerotic love in the Homeric epics.[80] It is due rather to the novel's role in reflecting contemporary morality.[81] Thus in Longus Book iv, the book which leads to the consummation of Daphnis' and Chloe's marriage, the homosexual parasite Gnathon looks like something from a different age when he crudely tries it on with the saintly Daphnis (iv. 11–12, 16–17). It is no surprise to discover that he 'had learnt the whole of his mythology of love in the symposiums of the dissolute' (iv. 17. 3), an obvious allusion to the Platonic ideal and to what it might lead in practice.

It must be readily admitted that reasons given to account for a change in sexual ethics will be speculative. There is naturally a desire to see the theory as a cause of practice. We may expect to find the change mirrored in 'real-life' behaviour, for example in legislation. But it is not clear whether the new conjugality is actually reflected in the progressive tightening up of imperial marriage law or in the reciprocal marriage contracts of local Greek law in Egypt, which are in fact known from the Hellenistic period onwards.[82] We can at least note the extent to which marriage and related areas had become the subject of official scrutiny and remark that the entry of marriage into the public domain represents a sharp change from the classical period; but we cannot say anything about the emotional place of the couple in these arrangements. We should also be wary of making the theory the result of any particular practice. One such reason advanced for the new moral direction is the changing political role of the senatorial elite in relation to the emperor.[83] The idea—that affection became more important in marriage as marriage became a less important locus for political

---

[80] Influence of Homer: Effe 1987. The absence of homoerotic love in epic does not imply (as it has often been felt to) that there was no homosexuality at all in Homer's time; cf. Sergent 1987: 207, 250 ff. on Achilles and Patroclus.

[81] Konstan 1994: 26–30 (cf. 113–25) well points out the 'asymmetry' of the homoerotic affairs in the novels.

[82] On Roman imperial law see Gardner 1986; Rouselle 1988: 78–106; Treggiari 1991. On marriage contracts (also attested at Dura-Europos) see Egger 1988: 56–9, ead. 1994: 266–71 with relevant literature and remarks on the novels' partial reflection of postclassical developments and preference for classical models of patriarchal control; the postclassical contracts are alleged to reflect 'die Auflösung des Oikos' as a sacral and legal institution in the Hellenistic kingdoms (see e.g. Modrzejewski 1970: 70 ff.).

[83] Veyne 1978.

advancement—is not totally implausible, at least for the minute
section of the male elite who constituted the imperial *Führungsschicht*. But the situation of the Roman 'service aristocracy' is not
relevant to the wider Greek elite who are the audience and compos-
ers of the novels. We must look for more general social and political connections, while allowing that something as complex as the
regulation of sexual behaviour can never be reduced to a single
cause or purpose.

One such connection may be made with the enhanced attention
among male thinkers in our period to male self-identity and to the
establishment of this inside marriage. The moralists and philosophers of our age—men like Seneca, Musonius, Plutarch, Dio,
Epictetus, Fronto, Aristides, Marcus Aurelius, Galen—devote much
space in their surviving writing to the art of successfully ruling
oneself and one's body.[84] Theirs is not the liberal-humanist idea of
the self as isolated individual. As we have seen, that has no place in
ancient society. Rather, this 'technology of the self' was practised
with an eye on the behaviour and advice of others as a taking stock
through observation and practice of the correct mode of living in
and with society. Above all, the desired poise and stability of the
self was rooted in the home and the marriage relation. This was to
be the centre of self-control in the crucial areas of sexual and emotional conduct. The crux of the matter, as Musonius put it, was this:
'if it seems neither shameful nor out of place for a master to have
relations with his female slave . . . let him consider how he would
like it if his wife has relations with a male slave . . . Yet surely one
will not expect men to be less moral than women, nor less capable
of disciplining their desires?' Here respect for oneself is best achieved
through showing respect to one's wife.[85] Similarly, Plutarch says
that anger must be controlled in the home in conduct towards our
servants and our 'wedded wives'. If a man is mild in his own house,
the more so will he be in public life, for under the influence of
those who live with him he has become a 'doctor of his own soul'.[86]

---

[84] Hadot 1981; Foucault 1988: 39–68. Seneca, Musonius, Fronto, and Marcus are
of course Romans, but are thoroughly imbued with Greek modes of thought, especially Stoicism.

[85] Musonius fr. xii = Lutz 1947: 84–8.

[86] Plutarch fr. 148 Sandbach ad fin. (reading ἰατρός after Sandbach 1969: 276 for
the incomprehensible ἀγαθός—the sense is in any case clear); cf. *Advice on Marriage*
144c 'a man who intends to bring harmony to the city, to the market-place, and to
his friends must have a harmonious household'.

His wife, as Xenophon's Habrocomes puts it, is quite simply 'the basis . . . of his whole life' (*Ephesian Story* v. 8. 2).

The elite in the Greek city was formed through intermarriage, that is, it depended upon the deployment of alliance. This was certainly designed to ensure control over the circulation of wealth and the government of the city. But more than this it is a fact that such alliance looks to the past and is founded upon the mystique of ancestry. It may be that greater attention to family life simply functioned as another outlet for elite energies in an age when overt aggression and ambition had to be channelled in more coded ways, such as competition for titles or displays of benefaction. But surely as important is the connection between past and present which the elite sustained through a symbolic joining of blood. In this regard it is no surprise to find the marriage relation becoming an important locus of self-identity for the Greek male. He married into a good family, firmly tied into the city's heritage. And by procreation he ensured the continuation of his own kind and therefore of the city he ruled. The order of his priorities was that 'we all know the families each of us come from, the education we have received, and the property and attitudes and way of life we have'.[87]

As far as the novel is concerned, it may be suggested that we are dealing with an extreme formulation of these changes. We have seen that the past setting of the novels fits perfectly with the place of the past in the Greeks' conception of themselves as heirs of the classical Greeks. The role of the city–country dialectic (which has a clear basis in 'real' social and economic organization) furthers this by asserting the centrality of civic life as the index of Greek civilization along traditional lines. Should not the ideal of married bliss be read, then, in terms of the way the Greeks saw themselves living and continuing to live their civic existence, the basic building block of which was the *oikos* (*oikia*) or household/family unit?[88] Conjugality emerges as part of a package of elements that allowed the novels to appeal to their audience's self-definition as Greeks whose life reached back into the past and was guaranteed to continue in the future. For though the feelings of the two elite individuals in the story are ostensibly private, they are in fact the subject of public display and commentary which marks their conjugality

[87] Galen, *On Precognition* xiv. 624. 8–11 (see below, 'Galen' nn. 15–18).
[88] Cf. Aristotle, *Politics* i. 2, 1252^a24–$^b38$.

out as the dynamic force underlying the public life of the city.[89] It must be significant that the novels place the new moral and ethical norms firmly in a world without Rome. The lived experience of the elite, the life of their friends and families, is expressed rather in an abstract political world that is their right by inheritance, even though it can exist only in the imagination.

One final point may now be made. It was suggested long ago that the novel's new ethical structure was responsible for its downfall, for a novel about lovers should not take virginity too seriously.[90] This is not so. If there was an in-built crisis in the ideal novels, it had to do with plot, not morals. The problem was always how to preserve spiritual union apart from physical union. Some authors put geographical distance between the protagonists to effect this. It was the genius of Longus and Heliodorus to be able to keep their heroes in close proximity—and chaste. And we cannot say that variation of plots would not have continued, if the novel had.[91] Yet the novel's demise is not without significance. It should not be doubted that it stopped being written when there was no longer a market for it. Its end coincides with the end of the second sophistic period and the transformation of Greek society into the world of late antiquity. As has been observed, on one level the fourth century in the Greek East does not look so different from the second. The world of the city and of the social network established on the claims of Greek culture goes on. In other ways—the visible Christianization, the bureaucratizing of the Empire and the vastly increased power of central government, the loosening of the ties which funnelled the wealth of the elite into the cities, the gradual

---

[89] In the novel the reciprocity of the couple is reinforced by the fact that the heroes are of much the same age and marry young (cf. Longus i. 7. 1 Daphnis and Chloe begin the story aged 15 and 13; Xenophon i. 2. 2 Habrocomes is 'about 16', i. 2. 5 Antheia is 14). Recent studies of gravestone evidence from the western half of the Roman Empire show that most men married some 5 to 10 years later than women and not before their mid-20s (Parkin 1992: 123–5; the custom among the Roman senatorial elite of marrying men in their early 20s and girls as young as 12 is peculiar); literary prescriptions for classical Greece show a slightly greater age difference with men marrying around 30 (Lacey 1968: 106–7, 162), while Egyptian census returns of the High Empire indicate a mean age gap of 7½ years with most males marrying around 25 and 60% of females by 20 (Bagnall and Frier 1994: 111–21).

[90] Schissel 1913: 47 ff.

[91] Cf. Hägg 1983: 73 ff., MacAlister 1994 on the revival of the novel in the Byzantine Comnenian period.

replacement of public generosity by charity, the founding of Constantinople, the challenge of Latin in offical usage—it is a very different world.[92] The demise of the novel must reflect these changes. For, if, as has been suggested here, the novel epitomized key ideological concerns of the elite in the second sophistic, it is clear that it would have had to change radically in order to survive. It did not. This is striking, because one might expect fashion and literary imitation to have had sufficient force to keep the novels going. They did not. Hence the novel's demise is further testimony of its particular relationship with the body of readers to whom it first appealed.[93]

[92] On continuity and change between the two periods see now Brown 1992.

[93] Clearly, the novels continued to be read—a different matter—and it may be that some were still written (see Appendix A on the dating of Heliodorus). It is worth noting that the known papyri of Chariton and Achilles Tatius fall between the 2nd and 4th centuries (with the exception of Wilcken's lost 6th- or 7th-c. codex of Chariton and the *Chione*; the Heliodorus parchment fragment is also 6th c.: Gronewald 1979). The fragmentary novels are apparently from second sophistic copies, except for one of the *Sesonchosis* papyri (*P.Oxy* 1826) which is a little later (*c*. early 4th c.), the *Chione* from late antiquity, and perhaps one or two others.

Regrettably this is not the place to discuss the Christian novel, a rather different creature (see Hägg 1983: 162–4 on the Ps.-Clementines), or the Apocryphal Acts such as those of Paul and Thecla (see Brown 1988: 154–9).

PART TWO

Greeks and Rome

5

Plutarch

INTRODUCTION

Plutarch of Chaeroneia in Boeotia is perhaps the most important author of the second sophistic period. He offers us detailed evidence of how an educated Greek aristocrat felt about Rome. Plutarch was born between 40 and 45. From his writings and from inscriptional testimony we know a good deal about his family and friends. We can see him engaged in local politics and other business, and active as a family man, a philosopher and author, and (perhaps) a farmer.[1] In literature he is best known for his *Parallel Lives*, the twenty-two paired biographies of 'noble Grecians and Romanes' (in North's words).[2] As with many, perhaps most, of Plutarch's surviving writings it seems certain that the *Parallels* were written after the reign of Domitian, when Plutarch, like Tacitus, again felt safe to express his opinions on the present and the past. But Plutarch was certainly active in literary creation before this period. Several single biographies including, notably, a series on the Roman emperors from Augustus to Vitellius, of which we have only the linked and rather disappointing *Galba* and *Otho*, were presumably written under the earlier Flavians.[3] Plutarch's many other surviving

[1] Jones 1971a: 3–64 gives an excellent account of his life and career; see also Ziegler 1951: 639–96; Russell 1973: 1–17; on farming as the family's economic activity—a likely enough assumption—note *How to Read the Poets* 33b–c ('our' philosophy, politics, and farming; this was written before Plutarch became a priest: cf. ibid. 34d, Jones 1966: 71). See also below, n. 6.
For my translations from Plutarch's *Moralia*, and especially for *Political Advice*, I have rested heavily throughout on Russell 1993.
[2] The best introductions to the *Parallels* are Jones 1971a: 81–109, and esp. Russell 1966, id. 1973: 100–42; Wardman 1974 is also serviceable. Thomas North's translation of Amyot's French version was published in 1579.
[3] The *Caesars*: Jones 1971a: 72–80; Georgiadou 1988. For a reasonable attempt at the chronology of Plutarch's works see Jones 1966, id. 1971a: 135–7; but the relative chronology of the *Parallels* themselves is difficult to determine because, though

works, collected together as the *Moralia*, were written at various times. These comprise essays of advice, consolation, literary criticism and education, philosophical pieces, conversation (the *Table Talks*), and crucial political essays, especially the *Political Advice*, which I shall be examining in detail below.[4] The titles of many other works now lost are known from the so-called *Lamprias Catalogue*, a list of Plutarch's works taken from the inventory of an unknown ancient library.[5]

A major part of Plutarch's life was religious activity. He believed in the gods worshipped in cult, but also like others thought philosophically in terms of a single divine principle which controlled the world of man and nature. His religious belief combines with his commitment to public service and his close relationship with the Greek past in his role as one of the priests of Apollo at Delphi. He held this office from about 90 or 95 till his death some time around 120 at the age of 75 or 80.[6] If we want a single label for Plutarch, we must call him a philosopher, which is how he thought of himself (cf. *Table Talks* 617f, *Political Advice* 798a–c). Most of his writing is about discovering to his fellow men and women a life that is morally excellent. As master he followed Plato (and his Successors in the Academy) in particular, though he was influenced also by the Stoics and the Peripatetics, especially in ethical and psychological matters. It seems that his dualistic faith in the operation of good and evil principles in the world led later Neoplatonist philosophers to ignore several of his more serious philosophical works, which were then lost. Those left to us are mostly the lighter pieces together with his strenuous attacks on the Stoics and the Epicureans, though two of the heavier Platonic enquiries remain.[7] Plutarch's stance as a philosopher naturally set him against sophists and rhetors and the cult of self-advertisement that so attracted the

there are numerous cross-references between them, not a few of these contradict each other (Brożek 1963: 70, 76; Pelling 1979: 80–1; for good discussion of the similar problem in Galen see Bardong 1942: 603 ff.).

[4] On the *Moralia* in general see Russell 1968, id. 1973: 63–99; esp. Ziegler 1951: 719–895.

[5] Text and history in Ziegler 1951: 696–702; Sandbach 1969: 3–29.

[6] Jones 1966: 66, id. 1971a: 13; Swain 1991c: 320–2. Religion: Brenk 1977, 1987; on Plutarch's moderate dualism (cf. below) Bianchi 1986.

[7] These are *Platonic Questions* and *On the Generation of the Soul in the Timaeus*. On Plutarch's Platonism see Dillon 1977: 184–230, id. 1988; Dillon 1982: 60–9 is also relevant. On his self-presentation within Platonic philosophy as an 'Academic' (at a time when the Academy was long since defunct) see 'Past' n. 88.

intellectuals of the age (cf. *On Listening to Lectures, How to Praise Oneself*). As has been noted, he was not a strict atticist. His approach to literary composition has more in common with that of Dionysius of Halicarnassus. His vocabulary is very wide, reflecting his wide range of interests and extensive reading of authors from all periods of Greek in prose and poetry. On the other hand, careful attention to style is clear from the long periodic sentences and from his marked aversion to hiatus. Within his own thesaurus he employs the Attic vocabulary we find in other second-century authors (tempered by a predilection for abstract nouns and compound verbs in the Hellenistic style), and in syntax and morphology displays a strong Attic stamp.[8] In all this he is not untypical of his age.

TWO PEOPLES — ONE CULTURE

Although my main concern in this chapter is with Plutarch's thoughts in *Political Advice* and other works on the meaning of Roman rule, the *Parallel Lives* are the obvious place to begin the search for his views of Rome and Romans.[9] For here more obviously than elsewhere in second sophistic literature we see expressed the notion of comparability between Greece and Rome. There is absolutely no doubt that Plutarch was very sympathetic towards Romans and highly interested and knowledgeable about Rome's history and institutions. This shows through clearly in the *Lives* (where his considerable reading of Latin sources should also be stressed).[10] It has been thought that Plutarch intended the series as a demonstration to Romans that the Greeks were their equivalents in deeds of statesmanship and war, and as a proof to the Greeks that the Romans were their counterparts in civilization.[11] Plutarch does indeed address the problem of how Hellenized Rome was (I shall return to this below), and in the *Parallels* and in the *Moralia* extols the great deeds of Greece's past. If the now lost *Epaminondas*

[8] Cf. Ziegler 1951: 928–38; Russell 1973: 18–41; above, 'Language' n. 25.
[9] In this section and the next two I am drawing rather heavily on my own earlier work on the *Lives*. This is necessary preparation for the treatment of the political writings. On one or two points of detail I have, naturally enough, changed my mind.
[10] Latin: Rose 1924: 11–19; Theander 1951: 68–9; Jones 1971a: 81–7. A useful list of Roman authors (writing in Greek and Latin) cited by Plutarch and of Latin terms explained by him can be found in Ziegler 1980: 13–15, 200–3.
[11] Ziegler 1951: 897.

and Scipio formed the first pair of the *Lives*, which is likely given Epaminondas' appeal to Plutarch's Boeotian patriotism, a conciliatory purpose may have been mentioned in a programmatic introduction.[12] But this seems unlikely from what Plutarch tells us in prefaces to the surviving pairs and from remarks in his moral essays. These make it plain that the purpose of the *Lives* was ethical.[13] A key part of Plutarch's plan for moral improvement, with the aim of constituting one's life according to philosophy, was the observation of others.[14] Comparison between past and present in one's own life and consideration of the views of those whose lives are examples from the past were equally important in this project.[15] It was the great actions of the men of the past that were particularly instructive.[16] Imitation and emulation of the virtues of the great men of history had to be accompanied by exploitation of our own resources of virtue (*Aratus* 1. 3–5). Thus, though it is 'fair actions that leave behind thoughts of them that are always delightful and fresh', bad actions could also serve as useful examples, so long as we are trained how to react to them.[17] In the introduction to the *Pericles and Fabius* Plutarch strongly expresses his belief that it must be statesmen we imitate rather than famous artists, for artistic representation does not presuppose virtue.[18] For this moral purpose Roman statesmen were as useful as Greeks. The reason for pairing Greeks and Romans was simply for interest value. The idea of comparison between the two races had been developed by the Roman authors Varro, Nepos, and Valerius Maximus. It is probably

---

[12] For Epaminondas see the surviving *Pelopidas* and the relevant portions of *On Socrates' Divine Guide* (where Epaminondas' brother, Caphisias, is a major player), as well as the excerpts in *Sayings of Kings and Commanders* 192c-194c. It is not known whether the paired Scipio was Scipio Africanus or Scipio Aemilianus (a single biography of one of these was also written); Scipio Africanus is more probable (Sandbach 1969: 74–5).

[13] Cf. *Aemilius* 1. 3 'for improvement of moral characters'. See Jones 1971*a*: 103–9; Wardman 1974: 18–26. Note also *On Progress in Virtue* 79b: real progress in philosophy shows when one's writings focus on 'character and emotion', precisely the subject matter of the *Lives*.

[14] *On Virtue and Vice* 101c, *How to Control Anger* 455f, *How to Praise Oneself* 547d, *On God's Slowness to Punish* 551a, etc. Cf. above, 'Novel' n. 84.

[15] See above, 'Past' nn. 54–5.

[16] Cf. *Demetrius* 1. 5, *Nicias* 1. 5, *Pompey* 8. 7.

[17] *On Contentment* 477b (quotation), *Pericles* 1. 4–2. 5, *Aemilius* 1. 5, *Demetrius* 1. 6, *How to Read the Poets* 26a–b, *On Moral Virtue* 452d.

[18] Cf. *How to Read the Poets* 18d and the declamatory attack on artists and writers in *On the Glory of the Athenians*.

right to hold that Plutarch was influenced by them, especially Nepos, though his precise idea of binary syncrisis—the detailed comparison of two things or people—is a very Greek one and was indeed a standard exercise in the schools (which accounts for the formal syncriseis that follow most of the *Parallels*).[19]

Various reasons may be put forward for the choice of individual heroes. Thus Plutarch tells us that he chose Lucullus and Romulus before deciding on their Greek pairs, Cimon and Theseus (*Cimon* 3. 1, *Theseus* 1. 5). Leaving aside these explicit statements it is obvious that the great men of Greece and Rome had to be included and that in most cases Plutarch would have thought of a Greek first (which is reflected in the normal order of the *Parallels*).[20] Knowing for certain only the relative position of three pairs in the series, it remains a matter of speculation whether Plutarch concentrated first on the great men of fifth-century Athens (nostalgic reasons have been suggested here), or if the lives of most of the great Republican heroes were chosen and prepared together (as common use of Asinius Pollio might suggest) and then coupled with the less prestigious Greeks.[21] Overall, simple chronological considerations go a long way to explaining the pairing of fifth-century Greeks with early or middle Republican Romans and of the later Greeks with the Romans of the late Republic.[22]

Whatever the reasons behind Plutarch's choice of heroes, there is no evidence that he thought one group of heroes superior to another. Rather, for the most part he judges both races with the same moral vocabulary and assumptions. However, it does seem that in the area of *paideia* ('education', 'culture') and in the effect of

[19] Nepos: Geiger 1985: 117–120, id. 1988. Syncrisis: cf. e.g. Theon, *Progymnasmata* 112–15 Sp. The first Greek–Roman comparison by a Greek is apparently Caecilius' stylistic assessment of Cicero and Demosthenes: cf. Plutarch *Demosthenes* 3. 2, Ps.-Longinus, *On the Sublime* 12. 4–5. On Plutarch's formal syncriseis cf. Pelling 1986b: esp. 84; Swain 1992b.

[20] The aberrant order of *Aemilius and Timoleon, Coriolanus and Alcibiades,* and *Sertorius and Eumenes* is perhaps to be explained by literary-structural considerations: Geiger 1981: 104; Pelling 1986b: 94.

[21] Geiger 1981: 88–94 for the first idea; Pelling 1979 argues intelligently for the simultaneous preparation of six late Republican heroes.

[22] Cf. *Themistocles and Camillus, Pericles and Fabius Maximus, Coriolanus and Alcibiades, Aristides and Cato Major* against *Pyrrhus and Marius, Lysander and Sulla, Sertorius and Eumenes, Agesilaus and Pompey, Alexander and Caesar, Phocion and Cato Minor, Agis-Cleomenes and Ti.-C. Gracchus, Demosthenes and Cicero, Demetrius and Antony, Dion and Brutus.* The exceptions are *Cimon and Lucullus* and *Nicias and Crassus.*

education on the production of virtue and vice in a man Plutarch examines Romans from a decidedly Greek point of view. We should recall how important the concept of *paideia* was to the Greeks of the second sophistic period and how readily the elite styled themselves 'the educated'. Plutarch's identification of this difference between his heroes is, then, highly significant. He did not follow Dionysius of Halicarnassus' contention that the Romans were the racial descendants of the Greeks. Indeed, unlike Dionysius, he makes surprisingly little effort to discover Greek origins behind Roman customs and religion and is very reluctant to accept the idea that the Latin language came from the Greek (cf. *Marcellus* 22. 7, *Numa* 13. 9–10).[23] In the important passage that follows his account of Quinctius Flamininus' announcement of the liberation of Greece in 196 BC Plutarch says that the Romans 'seemed to show slight sparks and insignificant traces of a common ancient race' (*Flamininus* 11. 7); but we should remember that these thoughts are attributed to the Greeks who were then present, even if much of what they say is Plutarch's own opinion, and that even these speakers refer to the Romans as 'foreigners' (*allophuloi*), a term used by Plutarch himself earlier in the same *Life* (2. 5).

Plutarch has a positive, genuine appreciation of Rome's *separate* development. But as a result of this he is aware that Romans, whatever their natural qualities, had had to learn to acquire Greek culture. The reason this was of such importance is that Plutarch's Platonic and Aristotelian idea of character formation is heavily dependent on the regulating effect of *paideia* or *logos* ('reason', 'rationality'), in other words on the successful interiorization of the educational, cultural, and linguistic systems of Greek society. For Plutarch this was the only way of ensuring the desired balance between the rational and irrational sides of the soul (*On Moral Virtue* 443c–d).[24] It is certainly not the case that Plutarch always examines the characters of the Roman heroes more closely than the Greeks from the angle of education. Often there is indeed more information about education on the Greek side of a pair than on the Roman.[25]

[23] See Swain 1990*b*: 126 nn. 2, 3, and above, 'Language' n. 68.

[24] Swain 1989*b*. *On Moral Virtue* is the subject of an admirable commentary by Babut 1969*a*; see also Dillon 1988: 362–4.

[25] Cf. *Alexander and Caesar*, *Coriolanus and Alcibiades*, *Lycurgus and Numa*, *Pericles and Fabius*, *Philopoemen and Flamininus*, *Solon and Publicola*, *Themistocles and Camillus*.

The point is precisely that Plutarch does little with this information, whereas in a number of Roman *Lives* (*Aemilius, Brutus, Cato Major, Cato Minor, Cicero, Coriolanus, Lucullus, Marcellus, Marius*) interest in the hero's *paideia* emerges prominently in a manner which is unrepresentative of the source material and generally independent of common thematic structures in the pair. Although it is reasonably clear that the Greek language was well known in Rome from the time of the Hannibalic War or earlier, it is true to say that higher Greek learning was not fully at home there until the time of Scipio Aemilianus in the mid to late second century.[26] And this is the picture of Roman civilization Plutarch himself worked with and which affects the presentation of his Roman heroes.[27]

Here I shall summarize what I have said in more detail elsewhere.[28] Consider first the early Roman king Numa. Pairing him with Lycurgus, the legendary Spartan lawgiver, Plutarch decides to make him into something of an ideal king who prefigures Plato in the purity of his virtue and who was probably acquainted with Pythagoras (*Numa* 8, 20. 8, 22. 5). But Numa's 'most beautiful and most just system' quickly failed after his death 'because it lacked the cohesive force of education' (*Numa and Lycurgus synkrisis* 4. 12).[29] In *Coriolanus*, perhaps in response to the place occupied by Socrates in the paired *Alcibiades*, Plutarch again comments on education in early Rome: not only is Coriolanus, despite his natural attainments, incapacitated by a lack of Hellenic education, but Rome itself is pictured as a place that lacks even the vocabulary for expressing the Greek term *aretê*, the 'excellence' or 'virtue' which is the summation of moral and philosophical achievement, since the Latin *virtus*, says Plutarch, signified at this time no more than 'manly courage' (1. 3–6, 15. 4, 21. 1). For Plutarch Hellenic culture began at Rome in the time of the Hannibalic War with the great general (Marcus Claudius) Marcellus. At the beginning of his *Life* we are rather surprised to find 'the sword of Rome' presented as 'an enthusiast of Hellenic learning and literature' (1. 3). It is difficult to say where Plutarch got this idea from. Marcellus' description of

---

[26] Kaimio 1979: 317; Gruen 1984: i. 250–72; Dubuisson 1985: 262–3.

[27] Contrast Dionysius of Halicarnassus, *History of Early Rome* vii. 71. 1, where Dionysius counters the 'improbable assumption' that Rome learned Hellenic customs after coming into contact with Greece in the 2nd c. BC.

[28] Esp. in Swain 1990*a* and 1990*b*. For further developments of these ideas see Pelling 1989.

[29] ἅτε δὴ καὶ τὸ συνδετικὸν ἐν αὐτῇ, τὴν παιδείαν, οὐκ ἔχουσα.

Archimedes, in which he alludes to the Greek culture of the
sumposion (17. 2), may have offered a clue, as may Posidonius'
narrative of Marcellus' campaign in Sicily (though there is no proof
of this). Marcellus' Hellenism goes closely with Plutarch's stress on
the (Hellenic) propriety of Roman religion at the time. Roman rites
'contain nothing barbaric or outlandish', but consist of proper, ancestral religious practices free from superstition (3. 5–6, 4. 7, 5. 1–7).[30]
This original presentation allows him to excuse Marcellus' war
crimes in Sicily and to congratulate him for introducing Hellenic
art and taste to Rome in the form of the spoils taken from Syracuse
(20–1). The special stress on Hellenism in the *Marcellus* is paralleled only in the *Lucullus* (on which see below), where the hero's
personal education is accorded great prominence and is connected
with his philhellenic command in the Greek world in the late Republic. For Marcellus, the first man to civilize Rome on the Hellenic model, a Greek education was not available, since the times
did not allow it (1. 2–5), and this is surely a reason why he suc-
cumbs in old age to the ambition (28. 6) that is properly regulated
by *paideia* (cf. *On Moral Virtue* 452d).

   Greek education becomes freely available at Rome from the second quarter of the second century. Thus Cato the Elder, who is
shown to be well versed in Greek life and letters, is an 'opsimath'
(*Cato Major* 2. 5), and Aemilius Paulus, a great philhellene, has a
'native and ancestral education', whereas it is possible for his sons
to be trained in Hellenic *paideia* (*Aemilius* 6. 8–9). By the time of
the Cimbric wars Plutarch knew there had been a real influx of
Greek philosophy and rhetoric at Rome (*On the Fortune of the
Romans* 318c, 322d). Hence he assumes that heroes of the late
Republican period have access to Greek education and judges them
accordingly, when he wishes, in a manner that is not easy to parallel
in the *Lives* of the Greek heroes. *Pyrrhus and Marius* shows this
particularly clearly. Although we know that Marius had a reasonably good Greek education and was not, it seems, hostile to Greek
culture, Plutarch presents him as wilfully ignorant ('he did not study
Greek literature and did not employ the Greek language for serious
subjects, thinking it laughable to study a literature whose teachers
were other people's slaves', *Marius* 2. 2). At *Marius* 2. 4 the wretched
end of Marius' highly ambitious career is specifically attributed to

[30] Hellenic propriety: cf. *On Superstition* 166b, *On the Face in the Moon* 935b.

his lack of Greek culture. Plutarch underlines this by making the theme a principal one of the *Life* (2. 4 'these matters should be examined right away in the facts themselves'). This is stressed again at the end (46). Plutarch might have made the point that, though Pyrrhus was a Greek and therefore had a Greek education (cf. *Pyrrhus* 1. 4; 8. 3, 6), he did not benefit from it in the least. But he does not, for though he almost always takes the *paideia* of his Greeks for granted, moral failing or success is explained without reference to it.[31] Romans are seen differently.

Demosthenes and Cicero is another good example of Plutarch's typical approach. Having in other respects a closely paralleled structure, it is all the more noticeable that of the two it is only Cicero who is scrutinized for the failings of his education. Plutarch presents Cicero as well educated (of course), but it is not until the period of his exile that he chooses to mention that Cicero liked to style himself 'philosopher', and when he does, he mentions it in the context of the unexpected failure of Cicero's lifelong association with education to bolster his morale at a difficult time (*Cicero* 32. 5–6).[32] No link is made between Demosthenes' ignoble conduct during his exile and his explicitly impoverished education (*Demosthenes* 4. 4, 26. 5–7). Cicero's surrender to a love of glory that is at variance with philosophical training is a major theme of his *Life*.

Plutarch, then, felt that Hellenic education could not be taken for granted in his Roman heroes. On account of this it was a useful criterion for bringing out Romans' characters when the information was available. It is well said that he thought that Romans had a 'potentiality for barbarism'.[33] This should not be read as anti-Roman. Rather, as we shall see in the rest of this book, it represents a view commonly held by educated Greeks that there was only one culture worth pursuing in the ancient world—not the modern notion of a unitary Graeco-Roman culture, but the Greek idea of Hellenic culture that Greeks were more likely to possess than Romans. The Greeks were more than happy if Romans adopted their culture. Indeed, as we shall be seeing, educated Greeks frequently judged Romans by their attitudes towards it and towards its exponents. Thus Plutarch's presentation of his Roman heroes

[31] On this particularly see Swain 1990*b*: 135.
[32] Among Romans only Cato the Younger, Nigidius Figulus, and Varro are called philosopher by Plutarch: Swain 1990*a*: 195, 197.
[33] Russell 1973: 132.

is not surprising or anomalous in any way but part of a familiar pattern.

It is worth observing—before passing on to his view of Greece under the Roman Republic—that Plutarch probably looked on the Roman addressee of the *Parallel Lives*, Q. Sosius Senecio, in a not dissimilar manner as a man who needed encouragement towards attaining the peace of mind that comes from Greek philosophy.[34] This emerges particularly from the essay he sent Sosius called *On Progress in Virtue*. The framework of the friendship between the two men is fairly well known. Sosius, who went on to become one of Trajan's closest allies (he was consul ordinarius in 99 and 107), must have met Plutarch first when he was quaestor of the province of Achaia between about 85 and 88. His career is known from an acephalous inscription well attributed to him by Jones, and suggests that he was born around 60.[35] This fits with Plutarch's description of him as a friend of his sons at *Table Talks* 734e; Sosius was indeed present at the wedding of Plutarch's eldest son Autobulus (ibid. iv. 3, 666d–667b). It is impossible to say at what point Plutarch wrote for Sosius *On Progress in Virtue*. Formally the work is a refutation of the Stoic belief that virtue is an absolute and does not admit of progress towards it. Sosius had plainly been disheartened by this rule (75d, 76e, 85b, 79c). But the essay is not a serious attack on Stoicism. Rather, it is a gentle protreptic to a friend encouraging him to carry on making progress towards 'improvement of moral character and alleviation of emotion' (79c).[36] Plutarch bids Sosius come over from Stoicism to the Platonic position. Sosius' Stoic leanings are confirmed by one of his appearances in the *Table Talks* which may be dated to around 92 or 93, when he was about 30.[37]

[34] It has been suggested by some that Sosius was in fact of eastern origin, something which would obviously affect the conclusions I draw here. There is, however, no evidence for this and he may be safely assigned to a provincial Italian background. On this matter see Appendix B.

[35] Jones 1971a: 55, 136. Career: Jones 1970 on *ILS* 1022 supersedes the still useful article of Groag in *RE* iiiA (1927), 1180–93; cf. also Puech 1991: 4883. Addressee of the *Parallels*: *Demosthenes* 1. 1, 31. 7; *Dion* 1. 1; *Theseus* 1. 1; cf. *Aemilius* 1. 6, *Agis-Cleomenes* 1. 3, *Agis-Cleomenes and Gracchi synkrisis* 5. 7.

[36] Cf. *Aemilius* 1. 3 (above, n. 13). Gentle protreptic: Babut 1969b: 47–8.

[37] *Table Talks* ii. 3, 637a (*spermatikos logos*, *SVF* index s.v.). The date depends on the setting. Of Sosius' six appearances in the *Table Talks* i. 1, ii. 1, iv. 3, and v. 1 are set in Greece; from what Plutarch says at i introduction, 612e, questions i. 5 and ii. 3 should be set in Rome. If that is so, 92 or 93 or shortly after, when Plutarch was certainly in Rome, is very likely: Jones 1971a: 23. Cf. also v introduction, 672d, with *On Moral Virtue* 441d.

An essay on making progress in virtue also seems to presuppose youth and this is suggested particularly by a remark about the young (*neoi*, i.e. those not much over 30) being unable as yet to understand Plato fully (79a, cf. 85c–d).

It is clear in general that Sosius was a highly educated man. Pliny the Younger felt able to write to him about the resurgence of poetry early in Nerva's reign.[38] In the *Table Talks* he appears fairly at home with the Greek poets and philosophers, though like the other major Roman participant Mestrius Florus, who obtained Plutarch's Roman citizenship, Sosius tends to ask questions here, not to answer them.[39] But Sosius' learning is not the point. Plutarch is concerned with his wisdom. If we remember his attitude towards the education of his Roman heroes in the *Parallel Lives*, we may say that the advice given to Sosius in *On Progress in Virtue* has a deeper significance than it would have done, had it been given to a Greek acquaintance. That is, in Plutarch's eyes there was a particular risk that Sosius as a Roman might not be able to use his education for his moral improvement (and indeed saw this happening). This is not just a view of Sosius as a younger man. For the message is amplified at vast length later on in the *Parallels* themselves (where the appeal of Stoicism to the Roman elite and its fatal dangers are explored in the *Cato Minor*).[40] Since Sosius had asked Plutarch to record the 'learned discussions' of the *Table Talks* (i introduction, 612e), it is not improbable that he was one of those who originally suggested to Plutarch the composition of the *Parallels* (cf. *Aemilius* 1. 1), perhaps in order to be able to flesh out Plutarch's earlier advice in *On Progress in Virtue* that he should picture before him the great men of the past and use them as mirrors in which he might adjust his own life (85a–b).[41]

CONQUEST OR LIBERATION

Plutarch's most important contribution to the history of the development of Greek and Roman relations is the *Philopoemen and*

---

[38] Pliny, *Letters* i. 13 of April 97 (Sherwin-White 1966: 114–16).
[39] Swain 1990*b*: 129–31, esp. 131 n. 47. Florus and citizenship—below, n. 99.
[40] Swain 1990*a*: 200.
[41] For the 'mirror' image cf. again *Aemilius* 1. 1; further *How to Tell a Flatterer from a Friend* 53a, *How to Control Anger* 456a–b (with Seneca, *On Anger* ii. 36. 1–3); and above, 'Past' n. 55.

Flamininus.[42] This is the only pair in the *Parallel Lives* where contemporaries are treated together and feature in each other's *Life*. The parallelism, of actions and of moral qualities, is heightened by the identical length of the narratives. Much of the subject-matter concerns the beginning of Roman domination in Greece following the defeat of Philip V of Macedon in the First Macedonian War. It is Plutarch's genius to be able to present Rome's involvement in Greece at this time from a Greek point of view in *Philopoemen*, where it amounts to domination, and from a Roman point of view in *Flamininus*, where it is seen as liberation from the Macedonians. In assessing this presentation we must remember that, as in all the *Lives*, fairness to the hero is a primary aim. Both men are put in the best possible light for the actions they take. This makes it difficult to determine where Plutarch's own sympathies lie (for Philopoemen resisting Rome or for Flamininus introducing her as a liberator). Nevertheless, it is clear to begin with that Roman involvement in Greece is the main historical circumstance Plutarch is interested in.

As with many other heroes Plutarch thought Philopoemen and Flamininus were really rather similar in their natures and shared particular ethical qualities. At the end of the formal syncrisis he says the difference between them is 'hard to define' (3. 5), a reference to the often reprehensible love of ambition both men displayed. Plutarch then asks Sosius to 'consider if we have not arbitrated fairly by awarding the Hellene the crown for military and strategic expertise, and the Roman that for justice and goodness of heart' (ibid.). These final qualities are only understandable against the background of Roman involvement in Greece. Only here—and quite definitely not in his domestic politics or in his action against Hannibal at the end of his *Life*—is Flamininus presented as a just liberator and benefactor (*Flamininus* 2. 5, 11. 4, 12. 6). Similarly with Philopoemen: most of his military actions were against other Greeks and are condemned on this basis by Plutarch at *synkrisis* 2. 3 (even if they did demonstrate his valour). It is only in his resistance to Roman involvement that Philopoemen is truly praiseworthy because of his fighting spirit, for which even the Romans later commended him (*Philopoemen* 16. 3; 17. 3, 7; 21. 12). Just before this division of merits Plutarch offers a clue to where his

---

[42] Jones 1971a: 94–9; Pelling 1986b: 85–8; Swain 1988 discusses the pair in more detail and with attention to Plutarch's sources; cf. Walsh 1992.

own emotional preferences lie. 'The reasonableness and humanity Flamininus showed to the Greeks were indeed noble, but the stubbornness and love of freedom Philopoemen showed to the Romans were more noble. For it is easier to confer favours on those who are asking for them than it is to annoy by opposition those who are more powerful' (*synkrisis* 3. 4).

For Plutarch Philopoemen is 'a late born child Hellas bore in old age as a successor to the virtues of her ancient commanders ... and a certain Roman ... called him "last of the Greeks"' (1. 6). That Plutarch considers this a great and accurate compliment is clear from his essay *On Having Many Friends*, where he says we should ask for one true and dear friend among our others who is in Homer's words 'much loved' and 'late born' (94a). In other words, Philopoemen is loyal to Greece, and Greece 'loved him exceedingly' in return, as Plutarch puts it. Before this comment he gives details of Philopoemen's education. Typically, these details are not connected with the good or the bad in his character during the rest of the *Life*. Rather, the theme that emerges here is his good service to Greece. The philosopher-politicians and expellers of tyrants, Ecdelus and Demophanes, 'certainly counted the education of Philopoemen among their other acts, thinking that by means of philosophy they had produced a man who was a common benefit to Greece' (1. 5). In the Nemean Games of 205 BC Philopoemen put on a military display of the troops he had led on behalf of the Achaean League against the Spartan tyrant Machanidas.[43] 'Just as they made their entrance Pylades the citharode happened to be singing the opening verse of the *Persians* of Timotheus, "Glorious the great crown of freedom he fashioneth for Greece". At which point ... the spectators turned their eyes on Philopoemen from all sides and applauded him joyfully. For in their hopes the Greeks were recovering their ancient dignity, and in their will they were coming closest to the spirit of the past' (11. 3–4).

Flamininus' announcement of his liberation of Greece at the Isthmian Games in 196 BC and the Nemean Games of 195 occupies a similar position in the text of the *Flamininus* (10–12). Plutarch records the resulting opinions of the Greeks in ch. 11 of this *Life*. Here Flamininus is contrasted favourably with Agesilaus, Lysander, Nicias, Alcibiades, and the other famous generals of the classical

---

[43] Errington 1968: 250.

period. Only Marathon, Salamis, Plataea, Thermopylae, and Cimon's deeds at Eurymedon and on Cyprus, the battles fought against Persia, had been creditable actions for the Greeks, since Greece's other wars were against Greeks. Now 'foreigners' with little obvious relation to the Greeks 'had undergone the greatest dangers and hardships to rescue Greece and to set her free from harsh despots and tyrants' (11. 7). These thoughts put in the mouths of others are largely Plutarch's own.[44] Plutarch speaks in his own right in the next chapter. 'In the case of Flamininus and the Romans the gratitude of the Greeks for the benefits they received led not only to expressions of praise, but also, and rightly [*dikaiôs*], to confidence among all men and to power.' Plutarch explains what he means by power and confidence by recording that peoples and cities and kings voluntarily put themselves under Roman control (cf. 5. 4–5). 'The result was that in a short time—and perhaps god was lending a helping hand—everything became subject to them. But he himself took most pride in the freeing of Greece' (12. 8–10).

This contrast between the facts of Roman rule and the policy of his hero Flamininus is, of course, a most important one to the biographer. With regard to the liberation of Greece itself, note first that Plutarch does not idealize Rome. The parallel versions in Livy and Polybius focus on Rome, her ideals, power, and virtue. There is, especially in Livy, an element of romance.[45] *Flamininus* 11 is different. Plutarch dwells on Greece and on the distinctive inability of her leaders to live in peace. In *Flamininus* 12 he describes how Roman power spread quickly throughout Greece, while Flamininus himself continued to take pride in his liberation. Plutarch preserves his hero's honour. At the beginning of the *Life* he had introduced Flamininus as 'a man who was young in years, humane in appearance, a Hellene in voice and language, and a lover of true honour … and a champion of freedom' (5. 7). There was indeed nothing barbaric about him or his army (5. 6–7). In this context Plutarch can report the views of all sides in Greece that the Romans 'had come to wage war not on the Greeks, but on the Macedonians on behalf of the Greeks' (5. 8). Now in ch. 12 Rome's domination of Greece is distinguished from the policy of Flamininus. Plutarch stresses that Roman power was achieved *dikaiôs*, 'rightly', both in

[44] Cf. *Phocion* 28. 3, *Pompey* 70, *Sulla* 12. 9–14.
[45] Livy xxxiii. 33. 5–8; Polybius xviii. 46. 13–15; cf. Appian, *Macedonian Wars* fr. 9. 4.

the sense that there was no injustice and that it was merited. After recording Flamininus' dedications at Delphi (12. 11–12), he notes finally that it was in Corinth 'in our own times' that the emperor Nero had once again 'made the Greeks free and autonomous' (12. 13).[46] Nero's action must have made a strong impression on the Greeks of the time. Whether Plutarch witnessed it or not, it certainly stuck in his mind. In the myth at the end of his important essay *On God's Slowness to Punish*, he humorously pictures Nero's soul being reshaped ready for birth in the body of a viper, when 'suddenly' a great voice instructs the craftsmen to adapt it for the body of a frog ('a milder kind . . . a singing creature') because he had paid for his crimes and in addition 'was owed some good from the gods for setting free from among his subjects the nation that was best and most loved by god' (568a). Some seventy or eighty years after Plutarch was writing Pausanias recalled with some bitterness Vespasian's abrogation of Nero's proclamation (vii. 17. 3–4). This action of Vespasian surely accounts for Plutarch's own deep hostility towards that emperor in the *Essay on Love* 771c. Plutarch was naturally aware that Flamininus' proclamation of liberty was really as short-lived as Nero's, and that, however just Flamininus' actions were, Roman intervention against Macedon entailed the subjection, not the liberation of Greece.

In *Flamininus* Flamininus' justness and personal disposition to win fame as a benefactor are crucial reasons for Greece's ready acceptance of Roman control (2. 5). The Greeks are grateful to Flamininus and the Romans. But in comparison with Philopoemen and the Achaeans they have no genuine popularity (cf. *Philopoemen* 1. 6, 11. 4, 15. 1–2, cf. 10. 13). The Romans had restored to the Greeks their freedom, but unlike Philopoemen they had not been able to restore to them their 'ancient dignity' (*Philopoemen* 11. 4). In *Philopoemen* 17 we hear of Philopoemen's opinions on the Romans' war against king Antiochus (III) of Syria: he begrudged them their victory over Antiochus in Greece (under M'. Acilius Glabrio in 191) because of the king's sloth and luxury. Plutarch now comments on Philopoemen's attitude to Rome. 'When the Romans had beaten Antiochus, they were already becoming more closely involved

---

[46] The text of Nero's speech at Corinth is known from a famous inscription, *SIG*³ 814 = *ILS* 8794 from 67 (or 66, canvassed by Halfmann 1986: 173–7). Cf. below, 'Pausanias' n. 33, for Pausanias' reference to Nero's liberation in his narrative of Rome's destruction of the Achaean League.

with Greek affairs, and were encompassing the Achaeans in their power as the demagogues inclined to their support. Their strength, with the help of the divine spirit [*daimôn*], was growing great in all areas, and the end was at hand, to which Fortune in its cycle was bound to come. Here Philopoemen, like a good helmsman contending against the waves, was on some matters compelled to give in and yield to the times. But in most he continued his opposition by attempting to draw those who were powerful in speech or action in the direction of freedom' (17. 2–3).

Philopoemen is presented as struggling against forces outside his control in the manner of Phocion and Cato the Younger (see *Phocion* 1–3). As the 'last of the Greeks' he certainly shared in the faults Plutarch criticizes in the Greek leaders of the past at *Flamininus* 11. He is liable to be contentious and angry (*Philopoemen* 3. 1), qualities Plutarch specifically reproves at the end of *Political Advice* (825e). Nevertheless, Philopoemen is not so crudely damned: the past leaders of Greece 'did not know how to turn their successses into legitimate gratitude and honourable conduct' (*Flamininus* 11. 5); whereas Philopoemen is judged at the end of his *Life* to have had precisely these abilities (21. 12). This attitude explains why Plutarch concludes in the formal syncrisis that Philopoemen's 'stubbornness and love of freedom' were more noble than Flamininus' 'reasonableness and humanity'. As we have seen, he is careful to protect the honour of Flamininus. But it is ultimately difficult to deny that his emotions side with Philopoemen. He never exalts the classical Greek empires of Athens or Sparta because he was fully aware of the disastrous consequences of Greek strife for Greek independence.[47] Philopoemen was in a different category. He was a true benefactor of Greece. Indeed, after the hero Timoleon of Corinth (to whom I shall return) it is Philopoemen who is represented as benefiting the Greeks most of all. His opposition to Rome is a vital part of this presentation.

---

[47] Two examples may suffice: first, the stringent criticism of Aratus, who earlier in his career had carried out 'the last, most recent deed of the Greeks' (*Aratus* 16. 4, 24. 2 on the liberation of Acrocorinth), for later bringing the Macedonians into the Peloponnese and barbarizing it in order to prevail over Cleomenes of Sparta (cf. above, 'Past' n. 58); second, the emotional outburst at Agesilaus' recall from Asia to fight Greeks, thereby leaving it to 'Alexander and the Macedonians' to conquer Persia, while the Greeks 'squandered the lives of their generals' fighting other Greeks: *Agesilaus* 15. 3–4.

DIVINE RULE AND ROMAN RULE

One of the most noteworthy features of Plutarch's account of how Roman power spread in the Greek world is his suggestion of divine support for Rome (*Philopoemen* 17. 2 'with the help of the divine spirit'; *Flamininus* 12. 10 'perhaps god was lending a helping hand'). On their own these statements would amount to no more than rhetorical flourishes in passages focusing on extraordinary successes. They are in fact part of a group of passages in the *Lives* which make it very likely that Plutarch thought the course of history was predetermined by divine providence and that he believed in particular that the rise of Rome and her continuing success were due to the operations of this power.[48] It is hardly surprising that Plutarch should hold such a theory, for both Platonists and (especially) Stoics accepted in their different ways that the world was governed by divine providence. We see this providence at work in history also in the essay on divine punishment, *On God's Slowness to Punish*, which offers support for the idea in a serious philosophical and religious environment. The extent of the belief, and its expression in the *Lives*, are not at all easy to determine. The *Lives* are not treatises on the workings of providence. Plutarch's belief in this power is expressed when and as it occurs to him that it was involved. It may be that we are dealing with more of a feeling than a certain and sure faith. As often with Plutarch's opinions about the gods there is caution (an important element in his thought), and occasionally incoherence. In many of the key passages in the *Lives* he speaks simply of *tuchê*, 'fortune'. Mostly, of course, talk of 'fortune' is part of the familiar rhetorical and dramatic scenery of ancient literary creation. Comments on fortune and chance occur frequently in the *Lives* because they are useful to the biographer in assessing stability of character (a prime example of this being the *Life of Aemilius*), or for pointing out the bizarre changes in a hero's career (the *Demetrius* is the best example here). It is very easy to lose sight of comments on providence by filing them under rhetoric. To do so is a natural observer prejudice. But where references to fortune cluster around major changes in history which do not concern character, we should be prepared to allow our author his belief in the involvement of the Platonic god.

[48] On what follows see Swain 1989c.

Plutarch sometimes makes the matter clearer for us, as in the *Philopoemen and Flamininus* passages, by talking of 'god' rather than 'fortune', or by styling fortune as 'divine' or 'heavenly'. Overall the terminology in the *Lives* is certainly confusing.[49] In his religious and philosophical works Plutarch distinguishes clearly between events that are guided by 'god', 'the divine', 'the divine spirit', or 'providence', and so on, and those which happen by 'chance' or 'accident'. In the *Lives* he excludes virtually all technical language. Thus the technical term *pronoia*, 'providence', which is common in the *Moralia*, is only used by Plutarch in the *Lives* in one passage in the *Pompey*.[50] Again, in serious writing the term *daimôn*, 'divine spirit', seems to signify one of the divine beings which function, among other things, as god's intermediaries for communicating with mankind. Plutarch's daimonology is extremely complex and unsure.[51] It is not clear whether he accepted the popular belief in the *daimôn* as a being which regularly interferes in human affairs and indeed takes a strong interest in particular individuals; but the idea of a personal *daimôn* is certainly handled seriously in *On Socrates' Divine Guide*. In the *Lives*, at any rate, the term *daimôn* is very common, so that it either stands loosely for 'god' or is used in the sense of an attendant spirit or 'genius'. Bearing all this in mind, is only when we have more or less unequivocal statements about changes of great importance that we are entitled to say Plutarch acknowledges the involvement of providence. The areas where this happens are for the most part in Roman history (the origin of Rome, Roman expansion in Greece and the East, and the establishment of monarchy at Rome by Caesar and Octavian). It would be easy to say that Plutarch knowingly or unknowingly confused what happened with what was destined to happen. That this is not so is shown by the fact that events Plutarch considers providential are associated by him with benefits for the world. He firmly believed in divine care for mankind and this is reflected in the way he imports providential interference into history.

It should be stressed before we go further that providence does not detract from free will. Rather, explanations in terms of divine causality are always complemented by explanations made in terms of human causality. So, for example, in *Flamininus* 12 god lends a

[49] For some guidance see Swain 1989c: 298–302.
[50] The non-technical sense of *pronoia* = 'foresight' is, of course, quite common.
[51] See Brenk 1986: esp. 2117–30.

hand, but the Greeks come over to the Romans voluntarily because of the benefits they see in Roman government. This dual causation is very clear in the one spectacular example of divine intervention in Greek history, Timoleon's liberation of Syracuse and Sicily from the tyranny of Dionysius II in the years after 344 BC.[52] This is a particularly clear test case for Plutarch's opinions. The *Timoleon* is shot through with references to *tuchê*'s support for Timoleon, though 'god' and *daimôn* are also used to indicate providence's guidance. Fortune in *Timoleon* has nothing to do with luck.[53] One of the strongest passages to stress it, *Timoleon* 16. 10–11, where it intervenes to save Timoleon from an assassin, resembles the story of the strange operation of divine power at *On God's Slowness to Punish* 558f. In his essay *How to Read the Poets* Plutarch suggests that we should speak not of 'fortune', but should name the god responsible wherever there is 'appropriateness, reason, and probability' behind the force of causation (24a–b). In the *Lives* the vocabulary is different. Here 'fortune' is named. In *Timoleon* providence is behind it. There was indeed plenty of reason for involving providential design in Sicily. Plutarch informs us that Timoleon's plans went smoothly because, unlike his great contemporaries Timotheus, Agesilaus, Pelopidas, and Epaminondas, whose deeds were marred by violence and labour, Timoleon's virtue merited the effective co-operation of fortune (19. 1, 21. 4–5, 36. 1–5).[54] The major reason for this is that he had fought tyrants and barbarians (the Carthaginians) and treated Greeks with justice (37. 4–6). His victory spoils were not from victories over Greeks, but showed both his valour and his justness (29. 6). The strong introduction of providential care in *Timoleon* is particularly significant because the events, though great, were of short duration. Although Plutarch's enthusiasm for his hero leads him to claim that the blessed state of Syracuse endured for a long time (*Timoleon* 39. 7—not the only historical distortion in the *Life*), he clearly knew this did not mean forever.[55] Thus in *Timoleon* Plutarch did not attribute providential care to an event simply because the change was permanent.

[52] Swain 1989*d*: 314–16, 327–34.

[53] So Babut 1969*b*: 479. This is the most obvious way in which Plutarch departs from the other favourable accounts of Timoleon, which presumably go back to Timaeus.

[54] Cf. Desideri 1989: 212.

[55] After Timoleon Syracuse was ruled by an oligarchy until the rise of the tyrant Agathocles in 317: Talbert 1974: 138–43.

We should remember this in the case of Rome where the changes were permanent and sustained. Divine assistance is not simply brought in to build empires. In this respect Rome contrasts notably with classical Athens. Plutarch tends to present the day-to-day politics of both imperial states in much the same way.[56] The picture of their historical development is also parallel.[57] The support of the divine is the crucial difference in their long-term successes. Rome clearly owes her birth and rise to her 'divine origin' (*Romulus* 8. 9; *Camillus* 6. 3 her 'fortune . . . could never have come to such heights of glory and power unless god had stayed by her').[58] No doubt in part these comments simply reflect Rome's good fortune (there is no idea of wider gains for the world in Rome's origin). On the other hand, if it is right to see in Plutarch's mind a connection between divine support for Rome and the benefits of Roman rule at a later stage, it is not too much to suggest that he may have viewed Rome's foundation and earlier history as part of god's overall plan in the same way that the divine had prepared for Timoleon's mission in Dion's rather less successful attempt to liberate Sicily in the 350s (*Dion* 4. 3–4, cf. 27. 1, 50. 4).

It is with Rome's expansion in the Greek East that Plutarch really begins to think in terms of providential care for the world. The Roman takeover of Greece is not the first time that Plutarch sees a divine cause behind Greece's loss of freedom. There are strong hints at *Demosthenes* 19. 1–2 before the battle of Chaeroneia and the beginning of Macedonian domination.[59] But it is only with the coming of Rome that the aims of providence become clearer.[60] In *Philopoemen* 17. 2 ('with the help of the divine spirit') and *Flamininus* 12. 10 ('perhaps god was lending a helping hand') Plutarch is referring not

---

[56] Aalders 1982*a*: 28, 30, 35, 37; Pelling 1986*a*: esp. 175 ff. on his fondness for using the Greek opposition of *boulê* ('Council'/'Senate') and *dêmos* ('People') at Rome.

[57] e.g. the idea of the people, virtuous in the early days of empire (e.g. *Aristides* 22. 1, 4; *Aemilius* 10. 1, 11. 3–4), arrogating power as the power of the state grows (*Aristides* 26. 2, *Cato Major* 14. 4), or the picture of the basically aristocratic constitutions of early 5th-c. Athens and 2nd-c. Rome being undermined by the later emergence of pernicious democratic elements (e.g. *Cimon* 15. 1–2; *Pericles* 7. 8; *Gracchi* 26. 3–4; *Caesar* 14. 2), as class differences open up (*Pericles* 11. 2–3, *Alcibiades* 13. 5; *Marius* 35. 1, *Pompey* 25. 7, *Cicero* 33. 2).

[58] Cf. Barrow 1967: 129; Aalders 1982*a*: 58; Barigazzi 1984: 270.

[59] Cf. *Phocion* 1–3, 28. 2–3 on fortune opposing Phocion (and Cato)—a good example of literary aims and belief in providential guidance coinciding.

[60] Cf. Babut 1969*b*: 477–83; Barrow 1967: 129; Jones 1971*a*: 69; Brenk 1977: 168.

to the liberation of Greece from Macedon in 197 BC, but to the period after this (and in *Philopoemen* explicitly to the years following the defeat of Antiochus III). There is no dramatic motive here for bringing in the divine (it should be noted that *Philopoemen and Flamininus* is in fact freer than usual from ordinary 'chance', etc.).[61] The *Philopoemen* passage, which rhetorically speaks of a 'cycle' of history,[62] seems to refer to the growth of Roman power in Greece only, since it introduces Philopoemen's opposition to Rome there (and so the phrase 'growing great in all areas' need not be pressed). But *Flamininus* plainly refers to the whole of the Greek East (peoples, cities, and kings). This may be why Plutarch is cautious about the role of the divine ('*perhaps* god was lending a helping hand'). There is also his desire to bring out human reasons for increasing Roman power. As we have seen, it is in *Flamininus* that he particularly stresses the impact of benefaction and justice in bringing the Greeks over to Rome. When he says Roman power increased 'rightly', this is firmly in his mind. To understand the role of the divine in *Philopoemen and Flamininus* we need to recall the reason for its assistance in *Timoleon*. It looks as if it is Rome's just behaviour and beneficial government that leads to divine support. In *Timoleon* Timoleon's actions were compared favourably with the struggles of his fellow-Greeks (36. 1–4). In *Flamininus* Flamininus is also compared favourably with leading Greek politicians who were unable to govern for the general good (11. 5). This is brought out further in *Timoleon* 29. 5–6 and *Flamininus* 12. 11–12 by the honourable dedications the heroes were able to make at Corinth and Delphi. It really mattered to Plutarch that these dedications did not mark victories over Greeks, as we can see from one of his Delphic essays, *On the Pythian Oracles*, where the main speaker Theon laments that 'on beautiful offerings you can read the most disgraceful of inscriptions', the testimonies to the Greeks' internal wranglings (401c–d).

It would seem to be god's interest in good government that is behind the change from democratic to monarchical government at Rome itself. The late Republican period was marred by *kakopoliteia* (*Pompey* 75. 5, *Caesar* 28. 4), 'bad government'. Unsurprisingly

---

[61] The only exception being the moralizing comments on the fate of Hannibal and of Marius at *Flamininus* 21. 9, 11–13.

[62] There is no evidence that Plutarch actually believed in 'cyclical' history: Brenk 1977: 168 n. 22.

Plutarch is particularly concerned with the effect of this on Greece. In the middle Republican period everything was fine. The good, philhellenic attitude of Flamininus is an important theme also in the *Life* of Aemilius Paulus, the victor over Perseus of Macedon in 167. Aemilius is a liberator in the mould of his pair, Timoleon. He frees and feeds the cities of Greece, and for Plutarch even frees the Macedonians (*Aemilius* 7. 3, 24. 1, 28. 1–29. 1). There is no mention of any Greek support for Perseus (contrast Polybius xxvii. 9. 1–10. 5, Appian, *Macedonian Wars* fr. 11. 1). In the late Republican period Roman power in Greece is a different matter. There are strong comments on maladminstration in *Sulla*, *Sertorius*, *Antony*, and *Lucullus*. Sulla is not one of Plutarch's favourite heroes. The main expression of his hostility comes in a digression during the narration of the siege of Athens (*Sulla* 12–14), which in Plutarch's eyes was conducted with unnecessary brutality (14. 5–10). The digression itself (12. 5–14) opens with an account of Sulla's sequestration of sacred funds and treasures, especially those of the Delphic Amphictyony, to pay for the siege. At 12. 9–14 Plutarch's own thoughts are put in the mouths of the Amphictyons. He attacks the bribery and corruption of the Romans and their generals. Sulla was particularly responsible for this new greed, he says. How different were Titus Flamininus, Manius Acilius, and Aemilius Paulus who had honoured, not robbed Greece's shrines. Plutarch does not say the late Republic ruined Greece—but he comes close to it, and his attitudes, as we shall see, may well have affected Pausanias' hostile view.

Later in *Sulla* Plutarch records details of the 'insolence and greed' of the soldiery billeted on the cities of Asia (25. 4–5). The difficulties of billeting exacerbated by the behaviour of the tax farmers are noted again at *Sertorius* 24. 5. There is further strong reproof of the economic deprivations of the Greek world during the triumviral period at *Antony* 24. 7–8, 62. 1, 68. 6–8. All these comments are, as usual, worked in with the characterization of the hero: that does not make them casual or detached criticism. The most interesting presentation is in *Lucullus*. Plutarch's characterization of Lucullus as strongly philhellenic is as surprising as his presentation of Marcellus, for Lucullus is known in other sources for his attachment to the material rather than to the intellectual side of Greek culture.[63]

---

[63] Petrochilos 1974: 85; Swain 1992c.

It is quite apparent that Plutarch has gone out of his way to rescue Lucullus from his vices. The reason for this is his aid and assistance to the Greeks in the period of the Mithridatic War. In particular, the introduction to *Cimon and Lucullus* begins with a lengthy anecdote about Lucullus' aid to Chaeroneia in these years.[64] *Lucullus* was, then, written out of gratitude (*Cimon* 2. 2). It was no doubt the close association of benefaction and Hellenism as well as purely literary reasons that encouraged Plutarch to suggest that Lucullus had divine support during his campaigns.[65] All of this responds well with the *Cimon*. And just as Cimon is excepted from the faults of his contemporaries (*Cimon* 11. 2, 18. 1, 19. 3–4; *synkrisis* 2. 1; *Flamininus* 11. 6), so Lucullus frees the Asian Greek cities from the depredations of the 'usurers and tax gatherers of the Romans', which Plutarch catalogues in detail at 7. 6–7 and 20. 1–6.

Providential fortune intervenes at Rome to end bad government by instituting a monarchy.[66] As usual rhetoric and drama call for observations about fortune and chance in the course of such momentous events. But there is also a consistency and aim behind what happens. Take first *Pompey*. Plutarch is keen to develop a political explanation of Pompey's fall and the rise of Caesar (46. 3–4) and traces their estrangement to the death of Julia (53. 7). He then brings in *tuchê* to account for Crassus' unexpected removal from the scene by his defeat at Carrhae (53. 8–9).[67] Later Plutarch pictures Pompey complaining to the philosopher Cratippus about the workings of 'providence' (75. 4–5). Keeping to the technical language here he adds in his own words that Cratippus might have answered, 'that events were already making a monarchy necessary due to the bad government'. Similarly at *Dion and Brutus synkrisis* 2. 2 Plutarch observes of the regret following Brutus' assassination of Caesar that 'it seems Caesar was provided by the *daimôn* like a most gentle doctor when events were making monarchy necessary'. Again, Lucullus was lucky to miss the change in the constitution which 'fate was devising by means of the civil wars' (*Cimon and Lucullus synkrisis* 1. 1). The civil wars were, of course, begun by

---

[64] Cf. Jones 1971*a*: 6–7.

[65] *Lucullus* 3. 8, 10. 1, 13. 5, 15. 3, 19. 6, 28. 7, 33. 1.

[66] Babut 1969*b*: 480–1; Brenk 1977: 164–5; Aalders 1982*a*: 59; Pelling 1988: 256–7 (rightly stressing the dramatic and rhetorical setting of these passages).

[67] Crassus was an 'obstacle' in the way of the civil war. In *Crassus* itself Plutarch is less interested in what is happening to Rome in general than in Crassus' own fate, and his comments on fortune look rhetorical.

men. This is stressed at *Pompey* 70. And human and political explanations are to the fore especially in *Cato Minor* and *Caesar*. Nevertheless, Cato, like Demosthenes and Philopoemen, is pictured as struggling against a fortune that 'destroyed the constitution through others' (*Phocion* 3. 4). In *Caesar*, the most political *Life*,[68] 'fate' is mentioned only in connnection with the unavoidability of Caesar's death (63. 1). After this Brutus, like Crassus earlier, is standing 'in the way' of the change to monarchy from democracy that 'events were making necessary' (*Brutus* 47. 7). After Brutus it is left to Antony and Octavian to fight it out. Narrating how Cleopatra and Canidius hastened on the war with Octavian against Antony's better judgement, Plutarch simply observes that 'it was necessary for everything to come to Caesar' (*Antony* 56. 6).

In his final years under Nerva, Trajan, and Hadrian, Plutarch was happy with the state of the world, its prosperity, and its peace. Clearly in human terms it was Rome and her empire which had brought this about. As we have seen, Plutarch certainly valued her role in ending Greece's internal wranglings (*Flamininus* 11. 3–7). For Rome to give the Greeks any more freedom in his own day was 'perhaps' undesirable (*Political Advice* 824c). Without reference to Rome he states that 'we currently enjoy the luxury of living in constitutional governments without tyranny or any war or siege' (*Should Old Men take Part in Politics?* 784f).[69] This was the 'democratic and legal regime of a man used to allowing himself to be ruled beneficially no less than to rule' (ibid. 783d). For Plutarch the divine takes pleasure in upholding justice and human happiness (see e.g. *How to Tell a Flatterer from a Friend* 63f). The providential aspect of god is like 'a good and kindly mother who provides and preserves everything for us' (*On the Decline of Oracles* 413c). The ruler who can emulate god in this is Plutarch's ideal. He pictures him at work in *Lycurgus and Numa* in the semi-mythical period, and examines the ideal in the short pieces entitled *Philosophers and Rulers* and *To an Uneducated Ruler*. He is the divine king who fully possesses the cardinal virtues and aims to make himself alike to the Platonic god in this manner (776e, 780e, 781a). It is impossible to determine whether Plutarch really believed Trajan or Hadrian was this man.[70] If he did, as the combination of these passages

[68] Pelling 1986a: 159–60.
[69] For this 'luxury' cf. *On the Pythian Oracles* 396f.
[70] Cf. Wallace-Hadrill 1981 on ideas of the virtues and on the actual deployment of these by the emperors.

might suggest, we must also remember that he thought of such a ruler as god's agent. Thus there is every reason to believe that on Plutarch's schema the current Roman administration would be supported because of Rome's continuing beneficial legality: just as god had earlier supported the growth of Roman power in the Greek East on this account, so also had he brought an end to the 'bad government' of the late Republic and initiated the principate. There is no doubt an element of wishful thinking here, since Plutarch was quite aware of past bad emperors.[71] The present good times would have made it easier to believe in the workings of providence—but there is no cause to imagine that Plutarch imported providence only on this basis. It is interesting to observe him again suggesting that the Roman civil wars were integrated into the divine plan in his essay *On the Decline of Oracles*, where it is implied that god in his wisdom made use of 'the earlier disorders and wars that affected practically the whole of the world' to effect a reduction in the population of Greece (413f–414b).[72] Further, it should be noted, as we might assume, that Rome is not god's sole agent in the world. The potential of divine aid working through man is hailed in the essay *On the Pythian Oracles*, where Plutarch concludes with a ringing celebration of Delphi's new affluence brought about, says his friend Theon, by co-operation between the god and 'the leader', quite likely a reference to Plutarch himself (409a–c).[73]

The areas where the divine interferes in Roman history in the *Lives* occur also—with one important exception—in the essay *On the Fortune of the Romans*. This is a rhetorical piece comparing the contribution of *Tuchê*, 'Fortune', and *Aretê*, 'Virtue', to Rome's rise to power.[74] Its rather strident tone reminds us of another declamatory work, *On the Glory of the Athenians*, which also features rival processions of the great men of the past. If it is right to suppose, as most do, that *On the Fortune of the Romans* is a youthful work (for in later writings Plutarch condemns this sort of display

[71] Cf. Flacelière 1963. The stress on *current* legality, etc., at *Should Old Men . . . ?* 784f and other passages (see n. 140) shows due caution towards the future.

[72] The comments are made by Plutarch's teacher Ammonius, arguing that god's present abandonment of many oracle sites is his 'demonstration of Greece's depopulation'; that this depopulation is part of god's plan seems to follow from the explanation that oracles were formerly fully staffed 'when by god's decision Greece grew strong in her cities and the area became populous' (414b; cf. *Political Advice* 824c, below, n. 139).

[73] Ziegler 1951: 661; Jones 1966: 63–6; Swain 1991c.

[74] Palm 1959: 34–6; Flacelière 1966; Barrow 1967: 122–30; Jones 1971a: 67–70; Brenk 1977: 157–63; Swain 1989e; Frazier, in Frazier and Froidefond 1990: 9–66, 201–15.

160 Greeks and Rome

oratory), we have an interesting forerunner of his ideas about providential guidance. The main difference between *Lives* and essay is
that in the essay fortune is more closely involved in Rome's success
and human causality is correspondingly further in the background.
Thus with Octavian it was 'fortune that built him up on Cicero,
Lepidus, Pansa, Hirtius, and Mark Antony; she raised him up to be
first and highest by their bravery, their hands' work, their victories,
fleets, and wars, then she threw down those through whom he rose,
and left him only' (319e), a rewriting of history not reflected in
Cicero or *Antony* (nor presumably in the lost *Augustus*).[75] More
importantly, aside from the first two chapters where God and Time
blend virtue and fortune to make Rome 'for all mankind a hearth
truly "holy and gift-bearing"' (316f) and a 'cosmos of peace' (317c),
in the rest of the essay the two powers look more like 'Providence'
and 'Courage', and in this general 'historical' part everything goes
Rome's way without consideration of any benefit for others.[76] It is
this absence that surely explains the one omission from Rome's
conquests under Fortune's lead, Greece itself.[77]

Plutarch's thoughts about providential interference in the world
are extremely important for understanding his approach to Rome.
They owe little or nothing to comparable earlier writers like
Polybius, Posidonius, Livy, or Dionysius of Halicarnassus. Polybius
seems to think of the Roman empire as a part of a wider organization of the world by 'fortune' in a Stoic manner (i. 4. 1 ff.), but he
never develops this notion in his *Histories*. For Livy there is an
ethical determinism at work—Roman good fortune followed on
from her virtues, but again no sign of providential interference. The
Stoic philosopher Posidonius, who continued Polybius' *Histories*,
is more interesting. For him the mutual harmony of the natural and
divine world led to a justification of Roman rule in the idea that

[75] For the language—without fortune—cf. *Pompey* 46. 4.
[76] Cf. above, in text after n. 29, on Plutarch's understanding of the root meaning
of Latin *virtus* as 'courage' rather than 'virtue'. The result of this is that *tuchê* and
aretê in *On the Fortune of the Romans* are quite different from the contrasted
'fortune' and (moral) 'virtue' in the two rhetorical essays praising Alexander, *On the
Fortune or Virtue of Alexander the Great* I and II.
[77] Though the Hellenistic kings Philip V and Antiochus III are victims of Rome's
'Great Spirit' at 324b–c. Plutarch's conception of Rome's fortune in this essay naturally has nothing in common with older Greek allegations that Rome owed everything to fortune (on which cf. Schnayder 1928: 46–8; Fuchs 1938: 2, 14–15; and the
comments of Polybius i. 63. 9, Dionysius of Halicarnassus i. 4. 2–3, Onasander,
Strategicus, proem 5–6).

Rome's power stemmed from her possession of the homeland most favoured by Nature. Even so, there is no sign of active intervention in the world at key moments. Dionysius is not interested in providence at all, except perhaps for a platitudinous reference to the 'universal law of Nature, which time cannot destroy, that the stronger shall always rule the weaker' (i. 5. 2).[78] Dionysius is, though, relevant to Plutarch's idea in another way. For while he speaks of a binding Law guaranteeing Rome's rule, we should not forget that Rome is for him a Greek foundation and remains a Greek city to the present day. This was his method of accommodating Rome's power to the traditional Greek desire of appropriation.[79] Plutarch, as has been noted, did not accept this idea. Rather, the economic and political stability of the Greek world of the later first century AD made another model available to a philosopher who anyway believed in god's constant intervention for man's welfare, that god himself had ordained the Roman empire as a means of bringing benefits to the world in general and to Greece in particular as 'the nation that was best and most loved by god' (*On God's Slowness to Punish* 568a). In its way this is an act of appropriation as great as that of Dionysius.

THE POLITICAL GAME

Plutarch's view of Rome in his political essays, to which I now turn, may appear to jar with these thoughts on the importance of divine support to the Empire's success. For the picture that emerges from the political works is of a man who will strongly uphold Greek freedom and who personally at any rate is against political integration with Rome. Again, this does not mean Plutarch was 'anti'-Roman. As has been remarked, it is well known that he was highly sympathetic to Romans. But he also had a strong racial and cultural identity as a Greek. If he believed that Roman government was good for the world in theory, there is no cause for *us* to find it odd that he was resistant to it in practice. Appreciation of Rome's

---

[78] Polybius: Walbank 1972: 63–5. Livy: Walsh 1958. Posidonius: Malitz 1983: 75 ff., 359, 420–1. Dionysius: Gabba 1991: 196 (for 'time' cf. above, 'Language', text after n. 21). Cf. Swain 1989c: 276–9. See also 'Arrian' n. 43 for Appian's probable belief in divine support for Rome.

[79] Cf. generally Bickerman 1952.

benefits does not automatically entail total acceptance of her rule. If there is contradiction, it represents the compromise and negotiation we must expect from someone living under a foreign power. The focus here will be restricted to those political pieces that comment on the relations between the Greek world and Rome. The work of the greatest importance, the *Political Advice* (*Praecepta gerendae reipublicae*, to give it its traditional Latin title), will be examined in most detail. Consideration will also be given to *Should Old Men take Part in Politics?* (*An seni respublica gerenda sit?*) and one or two other works. I shall have nothing to say on the *Philosophers and Rulers* (*Maxime cum principibus philosopho esse disserendum*) or the *To an Uneducated Ruler* (*Ad principem indoctum*), which deal (especially the latter) with Plutarch's thoughts on the ideal king, nor on the probably spurious fragment *On Monarchy, Democracy, and Oligarchy* (*De tribus reipublicae generibus*).[80]

Political Advice is an essay on the civic political life of a Greek politician under Roman rule.[81] It is perhaps the most important single expression of Greek elite views of living with Rome in our period, certainly the most detailed. Plutarch was well placed to speak on the subject. He knew important Roman and Greek politicians and was sufficiently experienced (by his own testimony) in local and international politics. The work was written late in his life when his fame as a philosopher and a writer had made him someone worth listening to.[82] In character *Political Advice* is very far from being a simple list of precepts. The structure shows great care. This is not only for literary reasons. Plutarch knew that careful writing could contribute to the reception of his message. Like a number of other works *Political Advice* had been requested. The addressee is a certain Menemachus of Sardis, who we may assume from the essay was a man of wealth (though the very rich are not always Plutarch's point of reference). Plutarch says that education and good family had directed him towards politics. But since he no longer had time to gain a knowledge of statesmanship by watching

[80] On the latter see Aalders 1982*b*.
[81] On it see esp. Jones 1971*a*: 110–21; also Renoirte 1951; Bleicken 1966: 231–2; Valgiglio 1976; Pavis d'Escurac 1981; Desideri 1986.
[82] The date is certainly after Domitian (815d) and before 114 when Plutarch's friend Cornelius Pulcher became procurator of Epirus and was already in possession of *Political Advice* (*How to Profit from One's Enemies* 86c–d; Bowersock 1965b: 269–70).

the example of those who are philosopher-politicians, he has turned to Plutarch for advice (798b).[83] The work is not, though, a private letter, but advice tendered to all who are thinking of entering the public arena.

One of Plutarch's lost works was a commentary on Theophrastus' *Responses to Crises* (*Politika pros tous kairous*). It is not unnatural to hold that Theophrastus' work was an important inspiration for *Political Advice*, the pragmatic nature of which obviously owes much to Peripatetic thinking.[84] We do not know for what occasion it was written. It may be that a particular problem had precipitated Menemachus into public life. All we may assume is that he knew Plutarch and that this is why he asked for the essay. It is worthwhile speculating on the connection between them. Another reader of *Political Advice* was Plutarch's Greek friend Cn. Cornelius Pulcher, a descendant of an old-established family of Epidaurus who was probably based in Corinth. Pulcher enjoyed a distinguished career as an equestrian officer, becoming procurator of Epirus under Trajan, *iuridicus* for Hadrian in Egypt, and probably first archon of the Panhellenion.[85] In the proem to the essay Plutarch sent him on *How to Profit from One's Enemies* he states he is sending his friend the text of a lecture from which he has removed material overlapping with *Political Advice*, 'since I see you often have that book close at hand' (86c–d).[86] A personal connection between Pulcher and Menemachus is suggested by an inscription (*IGR* iv. 1492) dating to the time of Hadrian which records a dedication to the emperor and his wife, Vibia Sabina, by one Cornelia Pulchra. The date is certainly before 128, for Sabina is called *Sebastê* ('Augusta').[87] The text was found near modern Kasaba (or Turgutlu)

[83] There are some parallels with the reading programme offered to a Greek politician by Dio of Prusa, *Or.* xviii (von Arnim 1898: 139–40).

[84] *Lamprias Catalogue*, no. 53 (52–3) Sandbach. Theophrastus' study (the title of which is not sure) was probably a collection of instructive examples rather than theory (cf. Fortenbaugh 1992: ii. 439–40); see Mittelhaus 1911: 29–55; Aalders 1982a: 64–5. Most of Plutarch's references in *Political Advice* to timing and sense of occasion come either in chs. 5–9 on public rhetoric (*kairos* being a technical term in the schools), or in chs. 17–19 dealing with Roman rule.

[85] Pflaum 1960–1: i, no. 81; Bowersock 1965b: 269–70; Jones 1971a: 45–6; Spawforth and Walker 1985: 84, 86 (for a different view—that Herodes Atticus was the first archon—see Bol and Herz 1989: 93).

[86] There is actually some repetition and inconsistency, notably the advice of Demos of Chios (commended at 91f–92a, slighted at 813a–b).

[87] The traditional date of 128 for Sabina's assumption of this title is much too late, the real date unknown: *RE* Suppl. xv (1978), 910–11 (Eck).

and came from an unknown ancient site called Tateikômê which lay near the Hermus valley between the ancient cities of Magnesia ad Sipylum and Sardis, being about twenty miles west of Sardis itself.[88] It is usual for dedications by women to be made on estates owned by them. Since there is no other known Cornelia Pulchra at this time in the Greek East, it is natural to take her as the daughter of the Cornelius Pulcher who was Plutarch's friend. This would mean that he too probably owned land in the Sardis area. There he would have known a notable such as Menemachus—they may not have been many years apart in age—and could have put Plutarch forward as a likely source of good counsel. And it would be natural that he too should come to possess a copy of the work sent to his Sardian acquaintance.

After the introduction Plutarch begins *Political Advice* by stressing the need for politicians to have a consistent policy (2, 798c–799a).[89] He recommends a thorough knowledge of the character of one's fellow-citizens (3, 799b–800a). Next he notes the very public nature of a public career and the consequent need of propriety (4, 800a–801c).[90] There follows a long section dealing with oratory (5–9, 801c–804c). Of interest to us are the remarks about the nature of political speaking: 'political oratory admits more generalization, more history, myth, and metaphor than you find in the courtroom, and those who make moderate and timely use of these will move their audiences very much' (803a). Examples are given and recommendations made of style, such as Demosthenes' *Philippics* (cf. 810d) and certain speeches in Thucydides' *History*. For the time being subject material is not discussed.

After preparation in the areas of policy and communication comes the entrance to political life itself (10–12, 804c–806f). There are two paths, the quick and the safe. The quick path demands participation in some action of public worth. The examples of how to do this are chosen carefully (804d–805a). Aratus destroyed the tyrant Nicocles, Alcibiades made the Mantinean alliance against Sparta, Pompey demanded a triumph from Sulla, and Scipio Aemilianus was elevated to the consulate at an election for aedile. These examples lead on to the present. 'These days, when the state of our

---

[88] For speculation about the exact position of Tateikômê see Buresch 1898: 5.

[89] Cf. similarly in private life: *How to Tell a Flatterer from a Friend* 52a, *On Progress in Virtue* 79a.

[90] Cf. *To an Uneducated Ruler* 782e–f.

cities requires no leadership in war, no dissolution of tyrannies, no acts of alliance, what starting-point can we find for a distinguished and brilliant career? There remain public lawsuits and embassies to the emperor which need a man of passion, daring, and intellect.' There are, says Plutarch, many other ways also of bringing oneself to public notice (805a–e). By contrast the surer and slower method is to attach oneself to a great man, so long as one is careful in one's choice (805e–806f).

Plutarch now passes to the politician's own friends (13, 806f–809b). The temptations of corruption on both sides are addressed. There are plenty of favours you can bestow that cause no bad feeling. 'Support a friend's candidacy for an office, entrust to him an administrative task that will bring him renown, or a mission of good will, such as conveying honours to a governor or an approach to another city concerning friendship and concord' (808b–c). It is also legitimate to enrich your friends, if they need it, by giving them well-paid court cases or contracts. Plutarch slips in praise of Menemachus' high standards: 'for not everyone is a Menemachus!' (808f–809b).

After a chapter on how to deal with political enemies (14, 809b–811a), Plutarch passes on to the service a politician should give his community (15, 811a–813a). Commenting on Epaminondas' successful supervision of a lowly office involving street-cleaning he notes that 'I myself no doubt give visitors something to laugh about when they see me engaged in such things in public, as I often am . . . standing by while tiles are being measured or concrete and stone is being delivered' (811c).[91] It is wrong to do these things out of ambition or if we are not suited to them,[92] but proper for the sake of the state. Next comes a brief statement on the desirability of co-operation with one's colleagues, including advice on how to conspire against the people (the *dêmos*) in case they are suspicious of 'some important measure that will save the situation', a cynical approach to preserving elite solidarity in the face of what Plutarch calls the people's 'malice and fault-finding' (16, 813a–c).

There follow three very important chapters in which Plutarch advises on relations with Rome (17–19, 813c–816a). These are rounded off in chapter 20 (816a–e) with a further exhortation to

[91] Cf. Dio of Prusa, *Or.* xl. 7, on his building projects.
[92] Cf. *Should Old Men take Part in Politics?* 794a.

concord with one's fellow-politicians. Following on from the previous section chapter 17 begins by advising against excessive ambition which takes the form of holding on to office continually (813c–d). On obtaining office Menemachus should recall Pericles' tag: 'Watch out Pericles—you're in command of free men, of Greeks, of Athenian citizens!' But he should also say this to himself, '"You're in command and you're under command: the city is subordinated to the proconsuls and to the procurators of Caesar. There are no 'lances of the plains', and this is not ancient Sardis or the historic power of Lydia". You must make your cloak more modest, and look out of your office at the tribunal, and don't put much pride or trust in your crown when you see the boots above your head.' The boots and the tribunal are those of the proconsul, the 'office' here is the *stratêgion* or headquarters of the *stratêgos*, 'general', as the chief magistrate of the Greek cities was often called.[93] To bring the matter home to Menemachus Plutarch reminds him of what happens to those forget these limits, like his fellow-Sardian Pardalas.

This sharp warning of the circumscribed power of the Greek city and its political leaders sets the tone for the rest of these chapters. Having established the relationship of the politician to those above him, Plutarch now turns to conduct with the people below. We laugh at small children trying on their fathers' shoes or crowns, he says. Parallel, however, are 'the magistrates in our cities who stir up the masses by foolishly urging them to imitate the deeds, spirit, and actions of their ancestors, when these are out of keeping with the present times and conditions. What they do is laughable, what is done to them is no longer a laughing matter, unless they are simply treated with contempt' (814a). The comparison of the politicians to naughty children does double work. They are not only small in relation to their own forefathers; their powerlessness is also measured against Rome's real paternal power. In his essay *On Brotherly Love* Plutarch warns against childish disputes which become serious, as happened to the 'most powerful Greeks in my time', who lost everything when they were sent into exile 'by the tyrant' (487e–488a; i.e. Domitian). Dio of Prusa also employs the children image with reference to the relations between Greek city and Roman empire.[94] It does not tell of unity or equality. Earlier in *Political*

[93] Jones 1971a: 133. *Stratêgos*: Liebenam 1900: 286–8, 558–64, cf. above, 'Past' n. 68.
[94] Dio, *Orr.* xxxii. 51, xxxviii. 21, 37. Cf. Quet 1978: 68, 70, 74.

Advice Plutarch had broached the problem of using historical and mythological examples in civic oratory (803a). Now he lists subjects which can 'form and correct the characters' of the people, and subjects which should be avoided. Athenian history is the source for both. At Athens, he says, we will avoid the history of the city's wars, but will recall things like the amnesty after the fall of the Thirty Tyrants, the fining of Phrynichus for his play about the capture of Miletus, the wearing of garlands when Cassander refounded Thebes, the expiatory sacrifice on hearing of the 'clubbing' of the aristocrats at Argos, and the time when they bypassed the house of newly-weds during the search for Harpalus' moneys. 'These are the ways in which we can still emulate our forefathers today'. To be avoided are 'Marathon, Eurymedon, and Plataea, and all other examples that make the many swell and snort with false pride—these we leave in the schools of the sophists' (814a–c).

Plutarch's remarks on the role of historical examples must be understood against the interrelation of Greek past and Greek identity in the second sophistic period. They show well enough that Plutarch thought it was possible to stir up the crowd by retelling historical glories. The reason for Roman intervention is certainly the unrest caused thereby, not the subject-matter itself, for, as we have seen, there is no evidence that Romans found the Greeks' interest in the past threatening. But the patriotic feelings the crowd displayed were obviously highly unwelcome. Plutarch glosses his remarks on examples from history at the start of the next chapter by saying, 'It is not enough to keep oneself and one's fatherland blameless in the eyes of our leaders' (18, 814c). And the comments follow on, of course, from the Romans' execution of Menemachus' fellow-citizen Pardalas for failing to realize 'the limits of the authority granted by those in control'. There is no need to imagine that patriotic feelings based on past glory were primarily directed by the politicians Plutarch has in mind against Rome (though this is of course possible). Rather, since chapters 17–19 are part of a larger section in *Political Advice* about harmony between political leaders in the cities, he probably envisages politicians trying to win popular support against other politicians or, perhaps (given the widespread inter-city rivalries of this time), against other cities.

In a different context, such as in the 'schools of the sophists', there was no danger from glorifying the Greek past. No disharmony would arise. Historical declamations as well as panegyrical and epideictic speeches like Aelius Aristides' *Panathenaicus* (with its massive retreatment of Athenian military might) fit in here. Plutarch would presumably include other literary evocations, like his own *Cimon* which celebrates the battle of Eurymedon, or *Aristides* which magnifies Aristides' role at Plataea.[95] His declamatory speech *On the Glory of the Athenians*, which resolutely argues for the pre-eminence of Athens' men of action over her artists and writers (a consistent viewpoint of the author of the *Parallels*) is another good example: it seems unlikely that the non-elite ever heard Plutarch so forcefully extolling Athenian military heroes (349b–350b). Nevertheless, what is striking about chapter 17 of *Political Advice* is not the warning against stirring up the masses and the consequences of so doing: it is that Plutarch does not focus on distributions of money or promises about giving games and shows and such like as vehicles for political infighting—though these are treated later in the work—but on Greek history. In this way he again brings to Menemachus' notice the contrast between Greece's former freedom and her present situation. The examples he chooses are highly revealing. For he does not pick Athenian local victories over Thebes or Sparta. He names two Athenian battles (Marathon, Eurymedon) and one pan-Greek action (Plataea) against the traditional national enemy Persia. These are among the battles he excepts from his condemnation of Greek warfare at *Flamininus* 11. 6. The spirit of the past was dear to Plutarch. In his warning about the potent feelings induced by reference to Greece's glories there is, it seems, something of his own patriotism and an awareness of the contexts in which it is safe to express it. I have noted already how strongly this patriotism comes out in his common defence of the Greeks' deeds during the same Persian Wars in *On the Malice of Herodotus*. Plutarch knew his own mind well enough to see that such matters were too open to exploitation to be safe subjects in civic discourse before the people.[96]

In chapter 18 (814c–e) Plutarch moves on from concern to protect one's city from blame to positive ways of getting on with the Romans. His advice is that 'one should always have a friend among the really powerful people up there, as a secure prop for one's policy (for the Romans are very keen to support their friends'

[95] Cf. *Aristides and Cato Major synkrisis* 5. 1 on 'the best, most brilliant, and most important actions of the Greeks, that is, Marathon, Salamis, and Plataea'.
[96] Cf. Jones 1971a: 114 n. 27. *On the Malice of Herodotus*: above, 'Past' n. 59.

political interests)'. After some examples he continues by asking, 'is there any comparison between this sort of favour and lucrative procuratorships and administrations of provinces which men pursue, growing old before other people's doors and neglecting their affairs at home?[97] Perhaps we should amend the verses of Euripides and proclaim that, "if you have to" lose sleep and frequent the court of another man and submit yourself to the familiarity of a leader, "it's best" done for a fatherland, "otherwise" embrace and preserve friendships based on equality and fairness.' Euripides' lines on gaining power (*Phoenician Women* 524–5 'if you have to do wrong, it's best to do wrong for absolute power [*turannis*], otherwise you must fear the gods') are nicely worked into the context.[98] It is wrong, says Plutarch, to demean yourself for the sake of obtaining jobs in the imperial service that bring high financial rewards (a moral and a political point). Preserving one's self-respect is far more important. And just as Euripides' play goes on to recommend equality against ambition, so Plutarch tells his addressee to seek friendships with Romans on a level.

Another passage where Plutarch seems to speak against taking up posts in Roman government—*On Contentment* 10, 470c—should be examined at this point. The context is men's desire always to obtain more than they have now. Thus prisoners envy those set free, those set free envy men born free, free men envy citizens, citzens envy the rich, the rich envy satraps, satraps kings, and kings the gods (470b). Plutarch next quotes Archilochus' lines about not wishing to be the fabulous Lydian king Gyges (fr. 19 West). He explains Archilochus' position by observing, 'For he was a Thasian. Yet there is another, a Chian, another, a Galatian or Bithynian, who is not content if he has obtained some share in glory or power among his own citizens, but weeps because he does not wear patrician shoes; and if he should wear them, he weeps because he is not yet a Roman praetor; and if he should be one of these, he weeps because he is not a consul; and on becoming a consul, he weeps because he has not been called first but later.' This is the only passage where Plutarch alludes to the fact that some of his contemporaries wanted to pursue a senatorial career to the top. It is not an attack on the possibility of men from the Greek East becoming

[97] Cf. *On Contentment* 466c, *Is Vice a Sufficient Cause of Misery?* 498c; Arrian, *Discourses of Epictetus* iii. 7. 31.
[98] For the idea of improving poetry see the essay *How to Read the Poets*.

senators or on those who were senators. Among this group were two of Plutarch's acquaintances (though he does not refer to their Roman careers).[99] More to the point, the essay is addressed to a Roman senator and orator, Paccius.[100] Plutarch's remarks in *On Contentment* are aimed primarily against those he identifies as having no chance of obtaining what they want and who are unhappy because of it. Archilochus and/or his speaker is content with his lot because he knows he is a Thasian.[101] Yet other groups—Chians, Bithynians, Galatians—do have unrealistic designs on power. It was under Nerva and Trajan that numbers of easterners first entered the Roman senate and this is plainly the social-political context of the passage in *On Contentment*.[102] There were senators from Galatia in Plutarch's lifetime, though with one exception from the Galatian/ Pergamene royal house all seem to have been descendants of Italian colonists. The first known Greek senator from Bithynia, Flavius Arrian, probably did not start his senatorial career until the end of the reign of Trajan or the very beginning of Hadrian's. No senators are known from Chios.[103] Still, the *On Contentment* passage shows Plutarch in touch with the developments of his time. He knew men who were senators and knew that many more now wanted to be. Yet it is noticeable that in *Political Advice* he does not even allude

[99] C. Julius Eurycles Herculanus, addressee of *How to Praise Oneself*, under Trajan (Halfmann 1979: no. 29); C. Julius Antiochus Epiphanes Philopappus addressee of *How to Tell a Flatterer from a Friend*, adlected *inter praetorios* under Trajan, suffect consul in 109 (Halfmann 1979: no. 36). The latter, a descendant of the royal house of Commagene, was known simply as 'King Philopappus' (*Table Talks* i. 10, 628a, cf. *How to Praise Oneself* 543e, *OGIS* 408–12, *ILS* 845; note similarly 'King Alexander', i.e. C. Julius Alexander *cos.* ?106 or 108 [*ILS* 8823, *IGR* iii. 173; Halfmann 1979: no. 25; Syme 1985: 357 n. 69]). In his own works Plutarch is silent on his own Roman citizenship (*SIG*³ 829A), which was obtained by the consular Mestrius Florus (*PIR*² M 531; Jones 1971a: 22, 48–9).

[100] An unknown associate of Pliny's friend, C. Minicius Fundanus (*cos. suff.* 107; major interlocutor in Plutarch's *How to Control Anger*): *On Contentment* 464d. See Jones 1971a: 59–60.

[101] There is no need to print Θάσιος γὰρ ἦν ἐκεῖνος as an imaginary objection— it is part of what Plutarch is saying (so rightly in the Budé vii. 1 [1975]). Archilochus' lines are attributed to a carpenter by Aristotle (*Rhetoric* 1418ᵇ30), but Plutarch is not making economic distinctions.

[102] Senate: Hammond 1957: 79; Halfmann 1979: 79; Syme 1985: 346–62, id. 1988; cf. Salmeri 1991: 569–71 on the relatively late appearance of eastern senators. Date of *On Contentment*: Jones 1966: 62–3 (plausibly suggesting the period after Fundanus' consulship, since he is referred to at the beginning of the essay as *kratistos*, 'excellent').

[103] Galatia: Halfmann 1979: 48–9, 69; no. 39 (C. Claudius Severus *cos. suff.* 112). Arrian: ibid. no. 56; Syme 1982: 183 (two Bithynian senators before Arrian hail from the colony of Apamea), 187–9 (Arrian himself); cf. below, 'Dio' n. 77.

to the possibility of a senatorial career for the budding politician. This is slightly odd because Sardis had already seen two Greek senators by the time Plutarch was writing to Menemachus.[104] This omission, together with Plutarch's condemnation of 'lucrative' posts in the equestrian service, suggests that he wanted to keep Greek politicians in Greek cities. This is not anti-Roman. But neither, one must say, is it pro-Roman. If friends embarked on a senatorial or an equestrian career (like Cornelius Pulcher), all Plutarch could do was to praise conduct in particular cases (*How to Profit from One's Enemies* 86b). His own advice is to stay at home and, in brief, not to integrate.[105]

Before we return to *Political Advice* one other matter requires investigation: did Plutarch break his advice to Menemachus by taking up Roman office himself? The eighth-century Byzantine historian George Syncellus records under Hadrian's reign that 'Plutarch of Chaeroneia the philosopher was appointed as an old man by the emperor to be procurator of Greece; Sextus the philosopher and Agathoboulus and Oenomaus were famous'.[106] There is comparable information in the *Suda*: 'Trajan, giving him [Plutarch] a share in the dignity of the consuls, ordered none of the governors in the area of Illyria to take any action without his opinion. He wrote many things'.[107] The *Suda*'s statement is clearly erroneous. The first part might be acceptable (for consular honours were awarded by the emperors Domitian and Maximinus to Quintilian and Apsines, the friend of Philostratus),[108] if it were not for the fact that the second part, with which it is connected in the Greek, is absurd and points to confusion with one of Plutarch's late Roman namesakes.[109] Syncellus definitely refers to Plutarch of Chaeroneia. It is tempting

[104] Ti. Julius Celsus Polemaeanus, *cos. suff.* in 92 (Halfmann 1979: no. 16), who endowed the remarkable Library of Celsus at Ephesus, and his son Ti. Julius Aquila Polemaeanus, *cos. suff.* in 110, who built most of it.

[105] So rightly Gabba 1959: 370, id. 1991: 55, 214.

[106] Syncellus 659 Dind. (= Eusebius *Chronicle* p. 415 no. 198a Helm²): Πλούταρχος Χαιρωνεὺς φιλόσοφος ἐπιτροπεύειν Ἑλλάδος ὑπὸ τοῦ αὐτοκράτορος [Ἀδριανοῦ] κατεστάθη γηραιός. Σέξτος φιλόσοφος καὶ Ἀγαθόβουλος καὶ Οἰνόμαος ἐγνωρίζετο.

[107] *Suda* π 1793: μεταδοὺς δὲ αὐτῷ Τραιανὸς τῆς τῶν ὑπάτων ἀξίας προσέταξε μηδένα τῶν κατὰ τὴν Ἰλλυρίδα ἀρχόντων παρέξ τῆς αὐτοῦ γνώμης τι διαπράττεσθαι. ἔγραψε δὲ πολλά.

[108] *PIR²* F 59; A 978.

[109] Cf. Jones 1971a: 29–30 (in favour of the *ornamenta consularia*); on the problem Babut 1975: 207. Later namesakes: note esp. the Plutarch who was proconsul of Achaia in the 4th c. (*PLRE* i. 707 PLUTARCHUS 3); cf. Millar 1969: 16–17.

to believe him.[110] But his information probably does not come from the fairly reliable pen of Eusebius in his *Chronicle*, as is often imagined, since (the original being lost) it is not to be found in the Latin translation of Jerome or in the Armenian version.[111] All things are possible. If Plutarch did hold the position of procurator, it could only have been nominal. But it seems better not to be tempted (perhaps Syncellus interpreted Plutarch's fame over-zealously?) and to allow Plutarch to practise what he preached.

The desire to avoid contacts with Roman government machinery is expressed again in the next chapter we come to in the *Political Advice* (19, 814e–816a). Here Plutarch commends the maintenance of as much independence as possible. 'In ensuring that your fatherland is obedient to those in control, there is no need to humble it any further.' Some politicians, says Plutarch, keep on referring all matters, great or small, to the governors. 'They bring on a reproach of slavery' (814e). Plutarch certainly did not think of Roman rule as slavery. But he expresses his fear that the charge will be made if the Greeks are too abject. Dio of Prusa gives similar advice to the Tarsians (*Or.* xxxiv. 38). The reason for the loss of independence is the greed and contentiousness of 'the first men' (*hoi prôtoi*): either they succeed in driving out their opponents or they bring in the Romans to help their side. In this way council, people, courts, magistrates all lose their power. The proper way to proceed is 'to mollify one's citizens by equal treatment, and the powerful by yielding to them in turn, and thus to keep them all within a constitutional framework [*politeia*] and to dissolve the difficulties' (815a). Plutarch instructs the politician in this passage to behave towards Rome as he presents Philopoemen behaving in the *Life of Philopoemen*. In the period of increasing Roman power after the defeat of Antiochus III Philopoemen 'was on some matters compelled to give in and yield to the times. But in most he continued his opposition' (*Philopoemen* 17. 3). Following Polybius, Plutarch contrasts Philopoemen's policy with that of his rival, Aristaenus of Megalopolis. Aristaenus thought the Achaeans should not 'oppose

---

[110] So Bowersock 1969: 57 n. 6, 112; Oliver 1970: 70–1 (amalgamating Syncellus with the *Suda*); Jones 1971a: 34.

[111] Jerome: 'Plutarchus Chaeroneus et Sextus et Agathobulus et Oenomaus philosophi insignes habentur' (Helm² 198. 1–3). Armenian version: ed. Karst (1911), 219, or in Eusebius ed. Schoene (1866), 164–5 (parallel texts). For a summary of the relationship between Eusebius and his translators see Barnes 1981: 112–13.

or displease' the Romans at all, whereas Philopoemen asked him in anger, 'Why are you in a hurry to behold Greece's fate?' (*Philopoemen* 17. 4–5; Polybius xxiv. 11. 1–13. 10). Again, in the *Life of Flamininus* Roman power is said to have increased because the Greeks 'actually sent for them and invited them and handed themselves over to them. And not only peoples and cities but also kings wronged by other kings sought refuge in their hands' (12. 9–10). It is the same sectional interests that are condemned in *Political Advice*. And Plutarch continues here by advocating control of problems within the city 'so that the city has not the slightest need of outside doctors and medicines' (815c).[112] He then gives some examples of crises and responses to them, concluding that 'we must pray that such times do not come upon us, but expect better'.

These three chapters, 17, 18, 19, are closed off in chapter 20 (816a–e) by another reminder to the politician of the need for co-operation and friendship with his colleagues (Plutarch includes an example of his own political behaviour in reporting the result of an embassy) and with the people. There is, he observes, at the end of this chapter and the beginning of the next, a mutual dependence of ruled and rulers (816e–f). He argues that in a 'democracy' all of us must learn 'obedience', even if some of us are sometimes office holders. Naturally Plutarch does not spell out the essential inequality in such a system. His 'democracy' is used in the sense developed by Isocrates and Hellenistic usage to mean an aristocratic constitution based on the rule of law. It has little to do with fifth-century Athenian or even modern notions of democracy in practice. Talk of lawful democracy or of the will of the people mediated through law was, however, of great importance to Plutarch and his contemporaries, for the ideology of consensual government in a legal regime was the most acceptable mode of manifesting their rule.[113] Thus the advocacy of harmony at and between all levels in the community is designed to perpetuate the status quo, the power of the elite. And this is Plutarch's main concern for the rest of the work.

He begins with the politicians. While out of office, they must obey those who are the current magistrates (21, 816e–817c), even if their behaviour should become insulting (22, 817c). Someone not in public office may nevertheless advise and take action 'for the

[112] Contrast the more realistic Polemo at Philostratus *VS* 532 advising the Smyrnaeans to refer only capital cases.
[113] Cf. above, 'Past' nn. 67–9.

common good', if the magistrates do not (23, 817c–f).[114] In chapter 24 (817f–818d) Plutarch returns to the politician's relations with the people. He should not constantly criticize them.[115] What he must resist are moves 'bringing others' property into public ownership or distributing common assets'. But 'if the many take the opportunity of an ancestral feast or the worship of a god to propose a show or a modest distribution, or some act of charity or display of one's generosity, let them enjoy their freedom and affluence in this way' (818c–d). Similarly, in the next chapter (25, 818e–819b) the politician's role is to turn the people away from 'inexpedient moves', often by 'a roundabout or circuitous method'. Inopportune embassies, useless building projects, and improper litigation are on Plutarch's list here. Next (26, 819b–e) he again stresses the need of co-operation between the men of power and influence to secure 'something important and useful' which is in fact controversial (cf. 813b). This co-operation should not lead to financial corruption. This advice is followed (27, 819e–820f) by a warning against *philotimia*, 'ambition' or 'display of ambition' (and so meaning a show or festival paid for by a man). Ambition becomes 'unmanageable and uncontrollable' when it is swept along by the will of the 'mobs'.[116] Thus statues and other honours granted by the many are not enduring or genuine. Plutarch goes on to contrast these with the 'true honour and favour' earned by 'trust in one's goodwill and a reputation for honour and justice'. This is the best way to achieve control (ch. 28, 820f–821e). Chapter 29 (821e–822a) continues the theme. Love from the people which is due to one's virtue is 'the strongest and most divine'.[117] That which comes from putting on shows in the theatre, distributing money, or staging gladiatorial fights is false.[118]

[114] Cf. *Lamprias Catalogue* 164 'Should a Citizen Give Advice, Knowing he will not Persuade?'

[115] Cf. *Phocion* 2. 6–9, *How to Tell a Flatterer from a Friend* 73a–c.

[116] Cf. *Agis and Cleomenes* 1–2.

[117] Cf. *How to Praise Oneself* 539e–f, *Philosophers and Rulers* 777e.

[118] Cf. 802d (where such entertainments must be controlled by oratory) and 822c, 823e (below). There is (perhaps surprisingly) no evidence for the plausible suppositions of Fuchs (1938: 49 n. 60) and others that criticism of Rome lurks behind criticisms of gladiation (Dio of Prusa *Or.* xxxi. 121–2; Lucian, *Demonax* 57; *Life of Secundus*, question 13 [p. 86 ed. Perry]; Tatian, *To the Greeks* 23; Philostratus, *Life of Apollonius* iv. 22). Plutarch is hostile (*On the Intelligence of Animals* 959c, *On Eating Meat* II 997b–c), but apparently felt gladiatorial shows sufficiently naturalized (on which see Robert 1940: 263) at least to be able to commend those gladiators

Plutarch 175

In chapters 30–31 Plutarch talks of financial responsibility. He speaks of the *philotimêmata*, the displays and donations which, as he notes, were an accepted part of political life (30, 822a–c). He appreciates that the expense could be unwelcome. You can compensate for this by choosing an 'attractive and honourable pretext, as when the worship of a god moves the whole community to piety'.[119] Resist 'those displays that arouse and nurture either brutal craving for blood or undisciplined vulgarity' (i.e. gladiatorial or wild beast shows or ribald comedy and satire).[120] In chapter 31 (822c–823e) there is advice on what the moderately rich politician should do in this respect. First of all he must not borrow to pay for 'liturgies'. By this Plutarch means the occasional but compulsory public services to which the rich in the Greek city had long found themselves nominated, and which they permitted because these were perfect occasions to display their ambition and munificence.[121] For Plutarch it is the 'foolish' politicians who use liturgies in the same way as they court the mob and divide the community (*Should Old Men take Part in Politics?* 796e); the true politician knows these displays have set purposes and that his love for his fellow men goes on regardless (ibid. 791c). The 'poor' man must not, then, seek to compete in the usual manner with 'racecourses and theatres and banqueting-tables' but should rival those who 'always try to guide the city by reason, relying on their virtue and spirit' (*Political Advice* 822f). He is on a level with his fellow-citizens (cf. 815a) and then becomes 'a sympathetic adviser, an unpaid advocate, and a kindly reconciler of husbands and wives and of those who are friends' (823b).[122] Unlike most people he does not look on public life simply 'as an interruption to leisure or as a liturgy' (823c). His is a way of life in which gladiatorial combats and stage shows have no part (823e).

---

whose behaviour showed they were 'Hellenes' at *Not even a Pleasant Life is Possible according to Epicurus* 1099b. Note also Favorinus' *For the Gladiators* (Philostratus VS 491), and see below, 'Conclusion' n. 4.

[119] Cf. *Should Old Men take Part in Politics?* 787b–c.

[120] On the latter see Aelius Aristides, *Or.* xxix *On the Prohibition of Comedy* (cf. Behr 1968a: 95–6).

[121] See, in addition to the references on euergetism at 'Past' n. 69, Liebenam 1900: 417–30; Jones 1940: 167–8, 175–6; Jones 1978a: 104–14.

[122] Cf. *Lamprias Catalogue* 156 'Should one Act as Advocate for Everyone [πᾶσι]?', 198 On Advocates (it is just possible that these belong rather to an anti-Stoic philosophical context—cf. *On Stoic Self-Contradictions* 1036a–d).

This section on the avoidance of debt in politics is clearly topical. As we shall see with Dio, the ideology of public display by the rich encouraged gross overspending. Rome was concerned to regulate the cities' finances in this respect.[123] Elsewhere Plutarch, as we have seen, blamed the late Republican tax collectors and moneylenders for crippling the Greek world with debt. In his vivid, probably youthful diatribe against debt, *Against Borrowing Money*, he again seems to allude to contemporary western moneylenders as a cause of the problem. Indebtedness under the Empire has nothing to do with the need to pay Roman taxes, which Plutarch must have known was the problem in the Republican period. Rather, in this thoroughly rhetorical piece indebtedness is revealed as a failing of personal morality. But the moneylenders themselves (*daneistai*) are also strongly attacked. Debtors are slaves not of the 'liquidators' (*aphanistai*) themselves but of 'rude, savage, barbarous slaves' (?freedmen agents), and 'just as Darius sent Datis and Artaphernes to Athens with chains and bonds for the prisoners, so they bring their chests full of contracts and bills like fetters against Greece and drive through her cities on their march' (828f–829b). The debtors are pursued forever by a 'usurer or a financier, one from Corinth, one from Patrae, one from Athens' (831a). A number of facts converge to suggest Plutarch is thinking of Roman or Italian financiers. First, Corinth, Patrae, and Athens were the economic centres of the Roman province of Achaia.[124] Second, the moneylenders are likened to foreign invaders. In particular they are likened to the Persians of old. One of the ways in which atticizing Greek coped with describing the administration of the Roman empire was to employ terms classical authors had used to describe the Persian empire. Governors turn into satraps or the emperor becomes the 'Great King'.[125] Thus at *Political Advice* 814c Plutarch recommends making friends 'among the really powerful people up there', i.e. at Rome, where 'up' recalls the manner of referring to Persia and upland Asia.[126]

[123] Cf. Dio of Prusa, *Or.* xlviii. 2; Pliny, *Letters* x. 17a 'nunc rei publicae Prusensium impendia, reditus, debitores excutio', etc.; Burton 1975: 104, id. 1979: 474–7, 480; Jones 1978a: 99. Below, 'Dio' n. 191 on financial and other forms of interference.

[124] Bowersock 1965c: 92–6; Alcock 1993: 75–7 on the significant numbers of western *negotiatores*.

[125] Mason 1970: 157; Bowie 1974: 201 n. 95; Jones 1986: 56. For the emperor as 'Great King' see Lucian, *Toxaris* 17, *Apology* 11, with 'Lucian' n. 80. On the problem of 'atticizing' Rome cf. Cassius Dio lv. 12. 4–5.

[126] Jones 1971a: 113 n. 22; *VS* 589. In Plutarch cf. esp. *Themistocles* 26. 1 *tois anô dunatois*, and note the example of 'the Persian' at *Political Advice* 815e and the significance of the Greeks' wars against Persia at 814c (above, n. 96).

In *Against Borrowing Money* this metaphor seems rather inappropriate for local, Greek usurers, and it is difficult to resist the idea that Romans/Italians are the target.[127] The passage attacking the moneylenders reminds us in quality of Plutarch's rhetorical denunciation of the assizes in Asia, probably at Smyrna, in a diatribe arguing that diseases of the soul are worse than those of the body.[128] The precise context and application of *Against Borrowing Money* is unknown, but it shows well enough how strongly Plutarch felt about the matter. This feeling carries through in *Political Advice* 822d–e, though here he is not concerned with the identity of the moneylenders. Rather, these comments about debt and benefactions serve the larger picture he wants to draw, his advice that the politician should work in the community for its benefit and his own. This is the message of the crucial final chapter.

Chapter 32 (823e–825f) is concerned with how to deal with civil strife (*stasis*) and the relation between private and public disputes. Plutarch begins by raising a problem. The politician 'will be at a loss to think what induced that great man [Solon] to decree that someone who attached himself to neither party in a time of civil strife should be deprived of his rights'. Before answering Plutarch dilates on the form of the city state. It is like the human body, and the diseased members are made well again by the influence of the healthy parts (824a). A very similar view is expressed at *Lysander* 17. 9. Throughout his works Plutarch makes use of medical analogies, especially the idea of the politician as the doctor who cures the state of its ills. These are employed in *Political Advice* too.[129] As he develops his ideas medical analogy comes to replace another prominent through the earlier parts of the work, which is drawn from the world of the theatre.[130] Most of these references (from 799a to 806a) fall in chapters 2–12 where Plutarch is giving advice on presentation and entry into politics and, in a word, on performance. Acting was an obvious analogy.[131] The later usage at 813e is especially interesting,

[127] Ziegler 1951: 780. Particular parallels between *Against Borrowing Money* and the later *Lucullus* may be noted: Swain 1992c: 310.
[128] *Are the Ills of the Mind or of the Body Worse?* 501e–502a. Smyrna: Jones 1971a: 14–15.
[129] 814f, 815a–c, 818b, 818d–e, 824a, 825d; cf. *Pompey* 55. 4, *Pericles* 15. 1, *Cimon and Lucullus synkrisis* 2. 7, *Dion and Brutus synkrisis* 2. 2, *Table Talks* viii. 1, 717d–e. Cf. Fuhrmann 1964: 238–40; Quet 1978: 64.
[130] 799a, 800b, 801f, 802e, 805d, 806a, 813e, 816f, 821c. Cf. Fuhrmann 1964: 241–4; Quet 1978: 65–6.
[131] The analogy is helped by the real use of theatres as places of assembly (cf. 799e). Note similarly the athletic metaphor in ch. 10 at 804d.

for here at a crucial point where he is calling to mind the power of Rome Plutarch stresses the other side—not the performance, but the need to get one's lines right with the aid of a 'prompter'.[132] At 816f the image of the protagonist coming on stage as attendant to a minor actor playing the part of a king illustrates the idea of co-operation with those who are magistrates. The medical analogy, though, is naturally more appropriate for the latter part of *Political Advice* where Plutarch is promoting the integrity and dignity of the state and the acceptance of corporate responsibility.[133]

And so to Plutarch's explanation of Solon's law. It was right, he says, to demand involvement in civil strife, but involvement should not be with one of two sides, but with both in the role of an arbitrator with the aim of restoring harmony (824b). Solon's precept is discussed also at *Solon* 20. 1.[134] There this 'very peculiar and surprising law' is taken as requiring involvement with the side whose policies are 'better and more just'. In this passage Plutarch is concerned with interpreting Solon's motives, not in making his own recommendations. In *Political Advice* recommendations must be made, and so he advocates the part of conciliation and refrains from questions of right and wrong. He now pursues his theme. 'The best plan is to take precautions to forestall civil strife, and to regard this as the greatest and noblest part of the art of statesmanship' (824b–c). There follows an important passage in which Plutarch lists what he considers to be the most important blessings 'the cities' can enjoy—'peace [*eirênê*], freedom [*eleutheria*], plenty [*euetêria*, literally "a good season"], populousness [*euandria*], and concord [*homonoia*, literally "like-mindedness"]'—and comments on how far they are enjoyed today. Peace and freedom, he says, are connected with current political arrangements. Plenty and a good population are in the hands of the gods and the wise man will ask the gods to grant them (824c). 'There remains for the politician only one of these great objects, but it is second to none: to ensure perpetual concord and friendship among one's fellows, and to remove all kinds of strife, dissension, and hostility.' Compare chapter 10, 805a–b ('there remain public lawsuits and embassies, etc.'). There

---

[132] Contrast *Demosthenes* 22. 5: statesmen should not behave like actors who have to follow 'the demands of the plot'.

[133] Note also the change in the athletic metaphors at 820d and 825e.

[134] Cf. also *On God's Slowness to Punish* 550b–c, *On the Intelligence of Animals* 965d. Cf. the thoughts of Plutarch's pupil Favorinus recorded by Gellius, *Attic Nights* ii. 12.

Plutarch was talking about functions of state still available, here he is concerned with the politician's general policy and ability to benefit the community at large through his rule. 'He will teach and explain to them individually and collectively the weak state of Greece,[135] which brings one great advantage to the wise, the chance to live one's life in peace and concord. Fortune has left no other prize to fight for. For what leadership, what glory can the victor expect? What power is it, that a short pronouncement from the proconsul undoes or transfers to another?' (824e). Rather, the politician must concern himself with resolving disputes, which often start in private and then inflame the state.[136] Plutarch offers a number of examples finishing with the enmity of Pardalas and Tyrrhenus at Sardis (825a–d). The role of the politician now resembles the poorer statesman in chapter 31. If he is conciliatory in his own disagreements, the more will he be so in public. In sum, 'if private enmities are removed, public ones cost little, and bring no unpleasant or irremediable consequences' (825e–f).

A number of points arise from this final chapter. The list of blessings the city typically desires finds an echo in epigraphical celebrations of priests' or magistrates' terms of office.[137] But equivalence between epigraphical texts of this sort and literary ones is problematic. The former tend to unreal, biased, and tendentious appreciation, and we have no controls for comparison. Literary texts may be equally tendentious, but at least in some cases can be carefully weighed in context and against what the author says elsewhere in a different texture.[138] So it is with Plutarch. The natural world is guided by god and has nothing to do with politicians, Greek or Roman. We pray for 'plenty' (*euetêria*) and 'populousness'

---

[135] For the language and sentiment cf. on the Hellenistic period *Philopoemen* 8. 3 and Pausanias i. 4. 1, vii. 17. 1, x. 19. 8; for similar observations of contemporary Greeks see Arrian, *Discourses of Epictetus* iii. 7. 3, Dio of Prusa, *Or.* xxxi. 157–60.

[136] Cf. fr. 148 Sandbach (from *On Anger*), and *Advice on Marriage* 144c quoted above, 'Novel' n. 86.

[137] See Jones 1971a: 115 n. 42 citing *IG* xii. 5. 906 (Tenos), Robert 1937: 257–8 (Bithynia), and further Andrei 1981: 104, for the blessings alleged to have been achieved by priests or *agoranomoi* during their terms. The ultimate origin of the list is Hesiod, *Works and Days* 225 ff. (peace, no war, no famine or calamity, blessings of nature), from which Plutarch (who wrote a commentary on the poem) quotes at 824c, and other similar passages.

[138] There is a similar difficulty involved in equating moral qualities (re-)commended by Plutarch with those displayed in honorific inscriptions, as done by Panagopoulos 1977 (cf. 232 where the problem is addressed briefly).

(*euandria*). These are the subjects people and cities ask the gods
about at *On the Pythian Oracles* 408c.[139] What of peace and freedom? Peace certainly exists. 'For peace our peoples [*dêmoi*] have
no need of politicians, at the present time at any rate, for every
Greek war, every foreign [*barbaros*] war has passed away from us'
(824c). Similar remarks occur in *On the Pythian Oracles, On Contentment*, and in *Should Old Men take Part in Politics?*[140] Plutarch
does not name Rome in these passages. Perhaps her role was simply
too obvious. But another factor is undoubtedly his belief that the
ordering of the natural world and of the world of man was ultimately under divine guidance, not human. It is very difficult for us
to envisage the possibility that in such passages Rome would not
always be in the forefront of a man's mind, especially in the case of
a man who knew so much about her history and so valued her
citizens. We cannot know for sure whether Plutarch was thinking
of Rome or not. But we can at least see that in *On the Pythian
Oracles* praise of the 'the current settled conditions' is definitely
not focused on Rome,[141] but in its context serves to explain the
simple questions now put to the oracle at Delphi and the simple
answers now given in accordance with 'the god's purpose' (28–30,
408b–409d). The same sort of thinking, which made Rome god's
agent in this matter 'at the present time at any rate', may well be felt
in the other passages, including *Political Advice*.

What of freedom? 'Of freedom our peoples have as much as
those in control allow them,[142] and more would perhaps not be
better' (824c). Plutarch knew well that a man could inherit freedom
and citizenship rights from his father (*Against Borrowing Money*
831c). Outside the city the freedom Rome offered was, of course,

[139] Cf. further *On Superstition* 166e ('wealth, affluence, peace, concord, success'),
On the E at Delphi 386c, *On the Decline of Oracles* 413b. On 'plenty' as a characteristic of terms of office see also Robert *BE* 1966. 137.

[140] *On the Pythian Oracles* 408b–c 'For my own part, I feel very content with the
questions men put to the god about the current [*nun*] settled conditions. All is peace
and quiet, war has ceased, there are no migrations or revolutions [*staseis*] or tyrannies, nor any of Greece's other disorders and evils demanding complicated medica-
tion, as it were.' *On Contentment* 469e 'Let us be grateful that we have life and
health and see the sun; that there is no war or civil strife, but that the earth supports
farming and the sea safe sailing for those who wish; and that we may speak and act,
or be silent and at rest' (cf. Tacitus, *Histories* i. 1. 4). *Should Old Men take Part in
Politics?* 784f.—above, n. 69.

[141] Contrast on this passage Hartman 1916: 174 'a *Romanis* se lectum iri speravit
Plutarchus'.

[142] For the language here cf. *Cato Minor* 61. 6.

not full freedom.[143] Who was affected by this? When Plutarch says it 'would perhaps not be better' for the 'peoples' (*dêmoi*) to have more, whose freedom is he talking about? The word *dêmoi* could refer to the lower class (as at 801a). But since it is used immediately before this meaning 'community' (the *dêmoi* do not need politicians for peace), it will bear the same sense here (picking up 'cities' a little before). Plutarch is saying that full freedom might give licence not only to the lower class, but to the 'first men' as well. There is no evidence that he wanted the lower class restrained by Rome, as has been suggested.[144] To be sure, he was no democrat. He wanted the Greek politicians—the city's own elite—to control the mass of their fellow-citizens, though not by violent means, but by the power of their own example (821a–b). We should not forget that he only says that full freedom would 'perhaps [*isôs*] not be better'.

It is easy to condemn Plutarch for naïvety in thinking that the local elite might be able to rule without strife. Still, we must allow him what he says. Part of this is that Rome should not be called in to city life. It is in this regard that the Greek politician is left only with the role of promoting 'concord'. This is not just a plea for a happy consensualism. In Plutarch's period, as we shall see with Dio of Prusa and Aelius Aristides, a whole ideological industry was established around this word. There is ample evidence from coins, inscriptions, and literary texts of interconnections between cities involving loose proposals to pursue concord and amity between their peoples. Such accord (which was never formalized in treaties) was a way of restraining local competition over titles and claims to heritage and of advertising and encouraging social and economic parity and common interests (hence the literal meaning of *homonoia*, 'like-mindedness'). Plutarch alludes precisely to the process at *Political Advice* 808c (missions to other cities 'concerning friendship and concord'). Much older than the idea of concord between cities was the notion of concord within the city. In Plato's *Republic* this took on an explicitly political formulation as a convenient method of empowering the rulers of the state against the ruled by enacting government through consent.[145] There is nothing quite as crudely explicit as this in Plutarch's general presentation. Nevertheless, for

---

[143] Cf. especially Dio of Prusa, *Or.* xliv. 12.
[144] Jones 1971*a*: 120.   [145] See below, 'Aristides' n. 147.

the most part concord and co-operation are focused within the city (805d, 819d for the term). This is the case too in the final chapter (824c–e). And, as we have seen elsewhere (16, 813a–c; 26, 819b–e), Plutarch is fairly open about the need to conspire against the ruled when 'something important and useful' is at stake. The general good government obtained through attention to concord and avoidance of disputes within the elite is a corollary of this. Concord, like peace and freedom, was good for the whole city (true enough); but naturally—as Plutarch does not have to remind Menemachus in his final remarks—the greatest benefit was for those who ruled the community like him.

Political Advice is restricted to local Greek politics. It disparages or ignores a significant area of contemporary political ambition, a career with Rome, not simply in terms of direct contacts as a procurator or a senator, but also indirect service such as being a priest of the local imperial cult or a delegate to a provincial organization with responsibility perhaps for the games or the cult at a higher level. There were Greeks in Plutarch's time who aspired to these tasks and made handsome careers out of them. Plutarch may not have approved.[146] Also notable is the fact that the emperor is hardly

---

[146] On Plutarch's attitude to the imperial cult see Bowersock 1973: 187–91 (arguing for blanket acceptance). In an official capacity 'Mestrius Plutarchus' erected a statue for Hadrian 'son of Trajan the god' and 'grandson of Nerva the god' (*SIG*³ 829A). It is not too difficult to say what Plutarch's real attitude was to the divinity of the deceased: at *Romulus* 28.10 he says that certain virtuous souls can progress after the death of the body through the stages of heroes and daimons to godhood but that this does not happen 'by civic law' (a passage perhaps in Pausanias' mind later, cf. 'Pausanias' n. 64). We cannot say whether Nerva and Trajan had passed these stages for Plutarch in a personal capacity. Living men could not have been gods in his eyes (his views on the Diadochi are significant in this respect: cf. the example of Demetrius at *Demetrius* 10. 4–11. 1, 12. 1, 13. 1–3, 24. 1–2, 42. 8–11). But the example of Numa shows the very close relationship he thought was possible between the divine and a man of consummate virtue. Thus Plutarch's attacks on the disreputable Demetrius and his type have no necessary bearing on the imperial cult as an institution (contrary: Scott 1929; Taeger 1957–60: ii. 531–2). There is no reason why a virtuous emperor could not have been accommodated within the existing religious system in this way. However, it is difficult to believe that Plutarch did not see a repeat of the Hellenistic monarchs in the case of an emperor like Domitian who claimed to be a god. In this case we cannot talk of acceptance. We should also bear in mind the force of collective ritual in the matter—Plutarch grew up with the imperial cult in existence and this was how it was, even for a thinking man (cf. Price 1984a: 7–11), especially in a public capacity. The point at issue in the text is that, whatever Plutarch's attitude, it seems unlikely—given what he says about procuratorships—that a career forwarded through this system would have met with his approval.

mentioned in the essay.[147] These omissions are the more obvious because Plutarch employs historical examples from Roman history quite freely (as he does in other essays of this sort).[148] *Political Advice* certainly voices Plutarch's frustration with the petty ambitions of the Greek elite, their stupidity and lack of real pride in their countries. These are faults he attacks elsewhere (*Flamininus* 11, *Agesilaus* 15. 3). Here it is perhaps no wonder that, although the advice is delivered in a spirit of optimism, i.e. that it can work, much of what is said has a negative tone: 'Do not appear too theatrical', 'Do not stir up the people', 'Do not be too ambitious', 'Do not fail to cooperate with your colleagues', 'Do not seek outside backers.' Despite this there is an overall message in the work which is positive. This is, 'Preserve your city's integrity and dignity.' As part of this it is clear that Plutarch did not want to find Roman government present in the cities of Greece. He valued Rome as god's agent in securing peace on earth. This was how he theorized Rome's success. In practice he wanted Greeks to retain as much power as possible. He wished for co-operation among Greece's politicians and for associated good behaviour among her peoples. Although he knew Rome would interfere if opportunity was offered, he also believed firmly that she did not want to control every aspect of civic life. It was Greek servility and factionalism that forced Romans to be 'masters more than they themselves want' (814f).[149] Plutarch's appeal and encouragement to preserve the vitality of the cities certainly squared with Rome's wishes for the smooth running of the Empire; but it is in accordance with his wishes for Greece, whose heritage he loved so much and whose loss of freedom he clearly regretted, rather than with Rome's wishes that the advice is tendered at all.

Two other works bearing on these issues may be considered, albeit rather briefly. First, mention must be made of *Should Old Men*

---

[147] Note 805a (embassies to the *autokratôr*), 813e (the procurators of *kaisar*). As a rule Plutarch does not use the word *basileus*, 'king', to mean emperor (as other authors do; on which see Wifstrand 1939: 531 ff.; contrast e.g. Plutarch's *Galba* and *Otho*), though it not correct to say he never does (Mason 1974: 120)—there is a clear example at *On the Decline of Oracles* 419e, and (as Mason observes) cognates of *basileus* can mean 'imperial' in Plutarch.

[148] He naturally found Rome rather less useful for illustrating his ethical and philosophical works.

[149] Cf. Dio of Prusa, *Or.* xxxi. 111.

take Part in Politics?, where Plutarch gives us some evidence for his own political aspirations and accomplishments. This essay goes closely with *Political Advice*. It was written at the very end of Plutarch's life around 115–20, and again shows an overwhelming desire to maintain the status quo in a world of local Greek politics without Rome.[150] The addressee (Flavius) Euphanes was a distinguished Athenian politician, archon eponymous between 105 and 110 and president of the Areopagus when Plutarch wrote to him (794b).[151] The main point of the essay is that older men should take part in political life because 'sense' is proper to old age (789f), but that they should not display inappropriate ambition.[152] Undertaking 'menial public services' (of the sort commended in *Political Advice*) after a career as agonothete, Boeotarch, or chairman of the Amphictyonic Council reveals a disgraceful ambitiousness (785c–d, 793d, 794a). The legal government Plutarch and Euphanes lived under made civic life with its 'shows, processions, distributions . . . and the constant worship of some god' unthreatening, indeed positively enjoyable (784f, 787b–c).[153] The only reference in all this to contemporary Roman political relations is Plutarch's criticism of old men who work their way on to embassies 'to governors or potentates' where there is no necessity but only 'flattery and currying favour' (794a). This is not anti-Roman, of course, but criticism of a Greek failing.

The other work that touches on political relations with Rome is the essay *On Exile*. It is not improbable that this was also addressed to Menemachus, since the exile is said to be a Sardian (who is perhaps now living in Athens).[154] In this traditional work of comfort Plutarch makes it plain how important regular contact with the Roman governor was for a Greek politician. The exile, he says, is now free from the demands made by the city: 'pay a contribution, go on an embassy to Rome, entertain the governor, perform a public service' (602c). He is free from 'orders issued by the governor, jobs undertaken in the city's interest, and public services that are hard to refuse' (602f). If he considers as a disadvantage the fact he is not

---

[150] Cf. Desideri 1986: 379, 381. Date of *Should Old Men . . . ?*: Follet 1976: 187; Swain 1991c: 320–1.

[151] Euphanes: Follet 1972; Kapetanopoulos 1976: 265–6 (archon in '110/1').

[152] Apparently a vice Plutarch particularly associated with elderly Romans: *Lucullus* 38. 3–4, *Marius* 2. 4, 34. 6, *Flamininus* 20. 1–2.

[153] Cf. *On Superstition* 169d; *Pericles* 11. 4.

[154] 599e, 601b, 607e. Cf. Ziegler 1951: 819; Jones 1966: 72.

in office, not on the Council, and not an agonothete (the good things in civic life), let him say to himself, 'We are not involved in civil strife, we are not spending our money, we do not hang on the governor's doors; it doesn't matter now who will be in charge of the province, or if he's easily angered or troublesome' (604b). The exile is lucky that there is no business or magistrate or governor to bother him (604d). To comfort his addressee Plutarch draws a rather gloomy picture of political life which contrasts with the sprightly humour of his essay on old men in politics. There is no reason to generalize from this. Of course Plutarch knew of difficult governors (cf. *On the Decline of Oracles* 434d); he is also happy to record a joke about the possibility of corrupt administration in his own province (*Table Talks* ii, 632a–b on Avidius Quietus).[155] As in *On Exile*, he was aware of the fact that governors and their entourage had to be entertained when they demanded it (*Table Talks* vii. 6, 708b); at the same he can mention this freely to his Roman friend Mestrius Florus as something everyone had to put up with.[156] Yet there is a further contrast that needs to be brought out. The rosy picture of politics in *Should Old Men take Part in Politics?* ignores Rome: contacts with Rome do not feature among the things Plutarch enjoys about political life in his old age. But in depicting the negative side of political life these contacts become routine chores along with the other demands of city politics. It is difficult, perhaps wrong, to compare essays with such diverse aims; but it does seem as if *On Exile* confirms key aspects of Plutarch's attitude towards Rome as expressed in *Political Advice*. Emphasis on the regularity of contacts with the governor in *On Exile*, which is as we find it, for example, in Dio of Prusa's civic speeches, makes the exclusion of Rome from *Political Advice* the more apparent; reference to these contacts in a negative context only provides confirmation of Plutarch's preference for keeping Romans out of Greek civic life.

Taking everything together, we can see that Plutarch did not in any way chafe at Roman rule, which he thought in accordance with divine planning, and yet was at heart a non-integrationist. While both Greeks and Romans were capable of producing men whose

---

[155] Cf. Jones 1971a: 52. Epictetus' advice (Arrian, *Discourses of Epictetus* iii. 7. 13) to the Roman corrector to steal from the 'ineffectual Greeks' (the Roman view), which is supposed to be ironic, may be compared.

[156] Cf. Eck in Drew-Bear, Hermann, Eck 1977: 365–83 on the granting of senatorial exemptions from such practices at the turn of the 3rd c.

lives were suitable for imitation in our own, there was a lurking suspicion that Romans lacked proper, Greek culture, which was the only path to philosophical happiness. Unlike Dionysius of Halicarnassus Plutarch accepted Romans for what they were—a much more respectful approach, but also one which involved a recognition that they were 'foreign'. He valued Romans highly for bringing the blessings of good government to the world. Yet we should not believe that he thought Greeks quite incapable of self-government. If he had done so, *Political Advice* would not have been written. Rather, Plutarch is possessed of an essential optimism founded on a faith in god's reliability and beneficence and a conviction that Hellenic virtues can triumph over Hellenic vices. It is these beliefs that encouraged him to welcome the stability and prosperity of the contemporary world—without ascribing its condition to the rule of Rome alone—and to promote the good government and independence of the cities of Greece—while trying to minimize the involvement of Roman power.

6

Dio of Prusa

INTRODUCTION

Dio of Prusa, a city in the Roman province of Bithynia, is known to historians principally for his speeches of advice to the Greek cities and for his four major *Orations on Kingship*. He also wrote many occasional pieces with an ethical or philosophical message. In this respect he follows on naturally from Plutarch. He was in fact born at about the same time and the two had many things in common—a rich background (though Dio was probably the richer), an interest in letters and philosophy (though Plutarch's work was at a higher intellectual level overall and his output was far greater), an involvement in politics and a belief in statesmanship (here Dio was more active in the rough and tumble of real civic life), and a considered relationship with Rome.

Plutarch and Dio must have known of each other's existence, but aside from two suggestive entries in the *Lamprias Catalogue* of Plutarch's works, there is no mention of the one by the other.[1] Perhaps this is not so surprising, if one considers key differences between them. Plutarch's self-image was that of the philosopher-scholar, a man who loved Hellas but also his own little town of Chaeroneia, someone who enjoyed serving in political life when necessary, but who preferred to leave it to others to seek glory, who thought often and deeply about god and passed his last years in prodigious scholarship and the worship of Apollo at Delphi. This was not Dio. He was an active politician in a number of cities where he held citizenship.[2] His important civic speeches at Prusa

---

[1] *Lamprias Catalogue* 204 'Speech (in Reply) to Dio at Olympia' (note Dio xii *Olympicus*), 227 'Discourse (in Reply) to Dio'; cf. Desideri 1978: 4–5.
[2] Apart from Prusan and Roman citizenship Dio mentions in concord speeches the grant of citizenship probably at Nicaea (*Or.* xxxix. 1) and certainly at Nicomedia (xxxviii. 1), Apamea, and other cities (xli. 2).

show us a man who understood power and who loved to exercise it. His battles with his rivals, which somewhat undermine his pleas for concord in the Bithynian cities, represent the sort of political behaviour Plutarch totally rejects in *Political Advice*. Nor was Dio a scholar. He indulged in belletristic activity (see especially the literary-critical *Orr*. lii, liii, lix) and wrote a now lost historical/ethnographical work on the Getae. There are a number of pieces which might be described loosely as moral philosophy (e.g. *Orr*. lxvi, lxvii, lxviii on different types of *doxa* ['glory', 'repute'], lxxiii, lxxiv on trust and the lack of it), and quite a few where he carefully pronounces on serious subjects (notably *Orr*. i–iv on the role of the king/emperor, and xii, xxx, xxxvi on the subject of man's relationship with the divine). The *Suda* records one apparently serious philosophical work, *Is the Cosmos Perishable?*, which confirms Dio's interest in Stoic cosmology.[3] But there is none of the painstaking philosophical enquiry or the sustained biographical/historiographical investigations that characterize Plutarch's work.

In trying to understand Dio and his attitude to Rome it is important first to consider his public persona, for it has often been thought that he changed or 'converted' from an earlier adherence to rhetoric and display to a later devotion to philosophy and instruction, and this has a bearing on his political activity. Dio, who testifies to the unauthorized circulation of his works during his lifetime,[4] was an immensely popular author after his death but presented later scholars with a problem of classification. Philostratus includes him in the category of the philosopher-sophists with which he begins his *Lives*.[5] In hedging his bets in this way he is recognizing Dio's varied literary output. He knew that Dio had written serious philosophical works aimed at improving the government of the cities; but Dio was also 'serious about themes of no importance', which were *sophistika* (*VS* 487), Philostratus' main interest. One of Dio's greatest admirers in late antiquity was Synesius, the late fourth- and early fifth-century Neoplatonist and bishop of Cyrene. He categorized Dio along different lines. Synesius took Dio as a model for his own dealings with monarchs and as an example of how inner freedom can be won through philosophy.[6] He introduces his work called

[3] *Suda* δ 1240. Cf. Brancacci 1985: 259–60.
[4] *Or*. xlii. 4–5; cf. below, n. 29.   [5] On this group see above, 'Past' n. 95.
[6] On the relationship see Asmus 1900; Treu 1958 (introduction and commentary to the *Dio*); Brancacci 1985: 137–97.

Dio by combating what he saw as Philostratus' rather light understanding of his hero. For Synesius Dio began his life as a sophist and ended it as a philosopher.[7] Towards the end of the work he says there is no cause for his addressee (his future son, whose birth was intimated during a reading of Dio) to be bothered if he has 'not improved Dio's writings'. The fact is that Dio needs no defence, as is also the case with the other authors whose philosophical worth he will maintain (16, pp. 274 ff. Terzaghi). Synesius was prepared to admit that Dio was good-humoured and was by no means always to be taken seriously (his only other use of Dio is in his *Encomium on Baldness*, which he tells us was written in response to Dio's *Encomium of Hair*). But for his own purposes he distinguished firmly between Dio's sophistic pieces like the lost *Encomium of a Parrot* and the works he regarded as serious like the *Euboean Oration* and the orations on kingship which he imitated.

According to Synesius the classification of Dio's works as philosophical or sophistic depended on whether they were written before or after his exile by Domitian (1–2, p. 238 Terz.). For Philostratus Dio's exile had been voluntary (*VS* 488). On the basis of Dio's own works and his frequent and very bitter references to Domitian it is plain that the exile was real enough and that Dio was barred from his own province.[8] And during this period, or shortly after it,[9] Dio did adopt the persona of a wandering Cynic philosopher. It is on this basis that he appears in speeches in the character of Diogenes, one of the founders of Cynicism, or as Heracles, that philosophy's great hero. This Dio, the Dio of the civic and kingship speeches, is admonitory and exhortatory and is more than happy to discourse on his personal sufferings and discomforts during an exile which had, as it were, given him the right to speak out.[10] But it is in fact doubtful that there was a real conversion. It looks very much as if

[7] The view essentially adopted by von Arnim 1898.

[8] Cf. *Or.* xiii. 1. The Roman friend of Dio whose downfall brought about his exile is unidentifiable (H. Sidebottom argues in an unpublished article, 'Dio of Prusa and the Flavian Dynasty', that he is more likely to be L. Salvius Otho Cocceianus, the nephew of Cocceius Nerva [Syme 1958: ii. 628], than the usual nominee, T. Flavius Sabinus; cf. Sidebottom 1990: 42–4). For speculation on this and other possible aspects of Dio's relationship with the Flavian emperors (for which there is actually no very good evidence) see e.g. Jones 1978a: 13–18, 45–6, *et al.*

[9] Von Arnim 1898: 260; Jones 1978a: 49–50.

[10] *Orr.* vi–x, xiii, xvi. The picture is not all gloom: cf. the introductory piece *Or.* xix. 1 on his visit to friends at Cyzicus (which was near but not too near the border with the province of Bithynia).

Synesius took Dio's propaganda about himself too literally.[11] There is nothing improbable about suggesting that Dio became more serious (or thought he did) as he got older. But the division between Dio the sophist and Dio the philosopher is simply too neat and must be rejected.[12]

What we see rather is Dio's skilful adoption of the personality to suit the occasion. It is almost certain, as we might expect, that Dio wrote sophistic pieces after his exile (the lost *Encomium of Hair* celebrates the cleaning of his hair after a long period of unkemptness), as well as before it.[13] The persona of the wandering Cynic philosopher, which Dio hit upon around the time of the exile, was maintained more as a convenient way of articulating his relations with the emperors Nerva and Trajan through the guise of a critical Greek sage, as a means of asserting philosophical self-righteousness before his Greek audiences, and for the purpose of commenting on his recent sufferings, than as a reflection of a true change of heart. To be sure, the political animal on view in the Bithynian speeches and in the letters of Pliny the Younger, which were written towards the end of Dio's life, does not stand out as a man of high moral probity. And it is Dio's political career that is the key to appreciating a life of continuity as a member of the Greek elite, not the manner in which he chose to package this at various times.[14]

Dio's attitudes were shaped by inherited wealth. His father had died leaving an estate which was owed the considerable sum of four hundred thousand drachmas (xlvi. 5–6).[15] This implies that he had

---

[11] It is perfectly possible that the partition of Dio's works into 'pre-exilic' and 'post-exilic', which was established in the schools before Synesius (as Synesius reports: *Dio* I, p. 238 Terz.), had already been extended to philosophical versus sophistic works; cf. the title of *Or.* xlvi *Before he Practised as a Philosopher, In his Fatherland.*

[12] So Momigliano 1969 (1950) and esp. Moles 1978; on Synesius' motives in making the division see Desideri 1973. Cf. in general on sophists and philosophers Stanton 1973.

[13] If we are right to suppose that pieces like *Encomium of a Parrot, Praise of a Gnat, Tempe* (praise of the famous beauty-spot; cf. Aelian, *Varied History* 3. 1), and *Memnon* (praise of the famous talking statue) were 'pre-exilic'.

[14] Later contemporaries of Dio took the view that he was a philosopher (Peregrinus according to Lucian, *Peregrinus* 18), a rhetor (Arrian, *Discourses of Epictetus* iii. 23. 18–19), or both (Fronto to Marcus at *On Eloquence* i. 4 [135 v.d.Hout²]), as it suited them. (The headless bust of a philosopher Dio found at Pergamum—cf. recently Brunt 1994: 41 n. 67—is a product of the Hadrianic era and therefore surely too late to represent a contemporary view of Dio of Prusa.)

[15] In Roman terms HS 1,600,000. The father is named in the tradition as Pasicrates (Photius, *Library* cod. 209, 165a, *Suda* δ 1240).

been, at least in part, a moneylender.[16] We do not know what proportion of the estate this sum represented. On his mother's side Dio's background was probably richer still.[17] His maternal grandfather had spent his first (inherited) fortune on public benefactions, according to Dio, but acquired another one from 'culture and the emperors [*autokratores*]'.[18] This accent on benefaction, spending lavishly to reinforce social and political dominance in the city, is very typical of the age, as is the interrelation between culture and power that Dio identifies. In this same speech, very probably composed before his exile, Dio says that he too had performed numerous expensive liturgies for the Prusans (xlvi. 6).[19] The Dio of *Orr.* xliii–xlv, xlvii–xlviii, and Pliny, *Letters* 81–2, who returned to Prusa after his exile and spent the next decade engrossed in grandiose schemes for embellishing the city, is the same man.

To determine Dio's attitude to Rome is no easy matter.[20] The speeches we must use as evidence are written for specific contexts and occasions and there is not nearly as much independent thought of the sort we can find in Plutarch against which we may judge them. Dio constantly shifts his ground to suit his audience's and his own changing prejudices; but at the same time he does have his own opinions and the attempt to recover them can and should be made. In general it is worth recalling that Dio had had the experience of being alternately promoted and blasted by Roman power. That he felt the benefits of Rome were less than secure is likely enough. This is confirmed by the fact that even in pro-Roman contexts he does not really eulogize Rome or enthuse about the benefits of Roman world rule. In some cases he is clearly hostile and irritated by the impuissance of the Greek cities and the Greek world in the face of Rome and, as we shall see, is severely critical of some of her provincial governors. As with Plutarch and the other intellectuals studied in due course, Dio puts a high value on Greekness and on the clearest expression of this, possession of Greek

[16] Jones 1978a: 6; Duncan-Jones 1982: 21. At *Or.* xlvi. 8 Dio denies, somewhat equivocally, that he was a usurer himself.
[17] For good accounts of Dio's finances and inheritances see Jones 1978a: 8–18; Salmeri 1982: 5–46; cf. MacMullen 1974: 50–1.
[18] *Or.* xlvi. 3. That this is his mother's father seems clear from Dio's remarks to the Apameans at *Or.* xli. 6 about 'the then *autokratôr* who was [his maternal grandfather's] friend', cf. xliv. 5.
[19] The date depends on the biographical information in the speech: see n. 69.
[20] Cf. Jones 1978a: 124–31.

culture, in his case in its highest form of philosophy. This comes through in almost all of what he says, and Greek ideals are particularly evident in the orations on kingship which were addressed (or alleged to have been addressed) to the emperor himself.[21]

DIVINE RULE AND ROMAN RULE

Of the four *Orations on Kingship* (*Orr.* i–iv) the first and third are addresses and are usually held to have been delivered before Trajan at Rome,[22] while the second and the fourth are in dialogue form and may have been sent to him (though proof is lacking). The focus here will be on the more important passages and on Dio's general ideas. The most important of these is his firm belief in the validity of monarchical rule as the ideal of government. For Dio the good king on earth looks to the model of the divine king in heaven. In attempting to steer Trajan towards this model of kingship Dio had no choice, of course, but to take Roman monarchy as the given form of monarchical rule among men. But there is no reason to suppose that he thought Roman monarchy and its emperor actually came close to or fulfilled the ideal of divine monarchy—the speeches are intended rather to establish what the ideal is. The orations are not straightforward flattery of Trajan and do not offer unequivocal confirmation of his right to power. Even if we restrict ourselves to the first and third speeches, we find that what flattery there is (and flattery is certainly present; see especially i. 36 and iii. 1–24) must be read against strong criticisms of prospective bad behaviour and warnings from Dio that the earthly king is only a mortal who will be destroyed by the divine king if he deviates from his example.[23] This admonitory Dio comes to the fore particularly in the dialogue

---

[21] Whether this identity as a Greek is racial (by blood) or cultural is our insoluble problem, not Dio's (cf. above, 'Introduction' n. 11): the 'native's point of view' is that he and the Prusans were Hellenes in all senses (*Orr.* xliii. 3, xliv. 10, xlviii. 8, l. 2).

[22] Cf. i. 5, 36, 49; iii. 1, 2, 3, 25. My interpretation of the kingship speeches here owes much to John Moles.

[23] i. 45–7, iii. 55, 82. Submission to the gods is the first duty of the king: i. 15–16, iii. 51–4. On Fears' mistaken belief that Dio thought Roman imperial power was divine (1977: 154–8) see Brunt 1979: 170; Salmeri 1982: 118 n. 115.

Or. iv between Diogenes (Dio) and Alexander (Trajan), in which—difficulties of interpretation notwithstanding—it is plain that Trajan's military ambitions are being sharply scrutinized.[24]

Dio's *Mentorhaltung* in the kingship speeches should not be seen only as advice for the emperor. The one piece of relatively independent evidence we have concerning the presentation of one of these to an audience, the short *Or.* lvii *Nestor*, indicates that at least on one occasion the important matter was Dio's presentation before Greeks of his relationship with the emperor.[25] Dio begins the *Nestor*, which is a familiar type of introductory speech,[26] by defending Nestor's boastful words in the first book of the *Iliad*, where the old man tells Agamemnon and Achilles that in the past he had had dealings with much better men than they and so they should listen to him as the men of old did (Dio quotes *Iliad* i. 260–8, 273–4). Having excused Nestor, Dio excuses himself for the speech he is about to rehearse (lvii.10–12). It is not boastful to say that on a previous occasion he has addressed 'other more powerful men [*kreittosi*], popular assemblies, or kings or tyrants'.[27] More to the point, why should he not repeat himself? After all, this is what Socrates often did, and the same thing has been happening with classical tragedies and comedies for many years. So, 'We are now going to report the words we spoke to the *autokratôr*', since it is important to know 'whether they are beneficial and useful for you and for the whole of mankind or whether they are trivial and useless' (lvii. 11).

Dio, then, claimed he was repeating before his Greek audience a speech he had addressed to Trajan. It is likely that the speech he chose was one of those preserved as *Orr.* i–iv,[28] though it is by no means certain that the version he gave his Greek audience was the one he offered the emperor. *Or.* iii with its flattery of the prince would have been particularly unsuitable. Nor of course do we know that *Orr.* i and iii (and ii and iv) were themselves delivered to

---

[24] See Moles 1983*a*; cf. Jones 1978*a*: 120–1.

[25] Cf. von Arnim 1898: 410–14 (variation of content to suit audiences).

[26] On this *prolalia* (and its type) see Mras 1949: 74–5.

[27] *Kreittones* perhaps means Romans specifically as at Plutarch, *Political Advice* 815a (cf. in Dio Or. xxxii *Alexandrian* 29, 59); on *dêmos* in the sense here of 'assembly' cf. Salmeri 1982: 58 n. 38.

[28] *Or.* ii has been suggested as the most likely candidate because of its extensive Homeric material: Lamar Crosby 1946: 417.

Trajan—if they were delivered—in the form that has come down to us. Other speeches must have been altered to suit different audiences and occasions (Dio speaks of repetition explicitly in the case of *Or.* xi),[29] and at least in the case of the fourth *Oration on Kingship* an alternative section seems to have been transmitted to us as *Or.* v (the *Libyan Myth*), which is alluded to at iv. 73–4 ('Have you not heard the Libyan Myth?, etc.'). It has been argued that the version of *Or.* iv addressed to Trajan must have been the existing one, where the Libyan myth is passed over in favour of Diogenes'/Dio's remarks on *daimones*, which were made in honour of the emperor's *genius*.[30] But it is perhaps right to wonder if the still rather frank tone of the final section (cf. 76 Alexander/Trajan 'was astounded at the man's courage and fearlessness') was not rather supposed to bolster Dio's self-presentation before *Greeks*, so complementing the rather aggressive Cynic core (4–72) which (on this argument) has been reinforced for Greek consumption.[31] For in repeating his kingship speeches in the Greek world Dio hardly wanted to appear to have flattered the emperor. He wanted to show that he had been tough at Rome and that he had drawn on Greek *paideia* to tell the emperor how to behave.[32] If this is accepted as a reason for the composition of the kingship orations, it is certainly consonant with their overall tone and their avowedly protreptic intention. We may compare Dio's robust reports of his visit to Trajan to secure benefits for Prusa, as he narrates the story in *Or.* xl. 13–15 (cf. xlv. 3, 7). Again, presentation to Greeks of his relations with the emperor is a principal reason why he brandishes before them imperial letters relevant to himself and his requests for Prusa in a context where

[29] See xi. 6 (von Arnim 1898: 183–204); note also Dio's comments in *Or.* xlii. 4–5 on pirated versions of his speeches (which were all well known—of course), complaints echoed by Galen in *On his Own Books* and *Synopsis of his Own Books on the Pulse*, by Arrian in the prefatory letter to the *Discourses of Epictetus*, and by Diodorus Siculus at *Library of History* xl. 8.

[30] Von Arnim 1898: 402–4, 412–14 (the 'Trajanic' version omitted iv. 72 ἀλλ᾽ ἂν ἀπαλλαγῇς to iv. 74 διηγήσαντο); Moles 1983*a*: 276–7 sharply refurbishes von Arnim here.

[31] Note that Lepper (1948: 195–7) thought the whole speech was too strong to offer Trajan and that its transmitted version is the product of a later change of heart against the emperor; the first part of this suggestion is not as silly as Desideri makes out (1978: 337 n. 8a).

[32] In this regard the question of whether Trajan could have understood the Greek of the speeches or not is irrelevant (he surely could have, since he was plainly educated well enough: Rawson 1989: 250; Moles 1990: 300 with n. 15 with literature; cf. 'Philostratus' n. 74).

friendship with the emperor is a vehicle for political praxis at home
(see *Orr.* xl. 5, xliv. 12, xlvii. 13).[33]

Let us look at Dio's idea of monarchy more closely. In the
Orations on Kingship, especially in the first (i. 37–47) and the third
(iii. 50–138), Dio presents monarchy as 'the happy and divine system now in force' (iii. 50), referring to the natural power of the
strong over the weak which shows that 'the government of the
universe' is 'under the control of the first and best god' (ibid.). As
has been said, the good king in Dio's conception is not a divine
king. He believes in the gods' rule in order to show that he himself
is ruled by 'worthy rulers'.[34] His *pronoia* ('forethought') for other
men is guaranteed by the gods' own care of him (51). Dio goes
on to hold out the promise that the good king may come to be
accepted as a *daimôn*, a 'divine spirit', or as a *hêrôs*, a 'divine hero',
after his death (54, apparently an allusion to the imperial cult).[35] But
he stresses that he remains mortal and under the rule of the gods.[36]
In *Or.* liii *On Homer*, where Dio draws close parallels between his
own life and Homer's (liii. 9), he says that Homer shows that good
kings should follow the example set by Minos, who was Zeus'

[33] There is nothing to suggest any warmth between Trajan and Dio apart from
Philostratus' report of Dio sitting in Trajan's chariot and charming the emperor with
his words (*VS* 488 'he would often turn to Dio and say, "I don't know what you
are saying, but I love you as I love myself"'), a story which reflects Philostratus'
culturalist assumptions (cf. *VS* 491 [Favorinus], 589 [Hadrian of Tyre]); on Trajan's
real cultural level see n. 32. I cannot find in Pliny, *Letters* x. 81–2, any sign of the
'favore' on Trajan's part which Desideri diagnoses (1978: 2); see below, n. 182.

[34] So Moles 1990: 356.

[35] The good king believes in *daimones* and *hêrôes* which are 'souls of good
men . . . In confirming this opinion [*dogma*] he does no small favour to himself.' The
idea that good souls become daimons is standard Greek thought and accords with
Plutarch's understanding of apotheosis at *Romulus* 28 (above, 'Plutarch' n. 146).

Dio mentions the workings of the imperial cult only in *Or.* xxxv *In Celaenae in
Phrygia* 10 (high priests of Asia), 17 (expenses connected with sanctuaries or rites).
The first passage criticizes the vanity of the 'blessed ones' (the priests; on 'blessed
[*makarios*]' in Dio as a generally sarcastic term see Desideri 1978: 353 n. 36), the
second reminds Celaenae (the literary name of Apamea Kibôtos) that it has no
temple itself (and thus no right to call itself by the much sought-after title of 'temple
warden [*neôkoros*]', on which title see Robert 1967: 46–64 [Ephesus and elsewhere],
id. 1969: 281–9 [Laodicea ad Lycum]; Johnston 1984*b*; Price 1984*a*: 65 n. 47).

[36] Cf. i. 65 where it is emphasized that Heracles, who is shown the difference
between kingship and tyranny, is a mortal. In *Or.* xxxii. 25–6, where Dio (probably
in the Trajanic period: see Appendix C) is referring to the model king, we hear of
'kings who have become gods because of their concern for the common safety, real
protectors, good and just champions'; nothing should be built on this—it is part of
Dio's exhortation to the Alexandrians to improve their behaviour (he later says that
it is quite absurd to call any man 'god' or 'saviour', xxxii. 50).

associate and pupil, and should 'direct their rule looking to him, assimilating their character to god, as far as is humanly possible' (liii. 11). Again, in the third *Oration on Kingship* the good king in his care for men must imitate god 'as far as he can' (82). In *Or.* i the desirability of human imitation of god is evident from the titles men have bestowed upon Zeus. 'Zeus alone of the gods is given the name father and king and is also called *Polieus*, *Philios*, *Hetaireios*, *Homognios* [the God of Cities, of Friends, of Comrades, of Families], and in addition to these *Hikesios*, *Phuxios*, and *Xenios* [the God of Suppliants, of Refugees, of Strangers] and thousands of other epithets, all of them good and the cause of good things' (i. 39). Dio goes on to explain Zeus' titles as various aspects of his care for men. Hence 'all these functions must from the start be part of the function and appellation of the king' (41). He continues this important passage by describing the 'administration' (*dioikêsis*) of the universe. 'It journeys through infinite time continuously in infinite cycles guided by the good soul and a like *daimôn* and by *pronoia* and by the justest and best rule and makes us like itself, for we are through our nature, which is common with it, marshalled by one ordinance and law and share in the same polity' (i. 42). In charge of this 'administration' is Zeus, from whom all kings derive their 'power and stewardship' (i. 45). The king who behaves unjustly and flouts the example of Zeus will end up as Phaethon did (i. 46–7).

Dio ends this section by saying that now is not the time to expatiate on the subject of Zeus and the universe, things which require a more detailed treatment 'there may perhaps be leisure to present in the future' (i. 48). This treatment is indeed provided elsewhere in *Orr.* xii and xxxvi and in less detail in *Or.* xl. If we are right in thinking that the first kingship oration was delivered in late 99 or in 100 (Trajan's first full year in Rome as emperor),[37] Dio's discussion of the subject does appear to have been later, though not by much.[38] Some of his thoughts on divinity are also paralleled in

[37] AD 99: Desideri 1978: 350 n. 1 (with further literature); cf. Moles 1990: 333–4. AD 100: von Arnim 1898: 325; Jones 1978a: 118, 138. 100 is also the date of delivery of Pliny's *Panegyricus*; notions that he influenced Dio (Trisoglio 1972) or that Dio influenced him (Morr 1915 [non vidi]) are unprovable and unlikely (Jones 193 n. 33; Desideri 1978: 350 n. 1, 357–8 n. 71). It was during this visit to Rome that Dio won important favours for Prusa, notably its appointment as an assize centre (see *Orr.* xl. 33, xlv. 3–4; cf. xliv. 11; and below, nn. 148 ff.).

[38] Jones 1978a: 53, 135; Desideri 1978: 120, 267, 308 (xxxvi and xii are an 'adempimento' of i. 48), 361 n. 1 (xxxvi); but note that AD 97 has also been canvassed for xii (e.g. Döring 1979: 91 n. 26).

what is presumably an earlier work, *Or.* xxx *Charidemus*, earlier because it (supposedly) reflects the ideas of a recently deceased pupil, Charidemus.[39] These works illustrate Dio's serious Stoicizing beliefs about the divine monarchy of the universe, the kinship of humans and gods, and the relationship between the divine model of government and its human counterpart, including Rome's world empire.

In the important *Or.* xii, the *Olympicus, or On the First Conception of God*, Dio addresses his audience at Olympia on the nature of god, speaking before Phidias' famed statue of Zeus. At xii. 27–37 he outlines to them a largely Stoic picture of god and the world. Men have an innate conception of the gods and of the 'leader of the universe' owing to their kinship with the divine (their souls being for the Stoics fragments of the divine spirit in charge of the world). Earlier men, Dio says, understood the nature of god better than we do now because they lived closer to him. After discussing various ways in which man has tried to comprehend god, Dio imagines a trial scene where Phidias has been accused of presumptuously daring to fix the appearance of the god (48–54) and defends himself by comparing his effort with the ideas of the poets, especially Homer (62–9, 73–9). Whereas Homer's gods are sometimes mild, sometimes terrible, Phidias says his Zeus is 'peaceful and altogether gentle, inasmuch as he is guardian of a Greece that is free of faction and lives in concord' (73–4). Phidias continues by giving a list of the titles which illustrate Zeus' role as king and as the true father of his people (75–6). This list and its wording is more or less the same as that given in *Or.* i. 39–41.

Kinship with god is emphasized also in two of the three explanations of the life of man offered in *Or.* xxx *Charidemus* (26–7, 28–44). But it is in *Or.* xxxvi, the *Borystheniticus*, that Dio's thoughts on the matter are developed to their fullest. The role of this speech in voicing Dio's Hellenism has already been considered.[40] At issue now is its exposition of his thoughts on the monarchical ordering of the divine and human worlds.[41] He tells his audience in Prusa of the words he delivered to the citizens of Borysthenes (Olbia) during

[39] Von Arnim 1898: 283 pronounced himself strongly against the authenticity of the work (cf. Nilsson 1955–61: ii. 401 n. 2; Desideri 1978: 248 n. 42); but see Hirzel 1895: ii. 111–12; and esp. Wilhelm 1918.

[40] Above, 'Past' nn. 50–3.

[41] See Russell 1992: 20–3 for an analysis. Desideri 1978: 362 ff. n. 12 gives the essential bibliographical information, esp. on the Platonic and Stoic background, Binder 1905 (also on *Or.* xii) and the detailed study in François 1921; also important is Schofield 1991: 57–92.

a recent visit.[42] At the request of a certain Hieroson ('Preserver of Sacred Things') he had expounded the Stoic ('our') conception of the cosmos as an eternal living creature under the control of Zeus.[43] The present *diakosmêsis*, 'world order', which is 'governed by a single soul and force', may be compared to the organization of the human city (29–32). Dio has already spoken of the city earlier in the speech: it is 'a multitude of humans dwelling in the same place controlled by law' (20). The true model of such a city is, however, only to be looked for in heaven (22). With regard to the present world order Dio stresses again that the city it resembles is quite unlike the lawless city which is torn apart and factionalized by tyrants, democracies (*dêmoi*), 'boards of ten' (*dekarchiai*), and oligarchies, 'and all other such infirmities'. Rather, it is like the city which is governed by the 'soundest and best kingship and is actually subject to royal power in accordance with law in complete friendship and concord'. This is ordained by 'the leader of all heaven and the master of all being', the one the poets call the 'father of gods and men' (31–2). The poets, especially the ancient ones, know these things well (32–5). Hence, since all rational creatures represent one family with god, the world is Zeus' house (*oikos*) or, better, his city (36–7).[44]

Dio sums up this part of the speech by affirming once again the Stoic idea of the community of gods and men. He then embarks on an exciting myth about Zeus' rule which, he says, the Persian Magi learnt from Zoroaster and sing in 'secret rites' (39–60). Dio himself is insistent about the strangeness of the myth.[45] However, in appending something of this sort he recalls Plato, as he had been invited to do by Hieroson before (27), and in content the myth, which was once taken all too eagerly as genuine 'Zoroastrian' or 'Mithraic' lore, is now better understood as a deliberately colourful product of Greek thought.[46]

[42] On the date of the visit cf. Jones 1978a: 135 ('ca. 98 or later'); further speculation in Sheppard 1984: 158–60.

[43] The significant name Hieroson rests on a sure emendation (Russell 1992: 225).

[44] As it is in the third (and much the longest) explanation of the origin of mankind in *Or.* xxx. 28–44.

[45] 43: 'I may appear strange chanting a barbarian song after songs that were Hellenic and elegant; but the attempt must be made'; cf. 61.

[46] Mithraic: e.g. Binder 1905: 62 following Cumont; Bidez and Cumont 1938: i. 91–7, ii. 142–53; see Russell's comments 1992: 22–3, 231 ff. The pseudo-Platonic *Axiochus* ends with a Magian myth (271a ff.).

Stoic influence is again to the fore here, especially in the ideas of *ekpurôsis*, the fire which periodically destroys the universe, and *palingenesia*, its subsequent rebirth.[47] These rather exotic theories were discarded by the middle Stoics Boethus of Sidon and Panaetius of Rhodes. But Dio believed in them, as is shown not only by this speech and by *Or.* xl. 35–7 (see below), but also by his lost *Is the Cosmos Perishable?*, one of the last attested works of Stoic cosmology, which presumably mounted a defence of the matter.[48] Myth was the perfect vehicle for expressing such difficult material (as Plato had shown). The first part of Dio's story symbolizes the motions of the universe through four horses, representing the four elements—earth, water, air, fire—which the Stoics believed formed the universe in four concentric spheres. Periodically the horse of Zeus (fire) and the horse of Poseidon (water) get out of control and cause natural catastrophes of flood and fire (47–50). This is one sort of 'driving'; but there is also another sort when all the horses fuse together by fire, overcome by the horse of Zeus. At this point Zeus is left alone as Soul or Mind and is filled with a desire to recreate the world as we know it. 'Having performed and completed his task he showed the existent world as something beautiful and extraordinarily lovely, far more brilliant indeed than we see it now' (50–60). At the end of the speech Dio apologizes to his Prusan audience for the obscurity of the myth (61), just as he apologized in the *Olympicus* (xii. 84, cf. 43), and as he does when he draws an analogy with the workings of the cosmos in *Or.* xl during his speech to the Prusans on concord with Apamea (xl. 36).[49]

What *Orr.* xii and xxxvi show is Dio's firm belief in the existence of a community of gods and men in the universe, which is under the rule of Zeus. *Or.* xxxvi also shows that Dio did not believe that the monarchical rule of Zeus (or Soul or Mind or whatever divine providence is called) was readily translatable into an ideal kingship

---

[47] For a basic account see Sandbach 1975: 78–9; Pohlenz 1947–9: i. 78–81, ii. 45–7 (on Dio).

[48] Boethus and Panaetius: Philo, *On the Eternity of the World* 76–8, Panaetius frr. 64–9 van Straaten. *Is the Cosmos Perishable?*—cf. above n. 3. The idea of *ekpurôsis* is accepted by the 1st- or 2nd-c. AD Stoic cosmologist, Cleomedes (*On the Circular Motion of the Heavenly Bodies*, p. 6 Ziegler).

[49] Cf. further xi. 6 ('some of these will not understand, some will pretend a feeling of contempt . . . others will try to refute' what Dio has to say about Homer and Troy), liv. 4 not many understand the words of Socrates (one of Dio's adopted personas).

among men. When he defines human organization in this speech in terms of a city, he stresses a thoroughgoing legality as the essence of true government, which can only happen under monarchical rule (xxxvi. 20, 31). However, 'a good city made from elements totally good no one knows to have existed before among mortals, nor is it worthwhile to imagine that it will ever exist in future (unless it is a city of the blessed gods in heaven)' (22). This limitation of the potential of human government is complemented at the end of the myth by Dio's remarks on the beauty of god's original creation and the decline of today's world. There is no reason why we should not take these thoughts as Dio's serious beliefs.

The combination of Dio's ideas on monarchy in the *Orations on Kingship*, the *Olympicus*, and the *Borystheniticus* makes it extremely doubtful that he ever believed Trajan was an ideal, divine monarch, or indeed that Trajan was a particularly close imitation of such. His real opinions about the qualities of this emperor are not recoverable, though we can say—for what it is worth—that his stringent criticisms of Roman governors never include direct criticism of the emperor. But many passages outside the *Orations on Kingship* make it plain that Dio did not see the Roman Empire itself as a perfect monarchy on earth, even potentially. The ending of the *Olympicus* is interesting in this respect, for, as we have seen, this is a speech where Dio exalts the operation of monarchical power in the universe. The final section of the work is a prosopopoeia by Zeus in which he praises the 'whole of Hellas' (?) and the Eleans for running the Olympic festival 'beautifully and properly',[50] and for 'offering sacrifices that are as magnificent as present circumstances allow [*ek tôn parontôn*], and above all for holding this most renowned trial of fitness, strength, and speed, as it was in the beginning, and because she preserves the customs of the festivals and of the mysteries which she inherits. But it worries me to see that, "no good care is taken of her, but wretched age is what you have and foul squalor to go with it and shameful dress"' (85). Dio leaves his audience here with Odysseus' remarks to his aged father Laertes, taken from *Odyssey* xxiv. 249–50. Although the pessimism of this ending accords with Dio's initial suggestion of the sadness of the

---

[50] There is a slight crux here: τάδε μὲν οὕτως, † Ἠλεῖοι δὲ καὶ † ἡ σύμπασα Ἑλλάς, καλῶς καὶ προσηκόντως ἐπιτελεῖ, κτλ. There is no cause to delete Ἠλεῖοι with von Arnim; cf. Russell 1992: 211.

speech to come (1), the editors have been puzzled.[51] What does Dio mean?

In the introductory section of the *Olympicus* (16) Dio tells his audience that he may seem as if he is 'straying in his words', just as he has in fact been leading the life of a wanderer (*alômenos*) during his exile. With these remarks he recalls the persona he adopted at that time when, as he puts it to the emperor, 'wandering in exile . . . I visited as many lands as I could with the appearance and dress of a vagabond, now among Greeks, now among barbarians, "begging for morsels, not cauldrons or swords"' (*Or.* i. 50). Here he also quotes from the *Odyssey*, in this case the lines describing Odysseus in disguise as a beggar on Ithaca (xvii. 217 ff.). At *Olympicus* 16, although there are other references for 'the educated' in his audience to catch (cf. 43),[52] the Odyssean persona is again relevant and important.[53] So, at *Olympicus* 85 Dio in the guise of Zeus addresses Greece using the words Odysseus also in disguise used to his father (remember that Dio has throughout been addressing Zeus as the divine 'father'). The context of the words Odysseus used is rather revealing. He begins by commending Laertes for the care he has lavished on his garden; so Zeus is made to praise the care Greece expends on the festival. He then asks him not to be angry if he says, as he does, that Laertes is not cared for himself (*Odyssey* xxiv. 244–50). Odysseus suggests as an explanation for Laertes' squalor that 'it is not because of your lack of work that your master does not care for you, still less is it clear that there is a slavish appearance or stature to be seen in you; rather you seem like a man who is a king, you seem like one who sleeps soft when he has bathed and eaten. For this is the way of old men. But tell me this and declare it truly, Whose slave are you?' (251–7).

The *pepaideumenoi*, the educated class who Dio trusts 'will keep up and share the labour till the end' (*Olympicus* 43), would certainly

---

[51] Cf. Geel 1840: 122–3; Russell 1992: 210–11. Geel quotes Morel's belief (repr. in Reiske 1784: ii. 642–3) that the lines ('mirum sane exitum orationis') applied to the statue itself; he was also attracted by the suggestion of Reiske 1784: i. 418 n. 34 that they were an allusion to Dio's own 'sordes vestitus'. Only Highet saw the way to the truth (1983: 76).

[52] Cf. Socrates—often Dio's model and *porte-parole* (*Orr.* iii, xiii, liv, lv; Döring 1979: 80–113)—at Plato, *Republic* 394d (wind-blown argument), *Theaetetus* 172d–e (take as long as you need to get to the truth—a passage alluded to at *Olympicus* 38).

[53] On Dio's use of this characterization see Höistad 1948: 94–102 (esp. its Cynic overtones); Jones 1978*a*: 46–8; Desideri 1978: 174–5 n. 2; Moles 1990: 319.

have recalled the context of the famous lines he quotes as his parting remarks. It is apparent from this context that when Dio comments on Greece's decline he is not suggesting she is suffering from a self-induced 'moral' slavery like that, for example, which he attributes to the Cilicians in *Or.* lxxx.[54] Rather, the message at the end of the *Olympicus* seems to be that Greece is tending her garden as well 'as present circumstances allow' for someone else's benefit. Her shameful apparel is due to her subjection to a master. Dio makes it perfectly clear on a number of occasions that the Greek world is firmly under Roman rule. In the second *Tarsian Oration* (*Or.* xxxiv. 39, 51) he comes close to implying that this rule will amount to slavery, if the Greeks let it.[55] In the *Olympicus* it is again a matter that 'worries' him. His words certainly recall what he has said at the beginning of the speech about the Romans' desire to exercise control over the Getae (xii. 20: Dio had gone to the war between the Romans and the Dacians 'in my desire to see men fighting for empire and power, others for freedom and fatherland').[56] Taken together with the explicit rejection in the speech of the violent side of Homer's Zeus, this may appear as an adverse comment on Roman imperialism under Trajan (cf. again *Or.* iv), though the passage is far too brief to support firm generalizations. We probably can go as far as saying, however, that Dio's allusion to continuing Roman imperial ambitions ('men fighting for empire and power') would hardly be obscure to his present audience, who are encouraged to think of this again in the rather abrupt ending which regards the Greek world itself.

Into the pessimistic ending of the speech we should also be prepared to read Dio's Stoic thoughts on the workings of the universe. In an earlier part of the speech he states that the first men knew god best and were best able to appreciate him (27–8). It is a common idea in antiquity that the first age is the best age. Some of the Stoics certainly held it. It is an idea that Dio himself develops in the *Borystheniticus*. As we have seen, in that speech he praises the monarchical government of Zeus and congratulates him on the

[54] The slavery in lxxx is voluntaristic. Note that the title of *Or.* lxxx is given by the MSS as *On the Freedom of Those in Cilicia*, with the exception of B (Parisinus 2958), where it is simply *On Freedom*.

[55] Below n. 118, text before n. 123. Cf. Plutarch, above, 'Plutarch' text after n. 111.

[56] For the wording here cf. *Or.* xxxii. 43. Dio's visit to the Getae is mentioned also by Philostratus *VS* 488.

creation of the 'present world-order'. The world, however, when newly created was 'far more brilliant indeed than we see it now. For all other works of craftsmen [*dêmiourgoi*] are better and brighter when they are new immediately from the artistic hands of their maker' (xxxvi. 58). Dio goes on in xxxvi to observe that this is true also of plants and animals, with human beings as the only exception. These remarks accord with his theory of the cyclical destruction of the world through fire and its rebirth from that element. At any stage after its (re-)creation the world is in a gradual, inevitable decline. Hence he envisages the present day as representing a less attractive and a less perfect version of what was once created. The particular expression of this idea in *Or.* xii is in the final focus on Greece's 'wretched age' and 'foul squalor', a condition Dio very strongly implies is due to her loss of political freedom and subordination to a master.

We can take this matter further—albeit tentatively—by suggesting that some implications of Dio's cosmology in *Or.* xxxvi are relevant to his view of the prospects of Rome's empire. Rather than hailing the birth of a new political era in a world freshly created,[57] Dio states in this speech, as we have just seen, that the world is currently at some point of decline in the inevitable cycle between creation and destruction (xxxvi. 58). This cycle rendered political apparatuses otiose. Compare *Or.* xl *In his Fatherland, On Concord with the Apameans.* Here Dio counsels the Prusans about the need for concord with their neighbours, the Apameans, as part of a defence of his own policies at home. Having lectured them on the evils of discord and the advantages to be gained from concord (xl. 25–34), he appends an extensive analogy with the workings of the natural world and the harmony that can be seen in operation there (35–41). As in *Or.* xxxvi the elements are under the control of 'the first and greatest god' (xl. 36; cf. xxxvi. 35). Mutual friendship and eternal concord ensure the permanence of this system. Even during the 'predominance' of the *aithêr*, wherein the psychic force dwells, friendship and concord are maintained and everything proceeds according to the 'law of reason' (37). The point of all this for the Prusans and Apameans is that there is an inevitability in the greater concordant processes of the natural world that makes their disputes with each other pointless and which they must learn to emulate.

[57] As is suggested by Russell 1992: 23, 233 (quoting Tacitus, *Agricola* 3. 1).

A passage in the *Rhodian Oration* (*Or.* xxxi) enables us to link this belief about the workings of the universe to Rome.[58] Dio is in the middle of attacking the Rhodians' habit of changing the names on their statues in order to honour Romans. The statues were originally erected, he says, 'because of benefits [to you], whereas many of those now receiving honour are being courted because of their might [*ischus*]'. He asks which of these is the better reason for bestowing honours. 'Assuming that not all of them have rightly been given these honours, the men themselves will not be unaware who is more likely to hold them uncertainly. For everyone knows that benefaction is far more permanent than power, since there is no might that time will not remove, but benefaction it cannot touch' (xxxi. 43). Dio's words here must be taken first in their context, of course. The *Rhodian Oration* deals with a Rhodian problem and its criticisms are largely of the Rhodians' actions. Criticism of Romans (41: the Rhodians may be honouring 'men who are not very decent [*epieikeis*] . . . which you will of course not say, if you are sensible', cf. 28, 135; 66–8 on 'that continuous and lengthy [civil] war'; 111: Roman interference in the Olympic games) can be set beside the stinging remarks about the Athenians (116–23). Nevertheless, there is a strongly voiced idea in the speech that today's men are simply not as worthy of honours as yesterday's, who were 'always . . . superior by nature' (75, 80, 93, 124, 126, cf. 163). Today's men are the Romans.[59] Here, then, Dio's belief in the decline of the present world clearly influences his attitude towards Rome. As men Romans are no worse than other groups today.[60] That said, they are the ones in power, which in this speech is why they are given the reinscribed statues Dio so deplores.

The Roman elite were keen adherents of Stoic morality.[61] The philosophy of a world system which stressed personal roles and

---

[58] On the date of *Or.* xxxi see below, Appendix C.

[59] xxxi. 93 'Suppose that all of those the city is courting are [good and worthy of honour]—and we must pray that all of them are good, especially the leaders [*hêgoumenous*; cf. 26, 105 *hêgemonas*, 110, 149; Robert 1960*b*: 327–30 (Lycia and elsewhere)]; but they are not equal to those great men [of the past]. How could they be? They themselves would not even claim to be only a little inferior to them, but would be afraid to say that sort of thing.' Interestingly, a lack of Roman influence has been noted on Rhodes in the early imperial period: Fraser 1977: 74–5.

[60] Dio's claim that the Rhodians alone preserve something of true Hellenic spirit (xxxi. 18, 163) is addressed to their 'orgoglio nazionalistico' (Desideri 1978: 112–13).

[61] Bodson 1967; Brunt 1973 (with specific discussion of Dio's attitudes), id. 1975; Rist 1982; Shaw 1985; Rutherford 1989: 59–80.

duties fitted in well with their conceptions of themselves and their needs. In adapting Stoicism to a Roman environment Posidonius had stressed the integration between man and nature and linked the fortunes of the imperial race with the blessings of Italian geography. His picture of the world under Roman dominion was drawn on by Strabo for his own pro-Roman account of world geography and influenced Livy's great history of Rome.[62] In theory orthodox Stoicism could also find room for an eternal Roman Empire, though not quite in the way it was usually imagined. For one of the peculiarities of the idea of an everlasting cycle of creation and destruction of the universe was that each successive world was more or less like the one before it, since it was made from the same elements on the same design.[63] In practice Roman Stoics rarely mentioned the orthodox cosmological features of the Stoic system; their interests centred on its practical ethical applications. When they did mention them, they took their lead from Panaetius, who was known for rejecting the idea of world conflagration.[64] How does Dio fit in here? If he did accept the idea that the world would be recreated with the same personalities and history (an idea which Origen quite reasonably says was embarrassing to some Stoics),[65] he would necessarily have accepted the recurrence of the Roman Empire. Further, the rational control of the world by Zeus might encourage us after all to say that he thought the Empire was for the best. However, the several passages where he criticizes Roman rule, including the end of *Or.* xii, make this rather unlikely. On his cosmological scheme Rome was necessary, but she was also—as he points out—a product of the world in decline. The recreation of the world would mean a long period of history with better people to come before the Romans.[66]

---

[62] Malitz 1983: 42 ff., 359 ff. Strabo—cf. esp. v. 3. 7–8 (C 234–6), vi. 4. 2 (C 286–8), xvii. 3. 24–5 (C 839–40). Livy—Walsh 1961: 53 ff.

[63] *SVF* ii. 624, 625, 626.

[64] Cf. Cicero, *On the Nature of the Gods* ii. 85: this cosmos (*ornatus*) is either everlasting or will endure for a very, very long time. Panaetius—cf. above, n. 48. The idea of world conflagration is still known to Seneca and Cornutus in the 1st c. AD, though they are not particularly interested in it: Lapidge 1989: 1401, 1404.

[65] *Against Celsus* v. 20 (*SVF* ii. 626).

[66] It may be that to go this far with Dio is to build on sand (especially given the loss of *Is the Cosmos Perishable?*). But it is worth noting that the Peripatetic Alexander of Aphrodisias later denounces the Stoics before Severus and Caracalla for holding ideas about providence, fate, and personal irresponsibility that are subversive of the emperors' own good intentions: see *On Fate* esp. 39 Bruns (repr. Sharples

Before moving on, it is worth remarking the differences between
Dio and Plutarch in these matters. Plutarch's notion of divine aid
in the formation of the Roman Empire is based on his faith that god
helps mankind and has assisted Rome because of her beneficial
government. Dio's joy in god's control of the universe is tempered
by an unease about the state of the present world, focusing on
Greece's decline under Rome. His thoughts are elusive, sketchy,
and difficult to interpret. But the interpretation here offered does
not jar with his views towards Roman government in Bithynia and
elsewhere as we see them in the speeches to the cities.

SPEECHES TO THE CITIES

I turn now to Dio's contacts with the Greek cities. I shall be concerned with passages which illustrate his view of Rome as a Greek.
Before moving to these a word may be said about the chronology
of the works which will be discussed or referred to. Dio's city
speeches are usually divided between the periods before and after
his exile. *Orr.* xxxi (the *Rhodian*), which I shall not be discussing
in any detail, and xxxii (the *Alexandrian*), which I shall not be
discussing at all, are mostly thought of as pre-exilic, especially the
former—though both speeches could and perhaps should be considered Trajanic.[67] The date of *Or.* xi (the *Trojan*) is unknown (and
not terribly important for my purposes). The other speeches, including those to the Bithynian cities (which offer the main interest
here and in the next section), are all post-exile.[68] It is worth observing, that if *Orr.* xxxi and xxxii are to be assigned to the earlier part
of Dio's career along with the one speech that must be early, *Or.*
xlvi *Before he was a Philosopher, In his Fatherland* (which I shall

1983: 212 with 270–1). As is usual in ancient polemic, Alexander does not name his
opponents, and the suggestion has been made that his silence is partly due also to
an awareness of the importance of Stoic morality to the Roman elite, which he
wished to keep secure from his attack on Stoic cosmology: Thillet 1984: p. xc.

[67] See Appendix C.

[68] The first *Tarsian Oration*, which Desideri dates to Vespasian (see Appendix C),
must be after the exile, since Dio refers to himself as like the wise, experienced
Odysseus going about in disguise (xxxiii. 14–15). On the second *Tarsian Oration* see
Jones 1978a: 136–7 (rightly rejecting the late dating by Kienast 1971 [AD 113], on
which see below, n. 115).

not be considering),[69] Dio's political activities and attitude to Rome
would seem to display a clear continuity.

I shall start this section with several pro-Roman comments Dio
makes (or comments which have been taken as such). The clearest
example of a pro-Roman stance can be found in *Or.* xli *To the
Apameans On Concord*, which forms a pair with *Or.* xl *In his
Fatherland, On Concord with the Apameans*. Apamea, a port on
the Sea of Marmara, was about fifteen and a half miles or twenty-
five kilometres from Prusa. The original foundation of Myrleia was
destroyed by Prusias I of Bithynia, who refounded the city and
named it after his wife. It thus shared the same founder as Prusa
itself. This explains Dio's identification of 'common ties of marriage
and children and constitutions [*politeiai*] and sacrifices to the gods
and festivals and spectacles' (xli. 10, cf. xl. 27). But Apamea was also
quite different from Prusa. At some time in the Roman Triumviral
period it had become a Roman colony with the name Colonia Julia
Concordia Apamea.[70] Since there is no sign of a 'double' foundation
or of a retention of Greek civic institutions,[71] Dio's talk of shared
politeiai must be seen as an appeal to history. He is well aware of
the differences, for as he points out to his audience at Apamea his
maternal grandfather and his mother had been made Roman citizens
and citizens of Apamea by the 'then *autokratôr*' and his father had
been elected a citizen of Apamea by the city itself (xli. 6).[72] Dio tells
the Prusans that the Apameans have in fact 'a special constitution'
and great influence with the governors ('if they behave' xl. 22).[73] To

---

[69] The title of *Or.* xlvi is part of the School tradition; see above, n. 11. The dating
rests on the biographical information that Dio has only a wife and a small child (xlvi.
13), whereas by the Trajanic perod he had an adult son (xl. 2; xliv. 8; l. 5, 10) and
several other children (xli. 6); see further von Arnim 1899: 374–6.

[70] Magie 1950: ii. 1268 n. 34; Jones 1978a: 91; Desideri 1978: 453 n. 1; Salmeri
1982: 15.

[71] Mitchell 1979: 436.

[72] See Desideri 1978: 454 ff. n. 9 on the problem of the relation between Apamean
citizenship and Roman citizenship (surely separate). The Pompeian *lex provinciae*
of Bithynia (on which see Sherwin-White 1966: 669–73, 718, 720–1, 724–6; de Ste.
Croix 1981: 529–30) forbade the sharing of citizenship between the Bithynian cities,
though as Pliny and Trajan noted in reinforcing it, this rule had long been ignored
by the curial class (Pliny, *Letters* x. 114–15), as we see in Dio's own citizenships at
Apamea, Nicomedia, and (probably) Nicaea (above, n. 2). Apamea's 'special constitution' perhaps exempted it from such restrictions.

[73] Apamea's most tangible privilege was its possession of *ius Italicum*, i.e. full
ownership of its land and complete immunity from tribute: Sherwin-White 1973:
318–21; Salmeri 1982: 15; Millar 1992: 407.

the Apameans he says he believes their character reflects the 'genuine character of those men and of that blessed city by which you
were sent here to live as friends among friends'. That city is superior to 'the rest of mankind' in fairness (*epieikeia*) and humanity
(*philanthrôpia*) more than it is in fortune and power. It 'both
shares citizenship, laws, and public offices [*politeiai, nomoi, archai*]
without reserve—considering no man of worth a stranger, and at
the same time it safeguards justice for all alike' (xli. 9). Dio exhorts
Apamea to live up to its foundation, since among other things it
has shared its own offices with Prusans. 'You have made common
these solemn privileges which are characteristic of the Romans'
city' (10).

These remarks look promising. But it must be remembered that
they are made in a particular context in a particular place: Dio
would hardly have come to Apamea and not have made traditional
pro-Roman comments of this sort. In this sense his praises are
compatible with those he addresses to the Nicomedians in *Or.* xxxviii
and to the Nicaeans in *Or.* xxxix. What Dio says of Rome in *Or.*
xli is comparable not with other comments in his own works but
with Aelius Aristides' *To Rome* (*Or.* xxvi), where Rome's willingness to share political benefits is heavily emphasized.[74] Aristides'
speech, as we shall see, was delivered at Rome before the imperial
family and is avowedly encomiastic. We have to be rather careful
about accepting what it says at face value. The same is true of Dio
here.[75] The favourable comments in *Or.* xli have to be seen in line
with the overall context of the speech.

As a Roman citizen Dio knew full well the advantages of sharing
the Roman franchise and the use of Roman law. There is no need
to think his praise of these items is insincere in any way. Thus he
spends much of the third *Oration on Kingship* advising Trajan to
keep a good retinue of friends about him (86–127).[76] General
reasons aside, selection from a wide pool of men is necessary to
find governors, commanders, and administrators (128–32), a clear
reference to the use of provincials in the equestrian and senatorial

[74] See below, 'Aristides' nn. 92, 99 (Aristides does not associate *epieikeia* with
Rome); cf. Galen's flattery of the sharing Severus and Caracalla at 'Galen' n. 40.
[75] Note e.g. Salmeri 1982: 112–13 backing up his pro-Roman interpretation of
Dio with Aristides' speech.
[76] Using the textual ordering of Emperius and von Arnim (i.e. here §§ 86–111 +
128–32 + 112–27). Cf. Salmeri 1982: 121–3, id. 1991: 558–61.

services and in the army. But how far he thought this was really possible or desirable, we do not know.[77] Above all it is noteworthy that neither at Apamea nor elsewhere in his works does he praise Rome for the benefits she brings provincials as a whole, except for 'justice' (xli. 9).

In this regard it is worth noting Dio's one definite allusion to the Roman peace, the benefit of Roman rule moderns often think Greeks should appreciate most.[78] Dio's reference—in the *Rhodian Oration*—is not very flattering. At xxxi. 125 in the course of his arguments to the Rhodians against reinscribing the statues of their old benefactors he notes that other peoples, unlike themselves, have demolished their city walls or let them fall down 'because of the peace and the slavery, of which all pray for the first, peace, while the other is no longer a sign of baseness [*kakia*]; but treating ancient benefactors like this is due to ingratitude'. Slavery (explicitly not 'moral' slavery) is the price of the world peace.[79] Nevertheless, Dio is quite aware that many cities did enjoy a fair amount of autonomy under Rome. As we shall see, he tried to obtain autonomy for Prusa itself. So here the Caunians are the slaves of Rome (and of Rhodes: 125); Phrygians, Egyptians, and Libyans are no better off (113–14); but Rhodes itself enjoys 'freedom' (*eleutheria*) (112).[80] Indeed, Dio informs his audience that the Romans are not 'so stupid and ignorant as to choose that none of their subjects [*tôn huph' hautois*] should be free and noble, but would rather rule over slaves' (111).[81] On the other hand, though Rhodes is prosperous and distinguished (40, 55, 62, 100 ff., 106, 157–9, 163), she is also afraid of Rome (113 'if it is the case that you are always in wait for their anger or hatred, then you are in a state of extreme wretchedness

---

[77] The first known senator from Bithynia was [Ca]tilius Longus adlected under Vespasian; he was from Apamea and so of Italian origin: Halfmann 1979: 29, 115 no. 18; *IK* xxxiii (Apamea) 2; Arrian (*cos. suf.* 129) is the first known Greek senator. Cf. above, 'Plutarch' n. 103.

[78] See e.g. Nutton 1978: 210.

[79] Cf. and ctr. Ps.-Longinus, *On the Sublime* 44 on the decline of great literature and the 'equitable slavery' (here probably moral slavery) of the present day (with e.g. Kennedy 1972: 450–2, who plausibly dates the work to the time of Augustus, though a mid- or late 1st c. date is possible; Russell 1964, id. 1981 for analysis).

[80] Dio was naturally aware of the precariousness of such 'freedom': *Or.* xliv. 11–12. The evidence for the real meaning of 'freedom' for cities under Rome is discussed by Bernhardt 1971; see also Millar 1992: 430–1. On the freedom of Rhodes, which was granted and removed by Rome several times, see Jones 1978a: 27–8.

[81] Reading μηδέν' (de Budé, Cohoon).

and total insecurity'), a feeling Dio tries to dispel. The *Rhodian Oration* is not crudely anti-Roman, as used to be believed;[82] but it is certainly ambivalent towards the merits of her rule.

A pro-Roman commentary has also been discovered at the end of the *Trojan Oration*. This speech was delivered at Ilium, the Greek city occupying the site of ancient Troy, which Roman official tradition sanctioned as the mother city of Rome.[83] In its way it is one of Dio's best speeches, a rhetorical *tour de force* where he argues at length (in what is his second longest surviving piece) that Troy was not captured by the Greeks, but was in fact the victor in the Trojan War. The speech is intentionally playful, as well as reflecting Dio's serious interest in exegesis of the poets and especially of Homer (cf. *Orr.* xii, xxxvi, liii, lv, lvii). Although he says his audience will not enjoy it (xi. 4 ff.), its influence (and the controversy it caused) in later literature suggests well enough that they did.[84] Towards the end Dio says he wishes to 'defend' Homer. There is nothing wrong in going along with his falsehoods because they were at least less serious than those he had told about the gods and because they gave encouragement to 'the Greeks of those times so they should not be alarmed, if there was a war between them and the people of Asia, as was expected' (147). Dio then points out that, if someone should object to what he says about the Greeks, he could say, 'but the situation is no longer as it was, and there is no fear that any of the inhabitants of Asia will ever come against Greece. For both Greece and Asia are subject to others [*huph' heterois*]' (150). With these words he refers, of course, to Rome. It is probably correct to hold that the occasion itself has prompted the comments.[85] This also accounts for the story of the Trojan origin of Rome, which Dio advances at 137–42. Hector sent Helenus and Aeneas to found colonies. Aeneas 'occupied Italy, the most fortunate land in Europe ... He was king of Italy and founded the greatest city of them all.' Hector told him that his descendants would rule Europe and Asia. 'From the strength and judgement and through the good fortune of its people the colony was powerful immediately and for

[82] See e.g. Schnayder 1927: 140–2 with reference to xxxi. 113; cf. Schmid 1887–96: i. 38–9 n. 13.

[83] Magie 1950: i. 82, 542.

[84] Brancacci 1985: 275 ff., cf. Kindstrand 1973: 141–62. Mantero 1966: 145–224 offers good comparative material from Philostratus' *Homerkritik*.

[85] Jones 1978a: 18.

ever more' (142). It cannot be ascertained how far Dio believed any of this (which is hardly lavish praise), since, as at Apamea, the remarks are heavily contextualized. For this reason there is no cause to see the speech as an attempt to ennoble Rome's origins.[86] Dio is telling his audience what it wanted to hear, and we can go no further than his rhetoric.

The contexts in which the Apamean and Trojan speeches were delivered, then, make it very difficult to interpret them as pro-Roman. True, Dio did not have to make the remarks he makes. But we will notice that it is not only the tone of the comments which is linked to the context: the particular items of praise (political participation in *Or.* xli, Rome's glorious foundation in *Or.* xi) are also context-specific. Which is to say that general praise of Rome is not on offer, as it surely should be, if there was genuine admiration behind the remarks. It is time now to consider other, less favourable verdicts, which recall Dio's comments in the *Rhodian Oration.* Since these are not given to cities at variance with Rome, the political context can be taken as relatively neutral, and it may be argued that what Dio has to say in these passages is a better guide to how he really felt about the Empire.

The works I shall be looking at here are *Orr.* xiii (*In Athens, On his Exile*) together with xxi (*On Beauty*), xxxiii–xxxiv (the *Tarsian Orations*), and xxxviii (*To the Nicomedians, On Concord with the Nicaeans*). These speeches, and those at Prusa which I shall look at in the next section, well show Dio's self-consciousness before an audience and his desire to be seen to give serious and profitable advice. As I have already suggested, claims of 'friendship' (*philia*) with the emperor look like a way of furthering Dio's standing and of controlling rivals. Criticism of Rome, including outright attacks on the governors, is a means of asserting his independence as a man who has the Greeks' best interests at heart. Importantly, these texts offer no confirmation of the suggestion that Dio was an agent of the emperor at Tarsus (or at Rhodes or Alexandria), or that he was carrying out a programme of urban renewal in Bithynia on his behalf.[87]

We can start with *Or.* xiii *In Athens, On his Exile.* This speech is post-exilic and may well have been delivered in AD 101 as Dio was

---

[86] Desideri 1978: 433.
[87] Among others Palm 1959: 132; Kienast 1971; Desideri 1978: 136, 399 with 450 n. 66. See further below, nn. 115, 147.

returning from Rome.[88] It is important for Dio's self-presentation
as a man who had survived exile through philosophy and who was
in demand by audiences to lecture on moral topics (1–13). Through
the mask of Socrates Dio upbraids the Athenians for their dependence on the traditional Greek educational diet of music, sport, and
literature, which has had no effect on their successes or failures
over the years (16–28). When he went to Rome, he says, he had
faced the same requests for lectures and spoke to 'many people
gathered together in the same place' (29–31). Dio advised the Romans to obtain teachers of morals 'not caring whether they were
Greeks or Romans, or a Scythian or an Indian (if any of them can
teach these things)' (32). 'Only then, I said, will your city be great
and strong and ruling according to truth. For now at any rate its
greatness is suspect and not at all safe' (34).

Dio's primary point of view here is a moral one, since he goes on
to speak of the Romans' expensive decorations and furnishings.[89]
On the other hand, since moral and political thought are intimately
linked in the Greek mind from the beginning, it seems muddled to
try to separate a moral attack totally from its political implications.
The point is sometimes made that there were many Romans who
criticized Rome's vices; but it is surely a different matter for a non-
Roman to do so, and we certainly should not brush aside such
reproaches by simply labelling them as 'moral'. We may in fact
have an example of criticisms Dio delivered at Rome in *Or.* lxxix
On Wealth, which is addressed to 'the greatest and most powerful
of cities' (1).[90] Here he discourses on 'our stupidity' in voluntarily
paying over silver to foreign peoples in return for 'little fragile
stones and animal bones', that is, for amber and ivory (5–6). He
then goes on to list the usual series of empires—Assyria, Media,
Persia, Macedon—which have each fallen prey to love of wealth.[91]
The next item on this list, which Dio leaves out, is by convention
Rome herself.[92] In this speech moral failings and political ones go

---

[88] Jones 1978a: 53–4.
[89] Cf. Musonius Rufus frr. xix–xx = Lutz 1947: 120–6.
[90] Delivery at Rome: Moles 1983b against Sheppard 1982. This is probably right,
though note that in one of the two major MSS through which Dio's works have
come down to us, B (Parisinus 2958), the title of the speech is *On Wealth of the
[Cities] in Cilicia* (Περὶ πλούτου τῶν ἐν Κιλικίᾳ—a similar ascription is added to the
title of *Or.* lxxx—Τῶν ἐν Κιλικίᾳ περὶ ἐλευθερίας—by all MSS except Parisinus 2958,
as noted above, n. 54).
[91] Cf. *Or.* xxxiii. 26–7.
[92] Desideri 1978: 175–6 n. 5, 233–4; in general Swain 1940.

together as love of money leads inexorably to the loss of political power. Regarding *Or.* xiii itself, we do not know, of course, that what Dio claims to have said to the Romans was actually said. What we can see is his concern to inform his Greek audience of his properly critical conduct towards their rulers.

Roman immorality and Roman power are closely associated in *Or.* xxi *On Beauty*, which may be examined at this point. This dialogue with two speakers has been dated to the period of Dio's exile because of the statement that everyone would 'now' like to see Nero still alive (xxi. 9).[93] A rather different point of view makes the speech pro-Domitianic because its arguments against male castration accord with a policy of that emperor.[94] There is certainly an attack in the work on Nero's treatment and castration of his catamite Sporus (6; not named), and Nero's downfall is ascribed to this (9).[95] But we are dealing here with Dio's own sexual politics and in particular his hatred of homosexuality (of which I have said something before and to which I shall return shortly). The work is plainly anti-Neronian but also—if it is pressed in this matter—hardly pro-Domitianic.

More interesting than the attack on Nero's depravity are the comments Dio makes on how the Romans choose their emperors. For a man who reached adulthood under Nero, witnessed the events of 68–9, then saw the reign of Domitian, a certain cynicism is only to be expected. The main speaker in the dialogue says, 'Wherever and whenever they have to appoint a king [*basileus*], they choose the richest man, the one from whom they expect to receive the most money. They do not care what sort of man he is in any other respect, even if he intends to castrate them all when he has taken office—all of them including those who have received cash—and to deprive them of everything they own' (8). It is difficult to reduce this to moral criticism devoid of political content. It is quite possible that we really should attribute the remarks made here to the period of the exile. In which case they are perhaps the views of a man temporarily embittered.[96] The minor speaker certainly criticizes the major one for 'finding out reasons to disparage human

---

[93] Von Arnim 1898: 296 with specific reference to the false Nero who received Parthian support in *c.*88 (Tacitus, *Histories* i. 2, Suetonius, *Nero* 57. 2).

[94] Desideri 1978: 190; cf. Suetonius, *Domitian* 7. 1.

[95] Cf. Tacitus, *Histories* i. 16 Galba on Nero: 'quem . . . sua immanitas, sua luxuria cervicibus publicis depulerunt.'

[96] Cf. Jones 1978a: 128.

affairs' (10). His point is in turn rebutted (11–12). What is more important is that forceful disparagement of wealth and luxury is voiced by Dio also in the kingship speeches, especially through the medium of Diogenes' remarks to Alexander/Trajan on the *philochrêmatos daimôn* (the 'avaricious spirit') in *Or.* iv. 91–100.[97] Again, moral criticism does not come down to vague generalizations about the state of the human race: in *Or.* xxi it focuses on the Roman king himself.[98]

I turn now to some of Dio's speeches of advice to cities, beginning with the *Tarsian Orations*. These two speeches (*Orr.* xxxiii and xxxiv) to the leading city of Cilicia are discrepant in tone. The first has much in common with the *Alexandrian Oration*, which reproves the Alexandrians for their addiction to theatre and racing. It is an attack on Tarsus' rumbustious morality carried out in a lighthearted and rather witty style. I include a discussion of it here because it shows well Dio's focus on morals in the political community. This touches on Rome, for there is a particular connection with a theme voiced in *Or.* xxi and with an anti-Roman remark Dio makes in *Or.* xxxvi. Dio spends much of his time in the first *Tarsian Oration* denouncing what he refers to allusively—or perhaps literally—as 'snorting' or 'snoring' (xxxiii. 33 *rhengkein*). He finishes by terming his speech 'this relaxed and weak message of encouragement' (62); but his subject at this point (and probably throughout), homosexuality, shows how serious he is.[99] As has been said, Dio

---

[97] Cf. i. 21, ii. 75, iii. 40.

[98] One other interesting point in *Or.* xxi is the major speaker's apology for talking 'not about Cyrus and Alcibiades, as the wise [*sophoi*, i.e. sophists] do even now, but about Nero and such things, fairly recent and inglorious topics'; the objection is apparently not just to recent subjects, but to a Roman one in particular.

[99] For some reason commentators have been wary of identifying the noise (cf. Jones 1978*a*: 73–4 with reference to Bonner 1942: 1–7 on numerous strong condemnations of snorting; Bonner in fact saw from these passages that Dio's noise referred to a 'sexual act', but felt that 'the subject is not one to be pursued here' [7], referring instead to F. Marx's edition of Lucilius [vol. ii. 106–7] and his explanation of Lucilius fr. 284 by *Greek Anthology* xi. 52 'snared by the love of a boy, etc.'; Welles 1962: 68 would have got to the point if his paraphrase of Dio had been more accurate). Highet 1983: 95 felt no such embarassment in identifying the 'heavy breathing of men engaged in sexual intercourse'.

Dio discourses on the Tarsians' noise throughout, and it is integral to the final attack on homosexual practices (where the Tarsians have gone as far as to depilate their whole bodies, including the genitals, 'to resemble boys' and 'would be really happy to borrow other female characteristics if they could' in order to be 'naturally androgynous'). Amongst other things the noise is a 'sign of the utmost hybris' (xxxiii. 50), *aporrhêton* 'unspeakable' (52), and made by *akolastoi* 'dissolutes' (23,

was strongly opposed to what he considered unnatural sex, that is, sex outside marriage and in particular male homosexual sex.[100] Here his attack focuses on the dress and gait of the Tarsian men and on their habit of depilation (52–64). What they do is 'against nature' (52, cf. 60, 63, 64). Dio recalls Plato's discussion of unnatural practices beginning at *Laws* 838a. But he is also certainly expressing his own strongly held beliefs.[101] That these were appropriately expressed at Tarsus is shown by the fact that in the second or third century AD the author of the *Amores* ascribed to Lucian chose it as the place where two friends discussed a conversation on the merits of homosexual and heterosexual sex during the festival of Heracles, deciding broadly in favour of the former (while stressing it involved a genital, not a 'Platonic' relationship).[102]

Dio's final attack on shaving and depilating the body recalls Musonius Rufus' remarks on what he too considers to be an effeminate practice.[103] It is again something Dio himself felt strongly about. In *Or.* lxxii head hair and beard are the mark of a philosopher (2).[104] They are also the mark of a true Greek.[105] This is expressed most forcefully at *Or.* xxxvi. 17, where Dio reports to the Prusans that the Homer-loving people of Borysthenes still had the long hair described by Homer ('a philosopher would have been

35); homosexuality is elsewhere condemned by Dio as *arrhêton*, 'hybristic', and characteristic of *akolastoi* (iv. 102, vii. 149, xxxvi. 8, lxxvii/lxxxviii. 36). The Tarsian noise is a real one which makes the city sound like a brothel (xxxiii. 36, cf. 54, 60). There may well also be a racial implication in Dio's attack on the noise, reflecting Tarsus' linguistically and racially mixed population (the favoured explanation of, amongst others, Desideri 1978: 125–6). But his efforts to get the Tarsians to be Greek (cf. below) focus on their conduct, not on how they speak.

[100] As opposed to sex 'in accordance with nature' (*Or.* vii. 135–6). Above, 'Novel' n. 79.

[101] The only favourable allusion to homosexuality is Epaminondas' establishment of the so-called 'sacred band' at *Or.* xxii. 2; but Epaminondas is something of special case for Dio—see below in text after n. 177.

[102] On Tarsus as the location see Jones 1984; cf. above, 'Novel' n. 71.

[103] Fr. xxi = Lutz 1947: 128. 29–30 (to attract women or boys). Cf. Arrian, *Discourses of Epictetus* i. 16. 9–12; Athenaeus, *Sophists at Dinner* 564f–565d; Buffière 1980: 614 ff.

[104] Cf. Arrian, *Discourses of Epictetus* i. 2. 28–9. Those with long hair are not necessarily true philosophers: Dio xii. 15, xxxv. 2; Arrian, *Discourses of Epictetus* iv. 8. 10 ff.

[105] *Orr.* vii. 4; xxi. 17; above all the lost *Encomium of Hair* preserved partly in Synesius' *Encomium of Baldness* 3 (193–5 Terz.). The most eloquent testimony to the care taken by men (and women) over hair in the second sophistic period is Galen, *On the Composition of Drugs by Places* xii. 421 ff. (cf. id. iii. 899. 13–14 on the dignity of the beard).

extremely pleased at the sight'). He makes this the opportunity for
an unexpected anti-Roman aside. 'Only one man among them was
shaved, and everyone reviled and hated him. And it was said that
he adopted this practice for no other purpose than to flatter Romans and to show his friendship for them, so that one could see
from that the disgracefulness of his action and how completely
unfitting it was for men' (17). The evidence of portraiture suggests
that first-century Romans generally shaved and that it was not until
Hadrian that beards became popular.[106] Dio is not necessarily
attacking this Roman style of appearance (nor does he seem to be
implying that the Borysthenites were unaware of it).[107] The point to
the Prusans—which is remarkably strong in the context of identifying the Borysthenites as idealized Hellenes—is that flattery of
Rome is wrong and deserves to be execrated.[108] It is also quite plain
that Dio preferred a traditional, 'manly' Greek appearance. This is
his main message to the Tarsians.[109]

The second *Tarsian Oration* (*Or.* xxxiv) is decidedly political and
is concerned with external and internal concord and with Tarsus'
problems with Roman government.[110] It is particularly interesting
for Dio's comments on class division in the city and on the need for
the citizens to integrate fully the guild of linen workers whose
members could not afford the 500 dr. necessary to gain the full
franchise. Dio, who claims elsewhere to have spoken for the poor
(xliii. 7), advises they be allowed immediate entry for free (21–3).[111]
Tarsus was also riven by disputes between the Assembly, the Council, the Gerousia, and the association of *Neoi*, the Youths (16–21).
Externally Dio advises on harmonious relations with neighbouring
cities, Aegeae, Mallus, Soli, Adana, and 'perhaps others' (7–14, 43–
53).[112] What concerns us now is Tarsus' relations with Roman power
(9, 15, 38–42). The Tarsians have a reputation for prosecuting
governors and have done so recently to 'some violent *hêgemones*'

[106] Cf. Strong 1988: 171 with n. 1 on the portraiture of Hadrian.
[107] As Jones 1978a: 63 suggests, reporting the evidence for Roman relations with
Borysthenes in the 1st and 2nd centuries (a military presence cannot be confirmed
before Trajan/Hadrian: Belin de Ballu: 1972: 172–3).
[108] Treu 1961: 150 accords Dio's remarks a familiar 'ethische Sinn'; this is inadequate.
[109] Cf. Robert 1977a: esp. 132 on Dio's efforts in this speech to persuade the
Tarsians to live up to their claims to a Greek (Argive) ancestry.
[110] There is a good analysis in Jones 1978a: 76 ff.
[111] On this and similar excluded groups see MacMullen 1974: 59–60.
[112] Cf. *Or.* xxxiii. 51, 'Past' n. 26 (Aegeae).

(9).¹¹³ Dio warns that, though it was good to prosecute these men 'so that their successors should be more reluctant to go wrong', the Tarsians could nevertheless acquire a reputation for litigiousness and malicious prosecution which would do them no good. The Tarsians also have current problems with the *stratêgos* (15; 38–42), a term that must be the equivalent of the word *hêgemôn* which Dio uses here for other governors (and/or possibly Roman officials) and elsewhere for current or past ones.¹¹⁴ Distrust between them (cf. *Or.* xxxii. 71) had been exacerbated recently by the Tarsians, who feeling slighted 'said' something (presumably as a body in the Assembly). The governor 'wrote in anger and acted thus, which he had never done before' (15).

Dio's advice in this situation is interesting. He has made it plain in a *captatio benevolentiae* at the beginning of the speech that he is presenting himself as a Cynic philosopher by dress and by practice (1–6). As at Alexandria and at Nicomedia he says that he has been sent by the gods (*kata to daimonion*).¹¹⁵ Thus he can speak freely and with authority. His advice on how to deal with the governor (38–42) follows a lengthy attack on the Tarsian elite,¹¹⁶ who are

¹¹³ Not '*strategoi*' (Jones 1978a: 76). On this prosecution (presumably by means of the Cilician *koinon*; cf. below) cf. Brunt 1961: 217, 220. On other arrogant governors of Cilicia see Plutarch, *On the Decline of Oracles* 434c–f, Philostratus, *Life of Apollonius* i. 12 (a story attributed to Maximus of Aegeae), and cf. Castritius 1971 on ?two earlier prosecutions.

¹¹⁴ The governors of Cilicia were in fact *antistratêgoi* (i.e. propraetors); see Thomasson 1972–90: i. 289–92. *Stratêgos* in Dio also has the common meaning of a city's chief magistrate (as in *Or.* xxxi), as well of course as that of general; see further Desideri 1978: 460–1 n. 3. On *hêgemôn* in Dio cf. above, n. 59, and see Desideri 1978: 149–50 n. 21; Robert 1960b: 329 n. 5 on the sense it may bear of 'Roman authorities'; Kienast 1971: 67–8 n. 27; in Dio the word can refer to local politicians (cf. *Or.* xlvi. 14); additionally, it has been suggested that it refers to the emperor at *Or.* xlv. 6 (Jones 1978a: 108), but this seems unlikely (it is a common meaning earlier, but as Mason 1974: 144–5 notes is rare after the Augustan period); see below, n. 163.

¹¹⁵ *Orr.* xxxii. 12, xxxviii. 51; Desideri 1978: 109, 166–7 nn. 86–8 maintains that these references to divinity are a way of alluding to the emperor (for him Vespasian or Trajan); there is nothing to suggest this is so—we are dealing rather with Dio's self-presentation as a philosopher whose message comes from god (so *Or.* i. 49 ff., esp. xiii. 9–10 where Dio interprets Apollo's message to carry on philosophical preaching 'until you come to the end of the earth' as a brief to wander like Odysseus, that is, as a Cynic philosopher). Kienast's analysis of *Or.* xxxiv (1971: 68, 74–5) is severely damaged by his unwarranted assumption that Dio was in the service ('Auftrag') of Trajan (and so the speech must belong to the start of the Parthian War).

¹¹⁶ *Hoi proestôtes*, as at Apamea (*Or.* xl. 18) or Prusa (*Or.* xlv. 6 [*proestêkotes*], where they are also criticized); at *Or.* xxxii. 69 they are the Romans (*proestêkotes*).

interested only in their own ambition and success (28–37). The
Tarsians are in a common situation. They should 'not submit in
every respect and simply hand themselves over to those in power
[*tois epi tês exousias*] for them to do what they like with you, however far they go in violence and greed'; on the other hand they
should not adopt a position where they will 'tolerate nothing at all'
or expect that 'some Minos' will come to them or Perseus (38).[117]
Dio the philosopher, the outsider with his odd dress and appearance, can give this advice, as he does elsewhere, that the Tarsians
must tolerate Roman rule but at the same time must not be 'slaves'
(*andrapoda*), nor decide, as 'those in Ionia' have (i.e. the *koinon* of
Asia),[118] to make no prosecutions. In a word, they should not be
'defenceless' (39).[119] With regard to the *stratêgos* they must stop
their chief magistrate (the *prutanis*) from threatening him—either
prosecute, if he is bad, or do not, if he is guiltless or relatively so
(40–2). Above all, the *dêmos* collectively cannot act like the citizen
who recently 'got a brilliant reputation for prosecuting two *hêgemones* in turn' (42).[120] What is noticeable here is that Dio scarcely
defends the real governor. In his remarks on the problem 'in general [*katholou*]' he simply says that at best he may be all right or
'not do much wrong [*mê megala hamartanein*]'; in any case the
Tarsians must put up with him or face worse (40–1). It is also
noticeable that in focusing on the governor's relationship with Tarsus
Dio pushes into the background the role of the *koinon*, which would
presumably carry out any prosecution (as in Bithynia).[121] Tarsus
was in fact the provincial capital and centre of the *koinon*.[122] It

[117] For Perseus as a mythological founder of Tarsus see *Or.* xxxiii. 1, 45, esp. 47
'don't you think that Perseus really would fly over the city now?'; there is a nice
discussion of this in Robert 1977a: 98–116 (esp. on the ties with Argos). Minos: cf.
Robert 1948b: 21, 1977a: 99 n. 49 for a comparison of a late Roman governor with
Minos, the archetypal honest judge.

[118] *Koinon*—cf. Brunt 1961: 220.

[119] *Anoplous*; on the idea of not putting up with everything cf. *Orr.* xxxiv. 26,
xl. 23.

[120] Cf. Castritius 1971 on Juvenal *Satires* viii. 92–94 'quam fulmine iusto | et
Capito et Numitor ruerint damnante senatu | piratae Cilicum'; Plutarch *Political
Advice* 805a on a brilliant start to a political career achieved through public prosecutions (*dikai dêmosiai*).

[121] Cf. Pliny *Letters* iv. 9; v. 20; vi. 5, 13; vii. 6, 10 on Julius Bassus and Varenus
Rufus; but the prosecution of Marius Priscus was carried out by 'una civitas publice
multique privati' (iii. 9. 4; Pliny's 'accusantibus Afris' [ii. 11. 2] and 'provinciales'
[x. 3a. 2] are unclear).

[122] *RE* ivA (1932) 2426, 2428 (Ruge).

clearly dominated the other cities. But Dio's earlier report that these were looking for another leader (14) is a reminder that Tarsus' independence of action against Roman control was dependent to some extent on the maintenance of amicable relations with its neighbours.

In the last section of the speech Dio brings the facts of Roman power to bear on Tarsus' local quarrels. He tells the Tarsians not to take their dispute with Mallus *epi tên exousian*, 'to the (Roman) authorities' (46). The quarrels of Tarsus and Aegeae, Apamea and Antioch, or Smyrna and Ephesus are 'over an ass's shadow, as the saying goes. For leadership and rule are in the hands of others' (48). Athens and Sparta wrangled over real issues in the past. Anyone seeing the present-day disputes would be ashamed. 'For they are those of fellow-slaves quarrelling with each other over reputation and primacy [*prôteia*]' (51), that is, to be officially recognized by Rome as the 'first' city in the province. Dio certainly rebukes the Tarsians (and the others) on this subject. On the other hand, the idea that the cities are 'fellow-slaves' does not suggest unity and consent in the running of the Empire. These doubts about the governors of Cilicia run parallel to the comments about the 'leading' Romans, whom the Rhodians felt obliged to honour. They are matched by very strong comments in the oration Dio delivered after his exile urging concord between the Bithynian cities of Nicomedia and Nicaea in the same matter he ends with at Tarsus, the cities' rivalry over the titles they claimed from Rome (*Or.* xxxviii *To the Nicomedians, On Concord with the Nicaeans*). To this oration I now turn.[123]

The speech to the Nicomedians is Dio's most elaborate contribution to the advocacy of harmonious relations, which was a characteristic task of Greek intellectuals in the second sophistic period. Cities too often advertised 'concord' (*homonoia*) on their coins with the aim of promoting or celebrating good reciprocal relations and,

---

[123] Date: Jones 1978*a*: 135; good discussion at 83–9. The thesis has been advanced by Sheppard 1984: 163–6 that *Or.* xxxviii dates to the start of Domitian's reign because xxxviii. 39 envisages that the title 'first' *will be* common to Nicomedia and Nicaea (a situation which did not occur until Domitian: Robert 1977*b*: 3–4; see below in text); rather Dio is speaking to the Nicomedians of an already *present* situation (§ 39 ἂν δὲ τὸ μὲν τῆς μητροπόλεως ὑμῖν ὄνομα ἐξαίρετον ᾖ, τὸ δὲ τῶν πρωτείων κοινὸν ᾖ, τί κατὰ τοῦτο ἐλαττοῦσθε; cf. §26 ἡμεῖς δὲ ἂν ἀπολάβωμεν τὸ πρωτεῖον ἀμαχεὶ παραδόντων αὐτὸ τῶν Νικαέων—that is, the Nicomedians do not wish to share the title with their rivals, as they do, but to take it for themselves).

less commonly, good internal relations between the people and the elite in the shape of the city council.[124] Dio spends a considerable amount of time in his speech explaining what concord is and what is to be gained by it (8–20). Along with Plutarch and Aristides he roots it firmly in the happiness of the family and home.[125] Interestingly, he asserts that no one has spoken to the Nicomedians on the subject before (4, cf. 51). Whether this is true or not, it is true that the concept was especially popular in the second century.[126] Dio tells his audience that it is the gods who enjoin good relations and that it is from the gods that his message comes (9, 18, 51). But his persona in this speech is not that of the philosopher, as it was at Tarsus. Here he is an insider, being in fact a citizen (1). He is speaking in his own interest.

From the reign of Claudius to that of Domitian Nicomedia and Nicaea had respectively the titles of 'metropolis' and 'first city'. Under Domitian Nicomedia was allowed to add the title 'first' and it was now trying to take this for itself from Nicaea (26).[127] Dio tells his audience that the issue they are concerned about is trifling. They are behaving like 'foolish children' (21).[128] In fighting for 'primacy' they are fighting for 'a name only' (24). As in his address to Tarsus Dio contrasts the 'primacy' over which Nicomedia and Nicaea are striving with the plans of Athens and Sparta in the past: the Nicomedians are merely fighting for 'vainglory' (24–9). Having put the matter in context, Dio next speaks of the role of Roman government. The aim of the Nicomedians should be to give the *hêgemones* grounds for respecting them (33). This can happen if Nicomedia and Nicaea co-operate and show that 'you care for the whole Bithynian race' (33). 'If you are together, you will rule all the cities [i.e. in the province], and the governors will feel greater reluctance towards you and fear, should they wish to commit crimes' (34). In other words, the power of the provincial council to prosecute corrupt governors will be upheld only through unity.

---

[124] See esp. Pera 1984; Klose 1987: 44–63. Sheppard 1984–6 offers a general account. Cf. above, 'Plutarch' n. 145, below, 'Aristides' n. 147.

[125] 15; Plutarch, *Political Advice* 824f; Aristides, *Or.* xxiv. 7–8.

[126] The term *homonoia* first appears in this sense on coins of the imperial period at Laodicea in the reign of Vespasian: Pera 1984: 120; for earlier evidence of the idea without the word, cf. *RPC* i. 1 (1992), p. 48 (Laodicea and elsewhere).

[127] On the history and development of the dispute from the numismatic evidence see Bosch 1935: 224–6; Weiser 1989: 55–8 on the Domitianic period; and esp. Robert 1977*b*.

[128] On the image cf. above, 'Plutarch' n. 94.

Dio then asks, 'what need is there to discuss with those who know it well the state of their relations with the governors? Or are you not in fact aware of the tyranny which your factionalism [*stasis*] gives to those who rule you?' (36). Dio warns that the governors can play one side off against the other. If they wish to do wrong, they can trade on the cities' desire to be loved by them (36).[129] They have made the Nicomedians look like children. 'Children are often offered the least important things in the place of the greatest. They in their ignorance of what is truly important and in their joy over trifles delight in what is a mere nothing. So with you also instead of justice, instead of not pillaging your cities and not seizing men's possessions, instead of refraining from arrogance against you, instead of not behaving with drunken violence, they hand you titles and in speech or letters call you 'first'. Then they are in no danger if they treat you for the future as the last of all! These titles which you take such pride in are spat upon by all those whose perception is correct, but especially among the Romans they excite laughter and, what is even more arrogant, they are called 'Hellenic failings'. Well, they are failings, men of Nicomedia, really, but not Hellenic ones, unless someone will say they are Hellenic in the sense that those Athenians and Lacedaemonians of old made rival claims to glory.' Their struggles had been, Dio repeats himself, for empire (*archê*)—'though you might think now that they fought gloriously for the right to lead the procession [*propompeia*]!' (37–8).[130]

We should not forget that in this passage Dio is primarily attacking the pig-headedness of the Nicomedians and the Nicaeans. That said, it is difficult not to take his remarks as extreme disparagement of Roman government as it was practised in Bithynia at this time.[131] Dio is as far from the ideal theory of kingship in the Roman empire as he possibly can be. The emperor is in fact absent from this speech—at least he is not named (I shall come back to this). Dio focuses rather on the relations between the cities and the governor and in particular how these are mediated through the provincial

---

[129] Cf. Philostratus, *Life of Apollonius* vi. 38 (the governor of Syria causes *stasis* at Antioch by sowing 'suspicions').

[130] 'Procession'—i.e. at the festival of the Eleutheria at Plataea: Robertson 1986; but also with relevance to Nicaea's and Nicomedia's struggle over primacy—see Merkelbach 1978: 290–2 on the prized right to lead the procession at the provincial games associated with the imperial cult.

[131] On the reality of the abuses catalogued by Dio in *Or.* xxxviii see Brunt 1961: 213–14.

council, the *koinon* (33–4). It is clear from Pliny's relation of the
trials of the governors of Bithynia, Julius Bassus and Varenus Rufus,
that the provincial assembly acted on behalf of the cities against bad
governors.[132] Aelius Aristides' address on concord to the provincial
assembly of Asia (*Or.* xxiii) suggests that the structure of the assembly there privileged the views of the three biggest cities over the
'many inferior ones'. Aristides reminds his audience at Pergamum
that, though Pergamum, Smyrna, and Ephesus had the right of
probouleuein, i.e. of 'voicing their opinions first', they could nevertheless be outmanœuvred by the smaller cities, if they were at
variance with each other (34). Thus Dio's point at xxxviii. 36–7 is
that the governor by the simple tactic of attributing titles can ally
himself with the 'party [*hetaireia*]' of the Nicaeans or that of the
Nicomedians in the provincial assembly 'so that he escapes prosecution . . . and doing wrong is protected by those who think they
alone are loved by him'.[133]

That Dio's fears are not groundless is shown by the Bithynian
assembly's change of mind regarding the prosecution of Varenus
Rufus. Pliny reports that the Bithynians dropped their prosecution
of Varenus 'ut temere inchoatam' (*Letters* vii. 6). The reason for the
change of heart is unknown. But Varenus was very keen to be
allowed to summon witnesses from Bithynia to back him (Pliny,
Letters v. 20. 2, 7; vi. 5. 1), a move which caused anger among the
Bithynian delegates and dissension in the Senate (v. 20. 2; vi. 5; vi.
13), since, as Pliny who acted for Varenus admits, it was strictly
speaking illegal (v. 20. 7).[134] Whether those who were sent by Varenus
to summon witnesses somehow caused the Bithynian change of
heart is a matter for speculation. Certainly, during the time allowed
him a pro-Varenus faction got the upper hand in the *koinon* and
sent a delegate to the emperor to announce the dropping of the
prosecution (vii. 6. 1). The original Bithynian delegate Fonteius
Magnus was then at variance with the second delegate, Polyaenus.
In the end the case was handed over to the *cognitio* of the emperor

---

[132] Pliny, *Letters*, as above, n. 121.

[133] On factions inside the Bithynian cities cf. Pliny, *Letters* x. 34, Dio xlv. 8, l. 3.
Cf. Philostratus' picture of a rich Cilician's relations with 'the rulers', i.e. the governors (*Life of Apollonius* vii. 23).

[134] The extortion laws (the lex Julia and the SC Calvisianum [Cyrene Edict V])
only allowed plaintiffs the right of summoning witnesses (Valerius Maximus viii. 1.
10; Ehrenberg–Jones 311. v).

(vii. 6, 10).[135] The result is unknown, but the solidarity of the Roman elite, their readiness to break their own rules, and Bithynian factionalism do not make it hard to guess the outcome.[136] Whether Dio is referring in *Or.* xxxviii specifically to the conduct of Varenus (and Bassus) is unknown.[137] Compared with his remarks in *Or.* xliii. 11–12 about an 'evil governor' he is surely speaking generally, as he does at Tarsus in *Or.* xxxiv.

It may be asked how absent the emperor is from *Or.* xxxviii. Consider the following. At some point during the reigns of Trajan and Hadrian Nicaea acquired in addition to the title of 'first city' that of 'metropolis', which had formerly belonged exclusively to Nicomedia.[138] It also, like Nicomedia, became 'temple warden' of the emperors. Nicaea proudly asserted in a dedication to Hadrian on one of its gates that its titles were *kata ta krimata tôn auto-kratorôn*, 'in accordance with the decisions of the emperors'.[139] A hundred years after Dio was writing we find the emperor Caracalla bestowing the title of 'three times temple wardens' on the Ephesians in response to a request by the Asian provincial assembly.[140] There is no need to look for such co-operation in the case of Nicaea and Nicomedia. We may assume that both cities lobbied hard to gain their additional titles. Nicaea's gains under Trajan and Hadrian parallel Nicomedia's acquisition of 'first' under Domitian. What the emperors gained by yielding to the cities is unclear. It is tempting to wonder whether some routine level of dissension was not of advantage to them in certain areas.[141] In the case of Nicaea the story is told by Herodian that its hatred of its neighbour led it to side with Pescennius Niger in the civil war against Septimius Severus,

---

[135] Garnsey 1970: 55–6 n. 2; Millar 1992: 348–9.

[136] On Varenus see Pliny, *Letters* vi. 13. 4 (senatorial solidarity; cf. ii. 11. 6, 13 [Priscus], iii. 4. 7 'quod in eiusmodi causis solet esse tristissimum, periculum senatoris' [Classicus], iv. 9 with vi. 29. 10 and Garnsey 1970: 55 [Bassus]), vii. 10. 2–3 on Trajan's decision to 'explorare provinciae voluntatem', to which Pliny adds smugly that the merits of the prosecution are in doubt owing to the uncertainty of whether there is a prosecution at all.

[137] The suggestion is made by Vielmetti 1941: 103 in his unexciting survey of the Bithynian speeches, and by Kienast 1964: 56–7.

[138] Though much earlier under Tiberius the title had belonged to Nicaea: Strabo xii. 4. 7 (C 565).

[139] Schneider 1938: nos. 11–12 (better texts in *IK* vii. 5ab); Robert 1977*b*: 8–9 (texts), 19 (Trajan and Hadrian), id. *BE* 1979. 541.

[140] Robert 1967: 48 (= *IK* xii. 212). NB Caracalla could also bestow a neocorate as a personal favour, as at Philadelphia: Buresch 1898: 16.

[141] Cf. the thoughts of Woolf 1993: 191.

which he says was another example of the age-old Greek factionalism that had made Greek affairs the 'easy prey of the Macedonians and slaves of the Romans' (iii. 2. 7–9). The result in this case was that Nicaea's titles were stripped from it and systematically defaced wherever they were inscribed, again by imperial will.[142] This involvement of the emperors is not unexpected or surprising to us.[143] Dio himself presents the awarding of petty titles as a mechanism used by governors to escape prosecution (xxxviii. 36–7). However, he must have been aware of the role of the emperors in supervising such titulature. The only criticism of the emperor in his works is in the *Orations on Kingship*, and it is very difficult to build anything on this. The positive remarks about Nerva and Trajan in speeches at Prusa (xl. 15, xlv. 2–3) are no more helpful, for the emperor, his virtues, and Dio's friendship with him are props for Dio's policies there. Again, in the *Alexandrian Oration* reference to the emperor's civilized conduct is simply a foil to the Alexandrians' undesirable frivolity (60, cf. 96). Dio's real views are not known. In the case of the titles of Nicaea and Nicomedia he was no doubt right to scrutinize the cities' own rivalries first: when it came to criticizing Rome's involvement, it was easier and safer to attack the annual governors. This at least focused his audience's mind on their own local factionalism and its consequences in their own backyard.

To some degree Dio's unidealized picture of Rome in *Or.* xxxviii contrasts with the idealized and (surely) deliberately naïve picture of the benefits of concord, which he presents to his audience at 8–20 and 41–8. He goes so far as to suggest to them that *philotimiai*, the displays of munificence through which the elite won honour, and *hupêresiai*, payments for public services (liturgies), will come to be shared between Nicomedia and Nicaea. He even imagines rich Nicaeans spending their money on Nicomedia (41). The reciprocity Dio envisages here is one of economic status and common culture, on which *homonoia* depended.[144] There are in fact many examples

[142] Robert 1977*b*: 21 ff.

[143] It is customary to cite Pius' diplomatic letter to the Ephesians on a related subject: *SIG*³ 849 (better in *IK* xv [Ephesos v], 1489–90), on the style of which see Williams 1976: 75; and the imperial letter found at Laodicea urging an end to 'vain contentiousness' over 'primacy' and bidding them be 'more dignified' (*MAMA* vi. 6; Robert 1969: 287–8). Cf. Roueché 1989: 217–18, and also the advice Cassius Dio has Maecenas give to Augustus on the cities' claims to titles at *Roman History* lii. 37. 10.

[144] There is nothing to support Kienast's suggestion (1964: 60) that pledges of *homonoia* were expressed in the manner of the formal agreements involving isopolity which are attested in the late classical and Hellenistic eras. See Jones 1978*a*: 84; Salmeri 1982: 91.

of rich men from one city spending their money in another. But Dio goes further than this in encouraging his audience to concord with what is apparently a flight of fancy—or wishful thinking—involving the possibility of more than Bithynian unity. The scale of his dreams is shown by the wish (*ôphelon*) that 'you could even make the *dêmos* of the Ephesians your brother, that you too could share the buildings of the Smyrnaeans!' (47–48).[145] There are parallels here with his grandiose scheme for making Prusa the population centre 'of the people of the region' and 'if possible' the political centre for 'other cities' at *Or.* xlv. 13–14.

This encouragement of fellow-feeling and unity is undoubtedly based on a perception of a shared Greekness, which is an essential part of all Dio's civic speeches.[146] As with Plutarch there is a strong element of optimism or faith at work. It is indeed remarkable, even laudable, that Dio did take the trouble to spread his politico-cultural message to the cities. It is not inconceivable that he really hoped for a greater political unification of Greek communities, as he suggests here at Nicomedia and at Prusa. One thing at least we can be pretty sure of: his missions were not undertaken on behalf of Roman government, however closely his desire for Greek vitality might coincide with Rome's wishes.[147]

DIO AND PRUSA

More information on Dio's relationship with Roman government and his thoughts on Greek unity can be found in the speeches in Prusa itself, to which I now turn. When he returned from exile Dio embarked on a programme of developing Prusa with the aim of enhancing its appearance and status. His grandfather had tried to use his good relations with an earlier emperor to secure the city freedom (xliv. 5). Others had tried to have the city appointed as an assize district (*dioikêsis*), but had been rebuffed (xlv. 6, 10). Dio aimed to secure both of these privileges, and in the case of the

---

[145] For the rhetoric cf. Isocrates, *On the Peace* 16.

[146] Clear encouragement of the Greek identity of Dio's audiences can be found for example at *Or.* xxxi. 18, 157–9; xxxii. 65; xxxiii. 1, 41; xxxiv. 38; xxxviii. 22, 46; xxxix. 1, 8; xliii. 3; xlv. 9; xlviii. 8; l. 2. See again 'Past' nn. 50–3 on Hellenism in the *Borystheniticus*.

[147] It is a curious argument that allows Greeks to promote the success of Greek states only as imaginary agents of Rome, and one that severely mars the interpretation of Dio's concord speeches, including *Or.* xxxviii, by Andrei 1981.

assizes he succeeded. But the first benefit he obtained from Trajan apparently concerned the strength of Prusa's city council.

The first relevant oration is *Or.* xliv *Speech of Greeting to his Fatherland for Proposing Honours to Him*. It is probable that Dio's greeting follows a return from an embassy to Trajan, since he implies at the beginning that he has been honoured recently at Rome and by 'all the Greeks'—specifically Athens, Argos, and Sparta (6)—and says that he prefers to be at home with the people of Prusa. Later in the speech (10–12) he remarks on benefits the Prusans can expect from the emperor. In this passage he stresses that good behaviour 'will benefit you more' than an enlarged council, the holding of assizes at Prusa, the provision of extra revenues, and freedom 'should you indeed obtain that too one day', which is in any case 'nominal and comes from those in control and in power' (11–12). Freedom is explicitly a future boon. It is not certain whether the other benefits already exist or are also potential: Dio has just spoken generally of 'the things which come from the rulers' as being potential—his audience must 'hope that they will happen and pray that some honour or glory or prosperity occurs'—in contrast to the ability they possess now to distinguish themselves from others by disciplined conduct (10). Nevertheless, some of these gains do seem to have been realized before the embassy. In the first part of *Or.* xl *In his Fatherland, On Concord with the Apameans* Dio defends his building programme at Prusa and reminds his audience of the other good things he has done for them. He mentions 'the embassy which you sent to thank [*eucharistountes*]' the emperor and his own part in it (13–15).[148] In *Or.* xliv the figure of the emperor is impersonal and is mentioned to show the audience the (hereditary) high standing Dio enjoys with him (xliv. 5 [cf. xli. 6], 12). This is again the case in *Or.* xl. The report of the emperor's actions serves to enhance Dio's standing with his Greek audience and in particular to deflect the allegations of his enemies. These alleged that the emperor had not listened to Dio and his fellow-ambassadors, but had preferred an embassy from Smyrna and had given Smyrna unbelievable benefactions 'along with [images of] the Nemeseis' (13–15).[149] Dio does not deny that the Smyrnaean embassy achieved its own aims (though in what is presumably a later

---

[148] On 'thanks' to senior officials see Robert 1977*b*: 19 n. 85.
[149] On the famous twin Nemeseis of Smyrna see Cadoux 1938: 220–3.

speech he asserts that only one city—probably Miletus—has been honoured more than Prusa).[150] His point in *Or.* xl is that his own embassy had also achieved its aims. Hence the emperor can be described as *philanthrôpotatos*, 'most benevolent', and *sunetôtatos hapantôn*, 'most intelligent of them all' (15). These characteristics reflect of course on Dio himself ('he gave me what I asked for').[151]

The main benefit gained for Prusa before the embassy was apparently the enlargement of the council by one hundred members (cf. xlv. 3, 7, 10) and perhaps also some financial improvement (xliv. 11), though elsewhere extra income is linked to the winning of assize status (xlviii. 11).[152] For the appointment of Prusa as the centre of an assize district is apparently something gained from the embassy itself, since Dio stresses in *Or.* xl the indignity of having to go elsewhere for trials as if one's city were 'a village belonging to others' (xl. 10), and reminds his audience at Prusa how much their new privilege ('what has now happened . . . that you receive trials') incites 'all others', especially the Apameans (33). Perhaps Prusa had formerly been within the district assigned to Apamea.[153]

The link between the two themes of *Or.* xl, Dio's defence of his plans for building at Prusa and his advocacy of better relations with Apamea, is clearly made through the concept of personal status, as Dio chooses to define it. He has brought Prusa respect through the embassy he led. He reminds his audience that the Apameans have power with Rome because they are a colony (22). Dio also has power with Roman government, inasmuch as it is he who has obtained benefits for Prusa (13–14), and it is he who is supported in his building programme by the emperor and the proconsuls (5–6). The message to those who are criticizing his plans for Prusa (8–9) is that Roman goodwill towards Prusa is channelled through Dio himself.

[150] *Or.* xlv. 4; Miletus: Jones 1975.
[151] Cf. *Or.* xlv. 2 'Nerva . . . a benevolent *autokratôr* who loved me and was a friend of old'.
[152] Cf. Jones 1978*a*: 109 on the possibility that Dio also secured the right to mint coins at Prusa.
[153] As Jones suggests plausibly (1978*a*: 108–9). Cf. Pius' refusal of assize status to Berenice in an inscription found in its rival Cyrene, perhaps originally from the meeting place of the provincial assembly: 'I replied that it is not clear how assize-holding cities will take it, if they no longer have assizes annually as they have had; for those who have to be deprived in order to give to those who do not seems to me to do a wrong, unless the establishment of such a shared system were made in accordance with your wishes' (Reynolds 1978: 114 ll. 74–7).

Dio explicitly associates his building plans with the dignity of being ranked as an assize district (xl. 10 'buildings and festivals and holding trials ourselves and not being examined before others . . . all of these enhance cities' pride and give them greater repute'). He seems to focus particularly on the assizes when he defines civic pride in terms of 'greater honour from strangers and governors' (ibid.), where the reference is to the annual/biennial court sessions presided over by the proconsul as part of his duties in the province. An assize centre benefited economically from the influx of people from other towns and from the presence of the governor. As Dio remarks in a rather ironic speech on the blessings of materialism in the major civic centre of Celaenae (Apamea Kibôtos) in Phrygia, 'having the courts is considered of the greatest importance to a city's strength and all men have made it their number one priority' (*Or.* xxxv. 15–17).[154] It is apparent that the assize districts—as the only administrative divisions in proconsular provinces like Asia and Bithynia—could also be used for wider administrative purposes, financial and other, outside the normal cycle of meetings.[155] Hence the economic benefits would not be limited to the biennial rush which Dio observes with disapproval at Celaenae.[156] In a speech in front of the proconsul Varenus Rufus in about 105 Dio emphasizes that the administrative reforms granted by Trajan were financially important: 'I have made my fatherland more valuable by providing financial capital, as it were, from the fees of the councillors,[157] and, by Zeus, by the increase in our revenues because of the assize district' (*Or.* xlviii. 11). The economic importance of assize centres like Prusa is recognized by the fact that in terms of the number of grammarians, sophists (rhetors), philosophers, and doctors who were

[154] Cf. xxxviii. 26. On Dio's speech at Celaenae see Jones 1978a: 65–70.

[155] On the uses of the assize (Latin *conventus*) system for administration see Robert 1949*b*: esp. 222 ff. (subscriptions for the temple of Caligula at Miletus); Habicht 1975: 90–1; Burton 1975: 102–6 (92 n. 5 on *dioikêsis* in Dio). Plutarch, *Are the Ills of the Mind or of the Body Worse?* 501e–502a is decisive on the annual cycle of the assizes in one part of the province of Asia (probably Smyrna: Jones 1971*a*: 15); Dio xxxv. 15–17 (παρ' ἔτος—cf. Pausanias vi. 26. 2, viii. 15. 2, esp. ix. 32. 3) indicates a biennial cycle in another part at Celaenae (there is no clear evidence of the relative chronology of these works).

[156] *Or.* xxxv. 17 'they say that the interval is now going to be longer, and that people are not prepared to be constantly driven all around the place'.

[157] On the fees paid by new councillors (*bouleutika*; Latin *honorarium decurionatus* or *summa honoraria*), especially at this time, see Garnsey 1971; Duncan-Jones 1982: 82–8 (84 on Bithynia, with reference to Pliny, *Letters* x. 112. 1–2), 147–55.

allowed immunity from public duties, assize centres were ranked second after metropolises.[158] This is why Dio was so concerned with obtaining the status. His attempts to do so show very well how such a man could use the Roman system for his own and his city's advantage.

Dio speaks about his embassy to the emperor also in *Or.* xlv *Defence of his Behaviour towards his Fatherland*. In this speech three emperors are characterized in relation to Dio and the benefits obtained for Prusa. The speech begins with a bitter attack on Domitian. He was 'an evil spirit [*daimôn*]' (1–2).[159] By contrast Nerva is named as a benevolent personal friend who gave Dio *agapê*, love', a particularly strong idea in the kingship orations (2).[160] The present emperor showed Dio extraordinary *philanthrôpia kai spoudê*, 'benevolence and interest'. Despite 'such honour . . . and familiarity and friendship' Dio did not (he says) ask for anything for his own benefit (such as wealth or 'some office or power'),[161] but had only the interests of Prusa at heart (3). I have already noted that Dio contrasts his own success with the emperor in this speech with the failures of others in the matter of obtaining assize status (6, 10). It is Dio's direct power with the emperor that must be stressed, power based on personal friendship and hence not available to all.

At this point (4–5) Dio underlines this message by reminding the Prusans of their previous unhappy dealings with earlier proconsuls over the benefits which he had now secured. '[I am saying] that you particularly desired this [i.e. greater influence], that there was a long period of hope while you were deceived, and you kept on giving excessive honours to those governors who did no more than promise (for certainly no private person ever either expected or promised). You came out to meet them in a body far from the city or waited for them in other cities. This perhaps is something worth reflecting on. And yet since these [false promises] were little things worth nothing, the man who was noble and above envy and malice should have said then, "You are mad and deluded making yourselves so dependent on men like that, cultivating people so low

---

[158] *Digest* xxvii. 1. 6. 2.
[159] Presumably in the sense Dio outlines in *Or.* xxv where political leaders are considered as *daimones*, 'divine spirits', of their peoples.
[160] Cf. especially iii. 112.
[161] Notice that Dio does not say he *was* offered—and turned down—a Roman office.

[*tapeinous*] in order to gain things that are neither needed nor great nor indeed clear, not to mention the fact that you have nothing definite." But, I think, it was difficult for them [the Prusans], however any of these things happened. Yet surely the fact that it was one or another of the governors who arranged and provided a benefit was not as distressing as that it was not one of our own citizens. Further, hope came upon them and beguiled them inasmuch as they were things that would never happen' (xlv. 4–5).[162]

These remarks are comparable with what Dio says about governors to the Nicomedians in *Or.* xxxviii. In that speech the emperor was not mentioned. Dio had no cause to appeal to higher authority to convey his message to Nicomedia. Here at Prusa Dio's friendship with the emperor is the crucial support he can invoke to bolster his building programme and to rebut his enemies. Governors it was possible to attack without criticizing the emperor (the more so in that their term of office was a year long only and allowed much readier comparison). Nor was Dio the only person at Prusa to attack the governors, as we see in *Or.* xliii where he fights allegations of collusion with a 'wicked governor'. In *Or.* xlv he goes on to mention a governor's letter written about an earlier attempt to obtain assize status. 'When the project failed many people laughed at the city, and I don't mean many of our neighbours (for that would have been less terrible), but of our citizens, as if the city was aiming at too much and showing that in stupidity it was no different from the sons of kings' (xlv. 6).[163] Again, Dio's message may be compared with that in *Or.* xxxviii. In the face of potentially negative treatment from the governors the Nicomedians and the Nicaeans were advised to stick together and to allow no opportunity of being abused. So, here in *Or.* xlv Dio criticizes disunity in Prusa. He then

---

[162] On the need to keep the MSS readings here against Emperius' exchange of ἡγεμόνων and ἰδιωτῶν (1844: 588 on xlv. 4 'neque enim provinciarum praesides infra [i.e. §5] οὕτω ταπεινοὶ recte appellabuntur'; the change is accepted by von Arnim and de Budé) see Desideri 1978: 440 nn. 22, 26. The reading of U ταπεινῶς ('submissively')—referring to the Prusans' behaviour—is possible, but cf. above, n. 59, on the inferior quality of 'the leaders' in the *Rhodian Oration*.

[163] Jones 1978a: 108 suggests the meaning of *hêgemôn* here is 'emperor' rather than 'governor'. This is possible (cf. Aristides, *Or.* xxvi. 26, 29; it is not clear that there is such a usage in Dio), but unlikely (i) after the attack on *hêgemones* = governors in §§4–5 for not conferring benefits, and (ii) given that Dio had only 'heard about this from many people', which implies an event of his exile, and, if this is so, Domitian as the emperor in question, for whom the description 'leader' is too mild an expression for Dio to have used (esp. in this speech: cf. 1).

brings this theme round to himself. He did not attempt to put placemen on the council when the extra councillors were chosen (7–8). Indeed, he deliberately absented himself when the voting took place (9–10). He could, he says, have cleared his name of allegations made about these matters 'by a single word . . . to you and to the governors, though you knew anyway. If you did not listen and the matter did not interest the governors, it wasn't hard to write to the *autokratôr*' (8).[164] Dio says he did not do this because he did not want to accuse anyone or malign the city (9–10). Rather, he kept quiet and put up with the injustices that had occured against him during his exile, just as Odysseus had done (11).

The reference to Odysseus is interesting for the interpretation of Dio's self-presentation, since the 'Cynic' Dio is largely missing from the civic speeches in Bithynia. As at Nicomedia Dio in Prusa is an insider. Orations xlvii and xlix are relevant in this regard. *Or.* xlix has a very different feel from those we have been looking at. In this short speech entitled *Refusal of Office before the Council* Dio expatiates on the (Stoic) duty of the philosopher to take part in public office. 'The function of the true philosopher is nothing other than to rule over men' (xlix. 13). Dio nevertheless goes on to excuse himself from the office of chief magistrate (*prôtos archôn*) on the grounds that he is soon to leave the city.[165] 'It is perhaps better neither for me nor for you that I should delay here' (15). The veiled or open threat to leave recurs in a number of Prusan speeches.[166] We do not have to read into his remarks here the promise of gains from Rome.[167] Rather, perhaps, Dio is complaining about having to undergo an 'examination' (*exetasis*), which he says he had not had to put up with when he was previously elected archon (15). The presentation of himself as philosopher marks him as a particularly valuable member of the community, because the philosopher is

[164] Interference in elections is noticed as an offence in the Flavian *lex Malacitana* §58 (McCrum–Woodhead 454. LVIII) and may well have been part of Bithynian provincial law.

[165] On the Bithynian *cursus honorum* and the various titles of magistracies in the Bithynian cities see Sherwin-White 1966: 671 on Pliny, *Letters* x. 79; Mitchell 1984: 123 on its Roman character.

[166] *Orr.* xliii. 8; xlv. 1, 14; xlvii. 2–3, 19 (a visit to the proconsul); l. 7 ('believe me that I am now speaking the truth'); cf. in rather different circumstances the early xlvi. 12. The only 'real' occasion may be *Or.* xliii. 8, below, n. 178; but we should also remember that Dio travelled to (certainly) Tarsus and (very probably) elsewhere (?Alexandria, Rhodes) during his last years in Bithynia.

[167] Von Arnim 1898: 384.

naturally close to god and is the trusted confidant and adviser of kings, who need the *pepaideumenoi* (3).

At the beginning of *Or.* xlvii (*Public Speech in his Fatherland*) Dio makes plain the Stoic influence on his conception of public duty, citing Zeno, Chrysippus, and Cleanthes (2). Mention of Odysseus' love for his homeland leads Dio to say that his remarks are those of 'a wanderer and a chatterer' (7–8). This phrase is part of the Cynic persona Dio adopts elsewhere.[168] Here, in a speech where he is defensive and bitter about the progress of his building projects and the attacks of his enemies, the characterization seems less convincing and Dio caps the final section, where he reports the (hostile) advice of a 'sympathizer' to stop playing the tyrant (20–4), by protesting that his 'foul cloak' and long hair are kingly rather than tyrannical (25). For Dio's enemies Dio is anything but a philosopher. For them his political aims at home are closely associated with his connections with Rome. Here the distance Dio puts between himself and the Roman governors of Bithynia is relevant. Dio's enemies, he reports, accuse him of 'cultivating governors' (xlvii. 21). This was not an isolated charge, as we see from *Or.* xliii where Dio vigorously defends himself against involvement with a 'wicked governor' (xliii. 11–12). In *Or.* xlvii he is also attacked for parading his close friendship with the emperor. 'Since there is familiarity between me and the *autokratôr*, perhaps even friendship, and with many others who are more or less the most powerful of the Romans, [he says] I should live with them in a position of honour and admiration' (xlvii. 22).[169] Dio's ambiguous self-characterization as now civic insider, now outsider, now promoting independence from the governors, now friend of the emperor, lent itself to such attacks. He could easily be seen as a hypocrite, extending his power at Prusa under a veil of philosophical detachment and using his influence at Rome for local political ends. The more obviously political Dio's schemes became, the more difficult it must have been for him to claim he was not simply out for himself. In this respect his denial, that he would complain to Rome about such allegations (xlv. 8–10),[170] must have appeared to his enemies more like a threat, as in this speech through exasperation it has indeed become (xlvii. 19).

---

[168] Cf. esp. i. 56, vii. 1, xii. 16.   [169] Cf. xlv. 3 on Dio's influence at Rome.
[170] Cf. the pre-exilic speech xlvi. 8.

Dio's most ambitious scheme for Prusa was his plan to amal-
gamate with it the smaller communities in its own territory and to
'force' other cities (presumably from other districts) into a political
federation with it, a process called *sunoikismos*. Dio associates this
proposal with 'the city's reconstruction, revenues, and countless
other benefits' at *Or.* xlv. 13–14. Synoecism happened at several
sites in the ancient world, sometimes where a 'core' city already
existed, sometimes where it did not. Military, political, or economic
considerations were the reasons behind it. In Dio's case financial
benefits to Prusa were clearly to the fore.[171] Dio (of course) presents
this idea as his own, though it would no doubt have needed the
emperor's permission (which is perhaps in his mind when he speaks
implicitly of his own lack of power at xlv. 14). If the idea was a
serious one—and is not to be seen alongside the wish he expresses
just before of being able to equip Prusa with 'harbours and dock-
yards' (an advertisement of his goodwill to the city)—we might
recall the hyperbole to the Nicomedians about the need to unite
not only with Nicaea but also with Ephesus and Smyrna (xxxviii.
47). Hyperbolic though this wish is, it nevertheless forms part of a
serious message that Greek political unity is not impossible. Dio's
advocacy of a synoecism in Bithynia centred on Prusa was impracticable, as he admits; that does not mean his desire was frivolous.[172]
It is not clear how he saw the proposal in relation to Roman power.
It is surely wrong, as noted several times already, to see it as an
official policy of Trajan's and to make Dio his agent.[173] Dio's promotion of unity at Nicomedia is closely connected with his severe
criticism of the practice of Roman government. Rome is not mentioned at xlv. 13–14. The main emphasis in the speech concerns the
obstruction of the governors over assize status (with the economic
benefits of which synoecism is associated at 14) and the support

[171] So Salmeri 1982: 33–4 n. 109 against Rostovtzeff's notion (1957: i. 257, ii. 654
n. 4; broadly accepted by Desideri 1978: 443 n. 11; for the truth of the matter see
Ameling 1985: 24–5) that Dio as a good liberal wanted to broaden the citizen base
with the peasantry. On synoecism for financial ends see Rostovtzeff 1941: i. 155–6
on the Hellenistic period, and for a Roman example see Garnsey and Saller 1987:
29–30 (*IGBulg* iii. 2, no. 1690).
[172] We should note Dio's regretful remarks at xlvii. 9–10 about his envy of Aristotle for being able to refound Stagira, and his own inability to do this at Prusa
because of his opponents (cf. also *Or.* ii. 79 where Dio cites the same event to assert
a claim to 'many large gifts' from the king/emperor).
[173] Desideri 1978: 399. On Trajan's limited policy of colonial urbanization see
Grelle 1972: 4 (to whose thesis Desideri 1978: 450 n. 60 is opposed).

and benefits Dio himself has directly from Trajan. There is nothing to suggest that Dio wanted independence from the emperor; rather, like Plutarch, he wants to preserve and increase Greek autonomy within the system he criticizes (a system necessary on his own cosmology). At least this is as far as we can safely go on a matter Dio describes as 'this passion [of mine]' (13, cf. 14 'like lovers do').

Dio had to be flexible in his relations with Rome. It is plausible to believe that his hostility (and hostility there sometimes is) was caused by Roman interference in the Bithynian cities. But the governors were not opposed to his plans in Prusa all the time. In addition to the crucial support of the emperor for his building projects (xlvii. 13),[174] Dio also stresses that of the governors (xl. 5–6), and even hints at it at the end of *Or.* xlv (15). *Or.* xlviii *A Political Speech in the Assembly* has been thought to give us a closer picture of Dio's relations with one governor, the notorious Varenus Rufus, who was in charge of Bithynia around 105/6. It was delivered in the presence of Varenus, perhaps while Dio himself was archon.[175] Dio spends much of this speech promoting internal concord between the people and the council (6–10, 13–17), incidentally defending the progress of his buildings (11–12). Concord was an apposite subject, since Varenus is thanked at the beginning of the speech for allowing assemblies again (1). The reason for their suspension is not mentioned, but was presumably due to strife between the masses and the elite in which—perhaps—Dio had aided the people (for reasons unknown).[176] Unfortunately nothing can be said about Dio's relationship with Varenus, especially if Dio has the official task of welcoming him and proposing a motion of thanks. This is a shame, because if friendship could be assumed (as has been

---

[174] On the necessity of the emperor's permission see Macer (writing under Caracalla/Severus Alexander) at *Digest* l. 10. 3. 1–2.

[175] If the inexperienced archon of xlviii. 17 is really Dio and not rather his son (on whose archonship see *Or.* l. 5, 10), as von Arnim held (1898: 390): for a balanced discussion see Desideri 1978: 277–8 n. 27; cf. Salmeri 1982: 34 n. 110. Date of Varenus Rufus' governorship: Eck 1982: 341.

[176] In any case in *Or.* l, a speech before the council, Dio justifies himself for having earlier taken the side of the people, before whom he pledges his support in the bitter *Or.* xliii (l. 3; xliii. 7); cf. Jones 1978a: 101–2 for this (admittedly insecure) reconstruction. For the subject of internal *homonoia* in Dio's speeches cf. also above, n. 111, and below, 'Aristides' n. 142 on *Orr.* xxxiv and xxxix. It is worth noting here the one epigraphical testimony to the problems which beset the Bithynian cities, *TAM* iv[1]. 3, a fragment from Nicomedia of an imperial letter which refers to disorder and *stasis* at some point when Bithynia was under proconsular rule (i.e. before the governorship of Lollianus Avitus from 159, below, 'Lucian' n. 99).

done), we might hold that the 'bad governor' who is alleged to have Dio's support in *Or.* xliii is Varenus. The identity of the 'bad governor', however, remains quite unsure.[177]

As to *Or.* xliii itself (*Political Speech in his Fatherland*), we again cannot be sure to what particular circumstances it belongs. Dio asserts his friendship for the people and is concerned especially to repudiate charges of collaboration with a tyrannous governor that are being disseminated secretly (xliii. 11). He begins the speech by noting that, whereas both he and 'the city' (here meaning the people) have the same enemies who 'hate' them, the latter is being 'accused' on the tribunal (i.e. of the governor), while Dio is accused 'here', i.e. before the assembly. The accusations against the people are again unknown, though abuses of their right of assemblage are the most obvious charges one can think of (cf. xlviii. 1). The rest of the speech consists of four sections, an 'illustration' from the career of the fourth-century Boeotian politician Epaminondas (3–6), a defence of Dio's stance towards the people (7–8), another historical example from the Athenians' treatment of Socrates (8–10), and finally the charges of abetting the corrupt governor (11–12). Epaminondas is one of Dio's favourite classical Greek politicians. In *Or.* xxii. 2 he is classed with Aristides, Lycurgus, and Solon as a philosopher-statesman. A similar verdict is delivered on him to the Prusan council in *Or.* xlix. 5–6. Epaminondas is also one of Dio's models for the idea of the political federation which he mentions to the people at *Or.* xlv. 13. In *Or.* xliii Epaminondas 'benefited' his country 'often and greatly'. He made it 'have first place' (4). But he was attacked by a man who had actively assisted the previous 'tyranny' in the city (that is, the Spartan occupation). The people rejected his slanders because they knew of Epaminondas' 'goodwill' towards them.

Dio breaks off now to remind his audience that he does not take part in prosecutions. He is not *barus*, 'threatening', to anyone. Why is his enemy 'displeased'? Because he wishes to prevent Dio coming to the aid of the *dêmos* 'should there be another crisis ... like the last one' (6–7). Dio says he is having to absent himself (*apodêmein*) on behalf of others (8). This 'absence' may imply no more than a

---

[177] For Varenus: Jones 1978a: 102 (following Dessau 1899: 86); Desideri 1978: 281 n. 76 (following Vielmetti 1941: 98). Alternatively for Julius Bassus: von Arnim 1898: 374–81; Salmeri 1982: 54 n. 27. Sherwin-White 1966: 275 allows the possibility of either, Brunt 1961: 214 n. 17 neither.

trip within the province.[178] Dio suggests that he is going in defence
of the people. He then brings in the story of Socrates, a figure with
whom he often likes to be compared. Socrates suffered for his
opposition to the tyranny installed at Athens by Sparta at the end
of the Peloponnesian War. But, unlike Epaminondas, 'he was put
to death by the people, on whose behalf he had incurred danger,
when it was flourishing later', because they believed the slanders of
malicious prosecutors. The charges of corruption and impiety towards the old gods were 'the very opposite of what Socrates used
to do' (8–9). Earlier in the speech Dio has exhorted the Prusan people
'to have a character that is Hellenic and to be neither ungrateful nor
unintelligent' (3). The Athenians' treatment of Socrates is a paradoxical reminder of this (which Dio mentions also at xlvii. 7).[179]

Dio turns finally to the 'secret' indictment against him. The first
charge of impiety against the gods is probably a means of tying
Dio's case to that of Socrates. He continues, '[Dio is charged] with
having persuaded a bad governor to torture the *dêmos*, to exile the
greatest number he could, and even to execute some, so making it
necessary for others to die voluntarily because as old men they
were unable to go into exile or bear leaving their country. Further,
[he is charged] with collaborating even now in everything with the
tyrant of our province [*ethnos*], specifically so that he will be successful in court [*kalôs agônieitai*] and shall take the cities by force,
and he is preparing the peoples, as far as he can. Further, he himself
is destroying the democratic government standing as its prosecu-
tor . . . and committing crimes against his own citizens and towns-
men, and doing many other things which I am ashamed to list. In
addition he is setting a bad example to young and old of indolence,
luxury, and treachery. He is bribing the masses, so that no one will
reproach him with what happened then but will somehow forget
his hatred and plotting' (11–12). It is clear from Dio's presentation
of the stories of Epaminondas and Socrates that he wishes his audience to apply these charges to his enemy rather than to himself.[180]
We should probably not read xliii. 11–12 in the light of Pliny's
report of the Bithynians' prosecution of Varenus, where the provincial assembly changed its mind after (it seems) a pro-Varenus

---

[178] Cf. *Or.* xl. 28.
[179] xlvii. 7 '[the Athenians] incur blame even now about Socrates, because their
behaviour towards the man was not just or pious'.
[180] So rightly von Arnim 1898: 368–71.

faction took control. For, though the governor in Dio's speech is to stand trial (*agônieitai*), presumably on a charge brought by the provincial assembly ('shall take the cities by force'), it seems implausible (though by no means absurd) to imagine that Dio could or would have denied his support in the *koinon* for the pro-Varenus faction. We would rather expect a justification of such action from him. Instead, the justification we have in *Or.* xliii is one that does not include support for Roman governors, a group to which Dio is fairly antipathetic.

Touching on these matters are two well-known letters from Pliny's special governorship in Bithynia in 110–112 (or so), *Letters* x. 81–2.[181] Pliny reports to Trajan that while he was at Prusa on 'public business' Flavius Archippus and his aide Eumolpus sought his judgement on two charges against Dio, the first that Dio should produce accounts for a building he had erected in the capacity of *curator operis* (the Greek *epimelêtês*)—the suggestion being 'quod aliter fecisset ac debuisset', the second that he had placed a statue of the emperor in a building complex in which his wife and son had been buried (*Letters* x. 81). Pliny is further requested by Dio's opponents to try the case in another city, Nicaea. Against Dio's wishes he allows an adjournment in favour of Eumolpus 'since the matter concerned precedent' (81. 5). Pliny's major worry is not the public accounts, but the potentially treasonable act of having placed the emperor's statue near a grave (81. 7–8), which is the first concern of Trajan's reply (x. 82. 1). Fear, terror, and charges of treason are not Trajan's way of securing reverence for his name ('as you knew very well'). As to the accounts, Trajan is content to observe that Dio 'does not and should not refuse' inspection (82. 2). Nothing can be said on this basis about Trajan's relationship with Dio. Trajan's rejection of the treason charge is merely part of the style of the age. He certainly does not profess (in this official correspondence) anything approaching Dio's claim of 'familiarity' or 'friendship' (*Orr.* xlv. 3, xlvii. 22).[182]

This correspondence is more interesting for the light it sheds on

---

[181] Pliny governed as Trajan's direct legate, breaking the usual government of the province of Bithynia and Pontus by annual proconsuls; on his dates see Sherwin-White 1966: 80–1.

[182] Style of the age: cf. e.g. Trajan in Pliny, *Letters* x. 55, 97. 2, Sherwin-White 1966: 557 for Pliny's similar expressions (x. 1. 2, *Panegyric* 18. 1, etc.). No real friendship with Dio: cf. Rawson 1989: 256 (Sura, Palma, and Senecio are named in Latin sources as Trajan's friends).

provincial 'use' of Roman government to pursue local rivalries. Flavius Archippus is known from three earlier letters of Pliny to Trajan (x. 58–60). When Pliny was enrolling jurors at Prusa (as part of his tour of the assize districts),[183] Archippus claimed he was a philosopher and was therefore exempt.[184] His enemies then alleged he should be removed from the list of jurors because he had been condemned to the mines for *falsum* (forgery).[185] What is interesting is the advantage taken of Pliny's visit to exact revenge on a foe. Archippus rebutted the allegations against him by handing Pliny several testimonial letters. Pliny subjoins two letters of Domitian showing Archippus his favour and an edict and letter of Nerva upholding the decisions of Domitian (x. 58). Unfortunately, the verdict of Velius Paulus, the governor who condemned Archippus,[186] which was also sent, has not been transmitted. It is noteworthy how careful both sides were to preserve Roman government documentation over the years. We are reminded of the testimonials Dio himself produces from time to time in Prusa. Why Archippus' enemies, especially the named 'accusatrix' Furia Prima (x. 59, 60), had waited until now to attack is unclear. The basis of their claim on Pliny's sympathy was perhaps Archippus' strong involvement with Domitian, who gave him an estate (x. 58. 5) and to Trajan's mind was probably responsible for his restitution (x. 60. 1). If so,

[183] The jurors were drawn equally from Roman citizens and non-Roman citizens in the province: Sherwin-White 1966: 640.

[184] The fact that Pliny mentions to Trajan the reason for Archippus' claim for exemption ('ut philosophus') has been held to show that there was no general exemption for philosophers at this time (Bowersock 1969: 33, broadly following Herzog 1935); but it should be noted that Pliny makes nothing of the reason once mentioned and that Trajan in his reply does not mention it at all (x. 60); further, Hadrian's exemptions (which included philosophers) are explicitly a confirmation of *already existing* regulations (*Digest* xxvii. 1. 6. 8). Despite Herzog 1935: 19–20, Charisius' slightly muddled statement at *Digest* l. 4. 18. 30 that the exemption was given to philosophers and others by Vespasian and Hadrian may contain the truth; that there is no mention of philosophers in the famous fragmentary edict of Vespasian exempting doctors and 'educators' printed by Herzog (= *FIRA* i. 73, cf. 77; McCrum–Woodhead 458) does not preclude the existence of other lost edicts or rescripts (nor is there cause to make Vespasian's ejection of philosophers from Rome a consistent policy: we only have to recall Hadrian's own caprice towards intellectuals). Cf. Griffin 1971: 280–1, I. Hadot 1984: 231–4.

[185] On the severity of this punishment, which one would not expect at this time for a member of the local elite (Archippus' then status is not of course known, though Pliny and Trajan speak of a 'restitution' of his 'status' by Domitian: x. 58. 3, 60. 1), see Garnsey 1970: 134.

[186] His governorship is dated to c.79/80 (Eck 1982: 302).

the case recalls another, Pliny's prosecution in 99 on behalf of the council of Baetica of the associates of Caecilius Classicus, the pro-consul of 97–8, who escaped prosecution by an early death (*Letters* iii. 4, 9). Among the ramifications of this trial was the indictment for prevarication (i.e. collusion with the defence) of one of the Baetican prosecutors, Norbanus Licinianus, by a witness presumably sympathetic to the defence party.[187] Licinianus was tried at once, which was as Pliny notes not legal, and was condemned largely for his behaviour under Domitian and relegated to an island, of all of which Pliny thoroughly approved (iii. 9. 29–35).[188] Licinianus undoubtedly suffered too from the natural hostility of the senate to provincial prosecutors (about which Dio warned the Tarsians at *Or.* xxxiv. 9). But we also see old scores among provincials being settled at the level of Roman government. The case of Archippus may be similar, except that he survived to bother Pliny a little later about Dio's building projects.[189]

The cases of Archippus and Furia Prima and Archippus, Eumolpus, and Dio are in one way good illustrations of Dio's (and Plutarch's) fears about Roman involvement in the cities of the Greek world. They also show its haphazard nature. Both times Pliny is involved we see him being sucked into local rivalries unwittingly.[190] Understandably he did not go looking for this sort of trouble and

[187] iii. 9. 29 'sive iratus quod evocatus esset invitus, sive subornatus ab aliquo reorum'.

[188] The penalty was far harsher than it should have been (ban on activity as an advocate under the SC Turpilianum): Sherwin-White 1966: 238; Garnsey 1970: 53.

[189] Julius Bassus, the disgraced governor of Bithynia defended by Pliny, was of eastern, almost certainly Pergamene, origin (being a descendant of Galatian and Pergamene royalty; Halfmann 1979: no. 19). Clearly that did not lessen the sympathy of the senate for him (cf. above, n. 136), but it might have been a factor in the Bithynian prosecution (Bassus asked Pliny to stress that his high birth laid him open to conspiracy and factional interest: iv. 9. 4–5; cf. vi. 31. 3 on Claudius Ariston 'princeps Ephesiorum').

[190] Cf. also Pliny, *Letters* x. 110–11, where Pliny's presence at Amisus leads to him being presented with an alleged misdemeanour which happened twenty years before. Later, around 174, years of rivalry between the leading families of Athens, the Herodes-Eucles family of Marathon and the Claudii of Melite, led to charges of tyranny being made against Herodes Atticus in a meeting of the assembly to which the Athenians had invited Marcus' special commissioners in Greece, the Quintilii (Philostratus, *VS* 559); the matter escalated to involve Marcus himself, whose res-olution of various connected disputes and attempt to reconcile Herodes with Athens is attested in a now famous series of texts found in the Roman agora at Athens (Oliver 1970; Ameling 1983: ii. 82–205, no. 189 incorporating Jones 1971*b*). Christians too realized the value of a governor's arrival for publicity and prophecy: Lane Fox 1986: 484, 487.

was unsure what to do when he found it. Yet on other matters the governor intervened more readily and without notice, such as the suspension of assembly at Prusa or the unadvertised convoking of the assembly to discuss Dio's building plans (Dio, *Or.* xlv. 15), which was on Dio's report of it an opportunity to gauge how much financial support the project really enjoyed (xlv. 16). It is perhaps surprising that we do not hear more from Dio about this sort of interference, which was mediated through procurators and curators.[191] Rather, his criticisms in the civic speeches focus on political interference by governors for their own ends (see especially *Orr.* xxxiv. 15, 38–42; xxxviii. 33–8; xliii. 11–12; xlv. 4–5), a far more serious matter.

It can scarcely be doubted that Dio was as aware as anyone else that governors' corruption was ultimately a symptom of imperial rule. Although there is no criticism of the emperor in these speeches (indeed, we find a few passages of favourable comment), the hostility and opposition Dio faced at home show well enough that many people did not believe he had any real influence with Trajan, and this makes it all the more likely that his own picture of the friendly emperor coming to his assistance and granting him favours is simply a prop for his domestic politics and not a genuinely held view. Despite their very different contexts and aims, it is probably right, then, finally to associate Dio's attacks on governors with the veiled but certain expression of distaste for Rome's control of Greece at the end of the *Olympicus*, the remarks on the low quality of today's 'leaders' in the *Rhodian Oration*, and the careful separation of the Roman king from the ideal monarch in the *Orations on Kingship*, with which we began. These criticisms should not be palliated by talking of philosophic 'freedom of speech' or 'concern with moral issues'. On a number of occasions Dio emphasizes the brutal facts of Roman power to his audiences. It is also relevant that he spent so much time and energy encouraging the Greeks and delivering to them the positive message of concord and unity. There

---

[191] Interference by Rome: cf. above, 'Plutarch' n. 123; cf. below, 'Aristides' n. 58 on the governor Severus' scrutiny of Hadriani's security arrangements; in general see Magie 1950: ii. 1391–2 n. 61, 1504 n. 29 (glossed by Oliver 1954); Burton 1979 esp. on the *curatores rei publicae* (Greek *logistai*) who were active from the reign of Domitian, if not before (Syme 1977: 43 on L. Caesennius Sospes; Philostratus, *VS* 512 on [Verginius] Rufus at Ephesus in the time of Nero [for his identity see below, 'Philostratus' n. 75]).

is nothing anti-Roman in this.[192] But the call to minimize Roman interference and the advice on how to handle the governors do go very closely with the reminder of the benefits of concord and unity at Tarsus, Nicomedia, and Prusa. This combination recalls (*mutatis mutandis*) Plutarch's *Political Advice* with its own positive message of unity, criticisms of the Greeks' failings in their dealings with Rome, and desire to minimize Roman rule. We cannot know for sure how Dio's policy in these matters went down with his audiences, significant numbers of whom may like himself have been Roman citizens or were perhaps employed in the military, equestrian, or even senatorial services of the Empire. But we must assume that he—like Plutarch—was not totally insensitive to their prejudices, and accept that his message was not out of step with their feelings.

[192] Indeed, Dio can preach it in front of the governor: xlviii. 9.

7

Arrian and Appian

ARRIAN—ROMAN POLITICS AND GREEK CULTURE

A complete contrast with Dio of Prusa is offered by his much younger contemporary Flavius Arrian of Nicomedia, who successfully combined Greek politics and literature with the exercise of Roman power. Arrian will not be discussed in detail here because in the main his several literary works do not touch on Greek perceptions of Rome. However, there are a number of key passages which are relevant to this subject and which may be examined to determine Arrian's self-perception between Greek culture and the Roman Empire. For Arrian, the first Greek senator we know of from Bithynia,[1] seems to be as perfect an example as we could want of the integration of the Greek elite into the highest levels of Roman government.

The key elements of Arrian's career are as follows.[2] He was born about 85–90. His praenomen, Lucius or Aulus, shows that the family was not given citizenship by the Flavians, as we would otherwise assume.[3] Some time around 108 he passed through Nicopolis, perhaps on his way to Rome, and heard the philosopher Epictetus, whose lectures on personal conduct he later wrote up as the famous *Discourses of Epictetus*.[4] His first service in Roman government was as a member of the *consilium* of the prominent consular C. Avidius Nigrinus (son of one of the brothers addressed in Plutarch's *On Brotherly Love*) during Nigrinus' correctorship in Greece around

[1] Cf. above, 'Plutarch' n. 103, 'Dio' n. 77. Arrian's family, as the names suggest, may have been Italian in origin, at least in part (Bowie 1974: 191); but little Italian immigration to Nicomedia is known of (Syme 1982: 184).

[2] Halfmann 1979: no. 56; Stadter 1980: 1–18; Syme 1982; Vidal-Naquet 1984: 311–22.

[3] Follet 1976: 34–5.

[4] Epictetus: Millar 1965; Brunt 1977: 19–30. Arrian and the philosopher: Wirth 1967 (Arrian's construction of the text); Brunt 1977: 30–48; Stadter 1980: 19–31.

112/13.[5] After apparently seeing service with Trajan on the emperor's Parthian campaign, Arrian almost certainly became praetorian proconsul of Baetica in the 120s, was then suffect consul probably in 129, and finally imperial legate in Cappadocia in 131–7, an important military post on the frontier of the Empire.[6] Arrian then retired to Athens, where he was archon in 145/6.[7]

Neither Arrian nor others saw any contradiction between his Roman military and political career and his profession of philosophy and literature, as is shown clearly by several contemporary inscriptions which celebrate both sides of his life.[8] Lucian, who himself identified with the aims of the Roman empire, saw Arrian in the same way.[9] Politically Arrian, like others from the Greek east who were in the equestrian or senatorial service, satisfied his ambition with a Roman career and was naturally proud of the status it gave him. The difficult question to answer is whether the Roman political and the Greek cultural sides had equal weight, not in the heavily contextualized public discourse of our epigraphic evidence— where they clearly did, but in Arrian's own writings and thought.

We will not find Arrian's views in his history of Trajan's Parthian war, the *Parthica*. The surviving fragments and the summary of Photius make it clear that this work was very much to Trajan's credit.[10] But there is as little of the personal here as there is in another Roman-contextualized work, the *Circumnavigation of the Black Sea*. This is a highly wrought description of official gubernatorial business from Arrian's tenure of Cappadocia written in the

---

[5] *SIG*³ 827A. On the family see Jones 1971*a*: 32, 53–4.

[6] See also Alföldy 1977: 238–9 for an identification of Arrian with the philosopher governor of Syria mentioned by Lucian at *Peregrinus* 14.

[7] Follet 1976: 209–12.

[8] *AE* 1971, 437 (containing Arrian's praenomen; literature at Stadter 1980: 2 n. 5): 'consular and philosopher'; *AE* 1968, 473 (erected by the Gellii of Corinth; cf. Arrian's letter to L. Gellius preceeding the *Discourses of Epictetus*; Stadter 1980: 14 n. 88): 'philosopher ... proconsul of the province of Cappadocia'; *AE* 1974, 370 (the Cordoba epigram composed by Arrian in honour of Artemis; Stadter 1980: 10 n. 61, 52): 'proconsul Arrian ... I offer to you, Artemis, these gifts of the Muses'. Note also the suggestion of Oliver 1982 that Arrian functioned as a sort of official watchdog over the philosophic schools at Athens in the 140s (there is of course no evidence for this).

On the vexed dating of Arrian's literary works see Stadter 1980: 179–87.

[9] *Alexander* 2 'a man who was among the first of the Romans and was associated with *paideia* for his whole life' (on the political reference see below, 'Lucian' nn. 107–8); Cassius Dio's *Life of Arrian the Philosopher* (*Suda* δ 1239) presumably also stressed (despite the title) the man's two sides.

[10] Photius, *Library* cod. 58; Stadter 1980: 135–44.

form of a letter addressed to Hadrian (and containing some gentle flattery of the emperor).[11] Rather, the search for personal comments leads us to the history of Alexander the Great, the *Anabasis*. Since this work is as Greek in its set-up as the *Parthica* is Roman, there is clearly a danger of not finding the balance we seek. On the other hand, the comments in the much discussed 'second preface' (i. 12. 1–5) are recognizably personal.[12] Further, their value for under-standing Arrian's cultural/political priorities is enhanced because his Roman side—despite the Greekness of the work—is not totally ignored. In this passage Arrian is narrating Alexander's visit to the tomb of Achilles and notes that the great man has thus far lacked a Homer to celebrate him in the way Homer had celebrated Achilles. He then says that he does not consider himself unworthy to write up Alexander's story. He goes on, 'As to who I am to make this judgement about myself, I do not have to record my name (for it is not at all unknown among men) nor what my fatherland [*patris*] is nor my family nor if indeed I have held any office [*tina archên*] in my own (land) [*en têi emautou*]; but I do record this, that father-land, family, and offices are found for me in these stories and have been from my youth. And for this reason I do not think I am unworthy of the first place in the Greek language just as Alexander was in arms'.[13] This is an exceptionally conceited passage: not to have to identify oneself is the ultimate privilege available. In par-ticular Arrian defies the conventions of ancient historiography (which encouraged the historian to give name and city), and plays instead on the recognized anonymity of Homer, whose genius he claims for his own.[14] A familiar Homeric model has been seen in the assertion that Arrian's real fatherland, etc., lies in 'these stories'.[15]

The question of importance for us is the meaning of 'my

[11] Cf. Bosworth 1993: 249 on ch. 23. 4 (Achilles' love for Patroclus) as a subtle reference to Hadrian and Antinous; but also note id. 245–6 on the role of Xenophon's *Anabasis* in the *Circumnavigation*. Given the context of the work not too much should be made of the first person plural verb after 'Romans' at 11. 2 ('Ῥωμαίοις . . . ἐξελοῦμεν), as some have wanted to do.

[12] See Moles 1985, Marincola 1989 for detailed comment.

[13] Aelius Aristides echoes this comparison at *Or.* 1. 49—either, then, a topos (Brunt 1976–83: ii. 540) and/or a reaction.

[14] A parallel also made by his contemporary Cephalion (Photius, *Library* cod. 68, 34a14–16); see further Marincola 1989: 188–90.

[15] Cf. Andromache's plea to Hector at *Iliad* vi. 429–30 ('you are for me father and lady mother, etc.'). For language closer to Arrian's see Aristides *Or.* xxxiii. 20.

fatherland' and the reference to office-holding 'in my own (land)'.
The first must be Nicomedia.[16] But the second has been claimed for
Rome.[17] Is this right? The suggestion is not to be dismissed out of
hand. Alexander was of course a quintessentially Hellenic subject,
but Arrian still finds room in the *Anabasis* to mention Romans (in
the third person) several times.[18] These passages reflect his own
interests and indicate one potential audience. Nevertheless, in the
second preface 'in my own [land]' should naturally be taken in the
Greek as a simple variation on 'my fatherland'.[19] This interpretation
depends on the question of what office Arrian says he is not mentioning. The sentence 'if indeed I have held any office in my own
[land]' should and could easily refer to local Bithynian office-
holding. One of Arrian's lost works is his *History of Bithynia* in
eight books from its beginnings down to the incorporation of the
kingdom into Rome's empire in 75 or 74 BC.[20] According to Photius'
summary Arrian gave full details of himself in the preface to this
work, which he described as 'a gift to his fatherland'. In particular
he spoke of having performed the priesthood of the chief deities of
Nicomedia, Demeter and Child. It is not difficult to imagine that he
performed other offices there too, such as being a representative to
the Bithynian provincial assembly in Nicomedia. It is difficult to
hold that Arrian's 'own [land]' is not Bithynia.[21] On the other hand,
when he goes on to speak of 'offices' in general, there is no reason
why he should not be referring to his *whole* career up to the point
of writing (whenever that is)—including Roman offices. For if Arrian
is as well known to men at large as he claims, one can hardly
exclude his Roman magistracies from among the reasons for his
fame.[22] Indeed, this was how he was identifiable to Lucian, and also

[16] So Bosworth 1980: 106. Brunt 1976–83: ii. 538 suggests Rome, citing Paulus at
Digest i. 9. 11, l. 1. 22. 6 on senators having domicile in their native lands and also at
Rome, since Rome is a common fatherland (cf. also 'Aristides' n. 96, 'Galen' n. 19);
this has nothing to do with the present passage of Arrian.
[17] Stadter 1980: 65 n. 19, 181; Brunt 1976–83: ii. 539.
[18] iii. 5. 7 (Rome learnt from Alexander how to govern Egypt); v. 7. 2–8. 1
(Roman pontoon bridges); vii. 1. 3 (Alexander was disturbed by Rome's fame); vii.
15. 5–6 (Rome never sent ambassadors to Alexander).
[19] For cogent reasoning see esp. Moles 1985: 165.
[20] See Photius, *Library* cod. 93; on summary and fragments see Stadter 1980:
152–61.
[21] Wirth 1964: 224 suggests Arrian's local office is his Athenian archonship; possible, but wrong. Bithynian assembly: Deininger 1965: 61 (it probably met elsewhere
too).
[22] Cf. Vidal-Naquet 1984: 320 (but beware his lacunose translation of i. 12. 4–5).

perhaps to Galen.[23] It is at this point that Arrian puts culture and power in context. He says clearly that career, family, and native land are nothing compared with 'these stories', i.e. the deeds of Alexander that he is now writing up. It is his lifelong devotion to these that earns him first place in the Greek language. It is plain that by saying what he does Arrian is according far more importance to cultural than political identity (where political is both local and Roman). His identity lies in playing Homer, the king of Greek letters, to Alexander, the king of Greek arms. This is a familiar but also very personal investment in the heritage of the Greek world.

Arrian's self-conscious association with classical Greece is shown most clearly elsewhere by his adoption of the name of Xenophon, the great Athenian general and author of the fourth century, in the extraordinary work which describes his response as governor of Cappadocia to the Alan threat of 135, the *Order of Battle against the Alans*.[24] The troops of various nations from the Empire are named fighting against 'the Scythians' not by legions but in 'phalanxes' (5, 6, 15, etc.); of Rome and her emperor there is no word.[25] This commander is interested only in himself as Xenophon—and Alexander—and in giving his present-day deeds a classical pedigree. In his treatise on hunting, the *Cynegeticus*, written when he was a citizen of Athens, Arrian again claims the name 'Xenophon'. Like Xenophon he prides himself on 'hunting, generalship, and wisdom' (*Cyneg.* 1. 4). Not surprisingly this work has an overt hypertextual relationship with the *Cynegeticus* by (or attributed to) Xenophon.[26] It has been supposed that 'Xenophon' was in fact part of Arrian's own name.[27] The epigraphical record, however, provides no support for this. Rather, we see in these and other works the constant

[23] Lucian: above, n. 9. Galen, *On the Use of the Parts* iii. 895. 17–18 'Arrian the consul' (written under Marcus: Ilberg 1889: 219); NB 'Arrianos' is Helmreich's correction of 'Adrianos' (cf. *PIR²* H 6) or 'Arianos' in the MSS; if 'Arrianos' is correct, Galen may be referring to Arrian's son mentioned by his granddaughter in *IG* ii² 4251/3 (Graindor 1922: 49–52; note her connection with Demeter).

[24] *Order of Battle against the Alans* 10, 22. Bosworth 1977: 247 ff.; Stadter 1980: 45–49; the work is distinctive for its constant use of the third person imperative or infinitive-imperative, as if Arrian were actually giving orders.

[25] For 'phalanx' = legion cf. Herodian vii. 8. 11, viii. 2. 2, 4. 6; on the Alexander imitation involved cf. Cassius Dio lxxvii. 7. 1–2 on Caracalla's 'phalanx' of Macedonians. Wheeler 1979 offers a literalist analysis of Arrian here.

[26] The authenticity of the Xenophontic work was not doubted in antiquity. On the relationship see Stadter 1976.

[27] Stadter 1967.

dialogue with the past that was so important to the identity of the Greek elite in our period. Arrian is strongly preferencing his Greek cultural identity through this. As in the *Anabasis* there is a hiding of his 'real' self—here not anonymously to recall Homer, but overtly to appropriate and masquerade as one of the most popular figures of the Greek literary canon.[28] It is true that the *Cynegeticus*, like the *Order of Battle against the Alans*, is not blindly rooted in the classical past. That is only as we should expect—the present living through the past. In the *Cynegeticus* Arrian celebrates the improved techniques and better hunting animals now available to the sportsman owing to the resources of the Empire (which is not named). Nevertheless, for Arrian in the second sophistic hunting is a Greek affair through and through and one particularly important to his own self-perception and self-presentation.

The suggestion has been made that Arrian wrote the *Anabasis* as an expression of his thoughts on the Roman empire. To write of the relation between Macedonians and Persians was to try to come to terms with the problem of integrating the two peoples of the Empire and the two sides of the writer himself.[29] The second preface at *Anabasis* i. 12 makes this idea, which is strained even as a reading of text, a most unlikely one to plant in the mind of the author. Arrian was a man of action as well as an intellectual. To satisfy the first side of his personality he took advantage of the possibilities offered by the new political ordering of the world. In his work on cavalry tactics, the *Tactica*, he praises the emperor Hadrian for his improvements and restyling of Roman cavalry techniques and finishes by applying to 'this present reign of Hadrian now in its twentieth year' a couple of lines attributed to Terpander which praise Sparta's devotion to war, the Muse, and justice (*Tact.* 44. 2–3).[30] This praise is far wider than matters tactical. In the same work Arrian includes a statement of what he liked about the Roman system (33). The Romans, he says, are to be congratulated for

[28] Arrian and Xenophon: see Münscher 1920: 124–6. Ameling 1984*a* compares honorary titles like 'New Homer', etc., which were awarded publicly for distinction in letters (Photius, *Library* cod. 58, 17b, says Arrian was called 'New Xenophon'); there may be something in this (cf. the double herm of Xenophon and ?Arrian: Oliver 1972).

[29] Vidal-Naquet 1984: 383–7.

[30] [Terpander] in Page, *PMG* p. 362. Cf. *Tact.* 32. 3 for a work on (?)infantry tactics written for 'the emperor himself' (on the text here see Bosworth 1993: 254 n. 147).

selecting for themselves whatever is good from any place. This practice of theirs is clear in the areas of war, religion, law (Arrian cites
the origin of the Twelve Tables from Athens), and other things—
'it would be a considerable effort to go through them'. The idea of
Rome's assimilation of the best discoveries of other peoples is well
known in Greek and Latin texts.[31] It is closely related to another
idea, that Rome assimilated different populations and made them
citizens.[32] It is not far from here to Dio of Prusa's advice to Trajan
(echoed by Aristides and Cassius Dio) to select for his friends the
best people from all over the Empire. In the *Tactica* Arrian does
not specify personnel. But the idea was surely in his mind, since it
was this policy which made possible his own Roman career. However, though Arrian plainly accepted political integration at this
level, it is nevertheless dubious to hold that Roman politics were
ultimately more important to him than his Greek culture.

Arrian is an important part of the process that was making real
the notion of a single political world for the eastern and western
elites. This was considerably advanced by the time of the *Constitutio
Antoniniana* in 212, when almost all free people within the Empire,
elite and non-elite, were created Roman citizens. The authors to be
considered in this book who saw this out and lived into the third
century—Galen, Cassius Dio, and Philostratus—accepted the political existence of the Empire as much as Arrian did. But cognitively
and spiritually not one of them doubted he was Hellenic. There is
no reason to think that Arrian was different.

APPIAN—ROMAN HISTORY AND LOCAL LOYALTY

With Arrian may be compared his slightly younger contemporary,
Appian of Alexandria, who was also a historian of Rome and whose
career prospered under Roman patronage, albeit at a much lower
level. A large part of Appian's *Roman History* survives and is important chiefly for the complete five-book narrative of the Roman

---

[31] Cf. *Ineditum Vaticanum* 3 (*FGrH* 839 dating to ? the 1st c. BC); Tacitus, *Annals*
iii. 27. 1. Posidonius, *FGrH* 87 F59 (Athenaeus 273e–f) is the likely source (though
cf. von Arnim 1892: 130 suggesting Fabius Pictor for the *Ineditum Vaticanum*).

[32] First in *SIG*[3] 543 (IV) (Philip V to Larissa); Gabba 1991: 87–8, 109–10, 208–
10 on Dionysius' praise of Rome in this regard. Cf. below at n. 38 with further
references.

civil wars from the Gracchi to the death of Sextus Pompeius at the beginning of 35 BC.[33] The story of the civil wars was completed in a further four lost books called the *Aiguptiaka* (*Egyptian Affairs*). The loss of these books, together with the loss of the tenth book of the *History*, which narrated Rome's conquest of Greece and Ionia, makes it very difficult to determine Appian's views of Rome's relations with the Greek world. Furthermore, the *History* is virtually devoid of personal comment. Nevertheless, some points can and should be made about this important author.

Appian's major interest in the *History* was ethical, as the structure of the work shows. For instead of adopting a chronological approach to the development of the Roman Empire, he treated Rome's conquests people by people (*kath' hekaston ethnos*). The aim was to compare Roman qualities with those of Rome's opponents (Preface 12. 46–9). For this purpose chronology was 'superfluous' (ibid. 13. 50). Despite Appian's own awareness of problems arising from his distribution of events, his chosen structure works remarkably well, and the continuity of the text is assisted by occasional pointers from one book to another.[34] From the fragments and from the surviving portions (*Celtic Wars* [in an epitome], *Spanish Wars, Hannibalic War, Carthaginian Wars, Illyrian Wars, Syrian Wars, Mithridatic War, Civil Wars*),[35] it is plain that he identified good sources and exercised his own judgement about the causes and progress of Rome's wars with intelligence and fairness. Appian certainly admired the Roman Empire of his own time. He was a friend of the prominent orator and consular Cornelius Fronto, who obtained an honorary procuratorship for him from the emperor Pius.[36] He mentions this office (without confessing its nature) at the

[33] On the *History* and its author see Gabba 1956 (*Civil Wars*); Kühne 1969 (Marxist materialism in the *Civil Wars*); Goldmann 1988; Brodersen 1993 (and other articles in the same volume). It is clear that the *History* was composed towards the end of Appian's life in the 150s.

[34] See e.g. the comments at *Spanish Wars* 14. 56; *Carthaginian Wars* 2. 10; *Illyrian Wars* 9. 25; *Syrian Wars* 52. 260 (a reference to the apparently uncompleted book of *Parthian Wars*); *Mithridatic War* 91. 415 (Pompey's campaign against the pirates cannot be accommodated in any other book), 119. 589 (difficulties of arranging the Mithridatic War by *ethnē*); *Civil Wars* i. 34. 151, v. 1. 2.

[35] These are books iv, vi, vii, viii (also containing the fragmentary *Numidian Wars*), ix (also containing the fragmentary *Macedonian Wars*), xi, xii, xiii–xvii.

[36] See Fronto, *Ad Ant. Pium* 10 (168 v.d.H.²) with Champlin 1980: 98–100. Two letters between Fronto and Appian in Greek are preserved as Fronto, *Epist. var.* (242–8 v.d.H.²); these are of no interest to the present enquiry (though cf. the sentiments of *Epist. var.* 245. 15–18 v.d.H.² with Preface 7. 26).

end of the Preface (15. 62), where he also stresses his prominent position in his 'fatherland' and his appearances as a barrister 'before the kings' at Rome.[37] In an important aside before his narrative of the Proscriptions under Octavian, Antony, and Lepidus, Appian says he is going to record a few examples of the various sorts of events 'to testify to each and to indicate the happiness of the present times [*es eudaimonisma tôn nun parontôn*]' (*Civil Wars* iv. 16. 64). He was, however, no panegyrist of Rome. His critical comment on the miscegenation of the Roman plebs at the time of the Liberators at *Civil Wars* ii. 120. 505–6 can certainly be read, as the tenses encourage, with a contemporary reference.[38] More importantly, throughout the *History* in authorial comments and speeches there are plainly stated examples of Rome's underhand diplomacy and aggressive imperialism in times past.[39] This record is not, however, obviously anti-Roman.[40] For the narrative always unfolds in a matter-of-fact way and each issue is taken on its merits. And Appian clearly also gives play to Roman virtues.[41] His statement in the Preface that he wanted to review Rome's actions 'in order to learn the peoples' weakness or powers of endurance and the virtue or good fortune of their captors' (12. 48) is borne out in the rest of the work. 'Good fortune' is an important factor in Rome's success because her enemies are very often no less courageous.[42] It is not in any way a slur on Rome. Indeed, Appian appears to believe that Rome had enjoyed the active support of the gods, though he hardly has a coherent scheme in mind in this regard.[43]

[37] Note too his final recommendation to readers who want to know more about him to turn to his autobiography. For Appian's career as a *causidicus* (to borrow Fronto's description), cf. Polyaenus *Strategems* ii Preface ('pleading suits before you', i.e. before Marcus and Lucius).

[38] Cf. 'Galen' n. 19 and 'Cassius Dio' nn. 18–19.

[39] On Appian's view of the static empire of the present cf. 'Aristides' n. 97.

[40] See, speeches aside, e.g. *Spanish Wars* 60. 253, 61. 256, 70. 297 (Viriathus); *Carthaginian Wars* 74. 343–6, 94. 442, 112. 528 (Third Punic War); *Macedonian Wars* fr. 11. 3–4 (Perseus); *Mithridatic War* 14. 48–9, 15. 50, 121. 598. Note the crudely anti-Roman Appian constructed by Hahn 1993.

[41] Note e.g. the significant 'reminder' of 'Roman virtue' in the dark days of the civil wars at *Civil Wars* v. 113. 472.

[42] For good examples see *Celtic Wars* fr. 1. 9 (Caesar and Ariovistus); *Spanish Wars* 75. 318–19 (Viriathus), 97. 419–21 (Numantia; contrast 98. 426 on Scipio); *Mithridatic War* 112. 540–50 (Mithridates).

[43] Cf. Preface 11. 43–4 (Rome's good judgement and good fortune); *Hannibalic War* 12. 49 (Hannibal led away from Rome by 'god'), 53. 224 (the Romans' victory at the Metaurus is divine 'compensation' for their disaster at Cannae); *Macedonian*

Although we do not have Appian's account of Rome's conquest of Greece, we may assume that the general presentation was no different from that adopted in the surviving books. That is to say, he would have been quite open about Rome's imperialist intentions in Greece. But it seems unlikely—though possible—that he would have commented in a personal and critical manner, as do Plutarch and Pausanias.[44] A more regrettable loss is that of the Egyptian books. Here there may well have been some expression of local patriotism, for elsewhere Appian speaks proudly of the power of the Egyptian kingdom under 'my kings', i.e. the Lagid dynasty.[45] Particularly revealing is his reason for narrating Rome's civil wars. These are useful to students of ambition and love of power. But 'it was especially necessary for me to narrate them beforehand, since they are the preliminaries of my *Egyptian History* and finish in it. For Egypt was captured as a result of this civil strife when Cleopatra became the ally of Antony' (*Civil Wars* i. 6. 24).

In trying to assess Appian's attitude to Rome it should be remembered that he never expresses the view that the Empire was a community of participating nations. Rome rules all the different peoples as an imperial power. Whether Appian thought that this was a good thing is unknown. But we cannot assume (as some have) that he felt 'Roman'. On a political level he must have identified with Rome as a citizen (though he does not mention his citizen name) and as an honorary procurator. But his decision to make a career in the Roman courts is an unsurprising use of opportunity. It is at a different level from the official Roman career of an Arrian or a Cornelius Pulcher,[46] but probably no different in intent. Alexandria remained Appian's 'fatherland' late in his life (Preface 15. 62), and it would be natural to assume (but impossible to prove)

Wars fr. 18. 2 (Perseus driven on by 'god'); *Syrian Wars* 37. 192 (Roman virtue and the aid of the gods); *Civil Wars* ii. 72. 299 (Pharsalus was used by god 'to start this present-day universal power'—perhaps a Plutarchan echo), iv. 134. 563 (the anger of the divine against Brutus and Cassius). Other passages—if not some of these—must certainly be seen as purely literary devices. See Goldmann 1988: 24–49 (rightly according the irrational in Appian a 'Zusatzfunktion' beside human causality).

[44] Elsewhere Appian writes of the Greeks factually as Rome's subjects: Preface 3. 10, 5. 17; *Carthaginian Wars* 135. 643 (Mummius' triumph); *Illyrian Wars* 5. 13; *Mithridatic War* 39. 151 (capture and regulation of Greece). Appian was naturally aware of the Roman Republican claim to have liberated Greece: cf. 'Pausanias' nn. 24, 37.

[45] Preface 10. 39–42, *Mithridatic War* 121. 600, *Civil Wars* i. 5. 21, i. 102. 477.

[46] On this prominent equestrian see above, 'Plutarch' n. 85.

that in this context he deplored Rome's rule, for Rome's control over the Empire's second city was highly restrictive.

Nor is it easy (again on the basis of what we have of this text) to establish an overt Greek identity for Appian. There are problems of evidence and interpretation here. First, it seems likely that Appian would anyway not have looked directly to a Greek background as his source of identity, but rather to a Graeco-Macedonian one. The status of the Macedonians as Greeks had long been open to dispute.[47] Alexander the Great was protected from scrutiny by his own merits. The Successors, the founders of the Hellenistic kingdoms and their heirs, were more exposed. Thus in our period Plutarch makes Alexandria a 'Greek city' in the *Life of Alexander* (26. 4) on account of its founder; whereas in his *Life of Antony* Ptolemaic Alexandria and its queen Cleopatra are explicitly Egyptian (25. 3, 29. 5, 31. 3, 50. 6–7).[48] It is clear from Appian's *Syrian Wars* that Appian himself had discussed the question of the relationship between Macedonians and Greeks. 'The affairs of the Macedonians and the Greeks were closely associated [*epimikta*] at various times and places, as I have demonstrated in my *Hellenic History*' (*Syrian Wars* 2. 5). In other words, being Macedonian was different (cf. ibid. 57. 297, *Mithridatic War* 41. 159), and very definitely a source of pride (cf. Preface 9. 33, 10. 37–42, 12. 45; *Civil Wars* ii. 149. 619–154. 649 for the digressive comparison between Caesar and Alexander), but not *too* different. Appian as an Alexandrian could legitimately claim the authority of Macedonian arms, as well as the intellectual inheritance of Greece.[49]

Second, while Appian clearly wrote for an audience which was not Roman, it is often said that he wrote in the *koine*.[50] If this were

---

[47] The problem continues to exercise the modern Greek state: cf. N. K. Martis' somewhat unluckily entitled *The Falsification of Macedonian History* (tr. J. Ph. Smith) (Athens 1984).

[48] For some of Plutarch's thoughts on Alexander and Macedonians see 'Plutarch' nn. 47, 76.

[49] There are no explicit comments of this sort, as there are with Arrian and Aristides, above, n. 13. It would be interesting to know what Appian thought of the Alexandrian Museum, which still attracted 'culturally distinguished men in every land' (*VS* 524). On Greek culture in Egypt cf. Quet 1992*b*, arguing that *OGIS* 709, the inscription in which the Alexandrians and other Greeks in Egypt honour Aelius Aristides ('Aristides' n. 115), should be read as a claim by these Egyptian Greeks to their membership of the Hellenic community.

[50] Greek audience—cf. the explanations of Roman customs/technical terms at *Carthaginian Wars* 66. 293–300; *Syrian Wars* 15. 63; *Civil Wars* i. 98. 457, ii. 2. 5, iii. 94. 389; see Goldmann 1988: 86 ff. Appian as a *koine* author—see e.g. Gabba 1967: p. xxxiii.

certainly so, it would have interesting consequences for his attitude towards the second sophistic elite and for his expectation of his audience. We might suggest that Appian rejected atticism because Athens and atticism meant nothing to him. The problem can be assessed under two headings: choice and ability. By one clear criterion of atticizing Greek—the use of the optative—Appian in fact plainly rejected the *koine*.[51] This is a matter of choice and a real indication of his desired appeal. In other areas he vacillates between non-classical and atticizing forms (cf. Plutarch and others). But this may be a matter of ability rather than choice, for it is well known that Appian kept a close stylistic eye on Herodotus, Thucyidides, and Xenophon.[52] In one respect Appian's language is indeed odd. His undoubted fluency in Latin affected his usage in Greek, and sure examples can be pointed to of contamination with Latin.[53] This to my mind is, again, a matter of ability: these usages had penetrated Appian's Greek and he was unaware of them. We should, then, take Appian as an atticizing author, if a rather unsuccessful one, recalling the inbuilt flaws in all atticizing Greek and the ultimate importance of displaying a social rather than a linguistic purity.[54]

All in all, without the personal statements of an Arrian, still less the information offered by a Plutarch or a Dio, Appian's preferences are hard to determine. He spent much time at Rome, and was proud of being honoured by the emperor. But there is no cause to discover in him a thoroughgoing identification with Rome. There is reasonable evidence of his local patriotism and his expectation of an educated Greek readership (with all that this entails). In short, his attitudes do not appear to be dissimilar to those of the other intellectuals studied in this book.

---

[51] 'Language' n. 42; Diel 1894: 22.

[52] Mention is made of Appian's non-classical use of prepositions, following Krumbholz 1885; but the increased frequency is no greater than in atticist authors like Arrian and the discrepant usage not necessarily deliberate.

Stylistic influences: respectively Zerdik 1886: 1–48 (somewhat exaggerated); Strebel 1935: 75–92; Goetzeler 1890: 25 ff. (though note Münscher 1920: 136 n. 4).

[53] Hering 1935 (generally convincing), cf. Gabba 1967: pp. xxxiv–xxxvii.

[54] Cf. again Preface 15. 62 'having attained first place in my fatherland'.

8

Aristides

INTRODUCTION

Aelius Aristides enjoyed enormous popularity for his rhetorical
prowess in his own lifetime and thereafter. His canonization as a
model of atticist style in antiquity itself and his popularity in the
Byzantine period have ensured that very many of his works survive.[1] Undoubtedly the most singular side of his character was his
devotion to the healing god Asclepius and his long struggle to be
well. I have already had occasion to say something about Aristides'
obsession with his health in the course of discussing the modern
conception of the second sophistic period as an 'age of anxiety'.
Aristides' recollections of his struggle were also famous in antiquity. 'He himself speaks of the nature of his disease . . . in the
Sacred Books, and these form some sort of diary for him, and such
diaries are excellent teachers of how to speak well on any subject.'[2]
The six *Sacred Tales* (*Orr.* xlvii–lii), as they are normally called, are
certainly one of the most interesting works to have come down to
us from this period.[3] They are records not so much of Aristides'
disease as of the treatments suggested for it by Asclepius. The title

---

[1] See Schmid 1887–97: ii. 7 n. 14, 14, id. *RE* ii (1896) 892; Boulanger 1923: 452–
7. On his reputation note the contemporary verdicts of Phrynichus, *Sophist's Stock-
in-Trade*, in Photius, *Library* cod. 158, 101a, and Hermogenes, *On Ideas* 353. 24 ff.
Rabe (comparability with Demosthenes), and the 3rd-c. views of Longinus *Excerpts*
6, 12 (214. 6, 215. 10 Sp.–H.) and Philostratus, *VS* 581–5.

Aristides is cited here by the text of Lenz and Behr (1976–80) for works i–xvi and
by the incomplete edition of Keil (1898) for the rest.

[2] Philostratus, *VS* 581.

[3] Behr 1968*a* is fundamental to understanding the background and structure of
the *Sacred Tales*; see also Misch 1949–62: i(2). 505–17; Dodds 1951: 109–10, 113–16,
id. 1965: 40–5; Festugière 1954: 85–104; Kee 1982: 129–34; Gourevitch 1984: 17–71;
Smith 1984; Bompaire 1989; Temkin 1991: 184–7. Useful notes are appended to the
translations by Nicosia 1984, Festugière 1986 (Saffrey), Schröder 1986, and Behr
1981–86: ii. 425 ff.

recalls the so-called 'sacred tales [*hieroi logoi*]' which were told to expound a god's deeds, and is used by Aristides in the sense of recounting his responses to divine revelation. The *Sacred Tales* are also important for assessing Aristides' views of Rome. For the fourth, the fifth, and the (mostly lost) sixth book tell of his return to health after ten years of severe illness, of his newly successful rhetorical career in Asia, Greece, and Italy, where he delivered the famous oration *To Rome* (*Or.* xxvi), and of his fight to avoid the responsibilities of various public offices enjoined on him by the cities and governors of the province of Asia. *To Rome* itself is often held to rank with Plutarch's *Political Advice* and Dio of Prusa's city speeches in its importance for understanding Greek attitudes to Rome in the second sophistic. It is of course an encomium (explicitly so at xxvi. 3), and because it is an encomium it is not in fact the best place to discover how Aristides really saw the ruling city. To do this it is necessary to compare what he says in *To Rome* with what he says in the rest of his work, including the *Sacred Tales*, where his thoughts are as private as we can hope for from a personality that was so publicly self-conscious.

Throughout his life Aristides styled himself as an orator (*rhêtôr*). As I have remarked, he was not a sophist (a type he had no respect for at all), though Philostratus was happy to classify him as one, and we should avoid the term when speaking of him, despite the fact he had some pupils.[4] His conception of oratory was drawn from Isocrates. It was something far removed from that of ordinary speakers, who indulged in disputatious and showy rhetoric for their own glory.[5] Aristides' oratory was god-given (as the *Sacred Tales* make plain) and above all serious in purpose and execution.[6] Prose was the medium, and Aristides, again following Isocrates, rated it (sometimes apologetically) as equivalent to poetry in diction and

---

[4] Cf. Behr 1968a: 106 n. 39, id. 1994: 1163 ff., and above, 'Past' n. 98. Festugière 1969: 148–9 is wrong to suggest that the word 'sophist' is used positively by Aristides (the examples he cites are simply taken out of context); that he has been believed by some against Behr discloses an unhealthy prejudice.

[5] See esp. *Or.* xxxiv *Against Those who Lampoon (the Mysteries of Oratory)* (Κατὰ τῶν ἐξορχουμένων). The image of 'initiation' into a mystery religion is borrowed here from the Platonizing philosophy of the period (Philo, Alcinous [Albinus], Heraclitus [the Homeric allegorizer, who is not as Stoic as he is sometimes held to be], Theon of Smyrna); see Dillon 1977: 300.

[6] Isocratean 'philosophic' rhetoric: *Or.* iii. 677–81; see Isocrates' *Against the Sophists* and *Antidosis* (for Aristides' wording cf. perhaps Isocrates *To Nicocles* 51).

power of expression.[7] Given this very close interest in his own art, it is not surprising that he chose to avoid the civic political duties that his social background called on him to perform.

Aristides was a citizen of Smyrna and was immensely fond of that city, as *Orr.* xvii–xxi testify.[8] He was born, however, in Mysia (the country above Pergamum) on 26 November AD 117 in the tribal area of the Olympeni.[9] It was not until 131 or 132, on the occasion perhaps of Hadrian's second visit to the area, that the city of Hadriani was established here, to which the family then belonged (and which was later to claim Aristides' services as its eirenarch or 'officer of the peace').[10] His father Eudaemon was evidently a leading man in the area (though there is nothing to suggest that he ever assumed the important tribal priesthood of Zeus Olympius), and he and his son were probably given Roman citizenship by Hadrian on this occasion.[11]

Eudaemon took care to have Aristides well educated. He certainly took lessons from Alexander of Cotiaeum, the grammaticus who taught Lucius Verus and Marcus Aurelius,[12] and probably studied with the eminent sophists Aristocles of Pergamum and Herodes Atticus of Athens.[13] Aristides was set on a rhetorical career from

[7] Cf. *Or.* xlv. 1–13; Isocrates, *Antidosis* 45–7, *Evagoras* 8–11. On Aristides' development of the 'prose' hymn see Russell 1990a (with reference to earlier discussions by Lenz and Gigli); in general Pernot 1993: i. 82 ff. It was never suggested that prose could do every poetical task—e.g. epic or drama.

[8] Smyrnaean citizenship: *Or.* l. 73, 103.

[9] Date (from the horoscope Aristides gives in *Or.* l. 58 together with the date of his birthday [cf. xlvii. 31]: Behr 1969, id. 1994: 1141–51, correcting id. 1968a: 1–2.

[10] Cf. Schwertheim 1987: 156–7 (on the basis of nos. 56 and 129; only one visit is allowed by Halfmann 1986: 200, in 124). The birthplace is given as Hadriani by Philostratus, *VS* 581; Behr's arguments (1968a: 3–4 n. 3) against the prevalent modern assumption that Aristides was born at nearby Hadrianutherae, where he made a dedication to Zeus (lost) and to Hera (Robert 1937: 211), now convince me (cf. Swain 1991a: 159 n. 57).

[11] Citizenship from Hadrian is assured by Aristides' full name P. Aelius Aristides Theodorus (*OGIS* 709 = *IGR* i. 1070; see below, n. 115). On the family's estates and the agricultural basis on their wealth see Behr 1968a: 4–8; generally Schwertheim 1987: 133–41. For the other side of the picture—the poverty and poor diet of the Mysian peasants—see Galen, *On the Powers of Foods* vi. 518.1 ff., vi. 522. 15 ff. (and for similar evidence cf. Garnsey 1988: 43–68). Zeus Olympius: Behr 1968a: 4–5 n. 6 (cf. the dedication referred to in n. 10; the temple is mentioned several times by Aristides, e.g. *Or.* xlvii. 43; Schwertheim 1987: 155–6).

[12] *Or.* xxxii *Funeral Speech for Alexander*; cf. Rutherford 1989: 52–3 on the differences between Aristides' and Marcus' views of him.

[13] This is implied by Philostratus, *VS* 582 'Athens trained him when Herodes was at his peak and Pergamum in Asia in the style [*glôtta*] of Aristocles'. Ti. Claudius Aristocles, a pupil of Herodes (*VS* 567; Ameling 1983: i. 130), was consul under Pius

the start and, had his health not broken down in the winter of 143/4, a condition which he exacerbated by his disastrous first journey to Rome in 144,[14] he would perhaps have gone on to combine rhetoric and politics along the lines of many another of the great public speakers. As it was, following his return to Asia he received his first revelations from the 'saviour' at the end of 144 (*Or.* xlviii. 7), and a year and some months after the beginning of the disease in the late spring or early summer of 145 'we came to the *kathedra* [literally 'seat'/'sitting', i.e. period of inactivity] in Pergamum' in the temple of Asclepius (xlviii. 70).[15]

The temple of Asclepius at Pergamum and the complex to which it belonged were from the time of their construction a meeting place for the elite group of Romans and Greeks who sought out the healing power of the god, especially through the habit of 'incubation', that is, spending the night in the sanctuary awaiting instructions given through dreams. There had been a temple of Asclepius at Pergamum from the middle of the fourth century BC and its fame was widespread.[16] The new second-century AD temple was built during the later years of Hadrian and the earlier part of the reign of Pius by L. Cuspius Pactumeius Rufinus (*cos. ord.* 142), a friend of Aristides (*Or.* l. 28, 43, 83, 84, 107) and of Galen's first teacher Satyrus, who was also known to Aristides and whose advice during the main period of his illness he found unwelcome (*Or.* xlix. 8–11).[17]

(probably) or Marcus and Lucius (Avotins 1978*b*: esp. 189–90; for the older view of his career see Halfmann 1979: no. 121); cf. above, 'Practice' n. 46. The Aristides *Prolegomena* 737 Dind. (112 Lenz) add as teacher the great Polemo of Smyrna.

[14] Dates: see below nn. 47–8.

[15] On the *kathedra* (for the word cf. xlix. 44; subscription to *Or.* xxx) see Behr 1968*a*: 26 n. 20, who is perhaps right in suggesting that Aristides picked the name thinking wistfully of an official chair of rhetoric. At this time, however, the chair seems to have been called the *thronos*: Avotins 1975; Rothe 1989: 21–7. *Kathedra* was in use later: *SIG*³ 845 (Nicagoras of Athens, *c.*240); at Eunapius, *Lives of the Philosophers and Sophists* 489 (Prohaeresius) it is not an official chair, but cf. 487 where *sophistikê*—i.e. *kathedra*—seems to be the Athenian municipal chair to which Prohaeresius is being elected; Penella 1990: 85.

[16] Edelstein and Edelstein 1945: i, no. 801, ii. 249; cf. Philostratus, *Life of Apollonius* iv. 34.

[17] Rufinus: Halfmann 1979: no. 66; Habicht 1969: 23 ff., no. 2; *PIR*² C 1637. Satyrus and Rufinus: Galen, *On Anatomical Procedures* ii. 224. 17–225. 1; Bowersock 1969: 60–1. Date of construction of temple and complex (which was formerly believed to be mainly the work of Pius; cf. Bowersock 1969: 86): Habicht 1969: 10–11, Le Glay 1976. Galen's reference to Rufinus as κατασκευάζοντος in the late 140s (ii. 224. 17; cf. Nutton 1973: 161 n. 4; Galen left Pergamum for Alexandria in 148/9: Nutton 1973: 162 n. 5), if the tense should stand, will refer to completion of the building. On the workings of the sanctuary as a cult site see especially Behr 1968*a*: 27–40.

The sanctuary was famed far into late antiquity as the 'grove of Rufinus'.[18] The presence of the elite sick of the second century is adequately attested through their dedicatory and honorary inscriptions.[19] Roman incubants must have felt especially at home, as the temple itself, which was circular and capped with a distinctively Roman brick dome, was almost certainly modelled by Rufinus on Hadrian's Pantheon at Rome (which was finished by about 128).[20] There was nothing parochial about the Pergamene Asclepieum where Aristides sought refuge during the *kathedra*.

Oration xxx, *A Birthday Speech to Apellas*, was written in this period, according to the subscription at the end of the text, when Aristides was 29 (i.e. in AD 147). The speech is a celebration in a highly artificial style of a pupil of Aristides (xxx. 27) on the occasion of his (?) fourteenth birthday.[21] It is not clear exactly why or how Aristides was persuaded to compose the speech.[22] But the connections it reveals well illustrate his social position in Pergamum during these years, complementing what we know from the *Sacred Tales*, and are a good introduction to his attitudes towards Rome. Aristides devotes the longest section of the speech to praising the ancestry of Apellas (6–15). He is descended from 'Kodratos', i.e. he is a member of the illustrious Pergamene and Galatian family of the Julii Quadrati, with which was connected also the corrupt governor of Bithynia, Julius Bassus. Aristides glories in the family's benefactions to Pergamum. These are so great that 'other families could claim to belong to the city but the city to this family' (9).[23] Aristides goes on, 'since this is the case, I think it would be all right, if I pass by the glorious deeds of his glorious descendants and sons and "sons of sons" (to use a poetic expression) since they obtained

[18] Ῥουφίνιον ἄλσος—*Greek Anthology* ix. 656. 13–14; Hepding 1933; see further Robert 1968*b*: 598–9 on *Greek Anthology* xiv. 72.

[19] Habicht 1969. It is curious that no text has been found in the Asclepieum honouring a poet: Bowie 1989*a*: 203.

[20] Ward-Perkins 1981: 277. The symbolic shape (cf. Cassius Dio liii. 27. 2 on the Pantheon) was no doubt intended to convey Asclepius' universalism.

[21] His sixteenth birthday—assumption of the *toga virilis*—is in the future (25). Fourteen is a guess of the scholiast included at the beginning of the text. Cf. Boulanger 1923: 333 n. 3.

[22] But cf. below, n. 76, for the suggestion that he was involved in the first of his immunity battles during the proconsulship of Antonius Albus at this time; in which case emphasizing his contacts with the prominent family of Apellas would have been advantageous.

[23] Cf. particularly the famous C. Antius A. Julius Quadratus *euergetês* of Pergamum (Halfmann 1979: no. 17).

Roman citizenship [*politeia*]' (10).[24] These achievements under the Principate are great, Aristides says, but this is not the time to speak of them. Instead the focus is turned on Apellas' immediate ancestry, his father Fronto, and his grandfather Apellas. Fronto is praised for the usual civic virtues and for 'the many provinces [*ethnê*] he governed and for the honours he gathered from the emperors [*basileis*]' (12). Fronto and Apellas senior are not as readily identifiable as has been assumed; nor can we say exactly how the family is related to the Quadrati.[25] What is known is known from Aristides, that the family did very well under Roman rule, that Apellas will soon assume the *toga virilis* (25 'as indeed royal law prescribes'), and that the emperor will then begin to accord him the (political) honours he deserves (ibid.). The speech ends with a prayer to Asclepius to grant to the boy from the emperor the honours the emperor's forbears had granted his ancestors and to 'grant to the emperor himself and the family of the emperor to govern for all eternity, as is their lot from Zeus' (28).

Or. xxx is an encomium but the views expressed about Greeks and Romans are typical of Aristides' feelings throughout his career.[26] Greeks should be proud of their inheritance; but the world is now a Roman one and it is to the Roman emperor that a family must look for advancement and honour. Aristides, unlike Dio, has nothing negative to say about Rome in any way. On the other hand, as with Plutarch, it would be wrong to classify him simply as a representative of an ideal Graeco-Roman *oikoumenê*. On a prosopographical basis his contacts, which as we shall see were developed in the period of the *kathedra*, show an acquaintance with many Romans. These were not, however, in the main western Romans, but members of old-established Greek (or Hellenized) families, the basis of whose association with Aristides is the

[24] Behr 1981–86: ii. 149 translates *politeia* (wrongly, I think) as 'office'; for 'citizenship' cf. *Or.* xxvi. 78.

[25] See Halfmann 1979: nos. 42 (C. Julius Fronto) and 43 (his brother C. Julius Nabus) and the stemma on p. 139; disregard the stemmata at Behr 1968a: 57 ff. n. 57 and 1981–6: ii. 390–1 n. 14 (amongst other things C. Julius Fronto flourished under Trajan and is unlikely to be the father of Apellas).

[26] On the Greek side of things we should compare *Or.* xxxi *Funeral Oration for Eteoneus*, delivered in the early 160s (Behr 1981–6: ii. 393) for a pupil of Aristides from Cyzicus (7, 15), who had died young. Nothing is known of his family except that it was eminent in the city and elsewhere (14 *psêphismata*), and that the boy would have gone on to 'council chambers, orations, glory, joy' (13)—the usual prizes, but at a lower key than Apellas.

enjoyment of a common and superior culture. As for Aristides himself, it will be difficult to dissociate his praise of Roman monarchy from the benefits he drew from it, not in terms of political or civic offices, but rather in his guaranteed security from these. That said, it is clear that he favoured the Roman system as it existed in practice in a way which is untrue of both Plutarch and Dio. There is only a very slight trace of any resignation about the Greek cities' dependency on Rome. There are a number of reasons for this. Aristides lived in a period of stable Roman politics. The transition from Hadrian to Pius to Marcus to Commodus was unproblematic. He knew that things had been different before. 'One of the *autokratores* of old, not of your house—nor may it be! nor could it happen under any of you!—but the story goes that one of the previous emperors in the middle of a game of draughts mentioned that he did not want the Nasamones to exist, and so the Nasamones perished' (*Or.* xix. 9).[27] But Aristides was too concerned with the present to look back at Roman history (as we shall see in *Or.* xxvi *To Rome*). When he praises Roman peace and urbanization, he meant it. The only political matters that worried him were the rivalries of the great Asian cities, which continued as they had in Dio's time, and the successful control of the masses.

THE POWER OF THE GOD

To explore Aristides' relationship with Rome further I turn now to the *Sacred Tales*. These begin with the advent of his illness (mental, physical, or whatever it was) and include material up until the time of their composition in the 170s.[28] They are remarkable as literary

---

[27] Referring to Domitian; cf. Cassius Dio lxvii. 4. 6 'I have prevented the existence of the Nasamones'.

[28] For a list of Aristides' symptoms see Behr 1968a: 162–70. According to Galen in his commentary on the *Timaeus* (preserved in Arabic; Schröder 1934: 33, 99 [text]) Aristides was one of those whose souls are naturally strong but whose bodies are weak, a weakness caused by excessive devotion to oratory, in which Aristides was pre-eminent. Galen's report is avowedly an eyewitness one (cf. Bowersock 1969: 61–2, 62 n. 1 against Behr 1968a: 162–3 who dismisses it), and he notes the unusualness of the case (cf. the man who almost lost his memory from study at *On the Affected Parts* viii. 165. 17 ff.).
For the chronology of the *Sacred Tales* I shall be relying heavily on Behr's labours (1968a: 121–8; his dates are conveniently printed in the margins of his translations in 1968a and 1981–6: ii. 278 ff.).

texts, excessively self-conscious not only about their content but
also about the writing process, factors which make interpretation of
their structure quite hazardous.²⁹ *Or.* xlvii = I was apparently composed early in 171 or 172, since Aristides says (59–60) he had not
bathed for over five years from the period covered by the extraordinary day-by-day account of his symptoms (the Diary), which
runs from 4 January to 15 February 166 or 167 (4–57).³⁰ The other
books were apparently composed a little later in 175, if the reference at xlviii = II. 9 to 'Salvius the present consul' stands; but it
may be an error of transmission or of Aristides, consciously or
unconsciously.³¹ Of the six *Sacred Tales* only the first three are
completely concerned with matters of health. The fourth book
narrates Aristides' battles with the proconsuls over his claims to
immunity from public duties, the fifth and the sixth (so far as we
can say) record Aristides' oratorical successes in the years leading
up to 165 and the period of the Diary set out in the first book. It
looks as though Aristides did not think of a project on this scale
until after the composition of the first tale around the Diary, for he
begins the first book with an apology for his necessary selectivity
(xlvii = I. 1–3, cf. xlviii = II. 1). The narration of the god's aid in the
first three tales is preparatory to the resumption of the rhetorical
career outlined in books four and five. It is the god who willed

²⁹ Cf. esp. xlvii = I. 1–4, xlviii = II. 1–4, 11, 24, l = IV. 13, 68–70; see Behr 1968*a*:
116 ff.; Pearcy 1988; Bompaire 1989: 36–9; Quet 1993; there is clearly much more
work to be done in this area.
³⁰ Behr 1968*a*: 109 n. 55. The year 166 seems more likely, since the emperor 'was
then in Syria' (xlvii = I. 33), a reference to the final stages of the Parthian War; but
the dream of the peace negotiations between the Parthian king Vologeses and the
emperor (xlvii = I. 36–9) is perhaps retrospective (and so 167 is more suitable); on
the other hand the dream may simply look forward to the end (cf. Lucian, *How to
Write History* 31, Iamblichus in Photius, *Library* cod. 94, 75b); see also below, n. 54
on 'Quadratus the governor' (xlvii = I. 22).
³¹ If the MSS lection stands, the reference is to P. Salvius Julianus *cos.* 175; but it
seems improbable that he should have been among the incubants at the Asclepieum
in 145 (this date is secured by Aristides having just arrived there) as the text goes
on to say, and so it is better to think of the famous jurist of the same name, the
consul of 148. In which case one can either emend the text (Behr: τοῦ τῶν ὑπάτων
[seen retrospectively]) or suggest confusion with the consul of the year of writing
(Bowersock 1969: 80). The matter is complicated by the part Salvius plays in the
writing process. In the passage under discussion, xlviii = II. 9, he appears in a dream
to Aristides' foster-father Zosimus, and 'discussed my speeches with him, particularly I think saying that he gave them a designation, "sacred tales"'. Here again
Salvius is linked to the time of composition in the 170s, since the particular application of this phrase is to the present text, and so the blurring between the past and
present Salvii may well be deliberate.

Aristides' recovery (l = IV. 1 ff.). Likewise it is the god who secured victory for him in his various battles in the courts (l = IV.
104, 108). In the *Sacred Tales* Aristides presents himself as someone
who is superior to his rivals because the god wanted it that way.
His skills have the best imprimatur available. Thus, rather than
seeing him as an ambitious man who was afraid of going too far,[32]
we would do better to say that he looks like someone who wanted
to go as far as he possibly could but was afraid he might not get
there on his own.

How odd was the relationship between god and man? In reading
the *Sacred Tales* we should remember that, however extraordinary
Aristides dreaming of his god seems to moderns who wish to psycho-
logize him,[33] contact with the gods through dreams (amongst other
things) was a normal and integral part of ancient culture.[34] Aristides
went further than anyone else in recording (or, it should be said, in
purporting to record) what he saw. But there was an abundant
oneirocritical literature in antiquity, and it so happens that the only
fully surviving example of it comes from the second-century author
Artemidorus Daldianus of Ephesus. His work is both a handbook
of 'real' dreams assiduously recorded from people in all walks of
life and also a treatise of interpretative modes.[35] The power dreams
could exert on rhetors has been alluded to already.[36] One example
reported by Philostratus will perhaps make Aristides seem less
unusual. The sophist and historian (P. Anteius) Antiochus of Aegeae
'spent many nights as an incubant in the temple of Asclepius [in
Aegeae], both for the dreams and also for the company of those
who were awake and conversing with one another. For the god
conversed with him while he was awake and made it a noble triumph of his art to keep diseases away from Antiochus.'[37] Only the

[32] Brown 1978: 41–5.
[33] For a report of various views of this sort see Smith 1984: esp. 32; Gourevitch
1984: esp. 22–59. Arch-psychologizers are Michenaud and Dierkens 1972, esp. in ch.
3, favouring a 'diagnostic psychanalytique de caractère rétentif anal' (115 ff.). Smith
1984: 41 (perhaps inevitably) equates Asclepius with the Father Figure.
[34] Lane Fox 1986: 150 ff., esp. 160–3.
[35] On Artemidorus (and comparisons with Aristides) see Behr 1968a: 171–204;
Lane Fox 1986: 155–8; Price 1986; Foucault 1988: 4–36; cf. Rutherford 1989: 195–
200. The very subject-matter of his text should warn against generalizing it as a
representation of social anxiety, as some have wished (e.g. MacAlister 1992), especially since Artemidorus himself is explicitly interested in dreams which predict the
future (*oneiroi*) rather than those which merely express present circumstances
(*enhupnia*).
[36] Above, 'Past' n. 87.   [37] *VS* 568. On Antiochus see above, 'Past' n. 28.

great Polemo dared to question the healing god's prescriptions (*VS* 536, to abstain from cold drinks: 'and what if you were treating a cow?'). Most patients, as Galen observed of Pergamene society, were only too happy to do what Asclepius said, no matter how absurd it might seem, because they believed [*pepeisthai*] it would help them.[38]

We may begin with some views of Marcus Aurelius in the first *Sacred Tale*. In one of his last speeches, *Or*. xlii *To Asclepius* (4, 10 written after the *Sacred Tales*), Aristides celebrates the cures the god enjoined on him which had brought his rhetoric to perfection and had led to his recent appearance before the imperial court at Smyrna in 176.[39] In the course of the Diary in the first *Sacred Tale* he says he dreamed of a meeting with the emperor (clearly Marcus) at which he was accompanied by Alexander of Cotiaeum (xlvii = I. 23). 'When I greeted him and stood there, the *autokratôr* expressed his amazement that I myself did not approach and kiss him [like Alexander]. I replied that I was a *therapeutês* of Asclepius. It seemed all right to me to say this much about myself. "In addition to other things," I said, "the god instructed me not to kiss in this way." And he said, "It is all right." And I was silent. And he said, "Asclepius is indeed better than all to worship."' Marcus was not in fact especially devoted to Asclepius,[40] but he was nevertheless receptive to other people's belief in him, if we may go by Galen's report that he had excused Galen from going to the German war when he was told by him that it was forbidden by the god.[41] Aristides' dream shows that it was obviously important for Aristides personally to believe that the emperor had recognized the superiority of the god and the right of the god alone to dictate his behaviour.

Some days later Aristides dreamed of Marcus again (xlvii = I. 36–9, here explicitly 'Antoninus the elder emperor'). This time the dream placed him in negotiations with the Parthian king, Vologeses. Lucius Verus, Marcus' co-emperor and the prince who really dealt with Vologeses, is supplanted.[42] Aristides dreams that he made a speech to the two monarchs, but was unsure whether to give 'the

---

[38] The doctor must instil the same confidence: *Commentary on Book Six of Hippocrates' Epidemics* xviib. 137. 7–12.

[39] Cf. Philostratus, *VS* 582–3. [40] Rutherford 1989: 200.

[41] *On his Own Books* xix. 19; see below, 'Galen' n. 66.

[42] It may be significant that Verus' favourite amusement, the pantomime, was denounced by Aristides in a lost work entitled *Against the Dancers* (attacked in turn in Libanius *Or*. lxiv: see Behr 1981–6: i. 416–19 [fragments], 501–3 [notes]; Mesk 1908).

king on our side' the greater part of it. Instead, he supposed he had 'astounded' them by offering them a choice of his writings. This picture of rhetor and emperor is not totally different from Philostratus' well-known dictum about Polemo, that he 'spoke to cities as a superior, to rulers not as an inferior, and to gods as an equal' (*VS* 535). There is a third major dream about the emperor in the first *Sacred Tale* (which contains the majority of such references). At xlvii = I. 46–9 Aristides imagines he is staying in the palace of Marcus and Lucius in Rome. Naturally they take the best possible care of him and assure him of his superlative rhetorical skills. The interest in the emperor in the dreams of this book invites speculation. People did think about the emperor (or perhaps rather the emperor-figure), though their dreams as mediated by Artemidorus at least are fairly free of him.[43] But Aristides seems to be claiming a more personal relationship, in which the emperor recognizes his specialities and the power of his god. These are the most important subjects throughout the *Sacred Tales*.

The second tale (*Or.* xlviii = II) begins by confessing the difficulties of writing the text that lies ahead. It dwells on the grave condition of the author during the first years of his illness, focusing on the serious consequences of his trip to Rome (5, 50–69). 'When I was brought from Italy, having contracted many varied physical ailments from constant sickness and from the constant wintry weather I had when I set out through Thrace and Macedonia, leaving home while I was still sick, the doctors were completely at a loss because they were powerless not only to help me but also to discover what the whole thing was' (5). These experiences are narrated at greater length and with greater intensity of suffering at 60–9. 'Perhaps someone would like to hear the basis of such great trouble? . . . I started out to Rome in mid-winter, being sick immediately I left home because of the rains and a cold'.[44] Owing to the time of year Aristides journeyed by land along the Via Egnatia. He stresses the constant rain, the icy river Hebrus, the lack of inns, the 'rush and haste out of keeping with the established season and my

[43] Dio of Prusa xx. 3 (gossiping about the emperor), Arrian, *Discourses of Epictetus* iii. 4. 7 (people abuse Caesar in the same way farmers abuse Zeus; 'what can [Caesar] do about it? he knows that, if he punishes everyone who abuses him, he won't have anyone to rule'); cf. Fronto, *Ad M. Caes.* iv. 12. 6 (v.d.H.² 66–7) on the ubiquitous painted models of the young Marcus in Roman shops. Artemidorus iv. 31, iv. 80, v. 16; cf. Lane Fox 1986: 157.

[44] Rains—cf. Schröder 1986: 57–8 n. 110.

bodily strength'. He arrived in Rome 'scarcely on the one hundredth day after I started from home'.[45] This is the only mention of Rome in the account, for Aristides now gets down to details of his illness. His intestines were swelling. The doctors' cures only made matters worse. 'It seemed I had to be taken home, if I could endure.' This time he went by sea, experiencing an *Odyssey* of bad weather. After about three weeks the ship reached Miletus and Smyrna 'beyond all expectation'.

The date of Aristides' Roman voyage can be determined without too much uncertainty. As the tenth year of his illness was 'coming round' he was commanded by the god to go to the same place where the disease began. This was the hot springs near the river Aesepus in Mysia in the region of Aristides' estates (*Or.* l = IV. 1–2). Aristides had a property at the small town of Baris on the banks of the Aesepus, and it was at this time that he here delivered the prose hymn *Or.* xxxvii *Athena*.[46] This information comes from the subscription appended to the end of the text, which also dates the speech by Aristides' age (35 years and one month) and by the proconsulship of Severus. Since the date of Aristides' birth is known to be 26 November 117, the proconsulship of (C. Julius) Severus, who plays an important role in the narration of Aristides' legal battles in *Or.* l = IV, can be fixed to 152–3.[47] Aristides was at Baris just after the winter solstice, in other words late December 152/ January 153 (l = IV. 1). Since the tenth year of his illness was 'coming round', i.e. beginning,[48] and the disastrous trip to Italy was undertaken shortly after the start of the illness (l = IV. 2), he plainly travelled to Rome in 144, or as he puts it, 'in the tenth year before' (l = IV. 2). Aristides' constant sickness at this time and his lack of any reference to oratorical performance before the imperial family

---

[45] Aristides states that he was not passed by any military couriers (*cursus publicus*); his exaggeration, but also the exceptional length of his travelling time, is shown by a journey of 36 days for a courier coming from Lycia to Rome in February–March by the Via Egnatia (Pflaum 1940: 386). See also *Or.* xxvi. 33 for a less jaded view of the imperial post.

[46] Baris and the springs: Behr 1968a: 6–7 n. 8d.

[47] Date of birth: see above, n. 9. The reference at *Athena* 29 'grant honours from both kings' refers then not to Marcus and Verus (Oliver 1968: 33, following Lenz 1963: 358–9) but (cf. l = IV. 75 'the kings, the *autokratôr* and his son' [same date]) to Pius and Marcus (rather than Athena and Zeus, as suggested by Bowersock 1969: 61 n. 3). The proconsul's year of office probably ran from August or September: Behr 1968a: 79 n. 62, id. 1994: 1177–82; Laffi 1967.

[48] ἔτει δεκάτῳ περιήκοντι—the 'tenth year' only comes round once.

make it quite unlikely that *To Rome* was performed during this trip, as is sometimes held.[49] The only work done at Rome was a short lyric poem on Apollo during the *ludi Apollinares* (6–13 July).[50] Typically this was attempted at the request of Asclepius. The god and the illness were the orator's sole interests in the capital.

Rome and Romans and the emperors are hardly mentioned in the third of the *Sacred Tales* (*Or.* xlix = III).[51] The fourth tale (l = IV) is quite different. Rome, the emperors, and the governors of Asia feature extensively, and all of them are in the hands of the god. The book is remarkable for the author's attention to its construction and for its triumphant, indeed happy tone, which forms a contrast with the catalogue of sickness and treatment in the first three tales. Aristides begins with the joyful trip he made back to the springs near the Aesepus where he had first caught a bad cold (l = IV. 1 ff.). 'The governor of Asia was then a very distinguished man, Severus, from Upper Phrygia. In his time wonderful things of importance to me were done by the god . . . At first, as I said, my idea was to go through his benefactions in this matter. Then it seemed better to go back to earlier times to narrate before this the other honours from the god as far as I could, first those which related to my speeches and such like, then those about the legal actions during the governorships' (l = IV. 12–13).

At l = IV. 14–70 Aristides duly reports at length the god's inspiration to resume his oratorical career. The god instructed him to compose not only speeches (14–30) but also 'songs' and lyric poetry, and commanded him to stage choral odes in honour of the gods (31–47). The revival of his career is confirmed by a series of dreams featuring among others Plato, Lysias, and Sophocles (48–69). In the first dream narrated here Aristides finds he is to share a tomb with Alexander the Great: 'I conjectured that both of us had reached the top, he in the power of arms, I in the power of words' (49).[52] At

---

[49] Oliver 1953: 886–7, followed by Klein 1981: i. 76–7, both holding also that 143 and not 144 is the date in question.

[50] *Or.* l = IV. 31 (cf. Bowie 1989*b*: 214 ff., esp. 214–15). For the idea that Aristides performed at this time *Or.* xxxv Εἰς βασιλέα, which is generally and rightly held to be spurious (Oliver 1978; Behr 1981–6: ii. 399–400, id. 1994: 1219–23; Stertz 1979; de Blois 1986; Pernot 1993: i. 261–2), see Jones 1972*b*, id. 1981 (replying to Stertz; cf. Birley 1987: 87–8 on Jones's 'brilliant re-examination').

[51] Cf. xlix = III. 21, a passing reference to the emperor in a dream about Asclepius; note also the presence here of Tyche γυνὴ ἐπιφανῶν—clearly another member of the Pergamene Quadrati (cf. *IGR* iv. 1687 Julia Tyche, mother of C. Antius A. Julius Quadratus; Halfmann 1979: 114).

[52] For the language cf. Arrian, *Anabasis* i. 12. 5, above, 'Arrian' n. 13.

l = IV. 63 ff. Aristides begins his transition to the second part of the speech. The complexity of the narrative is signposted and attributed to the god. 'I had decided to bring the story of these matters to a close, when another wonderful thing came to me, which if any other was worthy of no little thanks to the god' (63). Aristides had written to the governor Quadratus 'the rhetor' upon his assumption of the governorship of Asia, taking time to inform him of his name and profession, 'especially since I had had some troubles from earlier times, which will be told immediately' (63). Aristides refers obliquely to his legal troubles, which have already happened in real time but are still to come in the text. Rather, he reports now how he dreamed of the praise that was showered on him at gubernatorial headquarters on the day when Quadratus was to receive his letter, praise which was encouraged by the priest of Asclepius and his grandfather who were present in Quadratus' chamber.[53] The dream was confirmed by the letter's actual reception, which cannot be reported in case it seems like 'bragging' (67). Quadratus is the sort of governor Aristides wishes for. Even a first-time reader could guess this from his designation as 'rhetor'. His extreme goodwill to Aristides (67), the easy access of the priestly family to his bedroom (64), and the reference (almost certainly) to him as 'our *hetairos* [comrade]' (71) make him more likely to be the suffect consul of 139, C. Julius Bassus, a member of the same family of Quadratus as Apellas, than the other possible candidate, the consul of 142, L. Statius Quadratus of Athens.[54] Just as the story of Quadratus'

[53] On the family cf. Habicht 1969: nos. 45 ff.

.[54] C. Julius Bassus: Halfmann 1979: no. 63; his proconsulship would fall in 153/4 ('Severus ruled as governor of Asia, I think, a year before our comrade'), an unoccupied year in our *fasti* for the province (Syme 1983: 280); so, rightly, Behr 1994: 1195–7. L. Statius Quadratus: Halfmann 1979: no. 67. Halfmann and others (Alföldy 1977: 214–15; Syme 1983: 280–1) prefer to identify Aristides' Quadratus with the latter (cf. also Bowersock 1969: 84–5), who is presumably the proconsul under whom was executed the martyr Polycarp (*Martyrdom of Polycarp* 21; cf. Barnes 1967). Statius Quadratus is likely to have been governor around 156/7 (because of the usual number of years this office was assumed after the consulship; Syme 1983: 285; Birley 1987: 261), whereas Aristides' anxiousness to have his immunity confirmed after the battles with Severus strongly supports a direct successor (the 'I think' is common in the *Sacred Tales* and is very likely here to be simply stylistic; cf. l = IV. 97 on M'. Acilius Glabrio's presence at Smyrna in 152). See now Behr 1994: ibid.

The identity of 'Quadratus the governor' of xlvii = I. 22, who appears fixed by the narrative of the Diary to 165/6 (or perhaps 166/7), is even less sure (there is apparently no room for him in 165/6 given the tenancy of D. Fonteius Fronto—Alföldy 1977: 379; and 166–7 also has a respectable candidate in L. Sergius Paullus—Alföldy 1977: 216); it is possible, of course, that Aristides is not thinking of an immediate contemporary.

honour for Aristides is ushered in by a sudden vision, so also is it capped by one 'in the middle of writing', which again interrupts the narrative and presages oratorical preeminence (68–9). At l = IV. 70 Aristides sums up what has gone before, 'from which one can infer the rest'—not only what has been omitted, but also the following narration of his battles over his status with the other governors.

With Quadratus Aristides has begun the narrative of his law suits in reverse. The self-conscious tone of his inability to fit his notes 'into a proper chronology' at xlviii = II. 3 should remind us that he had a purpose in doing this. We already know that the god was responsible for 'wonderful things' relating to legal actions during several proconsulships (l = IV. 12–13). Each layer that is now peeled back reveals another victory, each of which takes place against the background of Aristides' refound success in oratory, which peaks with the decisions of governor Severus (1–12). When Aristides 're-turns' to narrate his legal difficulties it is with Severus' governor-ship that he begins. C. Julius Severus is the only one of the governors in *Or.* l = IV and the other *Sacred Tales* who receives a character sketch. He 'was proud in his ways and would not yield to anyone about any decision or policy' (71). He was a man 'so incorruptible that one could sooner stop the flow of the rivers than buy him, a man again so astute about things that he was least of all to be deceived' (82). The characterization is partly due to Severus' back-ground as yet another Pergamene descendant of the Pergamene and Galatian royal houses and younger cousin of the great C. Antius A. Julius Quadratus.[55] It also bolsters the justice of Aristides' case and his belief in the aid of the god working through Severus on behalf of his immunities.[56]

Under Severus (152/3) Aristides resisted nomination by Hadriani as 'warden of the peace' (*phulaka tês eirênês*), i.e. as eirenarch, and

[55] Severus: Sullivan 1978: 931–4; Halfmann 1979: no. 62; Syme 1983: 279; Mitchell 1993: i. 154–5; see esp. *IGR* iii. 173, 174 = *OGIS* 544, 543. His brother Julius Amyn-tianus dedicated an Alexander history to Marcus, cf. *PIR*² A 574. Similar reasons are behind the characterization of Severus by Cassius Dio, who calls him 'just, intelli-gent, and a man of rank' and who fondly recalled his legateship of Bithynia (lxix. 14. 4; Magie 1950: ii. 1486–8 nn. 54, 55, 1532–3 n. 7).

[56] On what follows see, with regard to Aristides' claims for exemption from public duties, Behr 1968a: 77–86, id. 1994: 1205–12; Bowersock 1969: 36–40; Nutton 1971: esp. 54 n. 19. See also in general on immunities and those eligible for them (especially grammarians, rhetors, doctors, and philosophers) Griffin 1971, I. Hadot 1984: 221–30.

by Smyrna as one of the prytaneis, the senior magistrates (72–94).[57] Aristides' story is immensely interesting not only for the workings of Roman government but also for his attitudes towards it. The office of eirenarch is the first problem. Presumably Hadriani had noticed that Aristides was now well again and that he had recently been nominated by Smyrna to the posts of revenue officer and high priest of Asia. The eirenarch was, if we may judge from the contemporary account in the *Martyrdom of Polycarp* (6–8), a fairly active head of police. The bluff Severus was presented with a list of names and chose Aristides.[58] 'I was in much doubt: it was not possible to make an appeal in the case, since there was no obvious adversary, but the same man both gave my name and confirmed it' (74). The god reassured Aristides, and letters arrived from the 'emperor and his son' and from 'the former prefect of Egypt', the rhetor, philosopher, and one time *ab epistulis* of Hadrian (C. Avidius) Heliodorus, who was perhaps a scion of the old royal house of Commagene.[59] These affidavits, as Aristides notes, had to do with his appeal against an earlier summons (75). They were quickly dispatched to Severus. Unfortunately Severus was as obstinate as Aristides. At the assizes in Ephesus the appeal was heard. Aristides stayed away, foolishly. The account fabricates direct speech. The governor, noting the testimonies, had added craftily, 'I invite him to share in my administration, though I confirm his rights of immunity and these remain in force' (78).

A parallel case some fifty years later involved the Smyrnaean sophist Claudius Rufinus. He had voluntarily undertaken the generalship in the city. The Smyrnaeans were now asking for more, but the emperors Septimius Severus and Caracalla confirmed his immune status and warned against turning his goodwill into a punishment.[60] Aristides' approach was not to appeal above Severus, since

---

[57] Aristides' avoidance of the non-Attic *eirênarchês* (*eirênarchos*) should be noted; cf. similarly l = IV. 96 where *eklogistês* is eschewed in favour of the classical form *eklogeus*.

[58] The governor's involvement in the matter is not simply a routine matter of security: the eirenarchs were not totally trusted by Roman government, which recognized their tendency to partisan behaviour: *Digest* xlviii. 3. 6. 1 (Pius as governor of Asia); see Magie 1950: i. 647, ii. 1514–15; Mitchell 1993: i. 196.

[59] Heliodorus: Pflaum 1960–1: i, no. 106; Halfmann 1979: no. 100a; Syme 1987: 216–18. He was prefect 137–42 and Aristides had presumably got to know him in Alexandria during his visit to Egypt in 141–2 (Behr 1968a: 15–16), a visit which resulted in his discourse on the Nile, *Or.* xxxvi.

[60] *SIG²* 876; see Lane Fox 1986: 466–7.

he was 'as it were asking for a favour and trying to begin some sort of friendship'.[61] Rather, he brought the forces of Greek culture to bear against him. Friends of Severus in Rome had already been approached (78). They are nameless, being unimportant. Now back in Pergamum 'Rufinus happened to be in town and he was concerned to honour us as much as he could' (83). Rufinus, as has been noted, was the builder of the new temple of Asclepius at Pergamum. He has been mentioned as such in this speech (I = IV. 28) and has been associated with Aristides' choral work for the god (43). Rufinus knew what to do. He wrote to Severus 'in his own tongue', that is, in Greek.[62] In his letter he gave advice to the governor and even dropped 'hints about what might happen, if he did not willingly exempt me' (84). This was not all Aristides did. Moving to Smyrna he next enrolled (L. Claudius) Pardalas, already introduced as 'that famous man who, I would say, of all the Greeks of our time was the foremost expert in the science of rhetoric' (27). More to the point Pardalas returned the compliment and crucially, as a devotee of Asclepius, recognized the divine nature of Aristides' illness and the promise of a divine cure (ibid.).

As Aristides knew, Severus was a boyhood friend of Pardalas, whose own family was not undistinguished (87).[63] At the festival of Dionysus at Smyrna in March 153 Severus gave judgement. Aristides' oratory was not on trial—he was, as the rhetor lovingly reports, 'first of the Greeks' in this respect. But there was, Severus said, a difference between professionalism and having pupils. Aristides had had pupils (cf. the speech for Apellas), but clearly not enough to satisfy the requirements of the immunity regulations, which were concerned to promote teaching.[64] The governor advised him to go to the city council of Smyrna to get himself put on the list of immune rhetors (who in the largest cities—metropolises—were five).[65] Clearly the Smyrnaeans had not wished the wealthy Aristides

[61] Severus was presumably inviting Aristides to share the burden of justice-giving as one of his *amici*; cf. *P.Oxy.* 2754 (AD 111) 'those who have obtained friends of the governor . . . as judges'.

[62] Behr 1981–6: ii. 440 n. 142 suggests the letter was in *Latin* because it was official correspondence between two Roman consulars; this is possible, but against the sense of the text and the tenor of the narrative.

[63] Habicht 1969: 142.   [64] *Digest* xxvii. 1. 6. 2, 4, 5; Bowersock 1969: 39.

[65] *Digest* xxvii. 1. 6. 2. Pius' limitation of the number of immune grammarians, rhetors, and doctors was presumably designed to protect civic finances (Bowersock 1969: 30–4; Nutton 1977: 201 on doctors), though it also guaranteed that cities did support these professions to a certain extent. Immunity for philosophers was also limited, not by a fixed number, but by Pius' dry remark about the rarity of true

to be on any such list. Previous events had made this clear, and Aristides must have based his claim to the emperor, which was confirmed by letter (75), on being included among 'those with exceptional knowledge'.[66] Nevertheless he now went to the council some time around July only to find he had been nominated as prytanis in the forthcoming election (88). Following the governor round on his assize tour Aristides next journeyed to Pergamum. Here he rose to the occasion and in a 'frank' speech lasting 'five measures' (of the water clock), i.e. about an hour and a quarter,[67] he 'intimated how one would appear making this speech in front of the emperor'. Severus now gave in, sent Aristides with a letter to the council of Smyrna, and simply forgot about 'the other office' of eirenarch (92–3).

'Thus was the god's prediction fulfilled'. This extraordinary narrative ends as it began (71) with a reference to the healing god. With the exception of the absent, epistolary emperor and his son, all the players are men of eastern origin, brought up with the same cultural outlook as Aristides. This is nicely illustrated by the oracle of which Aristides is reminded by the god when he is puzzling over who to resist: 'These things will be a care to me and the white maidens.' In context the 'white maidens' are the letters from the emperor. But educated readers would recall that the line was Apollo's famous reply to the Delphians during the invasion of the Gauls under Brennus in 279 BC.[68] Aristides, like Delphi, would escape unharmed; Severus, who hailed from Ancyra in Galatia and placed special emphasis on his royal descent from the Gauls who came to Asia at about the same time as Brennus invaded Greece,[69] would be defeated. It may be remarked that Severus himself, as we see him in Aristides, was certainly intent on his duty as a proconsul of Rome. But his eastern background was surely a significant factor in this stance: only a Greek would have dared to confront Aristides so doggedly, just as another Greek, Quadratus, praises him so highly.

philosophers and the expectation that those who were rich would contribute voluntarily, since they would show they were not practising philosophy if they disputed the extent of their wealth (*Digest* xxvii. 1. 6. 7).

[66] *Digest* xxvii. 1. 6. 10.
[67] Cf. Pliny ii. 11. 14 (16 slow running clepsydrae last 5 hours); Sherwin-White 1966: 167.
[68] Parke and Wormell 1956: ii, no. 329; *Paroemiographi Graeci* i. 403; Behr 1981–6: ii. 439 n. 128.
[69] For these ancestors see *IGR* iii. 173. 1 ff. (= *OGIS* 544) with Mitchell 1993: i. 38. Severus also emphasized his descent from the Pergamene royal house.

In the preceding governorship of the westerner (T. Vitrasius)
Pollio (151/2) Aristides had been nominated as a revenue officer
(*eklogeus* = *eklogistês*) at Smyrna (95–9).[70] If this officer had the
same responsibility as was given to the boards who are known to
have collected imperial taxes, it is likely that he would have had
to make up shortfalls in the revenue from his own purse.[71] The
election was confirmed by one of the governor's three legates (a
presbeutês).[72] Aristides promptly dreamed of Demosthenes' great
speech of self-defence, *On the Crown*, and of 'the great Glabrio
who would arrange everything' (97).[73] The westerner (M'. Acilius)
Glabrio began the year 152 as consul ordinarius. 'He happened
then, I think, to be in town.' Aristides may have got to know him
earlier at Rome or when he was legate in Asia and then *logistês*
(financial supervisor) of Ephesus not long before 152.[74] Fortunately
Pollio himself overturned the legate's decision and the council's
wish. 'I obtained immunity. From then on the magistrate [of Smyrna]
was a best friend, and the legate himself was a best friend too' (99).

'Come now, as if we were ever ascending higher on a ladder
[*klimax*], let us recall another of the things before these events. The
sophist, whom I mentioned a little earlier, was governor' (100–3).
Aristides narrates how a nomination by Smyrna to the provincial
highpriesthood ('the common priesthood of Asia') was checked by
a persuasive speech to the *dêmos* in the assembly, and then tells
how an election by the provincial assembly at the instigation of
delegates from Smyrna was overturned by 'a summons of the governor and a summons of the saviour to Pergamum' (100–3).[75] This

[70] Pollio: Syme 1983: 278–9. The date is summer 152.

[71] Cf. *Digest* l. 4. 3. 11; l. 4. 18. 26 on imperial taxes (Magie 1950: i. 648); but the
eklogistês may have been a municipal officer: Magie 1950: ii. 1514.

[72] The regular Greek term (Mason 1974: 153–4) can be used since it is a normal
classical Greek word ('envoy'); see Cassius Dio liii. 14. 6–7.

[73] Demosthenes (Aristides' favourite author: Sohlberg 1969: 187–91; Pernot 1981:
89–100) has already been surpassed by Aristides in his dreams: l = IV. 19.

[74] Glabrio: Syme 1980: 433–5, 446–8; he was *quaestor Augusti* about the time of Aristides' first visit to Rome. Cultural preferences are indicated for the prosopographically-
minded by his tribuneship under Arrian in Cappadocia in 137 and by the budding
but short-lived late 2nd-c. Cappadocian sophist Acilius Diodotus, whose family's
citizenship may be ascribed to Glabrio's patronage (Philostratus, *VS* 617; Habicht
1969: no. 35).

[75] Earlier Aristides had accepted the honour of the title 'asiarch' (l = IV. 53). If
this term means the same as the '*archiereus* of Asia' (Deininger 1965: 37–50; Rossner
1974; cf. above, 'Dio' n. 35 on Dio at Celaenae), Aristides' inconsistency may be
explained by the fact that the title is ascribed to him in a dream along with his
hieronym Theodorus ('for everything of mine was a gift of the god'); but the asiarch
may well be something different: Kearsley 1986.

is relatively straightforward apart from the identity of the 'soph-ist'.[76] Although the narrative here is short, the note of triumph is to be marked: *klimax* is a rhetorical term for an elaborate sentence pattern 'which seems to climb higher and higher', technically an 'epanastrophe' where the same word begins a clause that ended the preceding one.[77] Aristides' troubles and triumphs are similarly epanastrophic.[78] He goes on: 'Similar to this was that which hap-pened first of all these things' (105). He narrates an attempt under the (eastern) 'governor Julianus' by 'certain Mysians' to appropri-ate his Laneion estate.[79] Aristides dreamed of the emperor Hadrian 'honouring me who was recently acquainted with him'. Rufinus was on hand to help and the governor 'became so possessed that he immediately embraced me as if he was a best friend from of old' (107). Perhaps this final episode seems anti-climactic; until one

[76] Since he is certainly a governor (103 *hêgemôn*), he cannot be Glabrio, as has often been thought; nor in Aristides is it admissible to take *hêgemôn* in the sense of 'legate' (which it can mean: Mason 1974: 147–8) and think of Glabrio's legateship (Groag; cf. Bowersock 1969: 37); Aristides' word for 'legate' is always (the correct) *presbeutês*. The same reasoning invalidates the candidacy of Quadratus (be he Statius Quadratus—Syme 1983: 280–1—or Julius Bassus), since he was governor at least two years *after* Pollio. Nor is the case for Quadratus strengthened by the association between 'sophist' and 'rhetor' (which he is at l = IV. 63): Quadratus is painted in highly favourable colours, whereas 'sophist' is a term of disapproval in these pages. The consular *Kodratriôn* who 'was a sophist in the style of Favorinus' (Philostratus, *VS* 576) at about the right time has naturally come into the reckoning, but is hardly sure. Behr's former emendation of σοφιστής to Festus (*Φῆστος), the honorand of *CIL* ii. 6084, is best ignored, since the text at l = IV. 100 is sound. We could assume a name has dropped out somewhere (though not at 98 as Behr wants; cf. Behr 1981–6: ii. 469); if it has, the answer is perhaps the easterner L. Antonius Albus, proconsul in 147–8 (Halfmann 1979: no. 58; Syme 1983: 276), who is men-tioned in the previous *Sacred Tale* (xlix = III. 38—a reference to this passage itself would strain Aristides' 'a little before'; cf. the references at xlviii = II. 69 to xlviii = II. 5, l = IV. 43 to l = IV. 28, l = IV. 71 to l = IV. 63). Behr now (1994: 1202) also proposes Albus and suggests his name was corrupted to *allos*, 'another' and then corrected by a scribe to 'sophist'. There is, however, no overriding reason to remove 'sophist'—nothing prevents Aristides from accepting the governor's support and also criticizing his rhetorical posture. If a name has not been lost, the suggestion of Nicosia 1984: 258 that the sophist of §100 is the man who is 'one of the very distinguished sophists of our time' at §61 may well be right.

[77] Demetrius, *On Style* 270; Hermogenes, *On Ideas* 304 Rabe (both quoting the same passage of Demosthenes).

[78] The image of the ladder recurs in the *Sacred Tales* at xlvii = I. 48, xlviii = II. 30, xlix = III. 48, li = V. 65; in the first of these Marcus and Lucius assist Aristides to climb the ladder, in the third it conveys the possibility of access to Sarapis.

[79] The governor is perhaps Ti. Claudius Julianus, proconsul of Asia in 144–5 (Halfmann 1979: no. 57; Syme 1983: 274–5), grandnephew of the grandee Ti. Julius Celsus Polemaeanus, who was commemorated in the famous Library of Celsus at Ephesus; full name and date (Aristides did not return to Asia before spring 145) are not secure: Behr 1994: 1184–6.

realizes that it concerns Aristides' favourite piece of real property. Hence the familiar pattern is identified in the last utterance of the book: 'armed men and slingers and all those things yielded to the god' (108).

This remarkable story is continued in the fifth *Sacred Tale* by the narration of oratorical triumphs at Smyrna and Cyzicus, comparisons with Plato and Thucydides, and revelations about 'my future glory' (li = V. 67). In a dream Marcus Aurelius praises Aristides' rhetoric and prays for a good audience for him (44–5).[80] The incomplete sixth tale undoubtedly continued this line. Here in the twelfth year from the start of the illness visions led Aristides to Epidaurus, the original cult centre of Asclepius. He dreamed of encouragement from Musonius Rufus, the first-century AD Roman Stoic who wrote in Greek. He also heard voices: '"save yourself for the city of the Athenians", which meant for the Greeks'. Not only that: 'there were great predictions about things in Italy' (lii = VI. 3). At this point the text breaks off. Clearly Aristides refers to another visit to Italy via Athens. It is wrong to resist the notion that this trip was the occasion when he delivered his most influential oration, the *Panathenaicus* (*Or.* i), which is concerned with Athenian history and Athenian (Greek) culture, and the speech for which he is best known to moderns, *To Rome* (*Or.* xxvi).

TO ROME

To Rome has naturally attracted diverse judgements. For some it is nothing but rhetoric devoid of content, for others a blueprint of the Roman empire in the second century AD, while for others the speech reflects the part not of Rome but of the eastern elites and their desire to exercise local control through Roman support.[81] The speech

---

[80] Cf. the story in Philostratus, *VS* 583 '"Permit my students [γνωρίμους: Rothe 1989: 44] to be in the audience." "That is permitted," said Marcus, "for it is democratic." And when Aristides added, "Let them shout and clap as much as they can, O King," the emperor smiled and said, "That rests with you."'

[81] The various modern views are discussed by Klein in his very serviceable introduction (1981: 160–72). Rhetoric: see esp. Baumgart 1874 (for this speech and all the others) and Mesk 1909 (on Isocratean influence; but see also Sieveking 1919: 60–3). Blueprint: see Oliver 1953 and Klein 1981 and 1983 (notes). Local class concerns: especially Bleicken 1966 and Pavan 1962. Some might find use in de Leeuw 1939: esp. 6–26.

was originally delivered at Rome before the imperial family. Hence on a reasonable assumption (since Aristides was not Dio), it tells us a good deal about what the imperials wished to hear about themselves (rather than how Aristides wished them to act). Thus the great enthusiasm expressed in the oration for Roman rule cannot automatically be taken to represent the feelings of Aristides himself. As far as he is concerned, indeed, it appears, as we have been seeing, that his positive attitude towards Roman rule is closely connected with Rome's desire to benefit him personally in accordance with the wishes of the god and with her ability to protect and foster his friends. Readings of *To Rome* which find in it an affirmation of Rome's universal love for the world and a somewhat naïve praise of the universalizing of Roman citizenship and of the Roman name are at fault for a Romanocentrism which loses sight of Aristides and the rest of his work.[82] My interest is solely in Aristides' own viewpoint. Some commentators have been unhappy about what is not in the speech, remarking in particular that Aristides fails to mention Roman history and Roman cultural attainments.[83] We have noted already Aristides' lack of interest in Rome as a city when he reports his visit there in 144 in Or. xlviii = II. 60–9.[84] For a major author his total lack of interest in Roman history, including even the saintly Numa (who pops up in Dio of Prusa), is noteworthy. On the other hand it is right to emphasize that Aristides was doing

[82] The worst offender is Oliver 1953. Important as his commentary is, it is badly marred by his conception of the speech as an elaborate exposition of the Empire written under the influence of Plato's *Timaeus*, with Roman power presented as a reign of cosmogonic Eros (Roma = Amor), the emperor as the Demiurge, and the citizen as a lover protected by Love (874–8, 883–4, 946). These fantasies have been extensively criticized: Phillips 1954: 128; Vittinghoff 1957: 76; Bleicken 1966: 235; Vannier 1976: 501; Klein 1981: 165–6; other literature can be found in de Martino 1972–5: iv(1). 383 n. 44; they are accepted by Forte 1972: 407 (a work which is excessively pedestrian on this and all other matters), and developed by Ratti 1971, Méthy 1991.
[83] Boulanger 1923: 358; Palm 1959: 59. On other occasions Aristides does praise the education of emperors (*Orr.* xx. 8, xxiii. 73, xxvii. 23), a somewhat contexualized matter, of course, and in particular he identifies the African senator Maximus, almost certainly Q. Tullius Maximus *cos.* 168 (Alföldy 1977: 185), as being, 'according to those who are expert in these matters', a pre-eminent Roman orator and records that Maximus was with him at the Asclepieum where he welcomed his opinions on and knowledge of Demosthenes (*Or.* iv. 2–5); see Behr 1968a: 48 n. 26, id. 1981–6: ii. 469 suggesting without strong cause that Maximus' name should be read also at Or. l = IV. 18; and on Tullius Maximus' cultural pretensions cf. the poetic display *CIL* ii. 2660 = *ILS* 3259–60.
[84] At xlvii = I. 46 Aristides goes so far as to dream of the Tiber relief channel.

something different from the usual city encomium.[85] We cannot go as far as saying that he bypassed Rome because he felt there was now no difference between the Greek and Roman parts of the world (and hence the city itself was of no importance).[86] Nevertheless, in the speech he is praising the Roman Empire and not focusing on a single city.

To Rome does in fact start, after the initial expression of modesty, with a section on the great size of Rome itself and her ability to command the delights of world trade (6–13), though everything is kept suitably general. The rest of the speech may be summarized as follows. The section after this compares Rome with earlier powers, Persia, Macedon, the Greek cities (14–57). The aim is to show that only Rome had developed knowledge of government. The Persian kings had to be constantly on the move like 'nomads', enjoyed no real control of their comparatively small territory, and were essentially 'despots' rather than kings (15–23). Alexander 'could not establish his empire' (25), though he founded Alexandria as a 'kindness' for the Romans (26). His Successors were like 'satraps bereft of a king' (27). Rome is different. Her rule is over the whole world and is totally harmonious (30). 'The rulers who are sent to the cities' are themselves ruled by 'the great ruler and president of all' (31). 'If they have even some small doubt about the public or private legal cases and privileges of the ruled, whether some of them are indeed privileged, they immediately send to him to ask what should be done' (32). The emperor rules 'by letters' (33). Above all 'you are the only ones ever to have ruled over free men'. 'You appoint governors [*archontes*] as if by election', from whom appeals are readily made.[87] Aristides then suggests that the provincials are ruled 'to the extent that it pleases them' (36–7). Hence, 'how does this not go beyond every democracy?' (38). 'There is a great and fine equality between the small and the great, the unknown and the famous, between, indeed, the poor and the rich, and the noble and lowly' (39). Aristides next turns to *ta Hellênika*, at the risk of 'seeming to speak of trifles' (40). Rome has surpassed Greece in 'wisdom and moderation' (41), as is evidenced in the contentious behaviour of the states of classical Greece (40–50, cf. 14). This is

---

[85] Ratti 1971 (cf. n. 82); Klein 1981: 114–28; Pernot 1993: i. 330–1.

[86] Klein 1981: 129.

[87] Note that the usual word for provincial governor, *hêgemôn*, refers in *Or.* xxvi only to the emperor or to military commanders.

said not to condemn all the Greeks, but to prove that only Rome knows how to govern (51), something not even the Athenians managed (51–7).

The 'science' (*technê*) of empire was discovered when the greatest of empires had been formed (58). Aristides now goes on to discuss Rome's civil and administrative policy. 'What merits attention and wonder far more than anything else is the magnanimity of your government and of your conception, for there is nothing else like it. You have divided all the men in your empire into two parts . . . and everywhere you have made all the more accomplished, more noble, and more powerful into citizens or indeed kin,[88] while the rest you have made subject and governed' (59). 'No one is a stranger who is worthy of office or of trust, but there has been established a common democracy of the earth under one man, the best ruler and director' (60). Rome is the world's 'common town' (61), and 'you have made "Roman" the name not of a city but of a common race'; the world is divided not into 'Greeks and barbarians', but into 'Romans and non-Romans' (63). 'The greatest and most powerful men in each place guard their own fatherlands for you' (64). Nor is there any envy or hatred, 'not even from those who are left out', for the masses (*plêthê*) have security from the (local) *dunatoi* ('powerful') in the 'immediate anger and vengeance' which descends on these from Rome (65). The cities are free of garrisons. In fact, 'many of the provinces do not know where the garrison is'. 'If some city through its excessive size has lost the ability to control itself, you have not even grudged to these people men who will oversee and keep watch on them' (67). Now there is no 'dispute over empire and pre-eminence [*prôteia*]'. 'So great is your peace, even if warfare is ancestral to you' (71).

A brief summary of the ground already covered brings us to the Roman army (72–89). Aristides first observes the role of the provinces in the 'idea' (*gnômê*) of the army. That is, it was composed of provincials, 'so that the citizens were not disturbed'. 'You went to all your subject lands and searched for those who would perform this service [*leitourgia*].' Their return was citizenship (74–8). Defences of the empire are the next topic (78–85). The chain of command follows. Not all the top ranks are *eupatridai*, 'patricians'; 'merit' is the only important thing (85). Finally, training, tactics,

---

[88] Retaining πολιτικὸν ἢ καὶ ὁμόφυλον with Oliver 1953: 986 and Klein 1983: 36.

structure, and discipline are reviewed (86–9). Aristides next outlines the composition of the constitution. If one looks at the people,
it is a 'democracy', since 'the people easily obtains all its wishes and
requests'; but when one considers the senate, it will be seen that
there is no 'aristocracy more perfect'; but, again, when one sees the
'overseer and president', it will be apparent that 'he holds the most
complete monarchy, and is free of the tyrant's evils and greater
than the dignity of a king' (90–1).

Aristides now moves on to his final section before the perora-
tion, the peace and prosperity of the Antonine empire (92–106). He
notices the extensive urbanization (92–93), and in particular the
flourishing state of the Greek cities and of Ionia (94–95). 'You
constantly care for the Greeks as if they were your foster-fathers,
holding your hand over them and, as it were, raising them up when
they are down, giving freedom and self-rule to the best of them
who were leaders of old, guiding the others moderately and with
great consideration and care' (96). The whole world is enjoying a
festival (97) and is like a park (98–99). Freedom to travel in safety
is made possible by Roman roads and bridges (100–1). 'Common
and manifest security has been given to the earth itself and to those
who dwell in it' (104). All the gods confirm the empire and find joy
in its peace (105). Homer predicted it, and Hesiod, had be been as
mantic, would not have begun his account of man with the Golden
Age, but would have returned Justice and Reverence to earth at the
time of this empire (106). Aristides finishes the speech by praising
the emperor ('the great *archôn*'), apologizes for his inadequacy to
express the greatness of his theme ('it requires a time nearly as long
as the empire—which would be eternity'), and prays for the eternal
existence and safety of the empire, the 'great *archôn*, and his sons'.
'My daring is completed. Whether for better or worse is now a
matter for you to decide' (107–9).

It is apparent that some of Aristides' points in this ringing
laudation are quite personal and/or reflect particularly the Roman
government of the province of Asia. The stress on legal privileges
(*axiôseis*), the power of appeals, and the responses and government
of the emperor by letter (32, 33, 37) should be seen against his long
battles with the governors over immunity and status, in which the
emperor's epistolary support had been important. The particular
administration of the province of Asia may explain the generalization about the appointment of governors 'as if by election' (36),

since the proconsuls there were chosen through a (discreetly managed) sortition.[89] The situation of Asia also accounts for the comments about garrisoning (67), since no legions were stationed there.[90] And there is the explicit section on the prosperity of 'Ionia' (95).[91] What of the other, more general material? The most important stress on the democratic and shared equality of the Empire, on its citizenship, and on common ownership of the 'Roman name' (39, 63) is remarkable and appealing. It is unnecessary to suppose that Aristides believed all this. He no doubt thought the 'more accomplished, more noble, and more powerful' should—like himself—be offered citizenship (and so he would have been horrified by Caracalla's general extension of the citizenship in 212).[92] Roman offices were a natural consequence of this. But he never refers to himself as 'Roman' nor does he so describe any of his fellow-Greeks at the Asclepieum. Even if he had, the general orientation of the Greek elite in our period and the particular cases of the men studied in this book make it unlikely that anything other than politico-administrative loyalty would be at stake.

As for the suggestion that the world is now divided into 'Romans and non-Romans' rather than 'Greeks and barbarians' (63), it may be noted that Aristides does not say this is his own classification: rather, 'you divide'. Indeed, like all other Greeks under Rome Aristides continues to employ the familiar *Hellênes–barbaroi* shift (even here), and though in this speech the Romans stand outside the traditional division,[93] the old opposition of Greek versus barbarian is what constitutes Aristides' 'moral barrier', not the borders of the Roman Empire.[94] Aristides' sentiment, as we saw with Apellas and his family, is Greek, albeit one of a Greek favourable

[89] Alföldy 1977: 119, 122; cf. Syme 1983: 341; Philostratus, *Life of Apollonius* v. 36 (below, 'Philostratus' n. 48).

[90] That does not mean that there were no Roman troops to be seen; cf. MacMullen 1988: 145, 215–16 (some evidence of troops in this period in Asia); and see in general Mitchell 1993: i. 118–42 on the level of military activity and movement in Asia Minor at this time, esp. 141 for sharp remarks on Aristides' claim.

[91] Which of course compliments Pius who was himself governor of the province around 134/5.

[92] Cf. Bleicken 1966: 272; Klein 1983: 88–9. Just so was Cassius Dio, a man ever conscious of status (cf. lxxviii. 41. 2–4 on the equestrian emperor Macrinus), opposed to the change in his own thoughts (lxxvii. 9. 5, cf. lx. 17. 5–6; his flattery of Caracalla's constitution at lii. 19. 6 is a different matter: cf. Millar 1964: 104–5).

[93] 11, 14, 41, 96, 100.

[94] I borrow the phrase from Alföldi 1952 (whose thoughts are strangely reversed by Whittaker 1989: 16).

to Rome.[95] This is not unexpected; but it does make the statements in *To Rome* look a little different. The notion of Rome as the 'common town' must be treated carefully. It is a truism of the age (without legal significance—except for senators) and should be compared with Aristides' similar comments about the role of Corinth for Greeks.[96] The material on the army, especially the section on the fortifications which kept peace on the boundary of the empire (78–85), in other words the *limes*, will perhaps suggest a 'them and us' outlook to some. On the other hand, Aristides' near-contemporary Appian of Alexandria makes similar remarks about the defence of the Empire in his history but never comes close to suggesting any community of feeling between Rome and her subjects.[97] Aristides may again have admired Rome's military success without going as far as Lucian and talking of her armies as his own.[98]

What of equality (*isotês*)? Aristides knew (of course) that only 'a child or an old man would be so stupid as not to know that one city—the first and the greatest—holds the whole earth in its sway and that one house leads all' (*Or.* xxiii. 62). He applauded this situation. There is no need to make him believe what he says in *To Rome* about the operation of equality in the Empire. It may have amused his audience to hear that provincials were ruled 'to the extent that it pleases them' (37); but in *Or.* xxiii Aristides admonishes Pergamum, Smyrna, and Ephesus for sometimes venturing wrong opinions of this sort. Citizenship aside, Aristides makes little in the speech of political opportunities (cf. 60, quoted above; there are similar statements on power-sharing in the panegyrical

[95] Cf. Behr 1968*a*: 5.

[96] Nutton 1971: 58. Corinth: *Or.* xlvi. 23–4. Cf. 'Arrian' n. 16.

[97] Appian, *Roman History* Preface 7. 26–8 'they have encircled the empire with great encampments and guard all this land and sea as a fortress'; cf. 'Arrian', text before n. 46. On the static conception of the Empire (i.e. as having fixed borders) among its 'educated inhabitants' under the Principate see Millar 1982: 19–20. I doubt that either Appian or Aristides were equating the Empire with the sacred space of the Greek city (Nicolet 1983: 171; Whittaker 1989: 28) when they presented it in these passages as a territorial unit surrounded by fortifications; even if they were, we must not forget more importantly that Aristides' own 'us' does not necessarily comprise all those within the Empire.

[98] On Lucian see below, 'Lucian' nn. 56–7. Aristides, *Or.* xlvii = I. 38 (from the Diary) 'the king on our side' (*tôi par' hêmin basilei*), referring to Marcus as opposed to Vologeses 'the other [king]', should probably not be compared with Lucian's use of 'we', for Aristides does not prefer one king to the other. Beware Vidal-Naquet 1984: 341, where Aristides' 'you', etc., at xxvi. 26 (what Alexander did for you Romans) mysteriously becomes 'nous', etc.

speech at Cyzicus, *Or.* xxvii. 32, quoted below), and strangely says nothing about senatorial families from the east, though he was of course well aware of their aspirations.[99] More significant is his own (and, in the present context, very recent) disavowal of an essential part of equal gains, that is, equal responsibility, in his battles over immunity. Aristides wanted no part of the system he so lauds.[100] Thus, however far he may or may not voice the views of the Greek elite in this matter, he himself has a different intention.

What of 'democracy'? By Aristides' day the word had long since been shorn of its classical Greek meaning.[101] It is impossible to tell how cynical its application to the absolute monarchy of the Roman Empire actually is. The term was perhaps employed in this sense by Aristides, and perhaps first by him,[102] because it 'sounded good [*epieikes onoma*]', as Dio of Prusa puts it (*Or.* iii. 47 'if it was [only] practicable'). For a Roman audience it had the particular advantage of playing down the regal aspects of the system as well as corresponding to the imperial ideology of the empire as the empire of the Roman people.[103] Aristides himself may have been thinking especially of the legal aspects of the term, just as Plutarch was when he characterized the contemporary Greek city as a democracy in *Political Advice* ch. 21.[104] Popular influence over justice was held to be a hallmark of the classical Athenian democracy. *To Rome* lays much stress on the subject's right of appeal from mistaken governors. At 37 the phrase 'like an appeal from one's demesmen to the court' clearly recalls Aristotle on the resolution of disputed status in classical Athens.[105] Aristides' emperor is characterized as the 'great juryman' (38, 39) and by other 'civic' terms.[106] The only

[99] Cf. Sherwin-White 1973: 427 (in a discussion which, like that of many others, takes Aristides' oration as a fair summary of Aristides' thoughts and Aristides as a fair representative of everyone else). Aristides well aware of aspirations: see *Or.* xxx, above, nn. 23–6.

[100] His is not quite the 'Teilhabe' in the Empire that is discovered by Klein 1981: 135.

[101] De Ste. Croix 1981: 323.

[102] Cf. Starr 1952: 13–14 on Aristides and resonances of the idea in Cassius Dio lii. 14. 3–5 and Philostratus, *Life of Apollonius* v. 35 (but these passages are perhaps more concerned with modes of behaviour rather than with constitutional frameworks).

[103] On which see recently Millar 1988, id. 1989: 94. On Greek awareness of the Romans' aversion from the term 'king' see Appian, *Roman History* Preface 6. 22–3, cf. *Civil Wars* ii. 110. 461; Cassius Dio liii. 17. 1–18. 5 (on imperial titulature).

[104] Above, 'Plutarch' n. 113.   [105] *Constitution of the Athenians* 42. 1.

[106] The principal ones are: 'leader of the chorus [*koruphaios hêgemôn*]' (29); 'teacher [of the chorus]' (32); 'great magistrate' (39, 107, 109); 'director [*kosmêtês*]' (60);

other contemporary state to which he applies the term 'democracy' is Rhodes (*Or.* xxiv. 22), in reality of course an oligarchy, but referred to as a democracy.[107] There again the reference may be to legal aspects, as it is explicitly in Dio's *Rhodian Oration* (xxxi. 58). Really speaking, though, the emphasis on law in *To Rome* is no more than a common and essential underpinning in Greek thought of the idea of the good king (who would otherwise turn despot). And Aristides is kind enough to show that the imperial democracy rigorously excludes the mass, for only the 'the more accomplished, more noble, and more powerful' are citizens in it (59). (He all but ignores the Roman *plebs*, except in his 'Polybian' remarks on the mixed constitution at 90, cf. Polybius vi. 11. 12.) Thus, 'the greatest and most powerful men in each place guard their own fatherlands for you' (64). As he notes triumphantly with an eye on appeals, 'how does this not go beyond every democracy?' (38).

In keeping with the democratic ideology Aristides is careful to assert that the powerful do not contend for *prôteia* (69) and that the have-nots bear no hatred or envy toward the system (65). Naturally, he knew the truth was different. The strife of the leading cities is addressed in *Orr.* xxiii *To the Cities, On Concord* and xxvii *Panegyric in Cyzicus On the Temple*; awareness of the masses' dislike of the elite is to the fore in *Orr.* xxix *On the Prohibition of Comedy* (especially 4–6) and xxiv *To the Rhodians, On Concord* (32). *To Rome* suppresses what its audience would not have liked. There are certain places where the carefully structured celebration shows signs of strain. In praising the army, a section where he has been held to be particularly *au fait* with current Roman thinking (which would be surprising),[108] Aristides allows that the policy of local recruitment initiated by Hadrian made Roman citizens 'from the city' (i.e. Rome) a privileged extra-military group (74).[109] Rome's much celebrated discovery of the science of government follows the

'prytanis' (90, cf. 31, 109). He is conspicuously not *basileus*, 'king', the normal Greek word for the Roman emperor (cf. 90 'greater than the dignity of a king'); *autokratôr*, also used by Aristides, is avoided here for sounding too technical. Aristides elsewhere (xx. 1, xxi. 8) uses another 'civic' term, 'protectors'/'champions' [*prostatai*], to describe Marcus and Commodus (cf. xxvi. 106 'protection'); cf. above, 'Dio' n. 116.

[107] An oligarchy with a conscience for Strabo xiv. 2. 5 (C 652–3); democracy: cf. *IGR* iv. 1124 (Nero).

[108] Klein 1981: 138 ff.

[109] A Hadrianic reform: cf. Webster 1979: 108–9 summarizing the figures of Forni 1953: 187 ff. for the period from Hadrian to the end of the 3rd c. (under 1% of legionaries were Italian, new legions excepted).

establishment of the Empire (58), a truthful observation but in its allusion to the birth-travails one not quite consistent with the grosser flatteries of the speech. 'Freedom' bears, as it tends to, different meanings. The Romans rule free men (36), but freedom in the political sense is carefully measured out to the Greek cities (96 'giving freedom and self-rule to the best of them . . . guiding the others moderately and with great consideration and care').[110]

It is hardly surprising that there are inconsistencies of this sort in *To Rome*. Overall Aristides carried out rather well the task of presenting an autocratic regime as a participatory democracy where the elite are all Romans by name. It would be credulous to suppose he actually believed this picture. No wonder he acknowledges the difficulty of the speech in the preface. It is quite probable that the encomiums of Empire and emperor, which were accorded prizes in the festivals, were similarly flattering, but impossible to imagine what people thought of them.[111] With regard to Aristides the crucial factor in his praise of Rome seems to be Rome's guarantee of his own *axiôsis* and its support for the elite. This is surely a self-interested reason for welcoming the Empire and carries with it no unequivocal sign of deep loyalty.

When we look at Aristides in this regard, we must not forget his contrasting, genuine sympathy for Greek culture and for the history of Athens in particular.[112] Aristides styled himself 'first of the Greeks'. For him his speeches 'mean everything and signify everything. I account them my children, parents, work, play, all things' (*Or.* xxxiii. 20). The *Panathenaic Oration* (*Or.* i), which is three times the length of *To Rome*, contains an enormous central section glorifying Athens' deeds in war (75–321). *Or.* iii *To Plato, In Defence of the Four*, Aristides' longest work and controversial in later antiquity for style and content,[113] is an elaborate justification of the careers of Pericles, Cimon, Miltiades, and Themistocles against Plato's attacks in the *Gorgias*. His criticism of the Greeks in *To*

[110] Aristides characterizes Rome's relationship with the Greeks as one of honouring 'foster-fathers [*tropheis*]' (96), a word he usually applies to his favourite family retainers (Behr 1968*a*: 8–9).

[111] Cf. e.g. the encomia of the emperor at the Thespian Mouseia in Schachter 1981–6: ii. 176–9; see Price 1984*b*: 90 with literature. Pernot's notion (1993: ii. 739) that panegyrical literature celebrating Rome, often in official contexts such as addresses to governors, exemplifies the Greeks' general identification with the Empire is badly skewed.

[112] This aspect is well stressed by Stertz 1994 (whose ideas on Aristides and democracy are, however, rather muddled).

[113] Cf. Behr 1968*b*.

Rome, for which he carefully apologizes (51), is repeated before
Greek audiences (especially in *Or.* xxiii *To the Cities, On Concord*). It does not seem to detract from his overwhelming pride in
being and calling himself Greek. The same goes for the section in
To Rome on the failure of Alexander the Great to consolidate his
conquests (24–6).[114] We have seen that in his dreams Aristides knew
he was as great in oratory as Alexander had been in war (l = IV. 49).
Aristides clearly had a special fondness for Alexandria and was
honoured by (or on behalf of) that city (and other Egyptian Greeks)
under his full name, P. Aelius Aristides Theodorus, 'on account of
his bravery and his speeches'.[115] In *To Rome* Alexandria is the only
other city praised by the orator (26, 95).[116] That is interesting given
its traditional rumbustiousness (observed amongst others by Dio in
his *Alexandrian Oration*) and its habitual rebelliousness against
Roman rule.[117]

SPEECHES TO THE CITIES

It is time to move on to Aristides' city speeches. The works under
examination here are *Orr.* xvii–xxi (the Smyrnaean orations), xxiii

[114] Cf. Appian, *Roman History* Preface 10. 38 (and contrast perhaps Plutarch's
two rhetorical pieces *On the Fortune or Virtue of Alexander the Great* with their
emphasis on Alexander's successful philosophical government).

[115] *OGIS* 709 = *IGR* i. 1070 ἐπὶ ἀνδραγαθίᾳ καὶ λόγοις. The provenance of the
statue, which was found in Italy, is unknown. Behr 1968a: 111 speculates that behind the inscription lies gratitude for a supposed intercession by Aristides with
Marcus following Egypt's support for the rebel Avidius Cassius. More plausibly
Bingen 1987 equates *OGIS* 709 with the statue mentioned by Philostratus, *VS* 582,
as dedicated by Italy, Greece, and the Delta, suggesting the attestations of Italy and
Greece are lost and that the whole was erected in the form of a dedication by
Smyrna (hence the hieronym Theodorus, 'Gift of God', granted to Aristides here:
l = IV. 53–4) in gratitude to Aristides for his help after the earthquake of 177 or 178
(cf. below, n. 148). For another explanation see Quet 1992b (above, 'Arrian' n. 49).

[116] It is probably right to see a further allusion to it at 67 ('if some city through
its excessive size has lost the ability to control itself), as Oliver 1953: 932 and others
have pointed out. In 26 (Klein 1983: 76) Aristides alludes to the direct control
(*kratoiête*) exercised by Rome over the city, which notoriously was forbidden until
AD 200 to have its own city council. The extraordinary papyrus *BGU* 1210 (= *FIRA*
i, no. 99 = *Select Papyri* 206), which details a revision of the totalitarian rules of the
idiologus (one of the most senior financial officials in Roman Egypt), dates from the
same decade as *To Rome*.

[117] Aristides' attitude is perhaps due to the role ascribed to Alexander in the third
foundation of his beloved Smyrna (see *Or.* xxi. 4 where Alexander has 'these two
fairest and greatest memorials, this city and that by the Nile'; cf. Pausanias vii. 5. 1–3).

(*To the Cities, On Concord*), xxiv (*To the Rhodians, On Concord*), and xxvii (*Panegyric in Cyzicus On the Temple*). What do they tell us about his views of Rome?

It is as well to start with *Or.* xxvii, which was perhaps delivered in the autumn of 166 or 167.[118] In the fifth *Sacred Tale* Aristides tells us that he was sent by Asclepius to make this speech. The brilliance of his reception is predicted by a vision in which his doctor recalls Athena rousing the Phaeacians to welcome the travelling Odysseus.[119] Aristides goes on to record his somewhat difficult journey and the *spoudê*, 'enthusiasm', with which the speech was received before the council of Cyzicus and 'at the festival' (*Or.* li = V. 16).[120] The original temple had been established by Hadrian but was, it seems, destroyed, and Aristides' speech honoured the rededication (22 'you have inscribed on it the name of the best of the *basileis* up to that time [i.e. Hadrian], the work has come to completion for you in these times'). The temple, which was 'unquestionably a gigantic building',[121] is unlikely to have been dedicated principally to Hadrian, as was once thought, but to have accommodated the emperor's cult within it according to a familiar pattern. The major dedication is unknown.[122] Most of Aristides' speech is devoted not to the temple but praising the harmony of Marcus and Lucius and to exhorting the cities of Asia to follow their example (23–39). Aristides speaks of 'the abundance of all their culture' (23). They are friends who share everything in common (24). They are

[118] For 166—Behr 1968a: 101; Aristides went to Cyzicus (*Or.* li = V. 11–16) a year and a month (li = V. 11) after illness at his ancestral estate at Laneion (li = V. 1); the dating depends on identifying this illness with symptoms of the great plague, which Aristides contracted according to Behr in 165 (see esp. xlviii = II. 37–43, which refers in turn to xlviii = II. 18, a rather obscure passage in which Asclepius promises 17 years good health; this begins in 149 according to Behr 1968a: 71, who then reckons inclusively to arrive at summer 165). However, Lucian *How to Write History* 15 strongly implies that the plague was still in Parthia when he was writing in mid 166 (at the end of the war but before the triumph, 30–1; cf. Gilliam 1961: 229; Jones 1986: 60), and so Aristides' speech might rather be placed in the autumn of 167.

[119] *Odyssey* viii. 11 ff.

[120] The festival is connected with the Cyzicene Olympiad, the celebrations coinciding with the rededication of the temple: Behr 1968a: 101 n. 20; Schulz and Winter 1990: 41.

[121] Ward Perkins 1981: 282.

[122] The temple is a 'thank offering' to the gods for the bounty of the times (22, cf. 40). Hasluck 1910: 187 n. 7 suggested Persephone (Appian, *Mithridatic War* 75. 323 'the Cyzicenes worship her particularly'); Price 1984a: 146 ff., esp. 153–5 suggests Zeus, cf. Schulz and Winter 1990: 44. For bibliography on the subject see Price 1984a: 251–2.

brothers (28) who have extended their 'harmony' to mankind (31). In keeping with this is the constitution of their city. They have 'set out their goods as common possessions like prizes for the best people and it makes no difference whether you live in Europe, Asia, or Libya . . . All have a right to take charge of what happens . . . all the worthy to enjoy this common participation' (32). Here the panegyric is very close to what is said at *To Rome* 60, though the elitism is more pronounced. The emperors' government and its inspiration is divine, since friendship and sharing are the characteristics of the gods 'for ever' (35). The emperors are the gods' 'friends' just as they are of each other (36). They are like Sarapis and Asclepius the saviour gods (39).

The encomiastic tone of this section is clear enough as Aristides almost affirms the emperors' own divinity. It is very doubtful that he actually believed they were divine. In this speech prayers are uttered only 'on behalf' of the emperors and we are asked to 'congratulate them and join in prayer for them' (38, 40).[123] Marcus and Lucius are called 'divine [*theios*]' at *Orr.* xix. 5 (where there is a careful distinction between 'praying to the gods' and 'asking the divine rulers'), xxiii. 79, and xlii. 14; but it would be difficult to prove the designation was other than titular (though the usage in these passages is not without literary and political significance in context).[124] The imperial cult was a fact of life which Aristides felt free to mention.[125] The expression of imperial divinity becomes progressively more routine in provincial approaches to the emperor through the second century and beyond;[126] but routinization does not necessarily entail 'belief', and this is surely the case with Aristides.

[123] On *suneuchesthai* as 'join in prayer' rather than 'pray to' cf. Plato, *Laws* 687d, LSJ[9] s.v. Praying 'for' the emperors is part of the standard language of ordinary cult. The subject's 'double prayer' at *To Rome* 32 ('one to the gods for him [i.e. the emperor], one to him for himself') is a rhetorical development of this and is not meant seriously (Bowersock 1973: 200–1), nor is it relevant to the imperial cult as an institution.

[124] The emperors are never simply *theoi*, 'gods', as they mostly are in decrees and dedications (even of living emperors); cf. Bowersock 1973: 198–9; and on the language of inscriptions Price 1984*b* (suggesting that there is no change from the usual sense when *theos* is used of a prince; but note ibid. 81 on the third-c. preference for *theios* over *theos*). On the Aristides passages see below, nn. 139, 152.

[125] Note the reference to the Hadrianeion at Pergamum in the sanctuary of Asclepius (probably also the library of Flavia Melitine) at *Or.* xlvii = I. 29 and perhaps at l = IV. 106 where Aristides dreams of 'Hadrian the *autokratôr* in the court of the temple' (Price 1984*a*: 148; Habicht 1969: nos. 6, 38).

[126] Price 1984*a*: 239–48.

Towards the end of the Cyzicene oration Aristides makes some suggestive remarks about the relation between the cult and the exercise of imperial power. Pointing out to the assembled cities their good fortune to live under the Empire and the need to be grateful to the gods and to congratulate the emperors he says, 'for fair too are these adornments of buildings which are so wonderfully persuasive to the masses' (40). The reference is to the temple of the god including the shrine of the emperor. In a speech delivered according to its subscription during the games of the provincial assembly at Smyrna, *Or.* xxxiv *Against Those who Lampoon (The Mysteries of Oratory)* which dates probably to 170, Aristides and his audience in the council chamber there take immense pleasure, as he tells us at *Or.* li = V. 38–41, in a vicious attack on orators who flattered the masses. Aristides speaks of the intention of the true orator as being 'to persuade men and frankly to get them under his control' (xxxiv. 19). In particular, it is vitally important to know how to tell 'the many' what to do, since the many follow the opinion of a few experts (38–41).[127] The use of religious cult to propagate the elite's hold over the masses is an understandable part of this.

The last section of the Cyzicene oration turns aside from such crude political facts to the more laudable subject of harmony among the Asian cities. 'Now you must regard all the cities as sisters' (44). 'From the start this way has been the best and it is appropriate to the present times' (45). Especially noticeable is Aristides' claim that he is only putting into words what the cities are already practising (43, 46). In keeping with this restrained approach to the problem of the cities' rivalries is the absence of the key word *homonoia*, 'concord'. Throughout the speech Aristides has employed a musical analogy to stress the harmonious behaviour of the two fraternal emperors. Their music is a *harmonia* (30, 31).[128] The final section on the cities begins with a similar analogy (41). The emperors 'sing the same and share their music on behalf of all men and all the cities' (31); the cities must 'think the same' (43).

---

[127] For the real orator's way of handling the masses see particularly *Or.* ii *To Plato, On Rhetoric* 178–202. On the reference in the fifth *Sacred Tale* see Behr 1968a: 106–7.

[128] The omission of *homonoia* is slightly odd given the emperors' propaganda about their *concordia* at the beginning of their reign, which was then echoed in the local coinages of cities in danger from the Persian war (*RIC* iii [1930], M. Aurelius nos. 1 ff., 444 ff.; Robert, in Dupont-Sommer and Robert 1964: 76, no. 37; Robert 1980: 425–6).

Far more important thoughts about the relations between the
Asian cities are expressed in the speech which deals directly with
the subject, *Or.* xxiii *To the Cities, On Concord.* This is set before
the delegates of the provincial assembly at Pergamum some time
after the Parthian war, probably at the start of 168.[129] Aristides
presents himself as a fearless orator whose courage allows him to
address difficult subjects avoided by other speakers (xxiii. 1–4, 80).
This is a standard part of his oratorical persona, but also recalls for
us Dio of Prusa's remarks to the Nicomedians at *Or.* xxxviii. 4 ff.,
51. In this speech Dio spends a long time explaining what concord
is (xxxviii. 10–21), then comes to the specific discord between
Nicomedia and Nicaea over the titles which can be bestowed by
Rome, contrasting the Greeks' present vanity with the historical
rivalries of Athens and Sparta over real issues (21 ff., 24–5; cf. *Or.*
xxxiv. 49–51), making plain the need to stand firm against Rome
(33 ff.), and pointing out the material and spiritual advantages of
concord (41 ff.). Aristides' speech, which along with *Or.* xxiv to
Rhodes most shows political realism, is in many ways similar, but
reflects his own political prejudices and the more obviously stable
and acceptable Roman political situation of his time. He says that
he is following Isocrates in speaking of concord (xxiii. 2–3, referring to the *Panegyricus*). He is performing a useful service—he
knows 'what should be said and has the courage to say it' (4). The
speech is better than 'erecting a great number of very large buildings for you (temples excepted)' (80), a side of city politics of which
Aristides with no institutional political ambitions and no desire
to spend money is free to disapprove (cf. *Orr.* xix. 8, xxvii. 41).
His answer to the problem of the cities' rivalry for *prôteia*, a problem which is entirely natural (12), is to show that all three major
cities of Asia, Pergamum, Smyrna, and Ephesus, are equally praiseworthy and thus have no grounds to envy one another (13–25). Roman

[129] The date is indicated by the military success of Marcus and Lucius against
the barbarians (3, 53–7). Behr 1968*a*: 104 suggests the new year's meeting of the
assembly on the basis of *Or.* li = V. 26–9, Aristides' visit to Pergamum at the time
of '*epibdai*, when the Romans celebrate the first day of the year', and when assemblies and crowds cheered his oratory. This narrative is sequential to the visit to
Cyzicus and so perhaps one should think of 168 (above, n. 118) rather than 167
(Behr). The archaic *epibdai*, meaning properly the days following the great Athenian
festival of the Apaturia in early November, is confusing; but the precise Roman date
probably recalls an official occasion and perhaps refers specifically (cf. xxiii. 13) to
the duties of magistrates to 'pray and sacrifice on behalf of the emperor' on 3
January (Plutarch, *Cicero* 2. 1; Lucian, *The False Critic* 8; i.e. the *nuncupatio votorum*).

attributes are not ignored. Pergamum is the origin of 'the very things we are taking pride in' (13), a reference to the first temple of the imperial cult in the province of Asia, that of Roma and Augustus, founded at Pergamum in 29 BC.[130] Ephesus, the governor's seat, is on this account 'the common chancellery [*tamieion*] of Asia' (24).

This praise of the cities is followed by the 'useful' part of the speech (27–40), where Aristides outlines in generalities the advantages of concord and the problems of *stasis*. He then turns to the historical clash of Athens and Sparta (41 ff.) 'which you all know of'. In keeping with his earlier allusion to the speeches of Isocrates he applauds the unity of the Greeks against Persia and attacks the subsequent strife among the cities which, he says, led to Philip and Macedonian control (48–51). 'All those great things sank under the ground like water, and we ought to feel relieved that a small remnant of Greece has come down to you, restored by the virtue of the present rulers' (51), a reference to political rather than cultural power, as is plain from what follows. Aristides stresses that examples from the past which concern faction have a direct bearing on the present (53 ff.),[131] since faction and discord are worse during a period of peace. Like Dio he admits that the struggles of the ancient Greeks were at least about real things in contrast to those of the present: 'for what leadership are you doing this? or for which allies? or for what harbours, or triremes, or revenues, or districts?' (60). 'By Zeus, let me be granted some free speech [*parrhêsia*] right now!' (61). Aristides' exasperation (real or imagined) at this point recalls similar passages of Isocrates.[132] The 'disease' of the ancient Greeks 'made some sense' (59). Today, in the 'order established by good fortune' it does not (62). 'Why are we fighting over a shadow when it is possible for us to enjoy the peace?' (63).[133] Governors come annually 'by law'. The cities, however, 'mix wilfulness with flattery' in their dealings with them. Aristides ironically imagines that the governor's judicial progress is at the cities' behest—they continually

[130] On the temple see Magie 1953: ii. 1293–4 n. 52; Habicht 1973: 55–64; Price 1984a: 252.

[131] 'If anyone thinks these examples are waffle, because there is at present no war, he does not see that he is talking nonsense'. Cf. xxiv. 23 (the Greek past is especially relevant to pure Greeks like the Rhodians), further, above 'Past' nn. 61, 83.

[132] Cf. *Antidosis* 43, *Panathenaicus* 96. Aristides no doubt approved the advice at *To Nicocles* 28 to 'grant *parrhêsia* to men of sound judgement'. On *parrhêsia* in Aristides see Behr 1968a: 55 n. 53.

[133] Cf. Dio, *Or.* xxxiv. 48.

demand his presence and do not think that they as the real 'masters' have to do his bidding (64).[134] This is the only passage in Aristides where he comes at all close to commending some degree of self-respect to the Greeks. He then points out the essential contradiction in the cities' behaviour: 'I am amazed that while you accord yourselves the greatest airs for the temples and competitions you think of as common, it is over these very things that you have become divided' (65).

It is with this remark that the speech becomes rather interesting. For here Aristides identifies the crux of the cities' problem: they disputed over what was 'common' but over nothing that was actually theirs. As he puts it, if it is a case of separate possessions, disputes are understandable; as it is not, there is no cause for them (65). The irony of the situation is developed as Aristides plays on the word *koinon*, 'common', the name of the provincial league (the *koinon*) which was applied to its council chambers, temples, games, and 'everything so to speak that is most important' (66). 'If you are right to be proud of these things that are common, how can you not be ashamed that you wrangle because of them?' (66). Aristides is of course speaking before the *koinon*, perhaps on the main occasion in the year when prayers were uttered on the emperor's behalf,[135] and so has very much in his mind the imperial cult, its festivals and institutional sites, for which the provincial league had responsibility and which were the chief source of its identity.[136] On one level he is simply exploiting the discourse of community to get the Greeks to act harmoniously. But he was also surely aware of the ideological trap inherent in this discourse, that it was predicated not on the community of the cities, not on what they really had as common, but on the symbols of a foreign power whose attention the cities vied for; at any rate he will shortly make it clear that the concord which goes closely in his mind with communal relations

[134] Retaining the MSS reading κυρίους with Behr 1981–6: ii. 450 (κυρίως Keil). At *Or.* xvii. 5 the Smyrnaeans more diplomatically 'call' the governor to them.

[135] See above, n. 129.

[136] 65 'the temples and competitions you think of as common . . . you rejoice in as common'; 66 'you have called your council chambers common, common your temples and games, common everything so to speak that is most important . . . you take pride [*philotimeisthe*] in these as common'; 67 'you take pride in the designation', cf. 13 'the very things we are taking pride in had their origin from here' (referring to the cult). On the notion of 'commonness' in the speech in regard to the temples, festivals, and processions of the imperial cult see Moretti 1954; Merkelbach 1978: 292–6.

is directed by and towards Rome (73; see below). The complex exchange between central and local power that was present in the imperial cult, and which is part of the wider pattern of reciprocity between Greek culture and the needs and demands of Roman power and Rome's expectation of the Greek world, was ultimately, however serviceable to the Greek elite, a one-sided exchange.[137] This is part of the reason why provincial organizations like the Asian *koinon* did not bring the cities concord.

It is interesting to see how Aristides contrasts with Dio in the matter. Dio had singled out as the basis of concord between the Bithynian cities their shared cultural inheritance and present-day social ties (*Orr.* xxxviii. 22, 46; xl. 27; xli. 10). Aristides makes virtually nothing of these things during his speech to the Asian cities, and when he now returns to the advantages to be had from concord (67 ff.) his discussion is entirely general (cf. 27–40). The message is simply that concord and friendship are good for you. And he specifies the source of the communal ideology by reminding his audience that 'as I indeed remember, the best of the emperors who surpassed everyone in culture wrote to you explicitly about these matters right at the beginning and promised that he would judge those to be the best and the most excellent who voluntarily initiated concord' (73).[138] Aristides makes it clear to anyone who had not been listening that the ultimate reason for communal harmony is that it pleased Rome. There is nothing to suggest that he was in any way critical of this situation. The message is that Rome was in control, that the emperor and the governors were well disposed to the cities, that the cities could and should therefore live in harmony and enjoy the benefits of empire, and that, even if the Empire was not their own, they should at least take the discourse of community to heart. As he puts it earlier, 'How is it not likely that all would rejoice in the present situation, that all would be minded to think of their common blessings as if they were their own [*hôs huper oikeiôn*]?' (11). The cities' pursuits were by no means worthless, but were nothing in comparison with true friendship, which is their 'true adornment [*kosmos*]' (75–6; cf. *Or.* xxvii. 41). This is after all how the heavenly *kosmos* (in our sense of 'universe') functioned 'with concord prevailing' (76–7). The

[137] On the imperial cult in this manner see Price 1984*a*: 65–73.
[138] The reference is to Pius; for his interest in good relations between the Asian cities see *SIG*³ 849 (cf. 'Dio' n. 143).

analogy with the divine, standard in these contexts and too obviously punning on *kosmos* (which essentially means 'order'), has the advantage of moving the problem up and away from the awkward political sphere. Elevation also leads to the example of the 'kings who are best in everything' and who are, significantly, 'divine' (79 ff.). Count yourselves lucky to be ruled by them and imitate them, Aristides says (78; cf. xxvii. 40). 'Kings indeed would best govern human affairs by making themselves like the gods who are the masters of all, and cities would best be governed by moving as near as they can to the wishes of their rulers'. Hence, 'for the sake of the gods themselves and for the divine emperors . . . let it be our wish . . . to strive against each other in this one matter of who will be the first to initiate concord' (79).[139]

To the Cities, On Concord is an important gloss on *To Rome*. In that speech the Greek cities, and 'Ionia' in particular (xxvi. 95), have never had it so good (so also at xxiii. 8 ff.); but there is naturally no strife (and hence no need to mention concord). Roman control in the democracy of the world is played down. In *Or.* xxiii the facts can be mentioned, calmly (11: you are treated better than 'most of the ruled') or with more feeling (61–3: only 'a child or an old man would be so stupid as not to know that one city, etc.'). In particular, in *To Rome* the imperial cult was not mentioned because of the delivery of the speech before the court and because of the picture of the emperor as the Empire's first officer.[140] With the rites of the *koinon* before Aristides at Pergamum there was no need for silence, and indeed benefits of concord on the imperial design could be gained from advertisement.

Concord, as we have seen in Plutarch and Dio, has an internal aspect as well. This is the subject of Aristides, *Or.* xxiv *To the Rhodians, On Concord*, a written speech sent to 'the men of Rhodes' after a request for help (3), perhaps in the year 149.[141] Two speeches of Dio's concern internal concord. It is also a principal subject of Plutarch's *Political Advice*. Dio, *Or.* xxxix to the Nicaeans, is a celebration of internal concord on, as the title indicates, 'the cessation of faction'; but no clues are offered as to the origin of the trouble nor—generalities aside—to the nature of the cure. The second

---

[139] For the thought cf. Philostratus, *Life of Apollonius* iv. 8 (Smyrna).
[140] Cf. Klein 1981: 132 n. 24; see above, n. 123 on the 'double prayer' at *To Rome* 32. On the avoidance of the word 'king' in *To Rome* see above, n. 106.
[141] Behr 1968*a*: 73–4.

Tarsian Oration (xxxiv) is more helpful. This addresses amongst other problems the internal divisions in Tarsus between various enfranchised groups on the one hand (xxxiv. 16–21) and on the other the treatment of the unfranchised linen workers (xxxiv. 21–3). It was Dio's strength to appear as a mediator between all the groups in question. The problems at Tarsus did not stem simply from economic exploitation—that should be the explanation of the treatment of the linen workers, but in the case of the other groups Dio suggests peer rivalries, whether over status or wealth. In other words, internal *stasis* might reflect discord among the members of the elite as well as what one would expect, discord between elite and mass.[142] As we have seen, Plutarch's commendation of concord in *Political Advice* has like concerns. Harmony is certainly needed between the members of the elite, but it particularly involves the whole city, where it is invoked in the interest of the status quo. In Aristides' speech to the Rhodians economic and class divisions are the main problem. Aristides had no time for the masses and suspected (no doubt correctly) that they wished only to mock the activities of the elite and to be pandered to by flattering politicians (*Orr.* xxviii, xxxiv). Nevertheless, in promoting the ideology of civic harmony both sides had to be accommodated.

Much of the speech to the Rhodians, as Aristides notes (5), is taken up with traditional wisdom on the benefits of concord in the city, which is rooted in the harmony of the home and individuals, in Rhodes' heritage, and in the natural world (4–21, 41–57). Rhodes' 'freedom' and 'democracy' are now at risk, the former of deprivation, the latter of transformation into 'monarchy'. This would happen 'by force' (22). (The Rhodian ideology was a democratic one; in reality she was like others oligarchic.)[143] Discord, Aristides remarks, 'particularly harms the status quo' (4). The purpose of his missive is simply to reinstate the existing arrangements. Why had these failed? After some obligatory historical examples of concord and faction (23–7), the matter the Rhodians knew full well is broached. 'You do not have to help those who borrowed against

---

[142] Cf. 'Dio' n. 111. Literary references to internal discord often avoid diagnosis of the problem: Philostratus, *VS* 531 (Smyrna; rivalry between regions of the city), 603 (Naucratis), id. *Life of Apollonius* iv. 8 (Smyrna); Apollonius of Tyana, *Letters* lxxv (Sardis); Galen, *On Precognition* xiv. 622. 17, 648. 7 (Pergamum); Philip of Pergamum, *FGrH* 95 (if this really belongs to our period).

[143] See above, n. 107, for the views of Strabo and Dio.

your interests repay however many talents it was' (29). Aristides
goes on to say that, in the midst of the present 'happiness', they
should not 'deliberately give up "the portion that falls to you"
from, as it were, the theoric fund' (30). The theoric fund in classical
Athens was, in the words of the orator Demades, 'the glue of the
democracy', the mechanism which redistributed wealth to enable
the poor to attend festivals.[144] Aristides' own wording here recalls
one of his favourite speeches, Demosthenes' *On the Crown*.[145] If it
is not simply a gloss on the present prosperity, it may indicate that
those who had borrowed money borrowed against or from some
public fund.[146] Some people had suffered in the affair (which they
should refer to 'some occasional chance'); the perpetrators are warned
against displaying ambition and told to think themselves lucky for
escaping punishment (40). These two groups may be identified with
poor and rich or, as Aristides puts it, 'inferior' versus 'superior'
(32), for the former are advised to suspend their 'envy' against the
rich, the latter to give up their 'avarice' against the poor (ibid.).

Originally the concept of concord played an important part in
formulating the internal stability of the Athenian state in the difficult period at the end of the fifth century.[147] In the fourth book of
Plato's *Republic*, in the discussion of the cardinal virtues of civic
and personal life the careful social taxonomics of Socrates' city
depend particularly on *sôphrosunê* (sober, prudent, politically conservative behaviour) and *homonoia*, 'concord' (431d–432a). The city's
concord guarantees the status quo: 'it is the unison of the naturally
worse and the naturally better as to which of them should rule in
the city and in the individual'. The meaning of concord depends, of
course, on the political framework within which it is voiced. As has
been remarked, in the cities of the Empire it must have been a

[144] Demades fr. xxxvi de Falco²; Veyne 1990: 98.
[145] Demosthenes xviii. 254, cf. 113, 118.
[146] For large loans from public funds see e.g. *P.Oxy* 2848 (AD 225). Alternatively
the borrowing may have been against future revenue which did not materialize
(Behr 1981–6: ii. 369–70 n. 21 citing the well-known decree of the proconsul Paullus
Fabius Persicus [Smallwood 380] which *inter alia* forbids such practices and holds
the magistrate or priest personally liable to the lender). The borrowing at Rhodes is
plausibly connected with the earthquake of *c*.142, which called forth assistance from
the great Lycian benefactor, Opramoas (*IGR* iii. 739; Behr 1968a: 15–16 n. 15; Aristides xxiv. 3, 53, cf. 59; [Aristides] xxv goes into the gory details [the attempt of
Jones 1990a to attribute the speech to Aristides is again unconvincing]); other reasons
are possible, especially given Aristides' warnings about ambition, below in text.
[147] De Romilly 1972: 199–201.

convenient way of assisting elite power, by shoring it up if damaged or by simply reinforcing it against the masses, invoking always
a consensus between rulers and ruled. This is not to say that Aristides
(or anyone else) was not sincere in wishing to end strife. But having
observed that at Rhodes the rich were at fault and had escaped
punishment for their wrongdoing, he concludes that 'silence' is now
the best course and smothers the problems in general comments on
harmony (41 ff.); which leaves the sufferers without redress. Internal concord of this sort is the 'vertical' mode of the concord ideology, and was no doubt an essential preliminary to achieving the
'horizontal' concord that demonstrated the cities' ability to offer
each another parity in their social and economic institutions. We
see from the difference between Aristides' and Dio's treatment of
economic distinctions at Rhodes and at Tarsus that Dio's idea of
concord was more akin to a modern liberal outlook in wishing to
lessen internal divisions, while Aristides' was a familiar way of
perpetuating them by telling people how lucky they were to have
what they had.

The final group of speeches to be considered, albeit briefly, are
the Smyrnaean orations (xvii–xxi), which have some general items
of interest and suggest one or two important differences between
Aristides and his older contemporaries. *Or.* xvii *Political Speech in
Smyrna* and *Or.* xxi *Address in Smyrna* are closely connected pan-
egyrics of the city and of the arrival there of two Roman governors,
a father and some years later his son, who had very probably accompanied the father to Smyrna as his legate (xxi. 3, 16). *Or.* xxi
(which was not delivered in person) celebrates the reconstruction of
the city following the disastrous earthquake of 177 (or 178) and,
since Marcus and Commodus are ruling jointly (2, 8, 9) and the
work of reconstruction is well advanced, it should probably be
dated to 179. The proconsul of this year is unknown, hence his
father is not readily identifiable.[148] Both xxi and xvii offer elegant
welcomes. Their importance lies in Aristides' complimentary integration of Roman power and local Greek history.[149] The son had
heard of Smyrna's mythology and early history, especially the story
of its triple foundation, on his earlier visit with his father; he is

[148] Earthquake: Magie 1953: ii. 1537 n. 17 (178); Behr 1968a: 112 n. 68 (177).
Speech and addressees: Behr 1968a: 91–2 n. 1a; Burton 1992; Pernot 1993: i. 295–9
on the style of the *Smyrnaeans*.
[149] Cf. 'Past' n. 34. Cf. Calder 1906.

briefly reminded of it now (xxi. 3–4). He also saw the beauty of the city and its accord (5–6). All this refers to Aristides' own *Or.* xvii, where the father is given an extensive imaginary 'tour' (*periodos*) of the city (xvii. 1–22), recalling his own tour of duty,[150] before his powers of judgement are finally hailed for 'leading the people to what is finest' (23).[151]

Orr. xviii–xx concern the earthquake and its aftermath, the first (*Monody for Smyrna*) being Aristides' private lament for the city, the second his letter to Marcus and Commodus imploring their aid, the third (*Palinode for Smyrna*) celebrating the assistance of the Greek cities and of the emperors in the city's rebuilding. Important to take note of in *Or.* xix is the reference to the 'divine rulers' (xix. 5). The divinity of the emperors is also mentioned, as has been noted, at *Or.* xxiii. 79 in the context of their likeness to the gods.[152] In *Or.* xxiii the reference had additional significance because of the role of the imperial cult in that speech. Here in *Or.* xix the cult is again important. Having alluded to Smyrna's pro-Roman history (11) and its assistance to other cities in recent disasters (12), Aristides ends with the story of the city's first neocorate, the honour of erecting a temple to Tiberius, Livia, and the Senate in 26: 'Asia was preferred to the other provinces, Smyrna to the other cities so far that the rest of Asia received seven votes only whereas this city alone took four hundred' (13).[153] The story is capped with more praise of the emperors. It clearly illustrates the political worth of the imperial cult as a channel of communication between ruled and rulers and Aristides' understanding of how to exploit this.

The Smyrnaean orations also show certain crucial differences between Aristides and Plutarch and Dio. They are about his favourite city. But Aristides was not a local patriot. Like many an intellectual he felt himself at all times to be in a strong relationship

---

[150] At xxi. 16 the 'tour' is his son's tour of duty among the cities.

[151] Aristides' speech must have complemented the holiday atmosphere of the governor's arrival well—cf. *BGU* 362 col. 7. 20 = *Select Papyri* 404 (AD 215), which mentions payment for various items during the prefect's visit, including a speech of thanks by a rhetor—as well as being what the governor might expect: cf. Ulpian at *Digest* i. 16. 7. 1 advising that the proconsul 'pati debet commendari sibi civitatem laudesque suas non gravate audire'.

[152] At *Or.* xlii *To Asclepius* 14 where the 'divine kings' are spoken of, the context is again real divinity, since Aristides is thanking the god for enabling him to get to know the royals.

[153] Aristides refers to the votes of the Senate: cf. Tacitus, *Annals* iv. 56; Price 1984a: 258.

with central authority, be it the imperial family or the god Asclepius. Thus the speeches on the Smyrnaean earthquake and its aftermath reflect his own standing and aspirations more than the need of the city. Aristides behaves no differently now from the man who avoided public service there many years earlier. He had helped the city through his oratory and his contacts, but these are, one feels, to his own greater glory.[154] The earthquake speeches also show once more that Aristides liked the way the Romans ran the province of Asia. He certainly does not lament the end of the days of free Greece as Plutarch does, nor does he share in any way Dio's ambivalence and intermittent hostility to Rome. The Antonine emperors supported Greek culture and, as Aristides notes in *To Rome*, accorded the best sort of provincials appropriate status. This philhellenism and the Greeks' response to it (here the imperial cult) could be put to Smyrna's advantage. Nevertheless, there is no need to suppose that Aristides made the mistake of thinking the Greeks were equal partners in the Empire or that he personally identified with Rome for reasons other than that she allowed him to be what he wanted and protected his property. The picture we get from the *Sacred Tales* shows plainly that he himself interpreted his crucial battle over immunity as proof that all things 'yielded to the god', including the imperial system. Dio liked to present himself as having been tough with the emperor; Aristides delegated this role to Asclepius, whom even Marcus obeys.

All too often *To Rome* is taken to be representative not only of Aristides' views but of the whole Greek world in the High Empire. We should be very wary before making assumptions of this sort, even for Greeks with well-documented Roman careers. There was a basis for the picture Aristides draws of a happy accord between the Empire's elites; but the Greeks did not think or refer to themselves as Romans in this period except in obviously political contexts. As for Aristides, who had no interest in Roman history or culture, and wanted no part in the system he praised, we can scarcely doubt that his real loyalties, his cognitive and spiritual identity, lay firmly in Greece.

[154] The power of Aristides' 'keynote' (*endosima*) in persuading Marcus to allow the rebuilding of the city is also stressed by Philostratus at *VS* 582.

9

Lucian

INTRODUCTION—THE SEMITIC BACKGROUND

The satirist and essayist Lucian was born between 115 and 125 at Samosata, a city of Roman Syria.[1] Samosata had been the capital city of the independent kingdom of Commagene until AD 72, when on the basis of unfounded allegations king Antiochus IV was removed by the legate of Syria, Caesennius Paetus.[2] Antiochus and his family were well treated by the emperor Vespasian and enjoyed prominence in the Roman world. His grandson, Plutarch's acquaintance C. Julius Antiochus Epiphanes Philopappus ('Fond of Grandfather'), rose to a suffect consulship in 109, and his granddaughter Julia Balbilla the sister of Philopappus accompanied Hadrian and Sabina when they visited the 'singing' colossus of Memnon in Egypt on 19–21 November 130.[3] Commagene was thoroughly Hellenized

[1] Birth: Hall 1981: 13–16 (125) arguing from *Double Indictment* 32 (Lucian was 'already almost forty' when he changed his literary interests) and 2 where Zeus has to attend to the sacrifice at Olympia and to 'those fighting at Babylon', in other words the Olympic games of 165 occurring during the Parthian war; Jones 1986: 8 n. 10 notes the conventional nature of Olympia and Babylon (not to mention Zeus' other tasks of 'hailing among the Getae and feasting among the Ethiopians'); forty is a conventional age for a change in direction at *Hermotimus* 13. At Samosata: *How to Write History* 24.

[2] Josephus, *Jewish War*, vii. 219–43.

[3] See Halfmann 1979: nos. 36, 36a, 36b, and the stemma on p. 121. Balbilla owes her name to her other grandfather Ti. Claudius Balbillus, prefect of Egypt under Nero. For the four poems she inscribed on Memnon in 130 (and for those by other tourists) see Bernand and Bernand 1960: esp. nos. 28–31; Bowie 1990: 61–6; cf. Debrunner and Scherer 1969: §68 on the pseudo-Aeolic dialect she employed to recall Sappho. Another possible scion of Commagenean royalty, Avidius Heliodorus, was prefect of Egypt in 137–42, when his son Avidius Cassius who was proclaimed emperor at Alexandria in 175 was born (Syme 1985: 345, id. 1987: 215; against any relation with the royal house: Dörner and Naumann 1939: 47–51). On Lucian's own career in Roman government in Egypt see below, nn. 77–87.

at the elite level.[4] As in most of the 'Greek' East, the majority of its population was almost certainly not Greek, but in this case Semitic. It is very likely that Lucian's family was of the indigenous population. He refers to himself on several occasions not only as a Syrian but in particular as a 'barbarian'.[5] This Syrian background repays investigation, for Lucian's cultural and political identities seem to have much to do with it, and the material is still not well known.[6]

Samosata lay on the edge of the Roman world on the west bank of the Euphrates. Behind it were the Taurus mountains. Over the river lay the small kingdom of Osrhoene, which was not fully incorporated into the Roman Empire till 212/13.[7] The main difference between Commagene and Osrhoene was that the former looked south and west and was ruled by a mixed Iranian-Greek dynasty, while the latter looked south and east and was ruled, as the names of its kings suggest, by an Arab one.[8] From the second century onwards the capital of Osrhoene, Edessa (or Orhai, to give it its native name), developed as the centre of a vigorous Christian culture expressed in the emergent local dialect of Aramaic called Syriac. The earliest epigraphical text that can be defined as Syriac is a sepulchral inscription belonging to the year AD 6 found some fifty miles south west of Samosata on the east bank of the river near the crossing-point of Seleucia-Zeugma.[9] One of the earliest literary texts in Syriac is the dialogue on fate which features as principal speaker the second-century Edessan courtier Bardaisan, and which was

[4] Literature in Jones 1986: 6 n. 1, Metzler 1991 and other articles in the same volume.
[5] *Double Indictment* (where Lucian's character is 'the Syrian') 27 'he was still barbarian in language and was practically wearing a caftan in the Assyrian style', 34 'I myself am considered barbarian'; *Scythian* 9 'barbarian' and 'Syrian'; *Fisherman* 19 'a Syrian . . . one of those who live on the Euphrates', 'no less barbarian in *genos* [race/family] than me', 'barbarian in language'; *The Uneducated Book Collector* 19 'Syrian'; *On the Syrian Goddess* 1 'Assyrian'; note *On Hirelings* 10 where 'vile Syrian speech' is expected from a door-keeper. In these passages 'barbarian in language' probably refers to Lucian's usage of Greek (rather than his pronunciation of it), and this is clearly so at *The False Critic* 1, 11; see above, 'Practice' nn. 11–31. On his knowledge of Aramaic see below, n. 36. On 'Syrian'/'Assyrian' in Greek see Nöldeke 1871.
[6] Millar 1993 is now fundamental to all aspects of the culture and society of the Near East including Roman Syria.
[7] Millar 1993: 473.
[8] On Osrhoene and Edessa see additionally Segal 1970; Drijvers 1977: 863–96, 902–4.
[9] For translations of this important document (which still shows forms not found in the mature language) see Teixidor 1992: 19; Millar 1993: 458.

perhaps written by his pupil interlocutor in the early third century.[10] The dialogue (a characteristically, but by no means exclusively, Greek literary form) argues that the Christian god gives man free will, as is shown by the multiplicity of customs among various peoples, and that fate—and astrology, a particularly local habit—therefore has no power over us.[11] It was translated into Greek and much admired by Eusebius.[12] Religion and language seem to have sparked each other off in Edessa and from this time the use of Syriac spread rapidly in conjunction with Christianity until in the late antique world it achieved a position of self-conscious parity with Greek.

It is impossible to say for sure whether the rise of Syriac represents a challenge of any sort to Greek and to Greek traditions. Certainly the contents of Greek culture remained fully in use and the Greek language itself penetrated Syriac deeply, especially in late antiquity, when translation between the two tongues was common.[13] Nevertheless, given the central position of language in defining the Greek cultural heritage, the use of Syriac must be seen as a resistance of some sort. Greek culture was as closely allied to Greek and then Roman political power in this region as it was in Egypt. It was imposed, and this is true whether one argues for a 'strong' or a 'weak' Semitic underlay. For this reason a native point of view is hardly ever expressed, and it is difficult to know what it might look like. Those who were not of the master race were no doubt recognizable, as in Egypt, by linguistic performance.[14] Semitic cultural practices and habits may be a different matter from language. For as the Greeks knew, culture depends on tradition and, as Josephus observed, Greek domination of the local population was secured, at least in part, by wiping away the Semitic past.[15] The consequence of

[10] *The Book of the Laws of Countries*; text and translation in Cureton 1855, Nau, *Patr. Syr.* vi. 46 (Latin), Drijvers 1965; for the cultural setting see Drijvers 1966, Teixidor 1992 (a more accessible general introduction); and cf. Julius Africanus, *Kestoi* i. 20, for Bardaisan's display of archery at the court of Abgar the Great (in the last quarter of the 2nd c. or the first decade of the 3rd).
[11] On Lucian's mock *Astrology* see below, n. 31.
[12] *Preparation for the Gospel* vi. 9. 32–10. 48, cf. *Ecclesiastical History* iv. 30.
[13] Cf. Bowersock 1990: 29–40; Cameron 1991.
[14] Cf. *P.Giess.* 40, col. 2 = *Select Papyri* 215, Caracalla's instructions in 215 to purge Alexandria: 'the true Egyptians can easily be recognized among the linen weavers by their speech, etc.'
[15] Josephus, *Jewish Antiquities* i. 121 on the cultural Babel seen in the name changes of cities, some of which kept the name of their founder, while others did

this is that the Syriac culture that developed from the second and third centuries could never be rooted in a Semitic heritage of its own.

But we should not imagine that some did not or could not even so feel 'native'. Leaving aside the Jews as a separate and very well-studied case, there is the explicit reported comment of the second-century novelist Iamblichus (to whom I shall return) that he was 'not one of the Greeks who have settled Syria, but one of the natives [*tôn autochthonôn*]'. Syriac-speaking Christians in Iran living in the area of ancient Assyria made use of geography to enact some form of separate identity by calling themselves *Athorâyê* in memory of the ancient glories of Assur.[16] Regarding others, whether or not they are known to have used Aramaic, we can proceed only slowly. But ultimately, although it is impossible to get at the precise meaning of Syriac Christianity in the Roman Empire, we should not ignore the significant abandonment of the language of Roman power in the East. The well-attested use of a Semitic language in public and private contexts in the Nabatean kingdom before the creation of the province of Arabia and in Palmyra (a city which retained a remarkable degree of autonomy within the Empire) ended with the arrival of full Roman control. Syriac survived and prospered. Perhaps it was fortunate that Roman domination of its Osrhoenean heartland coincided with the appearance of a religion that was not Graeco-Roman, but Semitic (albeit from a different location and environment), and which was snapped up by the natives and later propagated in a largely monophysite form that remained distinct despite the attempts of westerners (from a local perspective, that is) to change it to their way of thinking.[17]

What has this to do with Lucian from Samosata on the west bank of the Euphrates? No Syriac inscriptions have been found at Samosata which, unlike Edessa, retained its original name (Aramaic

---

not: 'the Greeks were responsible for this, for in later times they were strong enough to make even the glory of the past [*tên palai doxan*] their own', and thus imposed new names along with new constitutions. Cf. Appian, *Syrian Wars* 57. 297–8, Ammianus xiv. 8. 6 on names being changed 'ad arbitrium... conditoris' (i.e. Seleucus).

[16] Cf. Millar 1993: 494 on and for references to the *Chronicle* of Karka de Bet Selok.

[17] Even so, Christianity did not and could not offer the natives the identity they had lost to the Greeks and perhaps this is why the region converted rapidly to Islam in due course; on all of this see the remarkable account of Crone and Cook 1977: 60–70, 85 ff.

Shemshat). But another very early Syriac literary text suggests that
the language was spoken there in Lucian's time, and also offers a
rather interesting non-Graeco-Roman perspective on Roman power.
The *Letter of Mara son of Sarapion* is a letter of encouragement
from a father to his son bidding him avoid materialism and trust to
the true wisdom of god.[18] It is tied to a particular historical context,
since Sarapion takes as his starting point the exile of certain of his
comrades from Samosata and says that he, also an exile, went to
meet them on their way to Seleucia. Seleucia could be the nearby
Seleucia-Zeugma, but the tone of the remarks about leaving homes
and family make it more likely to be Seleucia-Ctesiphon on the
Tigris in the Parthian kingdom. At the end of the letter Sarapion
names the Romans as the cause of the exile.[19] That the exiles seem
to be leaving Roman territory suggests a date after the annexation
of Commagene and before the mid-second century, since Osrhoene
was Roman-controlled after Marcus' and Lucius' Parthian campaigns and Mesopotamia was subject to Roman provincial administration after the 190s.[20] The Romans are implored to show their
'greatness' by restoring the fugitives. 'Let us obey that kingdom to
which time has given us—and let them not as tyrants treat us like
slaves.'[21] It is difficult to tell whether the text is in fact Christian,
as may be thought. There is no reference to Christ, but then again
there is only a passing one in *The Book of the Laws of Countries*
ascribed to Bardaisan. There is a reference to the Jews' 'wise king',
but this is perhaps rather to Solomon. More to the point the letter
has not a few exempla drawn from Greek mythology and history.[22]
And the tone is strongly Stoic.[23] It is a fascinating document of the
meeting of Semitic language, Greek culture, and Roman power.
The opinions expressed could have been readily expressed in Greek.
But this victim of Rome naturally enough avoided the language of

[18] Translated into English in Cureton 1855; into German in Schulthess 1897.
Inevitably I overlap to some degree with the comments of Millar 1993: 460–62
(whose identification of Seleucia I follow below).
[19] Cureton 1855: 76. 2–11.
[20] Birley 1979: 480–2. Cureton 1855: pp. xiv–xv suggests the addressee was the
distinguished Sarapion who became bishop of Antioch in 189 (Eusebius *Ecclesiastical History* v. 22).
[21] Cureton 1855: 76. 8–9, cf. 'tyrants' at 73. 29.
[22] Darius, Polycrates, Achilles, Agamemnon, Priam, Archimedes, Socrates, Pythagoras, Palamedes, Socrates–Athens, Samos–Pythagoras, Plato, Hera (Cureton 1855:
72. 27–34, 73. 31–74. 7).
[23] Schulthess 1897: 381–91.

the Roman government in the East and asserted his own identity in so doing.

Lucian, thus came from a cultural environment that was very different from that of an Aelius Aristides. Although it was not until much later that the possibility of making a career in the local language would have appeared attractive, a certain contemporary of his, the novelist Iamblichus, shows that the people of the region could look both east and west for their cultural inspiration at this time. Iamblichus' career is known partly from the summary of the *Babylonian Story* in Photius' *Library* and partly from the scholiast to Photius' text. According to Photius Iamblichus said he was a 'Babylonian' and 'flourished at the time of Sohaemus . . . who was a king and through his father a descendant of kings, but who nevertheless became a member of the senatorial council in Rome, was consul, and then once more a king of Greater Armenia'. Photius reports that Iamblichus said he was writing at the height of the Parthian War against Vologeses. 'He himself claims that he predicted that the war would happen and how it would end' (*Library* cod. 94, 75b).[24] The report of the scholiast presumably also comes from Iamblichus' novel but is fuller and apparently more accurate. Here Iamblichus is a *Suros*, 'Syrian', by birth, 'not one of the Greeks who have settled Syria, but one of the natives, and knew the Syrian language and lived by their customs until, as he says, he was taken up by a Babylonian foster-father and learnt the Babylonian language, their character, and their stories, one of these being, he says, the one he is now writing up'. The Babylonian is alleged to have been taken prisoner when Trajan 'invaded Babylon' and was then sold to a Syrian.[25] The scholiast goes on to report that 'he says he also acquired the Greek language by practice and usage so that he could become a good rhetor'.[26]

The link between the Parthian war of Trajan (to verify the

[24] Also in the edition of fragments by E. Habrich (1960). On what follows cf. Millar 1993: 489 ff.

[25] Trajan encamped at Babylon in autumn 116: Lepper 1948: 210.

[26] In Photius' judgement Iamblichus' style was too good for his subject matter (cod. 94, 73b–74a). The text of the scholium is printed in vol. 2, p. 40 n. 1, of the Budé edition by R. Henry (1960 = Habrich p. 2). To be compared is Josephus' account of his own mastery of Greek (retaining a deliberately faulty pronunciation) at *Jewish Antiquities* xx. 263–4, and his translation of the *Jewish War* into Greek from the (presumably) Aramaic vernacular original he says was available to the peoples of upland Asia (*Jewish War* i. 3, 6).

Babylonian's credentials) and the war of Marcus and Lucius, and the Babylonian teacher as a source for Iamblichus' own 'Babylonian' tale certainly make all of this information suspect; but Iamblichus' strong pride in his autochthonous Syrian background does not assist the story-line of his novel and there is no reason to disbelieve it. Sohaemus with his career changes from east to west and back again might also seem fictional, did we not know of him from Cassius Dio and Fronto. He is to be connected with the family of dynasts from Emesa (also in Roman Syria) who include as the last ruler of independent Emesa C. Julius Sohaemus.[27] Babylonian too continued in use as a language of lore, and so Iamblichus' claim for the paternity of his text is at least a plausible fiction.[28] As for Iamblichus himself, his birthplace cannot be identified, since *Suros* in Greek is vague, but Emesa is again very likely given his connection with Sohaemus, in whose time 'he says he flourished'.[29]

Lucian, like Iamblichus, achieved fame through Greek and made his career in the West. A Greek cultural-cognitive identity is extremely important to him.[30] But he also paid tribute to the culture of his own region in his *On the Syrian Goddess*. The goddess in question is Atargatis, and the essay describes her famous shrine at Hierapolis Bambyce, a city some ninety miles south-west of Samosata in the province of Syria, which retains its Semitic name Mabog/Manbog in the present-day Manbij. Lucian's usually irreverent attitude to religious beliefs (though not to belief in the divine itself), together with the fact that the work is written in the archaic Ionic dialect of Greek, formerly led scholars to consider *On the Syrian Goddess* spurious. The use of Ionic is in imitation of Herodotus. The only contemporary of Lucian to observe him at

[27] Halfmann 1979: no. 96; Birley 1988: 223–4, nos. 47–48; Shahid 1984: 41–2 on the name. C. Julius Sohaemus ruled Emesa from 54 and was installed by Rome in Sophene (the zone between Armenia, Cappadocia, and Osrhoene)—cf. his descendant's role in Armenia; he also took part in the annexation of Commagene with Paetus (Sullivan 1977: 216–18).

[28] See recently Geller 1983 on an incantation written in cuneiform and in the Greek alphabet and probably dating to the 1st c. AD.

[29] Iamblichus is also an Emesene dynastic name; cf. Iamblichus I and Iamblichus II (Sullivan 1977: 205 ff., 211–12). *Suros*: above, n. 5. If Iamblichus is Emesene, we might contrast the self-identity of another novelist of Emesa, Heliodorus, who writes of himself as a Phoenician (above, 'Novel' n. 60, and below, Appendix A), an identity which looks to the old Phoenician cities of the coast (and/or possibly reflects the existence in his time of the province of Syria Phoenice, which was created by Septimius Severus).

[30] On cultural-cognitive, etc., see 'Past', text after n. 9.

work, Galen of Pergamum, mentions him while discussing an inter-
polated passage of a work of Hippocrates (also of course in Ionic),
which had been fabricated, Galen suggests, in order to trick the
sophists. Lucian had similarly tricked a philosopher by getting some
accomplices to ask him to comment on a text purporting to be by
the early Ionian thinker Heraclitus.[31] Passages of Ionic pastiche
are found in Lucian's other works. And the authenticity of *On
the Syrian Goddess* is confirmed by the many reminiscences of
Herodotus' manner of recounting the stories of gods and temples,
since this sort of imitation is precisely in the style of the author and
his age.[32] This has its mischievous side. By recording the temple's
rites in a solemn and reverential style, so affectedly Herodotean,
Lucian injects a certain playfulness, which should not, however, be
taken as irony or condemnation. Rather, the careful writing and the
gentle humour are very much in the temple's honour.[33] We can thus
believe Lucian when he says he is writing as an 'eye witness' (1),
while also recognizing the studiedly Herodotean phraseology
(cf. e.g. Herodotus ii. 29. 2, 99. 1, 148. 5).

Many of the factual details Lucian mentions are corroborated by
other authors or by archaeology, though there are certainly distor-
tions and errors in the account.[34] He is careful to allude to the local
background, while thoroughly mixing in the traditions and expectations of Greek myth. One passage in particular is interesting
for elucidating his own background. At 31 ff. he describes the inner
sanctum wherein sit Hera and Zeus ('whom they call by another
name', i.e. Hadad). Between them stands another object called the

[31] Galen also records that Lucian tricked some grammarians with a similar ruse.
The remarks survive in Arabic (*CMG* v. 10. 1: 402. 31–42); see Strohmaier 1976;
Macleod 1979. Nutton 1993: 21 n. 39 plausibly suggests that Galen saw Lucian in
Alexandria, for his observations are made in the context of Alexandrian Hippocratism
(thus the date will be before Galen's return to Pergamum in 157, which easily fits
with what we know—or rather do not know—of Lucian's own movements).
[32] Ionic pastiche: *On the Hall* 20 (Herodotus speaking), *Lives for Sale* 3, 14
(Heraclitus), *Astrology* (on the authenticity of this work see Hall 1981: 381–7; but
note Jones 1986: 170 against, Bompaire 1958: 653–4 unsure); cf. the short introductory piece *Herodotus*.
  Authenticity of *On the Syrian Goddess*: Hall 1981: 374–81; Jones 1986: 41; Saïd
1994. Baslez 1994 once more denies Lucian's authorship; but see below, nn. 36 and
37.
[33] So Jones 1986: 42; Branham 1989: 159 on 'the comically qualified appreciation
that formal imitation alone makes possible'; the comic element is transferred to
Herodotus and away from the immediate subject.
[34] Oden 1977: 43–6; Baslez 1994.

'standard [*sêmêion*]' (33). It has been suggested that Lucian mistook the name of a goddess as the normal Greek word for a 'sign' or 'standard'.[35] But the 'standard' between Atargatis and Hadad is well known from representations of the cult at Hierapolis and from Hatra in central Mesopotamia. The object, which resembled a Roman legionary standard in form, was intended to symbolize the presence of the gods whose pictures it bore (as Lucian notes). The Semitic word for it is SMY'. It happens to be homophonous and synonymous with the Greek term, and the root from which it came had clearly coalesced with Greek *sêmeion* (and its cognates *sêmeia*, *sêma*) in a number of general senses. Lucian seems to be aware of this fusion when he records that 'it is called a *sêmêion* by the Assyrians themselves, and they gave it no name of its own'. In other words, it was simply the 'standard' and had no proper name. This homophony allowed him to include the Aramaic word in his Greek (contrast Hadad at §31).[36] Lucian ends *On the Syrian Goddess* with a

[35] Harmon 1925: 388–99 n. 2 following the mistaken *interpretatio* in the Syriac apologetic tract known as the *Oration of Meliton the Philosopher Who Was Before Antoninus Caesar* (text and translation in Cureton 1855: 44. 28, 45. 6); on this see Oden 1977: 149–55; Householder 1941: 95.

[36] See Chaquot 1955 on the Aramaic and Greek terms; Seyrig 1960: 241–6; Oden 1977: 133–55; Drijvers 1977: 834–5 (Hatra). The iconography of the standards at Hierapolis and Hatra (which was not in the Empire) does seem to have been influenced by the Roman military standard (Seyrig 1960: 245; Millar 1993: 247), for which *sêmeion* is the Greek term; but it is wrong to interpret Lucian as saying that the Assyrians themselves 'have no word for it' (Millar ibid.)—it is a proper name which he says is lacking.

With regard to Lucian's Aramaic note also Delchor 1987, who speculates that there is an Aramaic basis to the story of the 'sacred cockerel' and its breaking of the wax seals on the vessels of sacred water at *On the Syrian Goddess* 48. The cock is often taken to refer to a 'Gallus' (i.e. a priest of Cybele), but it is suggested that Lucian actually misheard the Aramaic for 'the Gallus broke [TR' GL']' as the word for 'cockerel' (TRNGL'). This is a rather desperate suggestion; for a slightly less implausible explanation see below, n. 75. This same tale has recently been held to show that the author of *On the Syrian Goddess* clearly knew no Aramaic—and is therefore not Lucian. Baslez 1994: 174 ascribes the cockerel to an interpreter's mistranslation of 'l'araméen *skwy*, signifiant tout à la fois "coq" et "inspecteur"', an error which would not be detected by someone who only spoke Greek. There are too many assumptions here. From the Semitic root SK', 'see', 'watch', comes the word SKWY, 'watchman', attested in Jewish Palestinian Aramaic; in late Hebrew there exists ŚKWY, 'cockerel' (the meaning of ŚKWY at Job 38. 36 is unclear, but the Vulgate takes it as 'gallus'); though written differently, these would be pronounced fairly similarly. But even if similar forms were found in the local Aramaic, it does seem far-fetched to make the interpreter's Greek quite so bad and the Greek-speaking author quite so stupid as not to question him further on the role of the cock. There is no need to deny Lucian's authorship on this basis, and the bird must rather be ascribed to his inventive ethnography.

personal note. Recounting the habit of dedicating locks of hair or beard clippings in vessels of silver or gold inscribed with one's name, he tells us that 'when I was still young I performed this rite and both my lock and my name are still in the temple' (60).[37]

Lucian's knowledge of Aramaic at Hierapolis may well be no more than that of the average tourist or Herodotean ethnographer. There is absolutely no proof that Aramaic was his first language. We can indeed proceed only cumulatively in building up a picture of his Semitic side.[38] But the Aramaic notice and the personal devotion at a shrine of such great regional importance do complement the several somewhat bitter references Lucian makes to his origin as a barbarian (As-)Syrian. These occur in contexts where he is defending his proficiency in Greek culture.[39] Chapter 14 of the *Double Indictment* is particularly revealing. Here Hermes and Justice are getting ready to try Lucian as 'the Syrian' for his bad treatment of Greek letters. Justice asks, 'Do we really have to try at Athens . . . cases from over the border that are better decided across the Euphrates?' The meaning of this seems to be that Athenian culture stopped at the river, leaving Osrhoene and Parthia beyond the pale. The Greek view might be that a native *Suros* came from the wrong side. The purpose of *Double Indictment* is to refute this. The same message is present at *How to Write History* 24, where Lucian complains that a historian of the current Parthian War had moved Samosata ('acropolis, walls, and all') to Mesopotamia 'with both rivers flowing round it', and that he might have to defend himself against the charge of being a Parthian or a *mesopotamitês*, i.e. a barbarian. This justificatory tone is absent from *On the Syrian Goddess*, where Lucian introduces himself as an *Assurios* (1). The lack of reticence may be due to the fact that Greek culture was always hospitable to non-Greek paganism. In the Syrian region itself, as Christianity grew and helped to relaunch the native language, Greek was indeed more and more closely identified with the pagan gods and effectively became the lingua franca of the old religion. On this public level we would not expect to find a Semitic

---

[37] Baslez's suggestion (1994: 173) that the offering reflects a purely Greek rite ignorantly imported to enhance the close of the text again seems to be wrong: hair and beard offerings by votaries are common enough in the region, and Lucian's report is accepted by Hajjar 1985: i. 91 in this context.

[38] Note Holzberg 1984: 169 on earlier racialist assumptions that Lucian must have been Semitic—and hence was no good.

[39] Above, n. 5, 'Practice' nn. 11–31.

religious and a Greek cognitive identity clashing, for they would complement each other in a familiar way. On the other hand, Lucian is particularly known for his biting satirical attacks on the traditional Greek gods and for his Epicurean leanings.[40] We are not dealing with a common paganism here. Rather, it is at the level of personal identity that *On the Syrian Goddess* shows a local, Semitic religious heritage being given leeway and favourable treatment not allowed to the Greeks. This is not surprising: since the native political tradition had been abolished by Greeks, religion was all that was left to anyone who considered himself indigenous, as Lucian apparently did, and who wished to make some acknowledgement of this.

GREEK CULTURE

We can take the matter further by looking at how Lucian presents his acquisition of Greek culture and what this culture meant to him, beginning with the *Dream, or Life of Lucian*. The very fact that Lucian feels the need to tell us of his struggle for education in this essay is significant. Here as elsewhere we can observe him combining his delight in his attainments with a certain justification and defensiveness. It seems likely that the work was read in Samosata, for Lucian tells his audience at the end that he now returns to them famous (18). He begins with his family's wish for him to go into the family business of sculpting. Fortunately a dream after a disastrous first day at work propelled him instead towards a life of culture. In the dream the personified Sculpture or Craft (*Hermogluphikê* or *Technê*) and Culture (*Paideia*) vie for Lucian's attention. Sculpture tells him he can be like Phidias, Polyclitus, Myron, and Praxiteles. She is built like a labourer and covered in dust and talks, of course, 'in a stumbling fashion with a good deal of barbarous language [*barbarizousa*]' (6, 8). Culture is quite different. She is refined in appearance and speech (6, 9–13). She will educate Lucian in the wisdom of the ancients, teach him the cardinal virtues, and more importantly will make him rich and famous the whole world over, 'worthy of office and a front row seat [*proedria*]', capable of helping his friends and his city.

[40] See below, n. 103.

On one level this story very clearly imitates Prodicus' parable of the Choice of Heracles, which was famous from Xenophon's *Memorabilia* ii. 1. 21–34 (= DK⁶ 84 B2). Lucian's audience could not have failed to recognize the reference; in case they did, Lucian thoughtfully mentions 'ancient and antiquated dreams' in the same breath as Xenophon at 17. In the parable the young Heracles is treated to a vision of Happiness or Vice (*Eudaimonia* or *Kakia*) and Virtue (*Aretê*), who contend for his allegiance. Lucian's version of this is intended to be amusing as well as 'useful' (5, 17–18). His Culture deliberately echoes the words of Prodicus' Virtue. Thus care is taken to stress the moral value of education (10), and even allusions to his present wealth (11, 16 cf. 1, 18) owe something to Virtue's talk of 'making money' (*Memorabilia* ii. 1. 28), though the element of toil is absent. Nevertheless, Lucian has deliberately moved Heracles' choice away from the purely moral register of the original and into the realm of social and economic status, and the literary-structural *mimêsis* of Xenophon should not disguise this important shift in values. Further, however humorous and exaggerated Lucian's report of his early struggles may be, there is no good reason to disbelieve entirely the family's involvement with sculpting nor even their attempt to enrol the young Lucian in a *technê*, 'craft' (1–2). What Lucian then wittily suggests in the main part of the work is his discovery of a prejudice against this sort of labour, observing in words which recall Plutarch that, despite the brilliance of Phidias' and Polyclitus' 'craft', no intelligent man would pray to be like them, since they used their hands to make a living (9).[41] Not all the ancient elite shared this bias. Galen for one did not, being obsessed by the value of all hard work. The pride taken by numerous trade-guilds in their crafts shows the more general attitude well enough.[42] Lucian, however, clearly thought it necessary to effect a social change along with an educational one in order to reach the level of the curial class and to become eligible for public office and for that particularly public honour, *proedria* or reserved seating in the theatre (11). His alignment with *Paideia* is a claim to social superiority.

Lucian began his Greek career as a rhetor. He does not say how

[41] Cf. Plutarch, *Pericles* 2. 1–4.
[42] See Galen's essay encouraging young men to learn a professional skill, the *Adhortatio ad artes addiscendas* (i. 1–39). In general MacMullen 1974: index s.v. 'Associations'.

this came about, but we may presume that the family's need of an extra wage-earner (*Dream* 1) was not nearly as pressing as is made out in his fiction: money was available for a training. In an entry attacking Lucian for his shocking attitude towards Christianity the *Suda* reports that he was a failed advocate in the great Syrian city of Antioch.[43] Lucian himself may allude to having been a forensic orator at *Fisherman* 9, 25 and *Double Indictment* 32, though the latter passage probably refers only to fictional forensic pieces. As has been noted, his self-consciousness regarding his Greek culture is much to the fore in the *Double Indictment*. The two indictments in question are made against 'the Syrian' by Rhetoric, who accuses him of having abandoned her for Dialogue, and by Dialogue, who complains of having been made into a fool by him. Rhetoric says she found the Syrian in Ionia, a natural place for a budding rhetor to be. She educated him and 'irregularly enrolled him' as a citizen, i.e. of Attic/Hellenic culture (27, cf. 30).[44] They travelled in Greece and Ionia with only 'moderate success', and then went to Italy, and finally to Gaul where, says Rhetoric, 'I made him rich' (27). In his *Apology* Lucian again speaks of the large amount of money he made in Gaul (15).[45] Lucian goes on to say in the *Double Indictment* that he had to leave Rhetoric because she became too boisterous (31). For 'a man who was already almost forty' it was time to abandon (fictional) forensic and sophistic oratory and turn to philosophical dialogues (32). This does not of course mean that Lucian abandoned rhetorical methods, which are important in all his works;[46] but we should probably hold that most of the overtly fictional sophistic pieces in his corpus do belong to the first period of his career.[47]

[43] *Suda* λ 683.

[44] Cf. *Toxaris* 57 'when I left home for Athens because of my desire for Hellenic *paideia*'. For the political metaphor of belonging to Athenian culture, cf. Aristides, *Orr.* i. 323, xxviii. 65.

[45] 'I received the biggest fees for public rhetoric [i.e. he was hired by local councils] . . . we were reckoned along with the big-earning sophists' (cf. Pollux, *Onomasticon* iv. 43, 'Past' n. 89). On the high standing of Hellenic culture in Gaul, especially Narbonensis, see above, 'Practice' n. 5; cf. Jones 1978*b* on the epitaph of an eloquent Syrian trader (if trader he be), who died at Lyon probably in the early 3rd c.

[46] He talks explicitly of giving rhetorical performances in his old age at *Hercules* 7; cf. *Bacchus* 6–8.

[47] Cf. *Encomium of a Fly*, especially the historical declamations *Phalaris* I and II, and the mock legal cases *The Tyrant Killer* and *The Disinherited Son*.

Lucian goes on in *Double Indictment* to advertise his new comic dialogues, which Dialogue objects to because they are not serious (33). Similar allegations and similar literary influences (Old Comedy and the Cynic satirist Menippus of Gadara) are brought forward by Diogenes in the *Fisherman* (25–6). Lucian heavily emphasizes the originality of these new writings. Two of the short introductory 'talks' (*prolaliai*), which he was so fond of as a genre, *You are a Prometheus in Words* and the *Zeuxis*, again dwell on his inventiveness and on audience reactions to this.[48] Literary commentators have been rather obsessed by the question of what works in the Lucianic corpus this new style refers to.[49] It seems best to take Lucian as speaking of a quite varied group of writings, ranging from the those which seem to owe something to real works of Menippus (*Menippus*; *Icaromenippus*) to the numerous comic dialogues (like the *Dialogues of the Sea Gods* or the *Fisherman*) to the less easily classifiable works like *Alexander* or *Peregrinus* to the diatribes like *The False Critic*. What all of these works have in common is a humour that is very often ironic and sometimes quite bitter.

As we saw in an earlier chapter, it is plain that even in his later career Lucian was unusually sensitive about his Greek.[50] The crucial importance of correct language and the status guaranteed by demonstrating *paideia* rule out any suspicion that this sensitivity was mere posturing. Lucian was not as happy in his cultural-cognitive identity as might be imagined. He certainly got cash from culture; but it seems that he was not fully accepted by the Greek elite. He admits to only 'moderate success' in Greece and Ionia. More to the point, though he talks theoretically about *paideia* as a way of gaining

[48] *You are a Prometheus in Words* 6 'we dared to combine and fit together elements which are quite disobedient and will not easily tolerate partnership'; another image used here is that of the Hippocentaur (5), the monstrous half-man, half-horse of myth, which is taken up again in *Zeuxis* (referring to Zeuxis' painting of one; cf. *Double Indictment* 33 where Dialogue uses it of a prose and verse mixture; *Runaways* 10 is a quite different usage). In *Zeuxis* Lucian stresses not only his inventiveness but also his 'good vocabulary, conformity to the classical canon, biting intellect, perception, Attic grace, construction, and art', which his audience does not properly appreciate (2).
[49] Cf. Helm 1906: 280–2 and Schwartz 1965: 132 arguing that *Prometheus* and *Zeuxis* refer to different developments from *Double Indictment* because they do not mention Menippus; Hall 1981: 29–35 is right to stress the shared elements in Lucian's report of what he was doing. See also Branham 1989: 38–46.
[50] Esp. in *A Slip of the Tongue During a Greeting* and *The False Critic*; see above, 'Practice' nn. 19–25.

public office and other privileges, he nowhere mentions that he acquired citizenship in Greece or Asia, though it was quite common in this period for cities to grant such rights to prominent men, and at the end of his life we still find him hoping for imperial offices in the future (*Apology* 12). The prosopography of Lucian is rather thin. He does not seem to have the rich Greek or Roman contacts that our other leading intellectuals do. Perhaps this is simply a matter of evidence, since there is no Philostratus or Gellius to put Lucian on the social map. But if our information from Lucian himself is reasonably accurate in this regard (and we may contrast Galen's record of his own extensive contacts with the eastern and western elites), this relative isolation might explain why Lucian does stand as a critical commentator on the culture of his contemporaries, observing its strengths and weaknesses, praising its good points and merits, and relentlessly probing its vanities and pretensions.

ROMAN POLITICS AND GREEK CULTURE

I believe this status as something of an outsider in the Greek world is also behind Lucian's favourable political attitude to Rome, to which I now turn. His relationship with the ruling power is hardly a simple one. Political identification is expressed in the particular context of the Parthian war and in his employment in imperial service later in life. We must set against this a good deal of criticism of Roman values, especially in *Nigrinus* and *On Hirelings*.

I begin with the four works that associate Lucian with the court of Lucius Verus at the time of the Parthian war, *How to Write History*, *On the Dance*, and the paired *Portraits* and *Defence of Portraits*.[51] These pieces have been well described as 'artful and indirect flatteries' of the emperor.[52] The first, and for us the most important, relates specifically to the Parthian war and can be dated to the middle of the year 166.[53] It is famous for being the only

---

[51] On these see Jones 1986: 59–77; Hall 1981: 20–4.

[52] Jones 1986: 67.

[53] Jones 1986: 60 on *How to Write History* 30–1, which show Lucian is writing after the start of the final campaign in Media under Avidius Cassius (not named) and before the triumph in October 166. Discussion: Bompaire 1958: 606–7; the commentaries of Avenarius 1956 and Homeyer 1965; Hall 1981: 312–24; Jones 1986: 59–67.

surviving work from antiquity to offer advice on what a history should contain (7–13, 33–63). This advice is interrupted with a section illustrating from contemporary historians how not to write history. Lucian says he had heard bad historians of the present war giving recitations 'recently in Ionia and only the other day in Achaia' (14), meaning Corinth (where he may have been based at the time of writing) and perhaps Ephesus (where Lucius Verus was based for part of the war and where Lucian did battle with the False Critic about this time).[54] Both advice and condemnation really relate to how a Greek should properly celebrate Rome's great victory, and mention of the great number of historians of Rome's war is very much to Rome's credit.[55] There is also a highly personal angle. This emerges in Lucian's protest about the mistaken geography of the historian who misplaced Dura-Europus away from the Euphrates and, as we have seen, transposed 'my fatherland Samosata' into Mesopotamia. More than this, Lucian identifies personally with the Roman side. He tells his addressee Philo (who is not known) that the work will be useful even for those who have written their histories of the present war 'in case some other war arises either between the Celts and the Getae or between the Indians and the Bactrians—for no one would dare to attack us, since they have all been beaten already' (5). He speaks similarly of 'our' side and 'our' commander (14, 17, 29), and when he looks forward to 'the triumph we have wanted so much' (31) we may believe that a native of Samosata really did welcome the Roman victory and was glad that his city was inside the Empire.

'We' had been used of Rome by a Greek before Lucian. It is found twice in that remarkably pro-Roman author Strabo.[56] But it seems particularly significant in the case of a second sophistic

---

[54] Corinth: *How to Write History* 3, 17, 29, 63. Ephesus: presence of Verus—Jones 1986: 166 n. 24 summarizes the relevant texts; Lucian and the False Critic—*The False Critic* 10, 22. As Jones observes, the emperor's presence was a likely stimulus to the writing of histories.

[55] 2 'there is no one who is not writing history.' We have one surviving work written for and sent to the emperors, the *Stratagems* of Polyaenus, which was compiled at the start of the war.

[56] Strabo ii. 5. 8 (C 116) the Romans have not bothered to invade Britain 'seeing that there is no reason to fear them at all, since they are not strong enough to cross over against us'; iv. 4. 5 (C 198) 'the Romans have put a stop to these customs [of the Gauls] as well as those concerned with sacrifices and divinations contrary to the usages among us'. See also Dubuisson 1985: 172–3, who claims the usage in Polybius (but note ibid. n. 246).

author.[57] We may be tempted to see this as a reflection of increasing political unification in the Empire. On the other hand we do not find the usage in Aristides,[58] Pausanias, Galen, or Philostratus. Presumably Lucian's friend Philo would not have been surprised to read it. We cannot tell. In the case of Lucian himself we can be a little more precise about its meaning. We have seen that Lucian's cultural-religious identity was probably a Semitic one of some sort (that is, as Semitic as centuries of overlaid Greek culture allowed); cognitively he had no real choice at this time but to be Hellene and to make his career in Greek letters; politically, since he does not claim to have been born into the elite of Samosata and was apparently not welcomed by the Greek elite, it may be suggested that he was naturally drawn towards a Roman identity. His fame and acceptance in the Roman West must have been significant in establishing this feeling. Lucian was clearly a Roman citizen by the time he composed *How to Write History* (though under what circumstances and when we know not). But we should not forget that the particular expression of this identity comes in an emperor-directed work partly celebrating Rome's protection of the region he came from. All of this makes generalization of Lucian's 'we' more difficult, and it would be a mistake to press the implied closeness of his political identification with Rome too far and too one-sidedly.

On the Dance, the second work connected with Lucius Verus, shows Lucian very much in tune with contemporary tastes.[59] The emperor was particularly fond of the pantomimic performances which it celebrates, and Antioch on the Orontes, where he was based for most of the war against Parthia, was a famous centre of the art. *On the Dance* is at once a description of pantomimic dancing and a defence of it from its many critics. If it was composed in Antioch, as the flattering reference to the people of that city suggests

[57] Palm 1959: 54–5. Cf. Lucian, *Alexander* 48 'our [soldiers]' in the context of Marcus' German wars. The first-person plural verb in Polyaenus, *Strategems* viii Preface, has been compared ('you yourselves [Marcus and Lucius] and the Roman Empire and the Greeks, whether we are at war or at peace'; but note well the accompanying flattery). See also above, 'Arrian' nn. 11, 17–19 on alleged comparable examples in Arrian.

[58] But see above, 'Aristides' n. 98 on *Or.* xlvii. 38.

[59] Social/cultural background: Robert 1930; Kokolakis 1959, 1960; Jones 1986: 68–75; other discussion: Robertson 1913 (authenticity); *RE* xiii. 2 (1927) 1759–60 (Helm, retracting earlier doubts); Bompaire 1958: 356–7 (doubts about authenticity). See further above, 'Past' n. 72.

(76), it may be seen as Lucian's way of seeking good will from the imperial court. There is no reason to think that Lucian was especially close to Verus himself. *Portraits* and *Defence of Portraits* have a more obvious aim. Both pieces are elaborate, clever flattery of Verus' mistress Pantheia.[60] The first compares Pantheia to an array of famous classical pictorial and literary portraits, combining the best from them to produce the perfect depiction of her. She is praised too for her intelligence and virtue, being compared to the 'portrait' of Pericles' mistress Aspasia in Aeschines of Sphettus' work of the same name. Aspasia, says Lucian, was, however, painted on a smaller canvas 'because the Athenian state was not equal to or even near to the present power of Rome' (17). In *Defence of Portraits* it is imagined that Pantheia has complained about the lavish praises of *Portraits*, alleging 'flattery' (1–2). A 'rewrite' is demanded (8, 12, 14), which is what we have. We are offered a rebuttal of any suggestion of flattery and further praise, which is 'as it were a cap and a crown' for the first piece (17 ff.).

Relevant to Lucian's general view of Rome (rather than to his relations with Lucius Verus) are *Nigrinus* and *On Hirelings*. These show a very different attitude from the works so far considered. In the past they have indeed been claimed as quite crudely anti-Roman pieces. The *Nigrinus* was even seen as a counterblast to Aelius Aristides' *To Rome*.[61] The works have also been associated with Lucian's alleged concern with the poor and the problem of class division in the ancient world.[62] More recent studies, however, have brought Lucian safely back into the bosom of the elite.[63] There is in fact nothing in Lucian's many writings to suggest that he was concerned with social problems—not even to the limited extent that Dio was. He certainly has much to say about money, either criticizing its moral effects or asking for it from patrons or simply

---

[60] Jones 1986: 75–7; on *Portraits* see Bompaire 1958: 275–6.

[61] Rohde 1914: 320 *Nigrinus* as a Greek 'Oppositionsschrift von der ästhetischen Seite'; Peretti 1946: esp. 73–80 on *Nigrinus* as a 'risposta polemica' following Lucian's conversion to philosophy and consequent antipathy to Roman morals; Highet 1962: 43.

[62] Marx and Engels 1845–6: 126 on Lucian's understanding of the contempt in which Greek philosophers are held by the *Volk* and the 'Roman capitalists' (i.e. in *On Hirelings*); perhaps the inspiration behind Peretti 1946: 128 ff., cf. Baldwin 1961: 207–8 deriding Bompaire's fears of 'une analyse marxiste de Lucien', Papaïoannou 1976: 235 ff. (but cf. 234–5—Lucian is not anti-Roman).

[63] Palm 1959: 44 ff.; Baldwin 1973: 114; Hall 1981: 221–51; Dubuisson 1984–6; Jones 1986: 78–89.

enjoying it.[64] But it would take a considerable leap of the imagination to believe that he was concerned with the plight of the poor in *Nigrinus, On Hirelings*, or elsewhere.[65] What these pieces are really interesting for is the light they shed on the relationship between Lucian's cultural cognitive and political loyalties.

Nigrinus purports to be a record of a conversation between Lucian and Nigrinus, a Platonic philosopher based in Rome, which is enclosed by a framing dialogue and has been written up as a letter sent to Nigrinus.[66] It is not known if Nigrinus existed or not.[67] In the framing dialogue Lucian says he went to Rome to see an eye doctor. He already knew Nigrinus and paid him a visit. Asked if he would be 'making the journey to Greece again', Nigrinus replied with a verbal 'ambrosia' which made Lucian 'sharper-sighted in my soul' (2–4). The philosopher begins his conversation with praise of Athens for her contempt of material values and for her tranquil life (12–14) and accent on *paideia* (13). He then attacks at length 'the city' he is living in, which is clearly Rome, for its size, its crowds, its vices of adultery, avarice, perjury, and falsity (15–21). Above all he attacks the rich themselves (21) and those who court them as clients and flatterers (22–5). Nigrinus concentrates his attack on false philosophers who work for money (24–5) and those that set ridiculous standards of asceticism (27–8). Lucian then reports another assault 'on the rest of mankind' and the bustle of 'the city' (29), including the elite Roman way of death (30–1), of dining (33 which particularly shows their 'want of education'), and of bathing

[64] Satire on wealth: esp. *Gallus, Timon, Menippus, Saturnalia, Dialogues of the Dead* nos. 3, 15–21 Macleod (= 2, 5–11); appeals for money: *Dipsades, Harmonides, Scythian*; cf. *Dream* 11, 18, *Apology* 12, 15 on Lucian's own wealth; see Hall's comments 1981: 225–32.

[65] Baldwin 1961: 202–3 also identified an anti-Roman drift in the *Saturnalia*, an attack (but a good-humoured one) on the rich during the festival of the *Kronia* (which was equivalent to and no doubt heavily influenced at this time by the Roman Saturnalia); but as Bompaire 1958: 318, 513 and Jones 1986: 87–8 note, the location is not of necessity Roman (cf. further Athenaeus, *Sophists at Dinner* 639b–40a, Timaeus Sophistes, *Platonic Lexicon* p. 3 Koch, Macrobius, *Saturnalia* i. 7. 36–7), and the general air of fantasy makes it extremely difficult to argue that the work is aimed 'against' Rome.

[66] On the structure note Anderson 1978 (comparing it to *Icaromenippus* and *Gallus*).

[67] He does not seem to be satirized; there is no need to think of the real Platonic philosopher Albinus of Pergamum (Galen, *On his Own Books* xix. 16. 14; he is not to be confused with Alcinous the author of the *Didaskalikos*—Whittaker and Louis 1990: pp. vii–xiii).

(34; which perhaps makes the rich, uncultured bather of 13 a Roman). Lucian finally reassures us of his rapture at everything that has been said.[68]

All of the vices identified in *Nigrinus* are attacked also by Roman authors, especially the satirical poets Horace, Persius, Juvenal, and Petronius in his *Satyricon*. It is reasonably certain that Nigrinus himself is Roman too, for he speaks of the horror he experienced at Rome 'when I first returned from Greece' (17). Nevertheless, his remarks come to us through Lucian. And, as with Dio of Prusa, the question to ask is whether Greek criticism of Rome differs from Roman criticism? As has been observed, we may surmise that Lucian felt Roman politically. On the other hand, his cultural outlook was thoroughly Greek. Whether or not Nigrinus is or is imagined to be Roman, the criticism put into his mouth is channelled through Greek culture and Rome is contrasted unfavourably with an idealized Athens. To say from this Greek perspective that 'the sons of the Romans only speak the truth once in their whole life—meaning what they say in their wills' (30), a comment highlighted by the use of 'Roman' here only, is surely in this context to make an anti-Roman remark (compare and contrast Seneca's *On Benefits* iv. 11. 5). Which is not to say that such a feeling must represent a speaker's dominant outlook. It certainly does not in the case of Lucian. But, for whatever reason, Lucian chose to compose this outburst, and it should not be ignored.

On Hirelings is rather similar to *Nigrinus* and indeed expands remarks made at *Nigrinus* 24–5 on 'philosophers for hire'. Here, though, Lucian speaks in his own voice. A lot of what he says is quite hostile towards the Roman elite; but there is again no cause to translate this into an overall 'profound aversion to the Roman world'.[69] We must be sensitive to the context of the remarks. Lucian is at pains at the beginning of the work to stress that the treatment of Greek *pepaideumenoi* by rich Romans really is as bad as he is making out.[70] He claims as his sources those who had suffered such treatment (a certain Thesmopolis is named in 33–4), and says he

---

[68] A recollection of the reactions of Apollodorus and Alcibiades to Socrates' teaching in the *Symposium*: Hall 1981: 159–60.

[69] Peretti 1946: 141 (a myopia Lucian later overcomes by entering Roman service). Peretti still has followers: e.g. Musti 1984: 14, Pinto 1974.

[70] Cf. *How to Write History* 14 for a similar assertion about his record of the bad historians; *True History* 4 (telling the truth that he is lying).

will add the 'logical conclusions' so that his addressee Timocles will
not make the same mistake and be taken in by the thought of
'having the best of the Romans as friends' (1–4). The victims are
grammarians, rhetors, musicians, and especially philosophers who
deserve preferential treatment from the *misthodotai*, 'paymasters'.
The 'blame' for what emerges from the book falls particularly 'on
those who do these things, then on those who put up with them'
(4). Lucian has blame in mind again at the end of the work: quoting
the ending of Plato's *Republic* he tells Timocles to remember that
'God is not to blame; the blame falls on the one that makes the
choice' (42). Here the reference is to the Greek hireling; at §4 the
doers are clearly the rich Romans. Lucian is not concerned with
'the rest of the mob, like trainers and flatterers'—they deserve what
they get and their masters are not doing anything wrong, 'if, as
they say, they piss in the pot'. His special task is to rescue the
pepaideumenoi (4).

He proceeds to discuss various causes of this 'voluntary slavery'
(5). There is strong moral criticism of the hirelings' desire for pleasure and luxury. They are like 'lovers' led on by their *erômenoi* (7).
At 10 ff. Lucian switches to a full description of what the Greek has
to put up with in his new master's house. This section forms the
bulk of the essay. A few examples will do. He must listen to Roman
complaints about the Greeks in the city (17).[71] He is even cheated
over his salary while being told he is 'the luckiest man in the city',
since he has been admitted 'into the first household of the Roman
Empire' (20). As he quietly observes the appalling bad taste of his
hosts, he stands out in his philosopher's cloak and is the only one
talking barbarous Latin (24). He suffers the stupidity of the rich
women (33–4, 36). Finally, after having been worn out by his work,
he is driven from the house on a trumped-up sex charge (39, cf. 29).
No one will believe him: 'your accuser is credible even if he remains silent; but you are a Greek, unreliable in character and pre-
disposed to all sorts of wrongdoing' (40). The Romans hold this
opinion about 'all of us', because they have experienced false philosophers who come to their homes and practise magic and display a
'servile attitude towards gain' (ibid.). And when the Roman masters

[71] Cf. notably Juvenal's disgruntled Roman client at *Satires* iii. 60–1; Hall 1981:
246–8 for discussion and other parallels (but Lucian was not drawing on Juvenal,
as the disparaging Helm 1906: 219–22 and others have wanted; see Jones 1986: 81
n. 15).

have thrown the hireling out, they are afraid of being exposed for what they are, realizing that he knows everything about their true natures (41, cf. 25). For they are in fact 'exactly like' expensive editions of books whose contents are 'Thyestes feasting on his children or Oedipus consorting with his mother or Tereus having sex with both his sisters at once' (41)—standard abuse but abuse all the same.[72]

In the final chapter Lucian paints an imaginary picture after the celebrated *Picture of Cebes*, a semi-philosophical work of unknown date which portrayed through the formal technique of an ecphrasis of a painting the choice between True *Paideia* and False *Paideia*.[73] In Lucian's picture we find at the top of a difficult ascent not True *Paideia*, as in the *Picture of Cebes*, but Wealth. His lover fights his way up to him but is waylaid by Hope, Deceit, Slavery, Labour, Age, Arrogance, Despair, and finally Repentance. The parallel works in several ways. The figure of the lover is drawn from *Picture of Cebes* 13, where it is used of those who pursue False *Paideia*. For the anonymous author this is the whole tribe of what Lucian (favourably) thinks of as *pepaideumenoi*, who are also pursuing a false goal. In Lucian's work the figure of the lover is also used, of course, of the deluded scholar's pursuit of his rich Roman *erômenos* (7), and the play on the commerce of education and sex is carried through in 27, 29, and 39.[74] Finally, the figures who bring the lover low in Lucian's picture answer to various named Virtues in the original (18–21), which are conspicuous by their absence among the rich Romans.

What does Lucian's outrage in this essay mean? Whatever one thinks about his general attitude to the Roman empire, his depiction here of the Roman rich of the city of Rome cannot be considered as anything but hostile. 'We' in *On Hirelings* is *not* 'Romans'. The explanation is provided by Lucian's cultural identity. Although he must have known Latin, he nowhere mentions Roman cultural activities (and has very little interest in Roman history).[75] In *On*

---

[72] Cf. Champlin 1980: 64–6.

[73] On the antecedents and influences of this work see Fitzgerald and White 1983: 16–27. For Lucian see esp. Joly 1963: 80–1.

[74] Cf. the unnatural sexual relations in 41. Lucian has much fun using the *Picture of Cebes* as a model in his combination of a genital and educational pursuit of Rhetorikê in the *Teacher of Rhetoric* 6 ff.

[75] Latin: note *A Slip of the Tongue During a Greeting* (to a Roman governor) 13 'you yourselves, if I know anything of the Roman language, when you exchange

Hirelings he is explicitly concerned with defending the dignity of Greek culture and concerned to stop its representatives from becoming Roman commodities (4). In this regard the literary ancestry of Lucian's jibes is far from irrelevant. But it is also important—as with any other author in any age—not to segregate literature from society (a mistake not made by Lucian's contemporaries). One does not have to lump all the criticisms crudely together under the label 'political' to see what is going on. *On Hirelings* certainly offers much in the way of moral criticism. The men who sign up for this 'voluntary slavery' are definitely to blame (5–9). The hosts have grown contemptuous because of the Greek charlatans they have experienced (40). The criticisms of the hosts' behaviour are also moral (10ff.). Again, the 'slavery' which Lucian speaks of throughout the essay is sometimes explicitly moral (cf. especially 7), though it also reflects the conduct of the other (real) slaves of the house and what they have to do (23–5). But Lucian's defence of the majesty of Greek culture must be seen as an essentially political rather than moral issue. The Greek scholar who works for the rich Romans is laying on the line his 'family, freedom, and ancestors' (23). Lucian stresses that it is Hellenic culture that is at risk: the hosts want nothing of Homer, Demosthenes, or Plato—but only the reputation of being a 'devoted student of Hellenic learning' (25, cf. similarly 36). In another diatribe, *The Uneducated Book Collector*, feigned *paideia* is again Lucian's subject. This work is aimed at a man whose cultural pretensions are located wholly within Greek culture, and hence there is no need to specify that he is faking 'Hellenic' *paideia*. In *On Hirelings* Lucian's indignation at the Roman hosts is precisely defined as their abuse of 'Hellenic learning', which they naturally

greetings often return the word *hugieia* ('health', alluding to the Latin *salve*, 'be healthy'). Cf. further *On the Dance* 67 'the Italiots [in Lucian mostly = 'Romans'] call the dancer a *pantomimos*' (a term common in Latin, but not really used in Greek literature—the contemporary usage in Athenaeus, *Sophists at Dinner* 20d, is an emendation, and epigraphical testimony is apparently lacking, though for an earlier example see *Inschriften von Priene* 113. 66 from the 80s BC).

Lucian has sometimes been thought to be playing on the Graeco-Latin *Gallos/ Gallus* = 'priest of Cybele' and Latin *gallus* = 'cockerel' at *On the Syrian Goddess* 48 in the story of the 'sacred cockerel' (where the Greek *alektruôn* lacks the double meaning; cf. *RE* vii (1910) 2160 (Dussaud), Delchor 1987: 60, and see above, n. 36, for alternative speculation. Note also the play on *kalos* 'beautiful' and **talos* (nonexistent in Greek but perhaps = Latin *talus*, 'ankle') at *Judgement of the Vowels* 11.

History: note the confusion of Scipio the Elder, who defeated Hannibal, with Scipio the Younger, who destroyed Carthage, at *Dialogues of the Dead* 25. 7 Macleod (= 12. 7); cf. Pinto 1974: 235.

lacked.[76] There is nothing in the essay to suggest that Lucian was especially worried by the wealth of the Roman hosts. For Lucian, as we have seen, culture entailed money; what he resented was money without culture. The idea that Lucian in *Nigrinus* and *On Hirelings* was a campaigning anti-Roman philosopher or a defender of impecunious Greeks is totally wrong. His concern is the wider one of protecting Greek culture and therefore (literally) protecting his own investments.

Late in life when the same Lucian became a member of the prefect's staff in Egypt, he wrote a short *Apology* for *On Hirelings*.[77] He describes the earlier work as a 'terrible indictment of that sort of life' (1, cf. 4). He imagines too that his present addressee, Sabinus, who is a philosopher, had a good laugh when he read it (1–2). Indeed, the work had long been admired (3 *palai*, cf. 1).[78] Lucian goes on to praise the style of the work and 'most importantly the fact it was useful to everyone, and especially the *pepaideumenoi*, in stopping them from subjecting themselves to a life of slavery out of ignorance' (3).[79] In the *Apology* there is no mention of 'Rome' or 'Romans' at all. Rather, when Lucian comes to the crux of the matter, his employment by the 'king' (11),[80] he says that the earlier work was written against 'entering the house of some rich man as a hireling' (ibid.), and that 'I pitied those who were slaves in houses under the pretext of giving instruction' (12). The *Apology* does not amplify *On Hirelings* as *Defence of Portraits* does the flattery of *Portraits*, nor modify it as the *Fisherman* does the blanket attack on

---

[76] See 25 on the contrast between the *apaideusia* ('want of education') in the Romans' souls and their desire to make a pretence of 'Hellenic learning'; cf. 13 'consider . . . whether anyone with even the slightest acquaintance with *paideia* could put up with [their behaviour]', *Nigrinus* 33 (Roman *apaideusia*). Lucian makes nothing of what he implies by saying that Greek education was fashionable, i.e. that some really did value it. Contrast Jones 1986: 82, Lucian's attack is 'directed at the patron's character, not at his nationality'; rather, both factors are important.

[77] Age: *Apology* 1 'one foot almost on the ferry'.

[78] The words 'close on your heels' and 'after a little' at §6 referring to the gap between *On Hirelings* and Lucian's new job should perhaps not be taken literally, since they occur in Sabinus' imagined indignation over Lucian first doing one thing, then the opposite. Sabinus may be the Platonic philosopher known from *IG* ii² 3803 (cf. Oliver 1950: 160).

[79] A good example of *pepaideumenoi* as a social term (there is no oxymoron with 'ignorance').

[80] Presumably Commodus. Note here the absence of the definite article in the Greek (παρὰ βασιλέως μισθοφορεῖν), the traditional way of referring to the Great King of Persia (cf. e.g. Lucian, *Toxaris* 17, Pausanias v. 1. 2, 'Plutarch' n. 125); cf. 12–13 (with and without the article).

philosophers in *Lives for Sale*. It leaves *On Hirelings* as it stands and defends Lucian himself from the charge of hypocrisy. That Lucian does not mention the explicitly Roman setting of the earlier work is hardly surprising and should not be taken as indicating that it was accidental. He also avoids mentioning Rome with regard to his present position. He says merely that he shares in and plays a part in 'the greatest empire' and that he is concerned with 'not the smallest part of this government of Egypt'.[81] He earns many talents and has hopes of a procuratorship or some other imperial post (12). Recalling a famous story in Herodotus he ends by saying that ultimately 'Hippocleides doesn't care!' (15).[82]

In some ways Lucian's defence in the *Apology* recalls the outlook of Dio and Aristides, in that he stresses his direct relationship with the 'king' rather than with Rome (11–13).[83] He shows himself favourably disposed towards the imperial system, while somehow dissociating himself from the Roman name. The presentation of his relationship with the emperor is especially interesting. Such comments as Lucian makes on emperors elsewhere are also favourable (as they must be in context).[84] In the *Apology* he compares his official salary to the emperor's receipt of rewards, which are not taxes and tributes: the 'king's greatest payment is praises and fame among all men, obeisance [*to proskuneisthai*] for his benefactions, and also the statues, temples, and sanctuaries which they have [*echousi*] from those they rule—these too are wages for the care and

[81] The post was evidently that of *eisagôgeus*, the man who 'introduced' cases to the prefect's court (*Apology* 12 *tas dikas eisagein*): Box 1935; vander Leest 1985; Jones 1986: 21 n. 80. The identification of the prefect by Schwartz 1965: 12–15 is an imaginary fact in a generally unreliable account (9–21).

[82] Cf. *Hercules* 8.

[83] There seems to be an allusion to the prefect at *Apology* 9 'if I said . . . I admired the intelligence, courage, and magnanimity of the man and wanted to play a part in his policies', where 'the man' is equivalent to 'the rich man' Lucian's philosophers go and work for as hirelings (4, 11), and he is also mentioned in the context of Lucian's duties at 12.

[84] See *Portraits* 22 (Verus is 'the great king, who is good and gentle'), *Peregrinus* 18 (Peregrinus attacked Pius who was 'most mild and most gentle'), *A Slip of the Tongue during a Greeting* 18 (Augustus' good sense). More interesting is *The Uneducated Book Collector* 22–3, where the (unnamed) king is 'a wise man who particularly honours *paideia*; if he should hear you are buying books and making a large collection, you think you'll soon get everything from him. But do you really think, you queer, that he is so steeped in mandragora he will hear of this but not know what sort of life you lead in the day, how much you drink, etc?' (referring to Marcus and the possibility of taking advantage of his love of education; see below, 'Galen' n. 43; by the way, inattention from drinking mandragora is not an allegation of addiction but a proverbial saying *pace* Witke 1965 [cf. below, 'Galen' n. 38]).

foresight they expend in continually watching over the common-wealth and making it better' (13). This is one of the most interesting references to the imperial cult in second sophistic literature.[85] Lucian is clearly in favour of the cult and clearly expects Sabinus to take the same view.[86] It is worth observing that he moves from speaking of the (present) emperor's enjoyment of fame to a generalizing plural—'they have'—when he comes on to mention the cult itself, presumably because he is thinking of past and present offerings to various emperors. Interesting too is the general idea of a quid pro quo, of gratitude, behind the cult, an idea which is not certainly articulated elsewhere by intellectuals, though cult and imperial bene-faction are linked in official epigraphic texts, and the idea of reci-procity certainly underlies the claims of Aelius Aristides in urging the emperors to rebuild Smyrna (*Or.* xix. 13).[87] 'Obeisance' seems rather 'oriental' but might be explained by a passage in *Nigrinus*, where the philosopher damns the hauteur of some of the rich at Rome who 'even expect obeisance—not at a distance and not in the Persian style, but you must approach bowing, humbling your soul and showing its feelings by holding your body to match, and then you must kiss his breast or his right hand' (21). It is quite possible that Lucian had done this himself to the emperor or to another grandee—and that he could also find it thoroughly absurd (which is the reaction he attributes to Nigrinus). In the *Apology* his accept-ance of the idea is entirely understandable.

I pass finally to the *Peregrinus* and the *Alexander*. The former is a denunciation of the Cynic philosopher and sometime Christian, Peregrinus of Parium, known also as 'Proteus', who attracted a good deal of publicity in his time and attained notoriety by immolat-ing himself at the Olympic games of 165.[88] Lucian wrote another piece attacking Peregrinus and his followers, the *Runaways*, set and

---

[85] Cf. Bowersock 1973: 201–2.

[86] Though cf. below, n. 97 on *Alexander* 48 'Marcus the god [*theos Markos*]'.

[87] Official texts: Price 1984*a*: 243. Aristides xix: above, 'Aristides' n. 153. Jones 1986: 84 n. 28 cites Aristides, *Or.* xxvii. 22, 24, 39, for a precise parallel; but it seems that the *charistêrion*, 'thank offering', of the temple in Aristides' speech (xxvii. 22) is a thank-you to the real gods (τοῖς θεοῖς cf. 39, 40 where 'thanks' is what the gods are offered, while the emperors—who certainly come close to divinity in the speech—are congratulated and prayed for).

[88] On *Peregrinus* see Schwartz 1963 (commentary); Hall 1981: 176–82; Jones 1986: 117–32; Edwards 1989. Another full-length work was apparently devoted to Peregrinus by the elder Philostratus: *Suda* φ 422 'Proteus Cynic or Sophist'. Lucian's hostile view is countered especially by Gellius, *Attic Nights* viii. 3, xii. 3 (Holford-Strevens 1988: 104–5).

apparently read in the important Thracian city of Philippopolis and fastening riotously on a certain Cantharus ('Dung Beetle').[89] The work holds no interest for Lucian's attitude to Rome. Nor is *Peregrinus* much more useful. An unknown governor of Syria who suspected that Peregrinus in his Christian phase was aiming at martyrdom and released him from prison is praised for his love of philosophy (14);[90] the emperor Antoninus Pius, who refused Peregrinus' petition for the restitution of his property (16), is praised, as has been noted, for his mildness in the context of Peregrinus abusing him at Rome (18); the prefect of Rome who expelled him from the city is a 'wise man' (18); and Peregrinus' advice to the Greeks to 'take up arms against the Romans' (19) is mentioned by Lucian in the same breath as his idiotic attack on 'a man outstanding in *paideia* and status', i.e. Herodes Atticus.

Alexander is far more interesting. It tells the story of a man called Alexander of Abonuteichos, a city of Paphlagonia in the Roman province of Bithynia and Pontus (cf. 57). Alexander set himself up as the *prophêtês* ('interpreter') of a fabricated snake-god he called Glycon, who was supposedly a reincarnation of the healing god Asclepius. This cult certainly existed and coins and images of Glycon have been found over a wide area. It has been noted already that the fraud (as Lucian saw it) ties in closely with the special place the second sophistic accorded to the Greek past, for one of Alexander's aims was to give his backwoods town a measure of respectability and wealth, and his activities can also be fitted into the usual pattern of inter-city rivalries perpetuated by the local elites.[91] Alexander must also be seen against contemporary religious trends, in particular the great influence now enjoyed by oracular shrines, for it was as a purveyor of oracles that he achieved his greatest fame and attracted the direct hostility of Lucian, who challenged him in Abonuteichos in 159.[92]

The work against Alexander was not written until after the death of the emperor Marcus (48), which must reflect in part the prophet's influence with the Roman court. This influence forms the centrepiece of the work (27, 30–7). To special petitioners Alexander

---

[89] Cf. Bowie 1980.   [90] Arrian has been nominated: above, 'Arrian' n. 6.
[91] Above, 'Past' n. 25–26.
[92] On *Alexander* see Weinreich 1921; Caster 1938; Robert 1980: 393–421; Hall 1981: 208–14; Jones 1986: 133–48; Lane Fox 1986: 241–50; Branham 1989: 181–210; Mitchell 1993: ii. 13 n. 24. Date of Lucian's visit—see below.

issued a special sort of oracle called an 'autophone', which was
alleged to be spoken by the god (26).⁹³ One of these oracles encouraged the Roman consular M. Sedatius Severianus to invade Armenia in 161, where 'that silly Celt' was disastrously defeated (27).⁹⁴
The main channel of Alexander's influence was the important consular P. Mummius Sisenna Rutilianus, *cos. suff.* 146 and governor of
Asia in 160/1.⁹⁵ He has been introduced early on and casually as
'his son-in-law Rutilianus' (4). Now (30) Lucian comments in detail. Alexander particularly attracted 'the most powerful men with
the greatest reputation in the city [of Rome]. The first and foremost
of these was Rutilianus, a man who in other respects was aristocratic and noble and had been tested in many Roman offices, but
was terribly sick in matters that concerned the gods and held strange
beliefs about them'. Lucian suggests that Rutilianus 'practically
abandoned the office to which he had been entrusted and flew to
Abonuteichos'.⁹⁶ He stresses that the Roman was the perfect con-
duit for the prophet, since he had 'very many most powerful friends'
(31). Alexander cultivated him so well that he was persuaded to
marry his daughter (35). In general Alexander's influence can be
presented as an 'attack' on the Empire (cf. 2, 30, 36, 37 'conspirators'). Later he causes disaster to the armies of Marcus in the
German wars (48 his 'greatest daring'), and has the 'daring' to petition the emperor to change the name of Abonuteichos to the more
respectable Ionopolis (58). Lucian makes no comment on Marcus.⁹⁷
Rutilianus was more of a problem. Lucian was clearly known to him.
He claims to have advised the consular against marriage (54–5),
which may explain Rutilianus' enquiry about Lucian and Alexander's
response.⁹⁸ Lucian had some familiarity with the governors: it is

⁹³ At 36 Lucian says an 'autophone' was sent to 'all the provinces' during the
great plague.
⁹⁴ Sedatius Severianus from Gaul, *cos. suff.* 153 (Alföldy 1977: 163; cf. *AE* 1981:
640; note that *Keltos* in Lucian apparently always refers to the Gauls rather than the
Galatians), is not to be confused with Aristides' friend, Sedatus (Aristides xlviii = II.
48, l = IV. 16, 43), on whom see Halfmann 1979: no. 78.
⁹⁵ Syme 1983: 282.
⁹⁶ The office in question cannot be the proconsulship of Asia, since Rutilianus is
already closely attached to Alexander by 159. On his career see also Alföldy 1977:
330.
⁹⁷ Though *Alexander* 48 is the only time a deceased emperor is referred to as 'god'
(contrast *Peregrinus* 18: Pius; *On the Dance* 34, *A Slip of the Tongue* 18: Augustus).
⁹⁸ 54: 'He delights in lovers' talks wandering at night and in unholy beds' (an
allegation of homosexuality).

here that he says the governor of Cappadocia, 'then a friend of mine', had given him an escort to take him to the sea (55). But Rutilianus was not a close acquaintance. After Alexander had attempted to murder Lucian and Lucian was preparing a prosecution, the governor of Bithynia in 159 (L. Hedius Rufus Lollianus) Avitus stopped him because of the influence of Rutilianus (57).[99] These details and the additional mention of meeting ambassadors from the Bosporan kingdom attest to the reality of the suggested prosecution, which the charge of murder (standard in ancient invective) would otherwise render suspect.[100] Lucian's disgruntlement is plain in his remarks about a 'judge in that state of mind' (57).

Alexander, then, was Lucian's most difficult enemy. In a way Lucian climbed down before him, since he left it till after the deaths of Alexander (59) and Rutilianus (34 of melancholia), as well as that of Marcus (48), before writing his exposé at the behest (he claims) of the addressee, an Epicurean called Celsus.[101] It is interesting that Lucian stresses his own affiliations at the start of the work. If anyone criticizes him, he says, for devoting a book to a man like Alexander, he can cite a precedent. 'Arrian the pupil of Epictetus, a man who was among the first of the Romans and was associated with *paideia* for his whole life, had a similar experience, and the defence he could make will do for us too, for he thought it worth writing up the life of the bandit Tillorobus.' Unlike Tillorobus Alexander 'filled the whole, as it were, of the Romans' empire with his banditry' (2). This comparison with Arrian works in a number of ways. It calls to mind Alexander of Macedon, whose history Arrian wrote.[102] Further, it emphasizes the devotion to

[99] Avitus: *cos. ord.* in 144 and *procos.* of Africa in *c.* 157/8 (Alföldy 1977: 147, 208). Avitus (Ἄυειτος is a certain correction of β's ἄυεκτος [γ has αὐτός]) is now known to have been governor in 159, not 165 as was long thought: see Marek 1985: 146–9 (= *SEG* xxxv. 1318), correcting earlier interpretations of *IGR* iii. 84 (cf. Jones 1990*b*: 62 n. 43); his office marks the beginning of permanent government of the province by imperial legates (Thomasson 1972–90: i. 249 with iii. 37; the end of his tenure is unknown).

[100] So Jones 1986: 146.

[101] For Celsus' Epicureanism cf. 17, 47. He may be 'Celsus the Epicurean' addressed in one of Galen's lost works on Epicureanism (*On his Own Books* xix. 48. 9); Hall 1981: 512–13; Jones 1986: 20.

[102] Cf. 1 where Lucian's task is equivalent to writing an Alexander history; 7, 16 for further association; Lucian's language ('thought it worth writing up') recalls Arrian, *Anabasis* i. 12. 4–5. See further Robert 1937: 98 n. 3 (Tillorobus' name), Vidal-Naquet 1984: 371–3 (on Arrian, promoting the fantastic idea of Tonnet 1988: i. 73 that Tillorobus is Lucian's derogatory name for Alexander the Great).

education and sense that is a key theme in the *Alexander* and is important to Lucian's reading of how Rome helped the spread of the cult. Just as Arrian is associated with *paideia*, so Lucian's audience consists of *pepaideumenoi* (2). Contrasting with them are the Paphlagonians, whose stupidity in accepting Alexander is stressed throughout (9, 11, 13–15, 17, 20, 45). The importance of Epicurean philosophy is also emphasized. Although it is difficult to be definite about Lucian's likes and dislikes, he does seem to have been sympathetic towards central Epicurean tenets and in particular to have welcomed their rejection of superstitious belief in the gods.[103] In the *Alexander* the Epicureans' opposition to the false prophet is mentioned in the context of Alexander's 'control of Italy' (38) and is then treated at length at 43–7. Two Epicureans are named, Lepidus at Amastris (25, 43),[104] and a certain Sacerdos from nearby Tium (43). Although Sacerdos is described as a 'comrade' of Lepidus, his conversation with Glycon/Alexander on the subject of his godhead, which was preserved in gold letters in Sacerdos' house, seems to earn him a rather adverse comment from Lucian about his 'intelligence'. Lucian ends this section on the Epicureans by praising the spiritual tranquillity and truth vouchsafed by Epicurus' doctrines (47), and he returns to the theme warmly at the end (61).[105]

Of the two Romans who are named as Alexander's victims (aside from Marcus), Lucian's description of Severianus 'the Celt' as 'silly' (27) recalls what he says about the 'silly' Paphlagonians (9). Rutilianus, who was Italian in origin, is described in similar terms (30 'they inflamed that wretched old man and drove him into real madness'; 33 it is difficult to blame Alexander for dealing with 'such homunculi'; 35 'that most intelligent Rutilianus'). Though Lucian mentions—without naming names—many others who were taken in by Alexander (especially 40 two 'wise morons'), his comments on these non-Greeks have a special significance. If we recall Lucian's complete disregard of Roman literary and artistic culture (an attitude he shared with most second sophistic authors) and especially his comments on Roman educational attainments in *On Hirelings*, it seems as though Rutilianus is suffering from an absence

[103] Cf. esp. the figure of Damis in the *Tragic Zeus*; Schwartz 1965: 145–8; Jones 1986: 26–8.
[104] This is Ti. Claudius Lepidus, high priest of the imperial cult: *PIR*² C 910.
[105] Branham 1989: 209 suggests an unintentional contrast between Lucian's advocacy of Epicurean tranquillity and his own 'moral rage'.

of Hellenic education (which is represented in *Alexander* by Epicurean philosophy), while Severianus is simply beyond the pale.
Lucian is not exactly being 'racial' here. It is just that Hellenic
learning—in particular the wisdom of Epicurus—is what confronts
and exposes Alexander; those that lack it are easy prey—and members of the Roman elite are among those like the Paphlagonians
who are liable to lack it. Consider again the introduction to the
Alexander and the characterization of Arrian. Arrian is famous for
his *paideia*, and in drawing a parallel with him Lucian is making a
like claim.[106] This is his Greek cultural identity. Arrian is also 'among
the first of the Romans'. This might seem a curious assertion for
one exponent of Greek culture to make about another. The remark
has of course a political bearing and refers to Arrian's accomplished
senatorial and military career.[107] In making it, Lucian is again alluding to himself and so to his own ability to identify with Rome on
a political level as a *civis* or an official. He seems to be saying that
Roman political status is important—but that a life-long devotion
to *paideia* is also relevant. It would seem that only Greeks like
Arrian—and Lucian—can combine the two. For both Severianus
and Rutilianus are prominent Romans who lack true culture and
the stability of mind gained thereby.[108]

---

[106] Cf. Macleod 1987.

[107] Cf. the anonymous 'helper [*boêthos*]' of the False Critic at *The False Critic* 21,
'a man who was among the best of the Romans'—if the critic is Hadrian of Tyre and
the anonymous is his fellow-Phoenician, Flavius Boethus (Jones 1986: 110–15), a
follower of Aristotelian philosophy with a distinguished Roman career (below, 'Galen'
n. 9), Lucian is again making a political identification. Compare and contrast *On
Hirelings* 3, 20 for 'best' and 'first' applied to Romans with rather less grace.

[108] Cf. criticisms of Greeks and Romans with political influence at Rome but
insufficient education: Lucian, *Demonax* 40: 'when a certain Polybius, a man who
was completely uneducated and ungrammatical [*soloikos*], said, "The king has honoured me with Roman citizenship", [Demonax] said, "If only he'd made you a
Hellene rather than a Roman!"' (see Jones 1986: 96 n. 43 for an identification of this
man with the Polybius who erected a bust of Cicero, Buckler and Robinson, *Sardis*
vii. 1 no. 49, where he is in turn put forward as the Polybius who wrote an *On
Solecism*); Arrian, *Discourses of Epictetus* iii. 7. 31 to the Roman corrector: 'let [Cae-
sar] write instructions for you so you can judge music and literature—and what
good will it do you?'; Cassius Dio lxix. 3. 5 for the sophist Dionysius' remark to the
imperial secretary (Avidius) Heliodorus: 'Caesar can give you money and honour,
but he cannot make you a rhetor'. Hadrian of Tyre's public celebration of Marcus'
son-in-law Cn. Claudius Severus of Pompeiopolis (*cos.* 167, 173; Halfmann 1979:
no. 101) as 'pre-eminent among the Greeks, select among the Ausonians' (*IK* xv
[Ephesos v], 1539) shares Lucian's positive approach to Arrian in the *Alexander*.

Lucian's attitude towards Rome is complex. He was a Roman citizen and on occasion (*How to Write History*, *Apology*) clearly expresses a political identification with the Roman system. But it is difficult to take him closer to Rome. To argue, for example, that his knowledge of 'actualités' makes him generally pro-Roman is rather simplistic.[109] Lucian no doubt knew a lot about Rome. But it is no great effort to suppose that he was intelligent enough to work out what was worthwhile about the Empire and at the same time to remain aware of where Roman rule had nothing to offer him. It was in fact particularly easy for him to identify politically with Rome in the contexts where he does this. He was not part of the Greek governing elite and owed no loyalty to it. Further, Rome had protected Samosata by fighting the 'barbarians' (*How to Write History* 2, 14, cf. 54). Finally, she accommodated him in her government and paid him handsomely (*Apology*), something always important to him. Culturally, though, Romans themselves looked philistine. Naturally Lucian knew of some who were highly educated in Greek *paideia*, such as Marcus (*The Uneducated Book Collector* 22) and probably the Platonist Nigrinus. But he plainly felt that many Romans displayed a quite shocking attitude towards Greek culture (*Nigrinus*, *On Hirelings*), and that even among the governing elite there were not a few who suffered from its absence (*Alexander*). For most of the time Lucian's adopted cultural identity as a Hellene did not clash with his loyalties to Rome's Empire. But in cases where Greek culture was abused by Roman power, it is clear where he stood.

[109] The approach adopted by Dubuisson 1984–6 against e.g. Reardon 1971: 17, 179 and the whole 'mimetic' tradition represented most clearly by Bompaire 1958.

10

Pausanias

INTRODUCTION

The next major figure to be studied is the periegete or 'guide', Pausanias, the author of the *Periêgêsis Hellados* or *Guide to Greece*. The work is famous in modern times, but it is not known whether it was much read by contemporaries. Certainly, it is not mentioned by surviving ancient authors until the sixth century, when it was used by the Byzantine geographer Stephanus, who found it a serviceable source for his own *Ethnica*. Stephanus gives us both the title of the work and the name of its writer. The *Guide to Greece* thus shows familiar symptoms of the death of the author.[1] The work, in ten books, was written over a long time. It was certainly commenced before 160 (or shortly after) and seems to have been published not much earlier than 180.[2] Extensive cross-referencing between books guarantees that it was planned and written as a whole.[3] These dates

---

[1] The quotation of Pausanias viii. 36. 6 at Aelian, *Varied History* xii. 61 is almost certainly an interpolation added after this part of Aelian was epitomized: Diller 1955: 272, id. 1956: 88 (it is still accepted as genuine by Pouilloux in Casevitz–Pouilloux–Chamoux 1992: p. x, cf. Musti 1984: 12).

[2] Regenbogen 1956: 1093; Heer 1979: 12; Habicht 1985: 9. The date is provided by the reference at v. 1. 2 to Corinth having been refounded by Julius Caesar 217 years before (i.e. written about 174) and at viii. 43. 6 to Marcus Aurelius' defeat of the Germans and the Sarmatians (i.e. after 175). There is no mention of Commodus. The start of work predates the death of Regilla, wife of Herodes Atticus, before 160 (Ameling 1983: ii. 9), since Pausanias later apologizes for not having mentioned in his first book on Attica the Odeum built by Herodes at Athens in her honour (vii. 20. 6).

[3] Cf. e.g. i. 24. 5 citing ix. 26. 2; x. 19. 5 citing i. 3. 5–4. 6. There are no references to any book beyond the tenth; a rogue reference in Stephanus to an eleventh book (pointing to a treatment of Euboea) seems to be an error (Regenbogen 1956: 1011; for a different view see Diller 1955: 274–5). There are signs of incompleteness in the 'false' reference of ix. 23. 7 (x. 38. 1 does not fulfill the promise), and many have felt signs of haste in the account of Delphi in Book x. For the idea that Book i was published separately see Frazer 1898: i. pp. xvii–xviii; against, Regenbogen 1956: 1010–11, Habicht 1985: 7–8.

suggest that Pausanias himself was a close contemporary of Lucian and Aristides. We can be reasonably sure from statements in the *Guide* that he came from Magnesia ad Sipylum in Lydia in the Roman province of Asia, an important city controlling one of the main routes into inland Asia Minor.[4] That he was a wealthy man is plain from his ability to spend many years travelling around Greece researching his book.[5] The nature of this wealth is unknown. Nor do we know who his friends were or in what circles we should place him.[6] All we have is the *Guide* itself.

Pausanias' preferences in his work are clear. The descriptions that interest him are mainly of cults and of the offerings or works of art in them. Secular buildings and their statues come a poor second. Above all he is interested in Greece's antiquity. He gives a good deal of historical background information for the areas he covered, information which is virtually restricted to the archaic, classical, or Hellenistic periods. In his account of Greece's heritage, history and religion complement each other naturally. Pausanias is very much rooted in the past. He includes hardly any monuments later than the third century BC. In terms of history Philopoemen in the late third and early second century is the last Greek worth mentioning (viii. 52. 1), while the Achaean League, which was destroyed by Rome in 146, is the last political organization of any merit (vii. 17. 2). He says he wrote 'from the beginning with the intention of selecting from the many uninteresting stories people tell about themselves those especially worth mention'. He adds that as he had given this policy proper consideration he

[4] Frazer 1898: i. p. xix; Habicht 1985: 13–15; see esp. v. 13. 7 'signs that Pelops and Tantalus dwelled with us . . . a throne of Pelops on the peak of Mount Sipylus'. On Magnesia, a free city following its resistance to Mithridates' general Archelaus (cf. i. 20. 5), but tributary in AD 17, see Magie 1950: i. 122–3, ii. 1336 n. 19, 1358–9 n. 23; Ihnken 1978.

[5] Habicht 1985: 17 well compares Apuleius' depletion of his inheritance of a million sesterces through travelling, studying, and liberality (*Apology* 23, cf. *Metamorphoses* xi. 28). Pausanias' travels were not restricted to Greece: he went as far as Italy in the west (e.g. v. 12. 6 Rome, v. 12. 3 Campania; perhaps even Sardinia, which is described at length because of the Greeks' 'extreme ignorance of it' at x. 17), the Euphrates in the east (x. 29. 4), and Egypt (e.g. i. 42. 3); see Gurlitt 1890: 87–90; Frazer 1898: i. pp. xx–xxii.

[6] Habicht 1985: 18. Emperors aside, the only identifiable contemporaries are Herodes (Atticus) (i. 19. 6; ii. 1. 7; vi. 21. 2; vii. 20. 6; x. 32. 1), (Sex. Julius Major) Antoninus (Pythodorus) (named at ii. 27. 6 as a benefactor of Epidaurus; Halfmann 1979: no. 89; cf. Aristides, *Or.* xlvii = I. 35), and (Ti. Claudius) [S]aethida (Caelianus) (iv. 32. 2 'Aithidas' is transmitted in the MSS; Halfmann 1979: no. 93a).

will not be departing from it (iii. 11. 1). Similar remarks are made elsewhere.[7]

It is clear that Pausanias' text with its cross-references and stated self-esteem is rather conscious of what it is doing. It asserts that it is a useful work for those who want to know what is most worth knowing about Greece. In this respect the debate over whether Greeks or Romans are the addressees is irrelevant. Anyone who wanted to learn about the Greek heritage, who understood the language and admired the history of the country, was a potential reader. That includes Romans; but it must be said that everything about the work points primarily to a Greek audience, and in particular one from outside old Greece.[8] Pausanias wanted to bring to their attention things that had been forgotten or that were not generally known (i. 6. 1, 17. 1). At the same time he was not interested in telling them what they already knew.[9] In the course of a digression on the colonization of Ionia from the mainland he claims that Ionia has the best climate and 'sanctuaries that cannot be found elsewhere' and that 'its many wonders are scarcely inferior to those in Greece' (vii. 5. 4, 6. 1). Yet it was old Greece and the antiquities of old Greece that attracted him. After a century and more of intensive archaeology in the sites he wrote about it is quite clear that earlier suspicions that he depended on literary sources and had very little original to say were totally unfounded.[10] Rather, he emerges as a faithful recorder of what he saw.

Spiritually and culturally Pausanias was totally Hellenic. Politically we cannot be quite sure. That he does not mention Roman citizenship for himself does not mean he did not possess it (and one passage—viii. 43. 5—suggests he might have had it); there was, after

[7] Cf. esp. i. 39. 3.

[8] Regenbogen 1956: 1013 ('kleinasiatische Griechen'), 1032, 1048, 1093; Bowersock 1985: 710. There is a good discussion of the matter in Habicht 1985: 24–6.

[9] So e.g. Regenbogen 1956: 1089 plausibly explains the very brief treatment of the Parthenon at i. 24. 5–7; the same might be said for much of the history or buildings of Athens that are passed over (including the Pnyx, which Meyer 1954: 564 suggested was omitted owing to Pausanias' antipathy towards democracy); see also Pausanias' excuse for not giving the story of king Pausanias of Sparta at iii. 17. 7, or his comment at viii. 42. 4 on the representation of Demeter at Phigalia: 'why they constructed it thus is plain to any intelligent man who is good on tradition.'

[10] As a further validation of his integrity Habicht's excellent book joins a distinguished tradition (Schubart 1883; Gurlitt 1890; Heberdey 1894; Trendelenburg 1914; Regenbogen 1956; Heer 1979). On the critics (especially Kalkmann, Wilamowitz, and to a lesser extent Robert 1909) see Gurlitt 1890: esp. 107–29; Regenbogen 1956: 1093–5; Habicht 1985: 165–75.

all, no particular reason to have commented on such a matter.[11] But, as with Lucian, we need not doubt where his preferences lie. More than this, although he shares contemporaries' highly favourable views of the Antonine emperors, his acute sense of 'Greece' as a source of identity makes him still resentful of Rome's conquest of Greece in the Republican period as well as of the way it was governed by Rome under the Julio-Claudians and Flavians. In assessing Pausanias' view of Rome and the Empire we must always bear in mind his deep interest in the history of Greece and the causes of its decline, together with his essential lack of interest in the present day. Importantly there are a number of direct passages of political comment on Roman rule from the beginning to his own lifetime and these must be studied in detail.

GREEK HISTORY AND GREEK FREEDOM

It is plain that Pausanias was familiar with Greek history and had read widely in the major historians.[12] Earlier scholars who carped at his mistakes, notably Holleaux,[13] missed the point that the historical information in the *Guide* is not of primary importance and that Pausanias very likely often wrote it from memory, not from research. These historical interests are not confined to free Greece, but cover a wide area of the history of the Greek world before the Roman conquest.[14] The first book contains digressions on the Hellenistic monarchs whose statues Pausanias saw at Athens.[15] Other major digressions are the story of Aratus (ii. 8. 2–9. 5), the very lengthy history of the hostility of Messene and Sparta (iv. 4. 1–29. 13), the rise and fall of the Achaean League and its consequences for Greece (vii. 7. 1–17. 4), the life of Philopoemen and his significance for Greek freedom (viii. 49. 1–52. 6), the Phocians and the Third Sacred War (x. 2. 1–3. 4), and the detailed narrative of the

[11] Similarly, there is no reason to expect comments on Latin language (cf. ii. 4. 5) and literature.
[12] Regenbogen 1956: 1070; Habicht 1985: 97–8.
[13] Holleaux 1895, 1898. On the main errors see Habicht 1985: 98–100, and below, n. 30.
[14] For a summary see Regenbogen 1956: 1063–9.
[15] i. 6. 1–7. 3, 9. 1–4 (Ptolemies); 8. 1 (Attalus); 9. 5–10. 5 (Lysimachus and others); 11. 1–13. 9 (Pyrrhus); 16. 1–3 (Seleucus). Philip and Alexander are 'too important' to form a mere digression (9. 4).

Greeks' resistance to the Gallic invasion of 279 (x. 19. 5–23. 14; cf.
i. 4. 1–6). In general Pausanias judges Greek states by their contributions to the welfare and liberty of Greece. Outside the digressions the decisive actions he wants his audience to know about are
those against Persia in 480 and 479, and especially those against
Macedon at Chaeroneia in 338 and during the Lamian war in 323/2,
and against the Gauls in 279. He carefully notes which states fought
in which.[16]

Of the major digressions in the work the enormously long account of the Messenians' wars with Sparta seems to be occasioned
by an interest in the 'sufferings' of the Messenians (and Spartans),
which are the will of the *daimôn*, the 'divine spirit' familiar from
Plutarch's musings on history (iv. 6. 1, 29. 13).[17] It also allows
Pausanias to give Messenia a book of its own. The story of the
Phocians' desecration of Delphi during the Sacred War was notorious in Greek history, and Pausanias' version stresses the bad end
which overtook the wrongdoers and their repentant behaviour in
helping to fight the Gauls. The other digressions are connected
with the theme of Greek freedom. Aratus, as in Plutarch's *Life*,
resists the Macedonians' interference in Greece but is eventually
forced to seek their help. Pausanias confines himself—unlike the
critical Plutarch—to a vague remark about 'necessity' (ii. 8. 6). The
treatment of the Gauls has been saved for the account of Delphi
'because the greatest actions of the Greeks against the barbarians
took place here' (x. 19. 5). The reason for Pausanias' interest in how
the Greeks were saved from the Gallic threat and how in particular

---

[16] Among the most important references for the Persian war: v. 4. 7 (Elis present);
v. 23. 1–3 (the famous list of the Greeks participating at Plataea copied without
comment); vii. 6. 3–4 (Achaeans absent for reasons of their own security); viii. 6. 1
(Arcadians present); ix. 6. 1–2 (Thebans forced to fight with Xerxes); x. 2. 1 (Phocians
deserted the Persian side and fought with the Greeks). For Macedon and the Gauls:
i. 25. 3–4 (participants in the Lamian war); iv. 28. 2–3 (Messene not at Chaeroneia
owing to its alliance with Macedon, participated in the Lamian war, prevented from
fighting against the Gauls); v. 4. 9 (Elis not at Chaeroneia owing to its alliance with
Macedon, participated in the Lamian war); vii. 6. 5–7 (Achaeans present at Chaeroneia,
not in Lamian war, and like 'the rest of the Peloponnesians' did not march against
the Gauls); viii. 6. 2–3 (Arcadians not at Chaeroneia, nor in the Lamian war, nor
against the Gauls, though they made up for this as members of the Achaean League);
x. 3. 4 (Phocians at Chaeroneia, in the Lamian war, fought most keenly against the
Gauls to 'atone for their old crimes'); x. 20. 1–5 (comparison of participants against
Persia and those fighting against the Gauls); x. 22. 13 (the Greeks who fought the
Gauls at Delphi).

[17] Cf. above, 'Plutarch' n. 51.

Delphi was defended valiantly and with divine assistance (i. 4. 4, x. 22. 12 ff.) is obvious. The accounts of Philopoemen and the Achaean League touch on the threat from Macedon but also on the consequences of Roman involvement in Greece. For his information on Philopoemen it is clear that Pausanias has largely followed Plutarch.[18] Philopoemen's career, including his resistance to Roman policy in Sparta regarding the tyrant Nabis, is narrated dispassionately (viii. 49. 1–51. 8). Two incidents are picked out to show his love of Greek freedom, the first the line from the *Persians* of Timotheus ('Glorious the great crown of freedom he fashioneth for Greece'), which happened to be played as Philopoemen was present at the Nemean Games (viii. 50. 3), the second Philopoemen's remark to the pro-Roman politician Aristaenus that he was 'hastening Greece's fate' by acceding to all Rome's demands.[19] Pausanias' own feelings are expressed in the chapter following the account of Philopoemen's deeds (viii. 52). In Plutarch's *Life* it is the Romans who call Philopoemen 'last of the Greeks' (1. 7). Pausanias seems to have this in mind in appending a list of Greece's benefactors, a breed of which Philopoemen was the 'last'.[20] Amongst those excluded are Aristides ('the Just') 'because he imposed tribute on the island Greeks'.[21] Tribute, as we shall see, is one of the things Pausanias resents about Roman rule. Significant is his appeal here to Athens as the centre of Greek civilization. Those who fought 'against' her in the Peloponnesian War, 'especially the famous among them', could be said to be the 'murderers and very nearly the wreckers of Hellas' (viii. 52. 3).

The narrative of the rise and fall of the Achaean League (vii. 7. 1–17. 4) is far more complex than the biography of Philopoemen. It again includes important reflections on Greece's undoing (vii. 10. 1–5) and ends with a chapter of musings on her decline (vii. 17). Pausanias begins by tracing the rise of the League in the second half of the third century, its bitter struggle with Sparta and its alliance with Antigonus Doson of Macedon against the Spartan king Cleomenes, and then records how the Athenians invited Roman

---

[18] Errington 1968: 238–40.   [19] Cf. Polybius xxiv. 13. 7.
[20] The benefactors are Miltiades, Leonidas, Themistocles, Xanthippus, Leotychides, Cimon, Conon, Epaminondas, Leosthenes, Aratus.
[21] The trial of Aristides for imposing tribute is envisaged and rejected as an implausible scenario in the schools of rhetoric—Hermogenes, *On Staseis* 33. 8 Rabe; *Introduction to the Staseis* vii. 22. 6 Walz; cf. the discussion in Philostratus, *Life of Apollonius* vi. 21.

power into Greece to assist them against Antigonus' expansionist successor Philip V (vii. 7). There are none of Plutarch's criticisms of the Achaeans' decision to prefer Macedonians to the truly Greek Spartans.[22] Pausanias next discusses the conduct of the war against Philip by the Roman generals 'Otilius' and 'Flaminius' (i.e. T. Quinctius Flamininus).[23] Philip is a blackguard in Pausanias' view (vii. 7. 5–6). But he also records criticism of the Roman generals for their 'cruel treatment of cities that were Hellenic and ancient and had done no wrong to the Romans', and further the fears of some of the Achaeans that the Romans were coming merely to take the place of Philip (vii. 8. 2). He next stresses the loyalty of the Achaeans as allies of the Romans against Philip, the Aetolians, and king Antiochus of Syria (vii. 8. 3). Then he narrates the breakdown of good relations between Rome and the Achaeans on the matter of Spartan incorporation into the League (vii. 8. 4–9. 7). In the course of this account he mentions the Romans' instructions to Philip to evacuate his garrisons from Greece (vii. 8. 7). Significantly he includes nothing of Flamininus' celebrated 'liberation' of Greece, which was announced at the Isthmian games of 196.[24] Far from noting Rome's avowed commitment to Greek freedom, Pausanias simply reports that Philip was offered a nominal peace 'at a huge price' (vii. 8. 8).[25] The omission of the liberation is surprising. Like every Greek Pausanias knew of it, of course, and in a later book when speaking of Elatea in Phocis he records that 'Titus [i.e.

---

[22] Cf. above on Aratus, 'Past' n. 58 for Plutarch.

[23] 'Otilius' (vii. 7. 8 'the most important of his names' [i.e. of the *tria nomina*]) is an error (perhaps for [P.] Villius [Tappulus]; Wachsmuth 1887: 276–8; Segré 1928: 232–6 offers the relevant *Quellenforschung*); Pausanias or his source is presumably thinking rather (see below in text) of the activities of Sulpicius Galba with king Attalus and the Aetolians in Greece in 208–207 (cf. Livy xxvii. 21. 10, xxviii. 5. 5 on Achaean worries); at vii. 17. 5 Pausanias reports that Sulpicius ('this man too being a Roman commander') sacked Dyme because Philip had made it subject to him.
The error of 'Flaminius' for Flamininus is also noteworthy (Cassius Dio's excerptors/epitomizers share it; cf. Plutarch, *Flamininus* 18. 3 *corr.* Reiske, 1. 1 where it is an alternative; further Cassius Dio's 'Titus' for Titinius Sisenna at Books xxx–xxxv fr. 100); outside Book vii Flamininus is called once 'Flaminius' (viii. 11. 11) and twice 'Titus' (viii. 51. 1, x. 34. 4), the name preferred by Polybius and Plutarch.

[24] Other accounts stress either Rome's high ideals (Livy xxxiii. 33. 5–8; Polybius xviii. 46. 13–15; cf. Appian, *Macedonian Wars* fr. 9. 4) or, again significantly, the failures of Greece (Plutarch, *Flamininus* 10–11); cf. 'Plutarch' n. 45.

[25] A reference to the penalty imposed on Philip of 1000 talents (Livy xxxiii. 30. 7). Pausanias' tone perhaps reflects the 'grumbling Aetolians', who in Plutarch's version suggest that 'peace had been sold to Philip' (*Flamininus* 9. 6, cf. Livy xxxiii. 31. 1).

Flamininus] was sent from Rome to free the whole Greek nation'.[26] In Book vii the tone of the account of the Achaean League and Pausanias' feelings about the loss of Greece's freedom expressed in ch. 17 precluded it.

Before coming on to the last years of the League Pausanias once more emphasizes the Achaeans' loyalty to Rome against Philip, the Aetolians, and king Antiochus (vii. 9. 7), a pointed reference, given every reader's awareness of their coming fate. It is at this point that Pausanias digresses on the traitors of Greece (vii. 10. 1–5), focusing on those who had betrayed panhellenic interests to the Persians, to the Spartans after the Peloponnesian war, and to Philip II of Macedon and his son Alexander the Great. 'Those who were sick with the disease of treachery never left Greece' (vii. 10. 5). The final traitor is the Achaean politician, Callicrates, who was behind the removal of the 1000 or so Achaeans who were deported to Rome in 167 on suspicion of having aided king Perseus in the Second Macedonian War (vii. 10. 6–12).[27] Pausanias next (vii. 11. 1–3) speaks with disgust of the arrogant behaviour of (C. Sulpicius) Gallus, envoy to Greece and Asia in 164, towards Argos and Sparta ('cities which had reached the peak of renown'),[28] and notes the Senate's brief to break up the League. He then narrates in detail the final actions of the Achaean League before its destruction (vii. 11. 4–16. 10). He concentrates on the folly of the politicians involved, especially Menalcidas, Diaeus, and Critolaus, and the petty squabbling over Sparta which ultimately brought Roman intervention. Critolaus, who began the war against the Romans, suffered from 'audacity combined with weakness', and his defeat is thus a matter of 'madness rather than bad luck' (vii. 14. 6). Diaeus is possessed of 'complete folly' (vii. 15. 8, 16. 1). Pausanias also dwells on the final battle with the Romans under Mummius before Corinth, on Mummius' sack and destruction of the city, the radical change in the constitutions of the Greek cities from democracies to 'magistracies based on a property rating', the imposition of tribute, the total abolition of the Achaean, Phocian, and Boeotian and other Greek

---

[26] x. 34. 4. Palm 1959: 65 makes this the basis of his claim that Pausanias did see the Romans as liberators.

[27] Cf. Livy xlv. 31. 9–11, Polybius xxx. 13. 6–11, 32. 1–12, xxxiii. 1. 3–8, 3. 1–2, 14. 1, xxxv. 6. 1–4. Pausanias explicitly compares the Romans with Philip II and Alexander, who allowed their enemies to 'defend themselves before the Amphictyons'.

[28] Cf. Polybius xxxi. 6. 5 ('deranged in mind').

Leagues, and the dispatch of a governor 'down to my time' (vii. 16. 1–10).

Although there are no other fully surviving accounts of these years, on the basis of what we do have for comparison we can be confident that Pausanias' detailed narrative reflects his own often expressed concern for Greece's freedom and dignity.[29] He is not writing history here. He did not research the story of the League carefully, as the several historical errors show.[30] His opinions were what mattered to him. Thus he rounds off his account at vii. 17 with personal comments on Greece's 'total weakness' after 146. Before the story of the Achaean League he had commented on the powerlessness of Sparta, Thebes, and Athens (vii. 6. 8–9) and then contrasted the isolation of the other Greeks with the successful alliance of the Achaeans (vii. 7. 1).[31] He now presses this home, adding the fate of Argos to that of Athens, Thebes, and Sparta (vii. 17. 1–2).[32] Finally, when the Achaean League 'was painfully growing up from the mutilated and mostly withered tree that was Greece, the cowardice [*kakia*] of its generals cut it short as it grew'. Pausanias next mentions Nero's famous liberation of Greece from tribute in AD 67, an event he marks out by a quotation from Plato (which he uses to suggest that Nero was essentially noble in his soul).[33] He then notes that 'the Greeks were not to gain from this gift', since in Vespasian's reign they 'became embroiled in civil war'. Tribute and governors were reimposed by Vespasian, who remarked that 'the Greek nation had unlearned freedom' (vii. 17. 3–4).

[29] That is, Pausanias clearly drew on Polybius for his history and language, but Polybius' (largely lost) account of the League's final years (an account written 'in pity' according to Strabo viii. 6. 23 [C 381], whose own account is matter of fact) was given by Pausanias a general colouring of pro-Hellenic patriotism (Regenbogen 1956: 1075 ff.; Lafond 1991: 40–2), which owes nothing to a hypothetical pro-Achaean corrector of Polybius (as suggested by Wachsmuth 1887—cf. Segré 1929: 483–8, Ferrary 1988: 202–3—who, however, amply demonstrates the step-by-step, selective, anti-Roman nature of the account).

On the history of the period see in addition to the works cited e.g. Briscoe 1967: esp. 15–19; Larsen 1968: esp. 486–98; Gruen 1976.

[30] On these (notably 'Otilius', and the misdating of the sack of Corinth to 140 at vii. 16. 10) see Wachsmuth 1887; Lafond 1991: 31–3; and below in text.

[31] Cf. Plutarch, *Philopoemen* 8. 3.

[32] We might contrast Arrian's carefully packaged list of Greek disasters at *Anabasis* i. 9, which does not stray from its context, Alexander's destruction of Thebes.

[33] Plato, *Republic* 491e, on great natures being ruined by bad training; another Plutarchan touch (*Demetrius* 1. 7 quoting Plato ibid.; *Flamininus* 12. 13, *On God's Slowness to Punish* 567f–568a on Nero). For Pausanias' admiration for Plato see i. 30. 3. On Nero's liberation cf. above, 'Plutarch' n. 46.

How should we take Pausanias' description of Rome's involvement in Greece in the years after 200? He is clear that Rome's role was one of conqueror, not of liberator. Apart from his silence on Flamininus' 'liberation' this is shown by his remarks on the Roman settlement after the sack of Corinth (vii. 16. 9–10). There is some evidence to back up the claim that Mummius and the Roman commissioners instituted constitutions based on property qualifications.[34] It is also true, as Pausanias notes, that certain of their requirements were later moderated ('the Romans took pity on Greece')—league assemblies were allowed to meet again and various fines were remitted.[35] Pausanias continues by saying 'the Greeks obtained this remission from the Romans, yet a governor was still being sent down to my time'. He was called governor of Achaia 'because they took the Greeks in hand [*echeirôsanto*] through the Achaeans, who were then leading the Greek nation'. We know that there were confiscations of land after the war (Corinth became *ager publicus*), and it is very probable that combatant districts were made tributary; but, though parts of Greece that fought with the Achaean League were officially subject to the will of the governor of Macedonia and no part can be said to have been free of his influence, no special governor was in fact sent to Greece proper until the separate province of Achaia was established (probably) by Augustus in 27 BC.[36] In the meantime 'liberation' seems to have continued to be a part of Rome's official ideology.[37]

Whether Pausanias' comments about the imposition of a governor

[34] Cf. Livy xxxiv. 51. 6 (Thessaly in 194 BC) with Briscoe 1967: 11.

[35] Leagues: Accame 1946: 16–18. At vii. 16. 9 Pausanias generalizes the abolition of the leagues, which apparently restricted to those of the combatants only (some of these were then reconstituted as before or with changes). Ferrary 1988: 186–99 argues from *SIG*³ 684, the letter of Q. Fabius Maximus to Dyme (which he convincingly redates to 144–143 from the earlier accepted dating of 115), that Fabius' remarks about the restoration of the Achaeans' (ancestral) 'constitution' suggest at least a formal restoration of their democracy (this is not mentioned by Pausanias at vii. 16. 10).

[36] Plutarch, *Cimon* 2. 1 explains the holding of a trial before the governor of Macedonia in 87 BC by saying that 'the Romans were not yet sending governors to Greece'. On interference by the governor see Accame 1946: 6–15, Ferrary 1988: 205–9; on tribute (again only applied to combatants rather than to 'Greece' as Pausanias has it) see Accame 18–27, Lafond 1991: 39 n. 29. On the establishment of Provincia Achaia cf. Strabo xvii. 3. 25 (C 840), Cassius Dio liii. 12. 4.

[37] Cf. Appian's Sulla at *Mithridatic War* 58. 237 contrasting 'our' Macedonia with the free Greeks; Gruen 1984: i. 155–6; but Ferrary's redating of *SIG*³ 684 (see n. 35) reduces the impact of one of the clearest expressions of this ideology.

represent ignorance or distortion cannot be known. It can be said, though, that they do represent a consistent picture of Roman intent.[38] If Pausanias got the facts wrong, the version he believed was certainly comfortable to him. He well knew that much of the blame for Roman control of Greece fell upon Greek politicians. Hence he strongly criticizes the Achaean generals for starting a war they could not win. Again, he identifies *stasis* as a reason behind Vespasian's reimposition of tribute and governors after Nero's liberation (vii. 17. 4).[39] In vii. 17 the discussion is of both internal wranglings and external control by Macedon and Rome. The difference, of which Pausanias is fully aware, between Greece's own wars and her struggles with Macedon on the one hand and Roman involvement on the other was that Roman rule, except for the interlude of Nero, meant a permanent loss of independence. He does not add that Greece was nevertheless well treated in his own day, something which is fully acknowledged by him on other occasions.[40] Rather, finishing by saying simply, 'I discovered that things happened like this', he completes his negative overview of the end of the Achaean League and the start of Roman rule by recording the Roman sack of Dyme in 208.[41] Philip had made it subject to him. 'And for this reason Sulpicius, another Roman commander, turned it over to his army to be sacked' (vii. 17. 5).

THE VIEW OF THE GODS

It is interesting that in his account of the origins of Roman rule in Greece Pausanias suggests divine providence played a part. At vii. 15. 6, recording the slaughter of 1000 Arcadian troops by the

---

[38] Pausanias does not share Gruen's view (1976: 69), that Rome did not intend to smash the League.

[39] Cf. *SIG*³ 796B honouring T. Statilius Timocrates for his assistance to the Panachaean League during a period of great difficulty 'after freedom was restored to us'. On the date—which must be c.AD 67/8—see Momigliano 1944: 115–16, cf. Touloumakos 1971: 41 n. 8, Spawforth 1994*b*: 223. See also Philostratus, *Life of Apollonius* v. 41, on Vespasian's allegation of *staseis* (which Philostratus, unlike Pausanias, does not admit).

[40] Contrast Zonaras ix. 31. 8 (and so very probably Cassius Dio) concluding after Polybius xxxviii. 18. 8–9 that the sack of Corinth was a harsh beginning of future bliss ('they said that, if they had not been captured so quickly, they would not have been saved').

[41] Date: Larsen 1968: 374 n. 1.

Romans at Chaeroneia, he notes that the 'justice of the Greek gods' was at work, since the Arcadians were slain at the very spot where they had deserted the Greek cause against Philip II of Macedon in 338. Pausanias' interest in the role of the Greek states during the various crises of Greece's freedom has been noted. The Arcadians' absence from Chaeroneia is mentioned elsewhere (viii. 6. 2, 27. 10). Talk of the 'justice of the Greek gods' may be merely a way of speaking. On the other hand, Pausanias was a firm believer in the power of the divine and certainly countenanced the idea of divine vengeance. Before asking if this involved Rome, we may explore his general attitudes.

He frequently speaks of divine power as 'fortune' and strongly asserts the universal influence of fortune over men.[42] But he also believed in a more focused side of divine might. He is willing to listen to stories that the gods had intervened to help cities.[43] This is a conventional view, to be sure, but conventional belief in the gods of Homer, Hesiod, and Herodotus in broad terms is Pausanias' belief (even if—see below—he also had some deeper conception of divinity).[44] The idea of divine punishment following the infringement of the gods' rights or property is no more dubious to Pausanias than it had been to Plutarch. A particularly striking example is the divine 'wrath' of Persephone and Demeter against the Megarians for having killed an Athenian herald, Anthemocritus, before the Peloponnesian war, i.e. some six hundred years previously. 'This wrath of the goddesses remains today, and they are the only Greeks whom not even king Hadrian could make more prosperous' (i. 36. 3).[45] Other good examples can be found (mythological ones aside) at iii. 12. 7 (the Lacedaemonians, Miltiades), iii. 23. 5 (Mithridates), viii. 7. 5–8 (Philip II and his relations, including Alexander the Great), and ix. 7. 3–4 (Cassander). Those involved with the plundering of Delphi in the Third Sacred War naturally come off badly (iii. 10. 5 Archidamus of Sparta), and the people of Ledon were punished because Philomelus was born there (x. 33. 2). The city of Helice was destroyed when 'some suppliants' were forcibly removed

---

[42] iv. 30. 5, viii. 33. 1–4; Heer 1979: 307–14.
[43] e.g. x. 23. 2, 30. 9, 32. 4 against the Gauls.
[44] Heer 1979: 127 ff. analysing each god/cult; Habicht 1985: 151–9.
[45] Cf. iii. 4. 6 where they suffer similarly for having cultivated sacred land. On Hadrian as a benefactor and second founder at Megara see *IG* vii. 70–4; cf. Halfmann 1986: 191 (his visit in 125); its lack of prosperity must be partly due to its proximity to Corinth, cf. Alcock 1993: 160.

from its temple of Poseidon, and other examples, says Pausanias, may be quoted to show the power of the God of Suppliants (vii. 24. 6–25. 4),[46] while the Spartan king Pausanias was refused assistance as a suppliant by the Goddess of the Bronze House because of a murder (iii. 17. 7–9).

None of this is to suggest that Pausanias believed wholesale all the stories that were told in connection with the gods, especially mythological ones. Indeed, in some cases he does not believe or will only partially accept such stories,[47] and complains that a 'foundation of truth'—for example, that Niobe was turned into a stone—has often been obscured by an edifice of lies, such as that 'Niobe on Sipylus sheds tears in the summer' (viii. 2. 6–7). In this passage Pausanias says that the gods are nowadays further removed from men and that divine wrath now 'comes late when sinners have departed'.[48] In another well-known passage in Book viii he says that when he first wrote he had inclined to the view that the mythological stories were rather foolish—in other words, he did not believe them[49]— but that he has now come to see that they are symbolic and represent a form of 'Greek wisdom' (viii. 8. 3).[50] In another comment on religion, the famous conversation with 'the man from Sidon' about the nature of Asclepius and Health, he again focuses on the symbolic meaning of the gods rather than on their anthropomorphic natures (vii. 23. 7–8).[51] This approach explains why

[46] Pausanias hurries over the details of the well-known story of Helice (cf. Diodorus Siculus xv. 48–9, also invoking Poseidon's wrath; Strabo viii. 7. 2 [C 384–5]; Prandi 1989).

[47] e.g. i. 41. 4–6; ii. 17. 4; iii. 15. 11; vi. 3. 8, 8. 2; ix. 16. 7; see Veyne 1988: 95–102.

[48] viii. 2. 5; cf. Plutarch, *On God's Slowness to Punish*.

[49] Cf. e.g. i. 38. 7.

[50] This injures Elsner's interesting presentation of Pausanias as a religious pilgrim (a basic definition of which must surely be someone who believes in full before going): Pausanias always believed in the divine, but there were many things about the shrines he visited that he did not believe and which he only later came to regard symbolically. It is difficult to say whether this change of attitude to myth really entailed a personal crisis, as Elsner seems to suggest in likening it to a *'rite de passage'* (1992: 21)—there is no reason to think Pausanias' belief in god changed rather than his reading of what allowed one to see god. Note also that the 'pilgrimage' was not in Pausanias' *'native land'*, an important part of Elsner's argument (ibid. 7, 9). Nor is Frazer's supposition warranted of a 'mental revolution' from a youthful (and better) scepticism (1898: i, p. lviii), a view which may be compared with the alleged 'conversions' of Dio and Lucian to philosophy ('Dio' nn. 4–14, 'Lucian' n. 61); cf. Heer 1979: 252–3.

[51] See Heer 1979: 250–4, Habicht 1985: 156–9, both diagnosing the influence of Stoic thought.

Pausanias feels able to continue using 'traditions' in matters 'pertaining to the divine' (viii. 8. 3). These stories were vitally important to him, and the *Guide to Greece* is built round them and the historical and geographical contexts to which they belong.

There is, however, no special place for Rome in the divine scheme. Plutarch (as we have seen) seems uniquely to have explained Rome's rise to power, including her control of Greece, as an act of divine providence which had lent special support to the Roman principate because of its benefits to the world.[52] But though Pausanias follows Plutarch closely on several occasions, there is no trace of this particular idea in the *Guide*. When Pausanias talks of providence's involvement in the fate of the Arcadian soldiers he stresses that it was the 'justice of the Greek gods' at work: the Roman forces were simply used to punish some of Greece's own traitors. The divine was in some conventional way responsible for Greece's decline (vii. 17. 1 'parts of Greece had been blighted and destroyed by the *daimôn* from the beginning'), but it was not working specifically through Rome. A not dissimilar example is Apollo's wrath against Mithridates for the impiety of one of his commanders and his consequent suicide 'when his empire had been destroyed and he was being pursued on all sides by the Romans' (iii. 23. 5). Romans themselves were liable to similar punishment from the gods. The gods caused the death of the general Sulla from the same disease 'as Pherecydes the Syrian' (i.e. being eaten by lice), because he had seized the Athenian leader Aristion from the temple of Athena, where he was a suppliant (i. 20. 7). Whether this is wishful thinking or whether Pausanias believed it is unclear; in either case it is an important part of his reading of Sulla's treatment of Greece. In the same passage he says that Sulla's horrible end was not in his opinion caused by his treatment of the Athenians, which was 'more savage than one would expect of a Roman';[53] the implication is that some might think it had been. Sulla is subject to divine chastisement elsewhere. At ix. 33. 5, having already noted his art thefts from the shrines of Boeotia and other places (ix. 7. 5–6, 30. 1),[54] Pausanias suddenly reintroduces him when he comes to the village of Alalcomenae: 'Sulla's uncivilized behaviour towards the Athenians

[52] 'Plutarch' esp. nn. 69–73.
[53] This is not a way of saying all other Romans behaved well, as Robert 1909: 32 seems to suggest.
[54] Cf. x. 21. 6. For ix. 7. 5–6 cf. Appian, *Mithridatic War* 54. 217.

was foreign to the Roman character, though in keeping with what he did to the people of Thebes and Orchomenus. He added to it in Alalcomenae by stealing the image of Athena herself. For his madness against the Greek cities and gods of the Greeks the most disgusting of all diseases attacked him' (ix. 33. 6). Here Sulla's actions against men as well as against gods are impugned. Pausanias' outrage over the theft of this Athena, which happened more than two centuries before he wrote, is due to the fact that the 'shrine was afterwards neglected inasmuch as it had been abandoned by the goddess'.

Two points may be made about these passages. First, there is (again) historical distortion or ignorance. According to other writers Aristion was not dragged out of the temple of Athena, but was starved out.[55] Whether this is ignorance or not, it is clear that Pausanias wishes to stress not only Sullan savagery,[56] but also—and this is most important to him—Sullan desecration. Second, Plutarch may be compared. His references to Sulla's removal of treasures from Epidaurus and Olympia and demands for money from the Delphic Amphictyons are the basis of very strong comments (ascribed to the Amphictyons) concerning the greed and rapaciousness of the late Republican generals (*Sulla* 12. 9–14). Pausanias' hostility to Sulla may well build on this, though it is primarily a like verdict reached from a like point of view.

Thefts from temples by Romans are in fact attacked regularly by Pausanias. Nero's thefts are remembered by him particularly.[57] Delphi suffered from his 'universal contempt [i.e. for the gods]' (x. 7. 1). Both he and Gaius had taken the image of Love from Thespiae, though Claudius had returned it. 'One of these sinners against the god made a soldier to whom he always gave the same suggestive, mocking password so angry that the man killed him as he was giving the password,[58] while in the case of Nero there are in

[55] Cf. Strabo ix. 1. 20 (C 398); Plutarch *Sulla* 14. 11; Appian, *Mithridatic War* 39. 151.

[56] Cf. his comments (ascribed to the Achaeans) about the brutality of 'Otilius' and Flamininus.

[57] Apart from Sulla see v. 25. 8, 26. 3 (Nero); vi. 9. 3; vii. 16. 8 (Mummius), 22. 5, 22. 9; viii. 46. 1–4 (Augustus); ix. 27. 3–4 (Gaius, Nero); x. 7. 1, 19. 2 (Nero). On Nero and his henchmen cf. Dio of Prusa, *Or.* xxxi. 147–9, Tacitus, *Annals* xv. 45. 3–4, xvi. 23. 1.

[58] Pausanias does not have to say that the password was sexual (Suetonius *Caligula* 56. 2, Cassius Dio lix. 29. 2).

addition to his treatment of his mother his unloving and accursed crimes against his wedded wives' (ix. 27. 3–4). Augustus is mentioned too, but neutrally. 'He was only following ancient precedent sanctioned by Greeks and barbarians', says Pausanias, 'in taking these things from the conquered' (viii. 46. 1, 4). Other religious intrusions naturally attract Pausanias' attention. He notes without obvious comment the erection of statues of the emperors in ancient shrines.[59] His comments on Mummius' dedications at the temple of Zeus at Olympia are instructive. His bronze Zeus from the spoils of the Achaean war is the first dedication in a Greek sanctuary by a Roman in a private or senatorial capacity (v. 24. 4). Here Pausanias may be mistaken, for we know of earlier dedications, beginning with those of Flamininus and Scipio Africanus in the 190s.[60] Mummius' dedication of twenty-one gilded shields on the outside of the temple shows Pausanias' prejudices. He has just recorded a dedication made by the Lacedaemonians and their allies after the battle of Tanagra in 457. As is usual, there is no comment on the futility of inter-Greek warfare (cf. here i. 29. 9). Mummius' shields came from 'his conquest of the Achaeans in war and from his capture of Corinth, when he drove out the Dorian Corinthians' (v. 10. 5). This comment accords with the tone of the narrative of the Roman–Achaean war in Book vii.[61]

The imperial cult also attracted Pausanias' attention. He notes temples of Octavia at Corinth and at Sicyon 'a precinct for the Roman emperors that was once the house of the tyrant Cleon' (ii. 3. 1, 8. 1).[62] His silence on its temples elsewhere has been noted.[63] More significant in this respect are his weary comments at viii. 2. 4–5 on the fact that the gods now keep away from mankind. So close were men to them in the past, he affirms, that some men became gods. Today there is too much vice for that to happen and

[59] e.g. i. 40. 2 (where the stress on the 'ancient shrine' perhaps reflects badly on recent statues); v. 12. 6–7, 20. 9; x. 8. 6.
[60] Guarducci 1937 (54–7 on Mummius); Gruen 1984: i. 167–72; Habicht 1985: 100. Pausanias might have remembered his Plutarch for some of these (*Flamininus* 12. 11–12, *Sulla* 12. 10). It has been suggested recently that he is specifying that Mummius was the first to dedicate a divine statue, in which case he may be right: Tzifopoulos 1993: 94–8.
[61] It also accords with a comment on Sulla's dedication of a Dionysus on Helicon, which he had taken from Minyan Orchomenus: 'this is an illustration of the Greek saying about "worshipping the gods with other people's incense"' (ix. 30. 1).
[62] The latter perhaps betraying irony: Elsner 1992: 19–20.
[63] Gurlitt 1890: 254 (Athens).

'no one any longer becomes a god from a man, except in the flattering words addressed to authority [*to huperechon*]'. This conventional remark is not directed against anyone in particular (Hellenistic
monarchs come to mind), and the context is not connected with
Rome. But it does refer to the present and must at least be seen
as relevant to Pausanias' feelings about the deification of the
emperors.[64]

Finally, there is the Amphictyonic League. In the context of the
Amphictyons Delphi is the assembly-point of Greece (x. 3. 3, 8. 1).
The history of the Amphictyony has four main stages (x. 8. 1–5).[65]
The original composition down to the Third Social War was rep-
resentative of pretty well all the Greeks.[66] After the war there was
a 'change' and 'the Macedonians found a way of belonging to the
Amphictyons'. The Phocians who had been the cause of the war
were expelled along with their allies, the Lacedaemonians. The
Phocians recovered their membership for their sterling aid against
the Gallic invasion of 279. 'King Augustus then willed that the
Nicopolitans . . . should also belong to the council'. The votes and
members were redistributed accordingly. The fourth stage is the
situation in Pausanias' own day. Pausanias lists the current division
of thirty Amphictyons. At first sight there is nothing overtly patriotic in this account. A little later in the Book Pausanias, as we have
seen, inserts a lengthy account of the Gallic invasion of Greece
because the Greeks' resistance against the barbarians at Delphi was
so praiseworthy.[67] Delphi (as one would assume) is of great historical and religious significance to him. It is certainly a focal point of
what he understands by 'Greece'.[68] The Amphictyonic League links
Delphi with the rest of Greece. In Pausanias' account the original
formation is an ideal which he is happy enough to ascribe to
Amphictyon, one of the mythical kings of Athens.[69] The second

[64] Gurlitt 1890: 33; Regenbogen 1956: 1089; Habicht 1985: 152 'acid criticism'. Cf.
above, 'Plutarch' n. 146: the actual practice of the cult for living emperors is a
different matter and we know nothing of Pausanias' views of it.
[65] See Daux 1975: 352–62, id. 1976: 63–71.
[66] x. 8. 2 'the following races . . . Ionians, Dolopians, Thessalians, Aenianians,
Magnesians, Malians, Phthiotians, Dorians, Phocians, Locrians who border Phocis'.
[67] x. 19. 5 ff.   [68] Bearzot 1988: 108–11.
[69] Pausanias also notes the rationalizing etymology proposed by Androtion (*FGrH*
324 F58; Strabo ix. 3. 7 [C 420]), which derived the word from elements meaning
'those who live around [the shrine]'.

stage was marked by the intrusion of the Macedonians. Pausanias' disapproval, which could anyway be inferred, is quite explicit. In the third stage Augustus deprived peoples represented in the original foundation of their votes and gave them to Nicopolis. As we shall see shortly, Pausanias strongly resented Augustus' establishment of this city because it involved depriving other cities of their populations. He does not comment on the removal of the votes, but it seems unlikely that he could have approved. The present-day structure of the League reflected further alterations by the emperors, probably by Hadrian.[70] The League continued to be heavily biased towards northern Greece. Pausanias does not say what he thought of this arrangement; but, again, it seems unlikely that he approved, for example, of the lack of representation accorded to the areas of Greece to which he devoted the *Guide*.[71]

CAESAR, AUGUSTUS, AND THE ANTONINES

Population changes caused by the Roman 'kings' particularly evoke Pausanias' indignation. Let us take Corinth first. At the start of Book ii he tells us that 'Corinth is inhabited by none of the ancient Corinthians, but by colonists sent by the Romans'. Pausanias briefly explains the final events of the Achaean war and records that the refoundation is said to be by Caesar 'who was first to establish the government in Rome that exists in our times', meaning Julius Caesar, who easily passes for an emperor in his eyes (ii. 1. 2, cf. 3. 1, iii. 11. 4, v. 1. 2). The incomers are the latest immigrants into the Peloponnese (v. 1. 2), and Pausanias later distinguishes carefully between them and the former inhabitants (v. 25. 1), who are marked out as 'Dorian' (v. 10. 5, i.e. as true Greeks). These few comments are difficult to evaluate in themselves; but it is legitimate again to bear in mind Pausanias' pro-Greek narrative of the war between Rome and the Achaean League and, generally, the enormous concentration in the *Guide* on the Peloponnese.[72] Further, in contrast to Favorinus and Aristides, who both stress the Greekness of second-

---

[70] Daux 1976: 71–7.   [71] So rightly Bearzot 1988: 109.
[72] Cf. the almost proud statement of completion at viii. 54. 7; Chamoux 1974: 85.

century Corinth, the keenness of Pausanias' memory of what had happened must be significant.[73]

He has more to say on Patrae and Nicopolis. Patrae, one of the key cities of Roman Achaia, was refounded by Augustus (vii. 18. 7).[74] Pausanias is not impressed by this,[75] perhaps because it involved the destruction of Rhypes ('he razed it to the ground'), one of the twelve ancient cities of Achaea (cf. vii. 6. 1) whose ruins he later notes in passing (vii. 23. 4).[76] He also notes that Artemis Laphria, whose peculiar cult at Patrae he describes in detail, had a 'foreign name', and that the image of the goddess in fact came from Calydon in Aetolia (vii. 18. 8, 9–13).[77] Pausanias' language becomes rather emotive. He asserts that Augustus' foundation of Nicopolis involved 'turning Calydon and the rest of Aetolia into a desert' and that the image of Artemis Laphria was given to the Patraeans 'from the spoils of Calydon'. This is plainly hostile, and there is only a little exaggeration. Nicopolis certainly took population from Acarnania, and western Aetolia suffered from the foundation too.[78] Later Pausanias repeats his allegation that the Aetolians 'had been driven out' (*anastatous . . . epoiêsen*) to make Nicopolis, adding that most of them went to Locrian Amphissa instead (x. 38. 4), a plausible consequence of the synoecism for eastern Aetolia.[79]

It is perfectly clear that Pausanias did not like what had happened in the past because of Roman imperialism and felt the need

[73] Favorinus, *Corinthian Oration* (= Ps.-Dio of Prusa, *Or.* xxxvii), Aristides, *Or.* xlvi. With Pausanias' feelings may be compared Ps.-Julian, *Letters* 198 Bidez—if this text does belong to the 1st or 2nd rather than to the 4th c. AD (cf. now Spawforth 1994b)—where the speaker complains that the Corinthians prefer the customs they have 'recently' adopted from 'the royal city' and its colony to the ways of their 'fathers' and 'ancient Greece' (409c–d). Note that Pausanias does also allude to the prosperity (*akmê*) of the Roman city (which had been using Greek for official purposes from the time of Hadrian: Kent 1966: 18–19) at ii. 2. 6.
[74] Bowersock 1965c: 92–3; Alcock 1993: 133 ff. on the disruption caused by both new colonies.
[75] 'Either thinking it was good for the coastal voyage [to Italy—recalling Thucydides i. 36. 2; cf. Strabo viii. 7. 5 (C 387)] or for some other reason'.
[76] Its desolation is not connected with Augustus in Strabo viii. 7. 5 (C 387). Note also vii. 17. 5 on Dyme's subordination to Patrae (on this passage see also n. 23).
[77] On the cult see Piccaluga 1981.
[78] The evidence of Pausanias and others (Strabo x. 2. 2 [C 450], vii. 7. 6 [C 325]; *Greek Anthology* ix. 553) is discussed by Kahrstedt 1950. The territory of Calydon seems to have been given to Patrae: Strabo x. 2. 21 (C 460).
[79] Kahrstedt 1950: 554. Pausanias would not have had much sympathy with Purcell's suggestion that the combination of Greek population and Roman administration at Nicopolis reflects the 'koine of the second century' (1987: 90).

to say so every so often. But as with our other authors the Antonine emperors are in a quite different category and receive much praise. Trajan's buildings at Rome attract very favourable comments (v. 12. 6). Hadrian is frequently mentioned and especially lauded. 'King Hadrian took very great care to honour the gods and contributed very much to the happiness of each of his subjects' (i. 5. 5, cf. 3. 2). Athens particularly benefited.[80] Pausanias' favour towards the emperor is for reasons such as his respect for the Greek gods (i. 5. 5, ii. 17. 6, viii. 10. 2, x. 35. 4), for restoring the ancient name of Mantineia (viii. 8. 12),[81] for his practical aid (i. 42. 5, ii. 3. 5, viii. 22. 3), and for honouring Epaminondas with an epigram (viii. 11. 8–9).[82] He also praises him for never having started a war (i. 5. 5), an important blessing given what Pausanias says a little later about Sulla's behaviour being 'more savage than one would expect of a Roman' (i. 20. 7). In such esteem does the periegete hold Hadrian that he comments in some detail on the cult of his favourite, Antinous, at Mantineia (viii. 9. 7–8, 10. 1). Earlier in Book viii Pausanias had spoken out against the deification of his contemporaries. Here in a different train of thought he suppresses his own objections, stating without reserve that 'they consider him a god' (9.7).[83]

Lavish praise is bestowed on Hadrian's successor Antoninus Pius in connection with the city of Pallantium in Arcadia. Pausanias reports the 'story' of Evander and other Arcadians from Pallantium who went to Italy and founded a colony on the Tiber called Pallantium, which in the course of time was changed to Palatium (i.e. the Palatine hill in Rome).[84] This was why Pius bestowed on Arcadian Pallantium freedom and immunity (viii. 43. 1–2).[85] Pius, like Hadrian, is then praised for never having gone to war willingly.

---

[80] i. 3. 2, 18. 6, 18. 9, 20. 7 (where Athens' prosperity under Hadrian is contrasted with its troubles under Sulla). Pausanias mentions Hadrian's honour of having a tribe named after him (i. 5. 5; 'Past' n. 21).

[81] Cf. Habicht 1984: 51.

[82] In Pausanias' view 'everyone should praise Epaminondas . . . or at least rank him second to none'.

[83] On the cult see Robert 1980: 132–46.

[84] Cf. Dionysius of Halicarnassus i. 31. 4. On Pausanias' real view of Rome's origins see below, nn. 93–4. Note that he here knows the spelling of Latin Palatium ('by omission of the letters l and n').

[85] Presumably in connection with the 900th anniversary celebrations of Rome's origins: Hüttl 1933–6: i. 173–4. Cf. viii. 27. 7: of the cities depopulated to found Megalopolis 'only Pallantium was destined to meet a kindlier fate' (probably—but in the case of Pausanias not necessarily—a conventional way of speaking).

As with Hadrian, the wars he undertook were against barbarians (viii. 43. 3–4, cf. i. 5. 5).[86] Pausanias also mentions gifts of money to Greek and other cities (including compensation for the disastrous earthquake of *c.*142) as well as building works. And he singles out for special praise an administrative reform which allowed 'Roman citizens among his subjects' who had married non-citizens and thus had peregrine children to make their children their heirs rather than having to 'leave their money to non-relatives or increase the wealth of the king'.[87] 'This king the Romans called Pious, because he showed himself particularly reverent to religion. In my opinion he might easily bear the name of Cyrus the Elder, who was called Father of Men'.[88] Finally, Pausanias mentions 'the second Antoninus' (i.e. Marcus) and his wars against the German barbarians and the Sarmatians, wars which were again forced on him (viii. 43. 6).

Perhaps the most interesting part of Pausanias' comments on the Antonines is his praise of this defensive strategy in the Empire and of their prosecution of wars of defence against barbarians. Here Pausanias might seem to display a 'them and us' mentality, as Lucian does in the context of Rome's Parthian war. That is, in political terms those inside the Empire (including the Greeks) are defended by the Romans against the barbarians beyond the gate. However, more careful analysis reveals a more traditional reading of the world. Pausanias like other second sophistic authors habitually divides mankind into 'Hellenes' or 'barbarians'.[89] The non-Greek population of the Empire is 'barbarian'.[90] Further, when he speaks of Pius' liberalizing reform of the inheritance laws for Roman citizens married to peregrines (a passage that just might indicate that he himself was a Roman citizen), though he seems at first to be interested in the position of provincial Roman citizens empire-wide ('citizen subjects'), he makes it plain that he is thinking only of how Roman government affects Greeks, since the peregrine children of this group 'belong to the Greek nation' (viii. 43. 5).[91] Pausanias' 'them and us',

[86] Note the imaginary British war between the Brigantes and the people of "Genounia" (viii. 43. 4), perhaps a misunderstood story about Brigantii and Genauni in Rhaetia: Hind 1977.
[87] Hüttl 1933–6: i. 110–12.
[88] Herodotus iii. 89. 3; cf. Pausanias viii. 51. 7, of Philopoemen by the Messenean *dêmos*.
[89] Cf. i. 16. 2, 21. 5; v. 22. 2; viii. 25. 13; ix. 40. 7; *et al.*
[90] So i. 5. 5, viii. 43. 4.
[91] Note the concept of Greeks (*to Hellênikon*) as a descent group; whether this is always in Pausanias' mind cannot be known.

then, is the traditional division of Hellenes versus the rest. Others like Dionysius of Halicarnassus, Plutarch, and Aristides got round the problem of what to do with Romans by (sometimes) classifying them as a separate group. This was made easier for Dionysius by taking over the idea of Rome's 'Greek' origin from Evander's Arcadians and other groups.[92] Pausanias also knew of this account, as we have seen, and may have accepted it; yet it is the Trojan origin of Rome under Aeneas that is in his mind in several passages of the *Guide*. He explains his comment that Pyrrhus was the first Greek to meet the Romans in war by saying that 'no further battle is said to have taken place between Aeneas and Diomedes and his Argives' (i. 11. 7).[93] In other words Aeneas stands here as a proto-Roman. At ii. 23. 5 Pausanias criticizes the Argives for alleging that the Palladium (the sacred image of Athena) was brought there from Troy: 'it is clear that the Palladium, as it is called, was brought to Italy by Aeneas'.[94] Pausanias knew (of course) of the usual Greek version of the legend, which held that the image was stolen from Troy by Odysseus and/or Diomedes.[95] He prefers the Roman account by which the image came to be lodged in the temple of Vesta in the Forum.[96] Dionysius' enthusiasm for the Greek provenance of all things Roman even led him to make the Trojans into Greek colonists (*History of Early Rome* i. 61. 1–62. 2). But Pausanias thought of the Trojans as *barbaroi*, as he makes plain at v. 22. 2, specifying amongst others Aeneas (again in relation to his Greek adversary Diomedes). This should not be taken as signifying that he believed in any way that the Romans themselves were now barbarians. The best one can do is to surmise that Pausanias also put them in a different category, neither Greek nor barbarian, as when, for example, he says that Augustus' art thefts were only what would be expected of any conqueror, Greek or barbarian (viii. 46. 4).[97] If this is a muddled view from a Greek perspective, it is a common one

[92] Above, 'Plutarch' n. 23, 'Aristides' n. 93, 'Language' n. 22.
[93] Other, that is, than their abortive engagement in *Iliad* v. Note in this passage Pausanias' great admiration for Pyrrhus' style of confronting Rome, even though he was 'no match' for them (i. 12. 2–3).
[94] For Aeneas and his men in Italy and the West see iii. 22. 11, viii. 12. 8, x. 17. 6.
[95] i. 22. 6; Apollodorus, *Library* epitome v. 13.
[96] Reported also in Dionysius of Halicarnassus i. 69. 4, ii. 66. 5; see Austin 1964: 83–5.
[97] Augustus ὑπό τε Ἑλλήνων νομιζόμενα καὶ βαρβάρων εἰργάσατο· Ῥωμαίοις δὲ τῆς Ἀθηνᾶς τὸ ἄγαλμα τῆς Ἀλέας ἐς τὴν ἀγορὰν ... ἐστὶν ἰόντι.

among the Greeks of the time and was perhaps the only way of dealing with the phenomenon of Rome.

'BY MISCHANCE OF ROMAN RULE'

To ask generally whether Pausanias welcomed Roman rule is perhaps too direct a question to be answered from the text he has left us. Clearly, he did not like Rome's subjugation of Greece in the Republic. His memory of those events is not innocent academic research; rather, as we have seen, his narrative of the final events of Greek freedom is certainly pro-Achaean. The imposition of tribute he liked neither in the Republican nor in the imperial period. Nor do the Julio-Claudians fare well. Against the bad side of Rome must be set Pausanias' high praise of the Antonine dynasty. It is difficult to know whether this can be translated by us into praise of the whole imperial system or whether we should see it more in terms of his praise of good kings like Seleucus Nicator or the Ptolemies or Attalus Soter.[98] In the case of Attalus it is worth noting that he is lauded particularly for fighting non-Greeks, Philip V of Macedon and especially the barbarian Gauls settled in Asia, an important element in Pausanias' estimation of the Antonine kings. If this is right, we may compare Dio's and Lucian's preference for the emperor-figure as the good part of the Empire. However, since Pausanias shared with Aristides and many others a familiar disparagement of the mass,[99] we may imagine that he found Rome's political bolstering of the elite congenial. And yet he had devoted his life to *ta Hellênika*. He knew this was to be a real labour of love. Right at the beginning he feels the need to hurry on from a digression on Greece's battle for freedom 'to continue describing all the things of the Greeks' (i. 26. 4).[100] His historical/topographical consciousness is totally Greek. However good the Antonine emperors were Pausanias had not forgotten that Rome was an imperial power

[98] Seleucus: i. 16. 3 ('particularly just and particularly religious'). Ptolemies: i. 9. 3–4. Attalus against Philip: i. 36. 5; vii. 8. 9, 16. 1, 16. 8; against the Gauls: i. 4. 5–6, 8. 1, 25. 2; x. 15. 2–3.
[99] Anti-democratic remarks: i. 8. 2–3 (Demosthenes' fate shows that no one who has trusted a democracy has 'ever had a happy end'); i. 29. 7 (faint praise of Athenian democracy); iv. 35. 5 (fate of Epirus without kings; Athens was the only prosperous democracy); cf. i. 3. 3 on the ignorance of 'the many'.
[100] Which is primarily a cultural conception of *ta Hellênika*—Bearzot 1988—but hardly unpolitical for that.

in his cultural home. He is certainly critical on various occasions of the leaders of the Greek cities.[101] Internal wranglings are certainly accorded blame for Greece's decline.[102] These criticisms are of Greece by a Greek. Pausanias' attacks on Rome are by a Greek against non-Greeks, which is—as we have seen with others—surely a different matter. In sum I find it hard to believe that Pausanias is not antipathetic to Roman rule in Greece, though we certainly cannot speak of a general hostility.

If this is right, we would probably do well, finally, to retain the reading of the manuscripts in the famous remark at viii. 27. 1 that 'Megalopolis is the youngest not only of the cities in Arcadia but of [all] those in Greece, with the exception of those whose inhabitants have been immigrants by mischance of Roman rule [*kata sumphoran archês tês Rômaiôn*]'.[103] Several commentators have suggested reading *kata sumphoran <epi> archês tês Rômaiôn*, 'by mischance <during> Roman rule', and have wanted Pausanias to refer to natural disasters that had occurred during (*epi*) the period of Roman control rather than disparaging Roman control in itself.[104] This is perfectly possible. On the other hand it is not possible to point to examples of natural disasters during this period recorded in the *Guide*.[105] When Pausanias says that Megalopolis was the

---

[101] Especially in the section on the traitors of Greece at vii. 10. 1–5; cf. Habicht 1985: 110. It is particularly noticeable how the leaders of the Peloponnesian War, amongst the most celebrated for later generations, are largely ignored by Pausanias and are conspicuously absent from the benefactors of Greece in viii. 52.

[102] See esp. vii. 14. 6 (the madness of the Achaean leaders in 146); viii. 52. 3 (the 'wreckers' of Greece in the Peloponnesian War). In contrast to Plutarch, Dio, Aristides, and Galen, there is nothing on rivalries in Pausanias' own time and no discussion of *homonoia*; this is not surprising given the *Guide*'s scope and aim.

[103] ἡ δὲ Μεγάλη πόλις νεωτάτη πόλεών ἐστιν οὐ τῶν Ἀρκαδικῶν μόνον ἀλλὰ καὶ τῶν ἐν Ἕλλησι, πλὴν ὅσων κατὰ συμφορὰν ἀρχῆς τῆς Ῥωμαίων μεταβεβήκασιν οἰκήτορες.

[104] See esp. Palm 1959: 72–4 following the suggestion of Clavier 1814–21: iv. 406; the emendation is accepted by the new Teubner editor, Rocha-Pereira ad loc. ii. 277, and by Habicht 1985: 119–20 ('earthquake or flood'); interestingly Adamantios Korais told Clavier to retract the additional *epi*, and he did (1814–21: iv, p. v). Palm (whose Pausanias, as I have noted, is rather pro-Roman) argued that the phrase *kata sumphoran* must be purely adverbial (as it is at vii. 25. 5 cited below n. 109); if this objection to the MSS reading is felt to be a real one (and Palm notes Pausanias' irregularity with the article, comparing ix. 12. 1 εἰκασμένον κύκλῳ τῆς σελήνης—cf. further on omission of the article with demonstratives Strid 1976: 86–7), it would be as easy to insert the article before (or perhaps after) συμφοράν as it is to insert ἐπί before ἀρχή.

[105] Palm 1959: 74 counters by observing, 'Naturkatastrophen waren nicht ungewöhnlich; Beispiele sind wohl unnötig.' But we might well expect mention of disasters involving destruction as serious as that envisaged (cf. the extensive comments on the inundation of Helice in 373 BC at vii. 24. 5–13).

'youngest' foundation he refers of course to its formation in the
360s through a synoecism of surrounding Arcadian communities,
some of which were forced to join. He goes into this process in
detail (viii. 27. 1–8).[106] At the end of his section on Megalopolis he
appends, as he sometimes does, some personal, generalizing thoughts
(viii. 33. 1–34. 1). The city, he says, had been founded with high
hopes, but was now mostly in ruins. This was due to the power of
to daimonion, 'the heavenly spirit', and of fortune. In these reflections Pausanias speaks particularly of the rise and fall of great city
powers like Mycenae and Babylon. Natural phenomena are exemplified briefly by the disappearance of islands, which show the power
of fortune to be even stronger than it is 'on the scale of mischances
and successes of cities'.[107] Pausanias' account of Megalopolis' rise and
his ruminations on its decline are not, then, about natural disasters,
but concern human affairs (even if he characteristically thinks that
the divine has played a hand in these). In the context of the new
foundation of Megalopolis the comment about changes of population under Rome at the beginning of this section refers, of course,
to similar new foundations after that of Megalopolis.[108] These new
foundations are Corinth and Nicopolis. The 'modern Corinthians
are the youngest of the Peloponnesians' (v. 1. 2). Nicopolis is clearly
younger still. That the new foundations under Rome were 'by
mischance of Roman rule' is explained by the hostility Pausanias
bears towards Rome for the destruction of old Corinth and the importation of a non-Dorian population, and for the brutal synoecism
by which (in his account) Augustus formed Nicopolis.[109]

[106] Cf. also vi. 12. 8, ix. 14. 4.

[107] viii. 33. 4 *kata sumphoras kai eupragias poleôn*.

[108] Habicht 1985: 119–20 strangely implies that Pausanias is speaking of cities
emptied of their populations.

[109] Cf. Hitzig and Blümner 1896–1910: iii. 206 quoting the interpretation of
Schubart. Augustus' refoundation of Patrae is also relevant here.

The sort of political change Pausanias has in mind occurred at Ceryneia in Achaea,
where the population was bolstered by 'Mycenaean settlers [*sunoikoi*] who came
here from the Argolid *kata sumphoran*', following an Argive siege (vii. 25. 5–6).
This is parallel to the case of Nicopolis, where the mischance is that of the Greek
immigrant population; in the case of Corinth the mischance is more from Pausanias'
own external viewpoint.

Note also Marcotte's suggestion (1988: 78) that *kata sumphoran* at viii. 27. 1
should be changed to *kata sumphoron* = 'pour servir l'intérêt de Rome'; apart from
the linguistic oddity, this transfers the phrase to a Roman perspective (for Pausanias
does not consider what has happened to be in his or Greece's interest), and Korais
would no doubt have asked Marcotte to change it back.

Pausanias' remark about the Romans at viii. 27. 1 should be care-fully contextualized. This properly limits its range to certain events, which is desirable because there is not enough evidence in the *Guide* as a whole to speak from this one passage of a general hostility.[110] But there is a feeling of antipathy to or aversion from Roman rule, a feeling with which viii. 27. 1 is not out of step. That said, the rulers of Rome as Pausanias wrote were civilized and philhellene in his eyes. It is important to note in this regard that he recognized, of course, that Romans were after all rather similar to the Greeks. It must have been of significance to him especially that they hon-oured the same gods.[111] In other ways too he could think syncritically of Rome and Greece.[112] But, like Plutarch, it seems that he does not like to see the exercise of Roman power in Greece. Benefactions by Romans are probably viewed on the level of the individual donor rather than as products of a system. Some comments Pausanias makes suggest, finally, that he did not think the system itself would last forever. Certainly, one aspect of his rather resigned approach to the power of fortune/fate in this world is that no earthly power could endure. This 'fatalism' is compatible with the famous Stoicizing conversation with the Sidonian visitor at vii. 23. 7–8.[113] So Pausanias comments on the present prosperity of Antioch and Alexandria at viii. 33. 3, implying that these great city states will not last, but will some day be brought down by fortune as others have been. A typically low-key comment earlier in the same book suggests he saw Roman influence in the same way. In Mantineia behind the theatre 'were abandoned as ruins the temple and image of Aphrodite who is called the "Ally" . . . The Mantineans made this sanctuary as a reminder for posterity that they fought with Rome at the battle

[110] As do Schubart 1883: 481–2, Gurlitt 1890: 87 n. 43, and Regenbogen 1956: 1069.
[111] A point stressed by Dio of Prusa, *Or.* lxxii. 5 (and reflecting the very common idea of the Greeks that foreigners' gods were identifiable with their own and vice versa); given this, Elsner's notion (1992: 29) that Pausanias sought refuge in a 'sacred world of initiation . . . not available to outsiders [i.e. Romans]', referring particularly to his favoured Eleusinian mysteries (cf. i. 37. 4, 38. 7; v. 10. 1; Heer 1979: 313; Elsner: 21), is somewhat undone by the emperors' sustained interest in the running of the rites and by their own initiations there (Millar 1992: 449–50; Spawforth and Walker 1985: 102–3; Mylonas 1961: 8 *et al.* on Hadrian, Pius, and Marcus; Kienast 1959–60).
[112] Cf. ii. 27. 5 on Roman and Greek theatres (Epidaurus comes out on top, but Roman ones are not inferior).
[113] Above, n. 51.

of Actium' (viii. 9. 6). Pausanias does not comment here; the juxtaposition of ruins and the idea of 'Roma aeterna' (which must have been known to him) is eloquent enough. The idea that Rome might not last would surely have appealed to our author, if only as a dream, for his love of the freedom of Greece should be recognized as another proof of his integrity as a hierophant of all things Greek.

II

Galen

The next major figure, the physician, medical writer, and philosopher Galen, is one of the most accomplished intellectuals of the second century, a man of standing in his own time and hugely influential afterwards.[1] Galen was born in Pergamum in 129 into the heart of second sophistic society. His father practised geometry and architecture among other learned subjects, and from an early age Galen was immersed through his care in a philosophical, literary, and scientific education of the highest quality.[2] Galen's numerous surviving writings—which are by no means restricted to medicine—show a man obsessed with two things: education and the furtherance of knowledge on the one hand, on the other his own attainments and talent. Since Galen lived at Rome for well over thirty years in the latter part of the second century and developed many contacts with the elite of the capital, including successive emperors from Marcus to Severus, he offers a particularly good opportunity for further discovering Greek attitudes to the Roman Empire.

GALEN IN ROME I

Galen was already a well respected doctor by 157 when he returned to Pergamum after a period of several years study in Alexandria,

---

[1] Galen's works are cited by volume and page of Kühn's edition (1821–33; repr. 1965), unless otherwise specified; the traditional Latin title will be given at the first occurrence. A concordance with modern editions of individual works can be found in Nutton 1981: 263–4, Hankinson 1991: 238–47, López-Férez 1991: 309–29.

[2] On his life see Nutton 1972, and esp. id. 1973. Galen's Roman name is unknown ('Claudius' is an early modern fiction); Kudlien 1986: 84–6 suggests he remained a peregrinus, but this seems implausible. Architecture, etc.: v. 42. 5–6, vi. 755. 11–12; that Galen's father Nico (*Suda* γ 32) was the learned Pergamene architect Aelius Nico (*PIR*[2] G 24; Bowersock 1969: 60) or his colleague Julius Nicodemus 'also called Nico' (cf. Nutton 1979: 183) is a likely assumption.

the desirable location for a proper medical training.[3] On his return his reputation was sufficient to secure appointment as doctor to the gladiatorial team of the Pergamene *archiereus*, the high priest who presided over the imperial cult and its games in the city (xiii. 599–600; xviiib. 567).[4] Galen says he got the job because it was noticed that he worked harder than other physicians.[5] During the next four years (from autumn 157 to autumn 161) he served five high priests. It was at this point that he went to Rome, where he arrived by September of 162. We do not know what took him there. Whether there were particular circumstances such as the rivalry of fellow-doctors at Pergamum (which has been suggested) is unclear. His journey looks more like a career move, the logical next step for someone of ambition and drive. Much of our information about Galen's earlier career at Rome, and particularly how he achieved fame and success in the city so quickly, comes from the short work called *On Precognition* (*De Praecognitione*), which was written about 178.[6] Far from being a technical medical work concerned with the prediction and progress of disease (*prognosis*)—a cornerstone of Hippocratic medicine—*On Precognition* is a history of the cases which brought Galen his immediate extraordinary success in the capital.[7] In many of these Galen's treatment did depend on his ability to determine how the patient would respond to various remedies, an ability which was used well at the expense of rivals. But the medical aspects of *prognosis* are of little importance compared with the power that prediction and cure could bring with them. Good writing was an important ingredient in this advertisement

[3] On Galen's later ambiguity towards this period of his life see Nutton 1993.

[4] Galen is silent on the cult itself.

[5] *How to Recognize the Best Doctor* (*De optimo medico cognoscendo*) in Iskandar 1988: 103. 10–105. 2; Galen alleges that none of his gladiatorial patients died bar two: 105. 14–19, cf. *On the Composition of Drugs by Types* (*De compositione medicamentorum per genera*) xiii. 600.

[6] See the useful edition and translation of Nutton 1979 (on whose text I rely). Date: Nutton ibid. 49–51 refines the discussions of Bardong 1942: 609–10 and Ilberg 1892: 493.

[7] The lecture *How to Recognize the Best Doctor* (Iskandar 1988) offers many parallels, though without the stress on social recognition that is to the fore in *On Precognition*; see Nutton 1990 for discussion. On the doubts expressed by Scarborough 1981 about the possibility of accepting Galen's information in this and other works without independent confirmation (he is, e.g., our only source for the consular Flavius Boethus, below n. 9; but note 'Lucian' n. 107) see Nutton 1984; Scarborough's main fear that Galen's fame is a creation of Galen himself (cf. also Kudlien 1986: 87–8) is largely unjustified.

of Galen's talents. Thus *On Precognition* is well stocked with the rhetorical devices that characterize second sophistic literature. On any account it is one of the most exciting texts written in the period.

The work opens with one of Galen's favourite topics, the decline of education, the disregard of philosophy, the prevalent laziness, and today's preference for fame and power, which sees dancers honoured with statues while hard work is despised (xiv. 599–605). These introductory remarks set the scene for Galen's first medical triumph at Rome, the cure of Eudemus. The Peripatetic philosopher Eudemus was an important contact in the city. He had been a friend of Galen's father and it is plausibly suggested that he had taught philosophy to Galen himself at Pergamum.[8] He was now in his sixty-third year and was suffering from a quartan fever (i.e. malaria). This cure is in effect the story of how Galen established his credentials, worsted his rivals, and made known his talents not only to the chief men of Rome but also eventually to the emperors Marcus and Lucius. It is narrated with the greatest pleasure (605 ff.). We are told that Eudemus was prepared to trust Galen because of the acquaintance with his father and because he knew that his father had been guided by dreams to have his son properly educated in both medicine and philosophy (608). It quickly emerges that Eudemus is not simply a familial or Pergamene friend, for the patient is visited by two members of the Senate, Sergius Paullus and Flavius Boethus. Both of these men were of eastern origin.[9] Boethus, from Phoenician Ptolemais, was 'devoted to the philosophy of Aristotle' (612), which would have endeared him immediately to Galen, himself a devotee of Aristotelian logic. Paullus was 'likewise' devoted to Aristotle. He came probably from Antiocheia ad Pisidiam, a Roman colony which by this time was no doubt Hellenized to a significant degree.[10]

---

[8] Nutton 1979: 157.

[9] L. Sergius Paullus: *cos. I* 151 (?), *procos.* of Asia (?) *c.*166/7, *praef. urbi c.*168, *cos. II (ord.)* 168. See Halfmann 1979: no. 77, Alföldy 1977: 161; and Mitchell 1993: ii. 6–7 on the meeting of his proconsular ancestor with St Paul. He is presumably not 'Paulus the rhetor' mentioned along with Eudemus at xv. 565, but may be the Paulus of Ps.-Galen *De venae sectione* xix. 525–7 (Scarborough 1981: 27 n. 133).

Flavius Boethus: *cos. c.*160–4, governor of Syria Palestina *c.*166–8; Halfmann 1979: no. 95; Alföldy 1977: 195. Galen dedicated a number of (mostly lost) works to him: *RE* vi (1909) 2535 (Kappelmacher).

[10] An eastern origin is suggested by Halfmann on the basis of the plausible stemma on p. 106; see also id. 1982: 645. On the gradual Hellenization of Roman colonies in the East see Levick 1967: 130–62 (Antiocheia ad Pisidiam and others).

Galen's first breakthrough was achieved with the prediction of
Eudemus' 'coming paroxysm'. The philosopher was so amazed at
the accuracy of the forecast that he spoke of Galen to all his friends,
who were the best educated and most socially eminent men in Rome.
Apart from Boethus and Paullus, who requested from Galen instruction and displays of his knowledge of anatomy, two more of
these friends are singled out for mention. These are Barbarus
and Severus, i.e. M. Vettulenus Civica Barbarus *cos. ord.* 157, uncle
of Lucius Verus (as Galen notes) and (probably) benefactor of
Pergamum, and Cn. Claudius Severus *cos.* 167 (?), *cos.* II *ord.* 173,
descendant of the former royal house of Galatia and son-in-law
of Marcus Aurelius.[11] Like Boethus and Paullus, Severus was 'devoted to the philosophy of Aristotle' (613. 5). Galen's success with
Eudemus led to the downfall of two prominent rivals, Antigenes
and Martianus. 'This was the start of the envy against me, marvelled
at as I was for the nobility of my life and for my exploits in the art'
(614. 7–9).[12] Galen was now perceived, he tells us, as a 'universal
blessing' in the city (619. 12). At this point he inserts a complaint
to Eudemus about the *kakonoia*, 'ill-will', of leading doctors against
him. There follows an important passage for his own view of Rome.
Into Eudemus' mouth is put a highly rhetorical denunciation of life
there, which is contrasted with a rosy picture of how things are
back home (620. 16–624. 10).[13]

'I told him how amazed I was by the ill-will of the leading doctors in the city of the Romans.[14] He said my experience was quite
understandable. He compared them with those in our country and

---

[11] Barbarus: Alföldy 1977: 328; *IGR* iv. 494 with Halfmann 1979: 209 (Ameling
1983: ii. 181 is against identification with the Pergamene benefactor).

Severus: Halfmann 1979: no. 101; Bowersock 1969: 83–4, 125–6; either he or
perhaps rather his father, Cn. Claudius Severus Arabianus (*cos. ord.* 146), talked
philosophy with Marcus (*Augustan History, Marcus* 3. 3; Marcus, *To Himself* i. 14),
introducing him to 'Thrasea, Helvidius, Cato, Dio, and Brutus' (where Dio is perhaps Dio Chrysostom rather than Plato's friend Dio of Syracuse—cf. Lucian,
Peregrinus 18, where Peregrinus likens himself as a philosophic martyr to Musonius,
Dio, and Epictetus, and Fronto, *On Eloquence* i. 4 [135 v.d.Hout²], offering Marcus
Dio as a philosopher-cum-rhetor). Both Severus and Barbarus were friends with
Herodes Atticus (Ameling 1983: ii, nos. 187, 188), who once apologized to Galen for
a poor rhetorical performance, as Galen records in *How to Recognize the Best
Doctor* (Iskandar 1988: 113. 15–115. 1).

[12] There was no reconciliation: 'Antigenes practically disappeared under the earth
because of the slanders he rashly uttered against me' (614. 16–18).

[13] The following translation is intentionally literal.

[14] Cf. *Über die medizinischen Namen*, Meyerhof–Schacht 1931: 21. 7.

said there were many causes for their excessive spite, going through all of them more or less in turn. "Do not think good men become bad [*ponêrous*] in this city; rather, those who start bad find a supply of business here to make profits far greater than they can in the cities outside [Italy]. They see that many like themselves have become rich and they copy their behaviour in its various forms, and from many causes they become totally bad. I shall tell you about some of them, having had many years' experience. The badness of those who are bad by nature does not grow from nature alone, nor is it even increased by the supply of profitable business; they learn from following the ways of wickedness [*panourgia*] that they see those like them practising on a daily basis, then they spend their time copying them. And if they are caught by someone practising their wickedness, they have only to move to some folk who know them not, whom they can attack in greater safety because of the first attempt at the evil behaviour [*prattontes kakôs*] which led to their being recognized, and this has no little influence in the fact that they never do stop practising wickedness. Those who live in small cities, not being tempted by the size of the gains, as they are here, and knowing that they are easily identified by their fellow-citizens, if they step out of line, refrain from exercising their theoretical plans. Here the fact that those who practise wickedness in any place are not known to all increases their natural evil. They can attack those who are unaware because they do not know them, particularly since their victims, because of the simplicity of their spirits, will not bite back in the way they bite each other, if they do anything wrong. Those who are conspiring against us here are acting in the same way as the bandits at home [literally 'with us'] who assist each other in their crimes against others and spare themselves, with the difference that the bandits carry out their evil-doing in the mountains, not in the city."'

'"But you have heard my plan often enough already," I said, "that when the faction [*stasis*] in my fatherland has stopped, you will immediately see me leaving this city, and I intend to make my stay here last only a little longer in order to escape more quickly from the wickedness of these nasty men." "But they do not know of your decision," said Eudemus. "And if they do know, just as they lie, so they will all think you are lying like them. And just as they cannot remain in their fatherlands because of their needy and uneducated background and because they are known for the wicked behaviour I have told you of, but come to this city, so they suppose that others who have come here will not want to quit before they have amassed money. And if they hear from the citizens of your family and property, and that you are not one of the needy, they will say that you have arranged everything to deceive the ears of your hearers. Whatever they do, they believe about all." This is what Eudemus said and more like it, and he suggested that if they were not able to harm me through wickedness, they would turn to plotting through drugs. Indeed, he told me the story of a young man who had come to the city about ten years before and was killed by drugs, along with the two servants who accompanied him, because he displayed his preparation in the art through deeds like mine. "I must thank you, dearest teacher", I said, "for telling me all about their badness. I shall keep myself safe, and having run in with them and having detected their ignorance, I shall leave this great and populous city for one that is small and thinly populated where we all know the families each of us come from, the education we have received, and the property and attitudes and way of life we have. Being concerned with this I have decided not to argue against their ignorance and badness." '

This harangue, in which Galen pays careful attention to rhetorical effects such as antithesis, balanced clauses, and the repetition of key words, is designed to bring out the hostility he faced at Rome and to magnify his achievement in overcoming it. It draws on traditional comparisons between sophistication and vice and the simple life (though the contrast is not, as is usual, that between town and country), and on a whole history of moralizing about wicked and vicious natures. But it also has specific reference to conditions in Rome. It makes it clear, that while many men come to live in Rome, Galen is different. He is from a rich and well-established family and, crucially, is not in Rome to make money. It is reasonable to read into Eudemus' remarks a denunciation of more than just rival doctors. Bad men in general are attracted to Rome for its opportunities of vice and greed. With reference to doctors in particular he says they can get away with what they do because at Rome no one knows his neighbour and there is consequently no control over anti-social behaviour. In *How to Recognize the Best Doctor* Galen again condemns Rome as a city where greed is rife and as a place where patients can die almost unnoticed and where the bad doctor who treats them will escape reproach.[15] Loneliness, isolation, false friendship, and lack of affection or family ties are not among the many vices attributed to the Hellenistic cities like Alexandria or Tarsus in Dio of Prusa's orations criticizing their habits (*Orr.* xxxii–xxxiv). And, though decline in friendship is part of the standard fare of moralists both Greek and Roman, there is evidence to suggest that it is Rome especially which is viewed as the unfriendly city where nobody knows anyone else. This is the Rome of Lucian's *Nigrinus* (e.g. 17 'feigned friendships') and of Soranus of Ephesus, who was there under Trajan (*Gynaecology* ii. 44. 1–2).[16] It is the Rome of Fronto and Marcus Aurelius too, who regret that the Greek virtue of 'affection' (*storgê*) is so rare among the Roman nobilty.[17] But, though Lucian's *Nigrinus* contrasts the hurly-burly of Rome with the peace and *paideia* of Athens (12 ff.), there is nothing quite like Galen's personal contrast between Roman isolation and the ties of family, culture, and wealth that he suggests are typical of Pergamum. This viewpoint is explicitly that of the local eastern elite.[18]

ROMAN PERSPECTIVES

It is perhaps a good idea to stop at this point and look at Galen's views of Rome before going on to further specific matters raised by

[15] Iskandar 1988: 47. 6–9 'this is because the city is great and populous: its inhabitants are very eager for, and occupied in, the pursuit of money and prestige.'

[16] [Injury to infants learning to walk] 'can be seen to happen more at Rome, because as some suppose the city has downpours of cold rain which easily lead to the [infants'] bodies being chilled, or as others say because women have continuous intercourse or have sex after drinking, but in truth it is because of their inexperience in child rearing. For the women in the city lack sufficient affection (*storgê*), as can be seen particularly by the contrasting behaviour of purely Greek women. Since, then, no one is watching the movements of the infants, the limbs of most of them become twisted.'

[17] Fronto, *Ad Ver. imp.* i. 6. 7 (111 v.d.H.²), *Ad Amic.* i. 3. 4 (173 v.d.H.²); Marcus, *To Himself* i. 11 (from Fronto on the 'eupatrids', cf. Fronto to Marcus in *De fer. Als.* 4. 2 [234 v.d.H.²]); Marcus alludes to the quality a number of times in *To Himself*.

[18] At *On the Diagnosis and Treatment of the Passions of the Soul* (*De propriorum animi cuiuslibet affectuum dignotione et curatione*) v. 49. 14–17 Galen estimated Pergamum's total population as some 40,000 male citizens (120,000 including wives and slaves), suggesting a total of ?180,000; but both in this passage and in *On Precognition* his eye is on a very much smaller and exclusive number.

On Precognition. His rather negative generalizations about the city here are a corollary of the topos that Rome is the city of the world, the place where all the different races mix and mingle, the common homeland of all mankind. This Roman idea is expressed or alluded to by a number of Greek writers of the second sophistic, and memorably by the great sophist Antonius Polemo, who described Rome as 'the epitome of the world'.[19] The negative side of this is that everyone in Rome is a foreigner and that the city lacks social integrity. Not that Galen is always negative about Rome's populousness. Polemo's *mot*, used without attribution by Athenaeus, is ascribed to him by Galen in the course of a discussion of the types of dislocations he had seen during his career (*On Dislocations Not Observed by Hippocrates* [*De humero iis modis prolapso quos Hippocrates non vidit*] xviiia. 347. 15 ff.). He says he was bound to have seen more at Rome and Ostia because of the sheer numbers of people. Previously he had seen only one of a particular type as a student at Smyrna, even though Smyrna was now bigger than it had been in Hippocrates' day; whereas one of Rome's quarters (an *amphodos*) has more inhabitants than all the cities in which Hippocrates spent his time. This cosmopolitan aspect of the capital, its potential for medical enquiry and for medical supplies appealed greatly to Galen.[20] Nor did he confine himself in this respect to the

---

[19] Cf. Plutarch, *On the Fortune of the Romans* 325e; Dio of Prusa, *Or.* lxxii *On Dress* 3; Aristides, *Or.* xxvi *To Rome* 61 (cf. 100–1); Athenaeus, *Sophists at Dinner* 3c, 20bc; Modestinus at *Digest* xxvii. 1. 6. 11. On the Roman idea see Christ 1938: esp. 81–3; on Modestinus and the Roman jurists Nutton 1971: 56–61; and for this and related ideas in Latin and Greek authors around the beginning of the 3rd c. see Unruh 1989: especially 97 ff.

[20] See esp. *On Antidotes* (*De antidotis*) xiv. 9 ff. (all manner of things are brought to Rome from all parts of the empire at all times; cf. Aristides, *Or.* xxvi. 11), 25. 1 ff. ('in Rome one has a better chance of being supplied with all the best drugs . . . such as Falernian wine, Hymettian honey, and 'Syrian' opobalsamum'), though not everything was available there (*On the Composition of Drugs by Types* xiii. 638. 10–11); cf. further *On the Power of Purgative Drugs* (*De purgantium medicamentorum facultate*) xi. 328. 9–12 (plentiful cases). In *On the Parts of the Medical Art* (*De partibus artis medicativae*) Galen notes that Rome is the only city big enough to support all the rival sects of doctors (*CMG* Suppl. Orient. II, p. 29. 21–4). In some passages the supply of *materia medica* at Rome is ascribed to the *truphê*, 'luxury', of Roman women (*On the Method of Healing* [*De methodo medendi*] x. 574. 6; *On the Composition of Drugs by Places* [*De compositione medicamentorum secundum locos*] xii. 512. 1–2), whose cosmetics Galen was required to write about (*On the Composition of Drugs by Places* xii. 435 ff.; see below); though this criticism is perhaps directed at rich women rather than rich Roman women (cf. *On the Method of Healing* x. 942. 10–13); cf. Lucian's remarks at *On Hirelings* 36.

city—he acquainted himself with *materia medica* in many parts of Italy (*On Antidotes* xiv. 30. 12), and Italian wines are often mentioned in the preparation of drugs.[21] He was, however, careful to keep in mind his total readership and to make sure that he did not appear to be preferencing Italians.[22]

These remarks on Rome as a source of supplies and observations are purely practical.[23] There is no warm admiration for Roman achievements such as we might expect from a man who stresses how closely the Roman elite took him to heart. Only in two passages does Galen mention Rome's material successes as distinct from her ability to command supplies. In his *Fourth Commentary on Book Six of Hippocrates' Epidemics* (*In Hippocratis librum vi epidemiarum commentarius iv*) xviib. 159. 2 ff. he praises Rome's water supplies: 'In Rome there is, among the many other advantages the city enjoys, an excellence and plentifulness in its sources (none of which contains any foul, poisonous, muddy, or hard water) such as we do not have even at home in Pergamum; while in many other cities the water is awful.' Again, this praise is practical rather than approbatory, for Galen goes on to say that the water brought from the 'Tiburtine mountains through stone channels' is, however, fine in other respects, hard and no good for cooking.[24] As for the water in the river Tiber, he remarks in another work that it is like any river running through a big city and ruins fish which are elsewhere good to eat (*On the Powers of Foods* vi. 722–3).

Another passage, *On the Method of Healing* x. 633. 1 ff., looks more promising when it is excerpted (as it sometimes is): 'almost all

[21] Especially in *On Antidotes*, *On the Powers of Foods* (*De alimentorum facultatibus*), *On the Composition of Drugs by Places*; cf. *On Distinguishing Pulses* (*De dignoscendis pulsibus*) viii. 774. 14–15 'I had never tasted the good Falernian wine before I came to Rome, but when I first encountered it I did not fail to recognize it from the signs I had read of'; it is on Italian wines that Galen makes one of the two speeches attributed to him in Athenaeus' *Sophists at Dinner* (26c–27d); cf. Robert 1980: 319 ff.

[22] *On Antidotes* xiv. 26. 8–9 'I am not writing only for those with access to royal abundance for such supplies'; similarly *On the Method of Healing* x. 363. 5 on the famous *Kurort* of Stabiae in Campania: 'I certainly must not treat only those in Italy, but as far as I can people everywhere.'

[23] Cf. similarly the comments at *On Antidotes* xiv. 7. 12 ff. on the opportunity he had of extracting minerals from the imperial mines on Cyprus owing to the acquaintance his 'very powerful friend there' had with the procurator.

[24] Strabo v. 3. 7–8 (C 235) is far more positive. On the praise of Pergamum's own water supplies cf. Aristides, *Or.* liii, with Jones 1991 (with reference to the researches of G. Garbrecht).

the roads in Italy faced these problems before the great Trajan repaired them, paving wet and muddy parts or carrying them on high causeways, cutting through scrub and heathland and throwing bridges over uncrossable rivers; where the road was unreasonably long, here he cut another short one, and where it was difficult due to the height of a hill, he diverted it through easier terrain; if the route was exposed to wild animals or isolated, he departed from it and joined with main highways, improving those which were rough.' The passage is certainly praise of Trajan and indirectly of Rome's government. But it would be a mistake to compare it, say, with Plutarch's celebration of G. Gracchus' road building programme (*Gracchi* 28),[25] for Galen uses Trajan's efforts as an elaborate, Platonic metaphor to praise his *own* progress in medicine since Hippocrates: 'all in all I can say that the whole road of healing has been cut by me, a project which, however, needed care to bring it to completion. Compare real roads on the ground—we see that some of the old ones have got muddy patches, are full of stones or bushes, are painfully steep or dangerous to go down, are full of wild animals, impassable because of the size of rivers, long, or rough. Almost all the roads in Italy faced these problems before the great Trajan repaired them . . .' It was this comparison which led the medical historian Daniel Le Clerc to exclaim, 'il se vante à tout coup dans ses écrits'.[26] *On the Method of Healing* was written in two stages.[27] At the beginning of Book vii (x. 456–8) Galen tells his friend and pupil Eugenianus (to whom he also sent *On the Order of his Own Books* [*De ordine librorum suorum*]) that he is resuming a project he had abandoned many years before owing to the death of the first addressee, Hieron, and his own antipathy towards fame. He has merely been interested in philosophy and Truth, which fame among 'the many' can only impede. 'For this reason I have never even written my own name on my own books, and I requested you, as you know, not to praise me in society too immoderately, as you tend to, nor to put my name on my writings.' It was in this conceited frame of mind that Galen in his old age likened his achievements to Trajan's road-building.

Galen's writings show that he believed he was the only man who had successfully combined medicine with philosophy and the only

[25] Or to Strabo's praise at v. 3. 8 (C 235), 3. 9 (C 236–7).
[26] Le Clerc 1723: 668–9, with Temkin: 1973: 58.
[27] Nutton 1991: 1–3 (Books vii–xiv composed in the 'late 190s').

one who had attained an unchallengeable intellectual superiority.[28]
This self-advertisement partly reflects the operating conditions faced
by all ancient medical practitioners, who worked in a world without professional controls or recognized standards. But Galen goes
beyond the norm. He felt that he had done mankind a service
through his discoveries and that he had brought us closer to understanding the workings of the great Demiurge, Nature.[29] The last
book of *On the Use of the Parts* (*De usu partium*) is a ringing
affirmation of his worth, which he says he has added to Books
1–16 as an 'epode' (iv. 346–66). This whole treatise, Galen asserts
here, is a work of initiation into which the philosopher must be
initiated, and gives a far clearer insight into the divine than the
mysteries of Eleusis and Samothrace (iv. 360–1, cf. iii. 576. 3 ff.).
On Precognition is in itself written with similar feelings in mind.
Given this, it is perhaps not surprising that Galen found no time to
praise Rome, but it is still noticeable that he lived there for so long
and did not. There is nothing on the peace which many other Greeks
welcomed (whether or not they ascribe it to Rome) or on the other
benefits which could have been attributed to Roman rule. Indeed,
in a highly interesting and well-known comment on the Antonine
economy at the start of *On Wholesome and Unwholesome Foods*
(*De rebus boni malique suci*) Galen talks about the 'continuous
famines' that have been occurring 'among many of the peoples
(*ethnê*) subject to the Romans' (vi. 749 ff.).[30] The urban populations
took all the wheat and even most of the leguminous produce. Hence
the country people had to go as far as boiling green grass, 'which
before they had never tasted even to try' (vi. 750. 9–10). A number
of passages in *On the Powers of Foods* speak of the poor diet of
the peasants and the removal of wheat and other foodstuffs to the
cities (esp. vi. 518. 1 ff., 523. 1 'food for pack animals not men') as

[28] See esp. *Protreptic to Medicine* (*Adhortatio ad artes addiscendas*), *That the Best Doctor is also a Philosopher* (*Quod optimus medicus sit quoque philosophus*), *On the Method of Healing* Books 1–2 (on which see Hankinson 1991; Barnes 1991); note too the lost *On Slander* 'in which there is also the story of his life' at *On his Own Books* xix. 46. 7.
[29] Walzer 1949 is of some use for Galen's religious belief; see also Kudlien 1981 on his 'personal faith' in Asclepius.
[30] This is Galen's normal phrase for the Empire (cf. e.g. *On the Composition of Drugs by Places* xii. 569. 17). NB *ethnê* does not necessarily mean 'provinces', as is sometimes assumed (cf. Sherwin-White 1973: 437–43 on the implications of the term for imperial unity): see Desideri 1978: 354–5 n. 53 with reference to Dio of Prusa; note also Deininger 1965: 137–9 on *ethnos* as a synonym for *koinon*.

normal.[31] But it is only in *On Wholesome and Unwholesome Foods*
that Galen speaks of a decline. Rome is not, of course, to blame for
this state of affairs. But the negative tone is interesting all the same.

Galen naturally had close relationships with individual prominent Romans (apart from the emperors). There is the consular C.
Aufidius Victorinus, the son-in-law of Fronto and general and friend
of Marcus, who hailed from Umbria. In one of his commentaries
on Hippocrates' *On Regimen in Acute Diseases* Galen mentions
him as *Biktôr* the prefect of Rome to whom a doctor had given false
information on Hippocratic regimen (xv. 723. 1).[32] The name should
perhaps be emended, for this is undoubtedly the same Victorinus
who is the addressee of a work surviving only in Arabic, the *On
Regimen in Acute Diseases According to Hippocrates* (*De diaeta in
morbis acutis secundum Hippocraten*). Galen's tone in the introduction is, however, somewhat testy. 'My brave Victorinus' had been
pestering the great doctor for some time to write for him something
on Hippocrates' treatment of acute diseases. Galen had told him
that personal conversation and instruction would be better and that
he had no wish to write concisely on a subject demanding a full
length commentary. He was now, however, giving in to pressure.[33]

A relationship of a different kind concerns the Piso who is the
addressee of *On Theriac to Piso* (*De theriaca ad Pisonem*), a work
often suspected of being inauthentic mainly because of Galen's flattery of Piso and the imperial family. There is, however, no good
reason to doubt that Galen wrote it.[34] Piso may be the consul
ordinarius of 175, L. Calpurnius Piso.[35] He is warmly commended

---

[31] See Mitchell 1993: i. 167–70 for a good account of Galen's descriptions of
peasant diet; Garnsey 1988 also makes good use of Galen on these matters.

[32] *Cos.* 155, *cos. II ord.* 183; *PIR²* A 1393; Champlin 1980: 27–8; cf. Pflaum 1966:
41–8 (but see Alföldy 1977: 361 ff.). One wonders whether Victorinus as *praefectus
urbi* was not the 'Herrscher' who arranged for the flogging of the charlatan doctor
whom Galen reported for taking advantage of his fame (Meyerhof 1929: 83 from a
fragment preserved in Arabic).

[33] *CMG* Suppl. Orient. II, 77. 3–79. 3; 'brave' presumably represents an original
κράτιστε (cf. xix. 8. 4) or ἄριστε (cf. xiv. 210. 4).

[34] See Appendix D.

[35] As suggested by von Premerstein 1898: 266; cf. *PIR²* C 295; this assumes he
survived into old age and that the son injured in the Troy Game in 204 (cf. below)
was a late one; if it is not this Piso, then another must be sought who was heavily
involved in public life (cf. xiv. 210. 9, 294. 4)—why not Claudius Piso, commander
of the 1st Adjutrix in Pannonia in 207 (*CIL* iii. 11082), whose grandfather is very
likely to be the eminent man from Prusias ad Hypium attested at *IGR* iii. 63
(Halfmann 1982: 638)?

in the introduction of the work and in the final remarks (xiv. 210–14, 294) for his education, reading, knowledge of medicine, his special affection for one of his sons, and for this son's philosophical endurance in an emergency operation made necessary by an accident during the equestrian spectacle of the Troy Game, an operation in which Piso himself was able to assist.[36] The passage which follows this is one of the most interesting for Galen's relations with Roman power. For he goes on to describe how the drug *thêriakê*, originally a sort of antidote, had taken on mythical health giving qualities among the Roman elite and had spread from them to all sections of society (214–19).[37] Marcus Aurelius had started the craze by using the drug every day as if it were a food.[38] 'Under the present greatest emperors' (Severus and Caracalla) everybody was using it.[39]

Galen continues as follows. 'We too can have good use of everything they have and can have this treatment freely ... since their superiority over men comes not only from the fact that they hold their royal power by divine right, but also from the pleasure they get in sharing all their goods with all men, just as the gods themselves do. The joy they feel is equivalent to the feelings of those who are saved because of them, and they think the greatest part of kingship is the common weal, which is something I have wondered at all the more in their case.[40] They not only take trouble about this

[36] The reference to the Troy Game puts the work after 204, the date of Septimius Severus' Saecular Games: Birley 1988: 159; cf. Fuchs 1990: 61–3 on the son's role in the performance.
[37] On theriac see Winkler's 1980 study of Galen's *On Antidotes*; Watson 1966 (a reasonable general account). Aristides also used theriac (though not as the doctors wished): *Or.* xlviii. 64, xlix. 27–8 (*pharmakon thêreion*).
[38] Cf. *On Antidotes* xiv. 3. 9–10; *On Precognition* xiv. 658. 6; *On the Affected Parts* (*De locis affectis*) viii. 355. 5 ff. (an imperial slave charged with collecting it). For the recipe Marcus liked, and which Severus ordered Galen to repeat (xiv. 65. 6–12), see xiv. 201. 9–14. On Marcus and theriac cf. Watson 1966: 88–9 and on the suggestion (Africa 1961; cf. Witke 1965) that he was addicted to the poppy juice used in some forms of it see P. Hadot 1984: esp. 33–41.
[39] xiv. 217. 5–7; for 'greatest emperors' cf. e.g. *IGR* i. 766. The suggestion of Nutton 1987: 49 n. 75 that the reference might be to Caracalla and Geta in February 211–January 212 is less likely to be right given the stress which follows on Severus' favourite sophist, Aelius Antipater (below in text), who fell out with Caracalla after the murder of Geta (Philostratus, *VS* 607, cf. Herodian iii. 15. 4 with Cassius Dio lxxvii. 1. 1).
[40] Cf. Alexander of Aphrodisias, *On Fate* 2, 39 (in Sharples 1983), on Severus and Caracalla as good *archontes* who aim only at the truth and *to beltion*, or Cassius Dio's Maecenas on the 'sharing' emperor (lii. 19. 5). Buraselis 1989: 25 ff. attempts to use Galen's remarks to recover Severan ideology.

drug, but are keen in all matters, so that if any of their friends
should have need of it, it is simply amazing how readily and with
what great enthusiasm they share their medicines. For they do not
wait for use to be necessary before supplying them, but in their zeal
to do well have prepared a stock of them which is ready against the
speed of fast developing crises' (217. 7–218. 5). Galen continues by
applauding three examples of cures attributable to the help of the
royal family. First there was (Aelius) Antipater, the great sophist
and *ab epistulis graecis* under Severus and Caracalla. He was 'greatly
honoured' by them for the magnificence of his character and for his
'perfect *paideia* in rhetorical studies'.[41] When he went down with
kidney disease, the royals showed their worth and 'fought against
the trouble with the finest drugs as if they were the best of doctors
and had been training in medicine for their whole lives' (218. 5–16).
Second, Arria, 'the dearest thing in the world to me'.[42] She was,
says Galen, 'praised by them particularly because of her command
of philosophy and her particular fondness for the writings of Plato'.
When she was ill and could not eat 'they took care of the woman
like the most experienced of doctors, giving her at my suggestion
some absinthe', which soon led to a full recovery. Finally Galen
comes back to the family of Piso himself: 'it is likely that you still
remember the case of your own son'. There was a nasty abscess and
'you were rather reluctant to allow an incision'. Fortunately, the
emperors came to the rescue and 'by giving him the drug freed us
from our great worry over him', for the ointment proved more
effective than surgery would have (218. 16–219. 17).

This elaborately written passage contains a good deal of flattery.
No other emperor is spoken of by Galen as *megistos*, 'greatest'.
Above all Galen could hardly have praised amateur doctoring genuinely. As to the fashionable use of theriac, we might note what he
says at *On Antidotes* xiv. 24. 14–18, where he recalls that its popularity among the rich during the reign of Marcus caused some of its
rarer ingredients to run out, and observes drily, 'how remarkable it
is that the rich emulate the emperors' tastes, or at least want to be

[41] Cf. Caracalla to the Ephesians in ?203: 'my friend and teacher who is entrusted
with the arrangement of letters in Greek' (*IK* xvi [Ephesos vi], 2026).
[42] She may just be the wife of M. Nonius Macrinus (from Brixia) who was proconsul of Asia in 170–1 and made an offering for his wife Arria's health (*ILS* 3986),
as Groag suggested (*PIR*² A 1115–16).

seen to do so'.[43] Regarding Antipater and Arria in particular, it is noticeable that Galen does not himself praise Antipater. As to Arria, he may have been fond of her, as he says. But did he seriously think her value to the emperors lay in her philosophic attainments? Perhaps he is here speaking of the 'circle' of intellectuals which Philostratus says was gathered around Severus' wife, Julia Domna.[44] Remarks elsewhere suggest that he did not recognize the philosophic pretensions of the imperial family. In the first book of *On the Composition of Drugs by Places*, which was written in the Severan period, Galen says he has been forced to write about beauty and hair treatments by the royal women and the emperors, who could not understand the difference between the job of the beautician and that of the doctor (xii. 435 ff.).[45]

Galen's praise of the learning of Piso himself is presumably also part of the flattery of Severus and his family and friends.[46] Why he considered this approach necessary we cannot say. We know that he involved himself in the events of the troubled year 193, though precisely how we know not.[47] Galen mentions most of Rome's emperors and in most cases he is entirely neutral towards them. This is notable in the case of Nero, who is mentioned because of his court doctor Andromachus the Elder (*On Antidotes* xiv. 2. 14).

[43] Cf. Cassius Dio lxxi. 35. 2 on the 'great numbers who pretended to study philosophy in order to get rich from [Marcus]' (Herodian i. 2. 4 expresses the same idea more charitably); Lucian, *The Uneducated Book Collector* 22 for a similar design on Marcus ('Lucian' n. 84).

[44] Philostratus, *Life of Apollonius* i. 3, VS 622. Claims about its members (including Galen) were wildly exaggerated before Bowersock 1969: 101 ff. pointed out the limits of our knowledge. Cf. below, 'Philostratus' nn. 34, 36.

[45] 'Sometimes the royal women also and the emperors themselves tell me to write about the art of beauty, and it is impossible to refuse by instructing them that there is a difference between the art of beauty and the cosmetic side of medicine', cf. xii. 443. 8–9. Galen got round his problem by borrowing at length from Trajan's physician, (T. Statilius) Crito, and from Archigenes of Apamea (also under Trajan). On the date of *On the Composition of Drugs by Places* see Ilberg 1889: 226–9, id. 1905: 296.

[46] Though Piso has been connected with the Piso addressed in the anti-Stoic *On Fate*, which survives among Plutarch's writings (*Mor.* 568b–574f): RE xx. 2 (1950) 1801–2 (Klass).

[47] Galen wrote a book 'On Public Speeches under Pertinax' (*On his Own Books* xix. 46. 9 περὶ τῶν ἐπὶ Περτίνακος δημοσίᾳ ῥηθέντων), which must have dealt with the period January to March 193. The work was presumably not hostile to Severus (who divinized Pertinax: Cassius Dio lxxiv. 4. 1–5. 5), for the addressee of *On his Own Books* is probably one of Severus' allies, below, n. 67.

Trajan, as we have seen, is praised in order to praise Galen. Hadrian, whom it is usual for second sophistic authors to applaud for Hellenic culture and philhellenism, is mentioned once in passing for having liked Artemidorus Capito's edition of Hippocrates, which Galen considered bowdlerized (*Commentary on Hippocrates' On the Nature of Man* [*In Hippocratis de natura hominis librum commentarius*] xv. 21. 9–10), and once for his wanton violence towards a slave, an example of how not to behave in *On the Diagnosis and Treatment of the Passions of the Soul*.[48] Marcus Aurelius by contrast is commended for his good character in *On Precognition*, as we shall see. He is said to have ruled 'lawfully' in *On Theriac* (216. 14–15). Apart from this last passage, which is embedded in Galen's flattery of Severus and Caracalla, there is nothing on the good government of the emperors or the Empire. Galen was clearly proud of his service to the *autokratores* (*On the Affected Parts* viii. 144. 7). But that is as far as it normally goes. The excessive praise of the Severans is abnormal. And, though it has been said rightly that Galen in the later 190s was more confident than ever with regard to his own knowledge and his progress over his rivals and predecessors in medicine,[49] he was also living in an increasingly monarchical regime and under emperors with a different style of government from that of the good Marcus. *On Theriac To Piso* may be taken as a reflection of these less certain times.[50]

[48] 'Hadrian the emperor, they say, struck one of his servants in the eye with a pen, and when he knew the blow had left him one-eyed, he called him and gave him permission to ask for a present in return for his suffering. When the sufferer remained in silence, Hadrian again told him to ask for what he wanted confidently. He asked for nothing other than an eye. For what gift could be equivalent to the loss of an eye?' (v. 17. 14–18. 4). Galen follows this anecdote with the extraordinary story of his angry Cretan friend ('although I have often spoken of it already'), who had attacked two of his servants and then begged Galen to whip him as a punishment; Galen declined but gave him a verbal whipping instead (v. 18. 5–20. 10)!

[49] Nutton 1991: 24. This is the period when a contemporary, who is probably Hippolytus of Rome, reports that 'Galen is perhaps even being offered obeisance' by followers of the Christian heretic Theodotus the Tanner who had a love of pagan logic (Eusebius, *Ecclesiastical History* v. 28. 14; Walzer 1949: 75 ff.; Connolly 1948 for Hippolytus).

[50] Galen was naturally aware that Commodus' rule was different too: in a passage of a commentary written during his reign he discusses patients who keep their worries and problems to themselves including those who 'fear imperial intrigue' (*Eighth Commentary on Book Six of Hippocrates' Epidemics*, CMG V. 10. 2. 2, p. 494. 22 [Arabic]), and in a fragment of *De moribus* he records the steadfastness of slaves who refused to testify against masters following the downfall of Perennis in 185 (Müller 1883).

GALEN IN ROME II

It is now time to return to the development of Galen's career in *On Precognition*. We left Galen telling Eudemus he would quit Rome and return to Pergamum when the *stasis* there had ceased. The trouble at Pergamum that kept Galen away is unknown. Ilberg's suggestion, that Galen was alluding obliquely to the ramifications of the Parthian War, cannot be right.[51] Rather, we are dealing with an instance of civil political unrest of the type attested as common by Plutarch, Dio, Aristides, and others.[52] Galen's involvement may have been personal or through family and friends. Meanwhile at Rome his fame grew apace.[53] Now he became embroiled in disputes with Peripatetics and Stoics, which he describes with relish. Eventually he was persuaded by Boethus to give an anatomical display before him and his teacher Alexander of Damascus.[54] Also present were Hadrian 'the rhetor' (that is, Hadrian of Tyre) and Demetrius of Alexandria, a pupil of Favorinus.[55] The display arranged by Boethus was broken off when Alexander questioned the possibility of belief in the senses before Galen had begun. Galen withdrew at this sceptical sophistry and the incident was reported to all the *philologoi* in Rome, especially Severus, Paullus, and Barbarus.

At this point (xiv. 630. 15) Galen begins to narrate in full and in the rather lively style that characterizes parts of *On Precognition* a

[51] Ilberg 1905: 288.
[52] Galen himself wrote a lost book on *homonoia* (*On his Own Books* xix. 46. 5).
[53] *On Precognition* xiv. 625. 10–11 'as you know, great was the name of Galen'.
[54] Cf. *On Anatomical Procedures* (*De anatomicis administrationibus*) ii. 218. 4 ff. Here Galen says that Alexander 'has now been adjudged worthy to give ·public instruction in Peripatetic doctrines at Athens'; because of this he is commonly identified (especially in the Arabic tradition) with Alexander of Aphrodisias (Nutton 1979: 189; Nutton himself 1984: 319 is against, cf. id. 1987: 45; Strohmaier 1978: 129 for Arabic sources), who was appointed by Severus and Caracalla to teach Aristotle in an unnamed city (presumably Athens), as he tells us at *On Fate* 1, some time after 198. Since Alexander is said to have been Boethus' teacher in *On Precognition* (xiv. 627. 2–3), he can hardly be the same Alexander of Aphrodisias; since *On Anatomical Procedures* was probably written 169–80 (Ilberg 1889: 223), we would have to assume that this Alexander was one of the first holders of the public chair of Aristotelian philosophy at Athens following Marcus' establishment of chairs of philosophy and rhetoric in 176 (and that *On Anatomical Procedures* was written nearer 180, which is likely), or alternatively hold that the note on Alexander is a much later addition (a known habit of Galen's) inserted around 200 by confusion with the later Alexander, as is suggested among others by Thillet 1984: p. xliv (see also Moraux: 1985: 81 n. 2; and Donini 1981: 678–87 who reclaims Galen's Alexander for Pyrrhonism).
[55] On Hadrian see 'Past' n. 90, 'Lucian' nn. 107, 108; on Demetrius Jones 1967.

case history he was obviously proud of and which he had already alluded to (xiv. 626. 2). This is the story of Justus' wife, whose pulse revealed that she was not ill but was in fact in love with a pantomime artist called Pylades.[56] It is consciously modelled on a similar observation attributed to (or by) the great Hellenistic physician Erasistratus.[57] Justus is unknown, but is presumably the same man as 'my dear Justus', to whom Galen sent *On the Parts of the Medical Art*.[58] If so, he is a non-medical man. At this stage in Galen's career it is not unnatural to imagine that he was an easterner, perhaps with political duties like Boethus, Severus, and Paullus.[59] Galen next narrates at some length his cure of Boethus' son, Curillus, and Boethus' wife. The malice against him grows much more serious after Boethus' gift of 400 *aurei*.[60] Worse, Boethus and Severus were now ready to tell Marcus Aurelius of his successes (xiv. 647. 15–16). 'When I saw their enthusiasm I was afraid in case they managed to do something which led to me being stopped from returning to Asia.' Galen asked them to hold back until he was more willing. He now learnt that the *stasis* at Pergamum had stopped and he could return home. The following narrative of his escape from Italy is again fast and dramatic (xiv. 648. 6 ff.). He gave out that he was going to visit Campania. He left a slave in his house with instructions to sell it as soon as a boat came in for Asia and then to embark immediately for Pergamum. Galen himself took the first ship he could from Brundisium, which brought him to the harbour city of Cassiope in Corcyra.[61] Until then 'I was afraid that one of the most powerful men or even the emperor himself on learning of my departure would send a soldier commanding me to return to Rome like a runaway slave'.[62]

[56] For Galen's attitude here cf. the fragment known as the *How to Detect those who Feign Sickness* (*Quomodo morborum simulantes sint deprehendendi*, in fact part of Galen's second commentary on *Epidemics* ii, which is preserved only in Arabic—see *CMG* V. 10. 2. 4, pp. 107–16).

[57] xiv. 630. 17 ff. On the famous story of Antiochus' love for Stratonice (to whom Galen oddly refers as 'the father's concubine') and the diagnosis attributed to Erasistratus see esp. Mesk 1913.

[58] *CMG* Suppl. Orient. II, p. 25. 1.

[59] Nutton 1979: 186 tentatively suggests the westerners C. Curtius Justus (*PIR*[2] C 1613) or C. Modius Justus (*PIR*[2] M 688).

[60] Galen, like Aristides, made a point of denying he took fees (Temkin 1973: 47 n. 84).

[61] On the problem of his itinerary here see Nutton 1973: 168.

[62] Much later in his life in *On his Own Books* Galen says he left Rome 'immediately' because of 'the great plague' (xix. 15. 16–17), an ambiguous statement that

It was not long before Galen did return at the behest of the emperors. Marcus and Lucius were looking for a man whose actions, not theories showed medical science (xiv. 649. 15–16).[63] Galen was summoned to the winter camp at Aquileia (168/9).[64] After the death of Lucius Verus, Marcus once more set off against the Germans and ordered Galen to go with him. 'Since he was a good and kind man I was able, as you know, to persuade him to leave me in Rome' (xiv. 650. 6–8). This story is told in more detail in *On his Own Books*. Here Galen says he had thought that he would be excused when he reached Aquileia (xix. 18. 2 ff.). 'I had heard that one of the [emperors], the older one, was both considerate and reasonable and gentle and mild.' But when he reached Aquileia the plague attacked as never before and both emperors fled to Rome. Galen remained to survive a hard winter and, following the death of Lucius Verus, was indeed excused from accompanying Marcus to the war.[65] Galen's success in this version of the story was due, however, not to Marcus' kindliness, but to Asclepius, who gave him instructions not to go, instructions Marcus felt he could not counter (xix. 18. 19 ff.).[66] This account may well be the more accurate one, which he could comfortably tell many years later to his friend Bassus,[67] while the version stressing Marcus' own generosity was published during the emperor's lifetime in *On Precognition*.

During Marcus' absence Galen was given the task of looking

Ilberg (1905: 294–5) thought convicted him of bad faith in *On Precognition*; but the earlier account, which states that Lucius Verus was still in the East when he left Rome (xiv. 647. 17–18, 649. 13; i.e. before August 166) and therefore implies that the plague had not yet arrived in Italy, is rightly preferred by Nutton 1973: 158–9.

[63] Cf. *On the Affected Parts* viii. 144. 5–7 'I was known from my actions in the art, not from sophists' speeches'.

[64] Cf. *On his Own Books* xix. 18. 1–2 'I journeyed by necessity'.

[65] Cf. *On Antidotes* xiv. 4. 11 ff.

[66] xix. 18. 20–19. 4 'he was persuaded to let me go in obeisance to the god, when he heard me say that my ancestral god Asclepius, whose devotee [*therapeutês*] I declared I had been since he had saved me from a potentially fatal abscess, was giving contrary orders.' Cf. Kollesch 1981: 7–8; Kudlien 1981: 120; while they are right to warn against interpreting this passage to mean that Galen ever held an official position at the shrine of Asclepius in Pergamum, a *therapeutês* was clearly more than the average visitor (cf. Behr 1981: 392 n. 33; Habicht 1969: 114, no. 79; Nicosia 1980; similarly Apollonius is described as a *therapôn* of Asclepius at Philostratus, *Life of Apollonius* i. 12). The god's effect on the emperor recalls Aristides' dream at *Or.* xlvii. 23.

[67] Bassus is probably the friend of Septimius Severus who was *praefectus urbi* in 193 (*PIR*² B 76, cf. Birley 1988: 106, 207); he presumably belongs to the Pergamene house of the Quadrati Bassi.

after the health of Commodus. He was also free to write up much
of his work. Disputes with rivals continued (*On his Own Books*
xix. 21–2). He successfully cured 'Hextos', who is probably Sextus
Quintilius Condianus *cos. ord.* 180 (*On Precognition* xiv. 651. 17 ff.)
and a member of a powerful first- and second-century family from
Alexandria Troas.[68] It is noteworthy that Claudius Severus also gives
attention to the sick 'Hextos' (653. 11 ff.). On Marcus' return Galen
was called in to cure the emperor himself (657. 16. ff.).[69] Marcus
was so pleased with him that he condemned all other doctors. 'He
kept saying about me, as you yourself know, that among doctors
I was the first, among philosophers unique' (xiv. 660. 10–16). Galen
then narrates the cure which he says was accounted his greatest
('but in truth is far from it'), that of Commodus' tonsilitis while
Marcus was still away (xiv. 661. 12–664. 13). In the midst of the
treatment Commodus was visited by Marcus' 'close relative' Annia
Faustina, who managed to embarrass Galen by pointing out his
success to a physician of the Methodist school, whom she had
brought with her (xiv. 662. 18 ff.).[70] Galen was not amused: 'You
have caused me to be hated by the doctors much more than I was
before.'

Galen ends *On Precognition* with two more triumphant cures,
one involving a prognosis of a forthcoming crisis through the observation of a nasal haemorrhage (xiv. 665–9),[71] the other the cure
of a bailiff with an intermittent pulse (xiv. 670–2). It is no coincidence that he finishes with a cure involving the pulse, which he
wrote about at length.[72] Questioned as to how he had done it, he
draws on Isocrates for his reply. This great man had been asked
whether a three-year training would suffice to gain knowledge of
all the rhetorical themes, and had replied, 'I would like to help you
grow to the point where you can learn to do what you ask even
in a day; but I would then convict myself of a natural want of

[68] Kollesch 1964–5; Nutton 1979: 213–14; Halfmann 1979: no. 119; Cassius Dio
lxxii. 5. 3.

[69] 176/7 seems a better date for this cure than 169, even though it is then out of
sequence; see Nutton 1979: 217–18, cf. Birley 1987: 196–7.

[70] Nutton 1979: 223 correctly identifies her with Marcus' cousin Annia Fundania
Faustina, wife of T. Pomponius Vitrasius Pollio (*cos. II ord.* 176), who was mur-
dered by Commodus in 190.

[71] Cf. Iskandar 1988: 61. 16–63. 2.

[72] See *Synopsis librorum suorum de pulsibus* for a survey of his own work;
Deichgräber 1956*b*: 3–30.

intelligence, since I have practised for many years' (xiv. 672. 9 ff.). There is, of course, no real modesty in the comparison with Isocrates, even if these words suggest it, for Isocrates was as highly self-conscious in his own praises as Galen.[73] So, typically, Galen's very last words are a recommendation to read his own work on the pulse and a further assertion of the power of prognosis.

The most striking thing to emerge from *On Precognition* and from Galen's other works is his insulation from the Roman world. Rome to Galen was an opportunity for his own success, it was the city where he could best of all fight his own academic corner and triumph. He went there in the first place to make his reputation. He then left because of the hostile academic climate. But after he was obliged to come back, he remained there, going home again only once (so far as we know).[74] And though late in life he still remembered that he had been forced back by Marcus and Lucius (*On his Own Books* xix. 18. 1–2), his own success and his own propaganda no doubt made it impossible to go or be elsewhere. In Galen's picture, as soon as he had come to the attention of Marcus, he and his preparation of the panacea theriac were indispensable. Marcus' son, Commodus, was less taken with the drug,[75] but by then its properties had touched the imagination of the Roman elite and Galen's formula was valued as highly as ever by Septimius Severus. Yet, though we can say that Galen needed Rome as much as he thought it needed him, Galen himself never puts it like this. He was proud to have served 'amongst others the leading men in Rome and all the emperors in turn' (*On the Affected Parts* viii. 144. 5–7). But there is no sense of attachment to the Empire in his writings or of a political identification with the Antonine regime (which we find in Lucian, Aristides, even Pausanias, and of course many others). It is difficult to know what this means. It could be argued, after all, that the Empire was simply a given for Galen, hence there was no need to comment on it. But though he had something to say about the events of 193, there does seem to be a feeling of indifference towards the Roman idea.

This contrasts with Galen's attitude toward the East. In his thoughts home (or as he puts it, 'with us') remained in Pergamum

[73] Esp. at *Antidosis* 101 ff. and *Panathenaicus* 200 ff.
[74] Nutton 1973: 167–8.   [75] *On Antidotes* xiv. 65. 3–4.

and its locality even after he had spent many years in Rome.[76] The
people he highlights in *On Precognition* are mostly eastern by origin and are certainly Hellenic by culture. Here a more familiar
pattern emerges. In his medical works Galen did not have much
cause to allude to the great writers of the past or to key events of
Greek history.[77] But, as we have seen, his stress on education was
not confined to the practice of medicine. He wrote widely on classical literature and philosophy (including, crucially, philosophy of
language and language purism). He mentions the authors of his
own time who we consider are among the most significant of the
second sophistic period, Plutarch, Favorinus, Lucian, and Aristides,
as well as the great rhetorical stars Polemo, Herodes Atticus ('the
most able orator of our time'), Hadrian, and (probably) Pausanias
of Caesarea.[78] In cultural terms Galen was avowedly Hellenic. His
whole medical output is a celebration of Hellenic philosophy and
learning. Thus it is no surprise to find that the newly rediscovered
complete version of his commentary on Hippocrates' *Airs, Waters,
Places* shows him remarking unfavourably on the Romans' ele-
mentary grasp of higher Greek culture. In this work Galen re-
counts that when he once explained to some educated Romans how
to determine the equinox, they had simply looked at him in amazement, as if he had been talking about 'white crows' (that is, about
something totally unheard of). He then pours scorn on one of their
number for consulting a Roman astrologer on the matter rather
than him. The trouble was that Romans only got as far as the basic
books of Euclid which they made their children read. The higher
mathematics needed by astronomers was beyond them.[79] There is
no need to conclude that Galen thought all Romans were stupid; he
is of course speaking of a very technical subject. Still, the remarks
do reveal a significant contempt. The achievements Galen really
valued were not appreciated at Rome to the same degree. In a very

[76] For the phrase *par' hêmin*, which is still found in works written under the
Severans, cf. the (very incomplete) list in Schöne 1917: 107–9; when it is used of
geography, as mostly, it never refers to Rome or Italy.
[77] Cf. Nutton 1990: 252.
[78] Plutarch: v. 300. 17. Favorinus: *On the Best Teaching* (*De optima doctrina*), and
above, 'Practice' n. 68. Lucian: 'Lucian' n. 31. Aristides: 'Aristides' n. 28. Polemo:
above, n. 19. Herodes: above, n. 11. Hadrian: above, n. 55. Pausanias: Iskandar 1988:
168.
[79] Strohmeier 1993: 162. The full commentary, which survives in Arabic, dates to
Commodus. The text will be edited in *CMG*.

real sense, in what mattered to him, Galen—who was never of
course a sophist—was not in the Roman Empire.[80]

---

[80] Regarding sophists it is interesting to find Aelius Aristides damning Galen's
teacher Satyrus as one at *Or.* xlix. 8; this is simply a term of abuse used in a sense
Galen himself often employs against rival doctors. On Bowersock's misleading presentation of Galen himself as a sophist (1969: 59 ff.) see Brunt 1994: 43–5, 51–2.

12

Philostratus

INTRODUCTION

Flavius Philostratus is the last author to be considered here in any detail. All his works reflect an active interest in the cultural history of the Greek world. He was a practising sophist and came from a sophistic family.[1] His wife was apparently of senatorial stock and at least one of his sons became a senator. He himself held the office of general at Athens during the first decade of the third century and was also close to the imperial court.[2] Philostratus did not live in the past. He was fully alive to the pleasures and the pressures the contemporary world offered to the educated elite. The Greek past was simply the way of preserving one's status in the present day. That is why the *Lives of the Sophists* often focuses, as has been observed,[3] not on the rhetorical output of the sophists or on their classicism, but on their economic and social standing, and on their relations with the cities and the emperors. In assessing Philostratus' attitude to Rome it is important to remember at all times that it is Greece's cultural inheritance that really matters to him now. This provides the frame of reference (as it were) through which his comments on Romans and on the Empire are mediated. It makes no difference that Philostratus' world was—after Caracalla's Empire-wide extension of the Roman citizenship in 212—necessarily Roman in political-administrative terms.[4] Culturally and spiritually it was as Greek as Plutarch's or Galen's.

---

[1] On the attribution of works between the various Philostrati and the divergent views of Münscher 1907 and Solmsen 1940 and 1941 see Anderson 1986: 291–6 and Flinterman 1993: 5–15. There is no dispute that the *Apollonius* and the *Lives of the Sophists*, the works examined below, are by the same man.

[2] Family: *IK* i (Erythrai i), 63 (cf. Jones 1989), where his son *c*.240 is 'kin and brother and uncle of senators'; *stratêgos*—*IG* ii² 1803 (Follet 1976: 101–2); see now Flinterman 1993: 16–29; in general Anderson 1986.

[3] Above, 'Practice' n. 3, 'Past' n. 99.

[4] *Constitutio Antoniniana*: above, 'Past' n. 8. On the equal treatment of East and West in the senatorial appointments of this age see Leunissen 1989: 89.

APOLLONIUS

The work of Philostratus which offers us most material on Greek perceptions of Rome is the *Life of Apollonius of Tyana*. The *Apollonius*, or to give it its correct title, *In Honour of Apollonius of Tyana* (*Ta es ton Tuanea Apollônion*), is an account in eight books of the historical holy man who flourished in the second half of the first century AD.[5] The work was written, it seems, after the death in 217 of Julia Domna, who inspired it (*Apollonius* i. 3), and before the composition of the *Lives of the Sophists* (very probably written in 237/8), where it is mentioned (*VS* 570).[6]

Like Lucian's enemy, the Cynic mystic Peregrinus,[7] the historical Apollonius attracted divergent publicity. We first hear of him in Lucian's *Alexander*, where he is damned as 'the famous Apollonius', one of whose pupils, also from Tyana, became the teacher and lover of the young Alexander (5).[8] It is interesting that Lucian later says he ranged himself against Alexander along with the followers of Timocrates of Heraclea, for Timocrates himself was a pupil of Apollonius' enemy, the well-known Stoic philosopher (Mestrius) Euphrates of Tyre.[9] At some time before Philostratus wrote there existed various letters ascribed to the sage, which have come down to us in a separate, amplified collection. It is very probable that these letters were originally embedded in a biographical treatment. This is suggested by a short passage of narrative preserved in one

[5] On the historical figure see Bowie 1978, Dzielska 1986 (the latter to be used with caution); also Anderson 1986: 175–97. The lengthy article of Grosso 1954 is largely unreliable (believing in the historical truth of most of what Philostratus says).

[6] After the death of Julia: Bowie 1978: 1670 n. 71. Bowie rightly notes that the lack of a dedication to Julia does not in itself mean she was no longer alive, since there is anyway no other dedication; but the way she is spoken of at i. 3 implies she was no longer living. *VS* 570 ('in my *In Honour of Apollonius*'; the title itself is ascribed to 'Damis' at *Apollonius* viii. 29): the particular reference in the *VS* (Apollonius did not fall in love with the mother of Alexander the Clay-Plato) has no basis in the *Apollonius*, but it can easily be taken as pointing to general comments on Apollonius' avoidance of sex (i. 13); cf. Bowie 1978: 1669 n. 70. On the date of the *Lives* see above, 'Introduction' n. 1.

[7] On whom note the work of Philostratus' father, above, 'Lucian' n. 88.

[8] Given the links between Apollonius and Asclepius and between Apollonius' own healing activities and Pythagoreanism, it is significant that Lucian makes Alexander's teacher a doctor and has Alexander passing himself off as a new Pythagoras.

[9] On Timocrates see Philostratus, *VS* 536; cf. Jones 1986: 148 n. 60. On Euphrates see Pliny, *Letters* i. 10 (a highly favourable picture); on his death *c*.121 see Follet 1976: 124. He presumably owed his citizenship (*IG* ii² 3945) to Plutarch's sponsor Mestrius Florus (above, 'Plutarch' n. 99).

manuscript and connecting two of them.[10] About the same time as
Philostratus was writing Apollonius was branded 'a wizard and a
magician' by the historian Cassius Dio, who reports that Caracalla
paid him honours during his Parthian expedition some time around
214/15.[11] A neutral reference occurs earlier in Dio's *History* in his
account of Domitian's assassination, which 'a certain Apollonius'
to Dio's amazement knew of in Ephesus as it was happening in
Rome.[12] Also in the second quarter of the third century, and perhaps as late as 248, can be placed the reference to Apollonius in
Origen's *Against Celsus*, where Origen cites the work on Apollonius
written by Moeragenes (also mentioned by Philostratus) as dis-
proving Celsus' assertion that philosophers were never taken in
by magic. Rather, 'respectable philosophers' like Euphrates and 'a
certain Epicurean' visited the sage *qua* wizard (vi. 41).[13]

According to the *Augustan History* the last of the Severan emperors, Severus Alexander (222–35), worshipped Apollonius alongside selected ancestors, Jesus Christ, Abraham, and Orpheus (29.
9). If this is true,[14] it nicely mirrors Caracalla's earlier interest; if
not, it anyway attests the possibility of pagan worship of Apollonius
in later antiquity.[15] This had or was given special prominence shortly
before the Great Persecution of Diocletian and Galerius, which was
initiated early in 303. It was now that the *vicarius Orientis*, Sossianus
Hierocles, used Philostratus' *Apollonius* to write a work comparing
the life and acts of Apollonius with those of Jesus Christ, with the
aim of demonstrating the sage's superiority. The tract was felt to be
dangerous enough to warrant a reply from Eusebius ridiculing the
credulity accorded to Philostratus' biography, which he said made
The Incredible Things beyond Thule look 'quite believable and

---

[10] The *Letters* is discussed below, nn. 64–9.
[11] lxxvii. 18. 4. Caracalla erected a *hêrôon* to the sage.
[12] lxvii. 18. 1. The different tone is perhaps explained by the varying times of
composition, though the actual dates of writing remain unclear (cf. below, 'Cassius
Dio' n. 5). Context is also important: Dio's great hatred for Caracalla led him to
assert that none of the gods would listen to the emperor (lxxvii. 15. 5–6)—hence,
perhaps, any divine being who was said to must be a fraud.
[13] Date—Chadwick 1953: pp. xiv–xv. On the 'Epicurean' note Edwards 1991: 565
(involving a pre-Philostratean Damis); cf. Anderson 1986: 300.
[14] Cf. MacMullen 1981: 92 for parallel, though less exotic, mixtures; rejected by
Syme 1968b: 61, 138. Apollonius and Moses are coupled for their closeness to god
in one of the Apolline oracles quoted in the late Christian collection known as the
Tübingen *Theosophia* §44 (p. 177 Erbse). See below, n. 63 on Severus Alexander and
Asclepius at Aegeae.
[15] On this see Dzielska 1986: 97 ff., 153 ff.

completely true'.[16] Further evidence for the influence of Apollonius at this time is detected in the destruction under Constantine of the shrine of Asclepius at Aegeae. Presumably this had been a focus of paganism during the Persecution and Christians were getting their own back. Apollonius seems to have been the particular irritant, for he had lived and taught in the temple with Asclepius' approval, according to Philostratus, *Apollonius* i. 7–13 (it is likely that Philostratus used a local source here in the shape of Maximus of Aegeae, on whom see below). Hierocles had turned Apollonius into a priest of the god.[17] A decisive Christian response was again required.[18] In this regard one should note the existence of the Egyptian poet Soterichus, who wrote *inter alia* an encomium of Diocletian and a *Life of Apollonius of Tyana* (*Suda* σ 877). Also to be connected with worship of Apollonius is the epigram now at Adana, which compares him to Apollo and praises him for removing men's troubles and errors.[19]

Philostratus' work on Apollonius thus came to play an important part in the response later pagans made to Christianity. He himself is unlikely to have been the first to write in favour of the sage. But of the three works he mentions as predecessors (i. 3), his main source, the memoirs of 'Damis' of Nineveh, must be seen as a feint. Aspects of the form and structure of the *Apollonius* correspond to distinguishing features of various of the ancient novels, especially the themes of travel in the mysterious East and the quest for wisdom, the 'historiographical' division into eight books, and the form of the title (*In Honour of Apollonius*).[20] The surprise 'discovery' of Damis' work recalls another fictional *topos*, that of finding source books,[21] and this in particular makes it clear that 'Damis' is simply

---

[16] On Hierocles see *PLRE* i. 432 (with Addenda 486) and esp. Barnes 1976: 243–5; Porphyry had already made use of Apollonius in his *Against the Christians* (frr. 4, 46, 60, 63 von Harnack). For Eusebius' *Against Hierocles* see de Labriolle 1950: 306–10 (also on Lactantius' view of Hierocles), Barnes 1981: 164–7, Hägg 1992 (on the chronologies of Barnes and M. Forrat, and suggesting that Eusebius was not in fact the author). Antonius Diogenes' *Incredible Things*: *Against Hierocles* 384. 20–2 Kayser.

[17] Eusebius, *Against Hierocles* 370. 29 Kayser.

[18] Eusebius, *Life of Constantine* iii. 56, with Lane Fox 1986: 671–2.

[19] See Dagron and Feissel 1987: 137–41, no. 88 for text, variant supplements, and discussion.

[20] Cf. Reardon 1971: 189 'presque un roman'; see Bowie 1978: 1663–7, Anderson 1986: 230–2 (novelistic traits, comparison with Xenophon's *Cyropaedia*).

[21] Speyer 1974: 50–2 compares Dictys Cretensis.

an invention of Philostratus and a vehicle for his own presentation.[22] The attribution to a Damis living under the Flavians has been plausibly explained as an elegant compliment to Philostratus' old tutor, the eminent sophist Flavius Damianus of Ephesus.[23]

A second favourable source mentioned by Philostratus is a certain Maximus of Aegeae, who wrote on Apollonius' life there. If he too is fictional, the reason for invention is not known. It is better to suppose he was real and to see his account of Apollonius as a product of local pride, as a vehicle for promoting the cult of Asclepius at Aegeae, and as a means of asserting the city's superiority over its neighbours.[24] Third comes Moeragenes' work in 'four books'. Origen describes this as 'reminiscences',[25] a title which should remind us of Xenophon's famous four books of *Reminiscences* about Socrates. Whether this means Moeragenes was favourable to Apollonius cannot be known for sure. Philostratus merely says that Moeragenes was ignorant of much of Apollonius' life. Origen's focus on 'magic' in his description of Moeragenes' version can easily be taken as reflecting Moeragenes' likes rather than any hostility.[26] Indeed, Moeragenes may simply have emphasized magic too much for Philostratus.[27] It is quite possible that his work was the

[22] The main debate about Damis goes back to Göttsching's youthful defence of his existence (1889: 66–74) and Meyer's strong denial (1917); see Koskenniemi 1991: 9–15, Flinterman 1993: 87–97, 175–80 (suggesting a pseudepigraphic source; cf. Speyer 1974: 49–52). Recently Anderson has over-confidently reargued the case in favour (1986: 155–73 with fantastic references to Middle Persian folk-tale; cf. Edwards 1991: 564). For a different approach (bypassing the stale question of existence) see Del Corno 1979 on Philostratus' literary use of 'Damis' as a 'schermo' for his own craft.

[23] Bowie 1978: 1670–1 (Damianus himself had been dead for some time when the *Apollonius* was written, but his three sons were all Severan senators; on them cf. Halfmann 1982: 629, Leunissen 1989: 192). Bowie's suggestion is more likely than Speyer's and Flinterman's idea of a pseudepigraphic neo-Pythagorean forgery issued to counter hostile views of Apollonius, since this leaves the question, Why 'Damis'?

[24] Meyer 1917: 402 supposed Maximus to be another Damis; but see Graf 1984–5. Apollonius' attack on Antioch at *Apollonius* i. 16 is typical of city rivalries in this period; cf. above, 'Past' nn. 26, 28.

[25] *Against Celsus* vi. 41 (*apomnêmoneumata*).

[26] So Bowie 1978: 1673–4. As Bowie points out, Moeragenes wrote of Apollonius as '*magos* and *philosophos*', a combination defended for men of great wisdom by Apuleius in his *Apology* 25–7 and with similar examples by the Apollonius of *Letters* 16–17. Bowersock's view (1970: 11–12) that Origen's report made Moeragenes a hostile witness is not necessarily wrong, of course; cf. Anderson 1986: 299–300 against Bowie.

[27] So Raynor 1984; cf. *Apollonius* v. 12, vii. 39.

biographical source in which, as has been said, there were embedded two of the *Letters of Apollonius*. It is not improbable that this account is also the one on which Philostratus based his own.[28]

As for Philostratus himself, use of the conventions of prose fiction should not lead us to suppose that he did not believe in Apollonius. Half way through the work he says his 'purpose' is 'to provide the life [*bios*] of Apollonius to those who do not yet know it' (v. 39), a handy biographical avowal.[29] In providing this information he was of course combating the views of those who regarded the sage as a charlatan. This aim is explicit at i. 2.[30] If we consider the conventions of ancient biography, so important a vehicle for the dissemination of religious and philosophical ideas in this period,[31] we are to expect that a character, once adopted, will not change. Thus Apollonius, philosophical ascetic, Pythagorean mystic, reformer of cults and morals, can easily end up in situations that are implausible to us or manifestly fictitious. But since Philostratus knew Apollonius was a 'divine man',[32] he did not have to ask whether a particular incident was true. The terrain of the true had already been decided by the gods. The 'sophistic' décor of the work, so obvious and (perhaps) intrusive to modern readers,[33] would not have been seen as distorting in this regard. Indeed, when at *Apollonius* i. 3 Philostratus mentions the desire of Julia Domna to have the work recast and informs his readers of her appropriate intellectual qualifications ('I belonged to the circle around her—for she greatly admired and welcomed all rhetorical writings'), he is informing them just how seriously Apollonius was taken by the

---

[28] Bowie 1978: 1678–9, connecting Moeragenes with a 1st/2nd-c. Athenian family with philosophical interests (one of whom appears in Plutarch, *Table Talks* iv. 6, 671c–672c discussing Jewish religion; cf. Teodorsson 1989–90: ii. 120–34; Puech 1991: 4861).

[29] Similar remarks are made about others in the *VS* (527–8, 574, 590–1). Cf. Eunapius, *Lives of the Philosophers and Sophists* 454 (ii. 1. 4 G.) 'Philostratus of Lemnos wrote a full account of him, entitling the books the *Life of Apollonius*, though they should be called *The Visit of God to Mankind*'.

[30] Cf. Smith 1978: 84–93 on the techniques employed by Philostratus to defend Apollonius and by the Gospels and other Christian writings to vindicate Jesus (many have accepted that Philostratus knew the Gospels—e.g. de Labriolle 1950: 180–8).

[31] Cf. Momigliano 1987.

[32] On the typology of the *theios anêr* (with some illustrations from Philostratus' Apollonius) see Bieler 1935–6. Belloni 1980 compares Apollonius from this angle with the traditional 'wise man' represented by Thales and Empedocles.

[33] See esp. Anderson 1986: 124–31.

ruling house at whose prompting he was writing a work of literature and in whose beliefs about Apollonius he himself shared.[34]

The reference to Julia Domna in the preface to the *Apollonius* tells us a lot about Philostratus' aims and his conception of his audience. Coming from a priestly dynastic family of Hellenized Syrians from Emesa, Julia was the first imperial wife to hail from the Greek East.[35] In the *Lives of the Sophists* Philostratus calls her 'the philosophic Julia', and again notes the existence of a group of intellectuals around her.[36] In the same passage he records that she secured the appointment of the Thessalian sophist Philiscus to the imperial chair of rhetoric at Athens.[37] This is exactly the sort of conduct which was bound to appeal to him. In the *Life of Apollonius* very great care is taken to stress Apollonius' Greek credentials, and the emperors Apollonius confronts are measured by their responses to Hellenic culture. Philostratus wrote at Julia's suggestion, but he wanted to be read by *pepaideumenoi* like himself. Thus, despite being a Cappadocian, Apollonius has a correct Attic diction without 'affecting hyperatticism' (i. 7, 17). One of the best things Damis can say of Apollonius is that through him he has become a *pepaideumenos* instead of a barbarian and is now fit to mix with Greeks as a Greek (iii. 43).

Other non-Greeks are similarly valued in the *Apollonius* for their acquisition of Greek culture. The Persian (i.e. Parthian) king Vardanes is naturally philhellene (i. 29). The whole Vardanes episode, tenuous as its roots in history are,[38] is indeed important in foreshadowing how a king should react towards 'a man who was Greek and divine', as the satrap of the Indus puts it (ii. 17). Coming to the Indian king Phraotes we are not surprised to find that he lives like a philosopher and speaks immaculate Greek (ii. 26 ff.). His philosophical utopia is underpinned (of course) by the Brahmans, led by his teacher Iarchas. Greek and the Greek character

---

[34] On the matter of prompting and belief cf. the *Heroicus* (a celebration of traditional Greek hero-cults): if it represents a response to Caracalla's restoration of the tomb of Achilles and admiration for Patroclus during his visit to Ilium (cf. Herodian iv. 8. 4–5; Münscher 1907: 504–8), it was a response on a level Philostratus surely found congenial (cf. *Apollonius* iv. 11–16; Mantero 1966: 13, 45–7, 225–7 sensibly distances him from court flattery here).
[35] On the background see Birley 1988: 68–72; *PIR*² J 663.
[36] 622 'geometers and philosophers around Julia'. See Bowersock 1969: 101–9. For Philostratus and Julia see also Philostratus, *Letters* 73, where her learning is elaborately complimented (Anderson 1986: 4–5).
[37] Cf. Avotins 1975: 323–4.   [38] Meyer 1917: 374–5.

command their highest respect (ii. 31; iii. 12, 16, 36). One particular point of interest may be noted here which shows the difference between Apollonius and other Greeks. In the course of a discussion of justice Iarchas contends that Greeks equate justice with the absence of injustice (a contention later supported by Apollonius, vi. 21–2). Iarchas declares, 'I once learned from Egyptians who come here that governors go out to you from Rome raising their axes [the *fasces*] naked over you, not yet knowing if they will be governing cowards, while you declare they are just if they merely do not sell their judgements' (iii. 25). We have already encounted a bad, pederastic governor at i. 12, an unhistorical incident showing Apollonius' expected aversion from homosexuality.[39] Iarchas' comment is general and a little more troublesome. In any of our earlier authors it might be hostile to Rome.[40] Here it is not. In context it is first and foremost a criticism of Greeks, the corruption of the Greeks of Apollonius' time being an important theme in the work. Second, it does, of course, purport to reflect conditions in the first century AD; in this respect it is not a comment on Roman governors at all times. But the real meaning of the comment lies in the presentation of Apollonius himself. His stance against imperial (Roman) authority in defence of true Greek culture is a most important theme in the *Life*. Thus Iarchas' relation of how some Greeks kowtow to Rome will not be applicable to him.

On his return to the West Apollonius rebukes the Ionian Greeks for their degeneracy. Much of what he is made to say is designed to promote concord among them (iv. 3, 8–9). Restoration of true Greek culture is also important (iv. 2, 5, 7, 19, 21–2, 27, 31–3). Some of his remarks are made by letter. The theme of moral decline, of which Apollonius is an arbiter *par excellence*, is voiced loudly in the collection of *Letters* ascribed to the historical Apollonius (to which I shall return). The tone of these is often abusive and obscure and shows the true philosopher's candour. The Philostratean commentator is saner and more constructive. However, one of Apollonius' criticisms is severe in both sources. This is the letter castigating the Ionians for falling from the Hellenic ideal by adopting

---

[39] Unhistorical (despite the information on the governor's fate): Meyer 1917: 401–2; but cf. Bowie 1978: 1684 n. 124.

[40] We might compare Plutarch's blunt remark about the governor's boots at *Political Advice* 813e ('Plutarch' n. 93), or Dio of Prusa's several bitter attacks on corrupt justice in the provinces ('Dio' nn. 117–22, 129–30, 162, 180).

Latin names.[41] Philostratus does not comment overtly; but calling the use of such names *barbarismos* in the *Apollonius* is his gloss and is not in the *Letters*. To suggest this is simply a linguistic matter is to miss the very close link between language and literature and cultural and political identity.[42] If Philostratus took the theme of degeneracy from the *Letters*, it is plain that it suited his own view about the development of contemporary Greek culture as we see it in the *Lives of the Sophists*. There he traces the resurrection of the type of rhetoric which characterizes the 'second sophistic' to Nicetes of Smyrna in the time of Nero. Previously 'the science had been reduced to great straits' (511). This fits well with his picture of Apollonius busily championing the revitalization of the Greek heritage in the mid-first century.

Soon after this Apollonius comes to Rome where he finds that 'Nero would not allow the practice of philosophy' (iv. 35). The details of Apollonius' stay in the capital (to iv. 47) are entirely unhistorical. The narrative consists of a series of syncrises between Apollonius and the tyrant-figure Nero, Apollonius and the friendly consul of AD 66 (C. Luccius) Telesinus, Apollonius and Tigellinus (who is frightened of him), and finally an exchange of letters with an imprisoned Musonius Rufus (who had in fact been exiled the previous year).[43] The defence of philosophy is all (iv. 38). Apollonius is now taken to the far West to Gades, where he remarks on Nero's failure to do what a king should do and on his abuse of the Olympic festival (v. 7),[44] and poses as a revolutionary 'all but taking up arms on behalf [note] of Rome' (v. 10).[45]

When Apollonius travels to Alexandria to meet Vespasian he is all ready to claim him as the good king on the Greek model (v. 27 ff.).[46] Introducing Vespasian Philostratus remarks that all previous emperors 'after the first *autokratôr*' (Augustus) had been harsh tyrants, with the possible exception of Claudius (v. 27). Vespasian

[41] *Apollonius* iv. 5; *Letters* 71 'Luculluses, Fabriciuses, and other blessed Lucanians' (cf. *Letters* 72).

[42] Flinterman 1993: 106–7; see Bowie 1974: 200.

[43] Bowie 1978: 1655–7.

[44] On Apollonius' remark that Nero cannot really win, because he altered the dates of the festival, cf. Pausanias x. 36. 9 with Habicht 1985: 83, Halfmann 1986: 174 on Nero's postponement of the 211th Olympics from 65 till the autumn of 66. Note also Gascó 1987–8: 440–2 on the extent of Philostratus' knowledge in this 'Spanish' section.

[45] Cf. Philostratus' portrait of Dio and Herodes at *VS* 488, 563.

[46] Cf. Bowie 1978: 1660–2.

demands to see Apollonius and is given a brief lecture on how to
be king (v. 28), which leads him to damn the emperors after Augustus
for shaming *ta Rhômaiôn* (v. 29, 32). The following debate between
the philosophers Dio of Prusa, Euphrates, and Apollonius before
Vespasian about the future government of Rome is a remarkable
assertion of Rome's need to be guided by men of Greek culture
(v. 33–5).[47] This belief, which is no surprise, is, of course, especially
visible in the thought of Plutarch (*On Progress in Virtue, Philosophers and Rulers, To an Uneducated Ruler*) and Dio (orations on
kingship). The *Mentorhaltung* fits a familiar pattern.

The debate itself differs from its prototype in the third book of
Herodotus' *Histories* by representing the choice of constitutions as
a simple one between democracy and monarchy (omitting oligarchy), Euphrates arguing for the former, Dio being made to suggest (somewhat mischievously) a referendum between the two, and
Apollonius arguing the case for monarchy, observing that it is a
foregone conclusion, praising the virtues of Vespasian as the good
pastor, noting his ability to found a dynasty and his need of many
friends. In the next chapter (v. 36) Apollonius follows this with
advice on how to be a good king: do not tax your subjects too
harshly, obey the law, reverence the gods, rule your sons, suppress
the vices of the city of Rome, and with regard to governors make
sure that those 'who are chosen by lot' (i.e. for the 'senatorial'
provinces) are 'suited to their provinces [*ethnê*] . . . and that Greek
speakers should rule Greeks and Latin speakers should rule those
who speak the same or similar languages'. Apollonius claims to
have in mind a governor of Achaia ('Hellas'), who was unsuccessful
precisely because he did not know Greek (*ta Hellênôn*) and the
Greeks could not understand him. There is no need to look for a
'historical' basis for this advice, though it is certainly worth noting
that the policy of Pius and Marcus which preferred easterners as
governors in provinces with a Greek-speaking population had been
given up by Commodus and the Severans.[48]

[47] It is of course unhistorical (cf. Levi 1981 on Grosso's fantasies), though
Philostratus' sense of history is good (Flinterman 1993: 152–61 on the setting).
[48] Pius and Marcus: Alföldy 1977: 78–9, 119–20 (Provincia Asia); Commodus and
the Severans: Leunissen 1989: 88–9 (n. 44 is especially revealing: 18 proconsuls with
a sure/probable western origin served in Provincia Asia in this period against only
3 with a sure eastern background, a situation which reflects not a conscious west-
ernization but the lower numbers of available eastern senators and the ending of the
policy of preferring them). For *ta Hellênôn* see n. 74.

Given the appeal of Apollonius to the Severan house, it may be wondered whether we should not be thinking of the parallels between Philostratus' Apollonius and Dio of Prusa's Socrates, Diogenes, and the other characters he uses in his speeches on the true king, and especially of his use of Heracles and Alexander, figures both dear to Trajan. In Dio's second speech on kingship the accent on Alexander's love of Greek literature and culture (ii. 32–3) is worth recalling.[49] It was in fact argued long ago that the young Severus Alexander and his powerful mother Julia Mamaea were in Philostratus' mind when he made Apollonius advise Vespasian.[50] Julia, like her aunt Julia Domna, was well respected by Greek intellectuals for her interest in culture and in the education of her son.[51] But though there is good evidence to link Severus Alexander with Asclepius at Aegeae (and so with Apollonius),[52] we should probably be thinking in general terms and not of a particular emperor.[53] Greek advice on the good king was many centuries older than Rome. In the *Lives of the Sophists* Philostratus has Hadrian and Marcus following the advice of Polemo and Aristides (*VS* 534, 583). It was natural to present Vespasian doing the same with Apollonius. One thing that may be remarked on here is the different type of exemplum offered by Dio and Philostratus. The use of Apollonius certainly shows an increasing tolerance for mystical and miraculous elements. This foreshadows the religious trends of pagan life and thought in later antiquity and ways of apprehending and revealing divine power that seem more and more 'irrational' to us. Once again, this does not constitute evidence of social 'anxiety'. It should be remembered

[49] Cf. Moles 1978: 84–5; Anderson 1986: 147–8.

[50] Göttsching 1889: 85–7 (where Philostratus even becomes one of the emperor's tutors).

[51] *PIR²* J 649. See for Cassius Dio Zonaras xii. 15 (= Boissevain's edition of Dio, vol. iii. 477 §2); Herodian v. 7. 5, vi. 1. 1–10 (not entirely favourable); Eusebius, *Ecclesiastical History* vi. 21. 3–4 'a most religious woman if ever there was one' (on her summons of Origen; she also received an address from Hippolytus: Richard 1963: 79–80); cf. *Augustan History, Severus Alexander* 3. 1–5 (education), 14. 7 (Julia's greed), 66. 1 (Julia's wisdom).

[52] See below, n. 63.

[53] Clearly there are several obvious contemporary references in the *Apollonius* for those who want to find them (e.g. i. 28—the warring sons of the wise Darius can be Severus with Caracalla and Geta; Vespasian is perhaps Severus; the good Titus and the bad Domitian can be Geta and Caracalla); see Göttsching 1889: 74–89, Koskenniemi 1991: 31 ff., Flinterman 1993: 241–56. Such evocations may have been in Philostratus' mind—without being of overriding importance to his portrait of his Hellenic sage.

that the figure of Apollonius is firmly rooted in a Hellenism which is perceived by Philostratus as restoring and continuing that of the classical age. Here there is no incompatibility with Dio.

There is one other incident in Book v that deserves comment. This is Vespasian's removal of Greek freedom after Nero had allowed the Greek cities to regain their 'Attic and Doric characters' (v. 41). Pausanias, as we saw, gives the reason for Vespasian's action as Greek *stasis*. This seems to be confirmed by epigraphic testimony. Philostratus, speaking as author, says 'Vespasian alleged *staseis* and other things which did not merit such anger'. Apollonius promptly sent him three letters (later incorporated in the collection) contrasting his behaviour towards the Greeks with Nero's.[54] Philostratus nevertheless adds that Apollonius continued to admire the rest of Vespasian's administration, which he took to be a blessing on himself (v. 41). In this way he brushes aside the jarring 'enslavement' (as Apollonius puts it), and re-establishes the Roman king's respect for the Greek sage.

Apollonius' final battles with Domitian are prepared for in Book vi by a visit to the Naked Philosophers in the marches of Egypt and Ethiopia,[55] and by favourable contacts with Titus (vi. 6–22; 29–34), including advice on how to be a good king (33) and a reminder to benefit the city of Tarsus (34). The confrontation with Domitian is, as with Nero, a test of true philosophy (vii. 1 [Philostratus on Domitian]; cf. iv. 38 [Apollonius on Nero]). Philostratus makes his point by listing and criticizing the struggles fifth- and fourth-century philosophers like Plato and Diogenes had with tyrants and monarchs. Apollonius stood above these and challenged Domitian 'on behalf of the ruled' (vii. 3–4). Most of Book vii is taken up with preliminaries for the contest: the summons to meet the charge of making a treasonable statement (9), conversation with the well-known Cynic philosopher Demetrius and with Damis, who both urge Apollonius to flee (11–14),[56] a favourable meeting with (Casperius) Aelianus (cf. Telesinus), Domitian's praetorian prefect (16–20), and finally Apollonius' imprisonment pending trial before

---

[54] Cf. nos. 42 f–h in Penella's edition of the *Letters* (drawn along with eleven others in series from the *Apollonius*; Penella 1979: 20). Pausanias: above, 'Pausanias' n. 39.

[55] On these Egyptian sages see Anderson 1986: 216–17.

[56] Demetrius' exile under Vespasian (Cassius Dio lxvi. 13. 3) naturally causes Philostratus no problem. On his pseudo-historical role in the *Apollonius* see Bowie 1978: 1657–9; further Kindstrand 1980: 85–98.

Domitian (21–42), in the midst of which Apollonius is interviewed and persecuted by the emperor (32–4). The final chapter is a rather crude moral tale of a rich Arcadian youth whose father failed him by not giving him a 'Hellenic education', but had sent him to Rome to study law (*êthê nomika*). Here his good looks led to advances from Domitian and, these refused, to his imprisonment. On a literary level the story perhaps prepares us for Apollonius' denial of having sacrificed an Arcadian youth 'of good parents' (viii. 7). Culturally the contrast between good, Hellenic behaviour and the hybristic behaviour expected of the tyrant is tied up with the dangers of foreign travel and the perils of bypassing Greek learning. There is nothing specifically hostile to Rome here, except inasmuch as anything that is good is Greek and only Greek. But it is worth observing that the story may represent an early example of criticism of the influence accorded to Roman law by the *Constitutio Antoniniana*.[57]

Book viii of the *Apollonius* is largely taken up with an imaginary defence speech of Apollonius that was never delivered.[58] Apollonius regards his trial as a 'discussion' (viii. 2). Philostratus' plot collapses almost completely when Domitian hesitates to press even the main charges, unexpectedly acquits Apollonius, and commands him to stay for a private conference. Apollonius, having denounced the wicked agents of Domitian's administration, promptly leaves (5). Philostratus then kindly gives us Apollonius' prepared apology (7. 1–16). The import of this is that Apollonius 'revealed the tyrant who had been an object of fear to all the Greeks and the barbarians as a toy of his philosophy' (10). The final incidents of the Book are Apollonius' magical appearance to his disciples, his visit to the holy

---

[57] There is nothing impossible about a Greek learning Roman law in the 1st c. (cf. Arrian, *Discourses of Epictetus* iv. 3. 12 for the ordinances of 'Masurius [Sabinus] and Cassius [Longinus]'—possibly addressed to Romans, of course), but the story rather presupposes conditions of Philostratus' own time; cf. *ILS* 7742 'd. m. T. Oclati Athenagorae Nicomedensis, iuris studiosi' (near Rome, late 2nd c. at the earliest; Kunkel 1967: 264, 344). On the spread of knowledge of Roman law in the East in the late 2nd and 3rd centuries see Jolowicz 1952: 545–7; Kunkel 1967: 354–65. Note the jurist Herennius Modestinus' *Excuses from Tutelage and Curatorship* explaining Roman law in Greek around the 230s (Schulz 1946: 250–2; Kunkel 1967: 259–61). For later complaints that Greek culture is being threatened by Roman law and Latin see e.g. Palm 1959: 84–6, Schulz 1946: 268–9 on Libanius.

[58] Interpreted by Lenz 1964 to support his belief that the *Apollonius* was written about 200 for the young Caracalla (for the obvious objections to this idea see Koskenniemi 1991: 42).

cave of Trophonius in Boeotia, his awareness of Domitian's assassination at Rome while he is in Ephesus, his death, and epiphany to a doubter (11–31).

Two items of interest may be mentioned. First, in the speech of defence Apollonius replies to the charge of having averted the plague from Ephesus (viii. 7. 8, cf. iv. 10, vii. 21, viii. 5) by saying that he could have saved from plague a barbarian city hostile to the emperor, something the emperor in his humanity could not have objected to. 'But let us assume that barbarians are of no interest and that we would not make them healthy, for they are our bitterest enemies and have no treaties with our race [*tôi peri hêmas genei*] —who would deny Ephesus its salvation?' The phrase 'our race' probably means 'Greeks' (referring to the Ephesians, who are descended 'from the purest Attic'). It is just possible that it means the people of the Empire (Greeks and Romans) as opposed to the barbarians outside it. One of the *Letters* (21) addressed to Domitian is relevant here. 'You should keep away from barbarians and not rule over them, for it is not right that they, being barbarians, should have good treatment.' If the *Letters* is a second-century work, this might be taken as evidence for the same 'them and us' mentality that we see in Lucian (in the context of the Parthian war) and that has often been discovered in Aristides' *To Rome*, where 'we' are Romans and 'they' are barbarians. However, the Apollonius of the *Letters* simply bids the emperor not to extend his benefits to non-Greeks (who could be non-Greek members of the empire).[59] There is nothing at all to suggest that he subsumes Greeks under 'Romans'.

The Apollonius of Philostratus in the context of his defence speech to the emperor explicitly places his barbarians outside the Empire and makes them its enemies. At first sight this may look more like the position adopted by Lucian. But elsewhere in the *Apollonius* 'barbarian' refers to peoples in the Latin West (v. 9), an assessment apparently of Philostratus himself (rather than his characters—if such a distinction is at all possible). Even if Philostratus is presenting Apollonius arguing before Domitian a distinction between those Greeks inside the Empire and those barbarians outside it, there is

---

[59] Cf. Pausanias i. 5. 5, viii. 43. 4 (both referring to imperial benefaction; 'Pausanias' n. 90). In a different context the Apollonius of the *Letters* argues that there are no real distinctions between Greeks and barbarians (44). For Philostratus' view see below in text.

no need to accord his Apollonius any form of Roman identity on this basis: one can easily applaud Rome for fighting a common enemy without identifying oneself—culturally, politically, or spiritually—with it. Overall, the Philostratean Apollonius is so overtly and self-consciously 'Greek' that it would be strange to imagine him advancing a communitarian viewpoint.[60] This is also the case with his thoroughgoing support of monarchy. It is monarchy on ideal, Hellenic lines that Apollonius wants, not the Roman Principate *per se*. A little earlier in Book viii he is made to say to Domitian, 'I corrected the cities for you' (viii. 7. 7). 'For you' is to be seen purely in the context of the defence speech. The sage knows Domitian will soon be removed and that Nerva will rule as a good king who respects Apollonius and wants his advice (vii. 8–9, 33; viii. 7. 10, 27).[61] In sum, reform of Greek cities and advice to Roman kings are part of the same Hellenic programme. Apollonius is certainly no revolutionary. He wants only to improve the status quo, not to abolish it. As Philostratus puts is, he has helped temples, cities, peoples, the dead, the sick, the wise, the unwise, and 'kings who made him their adviser in virtue' (vi. 43). Romans take their turn with the rest.

The second point of interest is the reference at the very end of the work to the imperial cult. As we would expect, the cult was taken for granted by Philostratus himself, as a passage in the *Lives of the Sophists* shows.[62] At *Apollonius* viii. 31 Philostratus says 'his shrines at Tyana are fitted out with royal offerings—for the kings would not deny him what they claimed for themselves'. The appeal of Apollonius to the imperial house is finally made explicit. More than this, Philostratus voices a now familiar demand for respect for Greek religion and culture, the superiority of which is the premiss of the whole work. It is nice to find that the shrine of Asclepius at Aegeae, with which Apollonius was so closely connected, was

[60] For a different view see Flinterman 1993: 133 (also citing for a 'we' mentality *Apollonius* v. 33, where Euphrates says that the Jews 'have long been in revolt not only from Romans but also from all men', do not share the rites and customs common 'to mankind', and 'are further from us than Sousa, Bactra, and the Indians beyond them', so that 'it was better never to have occupied them'; but here 'us' = men in general).

[61] Apollonius, like Dio of Prusa (*Or.* xlv. 2), does not get to visit Nerva as emperor, but goes one better in sending him a letter of precepts (viii. 28).

[62] *VS* 539–40 'Smyrna was contending about her temples and rights . . . she won *ta prôteia*' (i.e. the right to lead the procession in the games of the Asian *koinon*).

indeed patronized by third-century imperials, who associated themselves there with the god or with Hygieia (Health).[63]

LETTERS OF APOLLONIUS

Before passing to the *Lives of the Sophists* it is worth considering very briefly the *Letters of Apollonius*. Regrettably, nothing secure can be known about their origin except that some, and probably most, of them predate Philostratus, who clearly adapts a number of those found in our collection.[64] The *Letters* contains much material not in the biography,[65] and in the *Life* Philostratus, who was himself an author of surviving letters, no doubt invented where it suited him. That two of the letters in the collection came from another biographical treatment is suggested, as has been noted, by the narrative fragment preserved between them in one of the manuscripts.[66] This idea does not completely rule out the authenticity either of these letters or of others; good arguments have been put forward to support the idea that one of the *Letters* does indeed reflect the attitudes of the historical Apollonius and those he knew.[67] But it is easier to refer most of our collection of *Letters* to the ancients' liking for fictitious epistolography (which was particularly strong in the second sophistic).[68]

We can at least compare the collection's view of Hellenism and of Greek-Roman relations. The cities of the Greek world and their

[63] Robert 1973: 195–7 (Julia Domna, Severus Alexander, Valerian); Weiss 1982: 198–203 on the especially close links between the god and Severus Alexander. Note again Caracalla's *hêrôon* to Apollonius (above, n. 11).

[64] e.g., as noted, *Letters* 71 to the Ionians on their decline from Hellenic standards and their use of Latin names is summarized at *Apollonius* iv. 5 (where 'blessed Lucanians' is omitted).

[65] Especially in the letters taken from Stobaeus (79–100); Meyer 1917: 408.

[66] These are *Letters* 62 and 63 to the Lacedaemonians. See Meyer 1917: 412 with Diels 1918: 77–8 n. 1, Bowie 1978: 1677–88 (Moeragenes as the biographical author). Penella 1979: 4 n. 15 rejects the idea of a biographical fragment and ascribes the text to a scribal fancy.

[67] See Jones 1982 on *Letters* 53, the testimonial for Apollonius by a certain Claudius. Not many will go as far as the blanket belief in authenticity expressed by Lo Cascio 1978. Note Philostratus' report that some of Apollonius' letters were preserved in Hadrian's villa at Antium (*Apollonius* viii. 20).

[68] Note the glaring outsider *Letters* 59, from Garmus to Neogyndes. On the ancients' taste for epistolography see in general *RE* Suppl. v (1931) 186–220 (Sykutris), and for the second sophistic cf. above, 'Past' n. 72.

Greek culture are largely in decline.[69] The criticism is of moral and
political degeneration. Some of the *Letters* criticize Rome. The
cities are said to be getting worse under her rule, and the Roman
procurators of Asia are admonished for leaving the 'roots' of vice
intact (30, 31). The Roman administration is reproved for attending
to practical and material benefits rather than to the 'children, young
men, and women in the cities', who need moral instruction (54).
These criticisms are not especially grave, though they are less constructive than criticisms in the *Apollonius* (with which, of course,
they interact). They do not question the right of Rome to be ruling,
only the quality of her rule. In *Letters* 31 the Romans are at least
doing something about vice by 'lopping off the branches' of harm-
ful trees. Again, of the two letters to Domitian (20–1) the first is
moral counsel ('if you have power, as you do, you also need to
acquire prudence'), the second advice to keep imperial benefaction
away from barbarians (cf. above). At the same time the epistolary
Apollonius also displays the usual intellectual's aversion from the
benefits of Roman power (*Letters* 8 and 14 against Euphrates). But
again this is more a profession of asceticism than an anti-Roman
stance, as is shown by *Letters* 28, where Romans are deemed suitable to be friends of the semi-mythical saint, Zamolxis.

LIVES OF THE SOPHISTS

The basic attitude of the epistolary and the Philostratean Apollonius
is reformatory. There is no challenge to the existing order.[70] To
speak, however, of Apollonius' repeated intervention on behalf of
the established order is to raise the question of how that order is
perceived by its supporters.[71] Only if they believe they are supported by it as they wish is it in their interests to uphold it. The
Apollonius of Philostratus supports Rome so long as Rome hearkens
—as she does in Philostratus' picture—to the worth of Greek culture. Rome's material benefits are recognized (e.g. vi. 34 at Tarsus);
but it is Rome's recognition of Greeks' intellectual worth that

[69] *Letters* 25, 27, 32–4, 38–41, 56, 63–8, 71, 75, 76; see also Penella 1975: 308 = no.
75a in his edition. Praise for maintaining standards is awarded in 11, 12, 47, 69.
[70] Cf. Göttsching 1889: 88–9, Schmid 1887–97: iv. 569–70.
[71] Repeated intervention: Bowie 1978: 1682.

really counts. A similar picture can be seen in the *Lives of the Sophists*. Various aspects of this work have been commented on already.[72] Here it is as well to remind ourselves that the *Lives* offer a fairly reliable picture of an important section of the cultural and political elite of the second sophistic. They glorify Hellenism as the *Apollonius* does, but unlike that work they present it in the real world of men away from the divine. In the *Lives* fiction of the sort permissible in the *Apollonius* would have been inappropriate. But the characterization of Romans in the *Lives* again depends on their attitudes to the merits of the sophistic stars. If one follows the text through, the majority of appearances by emperors and others can be read along these lines.[73]

Take first Trajan. Philostratus tells a well-known anecdote about the emperor and Dio Chrysostom in which Dio is applauded by a Trajan who confesses to not understanding what he is saying (*VS* 488). Philostratus does not present the emperor as Greekless; but he does class him among those who 'have no exact knowledge of things Greek', i.e. Greek language and literature. This presentation, whether or not he knew it was exaggerated,[74] satisfies the biographer on two counts. First, Dio himself is presented as a sage who must be listened to and (literally) cannot be contradicted (Philostratus has just shown how necessary he was to Rome by having him exhort Roman troops to support the regime of Nerva). Second, it ties in with a wider theme in the *Lives* that presents the Greek language being loved by those at Rome who do not understand it (491, 589). There is nothing derogatory in this. Indeed, at *VS* 589 Philostratus says Hadrian of Tyre was applauded at Rome both by those who knew Greek (*ta Hellênôn*) and by 'those who were educated in the other language'. The key point is that Greeks and their language are respected by Romans.

The emperor Hadrian was bound to be a favourite in this regard because of his noted philhellenism (at which only Galen demurred). To Philostratus' mind he would relax from the burdens of office by

---

[72] Above, 'Practice' n. 3, 'Past' nn. 84–6, 89, 95–9.

[73] Cf. Flinterman 1993: 43–9.

[74] Cf. above 'Dio', nn. 32–3; but note Cassius Dio lxviii. 7. 4 'he lacked an exact education in rhetoric, but knew the practice of it and used it', a passage which Philostratus might have known (he would naturally gloss 'education' as 'things Greek [*ta Hellênôn*]', a phrase referring specifically to language also at *VS* 589 [below in text], *Apollonius* ii. 31, v. 36 [above, n. 48]).

turning to philosophers and sophists (490), just as the addressee of the *Lives*, Gordian, was intended to do with the text now before him (480). There are several other examples of such respect. The nasty governor Rufus comes to recognize how wonderful Nicetes is when he has him tried, and thus sends him home with high honours (512).[75] Domitian loads Scopelian with presents after his embassy speech on the vines of Asia (520). Hadrian honours Dionysius of Miletus (524) and admires Marcus of Byzantium, since 'of the kings of old he was the one who was most prepared to foster merits' (530).[76] Polemo was honoured and valued by Trajan, Hadrian, Pius, and implicitly by Marcus (531, 532, 534, 539).[77] Marcus' behaviour towards Gordian's ancestor, the great Herodes Atticus, in his trial before the emperor at Sirmium is especially philosophic (561). Marcus is naturally full of respect for Aelius Aristides (582–3), and showers gifts on the eminent Hadrian of Tyre (589). Even Commodus, damned for failing his education by Cassius Dio and Herodian,[78] is suitably deferential to Hadrian (590) and is charmed by Pollux (593). Severus praises and admires Hermocrates (611), though he also strips Heracleides the Lycian of immune status and awards it to Apollonius of Athens following a declamatory competition (601). Philostratus makes no comment here, but the failure of the same Heracleides before Severus in an extempore speech 'because he was afraid of the court and the bodyguards' leads him to apologize for sophists' typical sensitivity (614).

By contrast the emperor Caracalla does not have proper respect. Philostratus seems to criticize him for depriving Philiscus of Thessaly of his immunity because of his effete appearance (623),[79] and records that he had wanted to laugh when he witnessed him unexpectedly

[75] Philostratus probably refers to L. Verginius Rufus as governor of Germania Superior ('in command of the armies in Gaul'), a post he held in 67–8 (Eck 1985: 28 n. 1, 231–2).

[76] Philostratus plays down Hadrian's noted ambivalence towards intellectuals (*Augustan History*, *Hadrian* 15. 10, 16. 8; Cassius Dio lxix. 3. 1–4. 6; Syme 1985: 342; Swain 1989*a*); contrast his report of Hadrian's amiability towards Favorinus at *VS* 489–90 and honours to Dionysius with Cassius Dio's remarks on the two sophists and the emperor (lxix. 3. 4–6).

[77] Marcus' verdict in his correspondence with Fronto is rather more negative: *Ad M. Caes.* ii. 10 (29–30 v.d.H.[2]).

[78] See below, 'Cassius Dio' nn. 29, 31.

[79] 'We must not on account of [Philiscus'] failings in look, voice, and dress deprive him of his most important place in Greek rhetoric and composition'. Philostratus also notes here that Caracalla 'nevertheless even after this' gave immunity to Philostratus the Younger.

bestowing honours on Heliodorus 'the Arab' (625–6).[80] In one
of the *Letters* written by Philostratus Caracalla is attacked for
destroying his own house (72), a reference to the fratricide of Geta
in 212. In the *Lives* the fratricide is passed over without negative
comment when Philostratus reports the hostile reaction of Antipater.
The reason may be that he is simply not interested in moral comment, for the only important thing here was Caracalla's respect for
Greek culture. In this he was unreliable, as Philostratus stresses
with his ironic remarks on the magnificent power of fortune in
the case of Heliodorus.[81] The last emperor to be mentioned in the
Lives is Elagabalus (625). In his case Philostratus is not interested
in cultural relations, but in the sophist (Claudius) Aelianus, who
attacked 'Gynnis' (the 'little woman') for his debauchery and tyranny and who was attacked in turn by the younger Philostratus for
not daring to publish his accusations during the emperor's lifetime.
Cultural relations are mentioned with regard to the sophist himself,
since he was 'a Roman but talked Attic Greek like the Athenians of
the *mesogeia*'.

In their presentation of Greek relations with Rome the *Lives
of the Sophists* resemble epigraphical texts recording privileges or
benefactions. They concentrate on what is good in the relationship
between ruled and ruler, on successes rather than failures. An archetypal bad ruler like Commodus appears to support Greek culture.
An ambiguous philhellene like Hadrian is never ambiguous.
Further, the *Lives* in many ways simply present a relationship
between Greek culture and power rather than Greek culture and
specifically Roman power. Philostratus knew perfectly well that in
the Empire of his day there was no great political divide between
Greeks and other provincials—of the right class—and the central
power. Under the Severans the Roman empire was conspicuously
representative of the eastern and western elites. On the other hand
Philostratus was also aware that the pre-Severan emperors ('the
kings of old') were Italian or of Italian stock. They had to acquire
Greek culture. Thus the same feelings are in operation behind his

[80] If this man is the same as Heliodorus the novelist, Emesene origin (cf. *Ethiopian Story* x. 41. 4; above, 'Novel' n. 60, below, Appendix A) will explain Caracalla's
favour and appointment of him as *advocatus fisci*. For a known Emesene rhetor at
this time see *Suda* φ 735 on Fronto the uncle of Cassius Longinus and rival of one
of the Philostrati and of Valerius Apsines.
[81] Cf. again the verdicts of Cassius Dio and Herodian, below, 'Cassius Dio' nn.
30, 31.

presentation of Apollonius as adviser to the emperors of the first
century and the status of Polemo or Herodes before their emperors
in the *Lives*. The Greek sage must be needed by the Roman king.
Indeed, though Philostratus knew that the Roman elite in his time
was thoroughly versed in Greek,[82] he nevertheless emphasizes the
respect for Greek culture shown by non-Greeks throughout the
period of the sophistic.[83] Philostratus is excessively, though not
untypically, conscious of the superiority of Greek culture. It is
through this consciousness that he articulates the relation between
culture and power. No doubt he knew only one world in terms of
political power; in terms of culture he still lived in the world of
Greece.

[82] Cf. the assumptions in a story like that told by Cassius Dio lxxviii. 20. 2 where
the equestrian and senatorial order spontaneously assert the worth of Macrinus and
his son 'in Greek'.

[83] Cf. esp. Trajan (488), Favorinus (his own 489, his audience 491), Hadrian (589),
Aelian (his own 624).

13

Cassius Dio

INTRODUCTION

I want finally to amplify some of the attitudes of the Greek intellectuals I have been considering by turning very briefly to the historian Cassius Dio and his view of the place of Greek culture in the Roman Empire.

Coming from Nicaea in Bithynia Cassius Dio was a slightly older contemporary of Philostratus and lived from around 163/4 to after 229.[1] Politically he was fully committed to the Roman empire and enjoyed a distinguished senatorial career, being *consul II ordinarius* with the emperor Severus Alexander in 229. His first consulship was certainly under Septimius Severus.[2] Dio's relations with Severus show tensions similar to those felt by Galen. He had brought himself to the attention of the emperor by publishing and presenting to him a short work on 'the dreams and portents which gave Severus hopes of the imperial power'. Severus acknowledged this in complimentary terms (*Roman History* lxxii. 23. 1–2). This work has rightly been seen as a precaution taken by a man who wanted to keep secure under the new regime the honours granted him in the brief reign of Pertinax in 193, particularly his appointment as praetor for the year 194.[3] Similar is the study of the wars and civil disorders in the years after Commodus' assassination which also won imperial approval when it was published perhaps after the defeat of Severus'

[1] Cassius Dio lxxv. 15. 3; Millar 1964: 13, 24. For the Bithynian context see Ameling 1984*b*. On the *History* see, apart from Millar and amongst others, Manuwald 1979 (Augustus), Bering-Staschewski 1981 (from Marcus to Severus Alexander), Fechner 1986 (Rome's empire in the Republic).

[2] Millar 1964: 204–7.

[3] Another pressing reason was no doubt the assistance given by Dio's homeland Nicaea to the forces of Severus' rival, Pescennius Niger, at the end of 193 (Herodian iii. 2. 7–3. 1 gives the cause as civic rivalry with Nicomedia; cf. Robert 1977*b*: 22 ff. and Dio lii. 30. 3, 37. 9–10 [Maecenas' advice about the cities]).

last rival, Clodius Albinus, in 197.[4] When Dio came to write up his *Roman History* proper, perhaps in the reign of Severus Alexander,[5] this material was not discarded (as he says himself, lxxii. 23. 3), but now there was no flattery of the emperor and indeed much criticism, especially of his wasteful demolition of the walls of Byzantium (lxxiv. 14. 4), the trouble and expense caused by his acquisition of Nisibis (lxxv. 3. 2–3), and the self-destructive struggle with Albinus, which weakened Roman power and showed Severus' very worst side (lxxv. 7–8).[6] These and other criticisms are not negated by the sober assessment of Severus' personal characteristics at lxxvi. 16–17. The succeeding emperors, Caracalla, Macrinus, and Elagabalus, are all strongly criticized for personal or public policy or both. Under Severus Alexander, whose reign up till 229 is treated 'in summary' (lxxx. 2. 1), the situation in the empire remains critical in Dio's view owing to the rise of the Sassanian Persian dynasty to the East and the weakness and ill-discipline of the legions in Mesopotamia and elsewhere (lxxx. 3–4).

POLITICAL AFFILIATION

Dio writes the history of Rome as a Roman senator and governor. He says a good deal on the constitutional arrangements of the Empire. He praises the Republican government, which he refers to as 'the *dêmokratia*', for its achievements, while being fully aware of Roman expansionism and imperialism in the earlier period.[7] The size of the Republican empire and the rivalries of the late Republican dynasts made monarchy the only viable system of government. In a passage which blasts the Liberators Cassius and Brutus for not realizing this, Dio like his putative ancestor, Dio of Prusa,[8] says that democracy has a 'fair name' but is disastrous in fact. Even a bad monarch was better than the rule of the masses ('as the history

---

[4] lxxii. 23. 1–3; Millar 1964: 29.

[5] See Barnes 1984, arguing not unconvincingly against the traditional earlier dating.

[6] lxxv. 7. 3 'I am telling it as it really happened, not as Severus wrote [in his autobiography]'.

[7] 'Democracy': Manuwald 1979: 9 n. 10. Praise: see esp. xiii fr. 52. Imperialism: Fechner 1986: 216–46 (arguing correctly against the views of Gabba 1955: 306, 308 and others drawing on Caesar's speech at Vesontio—xxxviii. 36–46—that Dio sought to justify Roman imperialism as a defensive strategy).

[8] *Or.* iii. 47 (as Dio's ancestor: Millar 1964: 11–12; Ameling 1984*b*: 124–6).

of the Greeks, the barbarians, and of the Romans themselves shows'). For Rome, where 'moderation in a democracy was impossible', there was no choice. The key thing was that monarchy offered stability.[9] In this Dio's views are similar to those of Plutarch and the rest. He does not repeat Aristides' sophism that the Principate itself was a democracy. Monarchy was monarchy, whatever Romans liked to think.[10] Dio's ideal of monarchy was of course of a monarchy that would support its friends. This is expressed most clearly in the speech of Maecenas urging Octavian to become sole ruler of Rome (lii. 14–40), a major concern of which is the emperor's relations with the senatorial and equestrian classes, the offices they should hold, and the education they should obtain (19–28). The idea of political community in the Empire is expressed also in Dio of Prusa's kingship speeches and Aristides' *To Rome*. Whatever these authors believed on the matter, for Dio as a favoured Severan senator political community was, of course, a reality. He can, then, easily seem to be totally 'Roman'.[11] Though he never calls himself a 'Roman' as such, he certainly has no doubt that the Empire is 'ours' and that damage done to it hurts 'us'.[12]

The difficult question to answer is whether use of 'we' with regard to Rome should be seen as anything more than political affiliation. Dio, whose father was a Roman senator and governor and who was himself first in Rome at the age of 16 or 17, had certainly interiorized some Roman values and is perfectly able to represent others.[13] He plainly knew Latin well for work.[14] In the *History* he can build on Seneca's story about the conspiracy of Cn. Cornelius Cinna Magnus in *On Clemency* 1. 9 for his dialogue between Augustus and Livia at lv. 14–22.[15] Even more interestingly he is

[9] xliv. 1. 2–2. 5; cf. iii fr. 12. 3a, liii. 19. 1, liv. 6. 1, lvi. 43. 4, and the rhetorical flight at xlvii. 39.
[10] liii. 17–18 (the titles used instead of 'king'), cf. xliii. 44. 2, lii. 40. 2, lii. 41. 3–4. The perceived need of Dio's Augustus to develop a mask of democracy in liii is a different matter.
[11] So Gabba 1959: 378.
[12] xxxix. 38. 1 (our pride in Pompey's theatre at Rome), lxxv. 3. 3, lxxvi. 12. 5, lxxx. 4. 1–2 ('our armies . . . the soldiers I commanded').
[13] Father: Halfmann 1979: no. 123. In Rome for Commodus' arrival: lxxii. 4. 2. Roman values: cf. the idealization of virtue-loving northern barbarians at xxvii fr. 94. 2, lxii. 6. 2–5; the idea of the just war in Caesar's speech at Vesontio: above, n. 7.
[14] See liii. 18. 1, lv. 3. 4–5.
[15] He also seems to know Seneca's *Apocolocyntosis* (lx. 35. 3–4) and *Consolation to Polybius* (lxi. 10. 2).

able to paraphrase accurately three lines of the *Aeneid*,[16] the sort of knowledge (or at least the expression of it) that is extremely unusual among Greeks in this period.[17] Further, he presents the Roman empire as a given—he never compares it with earlier Greek powers (as even Aristides does). None of this is very surprising. By Dio's time the Empire had ceased to be 'Roman' in the old, exclusive sense of the term. But paradoxically it is for this reason probably illegitimate to call Dio 'Roman' except as a political designation. Over two hundred years before he was writing, Dionysius of Halicarnassus had pointed out the possible consequences for Rome (which he of course considered a Greek city) of centuries of immigration and miscegenation.[18] It was a danger which Dio himself voiced through the persona of Augustus: 'surely it cannot be right or good that our race should cease and the name of the Romans be extinguished with us, while the city is given over to other people, Greeks or barbarians?'[19] It was this same cosmopolitan aspect of Rome that Galen criticized. By Dio's own time the positive result of opening the Empire to provincials was that 'Roman' for a Greek was perhaps devoid of anything but political import, except in terms of history.

CULTURAL LOYALTY

Being Roman to Dio meant possessing major political status. (He is immensely self-conscious of his worth as a senator and of the

[16] lxxv. 10. 2 ('some verses of the poet Maro') referring to *Aeneid* xi. 371–3; Drances, who speaks here to Turnus, is not strictly speaking 'a certain soldier', as Dio has it.

[17] Cf. the senator (Cn. Claudius) Severus who discusses Roman philosophers with Marcus (above, 'Galen' n. 11), or the Greeks who claim to appreciate Catullus and Calvus (while disparaging all other Latin poetry) at Gellius, *Attic Nights* xix. 9. 7 (cf. 'Language' n. 68). A less exalted example is the Sardian Polybius who dedicated the 'sacred head' of Cicero (2nd-c. AD; above, 'Lucian' n. 108). Cf. further Swain 1991*b* on Greek translations of Latin literature. It cannot be proved that Dio himself used Roman historians as sources—cf. Manuwald 1979: 168–268—but see below, n. 24 on Cicero.

[18] *History of Early Rome* i. 89. 3 on the mixing of barbarians with the truly Greek Romans; cf. Appian's view at 'Arrian' n. 38, further 'Galen' n. 19 on positive and negative aspects of Rome's cosmopolitanism, and perhaps Plato *Laws* 949e–950a for the inspiration.

[19] lvi. 7. 5 (Augustus' speech to the unmarried knights).

need to maintain senatorial prestige.)²⁰ Culturally and spiritually there is no reason to think that Dio would have seen himself as anything other than Greek. So it is that 'we' is used also of his fellow-Bithynians and that at the end of the *History* he records his pleasure in going back to his 'fatherland'.²¹ Here he scarcely seems different from that other Roman senator and writer on Roman history from Bithynia, Arrian of Nicomedia. A comment preserved in Zonaras' epitome of Book xi which, given Zonaras' methods, is almost certainly attributable to Dio expresses his Hellenism with particular strength. Recording that the Romans despised the Lacedaemonian mercenary captain Xanthippus (who was employed by Carthage during the first Punic war) on the grounds that he was 'Greek' (*graikos*, a transliteration of Latin *graecus*), the text adds, 'for thus they call the Hellenes and they use the term against them as a racial slur [*eis oneidos dusgeneias*]' (Zonaras viii. 13. 7).²² That Greeks were aware of the pejorative associations of *graecus* is clear from Plutarch and Athenaeus.²³ The apparently anti-Roman nature of the remark here is reinforced by the context, where Xanthippus defeats the Romans owing to their contempt for him. Interpretation is hampered by the loss of the original text. But it seems very unlikely that the remark was as general as Zonaras makes it: Dio was probably talking about specific feelings towards Xanthippus and/or had in mind Roman Republican attitudes towards Greek culture—though it is quite possible that he was also thinking of the ever potential pejorative use of the Latin word.²⁴ In any case it shows again that Dio was Roman in political, not in cultural terms.

Dio makes expected assumptions about the merits of Greek culture. Like Plutarch he knows that Greek culture had not always

²⁰ All emperors are assessed for their attitude towards the senate; the most revealing comments are those on Macrinus' failure to sustain himself as emperor because he was only a knight (lxxviii. 41).

²¹ lxix. 14. 4 (our fond memories of C. Julius Severus; cf. above, 'Aristides' n. 55), lxxx. 5. 3. On Dio and the Greek world cf. Aalders 1986.

²² Cf. Boissevain's edition of Dio i. 161.

²³ See above, 'Past' n. 35; Plutarch, *Cicero* 5. 2 (*graikos* is used as an insult by 'the most banausic of the Romans') looks similar to Dio.

²⁴ It is not completely certain, of course, that 'racial slur' is also Dio's own point of view. Note that Dio is the only Greek author to quote the Latin word *graeculus* (xlvi. 18. 1 ὧ Κικέρων . . . ἢ γραίκουλε); the usage, occurring in a speech made against Cicero, is interesting because *graeculus* (which is by no means always pejorative, but like *graecus* takes its meaning from the context) was used particularly by Cicero in his speeches (Dubuisson 1991: 324); cf. Manuwald 1979: 268–72 on Dio's probable use of Cicero's *Philippics* (where *graeculus* is found at v. 14 and xiii. 13).

had a place in Rome.[25] In the time of the late Republic he still thinks it necessary to explain the difference between Cato the Younger and Cato the Elder by saying that the Younger 'had enjoyed a better Greek education' (xxxvii. 22. 1). He is quite interested in the education of the emperors.[26] Culture can include specific attainments in Latin letters,[27] but in most cases it ought to and surely does mean Greek culture. Thus Dio highlights Marcus' education under Fronto and Herodes Atticus and his lessons in Stoic doctrines. This education was of great benefit to him (lxxi. 35. 1).[28] The specific value of Greek culture is underlined by Dio's comment on Marcus' establishment of chairs of rhetoric and philosophy at Athens: here he did something 'for all mankind' (lxxi. 31. 3). By contrast Commodus and Caracalla failed to live up to the excellent education they were given (lxxi. 36. 4; lxxvii. 11. 2–3). No explicit link is made between their disastrous reigns and a rejection of *paideia*, but the assumptions Dio is making are plain enough. This shows particularly with Commodus in the much cited rhetorical assessment that follows on from Marcus' inability to educate him: 'the Roman empire and our history now descend from a kingdom of gold to one of iron and rust';[29] in the case of Caracalla Dio's one-sidedness emerges from inconsistencies in his own text.[30] Herodian has a similar perspective in his *History* of the period after Marcus (which was written around 250). He uses Marcus as a paradigm of the good king. An important part of this picture is Marcus

[25] Cf. xvii fr. 57. 62 on Scipio Africanus.
[26] There are direct comments at xlv. 2. 7–8 (Octavian); lvii. 1. 1 (Tiberius); lx. 2. 1 (Claudius); lx. 32. 3 (Nero); lxviii. 7. 4 (Trajan); lxix. 3–4 (Hadrian); lxxi. 35 (Marcus); lxxi. 36. 4 (Commodus); lxxvi. 16. 1 (Severus); lxxvii. 11. 2–3 (Caracalla); Zonaras xii. 15 = Boissevain, vol. iii. 477 §2 (Severus Alexander). These are part of Dio's biographical approach to imperial history (the biographical *Augustan History* is likewise interested in emperors' education).
[27] e.g. lxix. 18. 3 on Fronto's pre-eminence in the Roman courts; or on Octavian, Hadrian, and Marcus in the passages cited in n. 26.
[28] Dio clearly felt philosophy should uphold the status quo: lxvi. 12. 2 (criticism of Helvidius Priscus; cf. the attack on Seneca at lxi. 10. 2 for acting contrary to his philosophical endeavours).
[29] The proverb goes back to Hesiod, *WD* 110 ff.; contrast the inversion of the idea (now is the golden age) at Aristides, *To Rome* 106. Dio perhaps satirizes Commodus' own propaganda (lxxii. 15. 6; cf. Beaujeu 1955: 369–70). Contrast Philostratus' presentation of Commodus at 'Philostratus' n. 78 (text).
[30] Even as he condemns Caracalla he says that as emperor he continued to spend much time on education; later he has him honouring the 2nd-c. poet Mesomedes (lxxvii. 13. 7 with disapproval) and quoting some rather trite lines of Euripides at Dio himself (lxxviii. 8. 4).

as *pepaideumenos*.[31] In the case of Commodus, Herodian like Dio stresses Marcus' attempt to educate his son (i. 2. 1) and (going further than Dio) Commodus' later repudiation of education (i. 13. 7–8). With Caracalla again Herodian stresses his father's determination to give him a good education and again the son's rejection of this course (iii. 10. 2–4; iv. 3. 3–4).

Where he can Dio takes serious account of the effect of education or the lack of it on a ruler, a familiar perspective. Another perspective he shares with second-century intellectuals like Aristides, Lucian, and Pausanias is a concern with the defence of the Empire. This is hardly surprising for a governor; but it seems to be articulated through the traditional Greek mode of defence against *barbaroi*. Dio's ideal is, as in Aristides' *To Rome*, to have a standing army on the Empire's borders which is ready for defensive war.[32] His characterization of Marcus as the best emperor ever (lxxi. 34. 2) is in no small part to do with the continual wars he fought against barbarians, in which 'he survived himself and preserved the Empire'.[33] Dio's attitude towards the imperial cult has affinities with the likely feelings of Plutarch and Pausanias on making gods from the living, but is explicit. In regard to the cult of living emperors he notes that it is only 'Rome's subjects' who put up shrines and that emperors have not dared do this in Italy or Rome.[34] Dio has Maecenas advise Augustus to abolish the cult altogether.[35] This is his own view. Emperors are assessed accordingly, especially with regard to their attitude towards trials for 'impiety' (*asebeia*, i.e. *majestas*).[36] Dio's basic opinion, like Plutarch's and Pausanias', is (in Maecenas' words) that 'no man ever became a god by election' (lii. 35. 5).

Perhaps more important than any of these considerations for Dio's ties with the Greek world is the very language of the *History*. He was conscious of the need to atticize.[37] Thucydides was a

[31] Stressed heavily at i. 2. 3–4.
[32] lii. 27. 1–3, 37. 1 (Maecenas' speech); lxix. 9. 4–6 (on Hadrian). Herodian uses the *limes* system to criticize the softness of the Italians (ii. 11. 4–6).
[33] lxxi, esp. lxxi. 36. 3. Cf. Herodian i. 15. 7 where the Romans wished Commodus would have 'taken up soldiers' weapons against barbarians and proved himself worthy of the Romans' empire'.
[34] li. 20. 7–8. Cf. Fishwick 1990: 270 'The generalization scarcely holds true for Italy . . . [though] it is certainly true of the capital'.
[35] lii. 35. 3–36. 1.
[36] lvi. 46. 3; lvii. 9. 1–3; lix. 4. 3, 12. 1, 28. 1–8; lx. 4. 2, 5. 4; lxiv. 3. 4c; lxvi. 9. 1; lxvi. 19. 1; lxvii. 8. 1; lxviii. 1. 2, 2. 1; lxxii. 15. 2–16. 1; lxxiv. 4. 1–5; lxxviii. 12. 1.
[37] lv. 12. 5 'some of the books we read in order to write in Attic [*epi to attikizein*]'.

natural model here.[38] Thus it is not surprising that the very end of the work reveals Dio as a Greek back home in Bithynia, where the god closes his work and tells him that he has been preserved like Hector from out the dust of battle.[39]

---

[38] Litsch 1893; Kyhnitzsch 1894.   [39] lxxx. 5. 3 quoting *Iliad* xi. 163–4.

Conclusion

I began this work with a study of how the Greek elite used language to constitute themselves as a culturally and politically superior group. The role of language in the second sophistic is an intensification (as I called it) of an already existing polarization between the language of the educated and the non-educated. In the enlarged Greek world of the Hellenistic period we can identify a clear division between a Greek which stands in a relationship with the fossilized high standard of classical authors, especially those writing in Attic Greek (the classical dialect *par excellence* for prose and speech), and a Greek which effectively has no link with this standard. There is, however, little sign that educated speakers in this period were under any pressure to imitate closely and consciously the style or vocabulary and grammar of Athenian and other classical writers. The noticeable change in the second sophistic is that very great value was now placed on the ability to do both of these things and especially to achieve a proximity to Attic Greek.

The linguistic and stylistic purism that developed in the later first century AD can be seen as a progression from the stylistic concerns of Dionysius of Halicarnassus and others who promoted creative imitation of the classical Athenian orators towards the end of the first century BC. Dionysius' aims were both literary-stylistic, concerned, that is, with matters of taste, and also ideological and political. He believed that imitating the style of the great orator-politicians like Isocrates was the best way to guarantee correct political behaviour in the present day. In the second sophistic these political factors are again important. But the role of the classics in this period goes far beyond the aims and influence of Dionysius and his school. To Dionysius' concern with style was joined an overriding obsession with language itself. This obsession was due to the elite's need to give itself a clearer and more readily definable identity. Language became important for this purpose because it was the best way for them to demonstrate their social and political standing.

In its linguistic aspect language purism signalled the ability to use a vocabulary and grammar which appeared exactly to mimic that of classical authors. It was always a matter of dispute as to which of these should actually be imitated. But, while claims could be made for non-Attic classics like Homer, atticism was the most acceptable description of the process and the language of the Athenian classics the most acceptable model for general usage (leaving the non-Attic classical dialects as mediums for occasional belletristic display). It should be remembered that atticizing Greek was only employed for particular prestige occasions in speech and writing. It never supplanted the educated Hellenistic standard in general communication. It did, however, assist the maintenance of this standard, and since it was an extension of it, we may imagine that it would not have been too difficult for the educated to incorporate atticisms in their Greek, as they wished. But for others it would have been very difficult or impossible. The maintenance of language standards needed leisure and wealth which allowed continuous study of the classics. Atticizing Greek depended upon a battery of rhetorical and grammatical or lexicographical aids. For this reason it acted in its social aspect as a sure means of advertising membership of the elite, the multiplication of rule books reflecting on the one hand scholarly rivalries and the genuine difficulty of isolating and reproducing an ideal, and on the other the very great value attached to its possession and reproduction. Linguistic differentiation from the mass is another side of the same political function. The process of change which led to the formation of the modern demotic Greek language became more rapid after the first century AD. A compensatory reaction by those whose status depended amongst other things on their familiarity with the ancients might be expected. But the consciousness of the difference has again a social, not a linguistic significance. For by commanding access to a prestige language like classical Attic the second sophistic elite placed themselves in contact with the leaders of the most prestigious city of free Greece. They well understood the cultural litmus of language and deployed it to further their political-ideological control in the present.

Language purism, then, played a key role in establishing a coherent and recognizable identity for the Greek elite at this time. Complementary to it was the general role of the Greek past as a source of authority and commentary in the present. This past was centred on the myths and histories of Athens and other famous states of old Greece, but was by no means restricted to them. Tales and deeds of purely local relevance were extremely important too. Owing to the great diffusion of Greek culture and tradition in the Greek East, at Rome, and elsewhere, the Greek past as a model could not be exclusive to Greeks. Unlike atticism, which was supported by a complex array of theories and regulations, Greek culture, especially at the basic level of ordinary spoken Greek, could be acquired without any great technical expertise and was available as a ready-made medium of communication and government and/ or a sign of culture and learning to those that wanted it. It is perhaps because of this that the concept of descent through historical or mythological figures of the Old Greek world became such an important way of ensuring genuine contact with Greek antiquity among Greeks and those who claimed to be Greek. This was a matter of concern for cities in particular. Thus, although others could and did use Greek culture, the possession of a very old and relatively stable cultural-political heritage was obviously a source of identity and unity to the Greeks themselves and one which belied their equally old political segmentation and restricted local city-state patriotism.

It would again be wrong to read this wider classicism as a cultural phenomenon only. Since the chief beneficiaries of it were the same people who advertised their superiority through language, it would certainly be right to hold that internal Greek social divisions were entrenched by identification with the classics (which meant, of course, identification with the leaders of classical Greece). External relations are also important. For Greek identity had always been articulated through the opposition of Greeks and non-Greeks, who were called *barbaroi*. It was suggested in Chapter 1 that linguistic purism involved rejection of Latin interference in Greek, inasmuch as Latin exerted a noticeable influence on Greek below the educated standard. It seems very likely that in other areas too the intensified claim of the Greeks in the second sophistic period to be Greek is a reaction to Roman control. Greeks had always been aware of their language and history. What is new at this time is the level of exploitation of these existing cultural insignia and their consequent function as 'discursive structures' (as I put it in the Introduction) and mediums of articulating elite identity. Reaction to Rome is surely a key part of this development.

We must tread carefully in assessing the implications and

consequences of such a statement, remembering that in practical terms the identity adopted by the Greek elite had its effect in internal Greek politics and that there was no general hostility to Roman rule. A small—but growing—proportion of the elite were indeed politically involved with Rome. They held Roman citizenship or even administrative posts in the Empire. It is sometimes tempting to take the supposed feelings of this minority as the pro-Roman feelings of the Greek elite as a whole, and to draw the conclusion that the Empire was a political and cultural unit. This interpretation is understandable, but not necessarily correct either for the people concerned or, and particularly, for others. To be aware of the dangers of simplistic prosopographical linkage, one has only to remember, for example, how many members of the nationalist movement in British India in the nineteenth and twentieth centuries enjoyed an elite British education or were employed in the imperial Indian Civil Service. In the case of the Greeks we must never confuse the absence of direct political action against Rome with genuine political integration and harmony—the two do not necessarily go together; further, we must recognize that evidence of pro-Roman feelings so often comes from the public domain—being anything from epigraphic and numismatic celebrations of the emperors' divinity to the prevalence of Roman baths in the Greek cities—and is actually very difficult to use as proof of the real attitudes of people under foreign rule.

Rome's protection of the rich against political outsiders in the form of the urban and rural poor and especially against 'barbarians' is reason enough for the contentment of the eastern aristocracies. Their alignment with Rome was certainly political-ideological; but so was their cultural orientation. Their relationship with classical Greece, especially Athens, is an assertion of Greekness in the form that was possible under Roman control, that is, in the cultural arena. It may well be that this Greek cultural-political identity was always more important than the Roman political one, which often appears on inspection (where this is possible) to be local, temporary, and a matter of shared interests or self-interest.

A further general point may be made with regard to the identity the Greek elite constructed for itself: it was a totally male affair. The women of the establishment class in the second sophistic might well be property-owning and highly educated. There are good examples in the period of women practising euergetism and writing and performing belles-lettres.[1] But their opinions of the Greek world, let alone of Roman rule, are not expressed. (The activity of women in the public world of Christian discourse makes later antiquity very different in this respect.) In the period of the second sophistic expression of the male elite's identity through links with the classical past undoubtedly reinforced a deep-rooted patriarchy. Atticism contributed to this. Patriarchal attitudes are built into the very vocabulary and grammar of many, perhaps all, languages. Thus a language purism like atticism, which was so closely linked to social and political control by the male elite and which depended for its existence on an educational system dominated by men, cannot have failed to reinforce division of the sexes.

What, then, of the importance now assumed in male ethics by the marriage relation and the harmony of the household? These are not signs of a new commitment to sexual equality but are rather, as I suggested in the last chapter of Part One, reflections of a closer focus on the continuation of the city and its sustainability in an age of urban living. For in a society that is criss-crossed by links of patronage and kinship marriage must always be a matter of alliance, which in turn depends on ancestry and heritage and so again on links, real or imaginary, with the great men of the past. That the marriage relation became a locus of self-reflection for elite males in the second sophistic period, with particular attention to mutual respect between man and wife, is not wholly unexpected. For through its dependence on alliance and ancestry marriage assisted a very personal investment in the living past as a source of identity, quite as much as it satisfied a need for future reproduction. It is good to note that the expression of the new sexual ethics of the period, especially the accent on progress towards marital love, in the distinctive literature of the period, the Greek novel, is complemented there by a conscious or subconscious valorization of the world of the past, from which Greeks derived their power, and the worth of the city, on which they based their civilized existence.

My aim in the first part of this book has been simply to establish more clearly the meaning of the Greek past. It will be apparent to those who know the secondary literature in this area that much of what I have said is new and offers a different perspective that may

[1] Cf. Bowie 1994: 438–40, Egger 1994: 263–4 with literature, esp. Bremen 1996.

be disturbing to anyone accustomed to read the Roman Empire mainly from Rome. Fortunately, more sensitive approaches to Greeks and other provincials are becoming far commoner these days. Millar's *The Roman Near East* (1993) and Sartre's *L'Orient romain* (1991) are good examples of a non-Romanocentric approach to the wider Greek-speaking world. With regard to the Greeks of Old Greece and Asia Minor, Price's *Rituals and Power* (1984) has become a key work, as no doubt will Alcock's *Graecia Capta* (1993) and Mitchell's *Anatolia* (1993), to mention only three historians writing in English. Further, the current interest in Plutarch and the Greek novelists, though sometimes too narrowly literary, has introduced many more Hellenists to the Greeks of this time, a very important development indeed. In this regard I must pay tribute to a slightly older and justly influential article, Bowie's 'The Greeks and their Past in the Second Sophistic' (1974 [1970]), which remains the best exposition of the quality and extension of Greek classicism, especially in the literature of the period. Reardon's *Courants littéraires grecs* (1971) and Russell's *Greek Declamation* (1983) are among other works which deserve to be honoured here (and to be read more often by historians). The work of these and others notwithstanding, it must be said that much remains to be done.

The purpose of the second part of the book was to build on the general feelings and attitudes of the Greek elite and to examine the views of the leading intellectuals of the age with a particular question in mind. Clearly, there are major differences between these people regarding the contexts in which they wrote or spoke and their particular characters and aspirations. But there is no cause to suspect that as intellectuals they were eccentric in comparison with their peers or to suggest that they were somehow closed off from them. As members of the elite all of them either did or can be assumed to have had some (local) political experience or at least contact with power through relatives and friends. They were distinctive because they wrote; for this reason they account for a minuscule proportion. But in an age when possession of, or claim to, *paideia* ('education'/'culture') was how a man showed his integration into the higher levels of society, it would be wrong to argue that Plutarch and the rest were somehow unrepresentative of their fellows.

The particular question I set out to answer was how these figures saw Rome. This question is (ironically!) Romanocentric, for it can hardly be doubted that Greek intellectuals like Plutarch and Dio would rather have books written on their relationship with Greece than with Rome. Nevertheless the relationship with the ruling power rightly fascinates us. The interest second sophistic authors took in Rome varies (naturally). Plutarch and Dio have much to say. Their opinions were formed through their experience of the first-century Empire and the instability of that government. Plutarch wrote a good deal on Roman matters, had warm relations with prominent Romans, yet remained cool about Rome's control of the Greek world. Dio on occasions comes as close as any of our authors to hostility towards Rome. In contexts where there is no need to express his dislike of provincial administration we find that he does so forcefully. Presumably he was not totally insensitive to the audiences before whom he made these remarks (which may well have acquired some of their force in rewriting). Plutarch's coolness towards Roman government has to do with his Greek patriotism. He very much wanted the Greeks to govern themselves well without external assistance. With Dio personal bitterness resulting from his exile may be the primary motivation; but promotion of Greek unity is also important to a man whose concern with Greek politics was as great in practice as it was in theory to Plutarch.

The second-century authors I looked at started from a different perspective. For most of the period there was no obvious disruption at Rome or by Rome. Praise of the Antonine emperors is to the fore in Arrian, Appian, Aristides, Lucian, and Pausanias (as well as later writers like Philostratus, Cassius Dio, and Herodian). Each has his own agenda here. Arrian was a high-ranking imperial administrator. Praise of Hadrian in a work like the *Tactica* is public, though not apparently insincere. The *Anabasis*, however, reveals Arrian's Greek pride and his personal choice of what was important to him. Appian does not seem different. Sympathetic to the present emperors, working for many years in the courts at Rome, he nevertheless retained a loyalty to his fatherland, Alexandria, and through this looked to Macedon as a personal reference point. Aelius Aristides' priorities lie with himself and his god. His religious and cultural identity as a Greek is indisputable. Moderns habitually but inaccurately call him a 'sophist' after Philostratus. This may seem a venial error—it would not have done to Aristides, who emphasized the place the morally and politically useful rhetor like himself must occupy in the spiritual and structural life of the community. Far more serious mistakes stem from the assumption that the encomium he delivered before the imperial family, the *To Rome*, can be taken as the expression of the Greek aristocracies' love of Roman rule. Aristides certainly did owe political allegiance to Rome; but genuine feelings of loyalty—rather than local and temporary interests like his career and property—are in doubt. He craved authoritarian power; but the emperors were subordinate to the god in this regard.[2] Most revealingly he fought hard to stay out of the system his encomium lauds: the fourth *Sacred Tale* tells us more about Aristides' real feelings than *To Rome*.

What of Lucian? His avowedly non-Greek background surely had some imput into his complex and intriguing personality. Lucian acquired Greek culture (rather than being born into it), but apparently found himself rejected by the Greek elite on grounds that are familiar today. He shows a genuine identification with Rome in political matters. This loyalty was cemented perhaps by the reception of his work in the West, where he made his fortune, and certainly by the emperors' protection of his fatherland Samosata. Yet when his chosen cultural-cognitive identity clashed with his political one, there can be no doubt where he stood. For Lucian, as with Plutarch, Romans had a 'potentiality for barbarism' (to borrow Russell's phrase). As to Pausanias, it is clear that he bitterly resented Republican Rome's conquest of Greece and her destruction of the Achaean League. The 'mischance of Roman rule' led to the disruptive foundations of Corinth under Caesar and Nicopolis under Augustus. We must set against this the fact that Hadrian and Pius are praised by him highly and with affection. It is, however, difficult to know whether this is praise of the system as well as of the individuals. We are reminded of Galen's favourable remarks on Marcus Aurelius.

Galen himself towered above his second-century contemporaries in his erudition and productiveness, but also in his egotism and conceitedness. His opinions of Rome are spread through works largely untranslated into modern languages (with the exception of *On Precognition*), and this no doubt explains the comparative neglect of his views. He lived at Rome for many years but appar-

---

[2] Plutarch's positive and Dio's pessimistic (and somewhat elusive) thoughts on the relation between the Empire and the divine should be compared.

ently had no time for the system that guaranteed his prestige (as we would see it). The only story, for example, that he tells of Hadrian, the emperor Greeks loved most, concerns his disgraceful attack on a slave. Like Plutarch and Lucian, Galen had an observably low opinion of Roman education, an attitude elsewhere implicit in the more or less profound silence of Greeks on Roman cultural achievements. Galen had a very clear cultural identity as a Greek (an identity turning on the purity of his language and education), and an enduring local political attachment to the aristocracy of Pergamum, 'where we all know the families each of us come from, the education we have received, and the property and attitudes and way of life we have'; but towards Rome there is no interest or expression of participation.

It seems very likely that Galen lived into the reign of Caracalla and therefore witnessed the Empire-wide extension of the Roman citizenship in 212. But if the world was henceforth totally Roman in political-administrative terms, it is not clear that this affected personal attitudes and feelings. Philostratus and Cassius Dio lived a good part of their lives after Caracalla's measure. Yet there is nothing to suggest that their identification with Rome was any deeper than it had been for second-century authors. For Philostratus Greek culture is all. His assumptions about the correct relation between culture and power in the *Lives of the Sophists* echo what we find in the *Apollonius*. We can recognize a familiar pattern where the Greek elite's estimation of the emperor's support is in proportion to his acquiescence in their own chosen cultural-political identity. Cassius Dio, in so far as he provides information on Greek-Roman relations, displays a similar view. Like Aristides, Pausanias, and Lucian, he conceives the Empire militarily as a safe arena surrounded by protected borders. But as with them, there is no reason to imagine that his 'moral barrier' is reducible to an opposition between those inside versus those outside Roman territory. Dio's analysis of the personal qualities of the emperors is affected by their absorption of Hellenic culture. Despite or because of his prominent Roman career he seems 'Roman' in political affiliation only. For a man who was personally ambitious an imperial career was as natural now as it had been for Arrian; no further conclusions need be drawn from it.

The value accorded these attitudes will depend on one's idea of what sort of evidence is important or possible. They do not constitute 'data'. For that we must turn to information on age at marriage and death, calculations of life-expectancy, the male career, what people ate, their domestic space and architecture, how they spent their money, their mode of worship, their entertainments. The collation of such factual information is vitally important. But it must be said that there is a danger of ignoring people by concentrating only on the externals of their lives so that they become endlessly reproducible social facts and examples. This is where personal opinions, difficult to handle as they are, prove themselves very useful.

The obvious drawback with the intellectuals whose views I have been exploring is that they may seem to be out of touch with the rest of the population, whose habits and beliefs must be and (it is widely accepted) can be inferred from externals of the sort mentioned. There may be a particular problem with attitudes to Rome. Overall the identity the Greek elite constructed for itself involved a certain distance from Roman rule. We know from other sources, however, that Roman influences penetrated the Greek world deeply in areas which invite generalizations of 'Graeco-Romanism'. If we leave aside the institutional and the administrative and military sides of Roman life, what comes to our attention especially are certain cultural aspects of Rome in the East. There is the influence of Latin on non-educated Greek. There are the many festivals and processions bearing the names of the emperors (especially Hadrian and the Severans), or those to do with the imperial cult. There are the particular untraditional activities of these events—the gladiatorial combats and wild beast shows. The physical side of Roman culture is also remarkable. Changes in civic centres, especially the building or alteration of temples to house the imperial cult, were real and far-reaching. Above all there is the employment of the Roman-style building materials, brick and concrete. The most uncompromising constructions made from these must have been the curvilinear, vaulted bath houses, which became so prevalent in the Greek East.[3] To outside observers the admittance of such intruders is tangible proof of a Graeco-Roman *mentalité*.

But it is very difficult to know what the presence and use of such things did mean. It would in fact be reasonable to suppose that they did not impinge greatly on people's major cultural identity (allowing

[3] On architectural influences especially note Ward-Perkins 1981: 255 ff., 273 ff., the useful collection of papers in Macready and Thompson 1987, and Waelkens 1989.

always for the fact that the backing of real power makes their penetration seem deeper). The point of significance is that many of these aspects of Rome were accepted by the elite too or at least not attacked as Roman imports (and this applies to the intellectuals studied in this book). This is a process of naturalization, and one that is no more impossible than, for example, Frenchmen playing rugby and remaining fully French. We must remember that the Greeks had always been good at absorbing and appropriating cultural imports. Take the example of gladiatorial combats. It used to be imagined that elite Greek objections to such shows stemmed from proto-nationalistic feelings. In fact the objections that are made do not mention Rome. The shows are not apparently thought of as Roman, and their naturalization is revealed, for example, by Plutarch's observation of gladiators 'who are not altogether bestial but are Hellenes', and who remember to make arrangements for their women and slaves before they fight (*Not even a Pleasant Life is Possible according to Epicurus* 1099b). Elite and mass may divide on questions of taste and morality, but the origin of the practice is not an issue.[4]

This may be taken further with regard to baths, since the conversion of a cultural import into a natural pastime can be neatly illustrated from a short work of Lucian's called *Hippias, or The Bath*. Here Lucian praises the architect of a new bathing establishment.[5] 'The construction of a bath,' he remarks, 'is a common and really very usual idea in our world' (4). Hippias' bath is of the so-called 'imperial' type with an axial layout of halls and corridors built alongside palaestras, the cold rooms facing north and the hotter plunges ranged 'south, east, and west' (5–8). It has the usual Roman-style fittings of changing rooms, a warm room, a hot room, and finally 'without having to go through the same rooms' again the cold plunge, as well as other services such as reception rooms for the rich. The lavish use of different marbles marks it out as a standard product of affluence-led, Roman-influenced modern architecture. But the world of its origin is thoroughly Greek. Lucian plays on the obvious, that Hippias' name recalls that of the great

---

[4] See above, 'Plutarch' n. 118. Many members of the elite, of course, did not object at all. Note Athenaeus, *Sophists at Dinner* 154d, quoting the 3rd-c. BC scholar Hermippus on the Mantineans as the inventors (*heuretai*) of gladiatorial fighting.
[5] See Yegül 1979 for an interesting architectural reconstruction (though beware his 'Graeco-Romanism').

fifth-century sophist who was famous for his virtuosity in the arts and sciences. Thus Hippias himself is accomplished not only in geometry, mechanics, and other matters, but also in harmonics and music (3), and is 'truely *sophos* [wise]' (7). Moreover he reminds Lucian of Archimedes, Thales, and Epeius who made the wooden horse of Troy. Lucian's encomium, then, involved no clash with Hellenic culture; had it done, he would not have given it. For him entering Hippias' bath house did not even remotely involve taking a 'Roman' bath (there are no parallels with the nineteenth-century habit of taking 'Turkish' baths, where the foreignness of the experience was all part of the pleasure). Rather, a cultural habit we are tempted to cite as exemplifying a unitary imperial culture has been successfully attached to the traditional world of Greece.

Compare again the trans-class entertainment of the pantomime —elite Greeks were certainly aware of its popularity among the Romans (Lucian, *On the Dance* 34, Athenaeus, *Sophists at Dinner* 20d–e), but their attacks do not mention Rome.[6] Similarly, processions and festivals with Roman names would not necessarily have seemed 'Roman'. Whatever the names, they were essentially Greek in their organization and character. Instead of seeing their extension in this period only as a Graeco-Roman phenomenon, we might remember the need to create and extend traditional symbols of Greekness. There were varying degrees of compromise and accommodation with Rome in such areas—there had to be—but the major impetus is likely to be Greek. Even the imperial cult was closely integrated into the traditional religion of the Greek city, whatever reservations intellectuals had about its real meaning.

It would be a hard task to prove that the intellectual elite were out of step on these matters, at least so far as attitudes to Rome are concerned. Their acceptance is acceptance of the obvious, that aspects of Roman culture were widespread, and were therefore to be considered Greek. More importantly, though such things were a part of the pattern of cultural expression we find in the second sophistic and therefore reflect the self-confidence of the age and its leaders, they did not infringe the elite's ideological conception of themselves as heirs of the classics (except perhaps in language, where Roman influence was rejected by the elite, even if they might use

---

[6] See e.g. Plutarch, *Table Talks* 748c–d; Aristides, *Against the Dancers*, above, 'Aristides' n. 42.

a 'barbarian' Latin word to their menials). In this sense they did not matter.[7]

The real disjuncture between the elite and the non-elite turned, of course, on the familiar problems of access to education, power, and wealth and the less familiar divide caused by the function of language and history as the identity cards of society's superiors. This identity and the world that went with it did not last. It was challenged gradually but successfully by the emergence of Christian society, and it is tempting to enquire finally, and very briefly, what instruction hindsight gives from this perspective about its true appeal. In its vertical mode the elite's identity was thoroughly exclusive. Difficult rules about language joined looser ones about the use of classical authority. The mass of the population (and as far as we can tell most female members of the elite) were outsiders here. But the success of any group identity depends on securing the agreement of a very high proportion of potential members. Thus in its horizontal mode elite Greek culture sought to include as many recruits as it could by bringing and keeping the right sort of people inside through the educational system, and by emphasizing to the heirs of the classics the benefits that parity and 'like-mindedness' (*homonoia*) could bring them. However, the further it went in marking out this Greekness, the more obvious the possibility of transgression became. For Greek culture was not open only to the right sort. It was always possible to employ it without admitting to being Greek or wishing to claim that identity. In particular the effort to constitute oneself as a living link with the classical age involved a degree of artificiality that some had no reason or ability to tolerate. In this regard the divergence between the 'Syrians' Lucian and Iamblichus is instructive. Both men came from a region where it was in fact very difficult to connect with the Greek historical and mythological network. Lucian raises the problems associated with his claim to a Greek identity in contexts where his adopted Greek culture is under scrutiny from insiders. Iamblichus' identity was,

[7] Roman identity was by contrast heavily dependent upon particular material structures—civic constitutions, Roman Law, provision of amphitheatres and roads, etc. (cf. the importance of 'Parliament' and the 'Common Law' throughout English history). As Woolf 1994 rightly observes, these items radically transformed and 'Romanized' Gallic and Hispanic culture, but had a marginal effect on the identity of the Greek world.

by contrast, avowedly 'native': he used Greek culture simply to
make a career without borrowing the ideological baggage that went
with it.[8] But we do not have to look at 'non-Greeks' to find an
approach of this kind. In the Greek world proper, Christianity
raised the same questions and got the same answers.

The emergence in the East of Syriac Christianity in the lifetime
of Lucian and Iamblichus has been noted. Its appeal to those whose
gods, names, and cities had been appropriated or replaced by the
Greeks is obvious. (Indeed, in these regions it is less surprising that
the attractions of Greek identity palled than that they commanded
so much attention in the first place.) The more interesting question
is why the Greeks themselves gave up worshipping their old gods,
the start of the process which led to them assuming the name
Rhômaioi as a testimony of their new faith. Plural religion was an
intrinsic part of the Greek inheritance. One could hardly emulate
Pericles without accepting his gods. Yet it was through religion that
the whole classicizing edifice gave way. We have no real idea how
quickly Christianity spread in the ancient world. Recent work rightly
emphasizes the health of traditional belief well into late antiquity.[9]
Nevertheless, we may surmise that Christianity became increasingly attractive as a viable alternative in the period leading up to the
reign of Constantine and its official adoption as Rome's religion.
Whatever the causes of this in relation to spiritual life and other
areas, we should at least note in the Greek world the likely appeal
of a very different set of priorities and paradigms to those who had
no secure or direct interest in the Greek past and who were excluded from its benefits. To be sure, the traditional culture of the
male Greek elite continued to dominate civic life till the end of the
fourth century. But crippling defections from among those it sought
to control and from among its own ranks reveal the unsatisfactory
self-contradictions and cracks that were always present in it, even
in the relatively stable days of the second sophistic.

---

[8] 'Lucian' nn. 24 ff., 38 ff., 50.
[9] Cameron 1993: 69–71 with bibliography.

APPENDIX A

The Dating of the Greek Novels

The probable dates of the main Greek novels are: Chariton: ?mid-first century; Xenophon, Antonius Diogenes: ?mid-second century; Achilles Tatius: mid (cf. Willis 1990: 76) to late second century; Iamblichus: about 170; Longus: ?200–250; Heliodorus: third century (see below). See Reardon 1971: 333 ff., id. 1989: 5; Bowie 1985a: 684, id. 1994: 443.

Chariton (for whom papyrological evidence provides a *terminus ante quem* of the second century) has sometimes been placed as early as the first century BC, but most modern scholars put him in the middle or latter part of the first century AD on grounds of language and style. See Perry 1967: 343–4 n. 1; Ruiz Montero 1980; Baslez 1992; Jones 1992a (making him as late as Hadrian). Plot and literary history: Perry 1967: 96–148; Reardon 1971: 340–53, id. 1982; Müller 1976; Hägg 1987: 194–8. Language: Giangrande 1974, protesting at Papanikolaou's late Hellenistic dating; Ruiz Montero 1991, comparing his vocabulary with a partial atticist like Plutarch.

Heliodorus' novel has often been dated after 351 from a comparison of his siege of Syene (*Ethiopian Story* ix. 3–11) with the account of the real siege of Nisibis described by Julian in *Orr.* i. 27b–28d, 30a, and ii. 62b–66d. In fact Julian's account in comparison with other sources emerges as pretty fictional itself, and because it is precisely in its fictional details that it resembles Heliodorus, it is very likely that Julian imitated the writer of the novel (or a common source) rather than the other way round: see Lightfoot 1988: 115–19 with literature (to which add Bowersock 1994: 149–60, triumphant but unconvincing on the later dating, especially regarding the allegorical allusions to the siege in Ephrem). There is, then, no overriding reason against putting Heliodorus in the period of the second sophistic; the third century allows for his narrative's sophistication and advances over the other novelists (see e.g. Winkler 1982; Morgan 1989; Fusillo 1991: 147–65) as well as the 'late' elements that have been observed in his language, and ties him to the heyday of the priestly caste at Emesa to which he belonged (*Ethiopian Story* x. 41. 4; cf. *Thirteenth Sibylline Oracle* 150–4; Bowie 1985a: 696; Emesa went into decline after the 270s when the trade that came to it through Palmyra ceased following Palmyra's rebellion: Seyrig 1959). Since the founding families of Emesa were Arab chieftains (they were at any rate labelled as such in Graeco-Roman writers), it is not implausible to connect Heliodorus with the sophist called Heliodorus 'the Arab' who lived in the first half of the third century (Philostratus, *VS* 625-7—unless this man is the Palmyrene dedicant of IGR i. 45 in AD 235 [whom Philostratus could easily also call 'Arab'])—cf. above, 'Lucian' n. 29, 'Philostratus' n. 80. See also 'Novel' n. 2 with text on Iamblichus.

The fragmentary *Ninus* is perhaps the earliest recognizable example of the genre. Its teenage heroes, Ninus and Semiramis, are based on the legendary Babylonian royals who were well-known in Greek literature and were presented as lovers in the pantomime (Lucian, *The False Critic* 25). But, though familiar as entertainment, it may be right to suggest that these protagonists did not have the same appeal as the typically 'bourgeois' Chaereas and Callirhoe in the truly Greek setting of Chariton's novel (Dihle 1978: 55; Hägg 1987: 199 n. 78).

Nevertheless, in date *Ninus* is better placed in the first century AD than the first century BC, as Reardon 1971: 313 n. 10 (following amongst others Perry 1967: 153-4) suggests. We know it was written before AD 100-1, the date when *P.Berol.* 6926 which contains the main fragments A and B was reused. Reuse implies that the papyrus was recent (cf. Turner 1954 on the rapid reuse of documents dated on recto and verso; the one example where a document was reused for a literary text to which a terminus can also be applied [no. 22, Favorinus, *On Exile*] has a maximum interval of 25 years; *Ninus* is of course the original, not the secondary text). The hand of *P.Berol.* 6926 clearly belongs to the 'latter part of the first century' AD (Roberts 1955: no. IIa); the other important fragment, fr. C (*PSI* 1305), also belongs to this period (fr. D. *P.Gen.* 85, belongs to the Berlin roll). There is no good reason to think that the composition of *Ninus* was very much earlier. The partial correspondence of the plot with Xenophon's *Cyropaedia* again suggests an imperial date, given Xenophon's huge influence in this period (Münscher 1920: 106-81; cf. the possibly novelistic work based on the love story in the *Cyropaedia* mentioned by Philostratus as *VS* 524—*Araspas the Lover of Pantheia*—with Plutarch's comments on the pleasure of reading about Xenophon's Pantheia in *That Not even a Pleasant Life is Possible according to Epicurus* 1093c; further, the three Xenophons—including Xenophon of Ephesus—known to the *Suda* as novelists: ξ 49-51). Note too in *Ninus* the stylistic avoidance of hiatus (Reeve 1971: 536-7) and use of Attic vocabulary in the main (not all the words cited by Dihle 1978: 55 n. 32 are in fact non-atticist). Perry's date of 100 BC was based on his belief in the 'decline of drama on the stage after Terence' (1967: 154) and the consequent rise of the novel to fill the gap, a connection which even the imaginative will find difficult to sustain, nor in fact one based on a true premiss since in the Greek world productions of old and new plays, tragic and comic, remained very popular: see in our period e.g. Schachter 1981-6: ii. 176-9, nos. xvi-xviii for victory lists from the Thespian Mouseia.

The other important fragmentary novel, the *Metiochus and Parthenope*, should probably also be placed early on the basis of non-atticizing language: Dihle 1978: 47–54 (though there is no need to accept Dihle's pre-imperial dating; cf. again Reeve 1971: 536–7 on its stylistic avoidance of hiatus, not of course a sign of atticism in itself). See also 'Novel' n. 28.

APPENDIX B

Sosius Senecio's Alleged Eastern Origin

Opinion divides about the provenance of Q. Sosius Senecio, addressee of Plutarch's *On Progress in Virtue*, *Table Talks*, and *Parallel Lives*, between a western, Roman origin and an eastern, Greek one. The matter is important, since in his essay *On Progress in Virtue* Plutarch takes a special interest in his friend's philosophical education, and, if Sosius is a westerner, the essay (and the presentation of Sosius in the *Table Talks*) is further evidence of Plutarch's close interest in Romans' ability to absorb the spiritual and intellectual benefits of Greek culture.

It has been proposed that Sosius was a descendant of a Cilician dynastic family.[1] Alternatively his family has been located in southern Phrygia on the basis of an honorary inscription for his daughter, Sosia Polla (*RE* 15), and her grandfather, Sex. Julius Frontinus, the soldier and author who was Sosius' father-in-law.[2] Eastern origin has also been put forward for Sosius' son-in-law, Q. Pompeius Falco.[3] However, it is hardly secure. The only probable basis for Sosius' eastern origin are the two inscriptions from Phrygian Apamea honouring Sosia Polla and her husband Falco.[4] In the first of these among the reasons for honouring Sosia is 'the good will of her ancestors [*progonoi*] to the city'. Neither inscription names any member of Sosia's family before her grandfather Frontinus.[5] Frontinus was her maternal grandfather. If Sosius' own family is to be identified with the ancestral benefactors of Apamea, it would seem strange that it is not named outright. It also seems problematic to include Sosius in the term *progonoi*, 'ancestors'. A better candidate is Frontinus himself, whose *ekgonê*, 'granddaughter', Sosia is stated to be. During his proconsulship of Asia in 84–5

[1] Syme 1968*a*: 101 n. 127. Greek origin was posited to account for elements in the name of Sosius' son-in-law, Q. Pompeius Falco (see below), which derive from the Spartan C. Julius Euryclus Herculanus (Halfmann 1979: no. 29; cf. Plutarch, *How to Praise Oneself* 1); Sosius' connections with Sparta attested by citizens bearing his name (Ogilvie 1967: 114 n. 21) presumably derive from his quaestorship in Achaia.

[2] Jones 1970: 103.

[3] For literature see Halfmann 1979: 211 (who is against); further McDermott 1976: 242 (with some reservations).

[4] *IGR* iv. 779; *IGR* iv. 780 (= *ILS* 8820 = *MAMA* vi. 182 = *OGIS* 490).

[5] Cf. similarly *CIL* viii. 7066 (= *ILS* 1105) for Sosia Falconilla (*RE* 12), the granddaughter of Sosia Polla and Pompeius Falco.

he made dedications at Laodicea ad Lycum and Hierapolis to the west of Apamea.[6] He would certainly have called at Apamea itself during his term of office, since it was the capital of the next *conventus* district eastwards along the Via Sebaste.[7] It is reasonable to imagine that he benefited this city too. Who, if anyone, are the other ancestral benefactors in Sosia's family is not known.

Nor are there compelling reasons to assign an eastern origin to Falco. The suggestion that he did come from the East is based partly on the Euryclid items in his polyonymous name in an inscription from Tarracina near Rome,[8] partly on an inscription in his honour put up in the Cilician city of Hierapolis Castabala.[9] We do not know why the men who dedicated this inscription, A. Laberius Camerinus and his son Laberius Camerinus, chose Hierapolis. But the city was well known and visited for its cult of Perasia-Artemis,[10] and there is no cogent reason for it to have been Falco's birthplace. His connections are in fact with Italy. He was visited on his estate at Tarracina by M. Aurelius in 140,[11] and his descendants are attested in the west of the empire in southern and northern Italy and Africa.[12] As regards the link with the Spartan dynast C. Julius Eurycles one can say only that the nature of the connection is unknown.[13] Falco may after all be assigned to an Italian provincial background. In all probability Sosius Senecio can join him.[14]

[6] Proconsulship: Eck 1983: 208. Dedications: *IGR* iv. 847 (= *MAMA* vi. 2), *AE* 1969/1970, 593.

[7] Cf. *PIR*[2] J 322.   [8] *CIL* x. 6321 = *ILS* 1035.

[9] *CIL* iii. 12117 = *ILS* 1036.   [10] Dupont-Sommer and Robert 1964.

[11] Fronto, *Ad M. Caes.* ii. 9 (p. 29 v.d.H[2]); Birley 1987: 60.

[12] *CIL* x. 3724 (*RE* 115), x. 4760 (= *ILS* 6296; *RE* 117), x. 6322 (*RE* 118); xi. 405 (*RE* 115); viii. 7066 (= *ILS* 1105; *RE* 12). Cf. Sherwin-White 1966: 430 on Pliny, *Letters* vii. 22. 3; Halfmann 1979: 211.

[13] Cf. Doer 1937: 126.

[14] Cf. Sherwin-White 1966: 115; Halfmann 1979: 211 (both on the basis of Falco's descendants; Sosius had no son).

The Dating of Dio of Prusa's Rhodian *and* Alexandrian Orations

Dio's *Rhodian* and *Alexandrian* orations, especially the former, are mostly dated to the period before his exile. I append some arguments in favour of a Trajanic date.

In the case of *Or.* xxxi the evidence for the early dating is that Rhodes is currently free and that Nero's reign is 'very recent [110 *engista, eph' hêmôn*]'. Von Arnim 1898: 210–18 argued at length that the work was pre-exilic because of its 'sophistic' style and placed it in the reign of Titus, when Rhodes was free. The speech is certainly carefully composed and the sustained vigour of the treatment comparable perhaps only with the *Trojan Oration*; but unlike Dio's sophistic pieces it is a wholly serious work and not an *epideixis* in the usual sense; further, as we have seen, Dio's career cannot be so readily segmented into sophistic and philosophical parts (as von Arnim believed after Synesius), and so there is nothing on stylistic grounds that necessitates an early dating. As for Titus—rather than Vespasian—von Arnim made the weak point that Dio would have been too young to produce such a crafted work in the early seventies (1898: 215). However, if he were born around 40–45, as is widely believed, this objection cannot stand. Hence Jones 1978*a*: 133 argues with Momigliano 1951: 151 for an early Vespasianic date ('ca. 70–75 (?)') before that emperor deprived Rhodes of her freedom.

A Trajanic date is not, however, impossible. Von Arnim ruled it out because Dio expresses his hatred at xxxi. 150 for Nero rather than for Domitian, as he would have done (it is argued) after his exile. But Dio never mentions Domitian by name, though clearly referring to him as 'the tyrant' (see *Orr.* vi *Diogenes, or On Tyranny*, xiii. 1, xl. 12, l. 8) or 'despot' (*Or.* xlv. 1). Nero, who is mentioned or alluded to in *Orr.* iii. 134, xxi. 6, 9, 11, xxxi. 148, 150, xxxii. 60, xlvii. 14, lxvi. 6 (perhaps: von Arnim 1898: 277; or the Julio-Claudian dynasty: Cuvigny 1986 [somewhat dubious]), lxxi. 8–9, certainly behaved for Dio in a lawless and extreme manner, but is nowhere labelled 'tyrant'. Thus it is just possible that the reference at xxxi. 29 to the *damnatio memoriae* of 'tyrants and kings' (explicitly a contemporary happening) is to Domitian rather than to Nero. The collocation of Nero and 'the present ruler' at *Or.* xxxii. 60 (which is surely Trajanic; see below) might neutralize the reference to Nero's reign as 'very recent' at xxxi. 110, while *Or.* xlvii. 14 again shows Nero as a ready contemporary point of reference in the Trajanic period (cf. Syme 1958: ii. 518 with Dio xxi in mind), as he was later for the Philostrati (*Life of Apollonius, Nero*). A Trajanic date is now argued for by Sidebottom 1992.

Although the *Alexandrian Oration* hardly touches on relations between Greeks and Rome, it seems worthwhile to say something here on its dating. Jones's dating to the early seventies depends principally on identifying the military officer Conon (xxxii. 72 ὁ βέλτιστος) with a known prefect of Egypt, L. Peducaeus Colonus, referred to in the papyri as 'Kolôn' (Jones 1973, id. 1978a: 134; supported by Desideri 1978: 68–9; see also Desideri 116 ff. on literary correspondences between *Orr.* xxxi, xxxii, and xxxiii [of doubtful value]); but, although Dio's Conon looks like a Roman officer (he need not be one: Sidebottom 1992: 416), the identification with Colonus/Colon is forced and, further, the 'disturbance' Dio speaks of involving Conon (xxxii. 71–2) seems rather different from that recorded by Eusebius-Jerome for this period (so rightly Salmeri 1982: 97–8 n. 30). If a Vespasianic date cannot be upheld, we come back to von Arnim's Trajanic date (1898: 435–8; cf. Kindstrand 1978, rightly rejecting the notion that *Or.* xxxii is stylistically or by content inextricably related to *Or.* xxxi), which is based on Dio's philosophical stance in the speech (by no means a convincing reason in itself) and on the correspondences of thought between xxxii and the Trajanic kingship orations (cf. xxxii. 25–6 and *Or.* i. 23–4 and *Or.* iii. 45–9 concerning the character of the divine king and the tyrant and the good and bad democracy). A Trajanic date is not secure, but it is preferable.

APPENDIX D

Galen's On Theriac to Piso

The differences of approach and style between *On Theriac To Piso* (xiv. 210–94) and other works of Galen's are the basis of arguments against its authenticity among modern scholars. The objections were catalogued in a polemical outburst by the seventeenth-century French scholar Philippe Labbé.[1] Much of what he said reappears verbatim in Ackermann's useful *Historia literaria Claudii Galeni* reprinted in the first volume of Kühn.[2] Labbé's main points were that (i) *On Theriac* (alluding to Severus and Caracalla) failed to make mention of *On Antidotes* (which names only Severus as emperor: xiv. 65. 7, 66. 5–6), as it should have done in Galen's usual self-referential way, (ii) it refrained from mentioning rival doctors, (iii) it contained 'plurima verba' which were not used by Galen elsewhere, (iv) it contained stories, (v) its style showed excessive rhetorical posturing characteristic of youth (whereas Galen, if he were the author, would have been about 70), and (vi) it contained false information about the plants trifolium and helenium. Ackermann took over these points except for (iii), (iv), and (vi). He agreed with Labbé that the work was written 'ab aliquo nugatore, exercendi stili gratia, ex iis, quae apud Galenum in libris de antidotis legerat'. Above all, though he knew that a number of great scholars in the past had considered the work genuine, he could not see 'quo tempore scripserit Galenus eum librum', for it was totally alien to Galen's mature disposition. Among moderns the work is listed as false by Schubring, Ilberg, and López Férez.[3] Others have been unsure.[4] It has also been taken as genuine.[5]

---

[1] 1660: 22–35.   [2] pp. xxxiii–xxxviii.

[3] Schubring 1965: p. xlvii; Ilberg 1896: 193–4 Galen was 'schwerlich sein Verfasser'; followed by Winkler 1980: 11 (who gives a synopsis of opinion); López Férez 1991: 321.

[4] Von Premerstein: 1898: 261; Hankinson 1991: 244; Nutton 1976: 24, cf. id. 1984: 324 n. 45.

[5] Sudhoff 1915: 227; Watson 1966; Bowersock 1969: 84 n. 4; Nutton 1979: 164, id. 1993: 26 n. 64; P. Hadot 1984: 36 n. 31; Birley 1988: 198; Buraselis 1989: 25 ff. Sudhoff's testimony is no more than a brief reference; thus among serious medical historians Nutton alone is in favour, but he is also the only one to have devoted serious thought to the matter.

The real case against *On Theriac* is that it is out of character with Galen's self-presentation elsewhere, which is precisely what makes it interesting. So far as one can see, the linguistic usage of the work is no different from that of *On Antidotes*. The brief notices about trifolium and helenium (the former being especially important in Galen's pharmacology) do not apparently contradict what we learn in other works (xiv. 226. 19 ff., 244. 13 ff.). As for rivals, they are in fact mentioned (xiv. 250 ff. Asclepiades, xiv. 277–8 *methodikoi*). In regard to anecdotal material (the best example being perhaps the story of Cleopatra's death at xiv. 235. 7 ff.) *On Theriac* is hardly unique: Galen liked a good story and was adept at narrating one.[6] The lack of a reference to *On Antidotes* is more difficult, unless we assume—as is quite possible—that *On Antidotes* is the later work or that both were written around the same time.[7]

The character of *On Theriac* is different, because for reasons unknown Galen intended it as a complimentary piece to a man of public affairs who enjoyed a close relationship with the ruling family. The strong personal

[6] Cf. e.g. the tale of his violent Cretan friend, above, 'Galen' n. 48; Nutton 1991: 9–13 on storytelling from his case book.

[7] The existence of *On Antidotes* is referred to only in the third book of *On the Composition of Drugs by Places* (xii. 691. 11), which must have been written well into the Severan period (Ilberg 1889: 226–8). It is possible that this reference and the two to future work on theriac (*On the Composition of Drugs by Types* xiii. 451. 7, 909. 5–6) reveal common preparation of the pharmacological tracts rather than their order of publication (cf. Winkler 1980: 10; cf. the references at *On Antidotes* xiv. 8. 6, 80. 14 to *On Simple Drugs*).

Regarding relative dates, *On Antidotes* looks earlier than *On Theriac* because it speaks of 'our present emperor Severus' (xiv. 65. 6–7, 66. 5–6), whereas the words of *On Theriac* xiv. 217. 5–6 'under the present greatest emperors' can only really mean the joint rule of Severus and Caracalla, and the reference to the Troy Game (xiv. 212. 12–16) makes this after 204 (above, 'Galen' n. 36). However, as Ilberg noted (1896: 192–3), Galen's statement at *On Antidotes* xiv. 65. 11–12 that 'not even thirty years had been completed [μηδὲ τριάκοντα πεπληρωμένων ἐτῶν]' between the date of making theriac for Severus and the date at which he had first supplied it to Marcus strongly implies that Severus had theriac prepared when he was in Rome in the summer of 197 before leaving for the Parthian war (he had previously been in Rome in 193 and in the autumn of 196—this seems too early; he was not back there till 202—which seems too late), since Galen had first prepared the drug for Marcus after the death of Marcus' archiater Demetrius while Marcus was 'on the banks of the Ister' during the German war (*On Antidotes* xiv. 4. 11 ff.), i.e. in about 170 at the earliest. This means that *On Antidotes* can hardly have been written much before 200. If that is right, the references to Severus are without prejudice to the position of Caracalla at the time of writing, for Caracalla was co-emperor from January 28th 198 and had been *imperator destinatus* during the previous year (Birley 1988: 128 n. 23, 130–1 n. 4). When Galen refers to Severus, he is looking back a few years—he says that because of Commodus' neglect, when 'our present emperor Severus' ordered him to make theriac, 'I was forced' (aorist tense) to use stocks going back to Trajan and Hadrian (xiv. 65. 3 ff.). There is no reason why *On Antidotes* could not also be dated after 204.

slant makes a forgery by a *nugator* rather unlikely: the payer of compliments does not pass his praise off on another. Further, the new information embedded in an Arab commentator on Aristotle's *On Interpretation*, which quotes Alexander of Aphrodisias' verdict on Galen at the age of eighty, serves to confirm the belief of the Arab commentators on Galen himself that he had lived to 87 or 88 (and so beyond 215).[8] As Nutton observes, this strengthens the case for *On Theriac* by allowing it (and *On Antidotes*) more time for composition. It is the element of flattery in *On Theriac* that is surprising for Galen, who stresses in a harangue on recognizing the best doctor that he himself had never lost time waiting on the rich and powerful.[9] On the other hand no one would guess that the author of this same text who castigates the elite for their devotion to etymology and their obsession with how words were used in the past is the man who at another time wrote numerous philological works and literary commentaries (including no less than forty-eight books on the vocabulary of the Attic authors).[10] This last paradox shows how careful one must be before saying an author could not have written a particular work. We may compare Lucian, whose expression of implacable opposition to flattery of any kind (*Calumny, Timon, Toxaris, Nigrinus, On Hirelings*), is severely undermined by *Portraits, Defence of Portraits*, and other works aimed at Lucius Verus and his court (*On the Dance, How to Write History*), not to mention straightforward complimentary pieces like the *Harmonides* and the *Scythian*. If it is imagined that Galen was totally immune to pressures of power and status that affected all, that is to be duped by his own picture of himself as a ceaseless scholar toiling without regard for money or fame. It is also to fail to understand the markedly more authoritarian regime of the Severans. *On Theriac* shows that Galen was susceptible to pressures just as others were.[11]

---

[8] Nutton 1984: 320–4, especially 1987: 4–9. The *Suda* γ 32 reports that Galen died at around 70.

[9] *How to Recognize the Best Doctor*, Iskandar 1988: 103. 2; 113. 1, 10.

[10] Iskandar 1988: 129. 21–2 (with remarks 173–4 and Nutton 1990: 252–3); Galen, *On his Own Books* xix. 48. 11 ff.; above, 'Practice' nn. 64–6.

[11] In this respect the loss of Aelius Antipater's history of Severus (Philostratus, *VS* 607) and of Cassius Dio's pro-Severan pieces (Cassius Dio lxxii. 23. 1–3) is regrettable. Cf. again the prologue of Alexander of Aphrodisias' *On Fate* (above, 'Dio' n. 66, 'Galen' n. 40).

BIBLIOGRAPHY

Aalders, G. J. D. (1982*a*): *Plutarch's Political Thought* (trans. A. M. Manekofsky) (Amsterdam).
—— (1982*b*): 'Plutarch or pseudo-Plutarch? The Authorship of *De unius in re publica dominatione*', *Mnemosyne*, 35: 72–83.
—— (1986): 'Cassius Dio and the Greek World', *Mnemosyne*, 39: 282–304.
Accame, S. (1946): *Il dominio romano in Grecia dalla Guerra Acaica ad Augusto* (Rome).
Ackermann, J. Chr. G. (1965): *Historia literaria Claudii Galeni* (rev. from J. A. Fabricius [ed.], *Bibliotheca graeca*³ [rev. G. Chr. Harles], v [Hamburg, 1796], 377–500), in Kühn 1965: i. pp. xvii–cclxv.
Africa, T. W. (1961): 'The Opium Addiction of Marcus Aurelius', *JHI*: 97–102 (= 'Marc Aurels Opiumsucht', in Klein 1979: 133–43).
Albini, U. (1968) (ed., comm.): *[Erode Attico], ΠΕΡΙ ΠΟΛΙΤΕΙΑΣ* (Florence).
Alcock, S. E. (1993): *Graecia Capta: The Landscapes of Roman Greece* (Cambridge).
Alföldi, A. (1952): 'The Moral Barrier on Rhine and Danube', in E. Birley (ed.), *The Congress of Roman Frontier Studies, 1949* (Durham), 1–16.
Alföldy, G. (1977): *Konsulat und Senatorenstand unter den Antoninen: prosopographische Untersuchungen zur senatorischen Führungsschicht* (Bonn).
Allen, W. S. (1968): *Vox Graeca: A Guide to the Pronunciation of Classical Greek* (Cambridge).
—— (1973): *Accent and Rhythm* (Cambridge).
Altheim, F. (1951): *Roman und Dekadenz* (Tübingen).
Ameling, W. (1983): *Herodes Atticus*, i–ii (Hildesheim).
—— (1984*a*): 'L. Flavius Arrianus Neos Xenophon', *Epigr. Anatol.* 4: 119–22.
—— (1984b): 'Cassius Dio und Bithynien', *Epigr. Anatol.* 4: 123–38.
—— (1985) (ed.): *Die Inschriften von Prusias ad Hypium (IK 27)* (Bonn).
Anderson, B. (1991): *Imagined Communities: Reflections on the Origin and Spread of Nationalism*² (London).
Anderson, G. (1978): 'Lucian's Nigrinus: The Problem of Form', *GRBS* 19: 367–74.
—— (1984): *Ancient Fiction: The Novel in the Graeco-Roman World* (London).
—— (1986): *Philostratus* (London).

Anderson, G. (1989): 'The *Pepaideumenos* in Action: Sophists and their Outlook in the Early Empire', *ANRW* ii. 33. 1: 79–208.

—— (1990): 'The Second Sophistic: Some Problems of Perspective', in Russell 1990*b*: 91–110.

—— (1993): *The Second Sophistic: A Cultural Phenomenon in the Roman Empire* (London).

Andrei, O. (1981): 'Il tema della concordia in Dione di Prusa (Or. xxxviii, xxxix, xl, xli): Ceti dominanti ed ideologia nel II sec. d.C.', *Studi e ricerche* (Ist. di Storia, Florence), 1: 89–120.

—— (1984): *A. Claudius Charax di Pergameno: Interessi antiquari e antichità cittadine nell'età degli Antonini* (Bologna).

Angelomatis-Tsougarakis, H. (1990): *The Eve of the Greek Revival: British Travellers' Perceptions of Early Nineteenth-Century Greece* (London).

Anlauf, G. (1960): *Standard Late Greek oder Attizismus? Eine Studie zum Optativgebrauch im nachklassischen Griechisch* (Diss. Cologne).

Argyle, S. (1989): 'A New Greek Grammarian', *CQ* 39: 524–35.

Arnim, H. von (1892): '*Ineditum Vaticanum*', *Hermes*, 27: 118–30.

—— (1898): *Leben und Werke des Dio von Prusa* (Berlin).

—— (1899): 'Zum Leben Dios von Prusa', *Hermes*, 34: 363–79.

Asmus, J. R. (1900): 'Synesius und Dio Chrysostomus', *Byzant. Zeitschr.* 9: 85–151.

Austin, R. G. (1964) (ed., comm.): *P. Vergili Maronis Aeneidos liber secundus* (Oxford).

Avenarius, G. (1956): *Lukians Schrift zur Geschichtsschreibung* (Meisenheim am Glan).

Avotins, I. (1975): 'The Holders of the Chairs of Rhetoric at Athens', *HSCP* 79: 313–24.

—— (1978*a*): 'The Date and Recipient of the *Vitae Sophistarum* of Philostratus', *Hermes*, 106: 242–7.

—— (1978*b*): 'The Sophist Aristocles and the Grammarian Phrynichus', *PP* 33: 181–91.

Babut, D. (1969*a*) (ed., comm.): *Plutarque, De la vertu éthique* (Paris).

—— (1969*b*): *Plutarque et le Stoïcisme* (Paris).

—— (1975): 'Historia hoion Hylê Philosophias: histoire et réflexion morale dans l'oeuvre de Plutarque', *REG* 88: 207–19.

Bagnall, R. S., and Frier, B. W. (1994): *The Demography of Roman Egypt* (Cambridge).

Bakhtin, M. (1981): *The Dialogic Imagination: Four Essays* (ed. M. Holquist; trans. M. Holquist and C. Emerson) (Austin, Tex.).

Baldwin, B. (1961): 'Lucian as a Social Satirist', *CQ* 11: 199–208.

—— (1973): *Studies in Lucian* (Toronto).

Bannert, H. (1977): 'Caesars Brief an Q. Cicero und die Verbreitung von griechischer Sprache und Schrift in Gallien (zu BG 1, 29, 1. 5, 48, 4 und 6, 14, 3)', *WS* 11: 80–95.

Bardong, K. (1942): 'Beiträge zur Hippokrates- und Galenforschung', *NAG*, Ph.-hist. Kl., 1942, no. 7, 577–640.

Barigazzi, A. (1966): *Favorino di Arelate: Opere* (Florence).

—— (1984): 'Plutarco e il corso futuro della storia', *Prometheus*, 10: 264–86.

Barnes, J. (1991): 'Galen on Logic and Therapy', in Kudlien and Durling 1991: 50–102.

Barnes, T. D. (1967): 'A Note on Polycarp', *JTS* 18: 433–7.

—— (1976): 'Sossianus Hierocles and the Antecedents of the Great Persecution', *HSCP* 80: 239–52.

—— (1981): *Constantine and Eusebius* (Cambridge, Mass.).

—— (1984): 'The Composition of Cassius Dio's Roman History', *Phoenix*, 38: 240–55.

Barrow, R. H. (1967): *Plutarch and his Times* (London).

Baslez, M.-F. (1984): *L'Étranger dans la Grèce antique* (Paris).

—— (1992): 'De l'histoire au roman: la Perse de Chariton', in Baslez *et al.* 1992: 199–212.

—— (1994): 'L'Auteur du *De Dea Syria* et les réalités religieuses de Hiérapolis', in Billault 1994: 171–6.

—— Hoffmann, Ph., and Trédé, M. (1992) (eds.): *Le monde du roman grec* (Paris).

Baumgart, H. (1874): *Aelius Aristides als Repräsentant der sophistischen Rhetorik des zweiten Jahrhunderts der Kaiserzeit* (Leipzig).

Bearzot, C. (1988): 'La Grecia di Pausania: Geografia e cultura nella definizione del concetto di 'Ελλάς', *CISA* (Milan), 14: 90–112.

Beaujeu, J. (1955): *La Religion romaine à l'apogée de l'empire*, i (Paris).

Behr, C. A. (1968*a*): *Aelius Aristides and the Sacred Tales* (Amsterdam).

—— (1968*b*): 'Citations of Porphyry's *Against Aristides* Preserved in Olympiodorus', *AJP* 89: 186–99.

—— (1969): 'Aelius Aristides' Birth Date corrected to November 26, 117 AD', *AJP* 90: 75–7.

—— (1981–6) (trans.): *P. Aelius Aristides: The Complete Works*, i–ii (Leiden).

—— (1994): 'Studies on the Biography of Aelius Aristides', *ANRW* ii. 34. 2: 1140–1233.

Belin de Ballu, E. (1972): *Olbia: Cité antique du littoral nord de la mer Noire* (Leiden).

Belloni, L. (1980): 'Aspetti dell'antica σοφία in Apollonio di Tiana', *Aevum*, 54: 140–9.

Bering-Staschewski, R. (1981): *Römische Zeitgeschichte bei Cassius Dio* (Bochum).

Bernand, A., and Bernand, E. (1960): *Les Inscriptions grecques et latines du colosse de Memnon* (Paris).

Bernhardt, R. (1971): *Imperium und Eleutheria: Die römische Politik gegenüber den freien Städten des griechischen Ostens* (Diss. Hamburg).

Bianchi, U. (1986): 'Plutarco e il dualismo', in Brenk and Gallo 1986: 111–20.

Bickerman, E. (1952): 'Origines Gentium', *CPh* 47: 65–81 (= id., *Religions and Politics in the Hellenistic and Roman Periods* [Como, 1985], 399–417).

Bidez, J., and Cumont, F. (1938): *Les Mages hellénisés*, i–ii (Paris).

Bieler, L. (1935–6): *ΘΕΙΟΣ ΑΝΗΡ: Das Bild des 'göttlichen Menschen' in Spätantike und Frühchristentum*, i–ii (Vienna).

Billault, A. (1991): *La Création romanesque dans la littérature grecque à l'époque impériale* (Paris).

—— (1994) (ed.): *Lucien de Samosate*, Centre d'Études Romaines et Gallo-Romaines 13 (Lyons).

Binder, H. (1905): *Dio Chrysostomus und Posidonius: Quellenuntersuchungen zur Theologie des Dio von Prusa* (Diss. Tübingen).

Bingen, J. (1987): 'Aelius Aristide, *OGIS* 709 et "les Grecs d'Égypte"', in J. Servais *et al.* (eds.), *Stemmata: Mélanges de philologie, d'histoire et d'archéologie grecques offerts à J. Labarbe* (Liège and Louvain), 173–85.

Birley, A. (1979): 'Die Aussen- und Grenzpolitik unter der Regierung Marc Aurels', in Klein 1979: 473–502.

—— (1987): *Marcus Aurelius*[2] (London).

—— (1988): *The African Emperor, Septimius Severus*[2] (London).

Biville, F. (1990): *Les Emprunts du latin au grec: Approche phonétique*, i (Louvain and Paris).

Bleicken, J. (1966): 'Der Preis des Aelius Aristides auf das römische Weltreich', *NAG*, Phil.-hist. Kl., 1966, no. 7, 223–77.

Bodson, A. (1967): *La Morale sociale des derniers Stoïciens, Sénèque, Épictète et Marc Aurèle* (Paris).

Bol, R., and Herz, P. (1989): 'Zum Kultbild des Zeus Panhellenios: Möglichkeiten der Identifikation und Rezeption', in Walker and Cameron 1989: 89–95.

Bompaire, J. (1958): *Lucien écrivain: Imitation et création*, BEFAR 190 (Paris).

—— (1976): 'Les Historiens classiques dans les exercices préparatoires de rhétorique (*progymnasmata*)', in *Recueil Plassart: Études sur l'antiquité grecque offertes à A. Plassart par ses collègues de la Sorbonne* (Paris), 1–7.

—— (1989): 'Le Sacré dans les discours d'Aelius Aristides (XLVII–LII Keil)', *REG* 102: 28–39.

—— (1994): 'L'Atticisme de Lucien', in Billault 1994: 65–75.

Bonner, C. (1942): 'A Tarsian Peculiarity', *Harv. Theol. Rev.* 35: 1–11.

Bonner, S. F. (1939): *The Literary Treatises of Dionysius of Halicarnassus: A Study in the Development of Critical Method* (Cambridge).

Bosch, C. (1935): *Die kleinasiatischen Münzen der römischen Kaiserzeit, Teil II—Einzeluntersuchungen—Band 1: Bithynien, 1 Hälfte* (Stuttgart).

Bosworth, A. B. (1977): 'Arrian and the Alani', *HSCP* 81: 217–55.

—— (1980): *A Historical Commentary on Arrian's History of Alexander*, i (Oxford).

—— (1993): 'Arrian and Rome: the Minor Works', *ANRW* ii. 34. 1: 226–75.

Boulanger, A. (1923): *Aelius Aristide et la sophistique dans la province de l'Asie au IIe siècle de notre ère*, BEFAR 126 (Paris).

Bowersock, G. W. (1965*a*): 'Zur Geschichte des römischen Thessaliens', *RhM* 108: 277–89.

—— (1965*b*): 'Some Persons in Plutarch's *Moralia*', *CQ* 15: 267–70.

—— (1965*c*): *Augustus and the Greek World* (Oxford).

—— (1969): *Greek Sophists in the Roman Empire* (Oxford).

—— (1970): introduction to C. P. Jones (trans.), *Life of Apollonius* (Harmondsworth), 9–22.

—— (1973): 'Greek Intellectuals and the Imperial Cult in the Second Century AD', in den Boer 1973: 177–206.

—— (1974) (ed.): *Approaches to the Second Sophistic* (University Park, Penn.).

—— (1979): 'Historical Problems in Late Republican and Augustan Classicism', in Flashar 1979: 57–78.

—— (1985): 'Pausanias', in Easterling and Knox 1985: 709–10.

—— (1990): *Hellenism in Late Antiquity* (Cambridge).

—— (1994): *Fiction as History: Nero to Julian*, Sather Class. Lectures 58 (Berkeley).

Bowie, E. L. (1974): 'The Greeks and their Past in the Second Sophistic', in Finley 1974: 166–209 (repr. with some changes from *P&P* 46 [1970], 3–41).

—— (1978): 'Apollonius of Tyana: Tradition and Reality', *ANRW* ii. 16. 2: 1652–99.

—— (1980): 'Lucian at Philippopolis', *Mitteilungen des bulgarischen Forschungsinstitutes in Österreich*, Jg. III, 1 (Vienna), 53–60.

—— (1982): 'The Importance of Sophists', *YCS* 27: 29–60.

—— (1985*a*): 'The Greek Novel', in Easterling and Knox 1985: 683–99.

—— (1985*b*): 'Theocritus' Seventh Idyll, Philetas and Longus', *CQ* 35: 67–91.

—— (1989*a*): 'Poetry and Poets in Asia and Achaia', in Walker and Cameron 1989: 198–205.

—— (1989*b*): 'Greek Sophists and Greek Poetry in the Second Sophistic', *ANRW* ii. 33. 1: 209–58.

—— (1990): 'Greek Poetry in the Antonine Age', in Russell 1990*b*: 53–90.

—— (1991): 'Hellenes and Hellenism in Writers of the Early Second Sophistic', in Saïd 1991: 183–204.

—— (1994): 'The Readership of Greek Novels in the Ancient World', in Tatum 1994: 435–59.

Box, H. (1935): 'Philo: *In Flaccum* 131 (M. 2 p. 536)', *CQ* 29: 39–40.

Brancacci, A. (1985): 'Rhetorike Philosophousa: Dione Crisostomo nella cultura antica e bizantina (Naples).

Brandstaetter, C. (1894): 'De notionum πολιτικός et σοφιστής uso rhetorico', *Leipziger Studien*, 15: 129–274.

Branham, R. B. (1989): *Unruly Eloquence: Lucian and the Comedy of Traditions* (Cambridge, Mass.).

Brenk, F. E. (1977): *In Mist Apparelled: Religious Themes in Plutarch's Moralia and Lives* (Leiden).

—— (1986): 'In the Light of the Moon: Demonology in the Early Imperial Period', *ANRW* ii. 16. 3: 2068–2145 (with an index in *ANRW* ii. 36. 2 [1987], 1283–99).

—— (1987): 'An Imperial Heritage: The Religious Spirit of Plutarch of Chaironeia', *ANRW* ii. 36. 1: 248–349 (with an index in *ANRW* ii. 36. 2 [1987], 1300–22).

—— (1988): 'Plutarch's *Erotikos*: The Drag Down Pulled Up', *ICS* 13.2: 457–71.

—— and Gallo, I. (1986) (eds.): *Miscellanea Plutarchea*, Atti del I convegno di studi su Plutarco (Ferrara).

Briscoe, J. (1967): 'Rome and the Class Struggle in the Greek States 200–146 BC', *P&P* 36: 3–20 (= Finley 1974: 53–73).

Brixhe, Cl., and Hodot, R. (1993): 'A chacun sa koiné?', in Cl. Brixhe (ed.), *La Koiné grecque antique*, i. *Une langue introuvable* (Nancy), 7–21.

Brodersen, K. (1993): 'Appian und sein Werk', *ANRW* ii. 34. 1: 339–63.

Brown, P. (1978): *The Making of Late Antiquity* (Cambridge, Mass.).

—— (1988): *The Body and Society* (New York).

—— (1992): *Power and Persuasion in Late Antiquity* (Madison, Wis.).

Browning, R. (1978): 'The Language of Byzantine Literature', in Sp. Vryonis, Jr. (ed.), *The "Past" in Medieval and Modern Greek Culture: Byzantina kai Metabyzantina* 1 (Malibu, Calif.), 103–33 (= Browning 1989: xv).

—— (1983*a*): *Medieval and Modern Greek*² (Cambridge).

—— (1983*b*): 'The Continuity of Hellenism in the Byzantine World: Appearance or Reality?', in T. Winnifrith and P. Murray (eds.), *Greece Old and New* (London), 111–28 (= Browning 1989: 1).

—— (1989): *History, Language and Literacy in the Byzantine World* (Northampton).

Brožek, M. (1963): 'Noch über die Selbstzitate als chronologischen Wegweiser in Plutarchs Parallelbiographien', *Eos*, 53: 68–80.

Brunt, P. (1961): 'Charges of Provincial Maladministration under the Early Principate', *Historia*, 10: 189–227 (= *Roman Imperial Themes* [Oxford, 1990], 487–506).

—— (1973): 'Aspects of the Social Thought of Dio Chrysostom and of the Stoics', *PCPhS* 19: 9–34 (= *Studies in Greek History and Thought* [Oxford, 1993], 210–44).

—— (1975): 'Stoicism and the Principate', *PBSR* 43: 7–39.

—— (1976–83) (ed., trans.): *Arrian: Anabasis Alexandri and Indica*, i–ii (Loeb: Cambridge, Mass.).

—— (1977): 'From Epictetus to Arrian', *Athenaeum*, 65: 19–48.

—— (1979): 'Divine Elements in the Imperial Office', *JRS* 69: 168–75.

—— (1994): 'The Bubble of the Second Sophistic', *BICS* 39: 25–52.

Bubeník, V. (1989): *Hellenistic and Roman Greece as a Sociolinguistic Area* (Amsterdam).

Bürger, K. (1892): 'Zu Xenophon von Ephesus', *Hermes*, 27: 36–67.

Buffière, F. (1980): *Éros adolescent: La pédérastie dans la Grèce antique* (Paris).

Buraselis, K. (1989): Θεῖα δωρεά. Μελέτες πάνω στὴν πολιτικὴ τῆς δυναστείας τῶν Σεβήρων καὶ τήν *Constitutio Antoniniana* (Athens).

Buresch, K. (1898): *Aus Lydien* (Leipzig).

Burton, G. P. (1975): 'Proconsuls, Assizes and the Administration of Justice under the Empire', *JRS* 65: 92–106.

—— (1979): 'The Curator Rei Publicae: Towards a Reappraisal', *Chiron*, 9: 465–87.

—— (1992): 'The Addressees of Aelius Aristides, *Orations* 17 K and 21 K', *CQ* 42: 444–7.

Cadoux, C. J. (1938): *Ancient Smyrna: A History of the City from the Earliest Times to 324 AD* (Oxford).

Calder, W. M. (1906): 'Smyrna as Described by the Orator Aristides', in W. M. Ramsay (ed.), *Studies in the History and Art of the Eastern Provinces of the Roman Empire* (Aberdeen), 95–116.

Cameron, A. (1931): 'Latin Words in the Greek Inscriptions of Asia Minor', *AJP* 51: 232–62.

Cameron, A. (1991): 'The Eastern Provinces in the 7th Century AD: Hellenism and the Emergence of Islam', in Saïd 1991: 287–313.

—— (1993): *The Mediterranean World in Late Antiquity AD 395–600* (London).

Carney, T. F. (1973): 'Prosopography: Payoffs and Pitfalls', *Phoenix*, 27: 156–79.

Cartledge, P., and Spawforth, A. (1989): *Hellenistic and Roman Sparta: A Tale of Two Cities* (London).

Casevitz, M. (1994): 'La Création verbale chez Lucien: le *Lexiphanes*, Lexiphane et Lucien', in Billault 1994: 77–86.

—— Pouilloux, J., Chamoux, F. (1992) (eds., trans., comms.): *Pausanias: Description de la Grèce*, i (Budé: Paris).

Casson, L. (1974): *Travel in the Ancient World* (London).

Caster, M. (1938): *Études sur Alexandre ou le faux prophète de Lucien* (Paris).

Castritius, H. (1971): 'Ein bisher unbekannte Statthalter Kilikiens?', *Historia*, 20: 80–3.

Chabert, S. (1897): *L'Atticisme de Lucien* (Diss. Paris).

Chadwick, H. (1953) (trans.): *Origen: Contra Celsum* (Cambridge).

Chalk, H. H. O. (1960): 'Eros and the Lesbian Pastorals of Longus', *JHS* 80: 32–51 (= Gärtner 1984: 388–407).

Chamoux, F. (1974): 'Pausanias géographe', in R. Chevallier (ed.), *Littérature gréco-romaine et géographie historique: Mélanges offerts à R. Dion* (Paris), 83–90.

Champlin, E. (1980): *Fronto and Antonine Rome* (Cambridge, Mass.).

Chaquot, A. (1955): 'Notes sur le *Semeion* et les inscriptions araméennes de Hatra', *Syria*, 32: 59–69.

Christ, F. (1938): *Die römische Weltherrschaft in der antiken Dichtung* (Stuttgart).

Clark, D. L. (1957): *Rhetoric in Greco-Roman Education* (New York).

Clavier, E. (1814–21) (trans.): Παυσανίου Ἑλλάδος περιήγησις, i–vi (Paris).

Clogg, R. (1972): 'The Ideology of the "Revolution of 21 April 1967"', in R. Clogg and G. Yannopoulos (eds.), *Greece under Military Rule* (London).

—— (1985): 'Sense of the Past in Pre-Independence Greece', in Sussex and Eade 1985: 7–30.

Colson, E. (1975): *Tradition and Contract: The Problem of Order* (London).

Connerton, P. (1989): *How Societies Remember* (Cambridge).

Connolly, R. H. (1948): 'Eusebius *H.E.* v. 28', *JTS* 49: 73–9.

Costas, P. S. (1936): *An Outline of the History of the Greek Language* (Diss. Chicago).

Crone, P., and Cook, M. (1977): *Hagarism: The Making of the Islamic World* (Cambridge).

Cumont, F. (1929): *Les Religions orientales dans le paganisme romain*[4] (Paris).

Cureton, W. (1855): *Spicilegium Syriacum* (London).

Cuvigny, M. (1986): 'Une histoire de langue (Dion de Pruse, 66, 5–6)', *REG* 99: 361–6.

Dagron, G., and Feissel, D. (1987): *Inscriptions de Cilicie* (Paris).

Dalimier, C. (1991): 'Sextus Empiricus contre les grammariens: ce que parler grec veut dire', in Saïd 1991: 17–32.

Daly, L. W. (1950): 'Roman Study Abroad', *AJP* 71: 40–58.

Daux, G. (1975): 'Les Empereurs romains et l'Amphictionie pyléodelphique', *CRAI* 1975: 348–62.

—— (1976): 'La Composition du Conseil amphictyonique sous l'Empire', in *Recueil Plassart: Études sur l'antiquité grecque offertes à A. Plassart par ses collègues de la Sorbonne* (Paris), 59–79.

de Blois, L. (1986): 'The Εἰς Βασιλέα of Ps.-Aelius Aristides', *GRBS* 27: 279–88.

de Borries, J. (1911) (ed.): *Phrynichi Sophistae Praeparatio Sophistica* (Leipzig).

de Labriolle, P. (1950): *La Réaction païenne* (Paris).

de Lacy, Ph. (1966): 'Galen and the Greek Poets', *GRBS* 7: 259–66.

—— (1974): 'Plato and the Intellectual Life of the Second Century AD', in Bowersock 1974: 4–10.

de Lange, N. R. M. (1978): 'Jewish Attitudes to the Roman Empire', in Garnsey and Whittaker 1978: 255–81.

de Leeuw, C. A. (1939): *Aelius Aristides als Bron voor de kennis van zijn tijd* (Amsterdam).

de Martino, F. (1972–5): *Storia della costituzione romana²*, i–v (Naples).

de Romilly, J. (1972): 'Vocabulaire et propagande ou les premiers emplois du mot ὁμόνοια', in *Mélanges de linguistique et de philologie grecques offerts à P. Chantraine* (Paris), 199–209.

Debrunner, A., and Scherer, A. (1969): *Geschichte der griechischen Sprache*, ii. *Grundfragen und Grundzüge des nachklassischen Griechisch* (Berlin).

Deferrari, R. (1916): *Lucian's Atticism: The Morphology of the Verb* (Diss. Princeton).

Deichgräber, K. (1956a): 'Parabasenverse aus Thesmophoriazusen II des Aristophanes bei Galen', *SDAW*, Kl. f. Spr., Lit. und Kunst, Jg. 1956, nr. 2.

—— (1956b): 'Galen als Erforscher des menschlichen Pulses', *SDAW*, Kl. f. Spr., Lit. und Kunst, Jg. 1956, nr. 3.

Deininger, J. (1965): *Die Provinziallandtage der römischen Kaiserzeit* (Munich).

Del Corno, D. (1979): 'Lo scritto di Filostrato su Apollonio Tianeo e la tradizione della narrativa', in *La struttura della fabulazione antica*, Inst. Filol. Class. Med. 54 (Genoa), 65–87.

Delchor, M. (1987): 'Le Nature du coq sacré ('alektruôn 'iros) du *De dea syra* §48', *Semitica*, 37: 57–61.

Den Boer, W. (ed.) (1973): *Le Culte des souverains dans l'empire romain*, Entretiens Hardt xix (Geneva).

Derret, J. D. M. (1961): 'The Administration of Hindu Law by the British', *Comparative Studies in Society and History*, 4: 10–52.

Desbordes, F. (1982): 'Le Langage sceptique: Notes sur le *Contre les grammariens* de Sextus Empiricus', *Langages*, 16: 47–74.

Desideri, P. (1973): 'Il *Dione* e la politica di Sinesio', *Atti Acc. Sc. Torino*, 107: 551–93.

—— (1978): *Dione di Prusa: Un intellettuale greco nell'impero romano* (Florence).

—— (1986): 'La vita politica cittadina nell'impero: lettura dei *praecepta gerendae rei publicae* e dell'*an seni res publica gerenda sit*', *Athenaeum*, 74: 371–81.

—— (1989): 'Teoria e prassi storiografica di Plutarco: una proposta di lettura della coppia Emilio Paolo-Timoleonte', *Maia*, 41: 199–215.

Dessau, H. (1899): 'Zum Leben Dios von Prusa', *Hermes*, 34: 81–7.

Devereux, G. (1967): 'Greek Pseudo-Homosexuality and the "Greek Miracle"', *SymbOsl*, 42: 69–92.

Di Benedetto, V. (1958): 'Dionisio Trace e la techne a lui attributa', *ASNP* 27: 169–210 (continued in *ASNP* 28 [1959], 87–118).

Diel, H. (1894): *De enuntiatis finalibus apud Graecorum rerum scriptores posterioris aetatis* (Munich).

Diels, H. (1918): 'Hippokratische Forschungen V', *Hermes*, 53: 57–87.

Dihle, A. (1957): 'Analogie und Attizismus', *Hermes*, 85: 170–205.

—— (1977): 'Der Beginn des Attizismus', *A&A* 23: 162–77.

—— (1978): 'Zur Datierung des Metiochus-Romans', *WJA* 4: 47–55.

—— (1994): *Greek and Latin Literature of the Roman Empire From Augustus to Justinian* (trans. M. Malzahn) (London).

Diller, A. (1955): 'The Authors Named Pausanias', *TAPA* 86: 268–79 (= *Studies in Greek Manuscript Tradition* [Amsterdam, 1983], 137–48).

—— (1956): 'Pausanias in the Middle Ages', *TAPA* 87: 84–97 (= *Studies in Greek Manuscript Tradition* [Amsterdam, 1983], 149–62).

Dillon, J. (1977): *The Middle Platonists: A Study of Platonism 80 BC to AD 220* (London).

—— (1982): 'Self-Definition in Later Platonism', in Meyer and Sanders 1982: 60–75.

—— (1988): 'Plutarch and Platonist Orthodoxy', *ICS* 13.2: 357–64.

Dodds, E. R. (1951): *The Greeks and the Irrational*, Sather Class. Lectures 25 (Berkeley).

—— (1965): *Pagan and Christian in an Age of Anxiety* (Cambridge).

—— (1977): *Missing Persons* (Oxford).

Doer, B. (1937): *Die römische Namengebung* (Stuttgart).

Döring, K. (1979): *Exemplum Socratis*, *Hermes* Einzelschr. 42 (Wiesbaden).

Dörner, F. K., and Naumann, R. (1939): *Forschungen in Kommagene*, Istanbuler Forschungen 10 (Berlin).

Donini, P. (1981) 'Scetticismo, Scettici e cattedre imperiali', in G. Giannantoni (ed.), *Lo scetticismo antico*, i–ii (Naples), ii. 678–87.

Dover, K. J. (1978): *Greek Homosexuality* (London).

Drerup, E. (1923): *Demosthenes im Urteile des Altertums* (Würzburg).

Drew-Bear, T., Hermann, P., Eck, W. (1977): 'Sacrae Litterae', *Chiron*, 7: 355–83.

Drijvers, H. J. W. (1965): *The Book of the Laws of Countries: Dialogue on Fate of Bardaisan of Edessa* (Assen).

—— (1966): *Bardaisan of Edessa* (Assen).

—— (1977): 'Hatra, Palmyra und Edessa', *ANRW* ii. 8: 799–906.

Dubuisson, M. (1981): 'Vtraque lingua', *AC* 50: 274–86.

—— (1982*a*): 'Remarques sur le vocabulaire grec de l'acculturation', *Rev. belge de phil. et d'hist.* 60: 5–32.

—— (1982*b*): 'Y a-t-il une politique linguistique romaine?', *Ktema*, 7: 187–210.

—— (1984): 'Le Latin est-il une langue barbare?', *Ktema*, 9: 55–68.

—— (1984–6): 'Lucien et Rome', *AntSoc* 15–17: 185–207.

—— (1985): *Le Latin de Polybe: les implications historiques d'un cas de bilinguisme* (Paris).

—— (1991): '*Graecus, graeculus, graecari*: l'emploi péjoratif du nom des grecs en latin', in Saïd 1991: 315–35.

—— (1992): 'Le Grec à Rome à l'époque de Cicéron: Extension et qualité du bilinguisme', *Annales E.S.C.* 47: 187–206.

Duncan Jones, R. (1982): *The Economy of the Roman Empire*² (Cambridge).

Dupont-Sommer, A., and Robert, L. (1964): *La Déesse de Hiérapolis Castabala (Cilicie)*, Bibl. arch. et hist. de l'Instit. Français d'Arch. d'Istanbul 16 (Paris).

Dzielska, M. (1986): *Apollonius of Tyana in Legend and History* (trans. P. Pienkowski) (Rome).

Eagleton, T. (1984): *The Function of Criticism* (London).

Easterling, P. E., and Knox, B. M. W. (1985) (eds.): *The Cambridge History of Classical Literature*, i. *Greek Literature* (Cambridge).

Eck, W. (1980): 'Die Präsenz senatorischer Familien in den Städten des Imperium Romanum bis zum späten 3. Jahrhundert', in W. Eck *et al.* (eds.), *Studien zur antiken Sozialgeschichte: Festschrift F. Vittinghoff* (Cologne), 283–322.

—— (1982): 'Jahres- und Provinzialfasten der senatorischen Statthalter von 69/70 bis 138/139', *Chiron*, 12: 281–362.

—— (1983): 'Jahres- und Provinzialfasten der senatorischen Statthalter von 69/70 bis 138/139', *Chiron*, 13: 147–237.

—— (1985): *Die Statthalter der germanischen Provinzen vom 1.–3. Jahrhundert* (Cologne).

Edelstein, E., and Edelstein, L. (1945): *Asclepius: A Collection and Interpretation of the Testimonies*, i–ii (Baltimore).

Edlow, R. B. (1977): *Galen on Language and Ambiguity* (Leiden).

Edwards, M. J. (1989): 'Satire and Verisimilitude: Christianity in Lucian's *Peregrinus*', *Historia*, 38: 89–98.

—— (1991): 'Damis the Epicurean', *CQ* 41: 563–6.

Effe, B. (1982): 'Longos: Zur Funktionsgeschichte der Bukolik in der römischen Kaiserzeit', *Hermes*, 110: 65–84.

—— (1987): 'Der griechische Liebesroman und die Homoerotik', *Philologus*, 131: 95–108.

Egger, B. (1988): 'Zu den Frauenrollen im griechischen Roman: Die Frau als Heldin und Leserin', in Hofmann 1988: 33–66.

—— (1994): 'Women and Marriage in the Greek Novels: The Boundaries of Romance', in Tatum 1994: 260–80.

Einarson, B. (1952): 'Plutarch's Ancestry', *CP* 47: 99.

—— (1955): 'Plutarch's Ancestry Again', *CP* 50: 253–5.

444 Bibliography

Elsner, J. (1992): 'Pausanias: A Greek Pilgrim in the Roman World', *P&P* 135: 3–29.

Elsom, H. E. (1992): 'Callirhoe: Displaying the Phallic Woman', in Richlin 1992*a*: 212–30.

Emperius, A. (1844): *Dionis Chrysostomi opera*, i (Brunswick).

Epstein, A. L. (1978): *Ethos and Identity: Three Studies in Ethnicity* (London).

Erbse, H. (1949 [1950]): 'Untersuchungen zu den Attizistischen Lexica', *ADAW*, Phil.-hist. Kl., Jg. 1949, nr. 2.

Errington, R. M. (1968): *Philopoemen* (Oxford).

Fears, J. R. (1977): *Princeps a diis electus: The Divine Election of the Emperor as a Political Concept at Rome* (Rome).

Fechner, D. (1986): *Untersuchungen zu Cassius Dios Sicht der Römischen Republik* (Hildesheim).

Ferguson, C. A. (1972): 'Diglossia', in P. P. Giglioli (ed.), *Language and Social Context* (London), 232–51.

Ferrary, J.-L. (1988): *Philhellénisme et impérialisme*, BEFAR 271 (Rome).

Festugière, A.-J. (1954): *Personal Religion Among the Greeks*, Sather Class. Lectures 26 (Berkeley).

—— (1955): *Epicurus and his Gods* (trans. C. W. Chilton) (Oxford).

—— (1969): 'Sur les *Discours sacrés* d'Aelius Aristide', *REG* 82: 117–53 (= id., *Études d'histoire et de philologie* [Paris, 1975], 89–125).

—— (1986) (trans.): *Aelius Aristide, Discours Sacrés: Rêve, religion, médecine au IIe siècle après J.C.* (with an introduction by J. Le Goff and notes by H.-D. Saffrey) (Paris).

Finley, M. I. (1974) (ed.): *Studies in Ancient Society* (London).

Fischer, E. (1974) (ed.): *Die Ekloge des Phrynichos* (Berlin).

Fishwick, D. (1990): 'Dio and Maecenas: The Emperor and the Ruler Cult', *Phoenix*, 44: 267–75.

Fitzgerald, J. T., and White, L. M. (1983) (eds., trans.): *The Tabula of Cebes* (Chico, Calif.).

Flacelière, R. (1963): 'Rome et ses empereurs vus par Plutarque', *AC* 32: 28–47.

—— (1966): 'Plutarque, "De Fortuna Romanorum"', in J. Heurgon *et al.* (eds.), *Mélanges d'archéologie, d'épigraphie, et de l'histoire offerts à J. Carcopino* (Paris), 367–75.

Flashar, H. (1971) (ed.): *Antike Medizin* (Darmstadt).

—— (1979) (ed.): *Le Classicisme à Rome aux Iers siècles avant et après J.-C.*, Entretiens Hardt xxv (Geneva).

Flinterman, J.-J. (1993): *Politiek, Paideia en Pythagorisme* (Groningen).

Follet, S. (1972): 'Flavius Euphanès d'Athènes, ami de Plutarque', in *Mélanges de linguistique et de philologie grecques offerts à P. Chantraine* (Paris), 35–50.

—— (1976): *Athènes au IIe et au IIIe siècle* (Paris).

Forni, G. (1953): *Il reclutamento delle legioni da Augusto a Diocleziano* (Milan).

Forte, B. (1972): *Rome and the Romans as the Greeks Saw Them* (Rome).

Fortenbaugh, W. W. *et al.* (1992) (eds.): *Theophrastus of Eresus*, i–ii (Leiden).

Fortuna, S. (1986): 'Sesto Empirico, ἐγκύκλια μαθήματα e arti utili alla vita', *Studi class. ed orient.* 36: 123–37.

Foucault, M. (1988): *The Care of the Self: The History of Sexuality*, iii (trans. R. Hurley) (New York, 1986 [cited by the Penguin edition, London, 1988]).

François, L. (1921): *Essai sur Dion Chrysostome philosophe et moraliste cynique et stoïcien* (Diss. Paris).

Fraser, P. M. (1977): *Rhodian Funerary Monuments* (Oxford).

Frazer, J. G. (1898): *Pausanias's Description of Greece*, i–vi (London).

Frazier, F., and Froidefond, Chr. (1990) (eds., trans.): *Plutarque: Œuvres morales*, v. 1. *La Fortune des Romains, La Fortune ou la Vertu d'Alexandre, La Gloire des Athéniens* (Budé: Paris).

Frézouls, Ed. (1991): 'L'Hellénisme dans l'épigraphie de l'Asie Mineure romaine', in Saïd 1991: 125–47.

Frösén, J. (1974): *Prolegomena to a Study of the Greek Language in the First Centuries AD: The Problem of Koiné and Atticism* (Diss. Helsinki).

Fuchs, H. (1938): *Der geistige Widerstand gegen das Römertum* (Berlin).

—— (1990): *Lusus Troiae* (Diss. Cologne).

Fuhrmann, F. (1964): *Les Images de Plutarque* (Paris).

Fusillo, M. (1988): 'Textual Patterns and Narrative Situations in the Greek Novel', in Hofmann 1988: 17–31.

—— (1991): *Naissance du roman* (trans. M. Abrioux) (Paris) (= *Il romanzo greco. Polifonia ed Eros* [Venice 1989]).

Gabba, E. (1955): 'Sulla *Storia romana* di Cassio Dione', *RSI* 67: 289–333.

—— (1956): *Appiano e la Storia delle Guerre Civili* (Florence).

—— (1959): 'Storici greci dell'impero romano da Augusto ai Severi', *RSI* 71: 361–81.

—— (1963): 'Il latino come dialetto greco', in *Miscellanea di studi alessandrini in memoria di A. Rostagni* (Turin), 188–94.

—— (1967): *Appiani Bellorum Civilium Liber Primus²* (Florence).

—— (1991): *Dionysius and The History of Archaic Rome*, Sather Class. Lectures 56 (Berkeley).

Gärtner, H. (1984) (ed.): *Beiträge zum griechischen Liebesroman* (Hildesheim).

Gardner, J. F. (1986): *Women in Roman Law and Society* (London).

Garnaud, J.-Ph. (1991) (ed., trans.): *Achille Tatius d'Alexandrie: Le roman de Leucippé et Clitophon* (Budé: Paris).

Garnsey, P. (1970): *Social Status and Legal Privilege in the Roman Empire* (Oxford).

—— (1971): 'Honorarium decurionatus', *Historia*, 20: 309–25.

Garnsey, P. (1974): 'Aspects of the Decline of the Urban Aristocracy in the Empire', *ANRW* ii. 1: 229–52.

—— (1988): *Famine and Food Supply in the Graeco-Roman World: Responses to Risk and Crisis* (Cambridge).

—— and Saller, R. (1987): *The Roman Empire: Economy, Society and Culture* (London).

—— and Whittaker, C. R. (1978) (eds.): *Imperialism in the Ancient World* (Cambridge).

Gascó, F. (1987–8): 'Retórica y realidad en la segunda sofística', *Habis*, 18–19: 437–43.

—— (1992): 'Para una interpretación historica de las declamaciones en tiempos de la segunda sofistica', *Athenaeum*, 88: 421–31.

Geagan, D. J. (1967): *The Athenian Constitution after Sulla, Hesperia* Suppl. 12 (Princeton).

Geel, J. (1840) (ed., comm.): *Dionis Chrysostomi Ὀλυμπικός* (Leiden).

Geiger, J. (1981): 'Plutarch's Parallel Lives: the Choice of Heroes', *Hermes*, 109: 85–104 (= B. Scardigli [ed.], *Essays on Plutarch's Lives* [Oxford, 1995] 165–90).

—— (1985): *Cornelius Nepos and Ancient Political Biography, Historia* Einzelschr. 47 (Stuttgart).

—— (1988): 'Nepos and Plutarch: From Latin to Greek Political Biography', *ICS* 13.2: 245–56.

Geller, M. J. (1983): 'More Graeco-Babylonian', *Zeitschr. f. Assyriologie* 73: 114–20.

Gelzer, T. (1979): 'Klassizismus, Attizismus und Asianismus', in Flashar 1979: 1–55.

Georgiadou, A. (1988): 'The *Lives of the Caesars* and Plutarch's other *Lives*', *ICS* 13.2: 349–56.

Ghedini, G. (1926): *La lingua greca di Marco Aurelio Antonino*, i. *Fonetica e morfologia* (Milan).

Giangrande, G. (1962): 'On the Origins of the Greek Romance', *Eranos*, 60: 132–51.

—— (1974): rev. of A. D. Papanikolaou, *Chariton-Studien: Untersuchungen zur Sprache und Chronologie der griechischen Romane* (Göttingen, 1973), in *JHS* 94: 197–8.

Gibbon, E. (1896–1900 [1776–88]): *The History of the Decline and Fall of the Roman Empire*, i–vii (ed. J. B. Bury) (London).

Gignac, F. T. (1976): *A Grammar of the Greek Papyri of the Roman and Byzantine Periods*, i. *Phonology* (Milan).

Gilliam, J. F. (1961): 'The Plague under Marcus Aurelius', *AJP* 82: 225–51 (= 'Die Pest unter Marc Aurel', in Klein 1979: 144–75).

Glucker, J. (1978): *Antiochus and the Late Academy* (Göttingen).

Göttsching, J. (1889): *Apollonius von Tyana* (Diss. Leipzig).

Goetzeler, L. (1890): *Quaestiones in Appiani et Polybii dicendi genus* (Würzburg).

Goldhill, S. (1995): *Foucault's Virginity: Ancient Erotic Fiction and the History of Sexuality* (Cambridge).

Goldmann, B. (1988): *Einheitlichkeit und Eigenständigkeit der Historia Romana des Appian* (Hildesheim).

Goudriaan, K. (1989): *Over classicisme: Dionysius van Halicarnassus en zijn program van welsprekendheid, cultuur en politiek* (Diss. Amsterdam).

Gourevitch, D. (1984): *Le Triangle hippocratique dans le monde gréco-romain: le malade, sa maladie et son médecin*, BEFAR 251 (Rome).

Graf, F. (1984–5): 'Maximos von Aigai: Ein Beitrag zur Überlieferung über Apollonios von Tyana', *Jahr. f. Ant. u. Chr.* 27–28: 65–73.

Graham, A. J. (1974): 'The Limitations of Prosopography in Roman Imperial History (with Special Reference to the Severan Period)', *ANRW* ii. 1: 136–57.

Graindor, P. (1922): *Marbres et textes antiques d'époque impériale* (Ghent).

—— (1934): *Athènes sous Hadrien* (Cairo).

Grelle, F. (1972): *L'autonomia cittadina fra Traiano e Adriano* (Naples).

Griffin, M. (1971): review of Bowersock 1969, in *JRS* 61: 279–81.

—— (1993): 'Le Mouvement cynique et les romains: attraction et répulsion', in M.-O. Goulet-Cazé and R. Goulet (eds.), *Le Cynisme ancien et ses prolongements* (Paris), 241–58.

—— and Barnes, J. (1989) (eds.): *Philosophia togata* (Oxford).

Gronewald, M. (1979): 'Ein Fragment aus den Aithiopica des Heliodor', *ZPE* 34: 19–21.

Grosso, F. (1954): 'La vita di Apollonio Tianeo come fonte storica', *Acme*, 7: 333–552.

Gruen, E. S. (1976): 'The Origins of the Achaean War', *JHS* 96: 46–69.

—— (1984): *The Hellenistic World and the Coming of Rome*, i–ii (Berkeley).

Guarducci, M. (1937): 'Le offerte dei conquistadori romani ai santuari della Grecia', *Rend.Pont.Acc.* 13: 41–58.

Gurlitt, W. (1890): *Über Pausanias* (Graz).

Habicht, Chr. (1969): *Die Inschriften des Asklepieions: Altertümer von Pergamon*, viii.3 (Berlin).

—— (1973): 'Die augusteische Zeit und das erste Jahrhundert nach Christi Geburt', in den Boer 1973: 41–88.

—— (1975): 'New Evidence on the Province of Asia', *JRS* 65: 64–91.

—— (1984): 'Pausanias and the Evidence of Inscriptions', *ClAnt* 3: 40–56.

—— (1985): *Pausanias' Guide to Ancient Greece* (Berkeley).

Hadas-Lebel, M. (1984): 'Jacob et Esaü ou Israël et Rome dans le Talmud et le Midrash', *Rev.Hist.Relig.* 201: 369–92.

Hadot, I. (1984): *Arts libéraux et philosophie dans la pensée antique* (Paris).

Hadot, P. (1981): 'Exercices spirituels', in id., *Exercices spirituels et philosophie antique* (Paris), 13–58.

—— (1984): 'Marc Aurèle était-il opiomane?', in E. Lucchesi and H.-D. Saffrey (eds.), *Mémorial A.-J. Festugière: Antiquité païenne et Chrétienne* (Geneva), 33–50.

Hägg, T. (1983): *The Novel in Antiquity* (Oxford).

——(1987): '*Callirhoe* and *Parthenope*: The Beginnings of the Historical Novel', *ClAnt* 6: 184–204.

——(1992): 'Hierocles the Lover of Truth and Eusebius the Sophist', *SymbOsl* 67: 138–50.

Hahn, I. (1993): 'Appian und Rom' (rev. G. Németh), *ANRW* ii. 34. 1: 364–402.

Hahn, J. (1989): *Der Philosoph und die Gesellschaft: Selbstverständis, öffentliches Auftreten und populäre Erwartungen in der höhen Kaiserzeit* (Stuttgart).

Hahn, L. (1906): *Rom und Romanismus im griechisch-römischen Osten* (Leipzig).

Hajjar, Y. (1977–85): *La Triade d'Héliopolis-Baalbek*, i–iii (Leiden and Montreal).

Halfmann, H. (1979): *Die Senatoren aus dem östlichen Teil des Imperium Romanum bis zum Ende des 2. Jh. n. Chr.* (Göttingen).

——(1982): 'Die Senatoren aus den kleinasiatischen Provinzen des römischen Reiches vom 1. bis 3. Jahrhundert (Asia, Pontus-Bithynia, Lycia-Pamphylia, Galatia, Cappadocia, Cilicia)', in *Tituli*, iv–v. *Epigrafia e ordine senatorio* (Rome) v. 603–50.

——(1986): *Itinera principum* (Stuttgart).

Hall, E. (1989): *Inventing the Barbarian* (Oxford).

Hall, J. A. (1981): *Lucian's Satire* (New York).

Halperin, D. M., Winkler, J. J., Zeitlin, F. I. (1990) (eds.): *Before Sexuality: The Construction of Erotic Experience in the Ancient Greek World* (Princeton).

Hammond, M. (1957): 'The Composition of the Senate, AD 68–235', *JRS* 47: 74–81.

Hankinson, R. J. (1991): *Galen: On the Therapeutic Method, Books I and II* (Oxford).

Harmon, A. M. (1925) (ed., trans.): *Lucian*, iv (Loeb: Cambridge, Mass.).

Hartke, W. (1951): *Römische Kinderkaiser* (Berlin).

Hartman, J. J. (1916): *De Plutarco scriptore et philosopho* (Leiden).

Haslam, M. W. (1981) (ed.): 'Narrative about Tinouphis in Prosimetrum', in *Papyri Greek and Roman: Edited by Various Hands in Honour of E. G. Turner on the Occasion of his Seventieth Birthday*, Graeco-Roman Memoirs 68: 35–45.

Hasluck, F. W. (1910): *Cyzicus* (Cambridge).

Heath, M. (1994): 'The Substructure of *Stasis*-Theory from Hermagoras to Hermogenes', *CQ* 44: 114–29.

Heberdey, R. (1894): *Die Reisen des Pausanias in Griechenland* (Vienna).

Heck, H. (1917): *Zur Entstehung des rhetorischen Attizismus* (Munich).

Heer, J. (1979): *La Personnalité de Pausanias* (Paris).

Hein, A. (1914): *De optativi apud Plutarchum usu* (Diss. Breslau).

Helm, R. (1906): *Lukian und Menipp* (Leipzig and Berlin).

Henrichs, A. (1972): *Die Phoinikika des Lollianos* (Bonn).

Henry, M. M. (1992): 'The Edible Woman: Athenaeus' Concept of the Pornographic', in Richlin 1992*a*: 250–68.

Hepding, H. (1933): "*Ρουφίνιον ʼΆλσος*", *Philologus*, 88: 90–103, 241–3.

Herbst, W. (1911): *Galeni Pergameni de Atticissantium studiis testimonia collecta atque examinata* (Diss. Leipzig).

Hering, J. (1935): *Lateinisches bei Appian* (Diss. Leipzig).

Herzfeld, M. (1982) *Ours Once More: Folklore, Ideology, and the Making of Modern Greece* (Austin, Tex.).

—— (1987): *Anthropology through the Looking-Glass: Critical Ethnography in the Margins of Europe* (Cambridge).

Herzog, R. (1935): 'Urkunden zur Hochschulpolitik der römischen Kaiser', *SPrAW* (Sonderausgabe), ph.-hist. Kl. 32, 967–1019.

Higgins, M. J. (1945): 'The Renaissance of the First Century and the Origin of Standard Late Greek', *Traditio*, 3: 49–100.

Highet, G. (1962): *The Anatomy of Satire* (Princeton).

—— (1983): 'Mutilations in the Text of Dio Chrysostom', in *The Classical Papers of Gilbert Highet* (ed. R. J. Ball) (New York), 74–99.

Hind, J. G. F. (1977): 'The "Genounian" Part of Britain', *Britannia*, 8: 229–34.

Hirzel, R. (1895): *Der Dialog*, i–ii (Leipzig).

Hitzig, H., and Blümner, H. (1896–1910): *Des Pausanias Beschreibung von Griechenland*, i–iii (Leipzig).

Hobsbawm, E. (1985): *Bandits*[2] (Harmondsworth).

—— (1990): *Nations and Nationalism Since 1780: Programme, Myth, Reality* (Cambridge).

—— and Ranger, T. (1983) (eds.): *The Invention of Tradition* (Cambridge).

Hofmann, H. (1988) (ed.): *Groningen Colloquia on the Novel*, i (Groningen).

Höistad, R. (1948): *Cynic Hero and Cynic King* (Uppsala).

Holford-Strevens, L. (1988): *Aulus Gellius* (London).

—— (1993): 'Utraque lingua doctus: Some Notes on Bilingualism in the Roman Empire', in H. D. Jocelyn and H. Hurt (eds.), *Tria lustra: Essays and Notes Presented to J. Pinsent*, Liverpool Classical Papers 3 (Liverpool), 203–13.

Holleaux, M. (1895): 'Pausanias et la destruction d'Haliarte par les Perses', *RPh* 19: 109–15 (= id., *Études d'épigraphie et d'histoire grecques*, i [Paris, 1938], 187–93).

—— (1898): "*ʼΑπόλλων Σπόδιος*", in *Mélanges H. Weil* (Paris), 193–206 (= id., *Études d'épigraphie et d'histoire grecques*, i [Paris, 1938] 195–209).

Holzberg, N. (1984): 'Apuleius und der Verfasser des griechischen Eselsromans', *WJA* 10: 161–77.

—— (1986): *Der antike Roman* (Munich).

—— (1992) (ed.): *Der Äsop-Roman* (Tübingen).

Homeyer, H. (1965) (ed.): *Lukian: Wie man Geschichte Schreiben soll* (Munich).

Hopwood, K. (1989): 'Bandits, Elites and Rural Order', in A. Wallace-Hadrill (ed.), *Patronage in Ancient Society* (London), 171–87.

Horsfall, N. (1979): 'Doctus sermones utriusque linguae?', *EMC* 23: 79–95.

Householder, F. W. (1941): *Literary Quotation and Allusion in Lucian* (New York).

—— (1962): 'Greek Diglossia', *Georgetown University Monograph Series on Languages and Linguistics* no. 15: 109–32.

Howgego, C. J. (1985): *Greek Imperial Countermarks: Studies in the Provincial Coinage of the Roman Empire* (London).

Hüttl, W. (1933–6): *Antoninus Pius*, i–ii (Prague).

Hunt, E. D. (1984): 'Travel, Tourism and Piety in the Roman Empire: A Context for the Beginnings of Christian Pilgrimage', *EMC* 3: 391–417.

Hunter, R. (1983): *A Study of Daphnis and Chloe* (Cambridge).

—— (1994): 'History and Historicity in the Romance of Chariton', *ANRW* ii. 34. 2: 1055–86.

Ihnken, Th. (1978): *Die Inschriften von Magnesia am Sipylos* (*IK* 8) (Bonn).

Ilberg, J. (1888): 'De Galeni vocum Hippocraticarum glossario', in *Commentationes philologae . . . O. Ribbeckio* (Leipzig), 327–54.

—— (1889, etc.): 'Über die Schriftstellerei des Klaudios Galenos', *RhM* 44 (1889), 207–39; 47 (1892), 489–514; 51 (1896), 165–96; 52 (1897), 591–623 (repr. together as *Über die Schriftstellerei des Klaudios Galenos* [Darmstadt 1974]).

—— (1905): 'Aus Galens Praxis: Ein Kulturbild aus der römischen Kaiserzeit', *Neue Jarhb. f. das klass. Altertum*, 15: 276–312 (= Flashar 1971: 361–416).

Iliffe, J. (1979): *A Modern History of Tanganyika* (Cambridge).

Innes, D., and Winterbottom, M. (1988): *Sopatros the Rhetor: Studies in the Text of the Διαίρεσις Ζητημάτων, BICS* Suppl. 48 (London).

Iskandar, A. Z. (1988) (ed., trans.): *Galen: On Examinations By Which the Best Physicians are Recognized, CMG* Suppl. Orient. IV (Berlin).

Jacquemin, A. (1991): 'Delphes au IIᵉ siècle après J.-C.: un lieu de la mémoire grecque', in Saïd 1991: 217–31.

Jeffreys, M. (1985): Adamantios Korais; Language and Revolution', in Sussex and Eade 1985: 42–55.

Jenkins, R. (1963): *Byzantium and Byzantinism* (Cincinnati).

Jenkyns, R. (1989): 'Virgil and Arcadia', *JRS* 79: 26–39.

Jeuckens, R. (1907): *Plutarch von Chaeronea und die Rhetorik* (Strasbourg).

Johnston, A. (1984*a*): 'Greek Imperial Statistics: A Commentary', *RevNum* 6th ser. 26: 240–57.

—— (1984*b*): 'Hierapolis Revisited', *NumChron* 144: 52–80.

Jolowicz, H. F. (1952): *Historical Introduction to the Study of Roman Law*² (Cambridge).

Joly, R. (1963): *Le Tableau de Cébès et la philosophie religieuse* (Brussels).

Jones, A. H. M. (1940): *The Greek City from Alexander to Justinian* (Oxford).

Jones, C. P. (1966): 'Towards a Chronology of Plutarch's Works', *JRS* 61: 61–74.

—— (1967): 'A Friend of Galen', *CQ* 17: 311–12.

—— (1970): 'Sura and Senecio', *JRS* 60: 98–104.

—— (1971*a*): *Plutarch and Rome* (Oxford).

—— (1971*b*): 'A New Letter of Marcus Aurelius to the Athenians', *ZPE* 8: 161–83.

—— (1972*a*): 'Two Enemies of Lucian', *GRBS* 13: 475–87.

—— (1972*b*): 'Aelius Aristides, Εἰς βασιλέα', *JRS* 62: 134–52.

—— (1972*c*): 'Two Friends of Plutarch', *BCH* 96: 263–7.

—— (1973): 'The Date of Dio of Prusa's Alexandrian Oration', *Historia*, 22: 302–9.

—— (1975): 'An Oracle given to Trajan', *Chiron*, 5: 403–6.

—— (1978*a*): *The Roman World of Dio Chrysostom* (Cambridge, Mass.).

—— (1978*b*): 'A Syrian in Lyon', *AJP* 99: 336–53.

—— (1980): 'Apuleius' *Metamorphoses* and Lollianos' *Phoinikika*', *Phoenix*, 34: 243–54.

—— (1981): 'The Εἰς βασιλέα Again', *CQ* 31: 224–5.

—— (1982): 'A Martyria for Apollonius of Tyana', *Chiron*, 12: 137–44.

—— (1984): 'Tarsos in the *Amores* Ascribed to Lucian', *GRBS* 25: 177–81.

—— (1986): *Culture and Society in Lucian* (Cambridge, Mass.).

—— (1989): 'Τρόφιμος in an Inscription of Erythrai', *Glotta*, 67: 194–7.

—— (1990*a*): 'The Rhodian Oration Ascribed to Aelius Aristides', *CQ* 40: 514–22.

—— (1990*b*): 'Lucian and the Bacchants of Pontus', *EMC* 9: 53–63.

—— (1991): 'Aelius Aristides, "On the Water in Pergamum"', *Arch.Anz.* 1991: 111–17.

—— (1992*a*): 'La Personnalité de Chariton', in Baslez *et al.* 1992: 161–7.

—— (1992*b*): 'Hellenistic History in Chariton of Aphrodisias', *Chiron*, 22: 91–102.

Jüthner, J. (1923): *Hellenen und Barbaren: Aus der Geschichte des Nationalbewusstseins* (Leipzig).

Just, R. (1989): 'Triumph of the Ethnos', in Tonkin *et al.* 1989: 71–88.

Kahane, H., and Kahane, R. (1979): 'Decline and Survival of Western Prestige Languages', *Language*, 55: 183–98.

Kahrstedt, U. (1950): 'Die Territorien von Patrai und Nikopolis in der Kaiserzeit', *Historia*, 1: 549–61.

—— (1954): *Das wirtschaftliche Gesicht Griechenlands in der Kaiserzeit* (Berne).

Kaimio, J. (1979): *The Romans and the Greek Language* (Helsinki).

Kapetanopoulos, E. (1976): 'Three Athenian Archons (et alia)', Ἑλληνικά, 29: 248–67.

Kaster, R. A. (1988): *Guardians of Language: The Grammarian and Society in Late Antiquity* (Berkeley).

Kearsley, R. A. (1986): 'Asiarchs, *Archiereis*, and the *Archiereiai* of Asia', *GRBS* 27: 183–92.

Kedourie, E. (1971) (ed.): *Nationalism in Asia and Africa* (with an introduction by E. Kedourie) (London).

Kee, H. C. (1982): 'Self-Definition in the Asclepius Cult', in Meyer and Sanders 1982: 118–36.

Keil, J. (1953): 'Vertreter der zweiten Sophistik in Ephesos', *JÖAI* 40: 5–26.

Kennedy, G. (1972): *The Art of Rhetoric in the Roman World* (Princeton).

—— (1974): 'The Sophists as Declaimers', in Bowersock 1974: 17–22.

—— (1983): *Greek Rhetoric under Christian Emperors* (Princeton).

Kent, J. H. (1966): *Corinth*, viii. 3. *The Inscriptions 1926–1950* (Princeton).

Kerényi, K. (1927): *Die griechisch-orientalische Romanliteratur in religionsgeschichtlicher Beleuchtung* (Tübingen; rev. edn. Darmstadt, 1962).

Kidd, C. (1993): *Subverting Scotland's Past* (Cambridge).

Kienast, D. (1959–60): 'Hadrian, Augustus und die eleusinischen Mysterien', *JfNG* 10: 61–9.

—— (1964): 'Die Homonoiaverträge in der römischen Kaiserzeit', *JfNG* 14: 51–64.

—— (1971): 'Ein vernachlässigtes Zeugnis für die Reichspolitik Traians: Die zweite tarsische Rede des Dion von Prusa', *Historia*, 20: 62–80.

Kindstrand, J. F. (1973): *Homer in der Zweiten Sophistik* (Uppsala).

—— (1978): 'The Date of Dio of Prusa's Alexandrian Oration: A Reply', *Historia*, 27: 378–83.

—— (1979–80): 'Sostratus–Hercules–Agathion: The Rise of a Legend', *Ann. societ. litt. human. reg. Upsal.* (1979–80), 50–79.

—— (1980): 'Demetrius the Cynic', *Philologus*, 124: 83–98.

Klein, R. (1979) (ed.): *Marc Aurel* (Darmstadt).

—— (1981): *Die Romrede des Aelius Aristides: Einführung* (Darmstadt).

—— (1983) (ed., trans.): *Die Romrede des Aelius Aristides* (Darmstadt).

Klose, D. O. A. (1987): *Die Münzprägung von Smyrna in der römischen Kaiserzeit* (Berlin).

Kohl, R. (1915): *De scholasticarum declamationum argumentis ex historia petitis* (= E. Drerup [ed.], *Rhetorische Studien*, iv) (Diss. Paderborn).

Kokolakis, M. (1959): *Pantomimus and the Treatise Περὶ Ὀρχήσεως* (Athens).

—— (1960): 'Lucian and the Tragic Performances in his Time', *Platon*, 12: 67–109.

Kollesch, J. (1964–5): 'Aus Galens Praxis am römischen Kaiserhof', in E. C. Welskopf (ed.), *Neue Beiträge zur Geschichte der Alten Welt*, i–ii (Berlin), ii. 57–61.

—— (1981): 'Galen und die Zweite Sophistik', in Nutton 1981: 1–11.

—— and Nickel, D. (1993) (eds.): *Galen und das hellenistische Erbe*, Verhandl. IV. Intern. Galen-Symposiums, *Sudhoffs Archiv* Beiheft 32 (Stuttgart).

Konstan, D. (1994): *Sexual Symmetry: Love in the Ancient Novel and Related Genres* (Princeton).

Kortekaas, G. A. A. (1984) (ed.): *Historia Apollonii Regis Tyri* (Groningen).

Koskenniemi, E. (1991): *Der philostrateische Apollonios* (Helsinki).

Kramer, J. (1993): '*Ῥωμαῖοι* und *Λατῖνοι*', in G. W. Most, H. Petersmann, A. M. Ritter (eds.), *Philanthropia kai Eusebeia: Festschrift für A. Dihle zum 70. Geburtstag* (Göttingen), 234–47.

Kroll, W. (1915): 'Randbemerkungen XXXI', *RhM* 70: 607–10.

Krumbholz, F. (1885): *De praepositionum usu Appianeo* (Diss. Jena).

Kuch, H. (1965): *ΦΙΛΟΛΟΓΟΣ* (Berlin).

—— (1989): 'Die "Barbaren" und der antike Roman', *Das Altertum*, 35: 80–6.

Kudlien, F. (1981): 'Galen's Religious Belief', in Nutton 1981: 117–30.

—— (1986): *Die Stellung des Arztes in der römischen Gesellschaft* (Stuttgart).

—— (1989): 'Kindesaussetzung im antiken Roman: Ein Thema zwischen Fiktionalität und Lebenswirklichkeit', in H. Hofmann (ed.), *Groningen Colloquia on the Novel*, ii (1989), 25–44.

—— and Durling, R. J. (1991) (eds.): *Galen's Method of Healing* (Leiden).

Kühn, C. G. (1965) (ed.): *Galeni opera omnia* (Leipzig, 1821–33; repr. Hildesheim with a revised bibliography).

Kühne, H.-J. (1969): 'Appians historiographische Leistung', *Wiss. Zeitschr. Rostock*, 18: 345–77.

Kunkel, W. (1967): *Herkunft und soziale Stellung der römischen Juristen*[2] (Graz).

Kussl, R. (1991): *Papyrusfragmente griechischer Romane* (Tübingen).

Kyhnitzsch, E. (1894): *De contionibus, quas Cassius Dio historiae suae intexuit, cum Thucydideis comparatis* (Diss. Leipzig).

Labbé, Ph. (1660): *Claudii Galeni Chronologicum elogium* (Paris).

Lacey, W. K. (1968): *The Family in Classical Greece* (London).

Laffi, U. (1967): 'Le iscrizioni relative all'introduzione nel 9 A.C. del nuovo calendario della provincia d'Asia', *Studi class. ed orient.* 16: 1–98.

Lafond, Y. (1991): 'Pausanias historien dans le livre VII de la Périégèse', *JS* 1991: 27–45.

Lamar Crosby, H. (1946) (ed., trans.): *Dio Chrysostom*, iv (Loeb: Cambridge, Mass.).

Lane Fox, R. (1986): *Pagans and Christians In the Mediterranean World from the Second Century AD to the Conversion of Constantine* (London).

Lapidge, M. (1989): 'Stoic Cosmology and Roman Literature, First to Third Centuries AD', *ANRW* ii. 36. 3: 1379–1429.

Larsen, J. A. O. (1938): 'Roman Greece', in T. Frank (ed.), *An Economic Survey of Ancient Rome*, iv (Baltimore), 259–498.

—— (1968): *Greek Federal States: Their Institutions and History* (Oxford).

Lasserre, F. (1979): 'Prose grecque classicisante', in Flashar 1979: 135–73.

Latte, K. (1915): 'Zur Zeitbestimmung des Antiatticista', *Hermes*, 50: 373–94 (= *Kleine Schriften* [Munich, 1968], 612–30).

Lavagnini, B. (1921): 'Le origini del romanzo greco', *Ann. della Sc. Norm. Super. di Pisa*, 27: 1–104 (= *Studi sul romanzo greco* [Messina, 1950], 1–105).

Le Clerc, D. (1723): *Histoire de la médecine*[6] (Amsterdam).

Le Corsu, F. (1981): *Plutarque et les femmes* (Paris).

Le Glay, M. (1976): 'Hadrien et l'Asklépieion de Pergame', *BCH* 100: 347–72.

Lenz, F. W. (1963): 'Der Athenahymnos des Aristeides', *Riv. Cult. Class. e Med.* 5: 329–47 (= *Opuscula selecta* [Amsterdam, 1972], 355–73).

—— (1964): 'Die Selbstverteidigung eines politischen Angeklagten: Untersuchungen zu der Rede des Apollonios von Tyana bei Philostratos', *Das Altertum*, 10: 95–110 (= *Opuscula selecta* [Amsterdam, 1972], 433–48).

Leon, H. J. (1927): 'The Language of the Greek Inscriptions from the Jewish Catacombs of Rome', *TAPA* 58: 210–33.

Lepper, F. A. (1948): *Trajan's Parthian War* (London).

Leunissen, P. M. M. (1989): *Konsuln und Konsulare in der Zeit von Commodus bis Severus Alexander (180–235 n. Chr.): Prosopographische Untersuchungen zur senatorischen Elite im römischen Kaiserreich* (Amsterdam).

Levi, M. A. (1981): 'Il βασιλικὸς λόγος di Apollonio di Tiana', in L. Gasperini (ed.), *Scritti sul mondo antico in memoria di F. Grosso* (Rome), 289–93.

Levick, B. M. (1967): *Roman Colonies in Southern Asia Minor* (Oxford).

Liebenam, W. (1900): *Städteverwaltung im römischen Kaiserreiche* (Leipzig).

Lightfoot, C. S. (1988): 'Facts and Fiction—The Third Siege of Nisibis (AD 350)', *Historia*, 37: 105–25.

Litsch, E. (1893): *De Cassio Dione imitatore Thucydidis* (Diss. Freiburg).

Lo Cascio, F. (1978): *Sulla autenticità delle epistole di Apollonio Tianeo* (Palermo).

López Eire, A. (1981): 'Del ático a la *koiné*', *Emerita*, 49: 377–92.

López Férez, J. A. (1991) (ed.): *Galeno: obra, pensamiento y influencia* (Madrid).

Lukács, G. (1962): *The Historical Novel* (trans. H. Mitchell and S. Mitchell) (London).

Lutz, C. (1947): 'Musonius Rufus, The Roman Socrates', *YCS* 10: 3–147.

MacAlister, S. (1992): 'Gender as Sign and Symbolism in Artemidoros' *Oneirokritika*: Social Aspirations and Anxieties', *Helios*, 19.1–2: 140–60.

—— (1994): 'Byzantine Developments', in Morgan and Stoneman 1994: 275–87.

McDermott, W. C. (1976): 'Stemmata quid faciunt? The Descendants of Frontinus', *AncSoc* 7: 229–61.

Macleod, M. D. (1979): 'Lucian's Activities as a ΜΙΣΑΛΑΖΩΝ', *Philologus*, 123: 326–8.

—— (1987): 'Lucian's Relationship to Arrian', *Philologus*, 131: 257–64.

MacMullen, R. (1974): *Roman Social Relations 50 BC to AD 284* (New Haven).

—— (1981): *Paganism in the Roman Empire* (New Haven).

—— (1988): *Corruption and the Decline of Rome* (New Haven).

Macready, S., and Thompson, F. H. (1987) (eds.): *Roman Architecture in the Greek World* (London).

Maehler, H. (1976): 'Der Metiochus-Parthenope-Roman', *ZPE* 23: 1–20.

Magie, D. (1905): *De Romanorum iuris publici sacrique vocabulis sollemnibus in graecum sermonem conversis* (Leipzig).

—— (1950): *Roman Rule in Asia Minor*, i–ii (Princeton).

Maidhof, A. (1912): *Zur Begriffsbestimmung der Koine, besonders auf Grund des Attizisten Moiris* (Würzburg) (= M. von Schanz [ed.], *Beiträge zur historischen Syntax der griechischen Sprache*, xx = *Festgabe für M. von Schanz* [Würzburg, 1912], 277–373).

Malitz, J. (1983): *Die Historien des Poseidonios*, Zetemata Monogr. zur klass. Alt. 79 (Munich).

Mantero, T. (1966): *Ricerche sull' Heroikos di Filostrato* (Genoa).

Manuwald, B. (1979): *Cassius Dio und Augustus*, Palingenesia XIV (Wiesbaden).

Marache, R. (1952): *La Critique littéraire de langue latine et le développement du gout archaïsant au IIe siècle de notre ère* (Paris).

Marcotte, D. (1988): 'Le *Pausanias* de Christian Habicht: Notes de lecture', *LEC* 56: 73–83.

Marek, Chr. (1985): 'Katalog der Inschriften im Museum von Amasra', *Epigr. Anatol.* 6: 133–56.

Marincola, J. M. (1989): 'Some Suggestions on the Proem and "Second Preface" of Arrian's *Anabasis*', *JHS* 109: 186–9.

Martin, J. (1974): *Antike Rhetorik, Technik und Methode* (Munich).

Marx, K., and Engels, F. (1845–6): 'Die deutsche Ideologie', in eid., *Werke*, iii (Berlin, 1962), 9–530.

Mason, H. J. (1970): 'The Roman Government in Greek Sources', *Phoenix*, 24: 150–9.

—— (1974): *Greek Terms for Roman Institutions* (Toronto).

Meillet, A. (1935): *Aperçu d'une histoire de la langue grecque*[4] (Paris).

Melcher, P. (1906): *De sermone Epicteteo quibus rebus ab Attica regula discedat* (Diss. Halle).

Merkelbach, R. (1962): *Roman und Mysterium in der Antike* (Munich and Berlin).

—— (1977): *Die Quellen des griechischen Alexander-romans*[2] (Munich).

—— (1978): 'Der Rangstreit der Städte Asiens und die Rede des Aelius Aristides über die Eintracht', *ZPE* 32: 287–96.

—— (1988): *Die Hirten des Dionysos: Die Dionysos-Mysterien der römischen Kaiserzeit und der bukolische Roman des Longus* (Stuttgart).

Mesk, J. (1908): 'Des Aelius Aristides verlorene Rede Gegen die Tänzer', *WS* 30: 59–74.

Mesk, J. (1909): *Der Aufbau der XXVI. Rede des Aelius Aristides (Lobrede auf Rom)* (Vienna).

—— (1913): 'Antiochos und Stratonike', *RhM* 68: 366–94.

Méthy, N. (1991): 'Réflexions sur le thème de la divinité de Rome: à propos de l'*Éloge de Rome* d'Aelius Aristide', *Latomus*, 50: 660–8.

Metzler, D. (1991): 'Kommagene von Osten her gesehen', in A. Schütte *et al.* (eds.), *Studien zum antiken Kleinasien, Asia Minor Studien*, iii (Bonn) 21–7.

Meyer, B. F., and Sanders, E. P. (1982) (eds.): *Jewish and Christian Self-Definition, Self-Definition in the Greco-Roman World*, iii (Philadelphia).

Meyer, E. (1917): 'Apollonius von Tyana und die Biographie des Philostratos', *Hermes*, 52: 371–424 (= *Kleine Schriften* [Halle, 1924], ii. 131–91).

Meyer, E. (1954) (trans., comm.): *Pausanias: Beschreibung Griechenlands* (Zurich).

Meyerhof, M. (1929): 'Autobiographische Bruchstücke Galens aus arabischen Quellen', *Sudhoffs Archiv*, 22: 72–86.

—— and Schacht, J. (1931): 'Galen, Über die medizinischen Namen', *APrAW*, Jg. 1931, Phil.-hist. Kl., nr. 3.

Michenaud, G., and Dierkens, J. (1972): *Les Rêves dans les 'Discours Sacrés' d'Aelius Aristide, IIe s. ap. J.C.: Essai d'analyse psychologique* (Mons).

Mikalson, J. D. (1975): ' "ΗΜΕΡΑ ᾿ΑΠΟΦΡΑΣ", *AJP* 96: 19–27.

Millar, F. (1964): *A Study of Cassius Dio* (Oxford).

—— (1966): 'Epictetus and the Imperial Court', *JRS* 55: 141–8.

—— (1968): 'Local Cultures in the Roman Empire: Libyan, Punic and Latin in Roman Africa', *JRS* 58: 126–34.

—— (1969): 'P. Herennius Dexippus: The Greek World and the Third Century Invasions', *JRS* 59: 12–29.

—— (1982): 'Emperors, Frontiers and Foreign Relations, 31 BC to AD 378', *Britannia*, 13: 1–23.

—— (1983): 'Empire and City, Augustus to Julian: Obligations, Excuses and Status', *JRS* 73: 76–96.

—— (1988): 'Imperial Ideology in the Tabula Siarensis', in J. González and J. Arce (eds.), *Estudios sobre la Tabula Siarensis: Anejos de Archivo Español de Arqueología*, 9: 11–19.

—— (1989): ' "Senatorial" Provinces: An Institutionalized Ghost', *Ancient World*, 20: 93–7.

—— (1992): *The Emperor in the Roman World*² (London).

—— (1993): *The Roman Near East, 31 BC–AD 337* (Cambridge, Mass.).

Mirambel, A. (1937): *Les 'états de langue' dans la Grèce actuelle*, Conférences de l'Institut de Linguistique de l'Université de Paris 5 (Paris).

Misch, G. (1949–62): *Geschichte der Autobiographie*, i–iii (Berne and Frankfurt am Main).

Mitchell, S. (1979): 'Iconium and Ninica: Two Double Communities in Roman Asia Minor', *Historia*, 28: 409–38.

—— (1984): 'The Greek City in the Roman World: Pontus and Bithynia', in *Eighth International Congress of Greek and Latin Epigraphy, Athens 1982*, i (Athens), 120–33.

—— (1990): 'Festivals, Games and Civic Life in Roman Asia Minor', *JRS* 80: 183–93.

—— (1993): *Anatolia: Land, Men, and Gods in Asia Minor*, i–ii (Oxford).

Mittelhaus, K. (1911): *De Plutarchi Praeceptis Gerendae Reipublicae* (Diss. Berlin).

Modrzejewski, J. (1970): 'Zum hellenistischen Ehegüterrecht im griechischen und römischen Ägypten', *ZSS* (Rom. Abt.) 87: 50–84.

—— (1982): 'Ménandre de Laodicée et l'édit de Caracalla', in J. Modrzejewski and D. Liebs (eds.), *Symposion 1977: Vorträge zur griechischen und hellenistischen Rechtsgeschichte* (Cologne), 335–66 (= J. Modrzejewski, *Droit impérial et traditions locales dans l'Égypte romaine* [Aldershot, 1990], XII).

Moles, J. L. (1978): 'The Career and Conversion of Dio Chrysostom', *JHS* 98: 79–100.

—— (1983*a*): 'The Date and Purpose of the Fourth Kingship Oration of Dio Chrysostom', *ClAnt* 2: 251–78.

—— (1983*b*): 'Dio Chrysostom: Exile, Tarsus, Nero and Domitian', *LCM* 8: 130–4.

—— (1985): 'The Interpretation of the "Second Preface" in Arrian's *Anabasis*', *JHS* 105: 162–8.

—— (1990): 'The Kingship Orations of Dio Chrysostom', *Papers of the Leeds International Latin Seminar*, 6: 297–375.

Molinié, G. (1989) (ed., trans.): *Chariton: Le roman de Chairéas et Callirhoé*² (rev. A. Billault) (Budé: Paris).

Momigliano, A. D. (1944): review of S. A. Cook *et al.*, *The Cambridge Ancient History*, x (Cambridge, 1934), in *JRS* 34: 109–16 (= id., *Quinto contributo alla storia degli studi classici e del mondo antico* [Rome, 1975], ii. 986–1002).

—— (1951): review of Ch. Wirszubski, *Libertas* (Cambridge, 1950), in *JRS* 41: 146–53 (= id., *Quinto contributo* [1975], ii. 958–75).

—— (1969): 'Dio Chrysostomus' (unpublished lecture of 1950), in id., *Quarto contributo* (Rome), 257–69.

—— (1987): 'Ancient Biography and the Study of Religion in the Roman Empire', in M. Détienne *et al.* (eds.), *Poikilia: Études offertes à J.-P. Vernant* (Paris, 1987) 33–48 (= *Ottavo contributo* [1987], 193–210).

Moraux, P. (1985): *Galien de Pergame: Souvenirs d'un médecin* (Paris).

Moretti, L. (1954): *"KOINA 'AΣIAΣ"*, *RevFil* 32: 276–89 (= id., *Tra epigrafia e storia* [Rome, 1990], 141–54).

Morgan, J. R. (1982): 'History, Romance, and Realism in the Aithiopika of Heliodoros', *ClAnt* 1: 221–65.

Morgan, J. R. (1989): 'A Sense of the Ending: the Conclusion of Heliodoros' *Aithiopika*', *TAPA* 119: 299–320.

—— (1995): 'The Greek Novel: Towards a Sociology of Production and Reception', in A. Powell (ed.), *The Greek World* (London) (forthcoming).

—— and Stoneman, R. (1994) (eds.): *Greek Fiction: The Greek Novel in Context* (London).

Morgan, P. (1983): 'From a Death to a View: The Hunt for the Welsh Past in the Romantic Period', in Hobsbawm and Ranger 1983: 43–100.

Morr, J. (1915): *Die Lobrede des jüngeren Plinius und die erste Königsrede des Dio von Prusa* (Diss. Troppau [non vidi]).

Mouzelis, N. P. (1978): *Modern Greece: Facets of Underdevelopment* (London).

Mras, K. (1949): 'Die προλαλιά bei den griechischen Schriftstellern', *WS* 64: 71–81.

Müller, A. (1883): 'Zur Geschichte des Commodus', *Hermes*, 18: 623–6.

Müller, C. W. (1976): 'Chariton von Aphrodisias und die Theorie des Romans in der Antike', *A&A* 22: 115–36.

Münscher, K. (1907): 'Die Philostrate', *Philologus* Suppl. 10.4: 467–558.

—— (1920): *Xenophon in der griechisch-römischen Literatur*, *Philologus* Suppl. 13.2.

Musti, D. (1984): 'L'itinerario di Pausania: Dal viaggio alla storia', *QUCC* 17: 7–18.

Mylonas, G. E. (1961 [1962]): *Eleusis and the Eleusinian Mysteries* (Princeton).

Naechster, M. (1908): *De Pollucis et Phrynichi controversiis* (Diss. Leipzig).

Nestle, W. (1934): *Griechische Religiosität von Alexander d. Gr. bis auf Proklos* (Berlin).

Nicolet, Cl. (1983): 'L'Empire romain: espace, temps et politique', *Ktema*, 8: 163–73.

Nicosia, S. (1980): 'Un "Kultverein" di θεραπευταί nell'Asclepieio di Pergamo?', in M. J. Fontana *et al.* (eds.), *Miscellanea di studi classici in onore di E. Manni* (Rome, 1980), 1623–33.

—— (1984) (trans.): *Elio Aristide, Discorsi Sacri* (Milan).

Nikolaidis, A. G. (1986): '*Ἑλληνικός—βαρβαρικός*: Plutarch on Greek and Barbarian Characteristics', *WS* 20: 229–44.

Nilsson, M. P. (1955–61): *Geschichte der griechischen Religion*² i–ii (Munich).

Nöldeke, T. (1871): 'Assyrios, Syrios, Syros', *Hermes*, 5: 443–68.

Nora, P. (ed.) (1984–92): *Les Lieux de mémoire*, i, ii. 1–3, iii. 1–3 (Paris).

Norden, E. (1909): *Die antike Kunstprosa von VI. Jahrhundert v. Chr. bis in die Zeit der Renaissance*², i–ii (Leipzig).

Nutton, V. (1971): 'Two Notes on Immunities: *Digest* 27, 1, 6, 10 and 11', *JRS* 61: 52–63 (= Nutton 1988: IV).

—— (1972): 'Galen and Medical Autobiography', *PCPhS* 18: 50–62 (= Nutton 1988: I).

—— (1973): 'The Chronology of Galen's Early Career', *CQ* 23: 158–71 (= Nutton 1988: II).

—— (1976): *Karl Gottlob Kühn and his Edition of the Works of Galen* (Oxford).

—— (1977): 'Archiatri and the Medical Profession in Antiquity', *PBSR* 45: 191–226 (= Nutton 1988: v).

—— (1978): 'The Beneficial Ideology', in Garnsey and Whittaker 1978: 209–21.

—— (1979) (ed., trans.): *Galen: On Prognosis*, CMG V. 8. 1 (Berlin).

—— (1981) (ed.): *Galen: Problems and Prospects* (London).

—— (1984): 'Galen in the Eyes of his Contemporaries', *BHM* 68: 305–24 (= Nutton 1988: III).

—— (1987): 'Galen's Philosophical Testament: "On My Own Opinions"', in J. Wiesner (ed.), *Aristoteles: Werk und Wirkung* (Berlin), ii. 27–51.

—— (1988): *From Democedes to Harvey* (London).

—— (1990): 'The Patient's Choice: A New Treatise by Galen', *CQ* 40: 236–57.

—— (1991): 'Style and Context in the *Method of Healing*', in Kudlien and Durling 1991: 1–25.

—— (1993): 'Galen and Egypt', in Kollesch and Nickel 1993: 11–31.

Oden, R. A. (1977): *Studies in Lucian's De Syria Dea* (Missoula, Mont.).

Ogilvie, R. (1967): 'The Date of the *De Defectu Oraculorum*', *Phoenix*, 21: 108–19.

Oliver, J. H. (1950): *The Athenian Expounders of the Sacred and Ancestral Law* (Baltimore).

—— (1953): *The Ruling Power: A Study of the Roman Empire in the Second Century after Christ Through the Roman Oration of Aelius Aristides*, *TAPhS* 43.4 (Philadelphia).

—— (1954): 'The Roman Governor's Permission for a Decree of the Polis', *Hesperia* 23: 163–7.

—— (1968): *The Civilizing Power: A Study of the Panathenaic Discourse of Aelius Aristides Against the Background of Literature and Cultural Conflict, with Text, Translation, and Commentary*, *TAPhS* 58.1 (Philadelphia).

—— (1970): *Marcus Aurelius: Aspects of Civic and Cultural Policy in the East*, *Hesperia* Suppl. 13 (Princeton).

—— (1972): 'Herm at Athens with Portraits of Xenophon and Arrian', *AJA* 76: 327–8.

—— (1978): 'The Piety of Commodus and Caracalla and the Εἰς Βασιλέα', *GRBS* 19: 375–88.

—— (1982): 'Arrian in Two Roles', in *Studies in Attic Epigraphy, History and Topography Presented to E. Vanderpool*, *Hesperia* Suppl. 19 (Princeton), 122–9.

O'Sullivan, J. N. (1984): 'The Sesonchosis Romance', *ZPE* 56: 39–44.

Palm, J. (1955): *Über Sprache und Stil des Diodoros von Sizilien* (Lund).

—— (1959): *Rom, Römertum und Imperium in der griechischen Literatur der Kaiserzeit* (Lund).

Palmer, L. R. (1980): *The Greek Language* (London).

Panagopoulos, C. (1977): 'Vocabulaire et mentalité dans les Moralia de Plutarque', *DHA* 3: 197–235.

Papaïoannou, V. (1976): Λουκιανὸς ὁ μεγάλος σατιρικὸς τῆς ἀρχαιοτήτας (Thessalonica).

Parke, H. W. (1985): *The Oracles of Apollo in Asia Minor* (London).

—— and Wormell, D. E. W. (1956): *The Delphic Oracle*, i–ii (Oxford).

Parkin, T. G. (1992): *Demography and Roman Society* (Baltimore).

Parsons, P. (1971): 'A Greek Satyricon?', *BICS* 18: 53–68.

Patterson, C. (1991): 'Plutarch's "Advice on Marriage": Traditional Wisdom through a Philosophic Lens', *ANRW* ii. 33. 6: 4709–23.

Patterson, D. (1985): 'The Influence of Hebrew Literature on the Growth of Jewish Nationalism in the Nineteenth Century', in Sussex and Eade 1985: 84–95.

Pavan, M. (1962): 'Sul significato storico dell'*Encomio di Roma* di Elio Aristide', *PP* 17: 81–95.

Pavis d'Escurac, H. (1981): 'Périls et chances du régime civique selon Plutarque', *Ktema*, 6: 287–300.

Pearcy, L. T. (1983): 'Galen and Stoic Rhetoric', *GRBS* 24: 259–72.

—— (1988): 'Theme, Dream, and Narrative: Reading the *Sacred Tales* of Aelius Aristides', *TAPA* 118: 377–91.

Pelling, C. B. R. (1979): 'Plutarch's Method of Work in the Roman *Lives*', *JHS* 99: 74–96 (repr. with a postscript in B. Scardigli [ed.], *Essays on Plutarch's Lives* [Oxford, 1995], 265–318).

—— (1986*a*): 'Plutarch and Roman Politics', in I. Moxon, J. Smart, and A. Woodman (eds.), *Past Perspectives: Studies in Greek and Roman Historical Writing* (Cambridge), 159–87 (= B. Scardigli [ed.], *Essays on Plutarch's Lives* [Oxford, 1995], 319–56).

—— (1986*b*): 'Synkrisis in Plutarch Lives', in Brenk and Gallo 1986: 83–96.

—— (1988) (ed.): *Plutarch: Life of Antony* (Cambridge).

—— (1989): 'Plutarch: Roman Heroes and Greek Culture', in Griffin and Barnes 1989: 199–232.

Penella, R. J. (1975): 'An Unpublished Letter of Apollonius of Tyana to the Sardians', *HSCP* 79: 305–11.

—— (1979): *The Letters of Apollonius of Tyana* (Leiden).

—— (1990): *Greek Philosophers and Sophists in the Fourth Century AD: Studies in Eunapius of Sardis* (Leeds).

Pera, R. (1984): *Homonoia sulle monete da Augusto agli Antonini* (Genoa).

Peretti, A. (1946): *Luciano: Un intellettuale greco contro Roma* (Florence).

Pernot, L. (1981): *Les 'Discours Siciliens' d'Aelius Aristide (Or. 5–6)* (New York).

—— (1993): *La Rhétorique de l'éloge dans le monde gréco-romain*, i–ii (Paris).

Perry, B. E. (1967): *The Ancient Romances: A Literary-historical Account of their Origins*, Sather Class. Lectures 37 (Berkeley).

Petrochilos, N. (1974): *Roman Attitudes to the Greeks* (Athens).

Pflaum, H.-G. (1940): *Essai sur le cursus publicus sous le Haut-Empire romain*, Mémoires Acad. Inscr. 14 (Paris).

—— (1960–1): *Les Carrières procuratoriennes équestres sous le Haut-Empire romain*, i–iii (Paris).

—— (1966): *Les Sodales Antoniniani de l'époque de Marc Aurèle*, Mémoires Acad. Inscr. 15.2 (Paris).

Phillips, E. D. (1954): review of Oliver 1953, in *JRS* 44: 128–9.

Piccaluga, G. (1981): 'L'olocausto di Patrai', in O. Reverdin and J. Rudhardt (eds.), *Le Sacrifice dans l'antiquité*, Entretiens Hardt xxvii (Geneva), 243–87.

Pinborg, J. (1975): 'Classical Antiquity: Greece', in *Historiography of Linguistics = Current Trends in Linguistics*, 13: 69–126.

Pinto, M. (1974): 'Fatti e figure della storia romana nelle opere di Luciano', *Vichiana* (Naples), 3: 227–38.

Plepelits, K. (1976): *Chariton von Aphrodisias: Kallirhoe* (Stuttgart).

—— (1980): *Achilleus Tatios: Leukippe und Kleitophon* (Stuttgart).

Pohlenz, M. (1947–9): *Die Stoa*, i–ii (Göttingen).

Prandi, L. (1989): 'La rifondazione del "Panionion" e la catastrofe di Elice (373 a.C.), *CISA* (Milan), 15: 43–59.

Premerstein, A. von (1898): 'Das Troiaspiel', in *Festschrift für O. Benndorf* (Vienna), 261–6.

Price, S. R. F. (1984*a*): *Rituals and Power: The Roman Imperial Cult in Asia Minor* (Cambridge).

—— (1984*b*): 'Gods and Emperors: The Greek Language of the Roman Imperial Cult', *JHS* 104: 79–95.

—— (1986): 'The Future of Dreams: From Freud to Artemidorus', *P&P* 113: 3–37 (= Halperin *et al.* 1990: 365–87).

Puech, B. (1991): 'Prosopographie des amis de Plutarque', *ANRW* ii. 33. 6: 4831–93.

Purcell, N. (1987): 'The Nicopolitan Synoecism and Roman Urban Policy', in E. Chrysos (ed.), *Nicopolis I* (Preveza), 71–90.

Quass, F. (1982): 'Zur politischen Tätigkeit der munizipalen Aristokratie des griechischen Ostens in der Kaiserzeit', *Historia*, 31: 188–213.

Quet, M.-H. (1978): 'Rhétorique, culture et politique: le fonctionnement du discours idéologique chez Dion de Pruse et dans les *Moralia* de Plutarque', *DHA* 4: 51–118.

—— (1992*a*): 'Romans grecs, mosaïques romaines', in Baslez *et al.* 1992: 125–60.

—— (1992*b*): 'L'Inscription de Vérone en l'honneur d'Aelius Aristide et le rayonnement de la seconde sophistique chez les "Grecs d'Égypte"', *REA* 94: 379–401.

—— (1993): 'Parler de soi pour louer son Dieu: le cas d'Aelius Aristide', in M.-F. Baslez, Ph. Hoffmann, L. Pernot (eds.), *L'Invention de l'autobiographie d'Hésiode à saint Augustin* (Paris), 211–51.

Radermacher, L. (1899): 'Studien zur Geschichte der antiken Rhetorik IV: Über die Anfänge des Atticismus', *RhM* 54: 351–74.

—— (1947): 'Koine', *SÖeAW* 224.5 (Vienna).

Ranger, T. (1983): 'The Invention of Tradition in Colonial Africa', in Hobsbawm and Ranger 1983: 211–62.

Rattenbury, R. M. (1933): 'Romance: Traces of Lost Greek Novels', in J. U. Powell (ed.), *New Chapters in the History of Greek Literature*, 3rd series (Oxford), 211–57.

Ratti, E. (1971): 'Impero Romano e armonia dell'universo nella pratica retorica e nella concezione religiosa di Elio Aristide: una ricerca per l'*Εἰς Ῥώμην*', *Mem. Ist. Lombardo, Scienze mor. e stor.* 31.4: 283–361.

Rawson, E. (1989): 'Roman Rulers and the Philosophic Adviser', in Griffin and Barnes 1989: 233–57.

Raynor, D. H. (1984): 'Moeragenes and Philostratus: Two Views of Apollonius of Tyana', *CQ* 34: 222–6.

Reardon, B. P. (1971): *Courants littéraires grecs des IIe et IIIe siècles après J.-C.* (Paris).

—— (1973): 'The Anxious Pagan', *EMC* 17: 81–93.

—— (1982): 'Theme, Structure and Narrative in Chariton', *YCS* 27: 1–27.

—— (1989) (ed.): *Collected Ancient Greek Novels* (Berkeley).

—— (1991): *The Form of Greek Romance* (Princeton).

Reeve, M. D. (1971): 'Hiatus in the Greek Novelists', *CQ* 21: 514–39.

Regenbogen, O. (1956): 'Pausanias', *RE* Suppl. viii, 1008–97.

Reiske, J. J. (1784): *Dionis Chrysostomi Orationes*, i–ii (Leipzig).

Renoirte, Th. (1951): *Les "Conseils Politiques" de Plutarque* (Louvain).

Reynolds, J. (1978): 'Hadrian, Antoninus Pius and the Cyrenaican Cities', *JRS* 68: 111–21.

Richard, M. (1963): 'Quelques nouveaux fragments des pères anténicéens et nicéens', *SymbOsl* 38: 76–83.

Richlin, A. (1992*a*) (ed.): *Pornography and Representation in Greece and Rome* (Oxford).

—— (1992*b*): *The Garden of Priapus: Sexuality and Aggression in Roman Humor*[2] (New York).

Rist, J. M. (1982): 'Are You a Stoic? The Case of Marcus Aurelius', in Meyer and Sanders 1982: 23–45.

Robert, C. (1909): *Pausanias als Schriftsteller* (Berlin).

Robert, L. (1930): 'Pantomimen im griechischen Orient', *Hermes*, 65: 106–22 (= *Opera Minora Selecta*, i [Amsterdam 1969], 654–70).

—— (1937): *Études anatoliennes* (Paris).

—— (1940): *Les Gladiateurs dans l'Orient grec* (Paris).

—— (1948*a*): 'Épigrammes relatives à des gouverneurs', *Hellenica*, 4 (Paris), 35–114, 138–46.

—— (1948*b*): 'Épigramme d'Égine', *Hellenica*, 4 (Paris), 5–34.

—— (1949*a*): 'Sur une monnaie de Synnada τροφεύς', *Hellenica*, 7 (Paris), 74–81.

—— (1949*b*): 'Le culte de Caligula à Milet et la province d'Asie', *Hellenica*, 7 (Paris), 206–38.

—— (1960*a*): 'τροφεύς et ἀριστεύς', *Hellenica*, 11/12 (Paris), 569–76.

—— (1960*b*): 'Recherches épigraphiques', *REA* 62: 276–361 (= *OMS* ii [1969], 792–877).

—— (1967): 'Sur des inscriptions d'Éphèse: fêtes, athlètes, empereurs, épigrammes', *Rev. Phil.* 41: 7–84 (= *OMS* v [1989], 347–424).

—— (1968*a*): 'Les Épigrammes satiriques de Lucillius sur les athlètes: parodie et réalités', in *L'Épigramme grecque*, Entretiens Hardt xiv (Geneva), 181–295 (= *OMS* vi [1989], 317–431).

—— (1968*b*): 'Trois oracles de la théosophie et un prophète d'Apollon', *CRAI* 1968: 568–99 (= *OMS* v [1989], 584–615).

—— (1969): 'Les Inscriptions', in J. des Gagniers *et al.*, *Laodicée du Lycos: Le Nymphée* (Quebec and Paris), 247–389.

—— (1973): 'De Cilicie à Messine et à Plymouth', *JS* 1973: 161–211 (= *OMS* vii [1990], 225–75).

—— (1975): 'Nonnos et les monnaies d'Akmonia de Phrygie', *JS* 1975: 153–92 (= *OMS* vii [1990], 185–224).

—— (1977*a*): 'Documents d'Asie Mineure', *BCH* 101: 43–132 (= *Documents d'Asie Mineure*, BEFAR 239 bis [Paris, 1987], 1–90).

—— (1977*b*): 'La Titulature de Nicée et de Nicomédie: la gloire et la haine', *HSCP* 81: 1–39 (= *OMS* vi [1989], 211–49).

—— (1980): *À travers l'Asie Mineure: Poètes et prosateurs, monnaies grecques, voyageurs et géographie*, BEFAR 239 (Paris).

—— (1981): 'Une épigramme satirique d'Automédon et Athènes au début de l'Empire (*Anthologie Palatine* XI, 319)', *REG* 94: 338–61 (= *OMS* vi [1989], 432–55).

Roberts, C. H. (1955): *Greek Literary Hands 350 BC–AD 400* (Oxford).

Robertson, D. S. (1913): 'The Authenticity and Date of Lucian *De Saltatione*', in E. C. Quiggin (ed.), *Essays and Studies Presented to William Ridgeway* (Cambridge), 180–5.

Robertson, N. (1986): 'A Point of Precedence at Plataia: The Dispute between Athens and Sparta over leading the Procession', *Hesperia*, 55: 88–102.

Rogers, G. M. (1991): *The Sacred Identity of Ephesos: Foundation Myths of a Roman City* (London).

Rohde, E. (1914): *Der antike Roman und seine Vorläufer*[3] (Leipzig; repr. with a forword by K. Kerényi, Darmstadt, 1960).

Rohde, G. (1937): 'Longus und die Bukolik', *RhM* 86: 23–49 (= id., *Studien und Interpretationen* [Berlin, 1963], 91–116 = Gärtner 1984: 361–87).

Rose, H. (1924): *The Roman Questions of Plutarch* (Oxford).

Rosenmeyer, P. A. (1994): 'The Epistolary Novel', in Morgan and Stoneman 1994: 146–65.

Rossner, M. (1974): 'Asiarchen und Archiereis Asias', *StudClass* 16: 101–42.

Rostovtzeff, M. I. (1941): *The Social and Economic History of the Hellenistic World*, i–iii (Oxford).

—— (1957): *The Social and Economic History of the Roman Empire*², i–ii (ed. P. M. Fraser) (Oxford).

Rothe, S. (1989): *Kommentar zu ausgewählten Sophistenviten des Philostratos* (Heidelberg).

Roueché, Ch. (1989): 'Floreat Perge!', in M. M. MacKenzie and Ch. Roueché (eds.), *Images of Authority: Papers Presented to J. Reynolds on the Occasion of her 70th Birthday* (Cambridge).

Rousselle, A. (1988) *Porneia: On Desire and the Body in Antiquity* (trans. F. Pheasant) (Oxford).

Rudolph, L. I., and Rudolph, S. H. (1965): 'Barristers and Brahmans in India: Legal Cultures and Social Change', *Comparative Studies in Society and History*, 8: 24–49.

Ruiz Montero, C. (1980): 'Una observación para la cronologia de Caritón de Afrodisias', *Estudios Clásicos*, 24: 63–9.

—— (1991): 'Aspects of the Vocabulary of Chariton of Aphrodisias', *CQ* 41: 484–9.

Russell, D. A. (1964) (ed., comm.): *'Longinus', On the Sublime* (Oxford).

—— (1966): 'On Reading Plutarch's *Lives*', *G&R* 13: 139–54

—— (1968): 'On Reading Plutarch's *Moralia*', *G&R* 15: 130–46.

—— (1973): *Plutarch* (London).

—— (1979): 'Classicizing Rhetoric and Criticism: The Pseudo-Dionysian *Exetasis* and *Mistakes in Declamation*', in Flashar 1979: 113–34.

—— (1981): 'Longinus Revisited', *Mnemosyne*, 34: 72–86.

—— (1983): *Greek Declamation* (Cambridge).

—— (1990a): 'Aristides and the Prose Hymn', in Russell 1990b: 199–219.

—— (1990b) (ed.): *Antonine Literature* (with an introduction by D. A. Russell) (Oxford).

—— (1992) (ed., comm.): *Dio Chrysostom. Orations VII, XII, XXXVI* (Cambridge).

—— (1993) (trans.): *Plutarch: Selected Essays and Dialogues* (Oxford).

—— and Wilson, N. G. (1981) (eds., trans., comm.): *Menander Rhetor* (Oxford).

Rutherford, R. B. (1989): *The Meditations of Marcus Aurelius: A Study* (Oxford).

Saïd, S. (1987): 'La Société rurale dans le roman grec ou la campagne vue de la ville', in Ed. Frézouls (ed.), *Sociétés urbaines, sociétés rurales dans l'Asie Mineure et la Syrie hellénistiques et romaines* (Strasbourg), 149–71.

—— (1991) (ed.): *ΕΛΛΗΝΙΣΜΟΣ: Quelques jalons pour une histoire de l'identité grecque* (Leiden).

—— (1992): 'Les Langues du roman grec', in Baslez *et al.* 1992: 169–86.

—— (1994): 'Lucien ethnographe', in Billault 1994: 149–70.

St. Clair, W. (1972): *That Greece Might Still be Free: The Philhellenes in the War of Independence* (Oxford).

Ste. Croix, G. E. M. de (1981): *The Class Struggle in the Ancient Greek World* (London).

Sales, R. (1983): *English Literature in History 1780–1830: Pastoral and Politics* (London).

Saller, R. P., and Shaw, B. D. (1984): 'Tombstones and Roman Family Relations in the Principate: Civilians, Soldiers and Slaves', *JRS* 74: 124–56.

Salmeri, G. (1982): *La politica e il potere: Saggio su Dione di Prusa* (Catania).

—— (1991): 'Dalle province a Roma: il rinnovamento del Senato', in A. Schiavone (ed.), *Storia di Roma*, i–iv (Turin 1988–92 in progress), ii. 2 (1991), 553–75.

Sandbach, F. H. (1969) (ed., trans.): *Plutarch's Moralia* xv (Loeb: Cambridge, Mass.).

—— (1975): *The Stoics* (London).

Sartre, M. (1991): *L'Orient romain: Provinces et sociétés provinciales en Méditerranée orientale d'Auguste aux Sévères (31 avant J.-C.–235 après J.-C.)* (Paris).

Sasse, Chr. (1958): *Die Constitutio Antoniniana* (Wiesbaden).

Scarborough, J. (1981): 'The Galenic Question', *Sudhoffs Archiv*, 65: 1–31.

Scarcella, A. M. (1972): 'Testimonianze della crisi di un'età nel romanzo di Eliodoro', *Maia*, 24: 9–41 (= id., *Romanzo e romanzieri* [Perugia, 1993], ii. 329–56).

—— (1981): 'Metastasi narratologica del dato storico nel romanzo erotico greco', in *Atti del convegno internazionale 'Letterature classiche e narratologia'*, Materiali e contributi per la storia della narrativa greco-latina 3 (Perugia), 341–67 (= id., *Romanzo e romanzieri* [Perugia, 1993], i. 77–102).

—— (1993): 'Il romanzo greco d'amore e l'ideologia dell'amore in Grecia', in id., *Romanzo e romanzieri* (Perugia), i. 47–75.

Schachter, A. (1981–6): *Cults of Boeotia* i, ii, iv, *BICS* Suppl. 38. 1, 2, 4 (London).

Schissel von Fleschenberg, O. (1913): *Entwicklungsgeschichte des griechischen Romanes im Altertum* (Halle).

Schmid, W. (1887–97): *Der Atticismus in seinen Hauptvertretern*, i–v (Stuttgart).

—— (1917–18): 'Die sogenannte Aristidesrhetorik', *RhM* 72: 113–49, 238–57.

Schnayder, G. (1927): 'De infenso alienigenarum in Romanos animo', *Eos*, 30: 113–49.

—— (1928): *Quibus conviciis alienigenae Romanos carpserint* (Cracow).

Schneider, A. M., and Karnapp, W. (1938): *Die Stadtmauer von Iznik (Nicaea)* (Berlin).

Schöne, H. (1917): 'τὸ τοῦ Τραϊανοῦ γυμνάσιον bei Galenos', *Hermes*, 52: 105–11.

Schöpsdau, K. (1992): 'Vergleiche zwischen Lateinisch und Griechisch in der antiken Sprachwissenschaft', in C. W. Müller, K. Sier, J. Werner (eds.), *Zum Umgang mit fremden Sprachen in der griechisch-römischen Antike* (Stuttgart), 115–36.

Schofield, M. (1991): *The Stoic Idea of the City* (Cambridge).

Schröder, H. O. (1934): *Galeni In Platonis Timaeum Commentarii fragmenta*, *CMG* Suppl. I (Berlin).

—— (1986) (trans., comm.): *Publius Aelius Aristides: Heilige Berichte* (Heidelberg).

Schubart, J. H. Ch. (1883): 'Pausanias und seine Ankläger', *Jahrb. f. Cl. Phil.* 127: 469–82.

Schubring, K. (1965): 'Bibliographische Hinweise zu Galen', in Kühn 1965: xx, pp. xvii–lxii.

Schulthess, F. (1897): 'Der Brief des Mara bar Sarapion', *Zeitschr. d. deutsch. Morgenland. Gesellsch.* 51: 365–91.

Schulz, A., and Winter, E. (1990): 'Historisch-archäologische Untersuchungen zum Hadrianstempel in Kyzikos', in E. Schwertheim (ed.), *Mysische Studien, Asia Minor Studien*, i (Bonn), 33–82.

Schulz, F. (1946): *History of Roman Legal Science* (Oxford).

Schwartz, E. (1896): *Fünf Vorträge über den griechischen Roman* (Berlin; repr. with an introductory essay by A. Rehm, Berlin, 1943).

Schwartz, J. (1963): *Lucien de Samosate: Philopseudès et De morte Peregrini*[2] (Paris).

—— (1965): *Biographie de Lucien de Samosate* (Brussels).

Schwertheim, E. (1987): *Die Inschriften von Hadrianoi und Hadrianeia (IK* 33) (Bonn).

Scobie, A. (1973): *More Essays on the Ancient Romance and its Heritage* (Meisenheim am Glan).

Scott, K. (1929): 'Plutarch and the Ruler Cult', *TAPA* 60: 117–35.

Segal, J. B. (1970): *Edessa, The Blessed City* (Oxford).

Segré, M. (1928): 'La fonte di Pausania per la storia dei Diadochi', *Historia* (Milan), 2: 217–37.

—— (1929): 'Note storiche su Pausania periegeta', *Athenaeum*, 7: 475–88.

Sergent, B. (1987): *Homosexuality in Greek Myth* (trans. A. Goldhammer) (London).

Serrano Aybar, C. (1977): 'Historia de la lexicografía griega antigua y medieval', in F. R. Adrados *et al.* (eds.), *Introducción a la lexicografía griega* (Madrid), 61–106.

Seyrig, H. (1959): 'Caractères de l'histoire d'Émèse', *Syria*, 36: 184–92.

—— (1960): 'Les dieux de Hiérapolis', *Syria*, 37: 233–52 (= *Antiquités Syriennes*, 6th ser. [Paris, 1966], 79–98).

Shahid, I. (1984): *Rome and the Arabs* (Washington DC).

Sharples, R. W. (1983) (trans., comm.): *Alexander of Aphrodisias On Fate* (London).

Shaw, B. (1984): 'Bandits in the Roman Empire', *P&P* 105: 3–52.

—— (1985): 'The Divine Economy: Stoicism as Ideology', *Latomus*, 44: 16–54.

Shear, T. L. (1981): 'Athens: From City-State to Provincial Town', *Hesperia*, 50: 356–77.

Sheppard, A. R. R. (1982) 'A Dissident in Tarsus (Dio Chrysostom, Or. 66)', *LCM* 7: 149–50.

—— (1984): 'Dio Chrysostom: the Bithynian Years', *AC* 53: 157–73.

—— (1984–6): '*Homonoia* in the Greek Cities of the Roman Empire', *AntSoc* 15–17: 229–52.

Sherwin-White, A. N. (1966): *The Letters of Pliny* (Oxford).

—— (1973): *The Roman Citizenship*² (Oxford).

Sidebottom, H. (1990): *Studies in Dio Chrysostom On Kingship* (D. Phil., Oxford).

—— (1992): 'The Date of Dio of Prusa's Rhodian and Alexandrian Orations', *Historia*, 41: 407–19.

Siebenborn, E. (1976): *Die Lehre von der Sprachrichtigkeit und ihren Kriterien: Studien zur antiken normativen Grammatik* (Amsterdam).

Sieveking, W. (1919): *De Aelii Aristidis oratione εἰς Ῥώμην* (Diss. Göttingen).

Smith, A. D. (1976): 'Introduction: The Formation of Nationalist Movements', in id. (ed.), *Nationalist Movements* (London), 1–30.

—— (1986): *The Ethnic Origins of Nations* (Oxford).

Smith, M. (1978): *Jesus the Magician* (London).

Smith, R. C. (1984): 'Misery and Mystery: Aelius Aristides', in R. C. Smith and J. Lounibos (eds.), *Pagan and Christian Anxiety: A Response to E. R. Dodds* (Lanham, Md.), 29–52.

Snell, B. (1953): 'Arcadia: The Discovery of a Spiritual Landscape', in id., *The Discovery of the Mind: The Greek Origins of European Thought* (trans. T. G. Rosenmeyer) (Oxford), 281–309.

Sohlberg, D. (1972): 'Aelius Aristides und Diogenes von Babylon', *MH* 29: 177–200, 256–77.

Solmsen, F. (1940): 'Some Works of Philostatus the Elder', *TAPA* 71: 556–72.

—— (1941): 'Philostratos 9–12', *RE* xx.1 (1941), 124–77.

Sotiropoulos, D. (1977): 'Diglossia and the National Language Question in Modern Greece', *Linguistics*, 197: 5–31.

—— (1982): 'The Social Roots of Modern Greek Diglossia', *Language Problems and Language Planning*, 6: 1–28.

Spawforth, A. J. S. (1994a): 'Symbol of Unity? The Persian-Wars Tradition in the Roman Empire', in S. Hornblower (ed.), *Greek Historiography* (Oxford), 233–47.

—— (1994b): 'Corinth, Argos, and the Imperial Cult: Pseudo-Julian, *Letters* 198', *Hesperia*, 63: 211–32.

—— and Walker, S. (1985): 'The World of the Panhellenion: I. Athens and Eleusis', *JRS* 75: 78–104.

—— —— (1986): 'The World of the Panhellenion: II. Three Dorian Cities', *JRS* 76: 88–105.

Speyer, W. (1974): 'Zum Bild des Apollonius von Tyana bei Heiden und Christen', *JbAC* 17: 47–63.

Stadter, P. A. (1967): 'Flavius Arrianus: The New Xenophon', *GRBS* 8: 155–61.

—— (1976): 'Xenophon in Arrian's *Cynegeticus*', *GRBS* 17: 157–67.

—— (1980): *Arrian of Nicomedia* (Chapel Hill, NC).

Stanton, G. R. (1973): 'Sophists and Philosophers: Problems of Classification', *AJP* 94: 350–64.

Starr, C. G. (1952): 'The Perfect Democracy of the Roman Empire', *AmHistRev* 58: 1–16 (= *Essays on Ancient History* [Leiden, 1979], 262–77).

Stephens, S. A. (1994): 'Who Read Ancient Novels?', in Tatum 1994: 405–18.

—— and Winkler, J. J. (forthcoming) (eds., trans., comm.): *Ancient Greek Novels: The Fragments*.

Stertz, S. A. (1979): 'Pseudo-Aristides, ΕΙΣ ΒΑΣΙΛΕΑ', *CQ* 29: 172–97.

—— (1994): 'Aelius Aristides' Political Ideas', *ANRW* ii. 34. 2: 1248–70.

Stone, L. (1987): 'Prosopography', in id., *The Past and the Present Revisited* (London), 45–73 (repr. from *Daedalus*, 100.1 [1971], 46–79).

Strebel, H. G. (1935): *Wertung und Wirkung des Thukydideischen Geschichtswerkes in der griechisch-römischen Literatur* (Diss. Munich).

Strid, O. (1976): *Über Sprache und Stil des Periegeten Pausanias* (Stockholm).

Strohmaier, G. (1976): 'Übersehenes zur Biographie Lukians', *Philologus*, 120: 117–22.

—— (1978): 'al-Iskandar al-Afrûdîsî', in *The Encyclopaedia of Islam*² (Leiden), iv. 129–30.

—— (1993): 'Hellenistische Wissenschaft im neugefundenen Galenkommentar zur hippokratischen Schrift "Über die Umwelt"', in Kollesch and Nickel 1993: 157–64.

Strong, D. (1988): *Roman Art*² (London).

Strubbe, J. H. M. (1984–6): 'Gründer kleinasiatischer Städte: Fiktion und Realität', *AS* 15–17: 253–304.

Sudhoff, K. (1915): 'Vom "Pestsamen" des Galenos', *Mitt. Gesch. Med.* 14: 227–9.

Sullivan, R. D. (1977): 'The Dynasty of Emesa', *ANRW* ii. 8: 198–219.

—— (1978): 'Priesthoods of the Eastern Dynastic Aristocracy', in S. Şahin *et al.* (eds.), *Studien zum Religion und Kultur Kleinasiens* (Festschrift K. Dörner) (Leiden), ii. 914–39.

Sussex, R. (1985): 'Lingua Nostra: The Nineteenth-Century Slavonic Language Revivals', in Sussex and Eade 1985: 111–27.

—— and Eade, J. C. (1985) (eds.): *Culture and Nationalism in Nineteenth-Century Eastern Europe* (Columbus, Ohio).

Swain, J. (1940): 'The Theory of the Four Monarchies: Opposition History under the Roman Empire', *CPh* 35: 1–21.

Swain, S. (1988): 'Plutarch's *Philopoemen and Flamininus*', *ICS* 13.2: 335–47.

—— (1989*a*): 'Favorinus and Hadrian', *ZPE* 79: 150–8.

—— (1989*b*): 'Character Change in Plutarch', *Phoenix*, 43: 62–8.

—— (1989*c*): 'Plutarch: Chance, Providence, and History', *AJP* 110: 272–302.

—— (1989*d*): 'Plutarch's Aemilius and Timoleon', *Historia*, 38: 314–34.

—— (1989*e*): 'Plutarch's *De fortuna Romanorum*', *CQ* 39: 504–16.

—— (1990*a*): 'Plutarch's Lives of Cicero, Cato, and Brutus', *Hermes*, 118: 192–203.

—— (1990*b*): 'Hellenic Culture and the Roman Heroes of Plutarch', *JHS* 110: 126–45 (= B. Scardigli [ed.], *Essays on Plutarch's Lives* [Oxford, 1995], 229–64).

—— (1990*c*): 'The Promotion of Hadrian of Tyre and the Death of Herodes Atticus', *CPh* 85: 214–16.

—— (1991*a*): 'The Reliability of Philostratus' *Lives of the Sophists*', *ClAnt* 10: 148–63.

—— (1991*b*): 'Arrian the Epic Poet', *JHS* 111: 211–14.

—— (1991*c*): 'Plutarch, Hadrian, and Delphi', *Historia*, 40: 318–30.

—— (1992*a*): 'Antonius Diogenes and Lucian', *LCM* 17: 74–6.

—— (1992*b*): 'Plutarchan Synkrisis', *Eranos*, 90: 101–11.

—— (1992*c*): 'Plutarch's Characterization of Lucullus', *RhM* 135: 307–16.

Syme, R. (1958): *Tacitus*, i–ii (Oxford).

—— (1968*a*): 'The Ummidii', *Historia*, 17: 72–105 (= id., *Roman Papers*, ii [Oxford, 1979], 659–93).

—— (1968*b*): *Ammianus and the Historia Augusta* (Oxford).

—— (1977): 'The Enigmatic Sospes', *JRS* 67: 38–49 (= *Roman Papers*, iii [1984], 1043–61).

—— (1980): 'An Eccentric Patrician', *Chiron*, 10: 427–48 (= *Roman Papers*, iii [1984], 1316–36).

—— (1982): 'The Career of Arrian', *HSCP* 86: 181–211 (= *Roman Papers*, iv [1988], 21–49).

—— (1983): 'The Proconsuls of Asia under Antoninus Pius', *ZPE* 51: 271–90 (= *Roman Papers*, iv [1988], 325–46).

—— (1985): 'Hadrian as Philhellene: Neglected Aspects', *HAC Bonn* 1982/1983 (1985), 341–62 (= *Roman Papers*, v [1988], 546–62).

Syme, R. (1987): 'Avidius Cassius: His Rank, Age and Quality', *HAC Bonn 1984/1985* (1987), 207–22 (= *Roman Papers*, v [1988], 689–701).

—— (1988): 'Greeks Invading the Roman Government', *Roman Papers*, iv (Oxford), 1–20.

Taeger, F. (1957–60): *Charisma: Studien zur Geschichte des antiken Herrscherkultes*, i–ii (Stuttgart).

Talbert, R. (1974): *Timoleon and the Revival of Greek Sicily 344–317 BC* (Cambridge).

Tatum, J. (ed.) (1994): *The Search for the Ancient Novel* (Baltimore).

Taylor, D. J. (1987*a*): 'Rethinking the History of Language Science in Classical Antiquity', in Taylor 1987*b*: 1–16.

—— (1987*b*) (ed.): *The History of Linguistics in the Classical Period* (Amsterdam).

Teixidor, J. (1992): *Bardesane d'Édesse: la première philosophie syriaque* (Paris).

Temkin, O. (1973): *Galenism: Rise and Decline of a Medical Philosophy* (Ithaca, NY).

—— (1991): *Hippocrates in a World of Pagans and Christians* (Baltimore).

Teodorsson, S.-T. (1974): *The Phonemic System of the Attic Dialect 400–340 BC* (Göteborg).

—— (1989–90): *A Commentary on Plutarch's Table Talks*, i–ii (Göteborg).

Theander, C. (1951): *Plutarch und die Geschichte* (Lund).

Thillet, P. (1984): *Alexandre d'Aphrodisias: Traité du destin* (Budé: Paris).

Thomasson, B. E. (1972–90): *Laterculi praesidum*, i–iii (Göteborg).

Thompson, H. A., and Wycherley, R. E. (1972): *The Agora of Athens: The History, Shape and Uses of an Ancient City Center*, The Athenian Agora xiv (Princeton).

Threatte, L. (1980): *The Grammar of Attic Inscriptions*, i. *Phonology* (Berlin and New York).

Tonkin, E., McDonald, M., Chapman, M. (1989) (eds.): *History and Ethnicity* (London).

Tonnet, H. (1988): *Recherches sur Arrien: sa personnalité et ses écrits atticistes*, i–ii (Amsterdam).

Toohey, P. (1988): 'Some Ancient Notions of Boredom', *ICS* 13.1: 151–64.

—— (1990): 'Some Ancient Histories of Literary Melancholia', *ICS* 15.1: 143–61.

—— (1992): 'Love, Lovesickness, and Melancholia', *ICS* 17.2: 265–86.

Touloumakos, J. (1971): *Zum Geschichtsbewusstsein der Griechen in der Zeit der römischen Herrschaft* (Göttingen).

Toynbee, A. (1969): 'The Meanings of the Terms 'Barbarian' and 'Hellene' in Hellenic Usage', in id., *Some Problems of Greek History* (Oxford), 58–63.

Trapp, M. (1986): *Studies in Maximus of Tyre: A Second-Century Philosophical Orator and his Nachleben (AD 200–1850)* (D. Phil., Oxford).

4

Treggiari, S. (1991): *Roman Marriage* (Oxford).

Trendelenburg, A. (1914): *Pausanias in Olympia* (Berlin).

Treu, K. (1958): *Synesios von Kyrene: Ein Kommentar zu seinem 'Dion'* (Berlin).

—— (1961): 'Zur Borysthenitica des Dion Chysostomos', in J. Irmscher and D. B. Schelow (eds.), *Griechische Städte und einheimische Völker des Schwarzmeergebietes* (Berlin), 137–54.

Trevor-Roper, H. (1983): 'The Invention of Tradition: The Highland Tradition of Scotland', in Hobsbawm and Ranger 1983: 15–41.

Trisoglio, F. (1972): 'Le idee politiche di Plinio il Giovane e di Dione Crisostomo', *Il Pensiero Politico*, 5: 3–43.

Trouard, M. A. (1942): *Cicero's Attitudes towards the Greeks* (Diss. Chicago).

Tsigakou, F.-M. (1981): *The Rediscovery of Greece: Travellers and Painters of the Romantic Era* (London).

Turner, E. G. (1954): 'Recto and Verso', *JEA* 40: 102–6.

Tzifopoulos, Y. Z. (1993): 'Mummius' Dedications at Olympia and Pausanias' Attitude to the Romans', *GRBS* 34: 93–100.

Unruh, F. (1989): *Das Bild des Imperium Romanum im Spiegel der Literatur an der Wende vom 2. zum 3. Jh. n. Chr.* (Diss. Tübingen).

Valgiglio, E. (1976): *Plutarco: Praecepta Gerendae Reipublicae* (Milan).

vander Leest, J. (1985): 'Lucian in Egypt', *GRBS* 26: 75–82.

Vannier, F. (1976): 'Aelius Aristide et la domination romaine d'après le discours à Rome', *DHA* 2: 497–506.

Versteegh, K. (1987): 'Latinitas, Hellenismos, 'Arabiyya', in Taylor 1987*b*: 251–74.

Veyne, P. (1978): 'La Famille et l'amour sous le Haut-Empire romain', *Annales E.S.C.* 33: 35–63 (= id., *La Société romaine* [Paris, 1991], 88–130).

—— (1987): 'The Roman Empire', in P. Veyne (ed.), *A History of Private Life* (series eds. Ph. Ariès and G. Duby), i (trans. A. Goldhammer) (Cambridge, Mass.), 5–234.

—— (1988): *Did the Greeks Believe in their Myths?* (trans. P. Wissing) (Chicago).

—— (1990): *Bread and Circuses* (trans. B. Pearce) (London).

Vidal-Naquet, P. (1984): 'Flavius Arrien entre deux mondes', in P. Savinel (trans.), *Arrien: Histoire d'Alexandre* (Paris), 311–93.

Vieillefond, J.-R. (1987) (ed., trans.): *Longus: Pastorales* (Budé: Paris).

Vielmetti, C. (1941): 'I "Discorsi bitinici"' di Dione Crisostomo', *St. Ital. Fil. Class.* 18: 89–108.

Viscidi, F. (1944): *I prestiti latini nel greco antico e bizantino* (Padua).

Vittinghoff, F. (1957): review of Oliver 1953, in *Gnomon*, 29: 74–6.

Wachsmuth, C. (1887): 'Über eine Hauptquelle für die Geschichte des Achäischen Bundes', *Leipziger Studien*, 10: 269–98.

Waelkens, M. (1989): 'Hellenistic and Roman Influence in the Imperial Architecture of Asia Minor', in Walker and Cameron 1989: 77–88.

Walbank, F. W. (1972): *Polybius*, Sather Class. Lectures 42 (Berkeley).

Walker, S., and Cameron, A. (eds.) (1989): *The Greek Renaissance in the Roman Empire*, *BICS* Suppl. 55.

Wallace-Hadrill, A. (1981): 'The Emperor and his Virtues', *Historia*, 30: 298–323.

—— (1990): 'Pliny the Elder and Man's Unnatural History', *G&R* 37: 81–96.

Walsh, J. T. (1992): 'Syzygy, Theme and History: A Study in Plutarch's *Philopoemen* and *Flamininus*', *Philologus*, 136: 208–33.

Walsh, P. G. (1958): 'Livy and Stoicism', *AJP* 79: 355–75.

—— (1961): *Livy: His Historical Aims and Methods* (Cambridge).

Walzer, R. (1949): *Galen on Jews and Christians* (Oxford).

Ward-Perkins, J. (1981): *Roman Imperial Architecture*[2] (London).

Wardman, A. (1974): *Plutarch's Lives* (London).

—— (1976): *Rome's Debt to Greece* (London).

Watson, G. (1966): *Theriac and Mithridatium* (London).

Watt, I. (1957): *The Rise of the Novel* (London).

Webster, G. (1979): *The Roman Imperial Army*[2] (London).

Weinreich, O. (1921): 'Alexandros der Lügenprophet und seine Stellung in der Religiosität des II. Jahrhunderts n. Chr.', *Neue Jahrb. f. das klass. Altertum*, 47: 129–51 (= *Ausgewählte Schriften*, i [Amsterdam], 520–51).

Weiser, W. (1989): 'Römische Stadtmünzen aus Bithynia et Pontus', *Schw. Num. Rundsch.* 68: 47–84.

Weiss, P. (1982): 'Ein Altar für Gordian III., die älteren Gordiane und die Severer aus Aigeai (Kilikien)', *Chiron*, 12: 191–205.

—— (1984): 'Lebendiger Mythos: Gründerheroen und städtische Gründungstraditionen im griechisch-römischen Osten', *WJA* 10: 179–208.

Weissenberger, B. (1895): *Die Sprache Plutarchs von Chaeronea und die pseudoplutarchischen Schriften* (Diss. Würzburg).

Welles, C. B. (1962): 'Hellenistic Tarsus', *Mél. de l'Univ. Saint Joseph*, 38: 41–75.

Wendel, C. (1928): 'Die Überlieferung des Attizisten Moiris', *Philologus*, 84: 179–200.

Wesseling, B. (1988): 'The Audience of the Ancient Novels', in Hofmann 1988: 67–79.

Wheeler, E. L. (1979): 'The Legion as Phalanx', *Chiron*, 9: 303–18.

Whittaker, C. R. (1989): *Les Frontières de l'Empire romain* (Besançon).

Whittaker, J., and Louis, P. (1990): *Alcinoos: Enseignement des Doctrines de Platon* (Budé: Paris).

Wifstrand, A. (1939): 'Autocrator, Kaisar, Basileus', in *Dragma Martino P. Nilsson* (Lund), 529–39.

Wilamowitz-Moellendorff, U. von (1900): 'Asianismus und Atticismus', *Hermes*, 35: 1–52 (= *Kleine Schriften*, iii [Berlin, 1969], 223–73).

Wilhelm, F. (1902): 'Zu Achilles Tatius', *RhM* 57: 55–75.

—— (1918): 'Zu Dion Chrys. Or. 30 (Charidemus)', *Philologus*, 75: 364–83.

Williams, W. (1976): 'Individuality in the Imperial Constitutions: Hadrian and the Antonines', *JRS* 66: 67–83.

Willis, W. H. (1990): 'The Robinson-Cologne Papyrus of Achilles Tatius', *GRBS* 31: 73–102.

Winkler, J. J. (1980): 'Lollianos and the Desperadoes', *JHS* 100: 155–81 (rev. in R. Hexter and D. Selden [eds.], *Innovations of Antiquity* [New York, 1992], 5–50).

—— (1982): 'The Mendacity of Kalasiris and the Narrative Strategy of Heliodoros' *Aithiopika*', *YCS* 27: 93–158.

—— (1990): 'The Education of Chloe: Hidden Injuries of Sex', in id., *The Constraints of Desire* (London), 101–26 (abbreviated as 'The Education of Chloe: Erotic Protocols and Prior Violence', in L. A. Higgins and B. R. Silver [eds.], *Rape and Representation* [New York, 1991], 15–34).

Winkler, L. (1980): *Galens Schrift 'De antidotis': Ein Beitrag zur Geschichte von Antidot und Theriak* (Diss. Marburg).

Wirth, Th. (1964): 'Anmerkungen zur Arrianbiographie: Appian–Arrian–Lukian', *Historia*, 13: 209–45.

—— (1967): 'Arrians Errinerungen an Epiktet', *MH* 24: 149–89, 197–216.

Witke, E. C. (1965): 'Marcus Aurelius and Mandragora', *CPh* 60: 23–4.

Wörrle, M. (1988): *Stadt und Fest im kaiserzeitlichen Kleinasien* (Munich).

—— (1992): 'Neue Inschriftenfunde aus Aizanoi I', *Chiron*, 22: 337–76.

Wolanin, H. (1990): 'Quid Lucianus in dialogo iudicium vocalium de legibus ad litteras formamque verborum pertinentibus iudicaverit', *Meander*, 45: 3–11 (in Polish).

Woodward, A. M. (1929): 'Inscriptions', in R. M. Dawkins (ed.), *The Sanctuary of Artemis Orthia at Sparta*, Soc. Prom. Hell. Stud. Suppl. Paper 5 London), 285–377.

Woolf, G. (1993): 'Roman Peace', in J. Rich and G. Shipley (eds.), *War and Society in the Roman World* (London), 171–94.

Woolf, G. (1994): 'Becoming Roman, Staying Greek: Culture, Identity and the Civilizing Process in the Roman East', *PCPhS* 40: 116–43.

Wooten, C. W. (1987) (trans.): *Hermogenes' On Types of Style* (Chapel Hill, NC).

Yegül, F. K. (1979): 'The Small City Bath in Classical Antiquity and a Reconstruction Study of Lucian's "Baths of Hippias"', *Archeologia classica*, 31: 108–31.

Zeitlin, F. (1990): 'The Poetics of *Erôs*: Nature, Art, and Imitation in Longus' *Daphnis and Chloe*', in Halperin *et al.* 1990: 417–64 (rev. as 'Gardens of Desire in Longus's *Daphnis and Chloe*: Nature, Art, and Imitation', in Tatum 1994: 148–70).

Zerdik, A. (1886): *Quaestiones Appianeae* (Diss. Kiel).

Zgusta, L. (1980): 'Die Rolle des Griechischen im römischen Kaiserreich', in G. Neumann and J. Untermann (eds.), *Die Sprachen im römischen Reich der Kaiserzeit* (Bonn), 121–45.

Ziegler, K. (1951): 'Plutarchos', *RE* xxi. 1 (1951), cols. 636–962.

—— (1980): *Plutarchi Vitae Parallelae*, iv. *Indices* (rev. H. Gärtner) (Teubner: Leipzig).

Zilliacus, H. (1935): *Zum Kampf der Weltsprachen im Oströmischen Reich* (Helsinki).

—— (1936): *De elocutione M. Aurelii Imperatoris Quaestiones Syntacticae* (Diss. Helsinki and Leipzig).

Zimmermann, F. (1936) (ed.): *Griechische Roman-Papyri und verwandte Texte* (Heidelberg).

BIBLIOGRAPHICAL ADDENDA

Bremen, R. van (1996): *The Limits of Participation: Women and Civic Life in the Greek East in the Hellenistic and Roman Periods* (Amsterdam).

Brixhe, Cl. (1987): *Essai sur le grec anatolien au début de notre ère*[2] (Nancy).

Gleason, M. W. (1995): *Making Men: Sophists and Self-Presentation in Ancient Rome* (Princeton).

Jones, C. P. (1996): 'The Panhellenion', *Chiron*, 26: 29–56.

Nutton, V. (1995): 'Galen *ad multos annos*', *Dynamis*, 15 (1995), 25–39.

Rochette, B. (1997): *Le Latin dans le monde grec* (Brussels).

Schmitz, Th. (1997): *Bildung und Macht: Zur socialen und politischen Funktion der zweiten Sophistik in der griechischen Welt der Kaiserzeit* (Munich).

INDEX

Roman names are listed by *nomen* or *cognomen*

historical declamation 94–6
illness: as hypochondria 106–7, 254;
  kathedra 257, 258; start of/
  symptoms 257, 260, 264
Laneion estate 273
*Letter to the Kings concerning
  Smyrna* (xix) 296
Monody for Smyrna (xviii) 296
On the Prohibition of Comedy
  (xxix) 282
Palinode for Smyrna (xx) 296
Panathenaic Oration (i) 74, 168,
  283; delivery 274
Panegyric in Cyzicus On the Temple
  (xxvii) 282, 285–7; concord
  (*harmonia*) 287; date/context 285;
  harmony of the emperors 285–6;
  imperial cult and control of *dêmos*
  287
Plutarch and 259, 296–7
Political Speech in Smyrna (xvii)
  295–6
political-ideological identification
  with Greece 283–4, 297
religion/gods: Asclepius 257
  ('saviour'), 259, 262–3, 266, 268,
  272 ('saviour'), 274, 285, 297;
  emperors and divinity 259, 286,
  289, 292, 296; *see also* Aristides,
  rhetoric; Aristides, *Sacred Tales*;
  Asclepius; Asclepius, Asclepieum
  at Pergamum
rhetoric: god-given 256, 262;
  Isocrates 255, 288, 289; opposed
  to term sophist 99–100, 255;
  place and aims 95, 255, 256, 287;
  self-identity and 283
Roman citizenship 256, 284
Roman Empire: 'democracy' 279,
  281; equality/provincial
  participation 280–1; immunities/
  personal benefits 260, 266–74,
  275, 278, 283, 297; political-
  ideological identification/shared
  political interests 260, 280;
  terminology 259, 260, 263, 272,
  276, 278, 285; 'Them and Us'
  outlook 280
Rome, first trip 257, 265 (date)
Rome, second trip 274
Sacred Tales 260–74; composition/
  structure 260, 262, 264, 266, 268;
  dreams/psychology 262; Roman

governors, Asclepius' power over
  268–74; title 254–5; (I) Diary
  261; Marcus Aurelius/Lucius
  Verus 263, 264; (II) Rome, first
  trip 264–6; (III) 266; (IV) 112,
  266–74; composition/structure
  266, 268; nomination as eirenarch
  and prytanis 268–71, as provincial
  high priest 272, as revenue officer
  272; rhetoric, god-given 266;
  Roman governors and Greek
  culture 270, 271; (V) Marcus
  Aurelius 274; rhetorical
  triumphs 274
social network 259, 271
To Asclepius (xlii) 263
To Plato, In Defence of the Four
  (iii) 283
To Rome (xxvi) 208, 255, 266,
  274–84, 315; civic emperor 281;
  delivery/context 275; 'democracy'
  276, 277, 278; fault-lines 282–3;
  modern views 274–5, 297; Roman
  history/culture 275; summary
  276–8; *To the Cities, On Concord*
  (xxiii) compared with 292; §63:
  '"Roman" the name not of a city
  but of a common race' 277, 279
To the Cities, On Concord (xxiii)
  222, 280, 282, 284, 288–92;
  community, discourse of 290–1;
  concord and Roman control 291,
  292; date/context 288; imperial
  cult and Roman control 290, 291;
  To Rome (xxvi) compared
  with 292
To the Rhodians, On Concord (xxiv)
  282, 292
Aristides (the Just) 168, 235, 335
Aristion of Athens 343
Aristocles, Ti. Claudius of Pergamum
  256
Aristophanes 53
Aristophanes of Byzantium 22
Aristotle 53, 281
Arria 370, 371
Arrian (Flavius Arrianus) 11, 68, 78,
  170, 242–8, 251, 405, 415
  Alexander the Great, identification
  with 246
  Anabasis 247; i. 12. 1–5 (Second
  Preface) 244–6; Roman Empire
  interpreted by 247